P9-DFJ-436

The Complete Guide
to High-End Audio

Third Edition

The Complete Guide to High-End Audio

Third Edition

Robert Harley

Acapella Publishing

P. O. Box 1768

Tijeras, New Mexico 87059-1768 USA

Copyright © 1994, 1997, 1998, 2002, 2004 by Robert Harley

Third Edition
First Printing—2004

All rights reserved. No part of this publication may be reproduced or transmitted in
any form or by any means, electronic or mechanical, including photocopying,
recording, or by any information storage and retrieval system without written permission from the publisher, except for the inclusion of brief quotations in a review.

International Standard Book Numbers:
Hardcover: 0-9640849-7-X
Paper: 0-9640849-6-1

Cover Concept and Design: *Daniel Bish*
Cover Illustration: *Gregory Truett Smith*
Illustrations: *Rick Velasquez and Nancy Josephson,* except where otherwise credited
Copy Editors: *Richard Lehnert (first and second editions), Mark Lehman (third edition)*
Technical Reviewers: *A. J. Conti, Gary Gomes, Bill Low, Peter W. Mitchell,*
                Arthur Noxon (first and second editions)

Printed in the United States of America

Trademark Notice

This book comments on and describes various audio and video components. Many such products are identified by their tradenames. In most cases, these designations are claimed as legally protected trademarks by the companies manufacturing the products. Use of a term in this book should not be regarded as affecting the validity of any trademark or service mark. You should investigate a claimed trademark before using it for any purpose other than to refer to the product.

Warning Disclaimer

This book is designed to provide the most current, correct, and clearly expressed information regarding the subject matter covered. It is sold with the understanding that the publisher and author are not engaged in rendering audio/video system design.

It is not the purpose of this manual to reprint all the information otherwise available to the author and/or publisher, but to complement, amplify, and supplement other texts. You are urged to read all available material and learn as much as possible about audio, video, and home theater to tailor the information to your individual needs. For more information, readers are encouraged to consult with professional specialty audio and video retailers or manufacturers for information concerning specific matters before making any decision.

Every effort has been made to make this manual as complete and accurate as possible. However, there may be mistakes both typographical and in content. Therefore, this text should be used as a general guide and not as the ultimate source of audio and video information. Furthermore, this text contains information current only up to the printing date.

The purpose of this manual is to educate and entertain. The author and Acapella Publishing shall have neither liability nor responsibility to any person or entity with respect to any loss or damage caused, or alleged to be caused, directly or indirectly by the information contained in this book.

If you do not wish to be bound by the above, you may return this book to the place of purchase for a full refund.

Contents

Foreword

By Keith Jarrett

Music is the sonic motion of intention. With words, sound can be divorced from meaning by taking away the physical quality of speech. But music's meaning is *in* its physical quality: its sound. When a musician plays something a certain way and we can't hear the intent (the reason) behind it, we are hearing wasted motion, and register it as such because we haven't been given enough clues about the intent. We can then grow to think that everything is only gesture, and miss the real thing.

The media through which we hear music (our systems, rooms, etc.) cannot be separated from our ability to experience the music. It isn't the same *music* on a different system because we cannot separate music's rhetoric (its words) from its physical reality (its delivery). This makes the "delivery systems" (our stereos) more important than we might think they are. Can they *tell* us what the musicians on the recording are telling us?

As a musician, I often—too often—had the following experience: I would play a concert, hear the tape afterward, and wonder what was missing. I would remember incredible things in the concert that just weren't on the tape. The notes were there, but notes are not music. Where was the music, the *intention*?

We could think of it this way: On the tape, the rhetoric had no meaning. Had I trusted the tape and not my memory of the actual event, I would have never grown to understand that, even though the sound is on tape, it doesn't mean you've recorded the *music*. If you've heard a certain CD on a certain system, it doesn't necessarily mean that you've heard what's on the CD. We must learn to trust the responses of our own system—our ears—to music systems. Of course, this demands that we be in touch with ourselves—no easy thing.

People to whom music is important need to get close to the intention in a recording, and there's only one way to do this in the home: learn about the world of audio equipment. Use your (and others') ears to help remove whatever hinders you from the musical experience on the recording. Of course, it's not only the reproduction side that needs care—but that's the only side the listener has control over.

For instance, it's demonstrable that by merely flipping a two-pronged AC plug on a CD player, or even a turntable, a record you thought you didn't like can become a favorite—just because the polarity was wrong. Since music cannot be divorced from its emotional content, the *sound* of a record can determine whether you think you like the *music*. And vice versa, when you can't listen to music you really think you like because of how it was *recorded*.

Obviously, the musical experience is a delicate, complex thing, and we humans are more sensitive than we sometimes think. But we have the option to tune our music systems to better balance the equation. We can get closer to what we want if we *know* what we want.

There are stereo components that approximate the musical experience at many different price levels. We all know what our financial limitations are; but, given the desire to improve our systems, we *can* do it.

It by no means follows that musicians have to be audiophiles. Though I've been recording since 1965, I didn't seriously think about much of this until the last decade. But audiophiles and music lovers push the envelope, and we all benefit. Also, the more serious audiophiles are determined to keep their minds and ears open, keep learning, and try to remain patient during the process. Doing this thing right can take time.

There are a lot of people out there listening to all of these components for us. I recommend *using* this fact, and *carefully* reading others' evaluations, until you can tell whether a reviewer's preferences in sound match your own priorities. You *can* sort of get to know these guys over a period of time.

But, of course, it's *your* ears that count. I think you should pay attention to their needs. After all, we're talking nutrition in an age of diet soft drinks.

Preface to the Third Edition

Since the first two editions of *The Complete Guide to High-End Audio* were published in 1994 and 1998, respectively, some significant technological changes have affected the way we listen to music. This new edition has been updated, revised, and expanded to include these new technologies and trends. Perhaps the most important of these are the Super Audio Compact Disc (SACD) and DVD-Audio formats, the long-awaited replacements for the CD. Both of these formats offer the music lover sound quality vastly superior to that of conventional compact discs. It's not surprising that Chapter 8 ("Digital Source Components") underwent the most extensive rewrite and additions of any chapter in the book.

Conversely, some aspects of audio technology don't change much over time. Someone once said that "nobody has yet repealed the laws of physics," and that thought rang true as I approached the sections on room acoustics, audio and electronics basics, and critical listening. Nonetheless, I have incorporated my six additional years of experience garnered since the second edition's publication in addressing these subjects.

High-end audio is undergoing a sea-change with the recent availability of technology to deliver multichannel music reproduction. Although this is a controversial subject, I've included an entirely new chapter devoted to it. Even if you're a die-hard 2-channel enthusiast, I encourage you to approach Chapter 14 (entirely new for this edition) with an open mind.

This new edition also includes a revised, expanded, and updated version of a paper I presented at the 1991 Audio Engineering Society Convention, called "The Role of Critical Listening in Evaluating Audio Equipment Quality." The paper examines the philosophical foundation of observational listening as practiced in high-end audio, and takes on the "meter readers" who believe that everything that can be heard can be measured. I'm proud to say that since the paper's publication, it has become a touchstone for audiophiles and a lightning rod for attack by audio "objectivists." This newly expanded version appears for the first time in this book.

The biggest trend in high-performance audio since the second edition's publication is undoubtedly the integration of audio and video presentation, also known as home theater. Although *The Complete Guide to High-End Audio* is primarily a book about high-quality music reproduction, I've completely rewritten and expanded the home-theater chapter. This new chapter include tips for getting the best performance from a system that plays both music and films. For the 2-channel devotees—and there are a lot of you—Chapter 13, which covers home theater, is clearly marked so that you can skip it if you wish.

Home theater is, however, exerting an enormous influence on high-end audio. The booming demand for high-performance home theater is creating new business opportunities for high-end audio companies, and strengthening the entire industry. Moreover, home theater is serving as an introduction to high-performance audio; many home-theater consumers are surprised by how good reproduced music can sound, often drawing them back into their passion for music. Home theater also causes the average consumer, perhaps for the first time, to correctly position loudspeakers and consider the spatial aspects of reproduced sound.

The earlier editions of *The Complete Guide to High-End Audio* advised readers to have separate music and home-theater systems. Though that advice still has merit, it isn't practical for most readers. The reality is that many of today's systems must perform double duty. I share with you in this new edition my experience with adding video playback without compromising the system's all-important musical performance. Those readers whose interest is primarily in home theater may find useful my *Home Theater for Everyone: A Practical Guide to Today's Home Entertainment Systems*, also available from Acapella Publishing. For the serious home-theater enthusiast, *The Complete Guide to High-End Audio*, with its more in-depth technical content, can be used in conjunction with *Home Theater for Everyone*.

The Complete Guide to High-End Audio can be read by beginners as well as by seasoned enthusiasts. Each chapter progresses from the most basic information to deeper technical discussions; when you've reached your own comfortable depth in a given chapter, simply skip to the beginning of the next, where the material becomes easier. The extensive use of headings and subheadings throughout the text lets you access specific information more easily. For this new third edition, I've also segregated the most technical information ("Specifications and Measurements") for each component into its own section (Chapter 15).

Keep in mind that you don't need to understand the technical aspects of audio to enjoy music in your home. I've discussed this for those readers who want a deeper understanding of music-reproduction technology, and to make this book truly *The Complete Guide to High-End Audio*.

Robert Harley
Tijeras, New Mexico

About the Author

Robert Harley is the author of *Home Theater For Everyone*, and Editor-in-Chief of *The Absolute Sound* and *The Perfect Vision* magazines. *The Absolute Sound*, founded in 1972, is the world's most respected journal of high-end audio. Robert Harley's more than 650 published equipment reviews and articles on music and home-theater sound reproduction have helped thousands of enthusiasts improve their home-entertainment systems.

Robert Harley holds a degree in recording engineering and has taught a college degree program in that field. He has worked as a recording engineer and studio owner, compact disc mastering engineer, technical writer, and audio journalist. Before joining *The Absolute Sound* and *The Perfect Vision* in 1999, he was Technical Editor of *Stereophile* magazine for eight years, and also served in that capacity at *Fi: The Magazine of Music and Sound*.

Acknowledgments

A book like this one can never be brought to life by a single person. Instead, it is the culmination of the direct and indirect efforts of many individuals to whom I am indebted.

First, I thank my wife, Mary, for putting up with my long hours writing and laying out this new edition, and for proofreading the manuscript. I am grateful to the experts in specific fields of audio who provided technical review for the first editions of this book: Gary Gomes, A.J. Conti, Art Noxon, Bill Low, and, especially, the late Peter W. Mitchell, who seemed to be an expert in *every* area of audio.

My research for this book relied heavily on the writings of my audio journalist colleagues, particularly Martin Colloms, Dick Olsher, and Peter W. Mitchell. Their technical expositions in product reviews and articles over the past decade have been an invaluable source of information.

Special acknowledgment goes to *Stereophile* magazine founder J. Gordon Holt. He was the first audio writer to describe how an audio component *sounded* rather than how it *measured*. Gordon laid the foundation—more than forty years ago—for the entire field of subjective evaluation of audio equipment, and developed the unique language of describing reproduced music that we all take for granted today. Harry Pearson, founder of *The Absolute Sound*, deserves much credit for refining and expanding upon that lexicon, and for the idea that reproduced music should be judged in relation to "the absolute sound"—the sound of unamplified instruments in a real acoustic space..

I'd like to thank all my readers who have called me for advice over the years; your questions told me what I needed to include in this book.

The combination of my desire to write and my interest in music and audio technology springs from my family. My parents instilled in me a love of the printed word that has immeasurably enriched my life. My brother Stephen's willingness to share his stereo and record collection with his little brother was undoubtedly the seed that germinated, nearly thirty-five years later, into this book.

Many others contributed selflessly to this project. I thank Keith Jarrett for his eloquent foreword; Richard Lehnert for his valued editorial guidance, extensive typographical knowledge, and meticulous copy editing (the latter in the first and second editions); Mark Lehman for copy editing this third edition; Daniel Bish and Gregory Truett Smith for the unique cover; the many high-end equipment manufacturers who supplied graphics and photographs; *Stereophile* magazine for the Audio Precision and MLSSA graphs, and for allowing me to reprint short sections of text from my previous writings; and Larry Fine, author of *The Piano Book*, for sharing with me his insights into and experience in self-publishing. Special thanks go to Ruth Cooper who, in her own way, contributed to this third edition.

I'd also like to acknowledge the writings of Robert Pirsig. His reconciliation of two apparently disparate modes of thought makes it perfectly natural to describe, in the same article, an audio component's soundstage bloom as well as its reproduction of a –90dBFS, 1kHz undithered sinewave.

1 What Is High-End Audio?

High-end audio is about passion—passion for music, and for how well it is reproduced. High-end audio is the quest to re-create in the listener's home the musical message of the composer or performer with the maximum realism, emotion, and intensity. Because music is important, re-creating it with the highest possible fidelity is important.

High-end audio products constitute a unique subset of music-reproduction components that bear little similarity to the "stereo systems" sold in department stores. A music-reproduction system isn't a home appliance like a washing machine or toaster; it is a vehicle for expressing the vast emotional and intellectual potential of the music encoded on our records and CDs. The higher the quality of reproduction, the deeper our connection with the music.

The high-end ethos—that music and the quality of its reproduction matter deeply—is manifested in high-end audio products. They are designed by dedicated enthusiasts who combine technical skill and musical sensitivity in their crafting of components that take us one step closer to the original musical event. High-end products are designed by ear, built by hand, and exist for one reason: to enhance the experience of music listening.

A common misperception among the hi-fi–consuming public is that high-end audio means high-*priced* audio. In the mass-market mind, high-end audio is nothing more than elaborate stereo equipment with fancy features and price tags aimed at millionaires. Sure, the performance may be a little better than the hi-fi you find at your local appliance store, but who can afford it? Moreover, high-end audio is seen as being only for trained, discriminating listeners, snobs, or gadget freaks—but not for the average person on the street.

High-end audio is none of these things.

First, the term "high-end" refers to the products' *performance*, not their price. Many true high-end systems cost no more—and often less— than the all-in-one rack systems sold in department stores. I've heard many inexpensive systems that capture the essence of what high-quality music reproduction is all about—systems easily within the budgets of average consumers. Although many high-end components *are* high-priced, this doesn't mean that you have to take out a second mortgage to have high-quality music reproduction in your home. A great-sounding system can be less expensive than you might think.

Second, high-end audio is about communicating the musical experience, not adding elaborate, difficult-to-operate features. In fact, high-end systems are much easier to use than mass-market mid-fi systems. This is because the high-end ethic eliminates useless features, instead putting the money into sound quality. High-end audio is for music lovers, not electronics whizzes.

Third, *anyone* who likes music can immediately appreciate the value of high-quality sound reproduction. It doesn't take a "golden ear" to know what sounds good. The differences between good and mediocre music reproduction are instantly obvious. The reaction—usually pleasure and surprise—of someone hearing a true high-end audio system for the first time underscores that high-end audio can be appreciated by everyone. If you enjoy music, you'll enjoy it more through a high-end system. It's that simple.

Finally, the goal of high-end audio is to make the equipment "disappear"; when that happens, we know that we have reached the highest state of communication between musician and listener. High-end audio isn't about equipment; it's about music.

The high-end credo holds that the less the musical signal is processed, the better. Any electronic circuit, wire, tone control, or switch degrades the signal—and thus the musical experience. This is why you won't find graphic equalizers, "spatial enhancers," "sub-harmonic synthesizers," or other such gimmicks in high-end equipment. These devices are not only departures from musical reality, they add unnecessary circuitry to the signal path. By minimizing the amount of electronics between you and the musicians, high-end audio products can maximize the directness of the musical experience. Less is more.

Imagine yourself standing at the edge of the Grand Canyon, feeling overwhelmed by its grandeur. You experience not only the vastness of this massive sculpture carved deep into the earth, but all its smaller features jump out at you as well, vivid and alive. You can discern fine gradations of hue in the rock layers—distinctions between the many shades of red are readily apparent. Fine details of the huge formations are easily resolved simply by your looking at them, thus deepening your appreciation. The contrasts of light and shadow highlight the apparently infinite maze of cracks and crevasses. The longer and closer you look, the more you see. The wealth of sensory input keeps you standing silently at the edge, in awe of nature's unfathomable beauty.

Now imagine yourself looking at the Grand Canyon through a window made of many thicknesses of glass, each one less than perfectly transparent. One pane has a slight grayish opacity that dulls the vivid hues and obliterates the subtle distinctions between similar shades of color. The fine granular structure of the next pane diminishes your ability to resolve features in the rock. Another pane reduces the contrast between light and shadow, turning the Canyon's immense depth and breadth into a flat canvas. Finally, the windowframe itself constricts your view, destroying the Canyon's overall impact. Instead of the direct and immediate reality of standing at the edge of the Grand Canyon, what you see is gray, murky, lifeless, and synthetic. You may as well be watching it on television.

Hearing reproduced music through a mediocre playback system is like looking at the Grand Canyon through those panes of glass. Each component in the playback chain—CD player, turntable, preamplifier, power amplifier, loudspeakers, and the cables that connect them—in some way distorts the signal passing through it. One product may add a coarse, grainy character to instrumental textures. Another may reduce the dynamic contrasts between loud and soft, muting the composer's or performer's expression. Yet another may cast a thick, murky pall over the music, destroying its subtle tonal colors and overlaying all instruments with an undifferentiated timbre. Finally, the windowframe—that is, the electronic and mechanical playback system—diminishes the expanse that is the musicians' artistic intent.

High-end audio is about removing as many panes of glass as possible, and making those that remain as transparent as they can be. The fewer the panes, and the less effect each has on the information passing through it, the closer we get to the live experience and the deeper our connection with the musical message.

Each component in an audio system can be thought of as a piece of glass through which we experience music.

Courtesy AudioQuest

Why are high-end audio products more transparent windows on the musical event than mass-market "stereo systems"? High-end products are designed to *sound* good—that is, like the real thing. They're not necessarily designed to perform "well" according to some arbitrary technical specification. The true high-end designer *listens* to the product during its development, changing parts and trying different techniques to produce the most realistic sound possible. He combines technical skill with musical sensitivity to create a product that best conveys the musical experience. This dedication often becomes a zealous pursuit, involving many hundreds of listening hours and painstaking attention to every factor that influences the sound. Often, a more expensive part will be included to improve the product's sound, while the retail price remains the same. The higher cost of this musically superior part comes off the company's bottom line. Why? Because the high-end designer cares deeply about music and its reproduction.

Conversely, mass-market audio components are often designed to look good "on paper"—on the specification sheet—sometimes at the expense of sound quality. A good example of this is the "THD wars" of the 1970s and '80s. THD stands for Total Harmonic Distortion, a specification widely used by uneducated consumers as a measure of amplifier quality. (If you've done this, don't worry; before I learned more about audio, I, too, looked at THD figures.) The lower the THD, the better the amplifier was perceived to be. This led the electronics giants to produce products with vanishingly low THD numbers. It became a contest to see which brand had the most zeros after the decimal point in its THD specification (0.001%, for example). Many buyers bought receivers or amplifiers solely on the basis of this specification.

Although low THD is a worthy design goal, the problem arose in *how* those extremely low distortion figures were obtained. A technique to reduce distortion in amplifiers is called "feedback"—taking part of the output signal and feeding it back to the input. Large amounts of feedback reduce THD, but cause all kinds of other problems that degrade the amplifier's musical qualities. Did the electronics giants care that the large amounts of negative feedback induced to reduce their products' THD measurements actually made those products sound *worse*? Not a chance. The only thing that mattered was making a commodity that would sell in greater quantity. They traded musical performance for an insignificant technical specification that was sold to the public as being important. Those buyers choosing components on the basis of a specification sheet rather than listening ended up with poor-sounding systems. Ironically, the amplifiers that had the lowest THDs probably had the lowest quality of sound as well.

This example illustrates the vast difference between mass-market manufacturers' and high-end companies' conceptions of what an audio component should do. High-end manufacturers care more about how the product sounds than about how it performs on the test bench. They know that their audience of musically sensitive listeners will buy on the basis of sound quality, not specifications.

High-end products are not only designed by ear, but are often hand-built by skilled craftspeople who take pride in their work. The assemblers are often audiophiles themselves, building the products with as much care as if the products were to be installed in their own homes. This meticulous attention to detail results in a better quality of construction, or *build quality*. Better build quality can not only improve a product's sound, but increase its long-term reliability as well. Moreover, beautifully hand-crafted components can inspire a pride in ownership that the makers of mass-produced products can't hope to match.

High-end audio products are often backed by better customer service than mid-fi products. Because high-end manufacturers care more about their products and customers, they generally offer longer warranties, more liberal exchange policies, and better service. It is not uncommon for high-end manufacturers to repair products out of warranty at no charge. This isn't to say you should expect such treatment, only that it sometimes happens with high-end and is unthinkable with mass-market products. High-end companies care about their customers.

These attributes also apply to high-end specialty retailers. The high-end dealer shares a passion for quality music reproduction and commitment to customer service. If you're used to buying audio components at a mass-market dealer, you'll be pleasantly surprised by a visit to a high-end store. Rather than trying to get you to buy something that may not be right for you, the responsible high-end dealer will strive to assemble a system that will provide the greatest long-term musical pleasure. Such a dealer will put your musical satisfaction ahead of this month's bottom line.

Finally, most high-end products are designed and built in America by American companies. In fact, American-made audio components are highly regarded throughout the world. More than 40% of all American high-end audio production is exported to foreign countries, particularly the Far East. This is true even though high-end products cost about twice as much abroad as they do in the U.S., owing to shipping, import duties, and importer profit. The enthusiasm for American high-end products abroad is even more remarkable when one remembers the popular American misperception that the best audio equipment is made in Japan.

On a deeper level, high-end products are fundamentally different from mass-market products. From their conception, purpose, design, construction, and marketing. In all these differences, what distinguishes a high-end from a mass-market product is the designer's caring attitude toward music. He isn't creating boxes to be sold like any other commodity; he's making musical instruments whose performance will affect how his customers experience music. The high-end component is a physical manifestation of a deeply felt concern about how well music is reproduced, and, by extension, how much it is enjoyed by the listener.

The high-end designer builds products he would want to listen to himself. Because he cares about music, it matters to him how an unknown listener, perhaps thousands of miles away, experiences the joy of music. The greater the listener's involvement in the music, the better the designer has done his job.

A digital processor designer I know epitomizes this dedication. He had specified a premium-quality resistor at a certain point in his new design. This resistor cost $1 rather than the pennies most resistors cost. Just as the design was about to go into production, he looked even harder for any changes that would improve the product's sound. For fun, he tried an exotic $10 resistor in the circuit in place of the $1 resistor. He was surprised at how much better the product sounded with this change, and couldn't bear to see the product shipped with the $1 resistors. The company made the product with the $10 resistors although the retail price had already been established based on the parts cost using $1 resistors. High-end designers try to add quality to, rather than subtract cost from, their products.

To the high-end designer, electronic or mechanical design isn't merely a technical undertaking—it's an act of love and devotion. Each aspect of a product's design, technical as well as musical, is examined in a way that would surprise those unaccustomed to such commitment. The ethos of music reproduction goes to the very core of the high-end designer's being; it's not a job he merely shows up for every day. The result is a much more powerful and intimate involvement in the music for the listener than is possible with products designed without this dedication.

What *is* high-end audio? What is high-end sound? It is when the playback system is forgotten, seemingly replaced by the performers in your listening room. It is when you feel the composer or performer speaking across time and space *to you*. It is feeling a physical rush during a musical climax. It is the ineffable roller-coaster ride of emotion the composer somehow managed to encode in a combination of sounds. It is when the physical world disappears, leaving only your consciousness and the music.

That is high-end audio.

2 Choosing a High-End Audio System

Introduction

Choosing a high-quality music-reproduction system is one of the most important purchasing decisions you'll make. Unlike buying home appliances, your selections in components will influence how deeply you appreciate and enjoy an art form—music. A great-sounding system can even change your lifestyle as music assumes a greater importance in your life. A hi-fi system is a vehicle for exploring the world of music; the better the system, the further and wider that vehicle will take you.

Although selecting hi-fi components may seem a daunting task, a little knowledge and preparation will go a long way toward realizing your dream system—and staying within your budget. The informed shopper knows that choosing the right components, matching those components to each other, and setting them up careful are more important than a big bank account. This chapter will teach you to become a wise shopper and show you the path to assembling the most musically and aesthetically satisfying system possible for your money.

A high-end audio system is made up of many components, each with a specific job. These components generally fall into three basic categories: source components, control components, and playback components.

A source component is any device that recovers the audio signal from an information-storage medium. A compact disc player, which recovers an audio signal from a CD, is a source component. Other sources include DVD-Audio and SACD players, turntables, tuners, and digital-audio servers. Source components are also called the *front end* because they are the very beginning of the playback chain.

The control component is the preamplifier; it receives signals from the source components and controls which one is sent to the power amplifier for listening. The preamplifier is the heart of a hi-fi system; all of the source components run through the preamplifier, which also controls volume and signal routing.

Playback components are the power amplifier and loudspeakers, which work together to convert the preamplifier's output into sound. Fig.2-1 shows the basic configuration of source components, a preamplifier, power amplifier, and a pair of loudspeakers.

Fig. 2-1 A music playback system consists of source components, preamplifier, power amplifier (or integrated amplifier), and a pair of loudspeakers.

If you're a newcomer to audio, you may first want to read the introductory sections of Chapters 5–12 before shopping for a system. Each of these chapters is devoted to a specific component, with an introductory section explaining the component's function, terminology, and features.

Later sections in each chapter go into specific detail about selecting that component on musical and technical bases.

In this chapter, we'll look at how to choose a high-end system. The major topics include:

• *Setting your budget*

• *Complete vs. incremental purchases*

• *Choosing the system best suited to your needs*

• *Allocating your budget to specific components*

• *Upgrading a single component*

• *How to read magazine reviews of audio equipment*

• *System matching*

• *Do's and don'ts of selecting components*

• *Your relationship with the retailer*

• *Setting up your system for the best sound*

Setting Your Budget

How much you should spend on a music playback system depends on two things: your priorities in life and your financial means.

Let's take the priorities first. One person may consider a $2000 stereo system an extravagance, yet not bat an eye at blowing $7000 on a two-week European vacation. Conversely, another person of similar means would find a $7000 vacation a waste of money when there is so much great hi-fi on the wish list. The first person probably considers music as merely a dispensable diversion while driving to work. To the second person, however, enjoying and appreciating music is a vital aspect of human existence. How much of your disposable income you should spend on a hi-fi system is a matter of how important music is to you, and only you can decide that. Owning a good hi-fi system will probably elevate music listening to a much higher priority in your life.

The second factor—your financial means—can often suggest a hi-fi budget. Surveys of readers of audiophile magazines suggest that about 10% to 15% of one's annual income is an average expenditure. In one survey, the median system price was about $18,000, with 20% of readers owning systems costing more than $35,000. These are loose generalizations; high-end systems range in cost from less than $1200 to more than $200,000. And don't let these figures intimidate you: readers of audiophile magazines are dedicated enthusiasts who are not necessarily representative of all music lovers. You can put together a musically satisfying system for much less than the figures cited.

I strongly urge you, however, to establish a significant budget for your high-end system. The expenditure may seem high at the time, but you will be rewarded night after night and year after year with your favorite music wonderfully reproduced. A year or two from now, as you enjoy your system, the money spent will have been forgotten, but the pleasure will continue—a good music-playback system is a lasting and fulfilling investment. Moreover, if you buy a quality system now, you won't want to sell it or trade it in for something better later. It is sometimes false economy to "save" money on a less than adequate system. Do it right the first time.

There's another way of determining how much to spend for a hi-fi system: Find the level of quality you're happy with and let that set your budget. Visit your dealer and have him play systems of various levels of quality. You may find yourself satisfied with a moderately priced system—or you may discover how good reproduced music can sound with the best equipment, and just *have* to have it.

When setting a budget for your music system, you must also consider whether the system will be used only for 2-channel music reproduction, or will be called upon to reproduce movie soundtracks as part of a home-theater system. Maintaining high quality with home theater's six speakers instead of two, and buying a multichannel surround-sound preamplifier rather than a 2-channel preamp, can significantly increase the amount of money you'll need to spend. There are, however, ways to add multichannel music reproduction and film-soundtrack playback without greatly escalating the system cost. We'll briefly touch on this subject in this chapter, and delve into it in more detail in Chapter 13.

The Complete vs. the Incremental Purchase

After you've established a budget, you must decide which of the following three ways of buying a hi-fi is best for you:

1) Buy an entire system made up of the finest components.
2) Buy an entire system made up of components within a limited budget.
3) Buy just a few components now and add to the system as finances permit.

The first option doesn't require much thought—just a large bank account. The purchaser of this system needn't worry about budgets, upgrading, and adding components later. Other elements of buying a high-end system (I'll talk about these later) do apply to the cost-no-object audiophile: allocating the budget to specific components, dealing with the retailer, and home auditioning. But this sort of listener isn't under the same financial constraints that force the tough choices inherent in the other two options. Just choose a top-notch system and start enjoying it.

Most of us, however, don't enjoy such luxury, and must live within the set budgets of options 2 or 3. Option 2 is to spend the entire budget on a complete system now. In option 3, you'll spend your entire budget on just a few, higher-quality components and add the other pieces later as money becomes available. We'll call option 2 the *complete purchase*, and option 3 the *incremental purchase*. There are advantages and disadvantages to each approach.

Buying an entire system at once means that the overall budget must be spread among all the components that make up a hi-fi system. Consequently, you'll have less to spend on each component. You may not get the quality of components you'd hoped for, but the system will be complete and you can start enjoying it right away. This type of purchase is more suited to the music lover who doesn't want to think about equipment, but wants a system he can set up, forget, and use to enjoy music.

The listener more inclined to treat audio as a hobby, or who has her sights set on a more ambitious system, will buy just a few components now and add to the system as finances permit. This listener may spend the same amount of money as our first listener, but on just a pair of loudspeakers instead of on a whole system. She will use her old receiver or integrated amplifier, turntable, or CD player until she can afford the electronics and sources she really wants. Her system will be limited by the receiver's performance; she won't immediately get the benefit of her high-end loudspeakers. But when she *does* buy her dream electronics, she'll have a truly first-rate system. This approach requires more patience, commitment, and, in the long term, more money. But it is one way to end up with a superlative system.

The audiophile buying a system piece by piece can benefit from rapidly changing technology. She can start with components that don't change much over the years—power amplifiers, for example—and wait to buy those products likely to get better and cheaper over time: digital processors, CD players, CD transports, and so on.

Another benefit of adding components to your system one at a time is the ability to audition components in that system before buying. Rather than putting together a whole system in a store showroom based on your own auditioning or a salesperson's recommendations, the incremental buyer can carefully audition components and choose the best musical match for the rest of the system. This is a big advantage when assembling a hi-fi best suited to your musical tastes. This piece-by-piece approach is more for the hobbyist, and demands a deeper level of commitment to audio. It also requires a great deal more patience.

In short, if you want to get a good system, forget about the hardware, and just enjoy music, buy the entire system now. Given the same initial expenditure, you won't end up with the same-quality system as if you'd bought pieces slowly, but you'll be spending less money in the long run and can have the benefit of high-end music playback immediately. Moreover, you can go about your life without thinking about what piece of audio hardware to buy next. The complete purchase is recommended for the music lover who isn't—and doesn't want to be—an audio hobbyist. Many music lovers taking this approach, however, find themselves upgrading their systems piece by piece after discovering the rewards of owning a high-end audio system.

Conversely, the music lover on a budget who has set her sights on a more ambitious system, and who takes a more active role in audio equipment, will probably build a system gradually. This listener will more likely read product reviews in magazines, visit the dealer often, and take equipment home for evaluation. By doing so she'll become a better listener and a more critical audiophile, as well as develop a broader knowledge of audio equipment.

Whichever approach you take, the information in the rest of this chapter—selecting a system suited to your listening, allocating the budget to specific components, dealing with the retailer, and setting up the system in your home—applies equally well.

Choosing the System Best Suited to Your Needs

Just as a pickup truck is better suited to the farmer and a compact car to the city dweller, a hi-fi system ideal for a small New York City apartment would be entirely inadequate in a large suburban home. The hi-fi system must not only match your musical taste, as described in the next chapter, but must also suit your room and listening needs. (The following section is only an overview of how to choose the best system. More detailed information on how to select specific components is contained in Chapters 5–12.)

Many of the guidelines are fairly obvious. First, match the loudspeaker size to your listening room. Large, full-range loudspeakers don't work well in small rooms. Not only are large loudspeakers physically dominating, they tend to overload the room with bass energy. A loudspeaker that sounds fine in a 17' by 25' room will likely be thick, boomy, and bottom-heavy in a 12' by 15' room. The bass performance you paid dearly for (it's expensive to get correct deep-bass reproduction) will work against you if the loudspeaker is put in a small room. For the same money, you could buy a superb minimonitor whose build cost was put into making the upper bass, midrange, and treble superlative. You win both ways with the minimonitor: your room won't be overloaded by bass, and the minimonitor will likely have much better soundstaging and tonal purity. There are other benefits: minimonitors, with their limited low-frequency extension, are less likely to annoy neighbors. You can thus listen to music louder without bothering anyone. Further, placement is much easier in small rooms.

Conversely, a minimonitor just won't fill a large room with sound. The sense of power, dynamic drive, deep-bass extension, and feeling of physical impact so satisfying in some music just doesn't happen with minimonitors. If you've got the room and the budget, a full-range, floorstanding loudspeaker is the best choice.

Another important consideration is amplifier power. The amplifier should be matched to the loudspeakers and the room. A larger room requires more amplifier power, as does a loudspeaker of low sensitivity. These issues are described in detail in the power amplifier and loudspeaker chapters (6 and 7).

Value vs. Luxury Components

High-end audio components run the gamut from utilitarian-looking boxes to lavish, gold-plated, cost-no-object shrines. The packaging doesn't always reflect the quality of the electronics inside, but rather the manufacturer's product philosophy. Some companies try to offer the best sound for the least money by putting excellent electronics in inexpensive chassis. These are the so-called "value" products. Manufacturers of "luxury" components may put the same level of electronics in a lavish chassis with a 1"-thick front panel, lacquer-filled engraving, expensive metalwork, and custom machined input jacks or terminal posts.

A designer of *very* expensive electronics once told me that he could sell his products for *half* the price if he used a cheap chassis. He felt, however, that the level of design and execution in his electronics deserved no less than the ultimate in packaging.

Some buyers demand elegant appearance and a luxury feel; others merely want the best sound for the least money. To some music lovers, appearance and elegant packaging are secondary to sound quality; they don't care what it looks like so long as it sounds good. Conversely, some audiophiles are willing to pay for gorgeous cosmetics, battleship build quality, and all the trimmings that make some products exude elegance and luxury. There's an undeniable pride of ownership that accompanies the finest-built audio components.

When choosing high-end components, match your needs with the manufacturer's product philosophy. That way, you won't waste money on thick faceplates you don't care about, or spend money on a product that doesn't do justice to your home decor.

Another type of manufacturer puts mediocre or even poor electronics in a fancy, eye-catching package. Their market is the less musically sophisticated buyer who chooses on the basis of appearance and status (or the company's past reputation) rather than sound quality. These so-called "boutique" brands are not high-end, however, and should be avoided.

A related topic is convenience vs. cost. Some products include convenience features that add to the component's price without improving its sound quality. When choosing components, consider the tradeoffs between sound quality, convenience, and price.

Allocating Your Budget to Specific Components

There are no set rules for how much of your total budget you should spend on each component in your system. Allocating your budget between components depends greatly on which components you choose, and your overall audio philosophy. Mass-market mid-fi magazines have been telling their readers for years to spend most of a hi-fi budget on the loudspeakers because they ultimately produce the sound. This thinking also suggests that all amplifiers and CD players sound alike; why waste money on expensive amplifiers and digital sources?

The high-end listener makes different assumptions about music reproduction. A fundamental tenet of high-end audio holds that if the signal isn't good at the beginning of the reproduction chain, nothing downstream can ever improve it. In fact, the signal will only be degraded by any product it flows through. High-end audio equipment simply minimizes that degradation. If your CD player is bright, hard, and unmusical, the final sound will be bright, hard, and unmusical. Similarly, the total system's performance is limited by the resolution of the worst component in the signal path. You may have superb loudspeakers and an excellent turntable and cartridge, but they'll be wasted with a poor-quality preamp in the signal chain. Quality matching between components is essential to getting the most sound for your budget.

High-quality loudspeakers at the end of a chain containing a bad-sounding component can even make the system sound worse than lower-quality loudspeakers: The high-resolution loudspeakers reveal all the imperfections of the electronics upstream of them. This situation has been likened to having a large picture window in your home. If the view is of the Northern California coastline, you want that window to be as clean and transparent as possible. But if the window overlooks a garbage dump, you'd prefer that it somewhat obscure the view.

I've listened to $400 loudspeakers driven by $30,000 worth of electronics, and $9000 loudspeakers driven by budget integrated amplifiers. I can state categorically that the electronics and source components are every bit as important as the loudspeakers. Although the loudspeakers significantly influence the overall sound, high-quality source components (turntable and CD player) and good electronics (preamplifier and power amplifier) are essential to realizing a musical high-end system.

Since the first two editions of this book, however, I've had experiences with very good-sounding and affordable integrated amplifiers driving moderately expensive loudspeakers, and the results have been excellent. As explained in Chapters 6 and 7, loudspeaker sensitivity (how loudly the speaker will play for a given amount of amplifier power) greatly affects how large an amplifier you need to achieve a satisfying volume. High-sensitivity speakers need very little amplifier power. And because amplifier power is costly, it follows that a system with high-sensitivity speakers can be driven by lower-cost amplification—*provided that the amplification is of high quality*. Fortunately, manufacturers have recently responded to the need for relatively inexpensive high-performance amplification by designing integrated amplifiers with outstanding sound quality, but with lower output powers. By putting the preamplifier and power amplifier in one chassis and cutting back on power output, manufacturers can put their high-end circuits in lower-priced products. The trick is to find those bargain integrated amplifiers that deliver truly high-end sound, and mate them with loudspeakers that not only have the appropriate sensitivity, but are also a good musical match. This approach will get you the best sound for the least money. If, however, cost is secondary to sound quality—that is, you're willing to spend more for an improvement in sound—then buy the best separate preamplifier and power amplifier you can find.

For the following exercise, I assembled an imaginary 2-channel system of the components I'd choose if my audio budget totaled $10,000. This hypothetical system follows a traditional audiophile approach. Here are the costs per item:

> Preamplifier...$2000
> Power amplifier 2000
> Digital source 1300
> Loudspeakers...4000
> Interconnects and cables 700
> **Total** **$10,000**

As you can see, loudspeakers consumed 40% of the budget, the digital source took up another 13%, and the preamp and power amplifier each received 20%. The remaining 7% was spent on interconnects and cables. These numbers and percentages aren't cast in stone, but they're a good starting point in allocating your budget. If you wanted to include a turntable, tonearm, and cartridge, the budget for the other components would have to be reduced.

Another approach with this budget would be to buy an inexpensive CD player ($500) and put the $800 saved into better loudspeakers or electronics. Then, as finances permitted, you could add a digital processor and drive it with the CD player's digital output jack (see Chapter 8). You'll have music in the meantime, and end up with a better-sounding system in the long run.

The 40% figure for loudspeakers is very flexible. Keep in mind that there's an important threshold in loudspeaker performance at about $2500: Loudspeakers costing a little more than $2500 are often disproportionately better than those costing a little less than $2500, so you may want to adjust your budget allocations to cross this threshold. As described in Chapter 7, many moderately priced loudspeakers outperform much more expensive models. Use Chapter 7's guidelines on choosing loudspeakers to get the most performance for your loudspeaker dollar.

Following the earlier discussion of matching a superb but low-powered integrated amplifier with high-sensitivity speakers, here's another example of how I might allocate a $10,000 budget:

Integrated amplifier	$3000
Digital source	$1000
Loudspeakers	$5500
Interconnects and cables	$500
Total	**$10,000**

Again, the key to putting so much of the budget into loudspeakers is extremely careful matching of the amplifier's power output power to the loudspeaker's sensitivity (and impedance curve, explained in Chapter 7), along with finding those few integrated amplifiers that deliver the musicality of expensive separates, but simply have lower output powers. Here's an extreme case: I lived with a system for about a month (during a product review) that included $11,000 loudspeakers driven by a $1500 integrated amplifier and the result was musical magic. It takes a lot of searching to find these synergistic combinations—or a great dealer who has discovered these ideal matches for you. I must stress that this approach only works with certain components, and is useful for getting the best sound for the least money. It is not the ideal strategy when the best possible sound is your goal.

Here's another sample budget, this one based on a maximum expenditure of $2000:

Amplification	$750
Digital source	400
Loudspeakers	750
Interconnects and cables	100
Total	**$2000**

This system will use an integrated amplifier instead of a separate preamplifier and power amplifier, and a CD player instead of separate CD transport and digital processor. Again, I selected components that experience suggested would be a good match, and tallied the percentages after choosing the components. Interestingly, the breakdown was similar to that in the first example: 37% on loudspeakers, 20% on a digital source, 37% on amplification, and 5% on interconnects and cables.

I've heard systems at this price level that are absolutely stunning musically. When carefully chosen and set up, a $2000 high-end system can achieve the essence of what high-quality music reproduction is all about—communicating the musical message. I've even heard a whole system with a list price of $850 that was musical and enjoyable. The point isn't how much you spend on a hi-fi, but how carefully you can choose components to make a satisfying system within your budget.

These guidelines are for a dedicated 2-channel music system, not a multichannel music and home-theater system. The different requirements of home theater suggest a somewhat different budget allocation. If most of your listening time with a multichannel system is devoted to music, the budget guidelines are very similar to those described earlier, but with a shift of money from electronics to loudspeakers. That is, you should spend a bit more of your total budget on speakers. That's because home theater and multichannel music require five or six loudspeakers, and spreading out a fixed amount of money over five speakers rather than two inevitably results in compromised performance. If music is your primary consideration, put most of your speaker budget into the left and right speakers, with less devoted to the center, surround speakers, and subwoofer. Those readers who spend more time watching movies should spend even less on electronics and source and more on speakers. That's because the center channel loudspeaker plays an important role in the home-theater experience (it reproduces nearly all the dialogue), and choosing a quality model is of paramount importance.

In my experience, the sonic differences among amplifiers, preamplifiers, and source components are much less pronounced when we watch movies than when we listen to music. So much of our attention is taken away from the aural experience by the overwhelming visual sensory input. I've used audio/video receivers in my system (during product reviews) and found most of them lacking when reproducing music, but more than adequate for film-soundtrack playback.

Whether choosing a dedicated 2-channel music system or a combined music and home-theater package, you should save some of your budget for an AC power conditioner and accessories. I advise against buying a power conditioner and accessories when you buy the system. Take the system home, get it set up and optimized, *then* add a power conditioner and start experimenting with accessories. Here's why: AC conditioners don't always make an improvement. In fact, they can

degrade the sound. There are many variables with AC power conditioners, including the quality of AC from your wall, the method of AC conditioning, and the number and nature of the components plugged into
the conditioner. It is therefore best to try the conditioner at home before
buying.

There's another good reason for adding an AC line conditioner later:
By getting to know how your system sounds *without* an AC conditioner,
you'll be better able to judge if the conditioner is an improvement.
Remember that a change in sound isn't always for the better. The same
logic holds true for accessories such as cones, feet, and tube dampers:
You'll be in a much better position to judge their effectiveness—or lack
of it—by knowing your system intimately before installing accessories.
Set aside some of your budget—perhaps a few hundred dollars—for
accessories. If they don't make a difference, you've now got a few hundred dollars to spend on records or CDs. (A full survey of accessories is
included in Chapter 12.)

Upgrading a Single Component

Many audiophiles gradually improve their systems by replacing one
component at a time. The trick to getting the most improvement for the
money is to replace the least good component in your system. A poor-
sounding preamp won't let you hear how good your digital processor is,
for example. Conversely, a very clean and transparent preamp used with
a grainy and hard digital source will let you hear only how grainy and
hard the digital source is. The system should be of similar quality
throughout. If there's a quality mismatch, however, it should be in favor
of high-quality source components.

Determining which component to upgrade can be difficult. This is
where a good high-end audio retailer's advice is invaluable—he can
often pinpoint which component you should consider upgrading first.
Another way is to borrow components from a friend and see how they
sound in your system. Listen for which component makes the biggest
improvement in the sound. Finally, you can get an idea of the relative
quality of your components by carefully reading the high-end audio
magazines, particularly when they recommend specific components.

In Chapter 1, I likened listening to music through a playback system
to looking at the Grand Canyon through a series of panes of glass. Each
pane distorts the image in a different way. The fewer and more transparent the panes are, the clearer the view, and the closer the connection to
the direct experience.

Think of each component of a high-end audio system as one of those
panes of glass. Some of the panes are relatively clear, while others tend
to have an ugly coating that distorts the image. The pane closest to you

is the loudspeaker; the next closest pane is the power amplifier; next comes the preamp; and the last pane is the signal source (CD, SACD, DVD-A player or turntable). Your view on the music—the system's overall transparency—is the sum of the panes. You may have a few very transparent panes, but the view is still clouded by the dirtiest, most colored panes. This idea is shown graphically on page 3 earlier.

The key to upgrading a hi-fi system is getting rid of those panes—those components—that most degrade the music performance, and replacing them with clearer, cleaner ones. This technique gives you the biggest improvement in sound quality for the money spent.

Conversely, putting a very transparent pane closest to you—the loudspeaker—only reveals in greater detail what's wrong with the power amplifier, preamplifier, and source components. A high-resolution loudspeaker at the end of a mediocre electronics chain can actually sound worse than the same system with a lower-quality loudspeaker.

Following this logic, we can see that a hi-fi system can never be any better than its source components. If the first pane of glass—the source component—is ugly, colored, and distorts the image, the result will be an ugly, colored, and distorted view.

As you upgrade your system, you can start to see that other panes you thought were transparent actually have some flaws you couldn't detect before. The next upgrade step is to identify and replace what is *now* the weakest component in the system. This can easily become an ongoing process.

Unfortunately, as the level of quality of your playback system rises, your standard of what constitutes good performance rises with it. You may become ever more critical, upgrading component after component in the search for musical satisfaction. This pursuit can become an addiction and ultimately *diminish* your ability to enjoy music. The next chapter includes an editorial I wrote for *Stereophile* magazine examining this subject.

How to Read Magazine Reviews

I've deliberately avoided recommending specific products in this book. By the time you would have read the recommendations, the products would likely have been updated or discontinued. The best source for advice on components is product reviews in high-end audio magazines. Because most of these magazines are published monthly or bi-monthly, they can stay on top of new products and offer up-to-date buying advice. Many magazine reviewers are highly skilled listeners, technically competent and uncompromising in their willingness to report truthfully about audio products. There's a saying in journalism that epitomizes the ethic of many high-end product reviewers: "without fear or favor." The magazine should neither fear the manufacturer when publishing a negative review, nor expect favor for publishing a positive one. Instead, the competent review provides unbiased and educated opinion about the sound, build quality, and value of individual products. Because high-end reviewers hear lots of products under good conditions, they are in an ideal position to assess the relative merits and drawbacks and report their informed opinions. The best reviewers have a combination of good ears, honesty, and technical competence.

You'll notice a big difference between reviews in high-end magazines and reviews in the so-called "mainstream slicks." The mass-market, mainstream magazines are advertiser-driven; their constituents are their advertisers. Conversely, high-end magazines are usually reader-driven; the magazines' goal is to serve their readers, not their advertisers. Consequently, high-end magazines often publish negative reviews, while mass-market magazines generally do not. Moreover, high-end magazines are much more discriminating about what makes a good component that can be recommended to readers. Mass-market magazines cater to the average person in the street, who, they believe (mistakenly, in my view), doesn't care about aspects of music reproduction important to the audiophile. The high-end product review is thus not only more honest, but much more discriminating in determining what is a worthy product. If you're reading a hi-fi magazine that never criticizes products, beware. Not all audio components are worth buying; therefore not all magazine reviews should conclude with a recommendation. Also beware of so-called "consumer" publications that regard an audio system as an appliance, not as a vehicle for communicating an art form. In their view, the improvements in performance gained by spending more are not worth the money, so they recommend the least expensive products with the most features. They take a similar approach to reviewing cars: why spend lots of money on a depreciating asset when all cars perform an identical function—moving you from point A to point B? It is simply not within their ethos to value spirited acceleration, tight handling, a luxurious interior, or the overall feel of the driving experience.

As someone who makes his living reviewing high-end audio products, I'll let you in on a few secrets that can help you use magazine reviews to your advantage. First, associate the review you're reading with the reviewer. Before reading the review, look at the byline and keep in mind who's writing the review. This way, you'll quickly learn different reviewers' tastes in music and equipment. Seek the guidance of reviewers with musical sensibilities similar to your own.

Second, don't assign equal weight to all reviews or reviewers. Audio reviewing is like any other field of expertise—there are many different levels of competence. Some reviewers have practiced their craft for decades, while others are newcomers who lack the seasoned veteran's commitment to the profession. Consider the reviewer's reputation, experience, and track record when giving a review credence. Also consider the reviewer's standards for what makes a good product. Just as there's a big difference between a movie recommendation given by Joel Siegel (*Good Morning America*) and Andrew Sarris (*The Village Voice*), so too are there differences in product recommendations from high-end reviewers.

Finally, listen to the products yourself. If two components are compared in a review, compare those products to hear if your perceptions match the reviewer's. Even if you aren't in the market for the product under review, listening to the components will sharpen your skills and put the reviewer's value judgments in perspective.

A common mistake among audiophiles looking for guidance is to select a component on the basis of a rave review without fully auditioning the product for themselves. The review should be a starting point, not some final judgment of component quality. It's much easier to buy a product because a particular reviewer liked it than it is to research the product's merits and shortcomings for yourself. Buying products solely on the basis of a review is fraught with danger. Never forget that a review is nothing more than one person's opinion, however informed and educated that opinion might be. Moreover, if the reviewer's tastes differ from yours, you may end up with a component you don't like. We all have different priorities in judging reproduced sound quality; what the reviewer values most—soundstaging, for example—may be lower in your sonic hierarchy. Your priorities are the most important consideration when choosing music-playback components. Trust your own ears.

Sharp-eyed readers can find out which products a reviewer really thinks are special. Most reviewers list the reference system with which they audition new products. When a particular product shows up in the reference system in review after review, you can be sure that the writer thinks that product is especially good. Another sure sign of a superb product is if the reviewer buys the product him- or herself.

Some magazine readers view all reviews with suspicion because the reviewer enjoyed the free loan of the product. That is, they believe there's a *quid pro quo* that guarantees the manufacturer a positive review because the reviewer got to use the product for several months. This belief is patently false. Reviewers have access to virtually any products they want, and have no allegiance to the manufacturer who lent it to them. This may be hard to believe from a reader's standpoint, but after receiving, unpacking, setting-up, and learning about hundreds of products, getting new equipment often becomes a chore rather than cause for excitement.

I'd also like to address the issue of long-term equipment loans. Most reviewers have reference systems composed of products they don't own. The manufacturers or distributors of those products choose to allow the reviewer to keep the product for many months or even a year, giving the product exposure in issue after issue. Reviewers need reference-quality equipment with which to judge the product under evaluation—reference-quality equipment they can't afford to buy. The long-term loan is mutually beneficial; the reviewer has access to the best tools available, the manufacturer enjoys the prestige—and presumably increased sales—conferred by the reviewer's repeated mentions, and the reader gets the most accurate descriptions of the products reviewed within the context of the reference system. Moreover, because so many manufacturers see the value in long-term loans, reviewers have access to virtually any products they want. This removes the putative pressure to give positive reviews only to those manufacturers who agree to long-term loans. If a reviewer keeps a product in his system, it's because that product sounds good.

It would be a violation of journalistic ethics, however, if a deal were struck between manufacturer and reviewer that allowed the reviewer to keep the product as his own at the conclusion of the review. In my fifteen years' experience as a reviewer and magazine editor, I have never been approached by a manufacturer in an untoward way, and have never been aware of such behavior (at least on the magazines I've worked for), and would not tolerate any such ethical lapses by a writer on our staff.

A final word about product reviews: Don't stop enjoying music if a component you've already purchased gets a negative review. You enjoyed music through that product before the review appeared; why should another person's opinion diminish your musical satisfaction? Positive or negative, magazine reviews carry far too much weight in readers' minds and in the marketplace. (Remember, you heard this from a professional reviewer.)

In sum, reviews can be very useful, provided you:

- Get to know individual reviewers' sonic and musical priorities. Find a reviewer on your sonic and musical wavelength, then trust his or her opinions.

- Compare your impressions of products to the reviewer's impressions. This will not only give you a feel for the reviewer's tastes and skill, but the exercise will make you a better listener.

- Don't assign the same weight to all reviews. Consider the reviewer's reputation and experience in the field. How many similar products has the reviewer auditioned? If a reviewer has heard virtually every serious digital processor, for example, his or her opinion will be worth more than that of the reviewer who has heard only a few models.

- Don't buy—or summarily reject—products solely on the basis of a review. Use product recommendations as a starting point for your own auditioning. Listen to the product yourself to decide if that product is for you. Let *your* ears decide.

System Matching

It is a truism of high-end audio that an inexpensive system can often outperform a more costly and ambitious rig. I've heard modest systems costing, say, $1500 that are more musically involving than $50,000 behemoths. Why?

Part of the answer is that some well-designed budget components sound better than ill-conceived or poorly executed esoteric products. But the most important factor in a playback system's musicality is *system matching*. System matching is the art of putting together components that complement each other sonically so that the overall result is a musicality beyond what each of the components could achieve if combined with less compatible products. The concept of synergy—that the whole is greater than the sum of the parts—is very important in creating the best-sounding system for the least money.

System matching is the last step in choosing an audio system. You should have first defined the system in terms of your individual needs, set your budget, and established a relationship with a local specialty audio retailer. After you've narrowed down your choices, which products you select will greatly depend on system matching.

Knowing what components work best with other components is best learned by listening to a wide range of equipment. Many of you don't have the time—or access to many diverse components—to find out for yourselves what equipment works best with other equipment. Consequently, you must rely on experts for general guidance, and on your own ears for choosing specific equipment combinations.

The two best sources for this information are magazine reviews and your local dealer. Your dealer will have the greatest knowledge about products he carries, and can make system-matching recommendations based on his experience in assembling systems for his customers. Your dealer will likely have auditioned the products he sells in a variety of configurations; you can benefit from his experience by following his system-matching recommendations.

The other source of system-matching tips is magazine reviews. Product reviews published in reputable magazines will often name the associated equipment used in evaluating the product under review. The reviewer will sometimes describe his or her experiences with other equipment not directly part of the review. For example, a loudspeaker review may include a report on how the loudspeaker sounded when driven by three or four different power amplifiers. The sonic characteristics of each combination will be described, giving the reader an insight into which amplifier was the best match for that loudspeaker. More important, however, the sonic descriptions and value judgments expressed can suggest the *type* of amplifier best suited to that loudspeaker. By *type* I mean both technical performance (tubed vs. transistor, power output, output impedance, etc.) and general sonic characteristics (hard treble, forward presentation, well-controlled bass, etc.).

Let's say the reviewer drove the loudspeakers with four amplifiers: a low-powered but sweet-sounding integrated amplifier, a high-output-impedance tubed design, a medium- to high-powered inexpensive solid-state unit, and a massive solid-state amplifier that requires two people to lug it into the listening room. The reviewer reports that the integrated amplifier just didn't have enough power to produce sufficient volume, and that the sound lacked dynamics. The high-output-impedance tubed amplifier was mushy in the bass and had a reduced sense of pace and rhythm. The inexpensive solid-state amplifier had terrific bass control, but its forward presentation and grainy treble made it less than ideal with the loudspeaker under review. (All of these terms—like *forward*, *grainy*, and *pace*—are defined in the next chapter.) Finally, the reviewer concludes that the solid-state behemoth is the only amplifier suitable for this particular loudspeaker.

This doesn't mean that the most expensive amplifier will always work the best with all loudspeakers. I can think of loudspeakers in which this scenario would be completely different. Another loudspeaker would sound just fine with the integrated amplifier, suggesting that using the huge solid-state unit would be overkill. However, if the loudspeaker was a little tizzy in the treble and lean in the midbass, the tubed amplifier would tend to ameliorate these tendencies. Finally, if the loudspeaker wasn't that sensitive to treble grain, but needed to be driven by an amplifier with control and authority in the bass, the inexpensive solid-state unit would be a good choice—and the most cost-effective.

These reports of system matching can extend beyond the specific products reported on in the review. A fairly good idea of which type of sonic and technical performance is best suited to a particular product can be gained from a careful reading of product reviews. For example, you may conclude that a particular loudspeaker needs to be driven by a large, high-current amplifier. This knowledge can then point you in the right direction for equipment to audition yourself; you can rule out low-powered designs. You can also get a feel for how professional reviewers assemble systems in the annual Recommended Systems feature in *The Absolute Sound*.

By reading magazine reviews, following your dealer's advice, and listening to combinations of products for yourself, you can assemble a well-matched system that squeezes the highest musical performance from your hi-fi budget.

Do's and Don'ts of Selecting Components

Some audiophiles are tempted to buy certain products for the wrong reasons. For example, many high-end products are marketed on the basis of some technical aspect of their design. A power amplifier may, for example, be touted as having "over 200,000 microfarads (μF) of filter capacitance," "32 high-current output devices," and a "discrete JFET input stage." While these may be laudable attributes, they don't guarantee that the amplifier will produce good sound. Don't be swayed by technical claims—listen to the product for yourself.

Just as you shouldn't make a purchasing decision based on specifications, neither should you base your decision solely on brand name. Many high-end manufacturers with solid reputations sometimes produce mediocre-sounding products. A high-end marque doesn't necessarily mean high-end sound. Again, let your ears be your guide. I'm often pleasantly surprised to find moderately priced products that sound as good—or very nearly as good—as products costing two or three times as much.

You should, however, consider the company's longevity, reputation for build quality, customer service record, and product reliability when choosing components. High-end manufacturers run the gamut from one-man garage operations to companies with hundreds of employees and advanced design and manufacturing facilities. The garage operation may produce good-sounding products, but may not be in business next year. This not only makes it hard to get service, but also greatly lowers the product's resale value.

High-end manufacturers also have very different policies regarding service. Some repair their products grudgingly, and/or charge high fees for fixing products out of warranty. Others bend over backward to keep their valued customers happy. In fact, some high-end audio companies go to extraordinary lengths to please their customers. One amplifier manufacturer who received an out-of-warranty product for repair not only fixed the amplifier free of charge, but replaced the customer's scratched faceplate at no cost! It pays in the long run to do business with manufacturers who have reputations for good customer service.

Another factor to consider before laying down your hard-earned cash is how long the product has been on the market. Without warning, manufacturers often discontinue products and replace them with new ones, or update a product to "Mark II" status. When this happens, the value of the older product drops immediately. If you know an excellent product is about to be discontinued, you can often buy the floor sample at a discount. This is a good way of saving money, provided the discount is significant. You end up with a lower price, plus all the service and support inherent in buying from an authorized and reputable dealer rather than a private party.

The best source of advance information on new products and what's about to be discontinued are reports in audio magazines from the annual Consumer Electronics Show.

Your Relationship with the Retailer

If, in the past, you've bought audio equipment only from mass-market retailers, you should expect to have an entirely different sort of relationship with a high-end dealer. The good specialty audio retailer doesn't just "move" boxes of electronics; he provides you with the satisfaction of great-sounding music in your home. More than just an equipment dealer, he's usually a dedicated audio and music enthusiast himself—he *knows* his products, and is often the best person to advise you on selecting equipment and system setup.

Consider the very different relationships between seller and buyer in the following scenarios. In the first, a used-car dealer in downtown Los Angeles is trying to sell a car to someone from out of town. The seller has only one shot at the buyer, and he intends to make the most of it. He doesn't care about return business, the customer's long-term satisfaction with the purchase, or what the customer will tell his friends about the dealer. It will be an adversarial relationship from start to finish.

Then consider a new-car dealer in Great Falls, Montana, selling a car to another Great Falls resident. For this dealer, return business is vital to his survival. So is customer satisfaction, quality service, providing expert advice on models and options, finding exactly the right car for the particular buyer, and giving the customer an occasional ride to work when he drops off his car for service. He knows his customers by name, and has developed mutually beneficial, long-term relationships with them.

If buying a mass-market hi-fi system is like negotiating with a used-car dealer in downtown L.A., selecting a high-end music system should be made within a relationship similar to the one enjoyed between the Montana dealer and his customers.

Take the time to establish a relationship with your local dealer. Make friends with him—it'll pay off in the long run. Get to know a particular salesperson and, if possible, the store's owner. Tell them your musical tastes, needs, lifestyle, and budget—then let them offer equipment suggestions. They know their products best, and can offer specific component recommendations. The good stores will regard you as a valued, long-term customer, not someone with whom they have one shot at making a sale. Don't shop just for equipment—shop for the retailer with the greatest honesty and competence.

Keep in mind, however, that dealers will naturally favor the brands they carry. Be suspicious of dealers who badmouth competing brands that have earned good reputations in the high-end audio press. The best starting point in assembling your system is a healthy mix of your dealer's recommendations and unbiased, competent magazine reviews.

The high-end retailing business is very different from the mass-market merchandising of the low-quality "home entertainment" products sold in appliance emporiums. The specialty retailer's annual turnover is vastly lower than that of the mid-fi store down the street. Consequently, the specialty retailer's profit margin must be larger for him to stay in business. Don't expect him to offer huge discounts and price cuts on equipment to take a sale from a mid-fi store. Because the high-end dealer offers so much more than just pushing a box over the counter, his prices just can't be competitive. Instead, you should be prepared to pay full list price—or very close to it.

Here's why. After paying his employees, rent, lights, heat, insurance, advertising, and a host of other expenses, the specialty audio retailer can expect to put in his pocket about five cents out of every dollar spent in his store. Now, if he discounts his price by even as little as 5%, he is essentially working for free, and only keeping his doors open a little longer. If the dealer offers a discount or marks down demonstration or discontinued units, you should take advantage of these opportunities. But don't expect the dealer to discount; he deserves the full margin provided by the product's suggested retail price.

In return for paying full price, however, you should receive a level of service and professionalism second to none. Expect the best from your dealer. Spend as much time as you feel is necessary auditioning components in the showroom before you buy. Listen to components at home in your own system before you buy. Ask the retailer to set up your system for you. Exploit the dealer's wide knowledge of what components are best for the money. Use his knowledge of system matching to get the best sound possible on a given budget. And if one of your components needs repair, don't be afraid to ask for a loaner until yours is fixed. The dealer should bend over backward to accommodate your needs.

If you give the high-end dealer your loyalty, you can expect this red-carpet treatment. This relationship can be undermined, however, if, to save a few dollars, you buy from a competitor or by mail a product that your dealer also sells. If the product purchased elsewhere doesn't sound good in your system, don't expect your local dealer to help you out. Further, don't abuse the home audition privilege. Take home only those products you're seriously considering buying. If the dealer let everyone take equipment home for an audition, he'd have nothing in the store to demonstrate. The home audition should be used to confirm that you've selected the right component through store auditioning, magazine reviews, and the dealer's recommendations. The higher price charged by the dealer may seem hard to justify at first, but in the long run you'll benefit from his expertise and commitment to you as a customer.

If you don't live close to any high-end dealers, there are several very good mail-order companies that offer excellent audio advice over the phone. They provide as much service as possible by phone, including money-back guarantees, product exchanges, and component-matching suggestions. You can't audition components in a store, but you can often listen to them in your system and get a refund if the product isn't what you'd hoped it would be.

In short, if you treat your dealer right, you can expect his full expertise and commitment to getting you the best sound possible. There's absolutely no substitute for a skilled dealer's services and commitment to your satisfaction.

I recently realized my long-time goal of having a full-sized, professional-quality pool table in my home. The experience of shopping for the table, choosing a retailer, and having the table installed drove home some truths about the way high-performance audio equipment should be sold.

After reading billiard magazines, looking through brochures, and talking with retailers, I decided on a brand and model. The salesperson, Suzanne, knew pool tables inside and out. Her father had owned a billiard room, and Suzanne spent her teenage years repairing and maintaining a fleet of tables. With more than 20 years' experience in the field, she had the answers to all of my questions.

After settling on a model, I visited a second dealer in town who carried the same brand. He knew virtually nothing about his product; I had to tell him about certain options—information I had learned from Suzanne. I also met the installer, who seemed to have been hired for his ability to carry nearly a thousand pounds of slate up stairs rather than his knowledge of assembling pool tables. Nonetheless, this second dealer offered me a lower price than Suzanne had.

I was certainly enticed by the dealer's discounted price. After all, a table is a table; it doesn't matter where you buy it because they all come from the same factory, right? I told Suzanne about the lower price and asked her to match it. She stuck to her price, telling me that her installation was worth the price difference.

Only when Suzanne was installing the table did I realize what a wise decision I'd made. Unbeknownst to me, installing a pool table is a highly skilled and exacting procedure. How the table is assembled greatly influences the table's playability. For example, how tightly the cloth is stretched over the slate affects the table's "speed," or how easily balls roll across it. This is a crucial factor, because if the table is too "fast" or "slow," it throws off one's game when playing in tournaments, on other tables. In addition, the cloth must be stretched uniformly to ensure consistent speed over the entire table. Suzanne also was meticulous in matching the three pieces of slate for a perfectly smooth and level surface. In addition, she made sure the underside of the cloth was perfectly clean and free from fuzz before installing it over the slate, which ensures freedom from bumps. I learned these and many other intricacies because Suzanne was training another installer while I listened in. The result is that my table performs extremely well. I have no doubt that the other dealer would never have brought the table to the same level of performance that Suzanne did.

What really matters, whether the subject is pool tables or high-performance audio equipment, is the final, installed performance in your home. I had no idea how crucial setup is in getting the most out of a pool table, and very nearly made a costly mistake in going for the lower price.

The setup, matching, and connection of high-end audio components is a process even more exacting than the installation of a pool table. That's why your dealer's skill and knowledge are crucial to realizing the best possible sound for your budget.

Used Equipment

A used audio component often sells for half its original list price, making used gear a tempting alternative. The lower prices on used high-end components provide an opportunity to get a high-quality system for the same budget as a less ambitious new system. Moreover, buying used gear lets you audition many components at length. If you find a product you like, keep it. If you don't like the sound of your used purchase, you can often sell it for no less than what you paid.

There are two ways of buying used equipment: from a dealer, and from a private party. A retailer may charge a little more for used products, but often offers a short warranty (60 or 90 days), and sometimes exchange privileges. Buying used gear from a reputable retailer is a lot less risky than dealing with a private party (unless you're buying from a friend).

The audiophile inclined to buy used equipment can often get great deals. Some audiophiles simply *must* own the latest and greatest product, no matter the cost. They'll buy a state-of-the-art component one year, only to sell it the next to acquire the current top of the line. These audiophiles generally take good care of the equipment and sell it at bargain-basement prices. If you can find such a person, have him put your name at the top of his calling list when he's ready to sell. You can end up with a superb system for a fraction of its original selling price.

A few pitfalls await the buyer of used equipment, though the disadvantages listed below apply mostly to buying from a private party rather than from a reputable dealer. First, there are no assurances that the component is working properly; the product could have a defect not apparent from a cursory examination. Second, the used product could be so outdated that its performance falls far short of new gear selling for the same price—or less—than the used component. This is especially true of CD players, CD transports, and digital processors. Third, a used product carries no warranty; you'll have to pay for any repair work. Finally, you must ask why the person is selling the used equipment. All too often, a music lover doesn't do his homework and buys a product that doesn't satisfy musically or work well with the rest of his system. If you see lots of people selling the same product, beware—it's a sign that the product has a fundamental musical flaw. Finally, buying used equipment from a private party eliminates everything that makes your local specialty retailer such an asset when selecting equipment: You don't get the dealer's expert opinions, home audition, trade or upgrade policy, dealer setup, warranty, dealer service, loaner units, or any of the other benefits you get from buying new at a dealer.

Approach used components with caution; they can be a windfall—or a nightmare.

Product Upgrades

Many manufacturers improve their products and offer existing customers the option of upgrading their components to current performance. This is the "Mark II" (or III or IV) designation on some products. The dealer can usually handle sending your component back to the factory. Some manufacturers prefer to deal with the customer directly, saving the dealer markup and keeping the upgrade price lower.

I have ambivalent feelings about manufacturer upgrades. Some upgrade programs provide lasting value to a company's customers. Enjoying the benefits of a company's advances without selling a component at a loss and buying a new one can be a wonderful bonus. Conversely, some manufacturers think of an upgrade program as a profit center, charging large amounts for even minor improvements. Consider a company's track record when evaluating potential future upgrades. For products that are upgradeable via software updates, ask how much these revisions will cost. Some manufacturers charge nothing, or a nominal fee, for updated software.

Setting Up Your System for the Best Sound

How your system is set up and installed in your home can make a big difference in the system's musical performance. There are many setup techniques whose individual audible differences may be very small, but that can dramatically increase a system's performance when combined. System setup requires listening skill (covered in the next chapter), patience, and a desire to extract the last bit of performance from your system. There's nothing more satisfying than realizing a significant audible improvement without spending a dime.

All system setup should be based on a foundation of good loudspeaker placement. (This topic is so important that I've devoted a large section of Chapter 4 to it.) Once you've made this coarse adjustment, you can work on refinements. As your system's sound improves, you'll become more attuned to small performance variations.

Chapters 4–11 include specific setup procedures for each component in the playback chain; Chapter 12 covers the accessories that will help you get the most out of your system. Here's a summary of the system setup techniques detailed in those chapters.

- Position the loudspeakers and listening seat for the best sound. Without proper loudspeaker and listener placement, none of the other setup techniques will matter. (Chapter 4)

- Add acoustic treatments to the listening room. They can have profound effects on the system's performance, and can make the difference between mediocre and superlative sound. (Chapter 4)

- Keep interconnects away from AC power cords. If they must meet, position them at right angles to each other instead of parallel. (Chapter 11)

- Keep digital data interconnects (between a separate CD transport and digital processor) and analog interconnects between source components and your preamplifier separate from each other. The very high frequencies carried by digital cables can radiate noise and pollute analog signals. (Chapter 8)

- Turn off your digital components when playing LPs.

- Keep interconnects and loudspeaker cables as short as possible, but always the same length between left and right. (Chapter 11)

- Position components for adequate ventilation. Overheating will shorten product life.

- Ensure good contact between loudspeaker cables and binding posts. Get the spade lug fully on the binding post and tighten with a nut driver. (Chapter 11)

- Clean plugs and jacks periodically with contact cleaner. (Chapter 12)

- Maintain adequate distance between the preamplifier and power amplifier. The power amp's large transformer can radiate 60Hz hum. This is more crucial in preamplifiers with phono stages or with separate phono preamps. (Chapter 6)

- Install the equipment on a sturdy stand. Vibration can degrade system performance, particularly that of turntables. (Chapters 9 and 12)

- Don't use light dimmers or fluorescent lighting in the listening room. Dimmers put lots of noise in the AC line, which gets into your components through their AC cords.

- Experiment with AC power conditioners. They make a huge improvement in some systems, none in others, and can sometimes degrade system performance. Listen before you buy. (Chapter 12)

• Try accessories such as isolation feet and high-end AC power
  cords, but only with the provision that you can return them for a
  full refund. (Chapter 12)

Component Selection Summary

When choosing a high-end system or component, follow these ten guidelines:

1) Establish your budget. Buy a component or system you'll be
   happy with in the long run, not one that will "do" for now. Do it
   right the first time.

2) Be an informed consumer—learn all you can about high-end
   audio. Study magazine reviews, visit your local specialty retailer,
   and read the rest of this book. Do your homework.

3) Develop a relationship with your dealer. He can be the best source
   of information in choosing components and assembling a system.

4) Find components that work synergistically. Again, your dealer
   knows his products and can offer suggestions.

5) Select products based on their musical qualities—not technical performance, favorable reviews, specifications, price, or brand name.

6) Choose carefully; many lower-priced components can outperform
   higher-priced ones. Take your time and maintain high standards—there are some great bargains out there.

7) Buy products from companies with good reputations for value, customer
   service, and reliability. Also, match the company's product philosophy
   (i.e., cost-no-object vs. best value for the money) to your needs.

8) When possible, listen to prospective components in your system
   at home before buying.

9) Follow the setup guidelines in this and subsequent chapters to get the
   most from your system. Enlist the aid of your dealer in system setup.

10) Add accessories *after* your system is set up.

If you read the rest of this book, subscribe to one or more reputable
high-end magazines, and follow these guidelines, you'll be well on your
way to making the best purchasing decisions—and having high-quality
music reproduction in your home.

One last piece of advice: After you get your system set up, forget
about the hardware. It's time to start enjoying music.

3 Becoming a Better Listener

Critical listening—the practice of evaluating the quality of audio equipment by careful analytical listening—is very different from listening for pleasure. The goal isn't to enjoy the musical experience, but to determine if a system or component sounds good or bad, and what *specific characteristics* of the sound make it good or bad. You want to critically examine what you're hearing so that you can form value judgments about the reproduced sound. You can then use this information to evaluate and choose components, and to set up a system.

Evaluating audio equipment by ear is essential—today's technical measurements simply aren't advanced enough to characterize the musical performance of audio products. The human hearing mechanism is vastly more sensitive and complex than the most sophisticated test equipment now available. Though technical performance is a valid consideration when choosing equipment, the ear should always be the final arbiter of good sound. Moreover, the musical significance of sonic differences between components can only be judged subjectively. This is best expressed by Michael Polanyi in his book, *Personal Knowledge*:

> *Whenever we find connoisseurship operating within science or technology we may assume it persists only because it has not been possible to replace it by a measurable grading.*

Because connoisseurship is used in the evaluation of audio products, the process is more an aesthetic endeavor than a purely technical one. Good technical performance can contribute to high-quality musical performance, but it doesn't tell you what you really want to know: how well the product communicates the musical message. To find that out, you must listen. I have auditioned hundreds of audio products for review and measured their technical performance in a test laboratory. My experience overwhelmingly indicates that much more about the quality of an audio component can be learned in the listening room than in the test lab.

Many newcomers to high-performance music reproduction—and even a small fringe group of experienced audiophiles—question the need for listening to evaluate products. They believe that measurements can tell them everything they need to know about a product's performance. And since these measurements are purely "objective," why interject human subjectivity through critical listening?

The answer is that the common measurements in use today were created decades ago as design tools, not as descriptors of sound quality. The test data generated by a typical mix of audio measurements were never meant to be a representation of musical reality, only a rough guide when designing. For example, an amplifier circuit that had 1% harmonic distortion was probably better than one with 10% harmonic distortion. It doesn't follow that a harmonic distortion specification in any way describes the sound of that amplifier.

A second problem is that audio test-bench measurements attempt to quantify a variety of two-dimensional phenomena: how much distortion the product introduces, its frequency response, noise level, and other factors. But music listening is a *three*-dimensional experience that is much more complex than any set of numbers can hope to quantify. How can you reduce to a series of mathematical symbols the ability of one power amplifier, and not another, to make the hair on your arms stand up? Or the feeling that a vocalist is singing directly *to you*?

I once read that a motorcycle manufacturer attempted to quantify the "feel" of prototype motorcycles by attaching sensors at many positions around the motorcycle and putting the motorcycle on a dynamometer in a wind tunnel. The large amount of data collected was then processed to guide the engineers in designing improvements in the motorcycle's handling and overall riding experience. After investing a significant amount of money in the project, the company went back to relying on the comments of experienced test riders who could describe the experience, in "subjective" terms, of how the motorcycle "felt."

Judging music-reproduction equipment is no different. No matter how many measurements are gathered about the product's technical performance, they still don't tell you how well that product communicates the music. If I had to choose between two unknown CD players as my main source of music for the next five years, I'd rather have ten minutes with each player in the listening room than ten hours with each in the test lab. Today's measurements are crude tools that are inferior to the most powerful test instrument ever devised: the human brain.

A type of vacuum-tubed amplifier called "single-ended triode" (described in Chapter 6) illustrates the limitations of measurement to describe the musical attributes of audio components. All single-ended triode amplifiers have technical performance that is, by any standard, laughably bad. They have high distortion, absurdly low output power (often less than ten watts per channel), and can drive very few loudspeakers. Nonetheless, single-ended triode amplifiers can have a directness of musical communication that must be heard to be believed.

Richard Heyser, one of the greatest conceptual thinkers in audio, created a stunningly simple device that revealed the fallacy of relying solely on measurements to judge the quality of audio equipment. The device was a small box with an input jack on one end and an output jack on the other end. When connected to test equipment, the box measured perfectly; it had no distortion, no frequency-response aberrations, and no noise. Indeed, the measurements suggested that all the box contained was a piece of wire connecting input to output.

But when you listened to music through the box, the sound was so distorted it was nearly unintelligible. The secret to the Heyser Box is simple: when the box detected the pure, single-frequency sinewaves used in audio testing, a relay inside the box simply connected the input to the output. But when it detected a music signal, with its complex waveform, the relay was repeatedly opened and closed quickly so that the output "chattered." The Heyser Box brilliantly illustrates the danger of relying purely on measurement rather than listening when evaluating audio equipment performance.

I must point out, however, that some sophisticated audio designers have developed tests and measurements that are far more advanced than the decades-old parameters routinely used in the audio industry. These advanced measurements can, in some cases, reliably predict specific aspects of audible performance. As their creators are the first to admit, these measurements don't quantify the overall musical experience, nor are they a replacement for critical listening. The measurements are instead tools that help the designer more quickly or more reliably achieve some specifically sought sonic attribute in a product (less treble hardness, for example). Unfortunately, designers consider these sophisticated techniques trade secrets and don't share them with the audio engineering community at large.

Given a massive research budget, it may one day be possible to more reliably predict sound quality through measured performance. But that day is a long way off. Until then, we must listen. (The dichotomy between "subjective" and "objective" audio is addressed in Appendix D, a newly revised and updated version of my Audio Engineering Society Paper "The Role of Critical Listening in Evaluating Audio Equipment Quality."

Knowing what sounds good and what doesn't is easy; most people can tell the difference between excellent and poor sound. But discovering *why* a product is musically satisfying or not, and the ability to recognize and describe subtle differences in sound quality, are learned skills. Like all skills, that of critical listening improves with practice: The more you listen, the better a listener you'll become. As your ear improves, you'll be able to distinguish smaller and smaller differences in reproduced sound quality—and be able to describe *how* two presentations are different, and why one is better.

This chapter defines the language of critical listening, describes what to listen for, and outlines the procedures for setting up valid listening comparisons. It will either get you started in critical listening, or help you become a more highly skilled listener.

Audiophile Values

A general discussion of audiophile values is important in understanding the next sections of this chapter. Here are some broad statements about what distinguishes good from superlative sound quality, and audiophile value in reproduced music.

Good sound is only a means to the end of musical satisfaction; it is not the end itself. If a neighbor or colleague invites you over to hear his hi-fi system, you can tell immediately whether he's a music lover or a "hi-fi buff" more interested in sound than in music. If he plays the music very loud, then turns it down after 30 seconds to seek your opinion (approval), he's probably not a music lover. If, however, he sits you down, asks what kind of music *you* like, plays it at a reasonable volume, and says or does nothing for the next 20 minutes while you both listen, it's likely that this person holds audiophile values or simply cares a lot about music.

In the first example, the acquaintance tried to impress you with *sound*. In the second case, your friend also wanted to impress you with his system, but by its ability to express the *music*, not shake the walls. This is the fundamental difference between "hi-fi enthusiasts" and music lovers.

(You can use the same test to immediately tell what kind of hi-fi store you're in. If anyone pulls out a CD of trains, sonic booms, Shuttle launches, or jet takeoffs, run for cover.)

I've noticed an unusual trend when playing my system for friends and acquaintances not involved in audio. I sit them down in the "sweet spot" (the seating position that provides the best sound) and put on some music I think they'll like. Rather than sitting there for the whole piece or song, they tend to jump up immediately and tell me how good it sounds. They've apparently been conditioned by the kind of razzle-dazzle demonstrations in some hi-fi stores or friends' houses. When *you* begin listening—at someone's house or a dealer's showroom—don't feel the need to express an opinion about the sound. Sit and listen attentively with eyes closed, letting the *music*—not the sound—tell you how good the system is.

When listening in a group, don't be swayed by others' opinions. If they're skilled listeners, try to understand what they're talking about. Listen to their descriptions and compare their impressions with your own. In fact, this is the best way to recognize the specific sonic character-istics we'll talk about later in this chapter. But don't go along with what everyone else says. If you don't hear a difference between two digital cables, for example, don't be afraid to say so. In addition, you should be completely truthful when asked for an opinion about a system. If the sound is bad, say so.

All audio components affect the signal passing through them. Some products add artifacts (distortion) such as a *grainy treble* or a *lumpy bass*. Others subtract parts of the signal—for example, a loudspeaker that doesn't go very low in the bass. (Listening terms are defined later in this chapter.) A fundamental audiophile value holds that sins of commission (adding something to the music) are far worse than sins of omission (removing something from the music). If parts of the music are missing, the ear/brain system subconsciously fills in what isn't there; you can still enjoy listening. But if the playback system adds an artificial character to the sound, you are constantly reminded that you're hearing a reproduction and not the real thing.

Let's illustrate this sins-of-commission/omission dichotomy with two loudspeakers. The first loudspeaker—a three-way system with a 15" woofer in a very large cabinet—sells for a moderate price in a mass-market appliance store; it plays loudly and develops lots of bass. The second loudspeaker sells for about the same price, but is a small two-way system with a 6" woofer. It doesn't play nearly as loudly, and produces much less bass. While you need a refrigerator dolly to move the first loudspeaker, you can almost hold the second loudspeaker in your outstretched hand.

The behemoth loudspeaker has some problems: The bass is boomy, thick, and overwhelming. All the bass notes seem to have the same pitch. The very prominent treble is coarse and grainy, and the midrange has a big peak of excess energy that makes singers sound as if they have colds.

The small loudspeaker has no such problems. The treble is smooth and clear, and the midrange is pure and open. It has, however, very little bass by comparison, won't play very loudly, and doesn't produce a physical sensation of sound hitting your body.

The first loudspeaker commits sins of commission, *adding* unnatural artifacts to the sound. The bass peaks that make it sound boomy, the grain overlaying the treble, and the midrange colorations are all additive distortions.

The second loudspeaker's faults, however, are of omission. It *removes* certain elements of the music—low bass and the ability to play loudly—but leaves the remainder of the music intact. It doesn't add grain to the treble, thickness to the bass, or colorations to the midrange.

There's no doubt that the second loudspeaker will be more musically satisfying. The first loudspeaker's additive distortions are not only much more musically objectionable, they also constantly remind you that you are listening to artificially reproduced music. The second loudspeaker's flaws are of a nature that allows you to forget that you're listening to loudspeakers. In the reproduction of music, addition is far worse than subtraction.

Another audiophile value holds that even small differences in the quality of the musical presentation are important. Because music matters to us, we get excited by *any* improvement in sound quality. Moreover, there isn't a linear relationship between the magnitude of a sonic difference and its musical significance. A quality difference can be sonically small but musically large.

While reviewing a revelatory new state-of-the-art digital-to-analog converter, I listened to a piece of music I'd heard hundreds of times before. The piece, performed by a five-member group, had vocals and very long instrumental breaks. During the instrumental breaks, the vocalist played percussion instruments. Through lesser-quality digital processors, the percussion had always been just another sound fused into the music's tapestry; I'd never heard it as a separate instrument played by the vocalist. The group seemed to become a four-piece ensemble when the vocalist wasn't singing; I never heard the percussion as separate from the rest of the music.

The new digital processor was particularly good at resolving individual instruments and presenting them not as just more sounds homogenized into the overall musical fabric, but as distinct entities. Consequently, when the instrumental break came, I heard the percussion as a separate, more prominent instrument. In my mind's eye, and for the first time, the vocalist never left—she remained "on stage," playing the percussion instruments. By just this "small" change in the presentation, the band went from being a quartet to a quintet during the instrumental breaks. The "objective" difference in the electrical signal must have been minuscule; the subjective musical consequences were profound.

This is why small differences in the musical presentation are important—*if* you care deeply enough about music and about how well it is reproduced. "Small" improvements can have large subjective consequences. This example highlights the inability of measurements alone to characterize audio equipment performance. Measurements on the digital-to-analog converter in question indicated no technical attributes that would have contributed to my perceptions. More fundamentally, how can a number representing some aspect of the digital converter's technical performance begin to describe the musical significance of the change I heard?

Much of music's expression and meaning can be found in such minutiae of detail, subtlety, and nuance. When such subtlety is conveyed by the playback system, you feel a vastly deeper communication with the musicians. Their intent and expression are more vivid, allowing you to more deeply appreciate their artistry. For example, if you compare two performances of Max Reger's Sonata in D Major for solo violin—one competent, the other superlative—you could say that, on an objective basis, they were virtually identical. Both performers played the same notes at about the same tempo. The difference in expression is in the nuances—the inspired subtleties of rubato, tempo, emphasis, articulation, and dynamics that bring the performance to life and convey the piece's musical meaning and intent. This example is analogous to the difference between mediocre and superb music playback systems, and why small differences in sound quality can matter so much. High-end audio is about reproducing these nuances so that you can come one step closer to the musical expression.

The sad but universal truth about audio equipment is that, any time you put a signal into an audio component, it *never* comes out better at the other end. You therefore want to keep the signal path as simple as possible, to remove any unnecessary electronics from between you and the music. This is why inserting equalizers and other such "enhancers" into the signal chain is usually a bad idea—the less done to the signal, the better. The advent of digital technology, however, has made possible some beneficial signal processing. (An example is digital room correction, described in Chapter 4.)

Pitfalls of Becoming a Critical Listener

There are dangers inherent in developing critical listening skills. The first is an inability to distinguish between critical listening and listening for pleasure. Once started on the path of critiquing sound quality, it's all too easy to forget that the reason you're involved in audio is because you love music, and to start thinking that every time you hear music, you must have an opinion about what's right and what's wrong with the sound. This is the surest path toward a condition humorously known as *Audiophilia nervosa*. Symptoms of *Audiophilia nervosa* include constantly changing equipment, playing only one track of a CD or LP at a time instead of the whole record, changing cables for certain music, refusing to listen to great music if it happens to be poorly recorded, and in general "listening to the hardware" instead of to the music.

But high-end audio is about making the hardware disappear. When listening for pleasure—which should be the vast majority of your listening time—forget about the system. Forget about critical listening. Shift into critical-listening mode only when you need to make a value judgment, or just for practice to become a better listener. Draw the line between critical listening and listening for pleasure—and know when to cross it and when *not* to cross it.

There is also the related danger that your standards of sound quality will rise to such a height that you can't enjoy music unless it's "perfectly" reproduced—in other words, to the point that you can't enjoy music, period. Although it's not very high-quality reproduction, I get a great deal of pleasure from my car stereo—don't let being an audiophile interfere with *your* enjoyment of music, anytime, anywhere. When you can't control the sound quality, lower your expectations.

Sonic Descriptions and their Meanings

The biggest problem in critical listening is finding words to express our perceptions and experiences. We hear things in reproduced music that are difficult to identify and put into words. A listening vocabulary is essential not only to conveying to others what we hear, but also to recognizing and understanding our own perceptions. If you can attach a descriptive name to a perception, you can more easily recognize that perception when you experience it again.

A perfect example of the bond between words and perceptions is found in Michael Polanyi's *Personal Knowledge*. His description of the radiology student's experience is identical to that of the audiophile becoming a skilled critical listener:

> *Think of a medical student attending a course in the X-ray diagnosis of pulmonary diseases. He watches in a darkened room shadowy traces on a fluorescent screen placed against a patient's chest, and hears the radiologist commenting to his assistants in technical language, on the significant features of these shadows. At first the student is completely puzzled. For he can see in the X-ray picture of a chest only the shadows of the heart and the ribs, with a few spidery blotches between them. The experts seem to be romancing about figments of their imagination; he can see nothing that they are talking about. Then as he goes on listening for a few weeks, looking carefully at ever new pictures of different cases, a tentative understanding will dawn on him; he will gradually forget about the ribs and begin to see the lungs. And eventually, if he perseveres intelligently, a rich panorama of significant details will be revealed to him; of physiological variations and pathological changes, of scars, of chronic infections and signs of acute disease. He has entered a new world. He still sees only a fraction of what the experts can see, but the pictures are definitely making sense now and so do most of the comments made on them. He is about to grasp what he is being taught; it has clicked. Thus, at the moment when he has learned the language of pulmonary radiology, the student will also have learned to understand pulmonary radiograms. The two can only happen together. Both halves of the problem set to us by an unintelligible text, referring to an unintelligible subject, jointly guide our efforts to solve them, and they are solved eventually together by discovering a conception which comprises a joint understanding of both the words and the things.*

Just as the student learns to understand pulmonary radiograms at the moment he learns the language of pulmonary radiology, the audiophile learns to identify specific sonic characteristics when he learns the language of critical listening. The bond between words and ideas is inextricable. That's why listening with more skilled listeners is the best way to learn to identify differences yourself.

By describing in detail the specific sonic characteristics of how electronic components change the sound of music passing through them, I hope to attune you to recognizing those same characteristics when you listen. After reading this next section, listen to two products for yourself and try to hear what I'm describing. It can be any two products—if you have a portable CD player, hook it up to your system and compare it to your home CD player. Even comparing a CD and a cassette made from that CD will get you started. The important thing is to start listening analytically. If you don't hear the sonic differences immediately, keep listening. The more you listen, the more sensitive you'll become to those differences.

Each listener hears a little differently. What I listen for during critical listening may be different from another listener's sonic checklist. Moreover, the different values placed on different aspects of the sonic presentation are matters of taste. I notice this first-hand when I occasionally spend time listening critically in my listening room with visiting manufacturers and designers of high-end equipment—many of them highly skilled listeners. While we share many commonalities in determining what sounds good, there is a wide range of perception about what aspects of the presentation are most important.

For example, some listeners value correct reproduction of timbre above all else. A product may have outstanding bass, spectacular sound-staging, and clean treble, but if the timbre is synthetic or hard, those other good qualities won't matter to that listener. Another listener may find soundstaging of utmost importance. Finally, a layer of treble grain that is hardly noticed by one listener may be unacceptable to another. We all hear differently, and value different things in music reproduction. Not only that, but a single listener's musical perceptions and acuity vary with the time of day, as well as his mood and state of relaxation.

There's also evidence that people perceive soundstage information (the impression of music occupying a physical space) in two different ways. When you sit between two loudspeakers reproducing the same signal, your ears each send the same signal to your brain. You thus interpret the sound as coming from a point exactly between the loudspeakers. If the sound suddenly becomes slightly louder in the left loudspeaker, your brain concludes that the sound source is slightly left of center. This method of localization is called "intensity stereo": the information your brain uses to localize the sound is the difference in volume, or intensity, between your left and right ears.

A second method of localizing sounds and forming a soundstage in your head uses the phase (timing) information in a recording. Consider our two loudspeakers reproducing the same signal, which you hear as existing between the two speakers. If the left-channel signal is delayed slightly (a few thousandths of a second), you hear the image shift to the right. Although both loudspeakers are producing the same volume of signal, the image appears to come from the loudspeaker that produces the sound first. The two signals are said to have a different phase (timing) relationship to each other.

Some listeners are much more attuned to phase information than others. In recordings made in acoustic spaces (as opposed to recording studios), the phase information is enormously complex. As sounds reflect from the walls of the acoustic space, they create an almost infinitely dense pattern of very slight delays. It is this temporal (timing) information that cues your brain as to the depth of images, the focus of the images, and the overall size and scale of the concert hall. If a hi-fi system doesn't accurately resolve this temporal information, the sound-stage is foreshortened and image placement is vague—to some listeners. Other listeners may not hear the difference between a system that resolves these spatial cues and one that does not. That isn't to say that one way of listening is better than another, only that it appears that two separate mechanisms exist.

The recording that, in my experience, is most revealing of a system's ability to correctly preserve phase information is John Rutter's *Requiem* on the Reference Recordings label. When this disc is played back through a first-rate system, one's ability to hear the placement of individual images, along with the sense of the hall's size and characteristics, is stunning. Even a slight degradation of this recording's phase information reduces these qualities. (See Appendix A, "Sound and Hearing," for more on human hearing.)

The following description of what I listen for is a reflection of my own tastes, mixed with what I've learned from other skilled listeners. You may have your own sonic priorities, but the important thing is that we all hear and describe the same characteristics with the same language. The descriptive terms presented here can be found in my and other writers' product reviews for *The Absolute Sound*. There is general agreement about what these terms mean, but shades of meaning vary among individual listeners.

You should also know that recordings made with audiophile techniques are more revealing of some aspects of reproduced sound than recordings made for mass consumption. For example, a recording of classical music made in a concert hall with very few microphones, a simple signal path, and high-quality recording equipment will likely reveal more about a component's soundstaging performance than a pop recording made in a studio. Similarly, most mass-market recordings have little low bass and almost no dynamic range so that they sound "good" on a 4" car-stereo speaker. For these reasons, some of the sonic terms described in this chapter apply much more to audiophile-quality recordings than to mass-market ones.

When I listen critically to an audio component to characterize its sonic and musical performance and form judgments about that product, I first follow the setup procedures described later in this chapter. They are vital to forming accurate impressions of products, but secondary to the following discussion.

The sonic terms and characteristics defined here apply to audio components in general. Advice on what to listen for when choosing specific components is included in Chapters 5–13. Note that we often describe differences in terms of differences in frequency response (i.e., "too much treble"). The component may have a flat (accurate) measured treble response, but the distortions it introduces give the impression of too much treble.

It's also useful to understand the broad terms that describe the audio frequency band. The range of human hearing, which spans ten octaves from about 16Hz (cycles per second) to 20,000Hz, or 20 kilohertz (20kHz), can be divided into the specific regions described below. Note that these divisions are somewhat arbitrary; you can't say specifically that the lower treble begins at 2000Hz and not 2500Hz, for example. The table nonetheless provides a rough guideline for understanding the relationship between frequency ranges and their descriptive names.

Frequency Range		
Lower Limit	Upper Limit	Description
16	40	Deep Bass
40	100	Midbass
100	250	Upper Bass
250	500	Lower Midrange
500	1000	(Middle) Midrange
1000	2000	Upper Midrange
2000	3500	Lower Treble
3500	6000	Middle Treble
6000	10,000	Upper Treble
10,000	20,000	Top Octave

This rough guide will help you understand the following terms and definitions. A full characterization of how a product "sounds" will include aspects of each of the following sonic qualities.

Tonal Balance

The first aspect of the musical presentation to listen for is the product's overall *tonal balance*. How well balanced are the bass, midrange, and treble? If it sounds as though there is too much treble, we call the presentation *bright*. The impression of too little treble produces a *dull* or *rolled-off* sound. If the bass overwhelms the rest of the music, we say the presentation is *heavy* or *weighty*. If we hear too little bass, we call the presentation *thin, lightweight, uptilted,* or *lean*.

A product's tonal balance is a significant—and often overwhelming—aspect of its sonic signature.

Overall Perspective

The term *perspective* describes the apparent distance between the listener and the music. Perspective is largely a function of the recording (particularly the distance between the performers and the microphones), but is also affected by components in the playback system. Some products push the presentation *forward*, toward the listener; others sound more *distant*, or *laid-back*. The forward product presents the music in front of the loudspeakers; the laid-back product makes the music appear slightly behind the loudspeakers. Put another way, the forward product sounds as though the musicians have taken a few steps toward you; the laid-back product gives the impression that the musicians have taken a few steps back.

Another way of describing perspective is by row number in a concert hall. Some products seem to "seat" the listener at the front of the hall—in Row D, say. Others give you the impression that you're sitting farther back; say, in Row S.

Several other terms describe perspective. *Dry* generally means lacking reverberation and space, but can also apply to a forward perspective. Other watchwords for a forward presentation are *immediate, incisive, vivid, aggressive,* and *present.* Terms associated with laid-back include *lush, easygoing,* and *gentle.*

Products with a forward presentation produce a greater sense of an instrument's *presence* before you, but can quickly become fatiguing. Conversely, if the presentation is too laid-back, the music is uninvolving and lacking in immediacy. If the product under evaluation distorts the perspective captured during the recording, I prefer that it err in the direction of being laid-back. When a product is overly immediate, I feel as though the music is coming at me, assaulting my ears. The reaction is to close up, to try to keep the music at arm's length. The ideal midrange presentation has a sense of *palpable presence*, that feeling of the musicians existing right before you, but without sounding aggressive.

Conversely, a laid-back presentation invites the listener in, pulling her gently forward *into* the music, allowing her the space to explore its subtleties. It's like the difference between having a conversation with someone who is aggressive, gets in your face, and talks too loudly, compared with someone who stands back, speaking quietly and calmly.

In loudspeakers, perspective is often the result of a peak or dip in the midrange (a peak is too much energy, a dip is too little). In fact, the midrange between 1kHz and 3kHz is called the *presence region* because it provides a sense of presence and immediacy. The harmonics of the human voice span the presence region; thus, the voice is greatly affected by a product's perspective.

Untrained listeners who can't specifically identify whether a reproduced musical presentation is forward or laid-back will feel a tension that usually translates into a desire to turn down the music if the presentation is too forward. Conversely, a laid-back presentation can make the music uninvolving rather than riveting.

Note that the terms associated with overall perspective can be used to describe specific aspects of the presentation (such as the treble) in addition to describing the overall perspective. If we say the treble is forward, we mean that it is overly prominent, sounding as if it is closer to the listener than the rest of the music.

The Treble

Good treble is essential to high-quality music reproduction. In fact, many otherwise excellent audio products fail to satisfy musically because of poor treble performance.

The treble characteristics we want to avoid are described by the terms *bright, tizzy, forward, aggressive, hard, brittle, edgy, dry, white, bleached, wiry, metallic, sterile, analytical, screechy,* and *grainy.* Treble problems are pervasive; look how many adjectives we use to describe them.

If a product has too much apparent treble, it overstates sounds that are already rich in high frequencies. Examples are overemphasized cymbals, excessive sibilance (*s* and *sh* sounds) in vocals, and violins that sound thin. A product with too much apparent treble is called *bright.* Brightness is a prominence in the treble region, primarily between 3kHz and 6kHz. Brightness can be caused by a rising frequency response in loudspeakers, or by poor electronic design. Many CD players and solid-state amplifiers that measure as having a flat (accurate) frequency response nevertheless add prominence to the treble.

Tizzy describes too much upper treble (6kHz–10kHz), characterized as a *whitening* of the treble. Tizzy cymbals have an emphasis on the upper harmonics, the sizzle and air that rides over the main cymbal sound. Tizziness gives cymbals more of an *sssss* than a *sssshhhh* sound.

Forward, if applied to treble, is very similar to *bright*; both describe too much treble. A forward treble, however, also tends to be dry, lacking space and air around it.

Many of the terms listed above have virtually identical meanings. *Hard, brittle,* and *metallic* all describe an unpleasant treble characteristic that reminds one of metal being struck. In fact, the unique harmonic structure created from the impact of metal on metal is very similar to the distortion introduced by a power amplifier when it is asked to play louder than it is capable of playing.

I find the sound of the alto saxophone to be a good gauge of hard, brittle, and metallic treble, particularly lower treble. If reproduced incorrectly, sax can take on a thin, reedy, very unpleasant tone. The antithesis of this sound is *rich, warm,* and *full.* When the sax's upper harmonics are reproduced with a metallic character, the whole instrument's sound collapses. Interestingly, the sound of the saxophone has the most complex

harmonic structure of any instrument. It's no wonder that it is so revealing of treble problems.

White and *bleached* have meanings very similar to *bright*, but I associate them more with a thinness in the treble, often caused by a lack of
energy (or what sounds like a lack of energy) in the upper midrange.
With no supporting harmonic structure beneath it, the treble becomes
threadbare and thin, much like an overexposed photograph. Cymbals
should have a gong-like low-frequency component with a sheen over it.
If cymbals sound like bursts of white noise (the sound you hear between
radio stations), what you're probably hearing is a *white* or *bleached*
sound.

A particularly annoying treble characteristic is *graininess*. Treble
grain is a coarseness overlaying treble textures. I notice it most on solo
violin, massed violins, flute, and female voice. On flute, treble grain is
recognizable as a rough or fuzzy sound that seems to ride on top of the
flute's dynamic envelope. (That is, the grain follows the flute's volume.)
Grain makes violins sound as though they're being played with hacksaw
blades rather than bows—a gross exaggeration, but one that conveys the
idea of the coarse texture added by grain.

Treble grain can be of any texture, from very fine to coarse and
rough. (Think of the difference between 400-grit and 80-grit sandpaper.)
The more coarse the grain, the more objectionable it is. The preceding
discussion of grain applies in even larger measure to midrange textures,
which I'll discuss later.

Treble problems can foster the interesting perception that the treble
isn't integrated into the music's harmonic tapestry, but is riding on top
of it. The top end seems somehow separate from the music, not an integral part of the presentation. When this happens, we are aware of the
treble as a distinct entity, not as just another aspect of the music. If the
treble calls attention to itself, be suspicious.

The most common sources of these problems are, in rough order of
descending magnitude: tweeters in loudspeakers, overly reflective listening rooms, digital source components (usually the CD player or digital
processor), preamplifiers, power amplifiers, cables, and dirty AC power
sources.

So far, I've discussed only problems that emphasize treble. Some
products tend to make the treble softer and less prominent than live
music. This characteristic is often designed into the product, either to
compensate for treble flaws in other components in the system, or to
make the product sound more palatable. Deliberately softening the treble is the designer's shortcut; if he can't get the treble right, he just
makes it less offensive by softening it.

The following terms, listed in order of increasing magnitude,
describe good treble performance: *smooth, sweet, soft, silky, gentle, liquid,*
and *lush*. When the treble becomes overly smooth, we say it is *romantic,
rolled-off,* or *syrupy*. A treble described as "smooth, sweet, and silky" is

being complimented; "rolled-off and syrupy" suggests that the component goes too far in treble smoothness, and is therefore *colored*.

A rolled-off and syrupy treble may be blessed relief after hearing bright, hard, and grainy treble, but it isn't musically satisfying in the long run. Such a presentation tends to become *bland, uninvolving, slow, thick, closed-in,* and *lacking detail.* All these terms describe the effects of a treble presentation that errs too far on the side of smoothness. The presentation will lack *life, air, openness, extension,* and a sense of *space* if the treble is too soft. The music sounds closed-in rather than being big and open.

Top-octave air describes a sense of almost unlimited treble extension, which fosters the impression of hearing the air in which the music exists. A slight treble rolloff (a reduction in the amount of treble) in loudspeakers, for example, can diminish top-octave air. Loss of top-octave air is also associated with an opaque soundstage.

The best treble presentation is one that sounds most like real music. It should have lots of energy—cymbals can, after all, sound quite aggressive in real life—yet not have a synthetic, grainy, or dry character. We don't hear these characteristics in live music; we shouldn't hear them in reproduced music. More important, the treble should sound like an integral part of the music, not a detached noise riding on top of it. If a component has a colored treble presentation, however, it is far less musically objectionable if it errs on the side of smoothness rather than brightness.

The Midrange

J. Gordon Holt, *Stereophile* magazine founder and the father of subjective audio equipment evaluation, once wrote, "If the midrange isn't right, nothing else matters."

The midrange is important for several reasons. First, most of the musical energy is in the midrange, particularly the important lower harmonics of most instruments. Not only does this region contain most of the musical energy, but the human ear is much more sensitive to midrange and lower treble than to bass and upper treble. Specifically, the ear is most sensitive to sounds between about 800Hz and 3kHz, and to small changes in both low volume and frequency response within this band. The ear's threshold of hearing—i.e., the softest sound we can hear—is dramatically lower in the midband than at the frequency extremes. We've developed this additional midband acuity probably because the energy of most of the sounds we heard every day for thousands of years—the human voice, rustling leaves, the sounds of other animals—is concentrated in the midrange.

Midrange colorations can be extremely annoying. Loudspeakers with peaks and dips in the mids sound very unnatural; the midrange is absolutely the worst place for loudspeaker imperfections. Confining our discussion to loudspeakers for the moment, midrange colorations overlay the music with a common characteristic that emphasizes certain sounds. The male speaking voice is particularly revealing of midrange anomalies, which are often described by comparisons with vowel sounds. A particular coloration may impart an *aaww* sound; a coloration lower in frequency may emphasize *ooohhh* sounds; a higher-pitched coloration may sound like *eeeee*; another coloration might sound *hooty*.

Some midrange colorations can be likened to the sound of someone speaking through cupped hands. Try reading this sentence while cupping your hands around your mouth. Open and close your hands while listening to how the sound of your voice changes. That's the kind of midrange coloration we sometimes hear from loudspeakers—particularly mass-market ones.

In short, if recordings of male speaking voice sound monotonous, tiring, and resonant, it's probably the result of peaks and dips in the loudspeaker's frequency response. (These colorations are most apparent on male voice when listening to just one loudspeaker.)

Terms to describe poor midrange performance include *peaky, colored, chesty, boxy, nasal, congested, honky,* and *thick. Chesty* describes a lower-midrange coloration that makes vocalists sound as though they have colds. *Boxy* refers to the impression that the sound is coming out of a box instead of existing in open space. *Nasal* is usually associated with an excess of energy that spans a narrow frequency range, producing a sound similar to talking with your nose pinched. *Honky* is similar to nasal, but higher in frequency and spanning a wider frequency range.

Loudspeaker design has progressed so much in the past ten years that horrible midrange colorations are largely a thing of the past (at least in loudspeakers with high-end aspirations). Still, colorations persist—particularly in inexpensive loudspeakers—though they tend to be more subtle.

One type of lower-midrange coloration that still afflicts even moderately priced high-end loudspeakers is caused by vibration of the loudspeaker's cabinet. The loudspeaker will resonate at certain frequencies, launching acoustic energy from the cabinet when those frequencies are excited by certain notes in the music. Cabinet resonances are heard as certain notes "sticking out" or "jumping forward." This problem is clearly audible on solo piano; ascending or descending left-hand lines reveal that certain notes possess a character clearly different from the rest of the instrument's notes. These problem notes jump out because they have more energy; some of the sound is being produced by the loudspeaker cabinet, and not just by the loudspeaker's drive units (the cones that move back and forth to create sound). The same thing happens with musical instruments; the musician's expression "wolf tone" describes the same phenomenon. This problem also afflicts the upper bass. In Chapter 7 I talk in much greater detail about loudspeaker cabinet vibration.

As described previously under "Perspective," too much midrange energy can make the presentation seem forward and "in your face." A broad dip in the midrange response (too little midrange energy over a wide frequency span) can give an impression of greater distance between you and the presentation.

When choosing loudspeakers, be especially attuned to the midrange colorations described. What is a very minor—even barely noticeable—problem heard during a brief audition can turn into a major irritant over extended listening.

The preceding descriptions apply primarily to midrange problems introduced by loudspeakers. Expanding the discussion to include electronics (preamps and power amps) and source components (LP playback or a digital source) introduces different aspects of midrange performance that we should be aware of.

An important factor in midrange performance is how instrumental textures are reproduced. Texture is the physical impression of the instrument's sound—its fabric rather than its tone. The closest musical term for texture is timbre, defined by *Merriam Webster's Collegiate Dictionary, Tenth Edition* as "the quality given to a sound by its overtones; the quality of tone distinctive of a particular singing voice or instrument." Sonic artifacts added by electronics often affect instrumental and vocal textures.

The term *grainy*, introduced in the description of treble problems, also applies to the midrange. In fact, midrange grain can be more objectionable than treble grain. Midrange grain is characterized by a coarseness of instrumental and vocal textures; the instrument's texture is granular rather than smooth.

Midrange textures can also sound hard and brittle. Hard textures are apparent on massed voices; a choir sounds *glassy*, *shiny*, and *synthetic*. This problem gets worse as the choir's volume increases. At low levels, you may not hear these problems. But as the choir swells, the sound becomes hard and irritating. Piano is also very revealing of hard midrange textures, the higher notes sounding annoyingly *brittle*. When the midrange lacks these unpleasant artifacts, we say the textures are *liquid*, *smooth*, *sweet*, *velvety*, and *lush*.

A related midrange problem is *stridency*. I think of stridency as a combination of thinness (lack of warmth), hardness, and forwardness, all in the midrange. Strident vocals emphasize mouth noises and overlay the texture with a whitish grain. A saxophone can thus sound thin and reedy, though in a different way from that described as treble grain. A strident sax is hard, more forward in the mids, and granular in texture. Stridency can be caused by an apparent thinness in the lower midrange that makes the upper midrange too prominent. A product described as "strident" has been severely criticized.

Many of these midrange and treble problems are grouped together under the term *harshness*.

Other midrange characteristics affect such areas as clarity, transparency, and detail. These are discussed later, under more specific categories.

The Bass

Bass performance is the most misunderstood aspect of reproduced sound, among the general public and hi-fi buffs alike. The popular belief is that the more bass, the better. This is reflected in ads for "sub-woofers" that promise "earthshaking bass" and the ability to "rattle pant legs and stun small animals." The ultimate expression of this perversity is boom trucks that have absurd amounts of extraordinarily bad bass reproduction.

But we want to know how the product reproduces *music*, not earthquakes. What matters to the music lover isn't *quantity* of bass, but the *quality* of that bass. We don't just want the physical feeling that bass provides; we want to hear subtlety and nuance. We want to hear precise pitch, lack of coloration, and the sharp attack of plucked acoustic bass. We want to hear every note and nuance in fast, intricate bass playing, not a muddled roar. If Ray Brown, Stanley Clarke, John Patitucci, Dave La Rue, Dave Holland, or Eddie Gomez is working out, we want to hear *exactly* what they're doing. In fact, if the bass is poorly reproduced, we'd rather not hear much bass at all.

Correct bass reproduction is essential to satisfying musical reproduction. Low frequencies constitute music's tonal foundation and rhythmic anchor. Unfortunately, bass is difficult to reproduce, whether by source components, power amplifiers, or—especially—loudspeakers and rooms.

Perhaps the most prevalent bass problem is lack of *pitch definition* or *articulation*. These two terms describe the ability to hear bass as individual notes, each having an attack, a decay, and a specific pitch (these terms are explained in Appendix A). You should hear the texture of the bass, whether it's the sonorous resonance of a bowed double bass or the unique character of a Fender Precision. Low frequencies contain a surprising amount of detail when reproduced correctly.

When the bass is reproduced without pitch definition and articulation, the low end degenerates into a dull roar underlying the music. You hear low-frequency content, but it isn't musically related to what's going on above it. You don't hear precise notes, but a blur of sound—the dynamic envelopes of individual instruments are completely lost. In music in which the bass plays an important rhythmic role—rock, electric blues, and some jazz—the bass guitar and kick drum seem to lag behind the rest of the music, putting a drag on the rhythm. Moreover, the kick drum's dynamic envelope (what gives it the sense of sudden impact) is buried in the bass guitar's sound, obscuring its musical contribution. These conditions are made worse by the common mid-fi affliction of too much bass.

Terms descriptive of this kind of bass include *muddy, thick, boomy, bloated, tubby, soft, fat, congested, loose,* and *slow*.

Terms that describe excellent bass reproduction include *taut, quick, clean, articulate, agile, tight,* and *precise*. Good bass has been likened to a trampoline stretched taut; poor bass is a trampoline hanging slackly.

The amount of bass in the musical presentation is very important; if you hear too much, the music is overwhelmed. Excessive bass is a constant reminder that you're listening to reproduced music. This overabundance of bass is described as *heavy*.

If you hear too little bass, the presentation is *thin, lean, threadbare,* or *overdamped*. An overly lean presentation robs music of its rhythm and drive—the full, purring sound of bass guitar is missing, the depth and majesty of double bass or cello are gone, and the orchestra loses its sense of power. Thin bass makes a double bass sound like a cello, a cello like a viola. The rhythmically satisfying weight and impact of bass drum are reduced to shadows of their former power. Instruments' harmonics are emphasized in relation to the fundamentals, giving the impression of well-worn cloth that's lost its supporting structure. A thin or lean presentation lacks *warmth* and *body*. As described earlier in this chapter in the discussion of audio sins of commission and omission, an overly lean bass is preferable to a fat and boomy bass.

Two terms related to what I've just described about the quantity of bass are *extension* or *depth*. Extension is how deep the bass goes—not the bass and upper bass described by *lean* or *weighty*, but the very bottom end of the audible spectrum. This is the realm of kick drum and pipe organ. All but the very best systems *roll off* (reduce in volume) these lowermost frequencies. Fortunately, deep extension isn't a prerequisite to high-quality music reproduction. If the system has good bass down to about 35Hz, you don't feel that much is missing. Pipe-organ enthusiasts, however, will want deeper extension and are willing to pay for it. Reproducing the bottom octave correctly can be very expensive.

Just as colorations caused by peaks and dips in frequency response can make the midrange unnatural, bass can be colored by peaks and dips. Bass colorations create a monotonous, droning characteristic that quickly becomes tiring. In the most extreme example, *one-note bass*, the bass seems to have only one pitch. This impression is created by a large peak in the system's frequency response at a specific frequency. This pitch is then reproduced more loudly than other pitches. One-note bass is also described as being *thumpy*. Ironically, this undesirable condition is *maximized* in boom trucks. The playback system is tuned to put out all its energy at one frequency for maximum physical impact. The drivers of those vehicles don't seem to care that they're losing the wealth of musical information conveyed by the bass.

Many of the terms used to describe midrange colorations actually apply to the upper bass. *Chesty, thick,* and *congested* are all useful in describing colored bass reproduction. Bass lacking these colorations is called *smooth* or *clean*.

Much of music's dynamic power—the ability to convey wide differences between loud and soft—is contained in the bass. Though I'll discuss dynamics later in this section, bass dynamics bear special discussion—they are that important to satisfying music reproduction.

A system or component that has excellent bass dynamics will provide a sense of sudden impact and explosive power. Bass drum will jump out of the presentation with startling power. The dynamic envelope of acoustic or electric bass is accurately conveyed, allowing the music full rhythmic expression. We call these components *punchy*, and use the terms *impact* and *slam* to describe good bass dynamics.

A related aspect is *speed*, though, as applied to bass, "speed" is somewhat of a misnomer. Low frequencies inherently have slower attacks than higher frequencies, making the term technically incorrect. But the *musical* difference between "slow" and "fast" bass is profound. A product with fast, tight, punchy bass produces a much greater rhythmic involvement with the music. (This is examined in more detail later.)

Although reproducing the sudden attack of a bass drum is vital, equally important is a system's ability to reproduce a fast decay; i.e., how a note ends. The bass note shouldn't continue after a drum whack has stopped. Many loudspeakers store energy in their mechanical structures and radiate that energy slightly after the note itself. When this happens, the bass has *overhang*, a condition that makes kick drum, for example, sound *bloated* and *slow*. Music in which the drummer used double bass drums is particularly revealing of bass overhang. If the two drums merge into a single sound, overhang is probably to blame. You should hear the attack and decay of each drum as distinct entities. Components that don't adequately convey the sudden dynamic impact of low-frequency instruments rob music of its power and rhythmic drive.

Soundstaging

Soundstaging is the apparent physical size of the musical presentation. When you close your eyes in front of a good playback system, you can "see" the instrumentalists and singers before you, often existing within an acoustic space such as a concert hall. The soundstage has the physical properties of *width* and *depth*, producing a sense of great size and space in the listening room. Soundstaging overlaps with *imaging*, or the way instruments appear as objects hanging in three-dimensional space within the recorded acoustic. As mentioned previously in this chapter, a large and well-defined soundstage is most often heard when playing audiophile-grade recordings made in a real acoustic space such as a concert hall or church.

The most obvious descriptions of the soundstage are its physical dimensions—width and depth. You hear the musical presentation as existing beyond the left and right loudspeaker boundaries, and extending farther away from you than the wall behind the loudspeakers.

Of all the ways music reproduction is astounding, soundstaging is without question the most miraculous. Think about it: The two loudspeakers are driven by two-dimensional electrical signals that are nothing more than voltages that vary over time. From those two voltages, a huge, three-dimensional panorama unfolds before you. You don't hear the music as a flat canvas with individual instruments fused together; you hear the first violinist to the left front of the presentation, the oboe farther back and toward the center, the brass behind the basses on the right, and the tambourine behind all the other instruments at the very rear. The sound is made up of *individual objects* existing within a space, just as you would hear at a live performance. Moreover, you hear the oboe's timbre coming from the oboe's position, the violin's timbre coming from the violin's position, and the hall reverberation surrounding the instruments. The listening room vanishes, replaced by the vast space of the concert hall—all from two voltages.

A soundstage is created in the brain by the time and amplitude differences encoded in the two audio channels. When you hear instrumental images toward the rear right of the soundstage, the ear/brain is synthesizing those aural images by processing the slightly different information in the two signals arriving at your ears. Visual perception works the same way: there is no depth information present on your retinas; your brain extrapolates the appearance of depth from the differences between the two flat images.

Audio components vary greatly in their abilities to present these spatial aspects of music. Some products shrink soundstage width and shorten the impression of depth. Others reveal the glory of a fully developed soundstage. I find good soundstage performance crucial to satisfying musical reproduction. Unfortunately, many products destroy or degrade the subtle cues that provide soundstaging.

Terms descriptive of poor soundstage width are *narrow* and *constricted*—the music, squeezed together between the loudspeakers, does not envelop the listener. A soundstage lacking depth is called *flat*, *shallow*, or *foreshortened*. Ideally, the soundstage should maintain its width over its entire depth. A soundstage that narrows toward the presentation's rear robs the music of its size and space.

The illusion of soundstage depth is aided by resolution of low-level spatial cues such as hall reflections and reverberation. In particular, the reverberation decay after a loud climax followed by a rest helps define the acoustic space. The loud signal is like a flash of light in a dark room; the space is momentarily illuminated, allowing you to see its dimensions and characteristics.

To produce a realistic impression of a real instrument in a real acoustic space, the reverberation and hall sound must be distinct from the image itself. Better audio components place the image within, rather than superimposed on, the recorded acoustic. Poor-quality components don't resolve these spatial cues; they shorten soundstage depth, truncate reverberation decay, and fuse the reverberation into the instrumental images. When this happens, an audio system's ability to transport you to the original acoustic space is diminished.

Now that we've covered space and depth, let's discuss how the instrumental images appear within this space. Images should occupy a specific spatial position in the soundstage. The sound of the bassoon, for example, should appear to emanate from a specific point in space, not as a diffuse and borderless image. The same could be said for guitar, piano, sax, or any other instrument in any kind of music. The lead vocal should appear as a tight, compact, definable point in space exactly between the loudspeakers. Some products, particularly large loudspeakers, distort image size by making every instrument seem larger than life—a classical guitar suddenly sounds ten feet wide. A playback system should reveal somewhat correct image size, from a 60'-wide symphony orchestra to a solo violin. I say "somewhat" because it is impossible to re-create the correct spatial perspectives of such widely divergent sound sources through two loudspeakers spaced about 8' apart. Although image size and placement are characteristics inherent in the recording, they are dramatically affected by components in the playback system.

Terms that describe a clearly defined soundstage are *focused*, *tight*, *delineated*, and sharp. *Image specificity* also describes tight image focus and pinpoint spatial accuracy. A poorly defined soundstage is described as *homogenized*, *blurred*, *confused*, *congested*, *thick*, and lacking *focus*.

A related issue is soundstage *layering*. This is the ability of a sound system to resolve front-to-back cues that present some images toward the soundstage front and at varying distances toward the soundstage rear. The greater the number of layers of depth gradation, the better. Poor components produce the impression of just a few layers of depth: you hear perhaps three or four discrete levels of distance within the soundstage. The best components produce a sense of distance along a continuum: very fine gradations of depth are clearly resolved. Again, the absence of these qualities constitutes subconscious cues that what you're hearing is artificial. When this important spatial information is revealed, however, you can more easily forget that you're not hearing the "real thing."

Bloom—the impression that individual instrumental images are surrounded by a halo of air—is often associated with soundstaging. Although image outlines may be clearly delineated, a soundstage with bloom has an additional sense of diffused air around the image. It is as though the instrument has a little space around it in which it can "breathe." Bloom gives the soundstage a more natural, open, and relaxed feeling.

The term *action*, coined by Jonathan Valin, describes the sense of bloom expanding outward into space from the instrument, and the way in which the instrument's dynamic envelope grows. Action is bloom with a dynamic component. Think of how a trumpet sounds in real life, and the way the sound seems to expand in space as the instrument gets louder. Some audio components express this characteristic better than others; those with a good sense of action sound more realistic, vibrant, and alive than those that lack action.

A product's soundstaging performance should be evaluated with a wide range of musical signals. Some products may throw a superb soundstage at low levels, only to have that collapse when the volume increases during musical climaxes. Listen for changes in the spatial perspective with signal level.

Some products produce a crystal-clear, *see-through* soundstage that allows the listener to hear all the way to the back of the hall. Such a *transparent* soundstage has a lifelike immediacy that makes every detail clearly audible. Conversely, an *opaque* soundstage is *thick* or *murky*, with less of an illusion of "seeing" into space. *Veiling* is often used to describe a lack of transparency.

Soundstaging is toward the top of my list of sonic priorities (after tonal balance and lack of grain). The ability to present the music as a collection of individual images surrounded by space, rather than as one big image, is very important to the creation of musical realism. A soundstage with space, depth, focus, layering, bloom, and transparency is nothing short of spectacular.

To evaluate soundstaging and hear the characteristics I've described, you must use recordings that contain these spatial cues. Studio recordings made with multiple microphones and overdubs rarely reveal the soundstaging characteristics described. Recordings made in real acoustic spaces with stereo microphone techniques and a pure signal path are essential to hearing all aspects of soundstaging. In short, soundstaging is provided by a combination of the recording and the playback system. If soundstaging cues aren't present in the recording, you'll never know how well or how poorly the component or system under evaluation reveals them. Most audiophile recordings are made with purist techniques (usually two microphones) that naturally capture the spatial information present during the original musical event. Examples of these recordings are listed later in this chapter.

A term related to soundstaging is *envelopment*, a word that comes from the field of home theater and multichannel sound. Envelopment describes the feeling of immersion in a soundfield created by front and side- or rear-positioned surround speakers. Well-done surround sound can wrap around the listener, creating an almost seamless continuity between the front and rear sounds. (Envelopment is described in more detail in Chapter 13.)

Finally, superb soundstaging is relatively fragile. You need to sit directly between the loudspeakers, and every component in the playback chain must be of high quality. Soundstaging is easily destroyed by low-quality components, a bad listening room, or poor loudspeaker placement. This isn't to say you have to spend a fortune to get good soundstaging; many very-low-cost products do it well, but it is more of a challenge to find those bargains. The next chapter has many practical suggestions for achieving the best soundstaging possible from your system.

Dynamics

The *dynamic range* of an audio system isn't how loudly it will play, but rather the *difference* in level between the softest and loudest sounds that the system can reproduce. It is often specified technically as the difference between the component's noise level and its maximum output level. A symphony orchestra has a dynamic range of about 100 decibels, or dB (decibels are defined in Appendix A); a typical rock recording's dynamic range is about 10dB. In other words, comparatively speaking, the rock band is *always* loud; it has little dynamic range.

Dynamics are a very important part of music reproduction. They propel the music forward and involve the listener. Much of music's expression is conveyed by dynamic contrast, from *pp* (pianissimo) to *fff* (triple forte).

There are two distinct kinds of dynamics. *Macrodynamics* refers to the presentation's overall sense of slam, impact, and power—bass-drum whacks and orchestral crescendos, for examples. If the system has poor macrodynamics, we say the sound is *compressed* or *squashed*.

Microdynamics occur on a smaller scale. They don't produce a sense of impact, but are essential to providing realistic dynamic reproduction. Microdynamics describe the fine dynamic structure in music, from the attack of a triangle or other small percussion instruments in the back of the soundstage to the suddenness of a plucked string on an acoustic guitar. Neither sound is very loud in level, but both have dynamic structures that require agility and speed from the playback system.

Products with good dynamics—macro and micro—make the music come alive, allowing a vibrancy and life to emerge. Dynamic changes are an important vehicle of musical expression; the more you hear the musicians' intent, the greater the musical communication between performers and listener. Some otherwise excellent components fail to convey the broad range of dynamic contrast.

These characteristics are associated with *transient response*, a system's ability to quickly respond to an input signal. A transient is a short-lived sound, such as that made by percussion instruments. Transient response describes an audio system's ability to faithfully reproduce the quickness of transient signals. For example, a drum being struck produces a waveform with a very steep attack (the way the sound begins) and a fast decay (the way a sound stops). If any component in the playback system can't respond as quickly as the waveform changes, a distortion of the music's dynamic envelope occurs, and the steepness is slowed. Audio components described as *quick* or *fast* reproduce the suddenness of transient signals.

But just because a component or system can reproduce loud and soft levels doesn't necessarily mean it has good dynamics. We're looking for more than a wide dynamic range. The system must be capable of expressing fine gradations of dynamics, not just loud and soft. As the music changes in level (which, except in most rock recordings, it's doing most of the time), you should hear loudness changes along a smooth continuum, not as abrupt jumps in levels.

Another aspect of dynamics we seek is the ability to play loudly without the sound becoming *congested*. Many products—particularly CD players and loudspeakers—sound thick during musical climaxes. As the music gets louder, the sound becomes harder, timbre is obscured, and the soundstage degenerates into a confused mess. The word *congeal* aptly describes the homogenization of instrumental images within the soundstage. The nice sense of space and image placement heard at moderate volumes often collapses during loud passages. This produces a sense of *strain* on musical peaks that greatly detracts from your enjoyment. When a component doesn't exhibit these problems, we say it has *effortless* dynamics.

Detail

Detail refers to the small or low-level components of the musical presentation. The fine inner structure of an instrument's timbre is one kind of detail. The term is also associated with transient sounds (those with a sudden attack) at any level, such as those made by percussion instruments. A playback system with good resolution of detail will infuse music with that sense that there is simply more music happening.

Assembling a good-sounding music system or choosing between two components can often be a tradeoff between smoothness and the resolution of detail. Many audio components hype detail, giving transient signals an *etched* character. Etch is an unpleasant hardness of timbre on transients that emphasizes their prominence. Sure, you can hear all the information, but the presentation becomes too *aggressive*, *analytical*, and *fatiguing*: low-level information is brought up and thrust at you, and you feel a sense of relief when the music is turned down or off—not a good sign.

Components that err in the opposite direction don't have this etched and analytical quality, but neither do they resolve all the musical information in the recording. These components are described as overly *smooth*, or having *low resolution*. They tend to make music bland by removing parts of the signal needed for realistic reproduction. These kinds of components don't rivet your attention on the music; they are *uninvolving* and dull. You aren't offended by the presentation, as you are with an analytical system, but something is missing that you need for musical satisfaction.

Lack of detail is often an unintended consequence of removing treble brightness or grain. The design aspects that tame the aggressive treble also obliterate essential musical information. Such components are said to have low resolution. Some listeners prefer such low-resolution presentation to a more natural rendering. In fact, some products are actually designed to gloss over detail to make the products sound more "musical."

It is a rare product indeed that presents a full measure of musical detail without sounding etched. The best products will reveal all the low-level cues that make music interesting and riveting, but not in a way that results in listening fatigue—that sense of tiredness after a long listening session. The music playback system must walk the very fine line between resolution of real musical information and sounding analytical.

Pace, Rhythm, and Timing

The British audio reviewer Martin Colloms deserves the credit for identifying and defining important aspects of music reproduction he calls *pace, rhythm,* and *timing.* These terms refer to a system's ability to involve the listener in a physical way in the music's forward flow and drive. Pace is that quality that makes your body want to move with the beat, your foot to tap, and your head to bob—the feeling of being propelled forward on the music's rhythm. The sound of good pace and rhythm from an audio system can produce a sense of physical exhilaration.

Though the music's tempo doesn't change in an objective sense from component to component (one power amplifier to another, for example), the subjective impression of a timing difference can be profound. Some products put a drag on the rhythm, making the tempo seem slower or *sluggish.* Others are *upbeat,* conveying the music's rhythmic tautness and drive. In addition to apparently slowing the tempo, components with poor pace give the impression that the band is less tight and musically "up." The music has less vitality and energy, and the band is less locked-in to the groove.

Martin Colloms wrote this in his revelatory article on this overlooked aspect of music reproduction, published in the November 1992 issue of *Stereophile.*

> *While good rhythm is a key aspect of both live and reproduced music-making, it is not easy to analyze. It's as if the act of focusing on the details of a performance blinds one to the parameter in question. The subjective awareness of rhythm is a continuous event, registered at the whole-body level, and recognized in a state of conscious but relaxed awareness. Once you've learned that reproduced sound can impart that vital sense of music-making as an event, that the impression of an upbeat, involving drive can be reproduced again and again, you can't help but pursue this quality throughout your listening experience.*

Any random energy, such as in a power amplifier's power supply or a loudspeaker's cabinet—even a loosening of the bolts that secure drivers to loudspeaker baffles—can degrade pace and timing.

Rhythm and pace are more important in rock, jazz, blues, pop, than in classical music. Much of the feeling of propulsion comes from the bass drum and bass guitar working together.

Many listeners have heard examples of good pace or the lack of it without recognizing it as such. Instead, they may have felt an indefinable involvement in the music if the system had good timing, or a general apathy or boredom with the music if the system didn't convey pace and rhythm.

How do you listen for pace and rhythm? Forget about it; if you find yourself wanting to dance, the component probably has it.

Coherence

Coherence describes the impression that the music is integrated into a satisfying whole, and is not merely a collection of bass, midrange, and treble. The music's harmonic tapestry is integrally woven, not pieced together like a patchwork quilt.

Coherence also applies to the system's or component's dynamic performance, specifically the impression that all the transient edges are lined up with each other. This provides a sense of wholeness to the sound that we react to favorably. Coherence is more a feeling of musical "naturalness" than any specific characteristic.

A related term, coined by Harry Pearson, is *continuousness*, the impression that the music is harmonically whole across the spectrum.

Musicality

Finally, we get to the most important aspect of a system's presentation—*musicality*. Unlike the previous characteristics, musicality isn't any specific quality that you can listen for, but the overall musical satisfaction the system provides. Your sensitivity to musicality is destroyed when you focus on a certain aspect of the presentation; i.e., when you listen critically. Instead, musicality is the *gestalt*, the whole of your reaction to the reproduced sound. We also use the term *involvement* to describe this oneness with the music. A sure indication that a component or a system has musicality is when you sit down for an analytical listening session and minutes later find yourself immersed in the music and abandoning the critical listening session. This has happened many times to me as a reviewer, and is a good measure of the product's fundamental "rightness." Ultimately, musicality—not dissecting the sound—is what high-end audio is all about.

The following essay grapples with the conflict between analytical listening and musicality. It first appeared as an editorial in the November 1992 issue of *Stereophile*, and is reprinted with permission.

Between the Ears
by Robert Harley

Audiophiles constantly seek ways to improve the experience of hearing reproduced music. Preamps are upgraded, digital processors are compared, turntables are tweaked, loudspeaker cables are auditioned, dealers are visited, and, yes, magazines are read—all in the quest to get just a little closer to the music.

These pursuits have one thing in common: they are all attempts by physical means to enjoy music more. But there's another way of achieving that goal that is far more effective than any tweak, better than any component upgrade, and more fulfilling even than having *carte blanche* in the world's finest high-end store. And it's free.

I'm talking about what goes on *between* our ears when listening, not what's impinging on them. The ability—or lack of it—to clear the mind of distractions and let the music speak to us has a huge influence on how much we enjoy music. Have you ever wondered why, on the same system and recordings, there is a vast range of involvement in the music? The only variable is our state of mind.

Because audiophiles care about sound quality, we are often more susceptible to allowing interfering thoughts to get in the music's way. These thoughts are usually concerned with aspects of the *sound's* characteristics. Does the soundstage lack depth? Does the bass have enough extension? Is the treble grainy? How does my system compare to those described in magazines?

Unfortunately, this mode of thinking is perpetuated by high-end audio magazines. The descriptions of a product's sound—its specific performance attributes—are what make it into print, not the musical and emotional satisfaction to which the product contributes. The latter is ineffable: words cannot express the bond between listener and music that some products facilitate more than others. Consequently, we are left only with descriptions of specific characteristics that can leave the impression that being an audiophile is about dissection and critical commentary, and not about more closely connecting with the music's meaning.

A few months after I became an audio reviewer (and a much more critical listener), I underwent a kind of crisis; I found myself no longer enjoying music the way I once did. Listening became a chore, an occupational necessity, rather than the deeply moving experience that made me choose a career in audio. My dilemma was precipitated by the mistaken impression that whenever I heard music I had to have an opinion about the quality of its reproduction. Music became secondary to the sound. Music was merely an assemblage of parts, something to be dismantled and studied, not something that spoke to me emotionally.

I found, however, that only after I'd turned in the month's reviews did the party begin. I stopped being a critic and was a music lover again. I played favorite records, *not* those that would tell me what the equipment was doing. The music as a whole, not the sound as an assemblage of artifacts, once again became the object of my attention. It was as though an enormous burden had been lifted. I made up for lost time in those few days before the inevitable return to reviewing as the next month's products were set up for critical auditioning.

Here I was with a custom-built listening room, racks full of the world's finest audio reproduction equipment, and a job in which I spent a good deal of my time listening, yet most of the time I wasn't enjoying the music. My cheap car stereo gave more musical satisfaction. Something was dreadfully wrong.

This experience precipitated a catharsis that forced me to reexamine what music listening—among other things—was all about. I decided to forget about the sound for the vast majority of the listening time and let the music tell me which components were better than others. Critical listening and analytical reasoning became secondary to musical enjoyment. I began listening to music I *liked*, rather than diagnostic recordings that would tell me about the product's specific characteristics. The impulse to disassemble, listen to the *sound*, and constantly form judgments gradually disappeared. The result is that I now enjoy music more than at any other time of my life. Better sound *does* result in more music, but paradoxically, *only when the sound is forgotten*. Moreover, this conversion increased my listening and reviewing skills: I now have a much better feeling for which products will produce long-term musical satisfaction.

Nevertheless, analytical listening using particularly revealing recordings must remain a vital part of the reviewing process. Similarly, conveying the specific sonic characteristics of products under review is essential—potential purchasers should know what the product sounds like and decide if it's what they're looking for. But this type of diagnostic analysis no longer dominates—it has become merely one aspect of reviewing. Moreover, I came to realize that the information gained by analytical reasoning is a lower form of knowledge, and that the *feeling* about a product's quality—its ability to convey the music—is a higher form of knowledge.

These experiences point to a deeper problem of how rationality and the impulse toward dissection as the vehicle to understanding pervades Western thought. Traditional rationality views a whole as a collection of parts. The need to dissect, classify, and assign hierarchical structure is the very foundation of rationality. Our Western upbringing makes it seem so natural that any entity is merely an assemblage of component parts. Why should reproduced music be any different? Consequently, we hear in reproduced music treble, bass, midrange, soundstage, detail, and air. But how often at a live concert do you dismantle the sound the same way you do when listening to a hi-fi? I don't know about you, but I never experience live music in terms of tonal balance, depth, lack of grain, or other characteristics we assign to reproduced sound.

Consider two approaches to knowing a flower. Traditional rationality would pick it, dissect it, classify its parts, and attempt to understand and document its mechanisms. Another way to know the flower would be to just sit and look at it, appreciating its beauty, discovering subtleties in shape, color, smell, texture, and just absorbing its essence. The first method produces one kind of knowing—an important one, to be sure—but it isn't a complete knowledge.

Moreover, doesn't the first method destroy something in the process—namely, the flower? After the dissection is finished we find ourselves left with nothing. This is why I no longer enjoyed music; the analytical dismantling consumed the very thing I was trying to know. By allowing intellectual thought to intrude, the oneness between music and listener is destroyed.

The great accomplishments of rationality—making reproduced music possible in the first place, for example—produces a hubris that tempts one to overlook the virtues of nonrational experience. Rationality can point to its achievements as "proof" of its superiority. The kind of knowing produced by nonrational experience can point to no physical manifestations of its value. Instead, the worth is completely internal and unknowable by anyone who hasn't experienced it firsthand.

But it isn't just listening analytically to the sound that interferes with musical enjoyment. *Any* intellectual activity diminishes the experience. It is the quality of the listening experience that matters—the here and now—not an assignment of value as measured against some standard promulgated by hi-fi magazines, comparisons with other systems, or anything else that distracts from the music.

There's nothing wrong with being dissatisfied with your system; that's what fuels improvement. And a better system does produce a deeper musical experience. But you shouldn't enjoy music any less if your system falls short of a friend's system, or if you don't have the latest hot product, or if the sound doesn't equal that described in magazines. These things are artificial inventions *superimposed on* reality, not the reality itself. What really matters is the experience—immediate, here-and-now existence. All other thoughts or intellectual abstractions diminish our potential for a oneness with the music.

In this way of thinking (or, more precisely, *not* thinking), musical fulfillment is no longer dependent on external means. Yes, the technology that brings music into our homes is physical and external, but satisfaction cannot be experienced purely through the equipment, no matter how good it is. Instead, getting closer to the music is a special interaction between music and listener, the equipment merely serving as intermediary. Without this state of mind, no level of equipment will provide us with what we seek. My temporary lack of musical enjoyment, despite having a custom-built room filled with top-notch products, affirmed this truism.

By all means, continue critiquing and upgrading your system—it can be a path to more musical enjoyment. But when a favorite record goes on the turntable and the lights dim, forget about cables, preamps, tweaks, and magazines. At that moment, the only thing that *really* matters is the music.

Notes on Learning Descriptive Terms

By practicing critical listening, and adopting the language used here and in product reviews in high-end audio magazines, you will be much better able to assess the quality of audio equipment and make better purchasing decisions. By associating the descriptive terms with your own listening impressions, you can more tangibly characterize how good products and systems are, and *why* they are good or bad.

I recommend that you write down your listening impressions during or immediately after the listening session. This will not only solidify your impressions, but force you to find words to describe what you heard. Often we remember more strongly the memory of the impression, rather than the impression itself. I'm often asked how I can remember how a specific component sounds when I haven't heard that product for a year or more. Because I record my sonic experiences when writing product reviews for *The Absolute Sound*, I have formed a capsule impression of that product's basic character. I don't remember every detail, of course, but the mental image may be something like "slightly etched treble, very transparent and spacious soundstage, lean bass, somewhat lacking in dynamics, analytical rather than smooth." I also associate a general value judgment with that component: would I want to listen to it for pleasure over a long period of time?

By writing down these impressions, you'll not only have a written record of your experience, but also a more tangible mental impression, one that you can use when making later comparisons with other components.

Critical Listening Setup Procedures

Now that we've explored the lexicon of critical listening, let's look at the procedures required to reach valid listening judgments. These procedures are controls on the process that help ensure that our listening impressions are valid. It's easy to be fooled if you don't take certain precautions.

The following procedures are the result of my experience evaluating products professionally, and reporting those evaluations to a sizable audience. In my profession, the need to be right about products is paramount. Not only will readers buy or not buy products based on my opinions, but the fortunes of high-end manufacturers are greatly affected by reviews, positive or negative. Accurately describing a product's sound, and reaching correct value judgments about that product, are huge responsibilities—to readers, manufacturers, and the truth. The techniques described are essential to reaching the right conclusions. I wouldn't even consider forming concrete opinions about products without these safeguards. Neither should you.

By using these controlled procedures, you can stop second-guessing what you hear and concentrate on the real musical differences between components. Removing the variables that may skew the listening impressions will allow you to have greater confidence that the differences you're hearing are real musical differences between products, not the results of improper setup. If you follow these procedures and hear differences, you can have confidence in your listening impressions.

As you go into the listening session, turn your mind into a blank slate. Forget about the brand names of the products you're about to audition, their reputation for certain sonic characteristics, the products' prices, and whom you may offend if you like product A better than product B. Be completely receptive to whatever your ears tell you. If your impressions match your preconceived ideas about what the product sounds like, suspect bias. But if you find that your listening impressions contradict your prejudices, you've developed the ability to listen without bias. Removing bias is essential to reaching accurate value judgments.

The first rule of critical listening is that only one variable should be changed at one time. If comparing preamps, use the same source components, interconnects, AC power conditioner, power amp, cables, loudspeakers, music, and room. This is obviously impossible when comparing products at different dealers with different playback systems. But changing one variable at a time is an absolute requirement for arriving at valid opinions. This is why I stress taking the competing products home over the weekend for comparison. Not only can you evaluate them under the same conditions, but you get to hear how they interact with the rest of your system.

Changing only one component at a time is vital; big differences (two different pairs of loudspeakers, for example) will often swamp small differences. You can't separate what one new component is doing from what the second new component is doing. The ultimate expression of this mistake is someone who hears a system for the first time and remarks on how good (or bad) the loudspeaker cables are. It's ridiculous; you can't isolate what the loudspeaker cable is doing within the context of a completely unknown system.

The second rule is to match volume levels between components under audition. Level matching ensures that both products produce the same volume at the loudspeakers, and should become an integral part of critical listening sessions. All it takes is an inexpensive voltmeter and a few minutes of time. If you're comparing two CD players, for example, match their output levels to within, at most, 0.2dB of each other, and preferably to within 0.1dB. You'll be well rewarded for those few minutes spent level-matching with more accurate value judgments about the products. (The section at the end of this chapter explains how to match levels.)

Level-matching is crucial; slight level differences between products can lead you to the wrong conclusion. As described in Appendix A, the ear's sensitivity to bass and treble increases disproportionately with volume. That is, you hear more bass and treble when the music is loud. If product A is played louder than product B, product A may sound brighter, more forward, more detailed, more dynamic, and have more bass. If product A has a soft treble, lacks detail, and has a lean bass balance, you may not know it if the levels aren't precisely matched. If you *can* distinguish product A's character with mismatched levels, the degrees to which the treble is soft, the detail lacking, the dynamics missing, and the bass thin are much harder to gauge. With level matching, you'll know precisely how *much* these characteristics are present in the product you're evaluating; you can forget about trying to mentally compensate for different levels and concentrate on characterizing the sonic differences.

With the same playback system and matched levels, you're ready to compare products. The typical method is called A/B, in which you hear product A, then immediately afterward the same music through product B. One problem with A/B listening is called "The A/A Paradox." This states that when hearing two identical presentations (A/A), you tend to hear differences between them. The A/A paradox happens because music has meaning; you perceive it and react to it a little differently each time you hear it. Moreover, if the music is unfamiliar, a second hearing allows you to hear more detail. These factors combine to fool you into hearing differences that aren't there.

Fortunately, overcoming the A/A paradox is easy. When comparing products, listen to A, then B, then A again. The differences you heard between A and B are often solidified after hearing A again. After selecting another piece of music for further comparison, make the order B/A/B. This technique of hearing three presentations (or five, A/B/A/B/A) confirms or refutes first impressions. Usually, a characteristic heard in the first comparison is more apparent in a second comparison.

Selecting the right *source material* (i.e., recordings) is important in fully exploring a product's character. If the source material doesn't contain certain cues, you won't know how well the product reproduces those cues. For example, if you're comparing two power amplifiers and use only dry studio recordings of pop music, you'll never know how good the amplifiers are at resolving soundstage depth and other spatial cues. Similarly, if you listen to nothing but chamber music in evaluating loudspeakers, you can't tell how the loudspeaker conveys bass dynamics, punch, and rhythmic intensity.

Establish a repertoire of familiar music for evaluating components, each recording selected for some sonic characteristic that will tell you how a component behaves. Remember, this is diagnostic listening, not listening for pleasure. A range of source material should include: a full-scale symphonic recording, chamber music, orchestra with choir, solo piano, popular vocal, rock, blues, or other music with electric bass and kick drum, jazz with acoustic bass, and music with cymbals. Some of the jazz and orchestral recordings should be naturally miked; that is, recorded in a way that captures the original spatial aspects of the music and concert hall. Audiophile record labels will often describe how the recordings were made, and even include a photograph of the hall and where the microphones were placed. Get to know these recordings intimately. By hearing the same recording played back on many different systems, you can quickly characterize a component's sonic signature.

Another factor that can lead you astray in critical listening is *absolute polarity* (discussed in Appendix A). If one product under comparison inverts absolute polarity and the other one doesn't, you may be led to the wrong conclusions; or, at the very least, be confused about which product is better. Many owner's manuals will state if the product inverts polarity. If you know that product A does not invert polarity while product B does, reverse the positive and negative connections on *both* loudspeakers: the red wire goes to the loudspeaker's black terminal, and the black wire goes to the loudspeaker's red terminal when auditioning product B. If your preamp has a polarity inversion switch, you can just throw it instead of swapping loudspeaker leads. Fortunately, very few components invert absolute polarity.

It's also easy to be misled by a colored playback system. Say you have loudspeakers that are bright, forward, and a little rough in the treble, and you're comparing two digital processors to determine which one to buy. Processor A produces a sound through your system that is bright and forward in the treble. Processor B renders a smoother treble and is more musical in your system.

Is processor B inherently more musical? Not necessarily. It probably has colorations—an overly soft treble—that complement the loudspeaker's bright treble. Two products in the playback chain that have reciprocal flaws will often produce a musical result. And there's no reason not to buy processor B if you intend on keeping your loudspeakers. But don't make the mistake of thinking processor B is inherently better than processor A. In fact, processor A is probably more neutral and would be a much better choice with different, smoother loudspeakers. Although not ideal, choosing a product based on how it corrects other faults in your system is valid if the end result is a more musical presentation. Just recognize the situation when it occurs.

Recommended Recordings

I've found several recordings over the years that I rely on for reaching value judgments about audio components. Using the same music on a variety of equipment over a long period of time lets me more quickly and accurately determine the sonic characteristics of the component or system under evaluation. Although you may find different music that works for you, I'll list a few records I've found that are highly revealing of certain sonic traits.

For pure bass extension, the Rutter *Requiem* mentioned earlier in this chapter is a great test. The organ's pedal tones extend down to 16Hz, stretching the limits of any loudspeaker. This work is also a revealing indicator of soundstage size and image placement, particularly when played back through a CD player or digital processor with HDCD decoding.

The track "Wishing Well" from the CD *Speaking in Melodies* by Michael Ruff (Sheffield Lab) lets me immediately identify bottom-end dynamics (kick drum), bottom-end tautness (bass guitar), and pace and rhythm. This latter quality is indicated by how well the kick drum and bass guitar "lock in" to drive the track's propulsive rhythm. Some components dilute this quality, reducing the sense of drive and energy. Also listen for bass articulation: how well can you hear each note of the bass guitar, particularly during the piano break?

The snare drum on this track also contributes to the powerful drive and dynamic impact of the song. Lackluster dynamics are indicated by a reduced sense of snap; the snare doesn't "pop out" as dynamically through some components. I also listen for smoothness in the background vocals, the sense of space around the horns, and overall tonal balance in the relationship between the cymbals and bass guitar. Overall, this is a superb recording that tells me a lot about what a component or system is doing well or poorly.

Acoustic guitar is a good indicator of a component's transient ability and lack of hardness. The instrument shouldn't be overlaid with a metallic brightness that emphasizes the transient attack of the strings to the detriment of hearing the instrument's body. Some loudspeakers often add an unnatural edge that fosters the impression of hearing more detail, or of sounding "cleaner," but this presentation quickly becomes fatiguing. You should hear some transient zip (liveliness) that gives the instrument its life and vividness, along with a fast decay of the initial transient. Any energy storage in a loudspeaker (the speaker stores mechanical energy in its drive units or cabinet, then releases it as acoustic energy over time) is immediately apparent on well-recorded acoustic guitar. Acoustic guitar should be vivid, but without etch.

The three best acoustic guitar recordings I know of are the direct-to-disc LP *Michael Newman, Guitarist* (Sheffield Lab), Ralph Towner's instrument on the Oregon disc *Beyond Words* (Chesky), and *A Meeting by the River* with Ry Cooder and V.M. Bhatt (Water Lily Acoustics).

For macrodynamics, nothing has as wide a dynamic contrast or visceral dynamic impact as *Lauds*, by 20th-century composer Ron Nelson, on the HDCD-encoded disc *Holidays & Epiphanies* (Reference Recordings). The Dallas Wind Symphony, conducted by Jerry Junkin, pulls out all the stops in the climaxes of this wonderful piece. This recording is the ultimate test of dynamic range. Similarly, *Holidays & Epiphanies* also reveals to what degree a playback system congeals when pushed hard. Listen to see if the beautifully delineated soundstage degenerates into an undifferentiated roar, or if timbres harden on the musical peaks.

Another recording that collapses into a mess if not reproduced correctly is Frank Zappa's *The Yellow Shark* (Rykodisc). This disc, which solidifies Zappa's contribution to 20th-century "serious" music, contains such complex arrangements that any smearing in the playback system reduces the ability to hear all the fascinating intricacies of this chamber-orchestra arrangement, wonderfully performed by the Ensemble Modern.

When evaluating how well a particular loudspeaker placement integrates with the room, or judging the coherence between a subwoofer and main speakers, "Why Don't You Go Back to the Woods," from *Skip, Hop & Wobble* (Sugar Hill) by Jerry Douglas, Russ Barenberg, and Edgar Meyer, is particularly revealing. Bassist Meyer's virtuosic playing takes him all over the instrument's range, highlighting any bass discontinuities or room-induced boominess. Poor loudspeaker placement is instantly indicated by certain bass notes sticking out and hanging in the room, robbing Meyer's instrument of pitch definition and agility.

The ability of a component or system to resolve fine detail shows up in pianist Mike Garson's *The Oxnard Sessions, Volume Two* (Reference Recordings). Listen to the brushes on the snare drum on "All Blues"; good systems will let you hear the individual bristles moving on the drum head. Systems of lower quality blur the sound, making it hard to tell the mechanism by which the sound was created. Also listen for the wonderful sense of space surrounding Eric Marienthal's sax on "A Song for You," and the overall sense of spontaneous music-making that gives this record its musical and sonic magic. This recording is available on vinyl or HDCD-encoded CD. The vinyl is vastly better sounding, with better rendering of the piano's timbre (more "pianoness"), greater resolution of low-level detail (the snare brushes mentioned), and a bigger soundstage.

A favorite audiophile recording of female vocals is Jennifer Warnes' *Famous Blue Raincoat*. Although this is a great record, listen also to Diana Krall on her disc *Love Scenes* (Impulse!). Her voice has a purity and presence that immediately identifies a component's or system's overall perspective, degree of midrange purity, and amount of grain or hard textures.

In the SACD format, try *So Real*, a piano trio recorded in multichannel, on the DMP label. This hybrid SACD contains both 2-channel and multichannel mixes. One would think a piano trio an odd choice for a multichannel recording, but the presence of the surround channels enhances the space at the front of the soundstage and creates a feeling of being inside the studio's acoustic.

Perhaps the most stunning example of SACD's potential is the *Red Rose Sampler*. This disc contains various recordings made by Mark Levinson (the man) in the Manhattan showroom of his company, Red Rose Music. The tracks include, among others, piano, classical guitar, violin, sax, spoken word, and vocal with guitar accompaniment. The timbres on this disc are among the most natural of any recording I've heard.

JVC has released on its XRCD label two albums by Victor Feldman first issued on vinyl in the 1980s. The two titles, *Secret of the Andes* and *Soft Shoulder*, were of reference quality at the time and they remain reference quality today. The XRCD release, called *Audiophile*, maintains the original LPs' terrific sonics (I bought the LPs upon their release and have them for comparison to the CD). Engineered by the great Alan Sides, this disc contains stunning dynamics, resolution, space, and instrumental timbre. The drum sound and other percussion are startling. XRCD (Extended Resolution Compact Disc) is a mastering process that greatly improves sound quality, and JVC has released an impressive catalog of titles in the XRCD series.

If you have a DVD-Audio player, a must-have disc is *The Ultimate DVD Surround Sampler & 5.1 Set-up Disc* from Chesky records. In addition to containing test signals for calibrating a multichannel audio system, this disc features eight tracks recorded with 96kHz sampling and 24-bit resolution.

Two good sources for audiophile recordings are Music Direct (800-449-8333; www.amusicdirect.com) and Acoustic Sounds (800-716-3553; www.acousticsounds.com).

Single-Presentation Listening—What It's All About

The type of analytical listening I've described will reveal specific sonic attributes of components in relation to each other: CD transport A has deeper bass extension, smoother treble, and a deeper soundstage, while transport B has more inner detail, quicker transients, and a more focused soundstage. This kind of analytical listening will tell you a lot about the products' strengths and weaknesses, but it isn't the whole story.

What's missing from this dissection is how each product makes you *feel* about the music. Does your mind wander, thinking about what you're going to do next? Or are you riveted in the listening seat, playing record after record well into the night?

This ability to express the music in a way that compels you to continue listening is called a product's *musicality* and *involvement*. Musicality and involvement are rarely revealed in A/B comparisons and can't be described in terms of specific sonic attributes. Instead, this fundamental characteristic of a product's ability to provide long-term musical satisfaction is discovered only when listening for pleasure, without level-matching, selecting music for its sonic rather than musical qualities, or analytical thinking. Dissecting the music to characterize specific sonic attributes, as in A/B comparisons, destroys our receptivity to the music's meaning. Involvement comes only when you consider music as a whole, not as a collection of sonic parts.

This is why all critical listening should include not only A/B/A comparisons, but also what's called "single-presentation listening" and listening just for pleasure. Single-presentation listening is listening to the product under evaluation over a long time period—days or weeks rather than hours—with an unconscious ear to how the product affects the music. Listening for sheer pleasure involves no thinking about the sound, only about the music. If, after a long session, you feel exhilarated and fulfilled, you can be confident in the product's ability to convey the music's expression and meaning. In fact, this is without question the most important indicator of quality in an audio component.

There is a general correlation between a product's sonic performance as revealed during analytical listening and its musicality as discovered during listening for pleasure. Specific sonic flaws—grainy treble, hard textures, flat soundstage—will often distract you from the music in ways that prevent deep involvement. The less the presentation sounds artificial, synthetic, or affronts your ears, the easier it is to forget the hardware and hear only the music. Indeed, making the hardware disappear is the Holy Grail of high-end audio.

Your evaluative listening should thus include a mix of analytical A/B/A comparisons with single-presentation listening (with an ear to specific sonic attributes) and pure listening for pleasure.

Critical Listening Summary

I've summarized the setup procedures for conducting critical listening that will provide valid, useful information about the product under evaluation:

- *Use the same playback system for comparisons*

- *Change only one component at a time*

- *Match levels between products under audition*

- *Listen to A/B/A, not A/B*

- *Use very familiar music*

- *Select music that reveals specific sonic characteristics; i.e., bass, midrange liquidity, dynamics, treble, and soundstaging.*

- *Listen to the product for pleasure over a long period of time*

Do I follow all these guidelines every time I listen critically? No. But I don't reach firm opinions about products unless I do. If you're listening to make a purchase decision, follow these guidelines religiously. Be suspicious of any listening impression received in poor circumstances. And don't reach firm opinions unless all these guidelines have been followed.

By applying these techniques, you'll be more likely to reach accurate value judgments, and consequently buy products that will provide the greatest long-term musical satisfaction.

Level Matching

Level-matching procedures are identical for all electronic components, whether a digital processor, preamp, or power amp. First, play music at a comfortable level through the system to set the volume. Then play a test CD that has a 1kHz sinewave recorded at a low level. Measure the voltage across the loudspeaker terminals when the tone is playing, and note the voltage. Put a piece of masking tape on the preamp's face plate around the preamp's volume control and mark the position of the volume control.

After you switch components (power amp, CD player, etc.), play the 1kHz sinewave again and measure the voltage across the loudspeaker terminals. Adjust the preamp's volume control so that the voltage across the loudspeaker terminals is the same as what you measured for the first component. Mark the volume-control position on the masking tape. By setting the volume control at the first mark for product A and at the second mark for product B, you've got matched levels.

Some preamplifiers with detented (click stop) volume controls but continuous attenuation make level matching easier and more precise by removing the need for tape. Just count the number of steps necessary to achieve the same voltage across the loudspeaker terminals. Setting the volume control between detents is surprisingly accurate and repeatable. This technique doesn't work with detented volume controls that aren't continuously adjustable between the detents, however.

If you're comparing preamps, you don't need masking tape—just find the volume setting on both preamps that produces the same voltage across the loudspeaker terminals when playing the test tone, and leave the volume controls in the same position.

Matching levels for phono cartridges and phono preamplifiers is identical, except that a test LP replaces the test CD.

Level-matching isn't required when comparing products that don't affect the volume. These include interconnects, loudspeaker cables, CD transports, CD tweaks, digital interconnects, AC line conditioners, AC power cords, spikes, cones, vibration-damping devices, and equipment stands.

Ideally, the playback level between products should be matched to within 0.2dB, and preferably to within 0.1dB. To calculate the dB difference between two measured voltages, you need only a calculator with a "log" button. Here's how to do it.

First, find the ratio of the two measured voltages by dividing one by the other. Then find the logarithm of that ratio by pressing the calculator's "log" button with the ratio in the display. Next, multiply the result by 20. The answer is the difference in dB between the two voltages.

For example, if you measured 2.82 volts (V) across the loudspeaker terminals with digital processor A, and 2.88V across the loudspeaker terminals with digital processor B after level matching, you first divide 2.88 by 2.82, which gives you the ratio of the two voltages (1.0213:1). Next, push the "log" button on the calculator with 1.0213 in the display, and multiply the result, 0.00914, by 20 to get the answer: the levels are matched to within 0.18dB, or close enough for meaningful comparisons.

4 How to Get the Best Sound from Your Room

Introduction

The room in which music is reproduced has a profound effect on sound quality. In fact, the listening room's acoustic character should be considered another component in the playback chain. Because every listening room imposes its own sonic signature on the reproduced sound, your system can sound its best only when given a good acoustical environment. An excellent room can help get the most out of a modest system, but a poor room can make even a great system sound mediocre.

Fortunately, you can greatly improve a listening room with a few simple tricks and devices. The possibilities range from simply moving your loudspeakers—or even just your listening seat—a few inches, to building a dedicated listening room from scratch. Between these two extremes are many options, including adding inexpensive and attractive acoustical treatment products.

This chapter covers everything you'll need to know to get the best sound from your system, beginning with the most effective and least expensive acoustical technique of all—loudspeaker placement. Don't be intimidated by the technical information toward the end of the chapter— it's included for those wanting to know some of the theory behind the practical information presented in the beginning sections. (If you find this next section difficult, I've summarized it in "Acoustical Do's and Don'ts" later in the chapter.)

Loudspeaker Placement

The most basic problem in many listening rooms is poor loudspeaker placement. Finding the right spot for your loudspeakers is the single most important factor in getting good sound in your room. Loudspeaker placement affects tonal balance, the quantity and quality of bass, soundstage width and depth, midrange clarity, articulation, and imaging. As you make large changes in loudspeaker placement, then fine-tune placement with smaller and smaller adjustments, you'll hear a new-found musical rightness and seamless harmonic integration to the sound. When you get it right, your system will come alive. Best of all, it costs no more than a few hours of your time.

Before getting to specific recommendations, let's cover the six fundamental factors that affect how a loudspeaker's sound will change with placement. (Later we'll look at each of these factors in detail.)

1) The relationship between the loudspeakers and the listener is of paramount importance. The listener and loudspeakers should form a triangle; without this basic setup, you'll never hear good soundstaging and imaging.

2) Proximity of loudspeakers to walls affects the amount of bass. The nearer the loudspeakers are to walls and corners, the louder the bass.

3) The loudspeaker and listener positions in the room affect the audibility of room resonant modes. Room resonant modes are reinforcements at certain frequencies that create peaks in the frequency response, which can add an unnatural "boominess" to the sound. When room resonant modes are less audible, the bass is better defined, and midrange clarity increases. (Room resonant modes are described in detail later in this chapter.)

4) The farther out into the room the loudspeakers are, the better the soundstaging—particularly depth.

5) Listening height affects tonal balance.

6) Toe-in (angling the loudspeakers toward the listener) affects tonal balance (particularly the amount of treble), soundstage width, and image focus.

Let's look at each of these factors in detail.

1) Relationship between the loudspeakers and the listener

The most important factor in getting good sound is the geometric relationship between the two loudspeakers and the listener (we aren't concerned about the room yet). The listener should sit exactly between the two loudspeakers, at a distance away from each loudspeaker slightly greater than the distance between the loudspeakers themselves. Though this last point is not a hard-and-fast rule, you should certainly sit exactly between the loudspeakers; that is, the same distance from each one. If you don't have this fundamental relationship, you'll never hear good soundstaging from your system.

Fig.4-1 shows how your loudspeaker and listening positions should be arranged. The listening position—equidistant from the speakers, and slightly farther from each speaker than the speakers are from each other—is called the "sweet spot." This is roughly the listening position where the music will snap into focus and sound the best. If you sit to the side of the sweet spot, the soundstage will tend to bunch up around one speaker. This bunching-up effect will vary with the loudspeaker; some loudspeakers produce a wider sweet spot than others.

Fig. 4-1 The listener should sit between the loudspeakers and at the same distance from each loudspeaker.

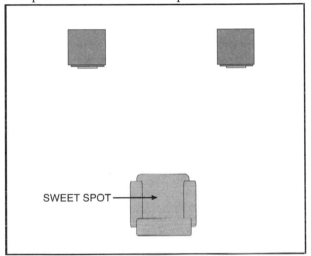

SWEET SPOT

Setting the distance between the loudspeakers is a trade-off between a wide soundstage and a strong center image. The farther apart the loudspeakers are (assuming the same listening position), the wider the soundstage will be. As the loudspeakers are moved farther apart, however, the center image weakens, and can even disappear. If the loudspeakers are too close together, soundstage width is constricted.

The best listening angle will produce a strong center image and a wide soundstage. You can experiment with angle simply by moving your listening chair forward and backward. There will likely be a position where the center image snaps into focus, appearing as a stable, pinpoint spot exactly between the loudspeakers. A musical selection with a singer and sparse accompaniment is ideal for setting loudspeaker spacing and ensuring a strong center image. With the loudspeakers fairly close together, listen for a tightly focused image exactly between the two loudspeakers. Move the loudspeakers a little farther apart and listen again. Repeat this move/listen procedure until you start to hear the central image become larger, more diffuse, and less focussed, indicating that you've gone slightly beyond the maximum distance your loudspeakers should be from each other for a given listening position.

Note that you should wait until after you've completed the entire loudspeaker placement procedure to install the loudspeaker's spikes.

A factor to consider in setting this angle is the relationship to the room. You can have the same geometric relationship between loudspeakers and listener with the loudspeakers close together and a close listening position, or with the loudspeakers far apart and a distant listening position. At the distant listening position, the listening room's acoustic character will affect the sound more than at the close listening position. That's because you hear more direct sound from the loudspeaker and less reflected sound from the room's walls. Consequently, the farther away you sit, the more spacious the sound. The closer you sit, the more direct and immediate the presentation. Some loudspeakers need a significant distance between the loudspeaker and the listener to allow the loudspeakers' individual drive units to integrate. If you hear a large tonal difference just by sitting closer, you should listen from a point farther away from the speakers.

2) *Proximity to walls affects the amount of bass*

The room boundaries have a great effect on a loudspeaker's overall tonal balance. Loudspeakers placed close to walls will exhibit a reinforcement in the bass (called "room gain"), making the musical presentation weightier. Some loudspeakers are designed to be near a rear wall (the wall behind the speakers); they need this reinforcement for a natural tonal balance. These loudspeakers sound thin if placed out into the room. Others sound thick and heavy if not at least 3' from the rear and side walls. Be sure which type you're buying if your placement options are limited.

When a loudspeaker is placed near a wall, its bass energy is reflected back into the room essentially in phase with the loudspeaker's output. This means the direct and reflected waves reinforce each other at low frequencies, producing louder bass. Fig.4-2 shows the difference in a loudspeaker's frequency response when measured in an anechoic chamber (a reflection-free room) and in a normal room. A frequency-response graph plots amplitude (loudness) vs. frequency. As you can see in the graph, not only is the bass boosted, but the loudspeaker's low-frequency extension is also increased. Each surface near the loudspeaker (floor, rear wall, and side walls) will add to the loudspeaker's bass output. The closer to the corners the loudspeakers are placed, the more bass you'll hear.

The loudspeaker's position in relation to the rear and side walls will also affect which frequencies are boosted. Correct placement can not only extend a loudspeaker's bass response by complementing its natural rolloff, but also avoid peaks and dips in the response. Improper placement can cause frequency-response irregularities that color the bass. That is, some frequencies are boosted relative to others, making the bass reproduction less accurate. The graph of Fig.4-3a is a loudspeaker's in-room response (the speaker's response as modified by the listening room) when placed equidistant from the rear and side walls. Note the 10dB notch (reduction in energy) at about 200Hz and the peak centered at 60Hz. The result will be a boominess in the bass and a leanness in the midbass. Moving the loudspeaker different distances from the rear and side walls can make the response much smoother (Fig.4-3b). The same loudspeaker's response at a different room position is shown in Fig.4-4.

Fig. 4-2 Comparison of a loudspeaker's anechoic and in-room responses

Fig. 4-3a Placing the loudspeakers the same distance from the rear and side walls produces peaks and dips in the bass response.

Fig. 4-3b Placing the loudspeakers different distances from the rear and side walls smooths the bass response.

Fig. 4-4
Response of
the same loud-
speaker in Fig.
4-3, but in a
different room
position
(Figs. 4-2, 4-3a,
4-3b, and 4-4
Courtesy Avalon
Acoustics, Inc.)

These graphs illustrate that a loudspeaker's room position affects the bass response, and that the loudspeakers should be positioned at different distances from the rear and side walls. A rule of thumb: the two distances shouldn't be within 33% of each other. For example, if the loudspeaker is 3' from the side wall, it should also be at least 4' from the rear wall.

Many loudspeaker manufacturers will specify the correct distance from the rear and side walls. When a measurement is specified, the distance is between the woofer cone and the wall. Start with the loudspeakers in the locations recommended by the manufacturer, then begin experimenting.

How close the loudspeakers are to the side walls affects the amplitude of the side-wall reflection. The closer the loudspeakers are to the side walls, the higher the level of the side-wall reflections reaching the listener—not a good thing. If you've treated the side walls as described later in this chapter, putting the loudspeaker closer to the side wall won't have as great an effect than if the side walls were left untreated.

A highly effective technique for finding the best distances from the rear and side walls was developed by David Wilson of Wilson Audio Specialties. Stand at the rear wall about the same distance from the side-wall as you expect the loudspeakers to end up. Bend over and begin speaking, moving in a line perpendicular to the rear wall. Listen to the timbre of your voice as you move. You'll hear different colorations as you move, and then suddenly, at one particular location, your voice will sound open, clear, and uncolored. There will be a small range (several inches) over which your voice sounds the most natural. Mark this area on the floor with masking tape. This is the best distance from the rear wall for your loudspeakers. Now repeat this exercise, but starting on the sidewall at the same plane at which you have placed the masking tape. The point at which your voice sounds the clearest is the best distance from the sidewall to locate your loudspeaker. The two points will intersect, indicating where you should position the loudspeaker. The intersection should be just behind the loudspeaker's front baffle and centered on the woofer. This technique is highly effective, and correlates very well with the placement suggested by computer modeling. The accuracy can be improved by having someone sit in the listening position as you move and speak, and confirm the point at which your voice sounds the least colored.

3) Loudspeaker and listener positions affect room-mode audibility

In addition to deepening bass extension and smoothing bass response, correct loudspeaker placement in relation to the room's walls can also reduce the audible effects of your room's *resonant modes*. Room resonant modes, described later in this chapter, are reinforcements at certain frequencies that create peaks in the frequency response. Room modes also create *standing waves*, which are stationary patterns of high and low sound pressure in the room that color the sound. The standing-wave patterns in a room are determined both by the room's dimensions and by the position of the sound source in the room. By putting the loudspeakers and listener in the best locations, we can achieve smoother bass response.

A well-known rule of thumb states that, for the best bass response, the distance between the loudspeakers and the rear wall should be one-third of the length of the room (Fig.4-5). If this is impractical, try one-fifth of the room length. Both of these positions reduce the excitation of standing waves and help the loudspeaker integrate with the room. Ideally, the listening position should be two-thirds of the way into the room.

Fig. 4-5 The "rule of thirds" says to place the loudspeakers and listening position a third of the way into the room. If this isn't practical, try one-fifth of the way into the room.

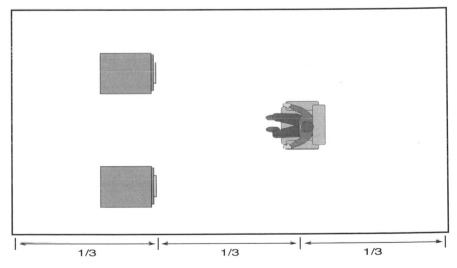

| 1/3 | 1/3 | 1/3 |

Starting with these basic configurations, move the loudspeakers and the listening chair in small increments while playing music rich in low frequencies. Listen for smoothness, extension, and how well the bass integrates with the rest of the spectrum. When you find the loudspeaker placement where the bass is the smoothest, you should also hear an increase in midrange clarity and definition.

An excellent test signal for evaluating bass and midrange sound in a room is the Music Articulation Test Tone (MATT) developed by Acoustic Sciences Corporation (ASC). This special test signal is a series of tone bursts that rise in pitch, with silences between the bursts. Ideally, you should hear the bursts and silences as separate events. When heard through headphones or with your ear near the loudspeaker, each burst is clearly articulated. But when the sound is modified by the listening room, certain frequency bands of the ascending tone bursts become smeared or garbled, indicating that the listening room is storing, and then releasing, energy at those frequencies. By moving the loudspeakers and listening to the MATT, you can easily discover where your loudspeakers work best in the room. (The MATT is available on *Stereophile*'s *Test CD 2*, which also includes more detailed information about how to use this unique test signal. This disc is available at www.tubetrap.com.)

The best way to find the right spots for your loudspeakers and listening chair with regard to reducing the influence of standing waves is a computer program called "Room Optimizer," created by RPG Diffusor Systems (www.rpginc.com). The program asks for your room dimensions, loudspeaker type and woofer location within the cabinet, and other information. The software performs multiple calculations to determine the optimum loudspeaker and listener location. "Room Optimizer" is highly recommended for this aspect of loudspeaker placement.

4) Distance from rear wall affects soundstaging

Generally, the farther away from the rear wall the loudspeakers are, the deeper the soundstage. A deep, expansive soundstage is rarely developed with the loudspeakers near the rear wall. Pulling the loudspeakers out a few feet can make the difference between poor and spectacular soundstaging. Unfortunately, many living rooms don't accommodate loudspeakers far out into the room. If the loudspeakers must be close to the rear wall, make the rear wall acoustically absorbent.

5) Listening height and tonal balance

Most loudspeakers exhibit changes in frequency response with changes in listening height. These changes affect the midrange and treble, not the bass balance. Typically, the loudspeaker will be brightest (i.e., have the most treble) when your ears are at the same height as the tweeters, or on the tweeter axis. Most tweeters are positioned between 32" and 40" from the floor to coincide with typical listening heights. If you've got an adjustable office chair, you can easily hear the effects of listening axis on tonal balance.

The degree to which the sound changes with height varies greatly with the loudspeaker. Some models have a broad range over which little change is audible; others can exhibit large tonal changes when you merely straighten your back while listening. Choosing a listening chair that sets your ears at the optimum axis will help achieve a good treble balance.

This difference in response is easily measurable. A typical set of loudspeaker measurements will include a family of response curves measured on various axes. The on-axis response (usually on the tweeter axis) is normalized to produce a straight line; the other curves show the *difference* between the on-axis response and at various heights. Chapter 15 ("Specifications and Measurements") includes a full description of how to interpret these measurements.

6) Toe-in

Toe-in is pointing the loudspeakers inward toward the listener rather than facing them straight ahead (see Fig.4-6). There are no rules for toe-in; the optimum amount varies greatly with the loudspeaker and the listening room. Some loudspeakers need toe-in; others work best firing straight ahead. Toe-in affects many aspects of the musical presentation, including mid- and high-frequency balance, soundstage focus, sense of spaciousness, and immediacy.

Fig. 4-6
Loudspeakers positioned with no toe-in (left) and with toe-in (right)

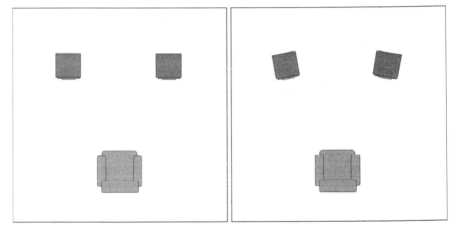

Most loudspeakers are brightest directly on-axis (directly in front of the loudspeaker). Toe-in thus increases the amount of treble heard at the listening seat. An overly bright loudspeaker can often be tamed by pointing the loudspeaker straight ahead. Some models, designed for listening without toe-in, are far too bright on-axis.

The ratio of direct to reflected sound increases with toe-in. That's because a toed-in loudspeaker will present more direct energy to the listener and project less energy into the room, where it might reach the listener only after reflecting from room surfaces. In a listening room with reflective side walls, toeing-in the loudspeakers can be a decided advantage. Moreover, the amplitude of side-wall reflections is greatly decreased with toe-in. Conversely, less toe-in increases the amount of reflected energy heard by the listener, adding to a sense of spaciousness and air. Reducing toe-in can open up the soundstage and create a feeling of envelopment.

Similarly, toe-in often increases soundstage focus and image specificity. When toed-in, many loudspeakers provide a more focused and sharply delineated soundstage. Images are more clearly defined, compact, and tight, rather than diffuse and lacking a specific spatial position. The optimum toe-in is often a trade-off between too much treble and a strong central image. With lots of toe-in, the soundstage snaps into focus, but the presentation is often too bright. With no toe-in, the treble balance is smoother, but the imaging is more vague.

Toe-in also affects the presentation's overall spaciousness. No toe-in produces a larger, more billowy, less precise soundstage. Instruments are less clearly delineated, but the presentation is bigger and more spacious. Toeing-in the loudspeakers shrinks the apparent size of the soundstage, but allows more precise image localization. Again, the proper amount of toe-in depends on the loudspeaker, room, and personal preference. There's no substitute for listening, adjusting toe-in, and listening again.

Identical toe-in for each loudspeaker is vital. This is most easily accomplished by measuring the distances from the rear wall to each of the loudspeaker's rear edges; these distances will differ according to the degree of toe-in. Repeat this procedure on the other loudspeaker, adjusting its toe-in so that the distances match those of the first loudspeaker. Another way to ensure identical toe-in is to sit in the listening seat and look at the loudspeakers' inside edges. You should see the same amount of each loudspeaker cabinet's inner side panel. Identical toe-in is essential to soundstaging because the speaker's frequency response changes with toe-in, and identical frequency response from both speakers is an important contributor to precise image placement within the soundstage.

Keep in mind that all loudspeaker placement variations are interactive with one another, particularly toe-in and the distance between loudspeakers. For example, a wide soundstage can be achieved with narrow placement but no toe-in, or wide placement with extreme toe-in.

Loudspeaker Placement in Asymmetrical Rooms

So far we've covered loudspeaker placement in an ideal room that is symmetrical and bounded on four sides. But what about those listening rooms in which one side is open to the rest of the house, or rooms in which proper loudspeaker placement is difficult? Fortunately, you can still get good sound in these odd-shaped rooms.

Let's first consider the room in which one wall is essentially missing, where the listening room opens to the rest of the house (Fig.4-7). The left loudspeaker will introduce more room gain than the right speaker because of its proximity to the corner. Remember that the closer the speaker is to walls, the greater the amount of bass. The right speaker has much less bass reinforcement, creating a bass imbalance.

The solution is two-fold. First, keep the speakers fairly far from the rear wall. This minimizes the room gain for the left loudspeaker, making

Fig. 4-7 A room in which one side is open can cause a bass imbalance.

OPEN
TO
HOUSE

its response more closely match that of the right speaker. Second, install a bass absorber (such as an ASC Tube Trap) in the corner behind the left loudspeaker. This trap will absorb bass energy rather than reflect it back into the room, and thus mimic the lack of room reinforcement from the right loudspeaker. You'll never be able to get a precise match, but these two techniques should get the two speakers close in bass output. I had a listening room for about two years that looked like Fig.4-7, and got good results with a 16" ASC Full Round Tube Trap in the left corner behind the loudspeaker.

Fig. 4-8 In angled rooms, the loudspeakers should be placed so that sidewall reflections are directed away from the listener.

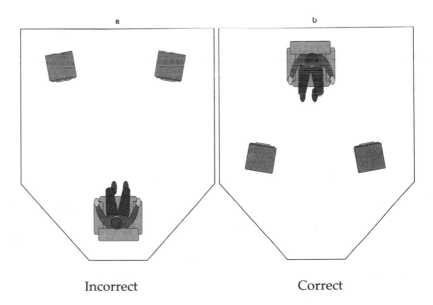

a   b

Incorrect   Correct

If a room has non-parallel walls, try to position the loudspeakers at the room's narrow end. Figs.4-8a and b show incorrect and correct loudspeaker placement in such a room. The problem with the placement shown in Fig.4-8a (left) is that detrimental sidewall reflections are directed at the listening position. In Fig.4-8b (right) sidewall reflections are naturally directed away from the listener. Many recording-studio control rooms are narrower at the speaker location for just this reason.

Short-Wall vs. Long-Wall Placement

The examples shown have all assumed that the loudspeakers will be placed on the room's short wall. This traditional method provides the maximum space for bringing the loudspeakers out into the room and away from the rear wall. But putting the speakers on the long wall (Fig.4-9) also has some advantages.

Fig. 4-9
Positioning the loudspeakers on the room's long wall reduces sidewall reflections at the listening position.

Long-wall placement results in more direct sound at the listening position and less sidewall-reflected energy. This confers a large advantage in tonal purity and soundstage accuracy, for reasons described later in this chapter. You hear more of the speaker and less of the room. The sound tends to be more immediate, detailed, and present.

Long-wall placement works only when the room is wide enough to accommodate some space between the speakers and the wall behind them, space between the speakers and listening position, and some space between the listener and the wall behind the listening position. If you sit with your head very near the wall behind you, the sound will likely be boomy. Consequently, you end up sitting fairly close to the loudspeakers with long-wall placement in all but very large rooms. As described in Chapter 7, speakers with first-order crossovers require significant space between speakers and listener for the sound of the individual drivers to properly integrate. If you sit too close to a speaker with first-order crossovers, the tonal balance will be wrong. Consider the room's width and the type of crossovers in your loudspeakers when deciding if long-wall placement is right for you. The reduction in reflected sound at the listening position with long-wall placement is a considerable advantage.

Finally, you may consider placing your loudspeakers at an odd angle in relation to the room, as shown in Fig.4-10. I've seen loudspeaker designers use this technique when trying to get good sound in a small hotel room at hi-fi shows. This placement, which works best for small speakers, has the advantage of reducing sidewall reflections at the listening position. The disadvantages are that it consumes much of the room's floor space and positions the speakers closer to walls, where the bass will be reinforced. That's why this technique is more successful with small speakers that have limited bass extension.

Fig. 4-10 Angled loudspeaker placement works best with small speakers.

Dipolar and Bipolar Loudspeaker Placement

Dipolar loudspeakers produce sound to the rear as well as to the front. An electrostatic speaker is a dipole because the vibrating diaphragm sits in open space rather than in a cabinet, launching sound equally to the front and rear. This rear wave from dipolar speakers is *out of phase* with the front wave; that is, when the diaphragm moves forward to create positive pressure in front of the diaphragm, it creates negative pressure behind the diaphragm.

A *bipolar* speaker typically uses arrays of conventional dynamic drivers on the front and rear of the loudspeaker enclosure. The front and rear waves from a bipolar speaker are *in phase* with each other. That's the difference between dipolar and bipolar: a dipole's rear wave is *out of phase* with the front wave, and a bipole's rear wave is *in phase* with the front wave.

Both of these speaker types are covered in detail in Chapter 7. What concerns us here, however, are the special placement requirements of bipolar and dipolar loudspeakers, along with the different ways in which they interact with the listening room.

The most important consideration when positioning dipoles is that the wall behind the speakers (the rear wall) has a much greater influence on the sound than it does with conventional point-source speakers (those that direct energy in only one direction). Conversely, how the sidewalls are treated is less important with dipoles because they radiate very little energy to the sides. (See Fig.7-4 in Chapter 7, which shows the dispersion patterns of point-source and dipolar speakers.)

Generally, dipoles like a reflective rear wall, but with some diffusing objects behind the speaker to break up the reflected energy. A highly absorbent rear wall defeats the purpose of a dipole; that reflected energy is beneficial, and you want to hear it. But if the wall is flat and lacks surfaces that scatter sound, the reflected energy combines with the direct sound in a way that reduces soundstage depth. Bookcases directly behind dipolar speakers help diffuse (scatter) the rear wave, as do rock fireplaces, furniture, and other objects of irregular shape. ASC Tube Traps can be positioned directly behind dipoles with their reflective sides out, or you can go all the way with RPG Diffusors. RPG's Skyline diffuser (Fig.4-11) is ideal for diffusing the rear wave from dipoles. These 2' by 2' squares are highly effective in scattering sound, and can be attached to a wall or mounted on a stand. A tall dipolar speaker benefits from two or three Skylines arrayed vertically directly behind each speaker.

Fig. 4-11 RPG's Skyline diffuser effectively scatters sound.

Courtesy RPG Diffusor Systems, Inc.

You still want to treat the sidewalls to absorb reflections with dipoles, but their narrow radiation pattern makes treating the sidewalls less important than with point-source speakers. This is particularly true of dipoles that sound their best toed-in toward the listening position. Similarly, dipoles have very narrow vertical dispersion, meaning they direct very little sound toward the ceiling and floor.

Dipolar loudspeakers also need to be placed farther out into the room than conventional point-source speakers. You can't put dipoles near the rear wall and expect a big, deep soundstage. Be prepared to give up a significant area of your listening room to dipolar speakers.

Subwoofer Setup and Placement

It's relatively easy to put a subwoofer into your system and hear more bass. What's difficult is making the subwoofer's bass *integrate* with the sound of your main speakers. Low bass as reproduced by a subwoofer's big cone can sound different from the bass reproduced by the smaller cones in the left and right speakers. A well-integrated subwoofer produces a seamless sound, no boomy thump, and natural reproduction of music. A poorly integrated subwoofer will sound thick, heavy, boomy, and unnatural, calling attention to the fact that you have smaller speakers reproducing the frequency spectrum from the midrange up, and a big subwoofer putting out low bass.

Integrating a subwoofer into your system is challenging because the main speakers may have small cones, and the subwoofer has a large and heavy cone. Moreover, the subwoofer is optimized for putting out lots of low bass, not for reproducing detail. The main speakers' upper bass is quick, clean, and articulate. The subwoofer's bass is often slow and heavy.

Achieving good integration between small speakers and a subwoofer is easier if you buy a complete system made by one manufacturer. Such systems are engineered to work together to provide a smooth transition between the subwoofer and the main speakers. Specifically, the crossover network removes bass from the left and right speakers, and removes midrange and treble frequencies from the signal driving the subwoofer. If all these details are handled by the same designer, you're much more likely to get a smooth transition than if the subwoofer is an add-on component from a different manufacturer.

If you do choose a subwoofer made by a different manufacturer, several controls found on most subwoofers help you integrate the sub into your system. One control lets you adjust the *crossover frequency*. This sets the frequency at which the transition between the subwoofer and the main speakers takes place. Frequencies below the crossover frequency are reproduced by the subwoofer; frequencies above the crossover frequency are reproduced by the main speakers. If you have small speakers that don't go very low in the bass and you set the crossover frequency too low, you'll get a "hole" in the frequency response. That is, there will be a narrow band of frequencies that aren't reproduced by the woofer *or* the main speakers.

Setting the subwoofer's crossover frequency too high also results in poor integration, but for a different reason. The big cone of a subwoofer is specially designed to reproduce low bass. When it is asked to also reproduce upper-bass frequencies, those upper-bass frequencies are less clear and distinct than if they were reproduced by the smaller main speakers. Finding just the right crossover frequency is the first step in achieving good integration. Most subwoofer owner's manuals include instructions for setting the crossover frequency. As a rule of thumb, the lower the subwoofer's crossover is set, the better.

Some subwoofers also provide a knob or switch marked *Phase*. To understand a subwoofer's phase control, visualize a sound wave being launched from your subwoofer and from your main speakers at the same time. Unless the main speakers and subwoofer are identical distances from your ears, those two sound waves will reach your ears at different times, or have a phase difference between them. In addition, the electronics inside a subwoofer can create a phase difference in the signal. The phase control lets you delay the wave generated by the subwoofer so that it lines up in time with the wave from the main speaker. When the sound waves are in-phase, you hear a more coherent and better-integrated sound.

One way of setting the phase control is to sit in the listening position with music playing through the system. Have a friend rotate the phase control (or flip the phase switch) until the bass sounds the smoothest.

But there's a much more precise way of setting the phase control that guarantees perfect phase alignment between the subwoofer and main speakers. First, reverse the connections on your main loudspeakers so that the black speaker wire goes to the speaker's red terminal, and the red speaker wire goes to the speaker's black terminal. Do this with both speakers. Now, from a test CD that includes pure test tones, select the track whose frequency is the same as the subwoofer's crossover frequency. Sit in the listening position and have a friend rotate the subwoofer's phase control until you hear the *least* amount of bass. The subwoofer's phase control is now set perfectly. Return your speaker connections to their previous (correct) positions: red to red, black to black.

Here's what's happening when you follow this procedure. By reversing the polarity of the main speakers, you're putting them out of phase with the subwoofer. When you play a test signal whose frequency is the same as the subwoofer's crossover point, both the sub and the main speakers will be reproducing that frequency. You'll hear minimum bass when the waves from the main speakers and subwoofers are maximally out of phase. That is, when the main speaker's cone is moving in, the subwoofer's cone is moving out. The two out-of-phase waves cancel each other, producing very little bass. Now, when you return your loudspeakers to their proper connection (putting them back in-phase with the subwoofer), they will be maximally *in-phase* with the subwoofer. This is the most accurate method of setting a subwoofer's phase control. Unless you move the subwoofer or main speakers, you need to perform this exercise only once.

The best integration comes from adding two (or more) subwoofers to your system. Two subwoofers drive the air in the room more uniformly, with fewer extremes of standing waves. The result is smoother bass throughout the room and better integration with the main speakers.

You can also get more dynamic impact and clarity from your sub-woofer by placing it close to the listening position. Sitting near the sub-woofer causes you to hear more of the sub's direct sound and less of the sound after it has been reflected around the room. You hear—and feel—more of the low-frequency wave launch, which adds to the visceral impact of owning a subwoofer. Bass impact is more startling, powerful, and dynamic when the subwoofer is placed near the listening position.

Subwoofer placement also has a large effect on how much bass you hear and how well the sub integrates with your main speakers. When a subwoofer is correctly positioned, the bass will be clean, tight, quick, and punchy. A well-located subwoofer will also produce a seamless sound between the sub and the front speakers; you won't hear the subwoofer as a separate speaker. A poorly positioned subwoofer will sound boomy, excessively heavy, thick, lacking detail, slow, and have little dynamic impact. In addition, you'll hear exactly where the front speakers leave off and the subwoofer takes over.

The simplest, most effective way of positioning a subwoofer is to put it near the listening position. Raise the subwoofer off the floor, if possible, so that it's close to where the listeners' ears would normally be. Play a piece of music with an ascending and descending bass line, such as a "walking" bass in straight-ahead jazz. Crawl around the floor on your hands and knees (make sure the neighbors aren't watching) until you find the spot where the bass sounds the smoothest, and where each bass note has about the same volume and clarity. Avoid positions where some notes "hang" longer, and/or sound slower or thicker, than others. When you've determined where the bass sounds best, put the subwoofer there. Now, when you're back in the listening seat, the bass should sound smooth and natural.

Some general guidelines for subwoofer placement: As with full-range speakers, avoid putting the subwoofer the same distance from two walls. For example, if you have a 20'-wide room, don't put the sub-woofer 10' from each wall. Similarly, don't put the subwoofer near a corner and equidistant from the side and rear walls. Instead, stagger the distances to each wall. Staggering the subwoofer's distance from each wall smooths the bass because the frequencies being reinforced by the wall are randomized rather than coincident.

Multichannel Loudspeaker Placement

So far, we've discussed the placement of two loudspeakers for stereo music reproduction. With multichannel music and home theater becoming increasingly common, let's expand on these loudspeaker-placement principles to include positioning more than two loudspeakers.

As described in Chapter 14 ("Multichannel Audio"), the optimum loud-speaker type (point source, dipolar) and configuration differ for multichannel music reproduction and home theater. For multichannel music, the ideal loudspeaker array is five identical full-range loudspeakers placed equidistant from the listener. For film-soundtrack reproduction, the center loudspeaker is typically smaller and lacks bass extension, and the surround speakers are dipolar types mounted on the sidewalls. Loudspeaker arrays optimized for home theater also include a subwoofer.

Let's first look at the ideal multichannel music loudspeaker array. The center loudspeaker should be positioned on the room's center-line directly in front of the listening position, and slightly behind the plane of the left and right loudspeakers. This placement creates a gentle arc, and puts the center loudspeaker at the same distance from the listener as the left and right loudspeakers. If the three front loudspeakers were lined up, the sound from the center speaker would reach the listener before the sound from the left and right speakers.

The rear-channel speakers should be located at 135–150° as shown in Fig.4-12 and at the same distance from the listener as the front three loud-speakers. This placement isn't always practical, however, so many multi-channel products provide a rear-channel delay for those situations in which the listener must sit closer to the rear loudspeakers. Delaying the signals to the rear channels causes the sound from the rear speakers to reach the lis-tener at the same time as sound from the front speakers.

Fig. 4-12 A typical multi-channel music loudspeaker array employs five identical full-range loudspeak-ers positioned equidistant from the listener at the locations shown.

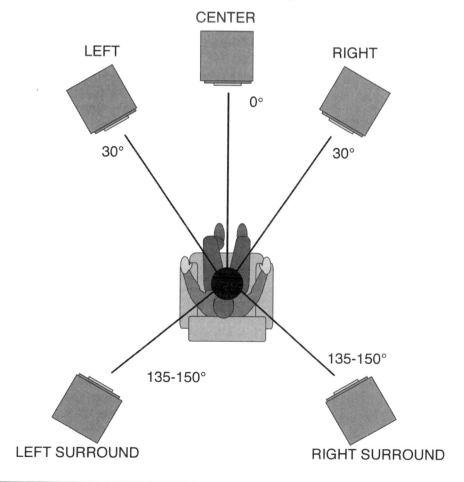

With this array, the front left and rear left loudspeakers can produce phantom images between them along the left sidewall, and the front right and rear right loudspeakers create phantom images along the right sidewall. Correct loudspeaker placement helps to achieve a soundfield that appears to be continuous from front to back, rather than as two separate soundfields at the front and rear of the room.

A multichannel music system can also employ seven speakers, with the two additional speakers located at the side positions. This array produces the greatest spatial realism because the side images are now "hard" rather than phantom, and the feeling of being immersed in a continuous soundfield is enhanced. Multichannel recordings made in a large acoustic and played back through a properly set up 7-channel system can be staggering in their ability to create a feeling of actually being inside the original acoustic space. It is even possible to hear discrete sidewall reflections localized along the sidewalls, just as one would hear at the original acoustic event.

Loudspeaker arrays optimized for film-soundtrack reproduction usually employ dipolar surround loudspeakers rather than point-source loudspeakers. Dipolar speakers produce sound equally to the front and rear; when positioned on the sidewalls, the listener hears sound from the surround speakers only after it has been reflected from the room's boundaries (Fig.4-13). This simulates the array of multiple surround

Fig. 4-13
Multichannel loudspeaker arrays optimized for film-soundtrack reproduction usually employ dipolar surround loudspeakers.

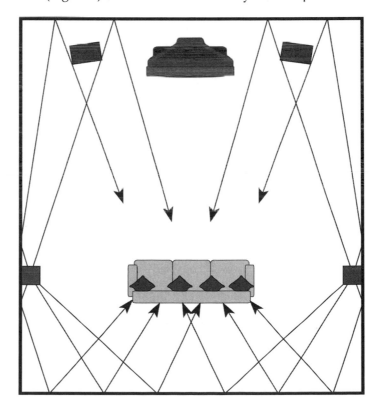

speakers in a movie theater from just two surround speakers, and creates a greater feeling of envelopment. (Chapter 13 includes more detailed information on multichannel loudspeaker placement.)

Loudspeaker Placement Summary

Loudspeaker placement is the single most important thing you can do to improve your system's sound. It's free, helps develop listening skills, and can make the difference between mediocre and spectacular sound with the same electronics and loudspeakers. Before spending money on upgrading components or acoustic treatments, be sure you've realized your system's potential with correct loudspeaker placement.

After you've found the best loudspeaker placement, install the carpet-piercing spikes (if any) supplied by the manufacturer. Level the spikes so that the loudspeaker doesn't rock: the loudspeaker's weight should be carried by all four (or three) spikes. If you have wood floors that you don't want to mar with spikes, place the round metal discs that are often supplied with the loudspeakers beneath the spikes.

You've seen how loudspeaker placement gives you precise and independent control over different aspects of the music presentation. You can control both the quantity and the quality of the bass by changing the loudspeakers' distances from the rear and side walls. The audibility of room resonance modes can be reduced by finding the best spots for the loudspeakers and listening chair. Treble balance can be adjusted by listening height and toe-in. The balance between soundstage focus and spaciousness is easily changed just by toeing-in the speakers. Soundstage depth can be increased by moving the speakers farther out into the room.

I've had the privilege of watching some of the world's greatest loudspeaker designers set up loudspeakers in my listening room for review. At the very highest levels of the art, tiny movements—half an inch, for example—can make the difference between very good and superlative sound. The process can take as little as two hours, or as long as three days. I've often had the experience of thinking the sound was excellent after half a day of moving the loudspeakers, only to discover that the loudspeaker was capable of much greater performance when perfectly dialed-in.

Loudspeaker positioning is a powerful tool for achieving the best sound in your listening room, and it doesn't cost a cent. Take advantage of it.

Common Room Problems and How to Treat Them

Treating your listening room can range from simply hanging a rug on a wall to installing specially designed acoustic devices. Large gains in sound quality can be realized just by adding—or moving—common domestic materials such as carpets, area rugs, and drapes. This approach is inexpensive, simple, and often more aesthetically pleasing than installing less familiar acoustic products. You can improve your room with existing household materials, or take the next step of installing dedicated acoustic-control devices. Here are some of the most common room problems, and how to correct them.

1) Untreated parallel surfaces

Perhaps the most common and pernicious of room problems is that of untreated parallel surfaces. If two reflective surfaces face each other, *flutter echo* will occur. Flutter echo is a "pinging" sound that remains after the direct sound has stopped. If you've ever been in an empty, uncarpeted house and clapped your hands, you've heard flutter echo. It sounds like a ringing that hangs in the air long after the clap has decayed. Flutter echo is a periodic repetition caused by the uncontrolled reflection of a sound back and forth between two surfaces. Imagine two mirrors facing each other, the reflections bouncing back and forth between the reflective surfaces to create the illusion of an infinitely receding distance. Flutter echo can blur transient attacks and decays and add a hard, metallic character to the upper midband and treble.

Try clapping your hands in various rooms of the house—particularly the bathroom or hallway. If your listening room has a pinging overhang similar to what you hear in the bathroom, you need to correct this problem.

Flutter echo is easy to prevent. Simply identify the reflective parallel surfaces and put an absorbing or diffusing material on one of them. This will break up the repeated reflections between the surfaces. The material could be a rug hung on a wall, a carpet on the floor (if the flutter echo is between a hard floor and ceiling), drapes over a window, or an acoustically absorbent material applied to a wall. Even small patches of highly absorbent acoustical foam, such as Sonex (described later), will kill flutter echo.

An effective material for controlling flutter echo without making the room too dead is a very thin carpet-like material used in airports and conference rooms. Although very expensive when sold as an acoustical treatment, this same carpet-like material is available from carpet mills for a fraction of the acoustic supply house's price. It is unobtrusive, easy to apply, available in a variety of colors, relatively inexpensive, and highly effective. Moreover, its absorption characteristics are just right for preventing flutter echo without absorbing too much energy and making the room "dead." The carpet can be glued or tacked into place; mounting it on Masonite backing allows you to move it around to find its most effective placement.

Flutter echo can be reduced or eliminated by a product called Flutterfree, manufactured by RPG Diffusor Systems. Flutterfree is a 4" wide hardwood strip available in 4' or 8' lengths in which wells of various depths and widths have been cut. The device acts as a reflection phase grating, diffusing sound impinging upon it. Flutterfree can be positioned horizontally or vertically on walls or ceilings, and grouped together or spaced.

Whatever solution works best for you, killing flutter echo is of utmost importance.

2) Uncontrolled floor and side-wall reflections

It is inevitable that loudspeakers will be placed next to the room's side walls and near the floor. Sound from the loudspeakers reaches the listener directly, in addition to being reflected from the side walls, floor, and ceiling. Side-wall reflections are the music signal delayed in time, colored in timbre, and spatially positioned at different locations from the direct sound. All these factors can degrade sound quality. Moreover, floor and side-wall reflections interact with the direct sound to further color the music's tonal character. Fig.4-14 shows how the sound at the listening seat is a combination of direct and reflected sound.

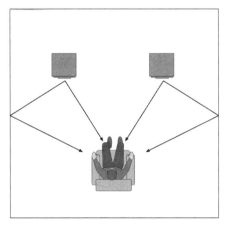

Fig. 4-14 The listener receives a combination of direct and reflected sound.

Side-wall reflections color the music's tonal balance in three ways. First, virtually all loudspeakers' *off-axis responses* (frequency response measured at the side of the loudspeaker) are much less flat (accurate) than their on-axis responses. The sound emanating from the loudspeaker sides (the signal that reflects off the side wall) may have large peaks and dips in its frequency response. When this colored signal is reflected from the side wall to the listener, we hear this tonal coloration imposed on the music.

Second, the side wall's acoustic characteristics will further color the reflection. If the wall absorbs high frequencies but not midband energy, the reflection will have even less treble.

Finally, when the direct and reflected sounds combine, the listener hears a combination of the direct sound from the loudspeaker and a slightly delayed version of the sound reflected from the side wall. The delay is caused by the additional path-length difference between the sound source (the loudspeaker) and the listener. Because sound travels at 1130 feet per second, we can easily calculate the delay time. If the additional path-length difference in Fig.4-14 was 4′, the side-wall reflection will be delayed by 3.5ms (3.5 milliseconds, or 3.5 thousandths of a second) in relation to the direct sound.

The result is a phenomenon called *comb filtering* (see Fig.4-15), a sequence of peaks and notches (hence its similarity to a comb) in the frequency response caused by constructive and destructive interference between the direct and reflected sounds. The phase difference between the two signals causes cancellation at certain frequencies and reinforcement at others, determined by the path-length distance. It all adds up to coloration of the signal at the listening position.

Fig. 4-15 Comb filtering is a sequence of peaks and notches in the frequency response caused by combining direct and reflected sound.

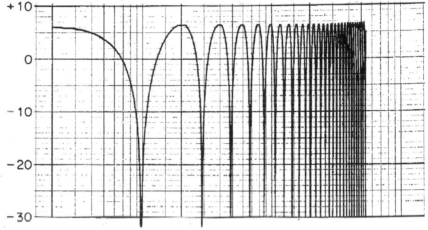

Courtesy *Audio Engineering Handbook*, K. Benson, McGraw-Hill, Inc., 1988

Comb filtering is used as a special effect in the recording studio. Adding a slight delay to a signal and mixing the direct and delayed signals is called *phasing*, characterized by a hollow sound. Darth Vader's voice in the *Star Wars* series undoubtedly includes some phasing. Continuously varying the delay causes the frequencies at which the reinforcements and cancellations occur to sweep the audio band for an effect called *flanging*. It's called flanging because in the days before digital-delay lines, the engineer used a tape machine to create the delay, and would put his thumb on the tape reel's flange to vary the delay time and create the characteristic sweeping sound. The most widely heard example of flanging is perhaps the Doobie Brothers song "Listen to the Music."

The result of these mechanisms—the loudspeaker's colored off-axis response, the sidewall's acoustic properties, and comb filtering—is a sound with a very different tonal balance from that of the direct signal from the loudspeakers. Side-wall reflections are one reason the same loudspeakers sound different in different rooms.

Side-wall reflections not only affect the perceived spectral balance, they also destroy precise image placement within the soundstage. The reflections present "virtual" images of the loudspeakers' signal that appear on the side walls. Although some degree of side-wall reflection adds spaciousness and size, strong reflections increase the *apparent* distance between the loudspeakers. This blurs the spatial distinction between individual images and makes the soundstage less focused and precise. When we hear a center-placed image as partially emanating from positions beyond the left and right loudspeaker boundaries, the tight image focus we seek is destroyed.

Sound also reflects from the floor and ceiling. Floor reflections tend to cause a reduction in mid bass energy, making the presentation a little leaner. The ceiling reflection affects the sound less than the side-wall reflections because of its greater path-length difference. Note that the sound of dipolar loudspeakers, which direct very little energy toward the ceiling, is less affected by ceiling reflections than is the sound of conventional loudspeakers. Finally, a sloped ceiling is advantageous with conventional loudspeakers when those speakers are placed at the short end of the room. The ceiling slope will tend to direct ceiling reflections away from the listening position.

Reflections reaching the listener from just one room boundary are called *first-order reflections*. These reflections have the greatest amplitude, and have the most effect on the reproduced sound.

Fortunately, treating side-wall reflections is simple: just put an absorbing or diffusing material on the side walls between the loudspeakers and the listening position. Drapes are highly effective, particularly those with heavy materials and deep folds. The floor reflection is even easier to deal with: carpet or a heavy area rug on the floor will absorb most of the reflection and reduce its detrimental effects. Low frequencies, however, won't be absorbed by a carpet or rug, leading to a cancellation in the midbass caused by interference between the direct and reflected waves. This is the so-called "Allison Effect," named after loudspeaker designer Roy Allison, who first publicized the phenomenon.

Interestingly, the type of carpet between you and the loudspeakers can affect sound quality. Specifically, wool carpet produces a more natural tonal balance than does synthetic carpet. That's because the fibers in wool carpet all have slightly different lengths and thicknesses, which makes them absorb different frequencies. Synthetic carpet, by contrast, is composed of identically sized and shaped fibers that absorb only a very narrow band of frequencies. You can demonstrate this to yourself at a carpet store by speaking into sample pieces of wool and synthetic carpet and listening to the sound of your voice. The wool carpet will produce a more natural timbre.

Side-wall reflections should be diffused (scattered) or absorbed. Diffusion turns the single discrete reflection into many lower-amplitude reflections spread out over time and reflected in different directions (see Fig.4-16).

Fig. 4-16 Sound striking a surface is absorbed, reflected, or diffused (or a combination of the three).

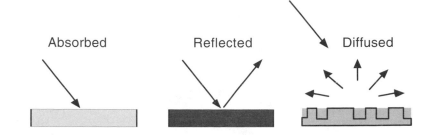

Absorbed   Reflected   Diffused

Fig. 4-17a An RPG Diffusor

Courtesy RPG Diffusor Systems, Inc.

Diffusion can be achieved with specialized acoustic diffusers such as those made by RPG Diffusors (shown in Fig.4-17a, and described later in this chapter), or an irregular surface. A open-backed bookcase full of books makes an excellent diffuser, particularly if the books are of different depths, or are arranged with their spines sticking out at different distances. Fig.4-17b shows RPG Diffusors installed behind loudspeakers. Note the rug on the floor between the loudspeakers and the listening position.

The second option is to absorb the side-wall reflection with an acoustically absorbent material. The acoustical foams described later in this chapter will work, but completely absorbing the side-wall reflection with an aggressive foam can make the room sound lifeless and constrict the presentation's sense of size and space.

There is some debate in the high-end community as to whether side-wall reflections should be absorbed or diffused. Diffusion proponents argue that the reflected energy is beneficial if converted to many lower-amplitude reflections spread out over time and space, the diffused reflections increasing the presentation's spaciousness and air.

Fig. 4-17b QRD
Diffusors, a
product of RPG
Diffusor
Systems, Inc.
installed at dmp,
(Digital Music
Products, Inc.),
Stamford, CT

Absorption proponents suggest that any reflections within the first 20ms
of the direct sound degrade the signal from the loudspeakers. Most
recording-studio control rooms are designed to provide a "Reflection
Free Zone" (RFZ) where the engineer sits, so that he or she hears only
the direct sound from the studio monitors. My experience suggests that
absorbing side-wall reflections is better than diffusing them, but that diffusing materials behind the listening seat are better than absorbing materials. Diffusing sidewall reflections tends to increase the spaciousness of
the sound; absorbing sidewall reflections reduces soundstage width, but
results in tighter image focus and a more spatially coherent presentation.
There is *no* debate, however, about whether or not uncontrolled side-
wall reflections degrade a room's sonic performance. They do.

An excellent product for controlling side-wall reflections is the
Tower Trap, also made by the Acoustic Sciences Corporation. This is a
tall, cylindrical device with absorptive and reflective (diffusive) sides.
Absorption or diffusion can be selected simply by turning the device.
When placed near the side wall with the reflective side to the room rear,
the absorptive side prevents the first reflection from reaching the listener
directly. Some of the energy striking the side wall is reflected into the
Tower Trap's rear (diffusive) side. Most of the side-wall reflection is
absorbed, while some is delayed in time, attenuated, and diffused—
exactly what we want.

Note that it isn't necessary to treat a listening room's entire side-wall
area; the reflections come only from small points along the wall. At mid-
and high frequencies, sound waves behave more like rays of light. We

can thus trace side-wall reflections to the listening seat and put the treatment in exactly the right location. As with light rays, a sound wave's angle of incidence equals its angle of reflection. That is, the angle at which a sound wave strikes a reflective surface is the same as the angle at which it bounces off that surface.

The technique for tracing side-wall reflections is shown in the series of photographs and illustrations in Figs.4-18, 4-19, and 4-20. First, mount a reflective Mylar strip on the side wall between the listener and the loudspeaker. The strip's center should be at the height of your ears when you're sitting in the listening chair. Next, put light sources (two lamps with their shades removed is ideal) where the loudspeakers are normally placed, as shown in Fig.4-18. When sitting in the listening chair, you'll see the two lamps reflected in the Mylar strip (Fig.4-19). The points along the Mylar strip where you see the lamps' bulbs are exactly the points where sound is reflected from the side walls to the listening seat. This is where to put the acoustic treatment. The photograph in Fig.4-20 shows how strategically placed acoustical materials (in this case, ASC Tower Traps) can kill side-wall reflections from both loudspeakers. Compare Fig.4-19 to Fig.4-20.

Fig. 4-18
Replace the loudspeakers with light sources and install a Mylar strip.

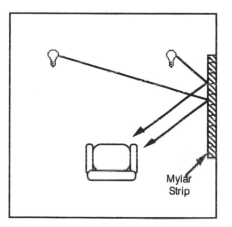

Mylar Strip

Repeat the process for the left side wall. If your listening room is symmetrical and the listening position is in the middle of the room, you need use this technique on only one side wall, then duplicate the acoustic treatment on the other. To maintain acoustical symmetry in the room, both side-wall treatments should be the same.

Treating the side-wall reflections from *both* loudspeakers on *each* side wall improves imaging. The right side wall will reflect sound from both right *and* left loudspeakers. The reflection of the left loudspeaker's signal from the right side wall confuses image placement and constricts soundstage width. This reflection can be thought of as a kind of "acoustic crosstalk"; we don't want left-channel information reflecting from the side wall into the right ear.

Note that a treatment placed away from the wall creates a larger apparent surface area than a treatment attached to the wall. The distance between the treatment and the wall causes the treatment to cast an acoustic shadow on the wall, widening the effective absorption area.

Fig. 4-19 The points of visual reflection are also the points of acoustic reflection.

Fig. 4-20 Acoustic treatments placed exactly at the reflection points kill side-wall reflections.

This technique can be applied to all reflections in the listening room. If you put a Mylar strip around the entire listening room, any point where you see a reflection of the light bulb itself is also a sound-reflection point. Additional absorptive or diffusive surfaces can then be placed and oriented exactly where they do the most good. You can also simply sit in the listening position and have a friend move a mirror along the sidewall. The point where you see the speaker's drivers in the mirror is the point where you should position absorbing or diffusing materials. This technique works for floor reflections; the point on the floor at which the mirror reflects the tweeter to the listening position is the place to add absorbing material.

Even if you don't go to the trouble of putting up a Mylar strip and lamps, you should do something to treat side-wall reflections. Bookcases, rugs, and drapes are all better than bare walls. If you really want to get the best from your system, however, there's no substitute for professionally designed acoustic treatments.

3) Thick, boomy bass

Thick, boomy bass is a common affliction that can be difficult to control. It often results from room resonance modes, poor loudspeaker placement, poor loudspeakers, or not enough low-frequency absorption in the listening room. As we will see in the later section on standing waves, listening-seat position can also exacerbate bass bloat.

If thick and boomy bass persists even after minimizing it with careful loudspeaker placement (the most effective method of alleviating the problem), you may want to consider different loudspeakers. If, however, the boominess is minor and you want to keep your loudspeakers, you can make the presentation leaner and tighter by adding low-frequency absorbers. These devices soak up low frequencies rather than reflecting them back into the room.

Passive low-frequency absorbers simply convert acoustic energy into another form—usually heat within a fibrous material. Low-frequency absorbers can be bought ready-made (such as ASC's Tube Traps and Tower Traps), built from common materials, or incorporated into an existing room structure. The easiest and most effective low-frequency absorber for the audiophile is ASC's 16" Full Round Tube Trap. These devices are extremely powerful, soaking up bass below 125Hz—the region below which most domestic materials stop absorbing. A pair of 16" Full Round Tube Traps in the corners behind the loudspeakers significantly tightens up the bass and removes boom and bloat.

Tube Traps employ a plastic sheet beneath the fabric exterior that covers about half the Trap. By rotating the trap, you can adjust the amount of high- and mid-frequency absorption; with the reflective side facing the listener, the Trap acts as a mid- and high-frequency diffusor. With the reflective side facing the wall, the Trap absorbs a broader range of frequencies. This variability is useful when tuning a room; rotating the Traps so that the reflective side faces the listener keeps the sound from becoming overdamped in the midrange and treble. (Tube Trap construction is shown in Fig.4-21.)

A very inexpensive and effective low-frequency absorber can be made in a few hours for less than $20. These devices, called *panel absorbers*, have very high absorption at low frequencies, and can be tuned to the exact frequency and bandwidth required.

Panel absorbers can stand free of or be built right into an existing wall. In a typical built-in absorber, a 4' by 8' frame of 2x4s is nailed on its edge to the existing wall. The inside is sealed with caulking where the wood meets the wall to make it airtight, then filled with Fiberglas insulation. Next, a sheet of Masonite or plywood is nailed over the frame. Many tiny holes are then drilled in the panel. *Voilà*—a low-frequency panel absorber. (This type of perforated panel absorber is also called a Helmholtz resonator.)

Fig. 4-21 Tube Trap construction. (Courtesy Acoustic Sciences Corporation)

US Patent #4,548,292

THREADED INSERTS FOR STACKING AND HANGING

COMPLETELY SEALED FOR SAFE, DUST-FREE PERFORMANCE

THREE SEPARATE COMPARTMENTS TO CONTROL STANDING WAVES

TREBLE RANGE REFLECTOR

ENTIRE SURFACE IS BASS ABSORPTIVE

STURDY EXOSKELETON CONSTRUCTION FOR STRENGTH AND DURABILITY

OUSTICALLY TRANSPARENT FABRIC

SIZES 9, 11, 13, 16, 20" IN DIAMETER AND UP TO 4' IN HEIGHT

©ACOUSTIC SCIENCES CORP.

Some panel absorbers have no holes, instead using a very thin sheet of material that flexes when struck by sound. The structure's absorption frequency is a function of the airspace depth (2x4s, 2x8s, 2x10s, or 2x12s may be used) and panel thickness. The Fiberglas inside the structure broadens the absorption peak. By changing the airspace depth and (in perforated absorbers) hole size, panel absorbers can be tuned to any low to mid frequency. Most rooms need broadband absorption in the bass, but panel absorbers can be narrowly tuned to absorb room resonance problems. A few panel absorbers, tuned to major resonance modes in the low-frequency spectrum, can greatly reduce bass problems in small rooms. To make these rather ugly contraptions palatable in a home, cover them with fabric. (Note that Helmholtz-type resonators shouldn't be covered directly with fabric: they need at least 1/4" of airspace to allow the holes to "breathe" freely.)

Free-standing panel absorbers are built the same way, but with a sturdy backing (3/4" particleboard, for example) instead of being attached to a wall. Specific details on building panel absorbers—material thickness, perforation size, spacing, etc.—can be found in F. Alton Everest's *The Master Handbook of Acoustics*.

Yet another way to get much-needed low-frequency absorption is by building a bass trap into an existing structure—a closet, say. Simply hanging an absorptive material such as acoustical foam or ordinary Fiberglas over the closet opening provides low-frequency absorption. This type of structure is called a *quarter-wavelength trap*. The trap will have peak absorption at the frequency whose 1/4 wavelength equals the distance between the closet back wall and the absorptive material, and also at odd multiples of the 1/4 wavelength. In fact, any absorptive material hung in front of a reflective surface will form a quarter-wavelength trap. Drapes in front of a window will work, but the distance between the window and drapes is so short that the lowest absorption frequency will be in the midband.

Let's calculate the absorption frequency for a closet 2' deep with absorptive material hung at the front. The formula is $F = 1130/4D$, where

F is the lowest absorption peak, 1130 is the speed of sound in feet per second, and 4D is 4 times the distance between the reflective closet wall and the absorptive material. The lowest peak absorption frequency for a 2'-deep closet is 141Hz. This structure will also have peak absorption at odd multiples of a quarter wavelength: for instance, at three (423Hz), five (706Hz), and seven (989Hz) times 141Hz, and so on. Drapes hung 6" from a window will provide peak absorption at 565Hz, 1695Hz, 2825Hz, 3955Hz, and so on. Slanting the absorptive material will skew these values along a continuum, making the absorption more even with frequency.

The quarter-wavelength trap is typically limited to providing mid-bass absorption because of the large dimensions needed to achieve deep-bass absorption. I must stress, however, that proper loudspeaker placement is the easiest and most effective technique for reducing bass thickness. These acoustic treatments should be tried only *after* exhausting every possible option in loudspeaker placement.

4) *Reflective objects near the loudspeaker*

Reflective objects near the loudspeakers—equipment racks, windows behind the loudspeakers, subwoofers or furniture between the loudspeakers, even power amplifiers on the floor—can cause poor image focus and lack of depth. The best solution is to remove the offending object. I gained a huge increase in image focus and soundstage depth in my system just by moving my equipment racks from between the loudspeakers to the side of the room. If this is impractical, move the reflective objects as far behind the loudspeakers as possible. Power amplifiers should not extend in front of the loudspeakers' front panels, for example. And for the best musical performance, don't put a big television monitor between the loudspeakers. This is one reason why a music system should ideally be separate from a video system: imaging is degraded by a large piece of reflective glass near the loudspeakers. Having said that, however, there are a few tricks you can use to minimize the deleterious effect a video monitor has on music reproduction. (These techniques are described in Chapter 13.) Systems that employ a front-projector system and separate retractable screen don't suffer this problem.

If you can't move the offending object, cover it with an absorbing material such as Sonex. Windows behind the loudspeakers should be draped, with the drapes closed when listening. There's a large window directly behind my loudspeakers; I hear a significant increase in soundstage depth with the drapes pulled closed.

A good test of whether imaging is degraded by reflective objects near the loudspeakers is the Listening Environment Diagnostic Recording (LEDR) found on the *Chesky Records Jazz Sampler & Audiophile Test Compact Disc, Vol.1* (Chesky JD37). The test consists of a synthetic percussion instrument processed to sound as if it is moving in an arc between and above the loudspeakers. A system and room with good imaging will make the sound appear to move smoothly and consistently in the intended direction. Any holes in the image will be characterized by the sound jumping from one spot to the next rather than a smooth, unbroken motion. Such holes could be due to poor loudspeaker quality or placement, but can often be corrected just by moving reflective objects away from the loudspeakers. Best of all, a potentially large improvement in imaging and soundstaging can be had for a few minutes of your time.

Acoustical Do's and Don'ts

I've summarized this chapter into a few simple guidelines for improving your listening room. This next section is a short course for those readers who don't want to read about absorption coefficients and off-axis response. If you just want some practical tips for getting the most out of your system, this is the section to read. More detail on each of these points can be found throughout the chapter.

1) Loudspeaker placement

Just as real estate agents chant "location, location, location" as the three most important things about the desirability of a house, the three most important ways to improve the sound in your room are loudspeaker placement, loudspeaker placement, and loudspeaker placement. Follow the suggestions in this chapter and spend a few hours moving your loudspeakers around and listening. You'll not only end up with better sound, but become more attuned to sonic differences. All acoustic treatments should be built on a foundation of good loudspeaker placement.

2) Start with good ratios between the room's length, width, and height.

This isn't always possible, but when you're out house-hunting, take your tape measure and the table on good room ratios on page 113. If you can build a room from scratch, or convert a garage or basement into a listening room, choosing optimum dimensional ratios gives you a significant head start in getting great sound from your system.

3) Avoid untreated parallel surfaces.

If you've got bare walls facing each other, you'll have flutter echo. Kill the flutter echo by facing one wall with an absorbent material. Use one of the acoustical foams described, RPG Flutterfree, a rug, or the carpet-like material described later in this chapter. Note that a product such as ASC Tube Traps can provide low-frequency absorption, sidewall diffusion, and reduce flutter echo all at the same time.

4) Absorb or diffuse side-wall and floor reflections.

Bare floors should be covered with carpet between the listening seat and the loudspeakers. Treat the side walls between the loudspeakers and the listening position with an absorbing or diffusing material. Avoid having reflective surfaces, such as bare walls and windows, next to the loudspeakers. ASC Tower Traps, the various acoustical foams, and RPG Diffusors are all effective in treating side-wall reflections. Bookcases on the side walls make good diffusers.

5) *Keep reflective objects away from loudspeakers.*

Equipment racks, power amplifiers, furniture, and other acoustically reflective objects near the loudspeakers will degrade imaging and soundstaging. Move them behind the loudspeakers, or cover them with an absorbing material.

6) *Choose a room with a high, sloped ceiling.*

This isn't always possible, but a high, sloped ceiling skews the floor-to-ceiling resonance modes and reduces the early reflections at the listening position, resulting in smoother bass and a more spacious and open presentation. The loudspeakers should be positioned in the low-ceilinged portion of the room.

7) *Balance high-frequency absorbing materials with low-frequency absorbing materials.*

Most rooms have lots of high-frequency absorption but little low-frequency absorption. Carpet, drapes, and soft furniture should be complemented with low-frequency absorbers (ASC Tube Traps or home-made panel absorbers) to keep the reverberation time flat across the band. Thick, slow bass results from such imbalances in reverberation.

8) *Move the listening seat for best low-frequency balance.*

Standing waves create stationary areas of high and low pressure in the room. Move the listening chair for best balance. Avoid sitting against the rear wall; the sound will be bass-heavy.

9) *Break up standing-wave patterns with irregular surfaces or objects.*

Strategically placed furniture or structures help break up standing waves. Large pieces of furniture behind the listening position diffuse waves reflected from the wall behind the listener.

A Short Course in Acoustical Theory

You don't need to know any acoustical theory to get good sound from your system. However, I've included the following survey of basic acoustical principles for those who want to take the next step in understanding how sound behaves in a room.

Listening-Room Resonance Modes

Resonance is the vibration of an object at its natural frequency, determined by the object's material and dimensions. Resonances surround us all the time—from a bell ringing at a certain pitch, to the sound made by blowing across the opening of a soda bottle. A singer breaking a glass with her voice is another example of resonance. It's not that the singer is that loud; when she hits the resonant frequency of the air in the glass, the reinforcement caused by the resonance adds energy to her voice.

As music lovers, we're interested in acoustic resonance: the reinforcement of certain frequencies within an enclosed volume of air, such as a listening room. When excited by the sound from the loudspeakers, the air in the listening room will resonate at particular frequencies, determined by the distances between the room's walls. These resonant points, called *room resonance modes,* can severely color the bass by creating large peaks and dips in the frequency response. Room resonance modes impose a sonic signature on the reproduced sound.

The room acts as an equalizer between your loudspeakers and ears, boosting certain frequencies and attenuating others. The result is degraded sound quality. In a poor room, the bass might lack specific pitch definition or sound slow and tubby, certain notes might be more prominent than others, dynamic impact could be reduced—or all of these at once.

Resonance modes also cause the room to selectively store energy at the resonant frequencies, and then release that energy more slowly than other frequencies. The result is a blurring and muddying of the sound tonally, along with a distortion of music's dynamic structure and reduction in transient fidelity.

Let's consider what happens along the length of a listening room when the air inside it is excited by sound from the loudspeakers. For now, we'll ignore the fact that the room has height and width, and consider only the resonance between the two walls that define the room's length.

A listening room's resonant frequencies are determined by the distance between the room's walls. The farther apart the walls are, the lower the resonant frequency. Specifically, the lowest resonant frequency, called the *fundamental* resonance, occurs when the room's length equals half the wavelength of the sound. Put another way, a resonant mode will occur when the sound's wavelength is twice the length of the room.

Other resonant modes occur at twice this frequency, three times this frequency, and so on. Whenever the length of the room is a multiple of half of the sound's wavelength, a resonant mode will occur. This phenomenon, along with the formula for calculating resonant mode frequencies, is shown in Fig.4-22.

Calculating your listening room's resonant modes is easy. (But remember: we're still considering only the room's length.) The formula is F1 = 1130/2L. F1 is the first resonant mode, 1130 is the speed of sound in air (in feet per second), and 2L is two times the room's length (in feet). If the room is 21' long, its first resonant mode will be 27Hz (1130/2 x 21).

Fig. 4-22
Resonant modes occur when the distance between the room's walls equals half the wavelength of sound. Resonant modes also occur at each multiple of half a wavelength.

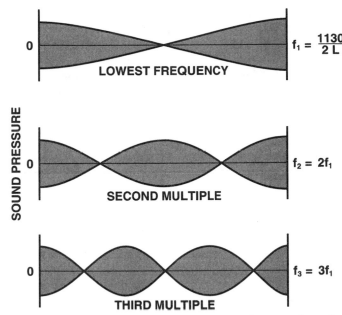

We know that the next mode will occur when the wavelength equals the room's length, at 54Hz (2 x F1), then again at the next multiple of half a wavelength (1-1/2 wavelengths) at 81Hz (3 x F1), again at 108Hz (4 x F1), and so forth. It is only necessary to consider room modes up to about 300Hz, after which they tend to become so dense that they don't cause problems.

The room's height and width will also create their own resonant modes. If we have an 8' ceiling, the resonant modes will occur at 71Hz (1130/2 x 8), 141Hz, 212Hz, and so on. If the width is 13', the resonant modes will be at 43Hz (1130/2 x 13), 87Hz, 130Hz, 174Hz, 217Hz, 261Hz, etc.

What this means to audiophiles wanting the most accurate reproduction possible is that those frequencies will be emphasized in a 21' by 8' by 13' room because of the room's resonance modes. These emphases, or peaks, in the frequency response color the sound. In fact, room resonance modes can cause bass peaks and dips as large as 30dB. Resonance modes are a significant source of coloration in listening rooms, causing poor bass articulation, boominess, and bass thickness.

You can hear (and identify) room resonance modes most easily by playing the swept sine wave test from the *AVIA Guide to Home Theater* test DVD. This test signal sweeps from a high frequency to a low frequency, accompanied by a readout from the video portion of the disc (when the DVD player is connected to a video monitor) showing the descending frequency of the test signal at any given moment. You can simply listen and hear how some frequencies get much louder than others, or use a sound-pressure level (SPL) meter to measure the effect.

We can see how resonances store energy at certain frequencies, and then release that energy over time, in Fig.4-23. This is an actual measurement of my listening room before and after acoustic treatment. The MATT test signal is played through the loudspeakers, a measurement microphone picks up the signal, and the result is plotted graphically. The MATT signal is a swept sine wave, spanning the range from 20Hz–1950Hz, and interrupted with silence every sixteenth of a second. The signal sounds like a series of blips of ascending frequency, as the signal is on, and then off, for that duration. The measurement result shows how the room modifies the signal, specifically the frequencies at which the room stores energy, and how severely the transient nature of the test signal is distorted. Acoustic energy "hangs" in the room during the silences between blips, filling in the nulls in the chart. The deeper the nulls in the trace, and the flatter the peaks, and the more regular the trace's shape, the better.

Fig. 4-23 Results of the MATT test on an actual room before (lower trace) and after (upper trace) acoustic treatment.

The upper trace looks almost like a square wave, with deep silences between blips, indicating that the room isn't storing and releasing much energy. The lower trace, the room's measured performance before treatment, shows that the nulls are much less deep. This indicates that the room is smearing the energy from the test signal over time, reducing articulation and degrading transient fidelity.

Optimizing Dimensional Ratios

We can minimize the frequency-response peaks and dips caused by room resonance modes by choosing a listening room with dimensional ratios that more evenly spread the resonant modes over the low-frequency band. Let's examine the resonance modes of two rooms of about equal volume. The first room has poor dimensional ratios, while the second room's dimensional ratios are excellent.

The first room is 24' long and 16' wide, with an 8' ceiling. If we calculate and plot the resonant modes for each distance (length, width, height), we end up with a chart that looks like this:

Mode	Length 24'	Width 16'	Height 8'
F1	24Hz	35Hz	71Hz
F2	48Hz	70Hz	142Hz
F3	72Hz	105Hz	213Hz
F4	96Hz	140Hz	284Hz
F5	120Hz	175Hz	355Hz
F6	144Hz	210Hz	
F7	168Hz	245Hz	
F8	192Hz	280Hz	
F9	216Hz	310Hz	
F10	240Hz		
F11	264Hz		
F12	288Hz		
F13	312Hz		

Notice that the third length mode (F3) at 72Hz coincides with the second width mode (F2) and the first height mode (F1). These three modes combine, piling up at 70Hz to create a huge peak in the response at this frequency. This undesirable situation occurs again at 140Hz, 213Hz, and 284Hz. The resonant modes coincide because the room's length, width, and height are multiples of each other. Actually, the three modes are perfectly coincident at 70.6Hz, 141.2Hz, etc. I've rounded them so they are slightly skewed, making the pileup more visible in Fig.4-24 (below). Moreover, there are no modes between 105Hz and 140Iz, which makes the pileup at 140Hz much more audible. The result will be a thick, peaky, and very colored bass reproduction.

We can also plot these modes graphically to better visualize room-mode distribution. This graph of mode vs. frequency is shown in Fig.4-24.

Fig. 4-24
Plotting the resonant modes graphically

Modes

As we can see, the modes are bunched together, with large spaces between them. The gaps between modes are just as detrimental as the coincident modes; they make the adjacent modes much more audible. Moreover, notes falling between modes are reduced in amplitude, making them sound weak and less prominent.

Let's see how this situation can be avoided by a room with better dimensional ratios. Our second room has approximately the same volume, but different distances between its walls. This room is 21' long and 14' wide, with a 10' ceiling. Calculating the resonant modes for each dimension, we see that they are much better distributed:

Mode	Length 21'	Width 14'	Height 10'
F1	27Hz	40Hz	56Hz
F2	54Hz	81Hz	113Hz
F3	81Hz	121Hz	169Hz
F4	108Hz	161Hz	226Hz
F5	135Hz	201Hz	282Hz
F6	161Hz	242Hz	339Hz
F7	188Hz	282Hz	
F8	215Hz	322Hz	

These data look like this in graphical form (Fig.4-25):

Fig. 4-25 Good dimensional ratios better distribute room-resonant modes.

We can see by comparing Fig.4-24 with Fig.4-25 that the resonant modes are more evenly distributed in the second room. Although there is some coincidence of modes, they are much less severe than in the first room. This second room will have smoother bass response, less coloration, and a more taut, punchy low end than the first room. Note that larger rooms have inherently more modes, and that the modes will therefore be more smoothly distributed—assuming good dimensional ratios. The smaller the room, the greater the challenge in distributing room resonance modes. Ideally, the room will have 20 or more axial modes below 325Hz, and the average spacing between those modes will be less than 15Hz. Distribution of axial modes along the width, length, and height can also be plotted as in Fig.4-26.

A sloped ceiling helps greatly in skewing the height modes along a continuum. The resonant modes are naturally spread out rather than occurring at the same frequency as with a flat ceiling. If a ceiling starts at 8' and slopes up to 12', calculate its modes assuming a height of 10' (the average of the two heights). The sloped ceiling doesn't eliminate resona-

Fig. 4-26
Another way of graphically representing modal distribution.

Mode Spacing

H
W
L

0   25   50   75   100   125   150   175   200   225   250   275   300   325

Frequency

Courtesy Acoustic Room Systems and A/V RoomService, Ltd.

nce modes, but does help to distribute them. Similarly, splayed walls tend to skew the resonance modes, but don't eliminate them.

Room resonant modes can be made less audible by avoiding square or cubical rooms—i.e., rooms of equal width and height, or width and length, or length and height, or whose measurements are equal in all three dimensions—or rooms whose long dimensions are multiples of its short dimensions. If the ceiling is 8', we want to avoid another dimension at 8', 16', 24', etc. Note that resonance modes will always occur; good dimensional ratios merely distribute them evenly rather than allowing them to coincide. The following chart shows, in descending order of quality, the best dimensional ratios (according to acoustician M.M. Louden):

Quality	Height	X	Y
1	1	1.9	1.4
2	1	1.9	1.3
3	1	1.5	2.1
4	1	1.5	2.2
5	1	1.2	1.5
6	1	1.4	2.1
7	1	1.1	1.4
8	1	1.8	1.4
9	1	1.6	2.1
10	1	1.2	1.4
11	1	1.6	1.2
12	1	1.6	2.3
13	1	1.6	2.2
14	1	1.8	1.3
15	1	1.1	1.5
16	1	1.6	2.4
17	1	1.6	1.3
18	1	1.9	1.5
19	1	1.1	1.6
20	1	1.3	1.7

(X can be length and Y width, or vice versa)

According to this chart, the ideal length and width of a room with an 8' ceiling is 15.2' by 11.2'. These dimensions are calculated by multiplying each dimension by 0.8. For a 12' ceiling, the optimum length and width are 22.8' by 16.8' (multiplying 1.2 by 19' and by 14'). Note that, although these dimensions are different for the three ceiling heights, the *ratio* between the length, width, and height are identical. It's the ratio that determines how smoothly the resonance modes are distributed.

Note also that a larger room with good dimensional ratios will sound better than a smaller room employing those same ratios. The larger room will produce more resonance modes, which can be more closely spaced in frequency and thus achieve a smoother distribution. Remember that good dimensional ratios don't prevent resonances; they instead distribute those resonances more smoothly over the audio band. Good ratios prevent the coincidence of resonance modes, and the attendant gaps in resonance modes that make the modes more audible.

If you don't have the luxury of choosing the dimensions of your listening room, you can use the techniques described earlier in this chapter to minimize the audibility of room resonant modes.

Computer software for calculating room resonance modes is available at a moderate price. For example: Given your room's dimensions, RPG's Room Optimizer software will run a full modal analysis and recommend loudspeaker and listener placement.

This explanation of room resonance modes and the examples given are greatly simplified. I've just covered what are called *axial modes*—those that exist between one pair of surfaces. Other modes resulting from two surface pairs (*tangential modes*) and three surface pairs (*oblique modes*, from all six walls of a room) aren't discussed. *The Master Handbook of Acoustics* provides greater depth on this subject.

Standing Waves

If you've seen a cup of coffee sitting on a vibrating surface, you've seen standing waves. The vibration excites the liquid, causing waves to spread out from the center and reflect or bounce off of the cup's perimeter. At some points, the waves reinforce each other; at other points, the waves cancel. The result is a stationary pattern of peaks and dips in the coffee. Although the two waves are in motion, they create a stationary wave that is formed by the interaction between the two moving waves. This is exactly what happens to sound in a listening room.

Standing waves are stationary areas of high and low sound pressure in a room. They are caused by constructive and destructive interferences between the incident (direct) sound and the reflected sound from a room boundary. For example, when the reflected waveform's positive pressure phase is superimposed on the incident waveform's positive pressure phase, the two waves will reinforce each other (constructive interference), producing a *peak*. If the reflected wave's negative pressure phase meets the incident wave's positive pressure phase, the two waves will cancel (destructive interference), producing a dip or *null*. These interactions produce a particular pattern of stationary areas of more and less bass for each resonant frequency in the room.

Let's look at how a standing wave is set up along the length of a 20'-long listening room. If we excite the air in this room at its lowest resonant frequency, the pressure maxima will occur at the room walls, the pressure minima in the center. (See Fig.4-27. This drawing is analogous to Fig.4-22, which showed how a resonant mode occurs when half a wavelength equals the room's length.)

Fig. 4-27 Maximum pressure occurs at room boundaries.

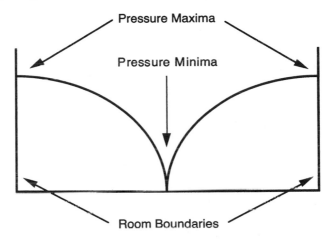

By playing a tone at the room's resonant frequency and walking around in the room, we can hear the sound get louder and softer. In practice, the model in Fig.4-27 isn't so neat; the effects of other room boundaries and objects (furniture) in the room skew this theoretical representation. In addition, the associated resonant modes at multiples of the modal frequency tend to make the pattern of standing waves more complex.

Nevertheless, standing waves create areas in the room in which the bass sounds heavier, and some in which it sounds thinner. Play music with continuous bass energy (organ music works well) and move your listening chair forward and backward; the presentation will be heavier in some areas, leaner in others.

Although this unequal pressure distribution is undesirable, we can use standing waves to our advantage. If your loudspeakers and room tend to be thick and heavy in the bass, try moving your listening chair forward or backward until the bass is a little smoother and leaner. Or use the same technique to add fullness and weight to a thin-sounding loudspeaker.

Reverberation

The sound in a room is a combination of three components: 1) direct sound from the loudspeakers, 2) discrete early reflections from the floor, ceiling, and side walls, and 3) later, more diffuse reflections, called reverberation. This concept of three components to sound is illustrated in Fig.4-28.

Fig. 4-28 Sound in a room is composed of direct sound, early reflections, and reverberation.

Reverberation is such a fundamental part of sound that we take it for granted. Although we don't hear it as a separate component of sound, reverberation adds warmth and space to music. If reverberation were completely missing from a sound, we would immediately identify the sound as being unnatural. You can hear how strange the absence of reverberation is on the *Denon Anechoic Orchestral Recording* (Denon PG 6006). The orchestra, recorded in an anechoic chamber (a room in which all sound reflections are completely absorbed), sounds completely different from even a recording made in a small, "dry" concert hall.

Reverberation in a room takes a finite time to decay into inaudibility (as shown in Fig.4-29). The time it takes for sound to decay by 60dB is called the room's RT_{60} (the RT stands for "reverberation time"). A small, acoustically dead rock recording studio may have an RT_{60} of 0.1 second; a cathedral may have an RT_{60} of six or seven seconds. A room's RT_{60} quantifies how acoustically "live" or "dead" the room is. In practice, sound in a room doesn't decay the full 60dB because the decaying sound becomes swamped by the room's ambient noise.

Although the concept of reverberation is less applicable to small spaces such as hi-fi listening rooms than to concert halls, it is nonetheless helpful in balancing sound-absorbing materials in the room. A room with reflective surfaces will have a longer reverberation time than a room with absorptive surfaces such as carpets, soft furniture, and drapes. These materials absorb sound rather than reflect it back into the room. You want to choose materials in the listening room that contribute to an optimum RT_{60}, and balance those materials so that the reverberation time is constant over the audio band.

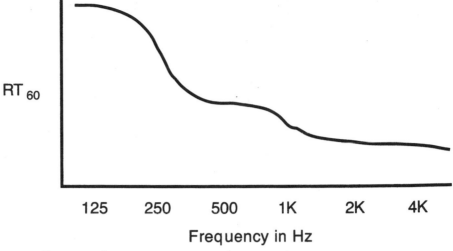

Fig. 4-29 Long reverberation time at low frequencies makes the sound heavy and muddy.

But what is the ideal reverberation time in a music listening room? And what combination of reflective and absorptive materials will produce the optimum reverberation time?

The quick answer is that optimum reverberation time in a listening room varies with the room's volume. For a 3000-cubic-foot room, a good reverberation time is about 0.4 second. For a 20,000-cubic-foot room, about 1 second is ideal. A surprisingly accurate measure of a room's reverberation time can be made with a handclap or balloon pop and a stopwatch. Have someone clap his hands loudly, or pop a balloon. Start the stopwatch when you hear the sound, and stop it when the sound has completely died away. Repeat the measurement several times and average the results. The measured result in seconds is a fairly reliable indicator of a room's RT_{60}.

Unfortunately, an optimum overall reverberation time isn't enough: we must ensure that the room's reverberation time is roughly the same at all audio frequencies. A room with thick carpet and heavy draperies materials that absorb high frequencies, yet do nothing to low frequencies—will have a longer reverberation time at low than at high frequencies. This condition, shown in Fig.4-29, can make a hi-fi system sound slow and thick in the bass, or dead in the treble. Reverberation time is thus specified at six frequencies: 125Hz, 250Hz, 500Hz, 1kHz, 2kHz, and 4kHz. Our goal is to make the reverberation time roughly equal at these frequencies by choosing the appropriate mix of acoustical treatments. We do this by mixing different materials, each having absorption characteristics that vary with frequency. Let's look at how these surfaces affect the sound impinging on them.

Every surface in a listening room will either absorb, reflect, or diffuse (scatter) sound. We'll deal first with absorption and reflection. The degree to which a surface absorbs sound is called its *absorption coefficient*. This is a measure of the percentage of sound it absorbs, specified at the six frequencies listed in the previous paragraph. An absorption coefficient of 1.0 means that 100% of the sound is absorbed. This condition is likened to an open window—no energy is reflected back into the room. An absorption coefficient of 0.1 means that 10% of the sound is absorbed and 90% is reflected back into the room. Absorption coefficients of more than 1.0 are possible with a material that presents a surface area to the sound field that is greater than its area of wall contact, such as some wedge-shaped foams.

The absorption coefficients for two common materials—heavy carpet over felt, and drywall on studs (1/2" thick on 2x4s, spaced 16" on center)—are as follows:

	125Hz	250Hz	500Hz	1kHz	2kHz	4kHz
Carpet	0.08	0.24	0.57	0.69	0.71	0.73
Drywall	0.29	0.10	0.05	0.04	0.07	0.09

We can quickly see that carpet absorbs virtually no energy in the bass, but a significant percentage of the energy in the treble—nearly 75% at 4kHz. Conversely, drywall absorbs (and leaks out of the room) a moderate amount of energy in the bass (29% at 125Hz), and reflects virtually all midband and treble energy. Drywall on studs absorbs low frequencies by diaphragmatic action: sound striking the drywall causes it to flex. This flexing converts mechanical motion into a minute amount of heat.

Now, suppose we built a room completely covered in thick carpeting—like a rock band's garage studio. The carpet would absorb nearly all the treble and reflect nearly all the bass. The result would be a very short reverberation time at high frequencies and a very long reverberation time at low frequencies. The room would sound thick, heavy, and congested in the bass, and be generally unpleasant. Moreover, the room would store energy in the bass through resonance and release that energy over time, smearing transient signals. A short reverberation time in the midband and treble, accompanied by boomy bass, causes a loss of intelligibility. In such a room, each band member keeps turning up his volume so that he can hear himself over the other band members. Turning up the volume only makes the problem worse.

At the other extreme, a room of bare drywall, a tile floor, and no high-frequency absorbing materials would sound bright, hard, and thin. The trick is to balance absorptive materials so that the amount of absorption is roughly the same at all six frequencies. In practice, it's difficult to get enough low-frequency absorption; most rooms have longer reverberation times in the bass. Fortunately, a slightly longer reverberation time at low frequencies is desirable to give the room warmth.

Reducing a room's reverberation time by adding absorbing materials also has the added benefit of broadening the resonances, making them less audible.

Fig.4-30 shows a computer model of my listening room's reverberation time. The upper plot is the reverberation time before installation of a complete room-acoustics package (described later in this chapter). The two lower plots are the ideal reverberation time and the actual reverberation time after room treatment.

Fig. 4-30
Computer model of my listening room showing reverberation time without treatment, with treatment, and the ideal.

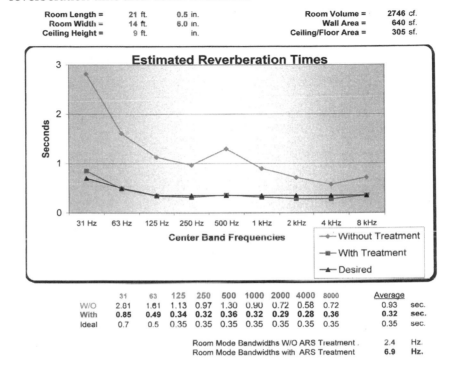

	31	63	125	250	500	1000	2000	4000	8000	Average	
W/O	2.81	1.61	1.13	0.97	1.30	0.90	0.72	0.58	0.72	0.93	sec.
With	0.85	0.49	0.34	0.32	0.36	0.32	0.29	0.28	0.36	0.32	sec.
Ideal	0.7	0.5	0.35	0.35	0.35	0.35	0.35	0.35	0.35	0.35	sec.

Room Mode Bandwidths W/O ARS Treatment .	2.4	Hz.
Room Mode Bandwidths with ARS Treatment	6.9	Hz.

Courtesy Acoustic Room Systems and A/V RoomService, Ltd.

You can calculate your room's reverberation time. First, multiply the absorption coefficient of every surface in the room by the square footage of that surface at the six frequencies. For example, if you have 294 square feet of carpet, multiply 294 x 0.73 (absorption coefficient of carpet at 4kHz) to get 215 absorption units. (These absorption units are called "sabines," after Wallace Clement Sabine, the American physicist who founded the science of architectural acoustics. Boston Symphony Hall, designed in 1900 by Sabine, was the first concert hall to be designed using the new field of architectural acoustics.)

Multiplying each surface area's square footage by the absorption coefficients at the six frequencies gives us a chart of every material in the room and how many sabines of absorption that material provides at the six frequencies: 125Hz, 250Hz, 500Hz, 1kHz, 2kHz, and 4kHz.

To convert the total sabines at each frequency into a reverberation time at that frequency, we use the following formula:

$$RT_{60} = \frac{(0.049)(V)}{(S)\ (a)}$$

where

RT_{60}	=	reverberation time, seconds
V	=	volume of room, cu ft
S	=	total surface area of room, sq ft
a	=	average sabine absorption coefficient

This method of calculating reverberation time works best with large rooms (and assumes that the materials are uniformly distributed throughout the room), but nevertheless will give you an idea of the balance between low- and high-frequency absorption. If you perform these calculations on your own room and find a large difference in the total sabines between 125Hz and 4kHz, you can add low-frequency absorbers to even out the reverberation time. The acoustical materials described earlier in this chapter can be used to achieve a smooth reverberation time with frequency. A full listing of materials and their absorption coefficients is included in *The Master Handbook of Acoustics*, mentioned earlier in this chapter.

Building a Listening Room from Scratch

This chapter cannot guide someone through the long and complicated process of building a dedicated listening room from the ground up. Instead, I recommend two approaches: The first is to study the subject and design the room yourself, bringing in an acoustician for consultation two or three times during the design process. You can end up with a good room without spending a fortune.

The second approach is to commission a full-fledged design from an architectural acoustics design firm. After I had built my room (from scratch) and treated it with freestanding (not built in) acoustic treatments, I had it completely treated with a built-in acoustics package from Acoustic Room Systems (ARS) and A/V RoomService, Ltd. ARS installs the treatments; A/V RoomService provides the computer modeling and design, as well as on-site voicing and fine tuning. This package is described later in this chapter.

Some acoustic-treatment manufacturers, notably RPG and ASC, also offer full acoustic design services. This way is ideal for those with large budgets or no time to learn acoustic design themselves. The design firm will often oversee construction, providing you with a completely finished room. This can be a *very* expensive proposition. RPG and ASC will, however, provide as much or as little help as you need. A little expert knowledge goes a long way.

Isolating the Listening Room

Many music listeners want to play music at high levels without disturbing neighbors or other family members, or to listen to music in a quiet environment without outside sounds intruding on the experience. This brings us to a specialized area of acoustics called isolation. Acoustic isolation prevents sound in one area from escaping into another area. A good example of successful isolation is the midtown Manhattan recording studio that records during business hours.

Keeping sound in the listening room from getting into the rest of the house is a daunting challenge. It requires good design, precision construction, and lots of money. There are, however, a few principles and techniques that can help minimize sound transmission.

Very briefly, some of the sound escapes from the listening room into the rest of the house through doors and other openings. Even small cracks, such as the space between the floor and door, allow large amounts of acoustic energy through. This phenomenon is called "flanking." To reduce flanking, use a solid-core door and seal its perimeter with weather-stripping or refrigerator seals. You can also buy acoustic doors, complete with jambs and seals, from acoustic supply houses. Look for the ads in the back of *Mix* magazine or other professional audio publications.

Second, isolating a room requires lots of mass between the sound source and the area to be protected from sound. Thick walls, double walls with unbridged air cavities, lead sheeting, and double solid-core doors are all fundamental prerequisites to achieving high isolation. Most audiophiles don't need such isolation, but if you do, it's very expensive. Half-hearted attempts at isolation just don't work; it takes a serious effort to achieve adequate isolation.

The effectiveness of a wall's ability to reduce the amount of sound it passes is expressed in its Sound Transmission Classification (STC). For example, a standard wall built with 2x4 studs and Sheetrock has an STC of 34dB without insulation (as you would typically find in a home's interior walls) and 36dB with 3.5" of Fiberglas insulation. Using a 2x6 plate with 2x4 studs staggered (studs alternating on each side of the wall) increases the STC to as high as 52dB (with insulation). A full double 2x4 wall with an unbridged air cavity has an STC of 58dB. As you can see, the more elaborate (and expensive) the construction method, the greater the wall's ability to attenuate sound passing through it.

A related subject is the room's *noise criterion*, a numerical rating of the background noise level present in the listening room. The lower the NC rating (NC20 is excellent, for example), the lower the room's ambient noise. A quiet room makes low-level detail more audible, contributes to the sense of space (reverberation decay is better resolved), and fosters the impression of a black background from which the music emerges.

The Walldamp Technique

The modern Western construction technique of drywall over a wooden stud frame introduces audible problems not found in other parts of the world that use thicker and denser building materials. Specifically, sound striking a drywall-over-stud wall causes the wall to resonate at about 70Hz. Sound is converted to mechanical energy (the wall moving), then back to acoustic energy (the vibrating wall acts just like a loudspeaker's diaphragm). The wall hums away along with the music, introducing a drone-like sound of a specific pitch. What's worse, the acoustic energy produced by the wall is released relatively slowly over time, changing the music's dynamic characteristics.

This phenomenon, called *wall-stud resonance*, introduces a specific coloration to the reproduced sound. You can demonstrate this by hitting a drywall-over-stud wall with the ball of your fist and listening to the resulting thud. The sound produced by the motion of the wall has virtually the same character, whether the initial sound was a double bass or an explosion in a film soundtrack. Consequently, the music is overlaid with a common signature that degrades fidelity. Homes built with thick plaster walls or concrete block don't suffer from this problem.

While acoustic absorbers can stabilize the air in a listening room, they do nothing to address wall-stud resonance. Keeping the room's walls stabilized under dynamic conditions (loud transient signals) requires careful attention to wall construction. If you're building or remodeling a home, you can greatly reduce wall-stud resonance and isolate the listening room at the same time. One method is to buy dual-layer drywall that has damping material between the layers. Unfortunately, this is a specialized material that must be custom-ordered and purchased by the truckload.

The second option is ASC's Walldamp material and construction technique, shown in Fig.4-31. The first step is to install a resilient channel between the studs and first layer of drywall. The resilient channel acts as a metal spring, isolating the wall from the studs and preventing the 70Hz wall-stud resonance from occurring. If left like this, however, the room would sound horrible; the entire wall would act as a drumhead, resonating whenever acoustic energy struck it.

This is where Walldamp and the second layer of drywall come in. The Walldamp in Fig.4-31 consists of squares of tarpaper coated on both sides with a special glue. When installed between two layers of drywall, the glue absorbs energy by a mechanism called *sheer stress damping*. That is, when the two pieces of drywall try to move relative to each other, the glue absorbs the energy on a molecular level. Specifically, the glue converts the mechanical energy of the wall's motion into a tiny amount of heat. Consequently, the acoustic energy striking the wall is absorbed by the damping action of the Walldamp instead of being reflected back into the room. Rather than shuddering when struck by sound, the wall behaves more like a thick plaster wall.

Fig. 4-31 ASC's Walldamp technique damps wall vibration and increases isolation.

RESILIENT CHANNEL SCREW TO STUD
16" ON CENTER
(12" ON CENTER FOR CEILING)

1" WALLDAMP™ STRIP ON RESILIENT CHANNEL

FIRST LAYER SHEETROCK
SCREW TO RESILIENT CHANNEL
(SCREW 6" OFFSET FROM STUD)

SECOND LAYER SHEETROCK
SCREW THROUGH FIRST LAYER
ONTO RESILIENT CHANNEL
(SCREW 6" OFFSET FROM STUD)

TARBOARD APPLIED TO
PERIMETER OF THE WALL
WITH PANEL ADHESIVE

1-1/2"X1/4" FELT AROUND
PERIMETER OF THE FLOOR
CALK BELOW FELT IF FLOOR IS IRREGULAR

4" WALLDAMP™ SQUARE
12" ON CENTER BETWEEN SHEETROCK

1" WALLDAMP™ STRIP AROUND
PERIMETER OF THE FIRST LAYER SHEETROCK

Courtesy Acoustic Sciences Corporation

In addition, the wall now acts as a large bass absorber at very low frequencies—just what most listening rooms need. Fewer freestanding bass absorbers are needed because now the entire *room* is acting as a bass absorber. Another benefit of this technique is that less of the sound inside a listening room escapes into the rest of the house: You can play music louder and later, without disturbing family members. Best of all, this construction technique adds very little to the cost of building or remodeling.

Complete Room Treatment: A Case Study

I recently had my listening room completely revamped by Acoustic Room Systems and A/V RoomService Ltd. I had built the room several years previously using good dimensional ratios (14.5' W x 9' H x 21' L) and solid construction techniques. The room's acoustics were improved by freestanding acoustic products, along with bookcases and open LP/CD cabinets for diffusion. The room sounded superb, and many high-profile loudspeaker designers who had set up their products in my room were favorably impressed.

Nonetheless, when asked to review a built-in, whole-room acoustics package from ARS and A/V RoomService, I jumped at the chance. (My full review appears in Issue 139 of *The Absolute Sound* and Issue 46 of *The Perfect Vision*.) ARS and A/V RoomService are an offshoot of Owens-Corning, which reportedly developed one of the world's most advanced acoustics laboratories. ARS installs a product developed by Owens-Corning, and A/V RoomSystems uses computer modeling software developed by the Fiberglas giant.

After I filled out a questionnaire that included my room's dimensions, construction, and interior finishing, along with my listening habits, A/V RoomService modeled my room and developed a layout for installing the Owens-Corning panels. These panels consist of 1.25" Fiberglas backed by a very thin Sheetrock layer. With the Fiberglas facing the room, the panel is absorptive above 300Hz. The the panels were installed so that the Sheetrock faces the room so that the is panel reflective above 300Hz while simultaneously acting as a diaphragmatic absorber below that frequency. Although the amount of diaphragmatic absorption is low, the large surface area has a cumulative effect. Nearly all the panels were installed in my room with the reflective side out. Only the corners and first-reflection points on the sidewalls and ceiling were absorptive.

A diffusive panel, made from molded plastic with a convoluted surface, was positioned in strategic locations to scatter sound. Every square inch of the room was covered by a panel or diffuser.

After installation, A/V RoomService visited to measure the room and compare the result to the computer model. After some adjustments to the panels, the entire surface was covered with a stretched fabric to completely hide the acoustic materials underneath.

Figs.4-32 and 4-33 show the ARS package being installed. The shiny surfaces are the diffusive elements. You can see some of the measured effects of this treatment in Fig.4-23 earlier, which shows the performance on the MATT test.

Fig. 4-32
Installation of the ARS system. Shiny areas are diffusers. View is looking toward the back of the room from the loudspeaker location.

Most ARS installations are in new construction, preventing a treated/untreated comparison. Fortunately, I'd been reviewing in this room for more than five years, and knew it well. The ARS and A/V RoomService package rendered a huge improvement in the overall sound. The bass was significantly cleaner, tighter, better defined, and had greater transient fidelity. The other significant improvement was in image focus and a sense of precision in the spatial presentation.

Fig. 4-33
Finished room (before large LP storage rack installation behind listening seat). The four loudspeakers attached to the wall are dipolar surround speakers for film-soundtrack reproduction.

DSP Room Correction

We've seen in this chapter that the listening room is a crucial link in the music playback chain. Every listening room, no matter how good, radically alters the sound produced by a pair of speakers. The room acts as an equalizer, boosting some frequencies and attenuating others. This change in frequency response can be as much as 30dB in the bass, adding large amounts of coloration to the music. Moreover, the room briefly stores and releases energy at certain frequencies, causing some bass notes to "hang" in the room longer. The result is a thickness and lack of clarity in the bass, along with a reduced sense of dynamic drive.

It's been said that a loudspeaker designer has 100% control over his product's sound above 700Hz, 50% control from 300Hz to 700Hz, and only 20% control below 300Hz. This aphorism reflects the increasing influence of the listening room on sound quality at lower and lower frequencies.

Although the listening room imposes far more severe colorations than any electronic component, we've grown to accept this musical degradation as an inevitable part of music listening. Even custom-built, acoustically designed rooms housing perfectly positioned loudspeakers will introduce significant colorations. All rooms introduce colorations: the better ones simply do less damage.

Attempts to reduce room-induced colorations with analog equalizers have met with limited success. Analog equalizers add their own audible problems, and are limited in resolution. Digital equalizers can have greater resolution than analog ones, but are still a crude tool for dealing with room problems.

The advent of Digital Signal Processing (DSP) provides a powerful new opportunity to remove the effects of the listening room on reproduced music. DSP is the manipulation of audio signals by performing mathematical calculations on the numbers that represent the music. DSP chips can be programmed to perform as filters or equalizers with many hundreds of frequency bands, and with characteristics impossible to realize with analog equalizers. The trick is putting this advanced technology to work to surgically correct room-induced colorations.

Far more sophisticated than a digital equalizer, a DSP room-correction system analyzes the response of your loudspeaker/room combination with high resolution, then creates digital filters to remove the room-induced problems. The room-correction system not only removes the room's effects, but also corrects for speaker colorations. If your speakers have a peak of energy at 2kHz, for example, the room-correction system can remove this coloration. In addition, the room-correction system will make the speaker/room response identical for each speaker. This new technology removes the room's effects on reproduced sound *electronically*, before it is reproduced by the loudspeakers. Put another way, the room-correction system distorts the signal in a way that counteracts the distortion imposed by the listening room. The result is flat response at the listening position.

Here's how room correction works: You (or your dealer) position the supplied measurement microphone at the listening seat, connect the room-correction system hardware to a personal computer, and run the supplied software on your PC. The room-correction system hardware puts out a series of pulses that are reproduced by your loudspeaker, then analyzed by the software running on your PC. The software then configures filters in the DSP chips that form an inverse of your room response. Peaks in the measured response become dips in the filter, and vice versa. The filter response is a mirror image of your room response. Newer, more sophisticated room-correction systems eliminate the need for the PC, and have greatly simplified the user interface.

Fig.4-34 shows the measured response of an actual loudspeaker in an actual room. The excess energy at 20Hz, along with the peaks at 120Hz and 180Hz, are the result of interaction between the loudspeaker's direct sound and reflections from the room's walls. Fig.4-35 shows the filter response, which you'll see is the inverse of the measured in-room response. The peak at 180Hz in the measured response becomes a dip in the filter response, and the broad reduction in energy through the midband in the measured response becomes a boost in the filter response. When these filters are applied to the music signal, the peaks and dips have been removed, as shown in Fig.4-36, the response at the listening position after correction. Only the response above 100Hz is shown; the rolloff below 100Hz occurs because this particular room-correction system employs a subwoofer crossover. The corrected subwoofer response is also flat.

The filter parameters calculated by the software are downloaded into the room-correction system's memory during the setup. The room-

Fig. 4-34 The frequency response of a loudspeaker in a room has severe peaks and dips.

Fig. 4-35 The room-correction system creates filters that form an inverse of the measured response.

Fig. 4-36 The filters remove the peaks and dips in the measured response, producing flat response at the listening position.

Courtesy Tact Audio, Inc.

correction system hardware stays in your rack and performs the filtering on all signals running through it. If you change speakers, speaker location, or listening spot, you'll need to re-measure the room and tell the computer to calculate new filter coefficients (about a 15-minute job, once you've been through it a few times). The filter parameters are unique to your speakers, room, speaker positions, and listening position.

At first glance, you might think that the room-correction system should produce perfectly flat response at the listening position. In practice, a flat response sounds thin, bright, and bass-shy. The ideal response has a rising response in the bass and a falling response in the treble. The room-correction system lets you choose or even create a "target curve," which is a response the room-correction system will create at the listening position. If the sound is too bright, for example, you can change the target curve so that less treble is reproduced. In fact, you can dial in any response you like by adjusting the target curve.

An important technical factor in a room-correction system is its *frequency resolution*. This specification indicates the correction system's ability to correct very narrow peaks and dips in the frequency response. For example, a room-correction system with a frequency resolution of 10Hz wouldn't be able to correct a peak or dip in your room that was 8Hz wide. Some room-correction systems have a frequency resolution of less than 1Hz, which is fine enough to follow any peaks and dips.

Room-correction systems can also reduce the detrimental effects of sidewall reflections described earlier in this chapter. The music signal driving the loudspeakers is pre-conditioned to contain signals that have the same delay as the wall reflections at the listening position, but of opposite polarity. The wall's reflections are thus canceled by a series of delayed waves from the loudspeakers that have opposite polarity from the wall reflections. The result is cancellation of reflections and removal of room resonance modes.

Note that because room-correction systems operate in the digital domain, analog signals from an LP front end must be digitized, then converted back to analog. That's why most room-correction systems include an integral analog-to-digital converter. Digital signals, such as from a CD transport, are input directly to the room-correction system, which either converts that digital signal to analog for driving a power amplifier, or outputs a digital signal for conversion to analog with an outboard digital processor. Although room correction can produce profound improvements in bass quality and image focus, some audiophiles will be reluctant to digitize LPs. The purity of an analog source is inevitably degraded by the digital conversion process. You must consider, however, whether the loss of quality from digitizing an analog signal is a greater or lesser evil than the degradation imposed by the listening room.

Room-correction systems are rare because the complexity of hardware and software requires a huge expenditure in development time and money. Make no mistake: correcting a room's response is an extraordinarily difficult task. Moreover, a room-correction system is as much a computer as an audio product, requiring specialized skills not normally found among audio engineers. Meridian Audio has tackled the field, offering a room-correction upgrade card to their 861 Multichannel Controller.

My experience with room correction suggests that the technology is extremely effective in removing colorations and restoring clarity to reproduced music. With room correction, the sound has a "lightness," agility, and clarity that are impossible to achieve in any other way. The overall presentation seems to have less midbass boxiness, and extreme low frequencies have greater dynamic impact. In addition, soundstaging improves because identical response from both loudspeakers is essential to precise image focus. (That's why each speaker must be toed-in by exactly the same amount.) Without room correction, image size and placement can change as an instrument moves between musical registers because the response of each speaker/room is different. With identical output from each speaker, image focus becomes tighter and the soundstage is better delineated. Once you get used to the sound of a system with DSP room correction, it's hard to go back.

A Survey of Acoustical Treatments

Although many of the products listed below are designed for professional applications such as recording studios, they are very effective in a domestic listening room. Still, they can often look more professional—even industrial—than domestic. The RPG Diffusors and ASC Tower Traps look like acoustic treatment devices, but are nicely finished. Sonex foam and Sonex ceiling tiles can also fit into many decors.

Sonex. Manufacturer: Illbruck, 3800 Washington Ave. N., Minneapolis, MN 55412-2197 Tel: (800) 662-0032. www.Illbruck.com.

Sonex is a popular—but expensive—acoustical foam used primarily in recording studios. It comes in a variety of colors and three thicknesses: 2″, 3″, and 4″. Sonex has a very high absorption coefficient, but the amount of low-frequency absorption varies with the thickness. 2″-thick Sonex has an absorption coefficient of 0.2 at 250Hz; the 4″-thick version has a coefficient of 0.7 at 250Hz.

Sonex comes in 4′ by 4′ squares that are usually attached to walls with panel adhesive. Sonex sheets are made in reciprocal pairs: one 4′ by 4′ sheet has wedges, the other matching indentations, but their function is identical. Sonex is also available in 2′ by 4′ sizes at the same price per square foot. A 2′ by 2′ version, the Sonex Junior, is also available in gray, beige, blue, and brown.

Illbruck also makes a huge range of other acoustic materials, described on its Web site.

Markerfoam. Manufacturer: Markertek, 4 High Street, Saugerties, NY 12477. Tel: (800) 522-2025. www.markertek.com.

Markerfoam is a lower-priced alternative to Sonex. Its surface structure is less aggressive than that of Sonex, but Markertek claims very high absorption coefficients (0.7 at 1kHz for 2″ thickness, 0.92 at 1kHz for 3″). Markertek sells a wide range of acoustic treatments, including Sonex products.

Tube Traps, Tower Traps, Cube Towers, Poly Elliptical Panels, Matrix Panels, Stud Stabilizer, and Acoustic Soffit. Manufacturer: Acoustic Sciences Corporation, P.O. Box 1189, Eugene, OR 97440. Tel: (503) 343-9727. Fax: (503) 343-9245. Web: www.tubetrap.com.

ASC makes a wide range of acoustic-treatment devices that are used in recording studios, churches, and hi-fi listening rooms. The company's Tower Trap is a low-cost alternative to ASC's popular Tube Trap. A new manufacturing technique allows ASC to sell Tower Traps for about half the price of Tube Traps. Both devices are cylinders with a reflective side and an absorptive side, allowing them to be tuned to the room's needs just by rotating them (see Fig.4-21 earlier). They absorb bass, kill side-wall reflections, absorb treble, or diffuse sound over a wide bandwidth. They are most effective as bass absorbers when placed in corners. Tower Traps (see Fig.4-20 earlier) are moderately priced, look good, and are highly effective. For the ultimate in bass absorption, ASC's 16" Full Round Tube Trap offers greater bass absorption at very low frequencies. Most rooms benefit from a pair of 16" Full Round Tube Traps in the corners behind the loudspeakers.

Cube Towers operate essentially as Tube Traps, but are square rather than round. Many find that these 14.5" by 78" traps look better in a room than round traps.

ASC's Poly Elliptical Panels combine low-bass absorption and mid- and high-frequency diffusion in a free-standing device. These rather large surfaces are extremely effective, are available in a variety of colors, and are a good alternative to building your own polycylindrical diffusers.

ASC's Matrix Panels (Fig.4-37) kill flutter echo and add some absorption and diffusion without making the room too dead. Matrix panels are available in two sizes, 2'x4' and 2'x2' and a variety of fabric colors.

Fig. 4-37 ASC's Matrix Panels combine absorption and diffusion in the same panel.

Courtesy Acoustic Sciences Corporation

The wall-stud resonance described earlier can be greatly reduced with Stud Stabilizer, a kind of shock absorber between the stud and Sheetrock. Stud Stabilizer needs to be installed during construction or remodeling. The product can be combined with Iso Damp to reduce wall-stud resonance.

Finally, ASC's Acoustic Soffit is a built-in bass trap that fits at the wall ceiling interface (Fig.4-38). The face of each vertical panel contains a specular diffuser that allows bass through (where it is absorbed) but diffuses frequencies above 400Hz. A big advantage of Acoustic Soffit is that it provides a large amount of bass absorption without taking up floor or wall space. Acoustic Soffit is the most decorator-friendly of all bass-absorption products.

Fig. 4-38 ASC's Acoustic Soffit provides bass absorption with minimal consumption of wall area.

Courtesy Acoustic Sciences Corporation

RPG Diffusors. Manufacturer: RPG Diffusor Systems Inc., 651-C Commerce Drive, Upper Marlboro, MD 20772. Tel: (301) 249-0044; www.rpginc.com. RPG makes such a wide range of diffusing products that I can't list them all here. The company offers professional individual acoustical components as well as complete packages designed for the home listening room. Acoustic Tools for Audiophiles, SoundTrac, and Concert Hall in a Box are a few of the complete acoustic treatment packages offered by RPG. The SoundTrac product includes complete acoustical consulting by RPG to achieve excellent acoustics with a visually appealing finish. RPG products are widely used in recording studios, concert halls, and auditoriums.

RPG's Skylines are 2' by 2' squares that provide a highly diffusive surface. These 6"-thick molded foam panels can be attached to walls with adhesive or double-sided tape. Skylines, shown earlier in Fig.4-11, work well behind the listening position, on a ceiling, or behind dipolar loudspeakers.

In addition to these specialized acoustical materials, mid- and high-frequency absorption is provided by common building materials. Standard acoustical ceiling tile, Fiberglas insulation, and glass-fiber boards (Owens-Corning Type 703 and Johns-Manville 1000 Series Spin-Glass, for example) are very effective absorbers.

5 Preamplifiers

Introduction

The preamplifier is the Grand Central Station of your hi-fi system. It receives signals from source components—turntables, CD players, SACD and DVD-Audio machines, tuners, tape decks—and allows you to select which of these to send to the power amplifier for listening. In addition to allowing you to switch between sources, the preamplifier performs many other useful functions, such as amplifying the signal from your phono cartridge (in some preamplifiers), adjusting the balance between channels, and allowing you to set the volume level. Fig.2-1, shown earlier, illustrates the preamplifier's role in a music-playback system. The preamplifier is the component you will most often use, touch, and adjust. It also has a large influence on the system's overall sound quality. (Note: preamplifiers are built into, or "integrated" with, integrated amplifiers and receivers, instead of being housed in a separate chassis.)

There are many types of preamplifiers, each with different capabilities and functions. Choosing the one best suited to your system requires you to define your needs. Listeners without a turntable, for example, won't need a preamplifier that amplifies the tiny signals from a phono cartridge. Others will need many inputs to accommodate tape decks, tuners, and some will need multichannel capability. Let's survey the various preamplifiers and define some common preamplifier terms.

Line-Stage Preamplifier: Accepts only *line-level* (low-level) signals, which include every source component except a turntable. Line stages have become much more popular as listeners increasingly rely on digital sources rather than LPs as their main signal source. If you don't have a turntable, you need only a line-stage preamplifier.

Phono Preamplifier (also called a *phono stage*): Takes the very tiny signal from your phono cartridge and amplifies it to line level. It also performs

RIAA equalization on the signal from the cartridge. RIAA equalization, named after the Recording Industry Association of America, is a bass boost and treble cut that counteract the bass cut and treble boost applied in disc mastering, thus restoring flat response.

A phono stage can be an outboard stand-alone unit in its own chassis, or a circuit section within a full-function preamplifier. If you play records, you must have a phono stage, either as a separate component or as part of a full-function preamplifier.

Pre-Preamplifier: Takes a very-low-level signal from a moving-coil phono cartridge and amplifies it to a level acceptable by a phono preamplifier.

Step-Up Transformer: Performs the same function as a pre-preamplifier, but uses a transformer rather than an amplifying circuit.

Full-Function Preamplifier: Combines a phono stage with a line-stage preamplifier in one chassis.

Tubed Preamplifier: A tubed preamplifier uses vacuum tubes to amplify the audio signal.

Solid-State Preamplifier: A solid-state preamplifier uses transistors to amplify the audio signal.

Hybrid Preamplifier: A hybrid preamplifier uses a combination of tubes and transistors.

Audio/Video Controller: A device analogous to a preamplifier that includes video switching, multiple audio channels (typically six), and surround-sound decoding such as Dolby Digital and DTS. (A/V controllers are described in Chapter 13, "Audio for Home Theater.")

Multichannel Preamplifier: A preamplifier with multiple audio channels (typically six) for playback of multichannel music. Differs from an A/V controller in that the multichannel preamplifier has no surround decoding, video switching, or other functions for film-soundtrack reproduction.

Digital Preamplifier: A preamplifier that accepts digital input signals (such as from a CD transport) and processes the audio signal in the digital domain. Digital preamplifiers usually include a digital-to-analog converter so that the digital preamplifier can drive a conventional power amplifier.

Passive Level Control: Sometimes erroneously called a *passive preamp*, the passive level control can replace a line-stage preamplifier in some situations. It is inserted in the signal path between a source component and the power amplifier.

Instead of amplifying the source, a passive level control merely attenuates (reduces) the signal level driving the power amplifier. It doesn't plug into the wall, and cannot amplify a signal as does an active line-stage preamplifier.

No Preamplifier: If you listen only to a single line-level source—no turntable, tape deck, tuner, or other source—a CD player, SACD machine, DVD-Audio player, or digital processor with a volume control can replace a preamplifier. The source component drives the power amplifier directly, with volume adjustable via its output level control.

How to Choose a Preamplifier

Once you've decided on a line-stage, a full-function preamp, or separate line and phono stages (the last are generally more expensive), it's time to define your system requirements. The first is the number of inputs you'll need. If you have only a CD player, the four or five line inputs on most preamps are more than enough. But let's say you have a turntable, CD player, tuner, two cassette decks, Hi-Fi VCR, and a DVD machine. You'll need a phono input, five line inputs, and two tape loops—at the minimum. A tape loop is a pair of input and output jacks for recording onto a tape deck and receiving a signal from a tape deck. When you press the Tape Monitor button on your preamplifier, you are routing the signal from the Tape Input jacks to your power amplifier for listening. Other preamplifier features this complex system may need are the ability to copy from one tape deck to another, or to listen to one source while recording another. Preamps with tape copy will usually have the legend "2–1" or "1–2" inscribed on the front panel, meaning tape deck #1 can feed tape deck #2, and vice versa. If the preamplifier has separate selector switches marked "Listen" and "Record," this means one source can be recorded while another one is listened to. An example of this is recording a cassette for the car stereo from CD while listening to the turntable.

I've included these examples for the sake of completeness; most high-end preamps have few features—and for good reason. First, the less circuitry in the signal path, the purer the signal and the better the sound. Second, the preamp designer can usually put a fixed manufacturing budget into making a preamp that either sounds superb or has lots of features—but not both. Mass-market mid-fi equipment emphasizes vast arrays of features and buttons at the expense of sound quality. Don't be surprised to find very expensive preamps with almost no features; they were designed, first and foremost, for the best musical performance. Most high-end preamps don't even have tone (bass and treble) controls. Not only do tone controls electrically degrade the signal—and thus the musical performance—but the very idea of changing the signal is antithetical to the values of high-end audio. The signal should be reproduced with the least alteration possible. Tone controls are usually unnecessary in a high-quality system.

Another school of thought, however, holds that a playback system's goal isn't to perfectly reproduce what's on the recording, but to achieve the most enjoyable experience possible. If changing the tonal balance with tone controls enhances the pleasure of listening to music, use them. If you're comfortable with the latter philosophy, be aware that tone controls invariably degrade the preamplifier's sonic quality. (Some preamps with tone controls do allow you to switch them out of the circuit when they're not being used, a feature called "tone defeat.")

A similar debate rages over whether or not to include balance controls in a high-end preamp. A balance control lets you adjust the relative levels of the left and right channels. If the recording has slightly more signal in one channel than the other, the center image will appear to shift toward the louder channel, and the sense of soundstage layering may be reduced. A similar problem can occur if the listening room has more absorptive material on one side than the other, pulling the image off-center. A small adjustment of the balance control can correct these problems. Like tone controls, balance controls can slightly degrade a preamplifier's sonic performance. It isn't unusual to find a $10,000 state-of-the-art preamplifier with no tone or balance controls, and a $199 mass-market receiver with both of these features.

When making a purchasing decision, you should also consider the preamplifier's look and feel. Because the preamplifier is the component you'll interact with the most, ask yourself: Are the controls well laid out? Is the volume control easy to find in the dark? Does the preamp have a mute switch? A mute switch is handy when your listening is interrupted, for protecting the rest of your system when disconnecting cables, or for maintaining the same volume level when comparing two other components, such as digital sources or cables.

One convenience feature once found on only a few preamps but is now ubiquitous is remote control. The ability to adjust the volume (and sometimes absolute polarity) from the listening seat is a huge advantage. Remote volume control let's you set the volume exactly for the particular recording, enhancing the musical experience.

Balanced and Unbalanced Connections

Some preamplifiers have *balanced* inputs, balanced outputs, or both. A balanced signal is carried on a three-pin XLR connector rather than the conventional RCA plug. (Balanced and unbalanced connections are described in Chapter 11.) Fig.5-3 later in this chapter shows the rear panel of a preamplifier with balanced inputs and outputs on XLR jacks and unbalanced inputs and outputs on the familiar RCA jacks. If you have a balanced source component—usually a CD player or digital processor—you should consider choosing a preamplifier with a balanced input. Nearly all source components with balanced outputs also have unbalanced outputs. You can use either output, but you may not get the best sound quality unless you use the balanced output option. (See Chapter 8, "Digital Source Components," for the reason why.) In addition, not all "balanced" preamplifiers are created equal, as we'll see.

A preamp with unbalanced inputs and a balanced output can accept unbalanced signals but still drive a power amplifier through a balanced interconnect. If your power amplifier has balanced inputs, getting a balanced-output preamplifier is a good idea. You can listen to the system through both balanced and unbalanced lines and decide which sounds better. Some products sound better through balanced connections; others perform best with unbalanced lines. (A more technical description of balanced preamplifiers is included later in this chapter.)

Other Considerations in Choosing a Preamplifier

In addition to providing volume control and letting you select which source component you listen to, the preamplifier is a *buffer* between your source components and power amplifier. That is, the preamplifier acts as an intermediary, taking in signals from source components and conditioning those signals before sending them on to the power amplifier. Source components can easily drive a preamplifier, with the burden of driving a power amplifier through long cables falling on the preamp's shoulders. By buffering the signal, the preamplifier makes life easier for your source components and ensures good technical performance.

Some line-stage preamplifiers let you completely bypass all the active electronics (tubes or transistors) in the unit for purer sound. The preamp then becomes a passive level control, doing nothing more than controlling the system's volume. Although removing the active electronics from the signal path has certain sonic advantages, the preamplifier no longer acts as a buffer between source components and the power amplifier. The result can be poor technical performance (for reasons described later in this chapter) and degraded sound quality (primarily soft bass and loss of dynamics). Conversely, some systems will work just fine without the preamplifier acting as a buffer, and will benefit from bypassing the preamplifier's active electronics. Fortunately, you can try such a preamplifier in both modes (called *active* and *passive*) just by throwing a front-panel switch. When in the passive mode, the preamplifier suffers all the limitations of passive level controls, described later in this chapter. If you see a front-panel switch marked Bypass, you'll know what that means.

Another approach is the minimalist preamplifier that includes tubes or transistors that are always in the signal path, but provides no gain (amplification). This variety of preamplifier functions as a buffer between your source components and power amplifier, but cannot amplify signals. Some designers feel that these so-called *unity gain* preamplifiers sound better than conventional preamplifiers that amplify source signals. Your source components must put out enough voltage to adequately drive a power amplifier when using a unity-gain preamplifier.

Yet another technique uses a unity-gain buffer when the preamplifier's volume control is set to a low level, and kicks in a simple gain stage (amplifying circuit) only when the volume is turned up. You can see a commonality in these disparate approaches: keeping the preamplifier's signal path as short and clean as possible so that it has as little effect on the musical signal as possible. Preamplifiers using these techniques are not the norm; most preamplifiers always amplify and buffer the signal.

After you've decided on your functional needs, determine how much you can spend on a preamp using the guidelines in Chapter 2. Then put together a short list of preamps worthy of serious auditioning. Use dealer recommendations, read reviews in responsible audiophile magazines, and ask friends who have high-end systems. If possible, try the preamp in your own system before you buy.

Note that these recommendations for choosing the preamp best suited to your system also apply to integrated amplifiers. Think of an integrated amplifier as a preamplifier that also happens to have a power amplifier built-in. An integrated amplifier is nearly identical functionally to a preamplifier. The only difference is that, instead of connecting the preamplifier output to a power amplifier, you attach speaker cables to the integrated amplifier. (See Chapter 6 for more information on integrated amplifiers.)

Now that you know what features and functions you're looking for, it's time to begin listening.

What to Listen For

The preamplifier has a profound effect on the music system's overall performance. Because each of the source signals must go though the preamp, any colorations or unmusical characteristics it imposes will be constantly overlaid on the music. You can have superb source components, a top-notch power amplifier, and excellent loudspeakers, yet still have mediocre sound if the preamp isn't up to the standards set by the rest of your components. The preamplifier can establish the lowest performance level of your system; careful auditioning and wise product selection are crucial to building the best-sounding playback system for your budget.

A preamplifier's price doesn't always indicate its sonic quality; I know of one $1500 model that is musically superior to another preamp selling for nearly $8000. If you do your homework and choose carefully, you'll avoid paying too much for a poor-sounding product.

In addition to the usual listening procedures described in Chapter 3, preamplifiers offer several methods of sonic evaluation not possible with other components. We can therefore more precisely evaluate preamps and choose the best one for the money.

We'll start with the standard listening-evaluation techniques. First, the same musical selection can be played on the same system, alternating between two competing preamps. Be sure to match levels between the two preamps under audition. Listen for the presentation differences described in Chapter 3—particularly clarity, transparency, lack of grain, low-level detail, soundstaging, and a sense of ease.

The most common sonic problems in preamplifiers are a bright and etched treble and a thickening of the soundstage. Many preamps, particularly inexpensive solid-state units, overlay the midrange and treble with a steely, metallic hardness. These preamps can give the impression of more musical detail, but quickly become fatiguing. The treble becomes drier, more forward, and etched. Cymbals lose their sheen, instead sounding like bursts of white noise. Vocal sibilants (*s* and *sh* sounds) become objectionably prominent; violins become screechy and thin. The poor-sounding solid-state preamplifier emphasizes the brightness of the strings and diminishes the resonance of the violin's wooden body. Such preamps also reduce the saturation of tonal color, sounding thin and bleached.

The preamplifier that thickens the sound makes the soundstage more opaque. The transparent quality is gone, replaced by a murkiness that obscures low-level detail and reduces resolution. Instruments and voices no longer hang in a transparent, three-dimensional space. Instead, the presentation is thick, confused, congealed, and lacks clarity. Even some expensive models impose these characteristics on the music.

Beware of the preamplifier that tends to make all recordings sound similar in timbre, tonal balance, or spatial presentation. The best preamplifiers let you hear changes in the size of the concert hall, how closely the microphones were positioned, and can clearly resolve the differences between a Steinway piano and a Bösendorfer, among other such subtleties. In addition, listen for how well the preamp resolves the fine inner detail of instrumental timbres.

Compare the preamps under audition to the very best preamp in the store. Listen for the qualities distinguishing the best preamp, and see if those characteristics are in the preamps you're considering. This will not only give you a reference point in selecting a preamplifier for yourself, but will sharpen your listening skills. The more experience you have listening to a variety of products, the better your ability to judge component quality.

A useful way of evaluating preamplifiers—one not possible with other components—is the *bypass test*. This technique compares the preamplifier to no preamplifier, revealing the preamplifier's editorial effect on the music. This most revealing of comparisons leaves the preamplifier's shortcomings nowhere to hide.

To conduct a bypass test, drive a power amplifier at a comfortable volume with a known high-quality preamplifier, or directly from a CD player or digital source that has an output level control. Using a voltmeter and a test CD with test tones, set the preamplifier under evaluation for unity gain—the volume position at which the input level is identical to the output level (usually a third to halfway up on the volume control). Put the preamplifier under evaluation in the signal path between the known preamp and the power amp. Compare the system's sound with and without the preamp in the playback chain. Did the preamp thicken the sound? Did the treble become dry and brittle with the preamp in the system? Was the sense of space, clarity, and transparency replaced by an opaque thickness that homogenized the individual instruments? Did the preamplifier impart a common sonic characteristic over varied recordings? Most important, was the music less involving? The bypass test provides a quick and accurate assessment of the type and amount of coloration imposed by a preamplifier.

If you're comparing two preamplifiers, use preamp A to drive the power amplifier; listen, then put preamp B in the signal path at unity gain between preamp A and the power amplifier. Listen for the difference between the presentations with and without preamp B in the signal path. Then reverse the roles of the two preamps, listening for preamp A's effect on the presentation. This technique, shown in Fig.5-1, quickly reveals exactly what each preamp does to the music. This method, however, doesn't provide listening conditions of the highest resolution; the colorations of the first preamplifier can obscure qualities in the second preamplifier. It also adds another run of interconnects and terminations to the signal path.

Fig. 5-1 The bypass test for evaluating preamplifiers

You can also conduct a bypass test by substituting a passive level control for the preamplifier. Although passive level controls can reduce dynamic contrast and soften the bass in some systems, they rarely add grain and etch, or reduce soundstage depth and clarity, as do most active preamplifiers.

A less analytical method is to borrow the preamp from your dealer for a weekend and just listen to it. How much more exciting and involving is the music compared to using your existing preamp? Does the new preamp reveal musical information you hadn't heard before in familiar recordings? How much does the new preamp *compel* you to continue playing music? These are the best indicators of the product's ability to provide long-term musical satisfaction. Trust what your favorite music tells you about the preamplifier.

Tubes vs. Transistors

Of the many components that make up a hi-fi system, the preamplifier is the most likely to use vacuum tubes instead of solid-state devices (transistors). This is because preamplifiers handle only low-level signals, making tubes more practical and affordable there than in power amplifiers. Power-amplifier tubes are large, expensive, run hot, and require replacement. Further, one theory of audio design holds that if the system is to include tubes, they are best employed closest to the signal source such as in the preamplifier.

Moreover, the qualities that have endeared many music lovers to the magic of tubes are much more affordable when used in a preamplifier. Tubed audio components are more expensive to build and maintain than solid-state units, but that cost differential is much lower in preamplifiers than in power amplifiers. If you want the special qualities of tubes but not their heat, greater expense, and higher maintenance, the tubed preamplifier is the way to go.

Tubes are often claimed to sound sweeter and warmer, and to have a more natural treble. Many solid-state preamps tend to make the treble dry, brittle, metallic, and etched. The result is steely-sounding strings (particularly violins), unnaturally emphasized vocal sibilants (*s* and *sh* sounds), and cymbals that sound like bursts of high-frequency noise rather than a delicate brass-like shimmer. Because these unpleasant artifacts can be introduced by many components (digital sources, power amplifiers, cables, tweeters), a natural-sounding tubed preamplifier can tend to ameliorate the system's tendency toward these amusical characteristics.

The popularity of tubed electronics has nothing to do with nostalgia and everything to do with sound quality. Tubes have several advantages in their favor as audio amplifying devices. First, the circuitry associated with a vacuum tube—the ancillary parts that make the tube work—is generally much simpler than a circuit using transistors. Second, the distortion tubes produce is very different from the distortion created by solid-state electronics. Harmonic distortion, introduced by all active electronics, adds spurious frequencies to the signal being amplified. For example, if a preamplifier is passing a 1kHz signal, the preamp will generate distortion at 2kHz (second harmonic), 3kHz (third harmonic), 4kHz (fourth harmonic), and so forth. Tubed circuits generally produce lower-order harmonic distortion components such as second and third harmonic, in contrast with the higher-order distortion (seventh and ninth) introduced by transistors. Lower-order distortion is much less musically objectionable than the upper-order harmonics. Moreover, a large amount of second-harmonic distortion (say, 5%) is harder to hear than a very small amount (say, 0.5%) of seventh-harmonic distortion. Tube proponents point to these facts as evidence of the superiority of tubed preamplifiers.

Be aware, however, that some tubed preamps are intentionally designed to sound very colored. Rather than present the music with the least added effect, tubed preamps often add significant amounts of *euphonic coloration*. This form of distortion can at first be pleasing to the ear, but represents a departure from the original signal. This type of "tubey" coloration is characterized by a soft treble, an overly laid-back and easygoing presentation, lack of detail, and a "syrupy" sound. Many audiophiles, in their attempts to avoid the worst characteristics of solid-state, turn to euphonically colored tubed preamps to make their systems listenable.

It is a far better approach, however, to make sure that each component in the chain is as transparent as possible. If this is achieved, there will be no need for "tubey" preamps. Ideally, the listener shouldn't be aware that she is listening to tubes; instead, she should be aware only of the music. Just as poor solid-state preamps color the sound by adding grain, treble hardness, and etch, the poor tube preamp will often err in the opposite direction, obscuring detail, adding false "bloom," and reducing resolution. Be equally aware of both forms of coloration.

It's a mistake to "fall in love" with either solid-state or tubes for the wrong reasons. The solid-state lover may think he is getting "more detail," and the tube aficionado may fall for the "lush sweetness." Both extremes are to be avoided in the pursuit of a truly musical playback system. The overly "sweet" preamplifier may become uninvolving over time because of its low resolution; the "detailed" and "revealing" solid-state unit may eventually become unmusical for the fatigue it produces in the listener. Not all tube and solid-state preamps can, however, be categorized so neatly. Many tubed preamps are extremely transparent and neutral, having very little effect on the sound.

Nor should you buy a preamp purely because it uses tubes. Certain circuits are better implemented with tubes, others with solid-state devices. There are no magic components or circuit designs that will ensure a product's musicality. Worthy—and unworthy—products have been made from both tubes and transistors. That's why some companies design tubed, solid-state, and hybrid tubed/solid-state preamplifiers. The designer picks the best device for the particular application.

Ideally, both tubed and transistor preamplifiers strive for musical perfection, but approach that goal from different directions. The gross colorations I've described are largely a thing of the past, or relegated to fringe products that appeal to a minority of unsophisticated listeners. Today's reality is that tubed and solid-state designs sound more and more alike every year. The best preamplifier will be a transparent window on the music—no matter what its design.

The best advice is to choose the preamp that has the least effect on the music; you'll get much more musical satisfaction from it for a longer period of time. And remember: The perfect tubed preamp and the perfect solid-state preamp would sound identical.

Tube Life and Replacement Options

The small-signal tubes found in preamplifiers (generally between two and eight tubes) need replacing after 1000 to 2000 hours of use. Any time the preamplifier is turned on, the hour meter is ticking. This fact, along with the heat produced by tubes, encourages many owners of tubed preamplifiers to turn their units off when not listening. Although this extends tube life, an electronic component doesn't sound its best until it's been on for a few hours. The best advice is to turn on the preamplifier an hour or so before a listening session, if possible. If you know you'll be listening at night after work, turn on the preamplifier in the morning and it will be at peak performance when you get home. Another alternative is to buy a mechanical AC timer (about $10) from a hardware store and set it to switch on the preamp two hours before you expect to come home. Solid-state preamplifiers, on the other hand, draw very little current, run cool, and don't need tube replacement—they can be left on continuously.

Replacement tubes vary in cost from $10 for an untested generic type to $80 for a premium-grade tube that has been thoroughly tested and selected for best electrical performance. You may also want to consider paying a premium for matched pairs of tubes that have the same gain (amount of amplification). If the preamplifier's channel balance (similarity of gain between left and right channels) is determined by the gain of separate tubes, it's worth the extra cost for matched pairs. This ensures that one channel won't be louder than the other.

Because tube quality has a big effect on the preamplifier's sound, high-quality tubes are worth the money. New Old Stock (NOS) tubes (tubes that are unused but that haven't been manufactured in a long time) carry the highest prices because of limited supply and high demand. Different brands of tubes equal in technical performance will also sound different, making choosing difficult. Your local dealer is the best guide in selecting the optimum replacement tubes for your preamplifier. Equipment reviews of tubed preamplifiers will sometimes include the reviewer's opinions about different tube brands used in a particular preamplifier.

Fortunately for the tube aficionado, the supply of reliable, high-quality tubes has never been better. In fact, the increasing popularity of tubed audio products is partially due to the recent availability of great tubes from the former Soviet Union. Their technology was heavily reliant on vacuum tubes (which are still used in MIG fighter jets), and their factories produced excellent products. With the end of the cold war, this large supply of superb, reasonably priced tubes has fueled the recent growth of the tubed audio industry.

Before leaving the subject of tubed preamplifiers, I should tell you that I've had tubed preamplifiers in my system nearly continuously for the past eight years. I haven't made a conscious decision to use tubed preamps, but they somehow wind up staying in my system for extended periods.

The Line-Stage Preamplifier

A typical minimalist line-stage preamplifier is shown in Fig.5-2. This model, an Audio Research LS2B, has five unbalanced line inputs (labeled Tape, Tuner, CD, Video, and Aux) and one balanced line input (labeled Direct). A front-panel input selector switch selects which input is routed to the output. A mute switch shuts off the signal at the preamplifier output. (This is useful when changing records or disconnecting and connecting source components—engaging the mute switch prevents a loud

Fig. 5-2 A line-stage preamplifier's front panel

Fig. 5-3 A line-stage preamplifier's rear-panel connections

Courtesy Audio Research Corporation

thump from going through your system.) Note that this preamplifier has no balance control for adjusting the relative levels between left and right channels.

The rear panel, shown in Fig.5-3, has one Tape Out for driving a tape-deck input, an unbalanced Main Out, and two balanced Main Out pairs. One of the pairs of Main Out jacks would be connected to the power amplifier through a pair of interconnects. Whether to use the balanced or unbalanced outputs depends on whether the power amplifier has balanced or unbalanced inputs. It's best to try both interconnect types and choose the one that sounds best. (Your dealer should lend you interconnects for this purpose.) The tape outputs on this particular preamplifier are *buffered*, meaning that there is a separate amplifier for driving the tape recorder's inputs. The front-panel Defeat switch turns off this buffer amplifier.

The Direct input has a shorter signal path, bypassing the input selector switch for maximum sonic purity. Though this is a small refinement, such details are audible at the very top levels of performance.

The Phono-Stage Preamplifier

The phono stage amplifies the very tiny signal (between a few tens of microvolts and a few millivolts) from the phono cartridge to a line-level (about one volt) signal. This line-level signal can then drive a line-stage preamplifier, just as any other source component would. A phono stage can be an integral part of a full-function preamplifier, an optional board that plugs into some line-stage preamplifiers, or an outboard unit in its own chassis. Outboard phono stages have no volume controls; they usually feed a line input on a line-stage preamplifier.

In the days before CD, virtually all preamplifiers included integral phono stages. In many of today's preamplifiers, however, a phono stage is an option (usually about $200–$800) for those listeners who play LPs. This arrangement reduces the preamplifier's price for those needing only a line-stage preamplifier. It's also less expensive to buy a preamplifier with an integral phono stage than buying separate line and phono stages. With one chassis, one power supply, one owner's manual, and one shipping carton, a full-featured preamp is less expensive. These integral phono stages can also offer exceptional performance.

Not all line stages accept a phono board; if you think you'll want to play records in the future, be certain the line-stage preamp you buy will accept a phono board. If the preamp's rear panel has an input marked Phono, a ground lug, and a front-panel input selection position marked Phono, you can be confident that the preamp has a built-in phono stage or will accept a phono board. Note, however, that some line-stage preamps have a line-level input marked Phono but no phono stage. Look on the rear panel for the ground lug—a post for connecting a ground wire between the preamplifier and the turntable. If the preamp has a ground lug, it probably has provisions for accepting phono signals.

RIAA Equalization

In addition to amplifying the cartridge's tiny output voltage, the phono stage performs RIAA equalization on the signal. RIAA stands for Recording Industry Association of America, the body that standardized the record and playback equalization characteristics. Specifically, phono-stage RIAA equalization boosts the bass and attenuates the treble during playback. This equalization counteracts the bass cut and treble boost applied to the signal when the record was cut. By combining exactly opposite curves in disc mastering and playback, a flat response is achieved. RIAA equalization curves are shown in Fig.5-4. The dotted trace is the curve applied when the lacquer master is cut; the solid trace is the curve applied in the phono preamplifier. The combination of these complementary curves is flat response.

Fig. 5-4 RIAA equalization curves

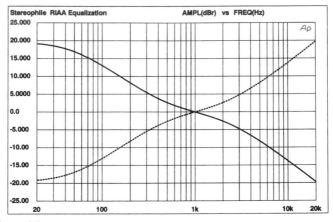

Courtesy *Stereophile*

Attenuating bass and boosting treble when the disc is cut allows more signal to be cut into the record groove and increases playing time. Because bass takes up more room in the groove than does treble, reducing the amount of bass in the groove allows the grooves to be spaced closer together. In addition, the treble boost in disc cutting and subsequent treble cut on playback act as a noise-reduction system: attenuating treble on playback also attenuates record-surface noise. RIAA equalization is why you can't plug a line-level source into a preamplifier's phono input. Similarly, a phono cartridge can't be plugged into a preamplifier's line input.

One aspect of a phono preamp's technical performance is its *RIAA accuracy*. This measurement or specification indicates how closely the phono stage's RIAA equalization circuit matches the standard curve used in disc mastering. Typical performance is 20Hz–20kHz, ±0.5dB. That means the phono preamplifier will exhibit frequency-response variations (some frequencies are emphasized over others) of no more than 1dB (plus half a dB and minus half a dB) over the audioband of 20Hz to 20kHz. Because RIAA errors are essentially frequency-response errors, they can greatly affect the phono stage's sound. A positive RIAA error in the treble can make the phono stage bright and etched; a negative error in the treble can make the sound dull and lifeless. Examples of RIAA errors are shown in Chapter 15, "Specifications and Measurements."

Note that European audio equipment often has a low-frequency rolloff curve built into the phono stage's RIAA circuit. That is, low frequencies are intentionally reduced in volume. This prevents the very low frequencies (below about 30Hz) generated by warped records from getting into the rest of the system, but can also reduce bass extension on playback systems capable of reproducing frequencies down to 20Hz.

Phono-Stage Gain

The amount of amplification provided by a phono stage (or any other amplifier) is called its *gain*. Gain is specified either in decibels (dB), or as a number expressing the ratio between input and output voltages. Phono stages have much more gain than line stages. Where a line stage may have 10 to 20dB of gain, a phono stage typically amplifies the signal by 35 to 60dB.

The amount of phono-stage gain required depends on the type of phono cartridge driving the phono preamplifier. Phono stages are of two varieties, each named for the type of cartridge with which it is designed to work. The first is the *moving-magnet* phono stage. Moving-magnet phono stages have their gain optimized to work with the relatively high output voltages from moving-magnet cartridges. Moving-magnet cartridges have high output voltages as cartridges go, on the order of two to eight millivolts (2–8mV). Consequently, they need less gain; a moving-magnet phono stage's gain is toward the lower end of the range, typically about 35dB.

Moving-coil cartridges have much lower output voltages due to their different method of generating a signal. Moving-coil output levels range from 0.15mV to 2.5mV. Consequently, they need more amplification (gain) in the phono preamplifier to reach line level than do moving-magnet cartridge signals. Moving-coil phono preamplifiers have about 40–60dB of gain. Note that moving-coil output voltages vary greatly with the cartridge design, with some so-called "high-output" models reaching moving-magnet levels.

Because of this wide variation in cartridge output level, a gain mismatch can occur between the cartridge and phono stage: The phono stage can have either too much or too little gain for a specific cartridge output voltage. If the phono preamp doesn't have enough gain, the volume control must be turned up very high for sufficient playback levels. This raises the noise floor (heard as a loud background hiss), often to the point of becoming objectionable. Conversely, a high-output cartridge can overload a moving-coil phono stage's input circuitry, causing distortion during loud musical passages. This condition is called *input overload*. A high-output cartridge driving a high-gain phono preamplifier can also make the preamplifier's volume control too insensitive. A moderate listening level may be achieved with the volume control barely cracked open; this makes small volume adjustments difficult.

Correctly matching the cartridge output voltage to the phono-stage gain avoids excessive noise and the possibility of input overload. A moving-coil cartridge specified at 0.18mV output needs about 55dB of gain. A typical moving-magnet output of 3mV should drive a phono stage that has about 35dB of gain. Some phono stages and full-function preamps have internal switches that adjust the gain between moving-magnet and moving-coil levels.

A pre-preamplifier is a small stand-alone component that can boost a moving-coil signal up to moving-magnet levels. If you have a moving-magnet phono input and upgrade to a moving-coil cartridge, you can add a pre-preamplifier instead of getting a new phono stage. Similarly, a *step-up transformer* increases a moving-coil's output voltage to a higher level. A transformer can improve the phono system's signal-to-noise ratio, or allow a moving-coil cartridge to drive a moving-magnet phono input.

High phono-stage gain carries the penalty of increased noise. Although phono stages in general have poorer signal-to-noise specifications than other components, very-high-gain phono preamps can be objectionably noisy. All other factors being equal, the greater the gain, the higher the noise. Select a phono preamp with just enough gain for your cartridge.

Cartridge Loading

Cartridge loading is the impedance and capacitance the phono cartridge "sees" when driving the phono input. Cartridge loading, specified in both impedance and capacitance, has a large effect on how the cartridge sounds, particularly moving-magnet types. Improper loading can cause frequency-response changes and other undesirable conditions. Many preamps allow you to adjust the input impedance and input capacitance to match the phono cartridge by adding resistors and capacitors to the phono stage's input circuit. These adjustments usually require a soldering iron, however, and should be done by your dealer. Some preamps have tiny internal switches to adjust cartridge loading, while others provide front-panel adjustments. One model even allows cartridge loading by remote control while in the listening seat. Note that the tonearm cable's capacitance must be added to the phono preamplifier's input capacitance to find the total capacitance loading the cartridge. More discussion of cartridge loading is included in Chapter 9 ("The LP Playback System").

The Digital Preamplifier

As music reproduction systems become more and more digital, the logical step is for the preamplifier to become digital also. A digital preamplifier takes in digital signals from a source component such as a CD transport, adjusts the volume and performs other signal processing in the digital domain, then converts the digital signal to analog for output to your power amplifier. A digital preamplifier is shown in Fig.5-5.

Fig. 5-5 A digital preamplifier operates on signals in the digital domain.

Courtesy NAD Electronics, Inc.

The term "preamplifier" is really a misnomer because the device we're talking about doesn't "preamplify" signals. The device could just as well be called a digital-to-analog converter that has built-in source switching, volume control, and sometimes tone and balance adjustments. The product is, however, called a digital "preamplifier," and is built to look and feel like a traditional analog preamp because that's the product it replaces. Just as we "open files" in our computers and adjust the "leading" of type, the digital product we're describing is a "preamplifier."

Because it operates in the digital domain, the digital preamplifier can perform some kinds of signal processing we'd never attempt in the analog domain. For example, the product shown in Fig.5-5 includes an equalizer, dynamic-range compressor/expander, soundstage width control, and other functions not possible in analog preamps. These processes are largely to correct recordings that have sonic deficiencies; most of the time, you leave them switched out of the circuit.

Digital preamplifiers can have a few analog inputs that bypass all the digital circuitry (and forgo the signal processing just described) and function as a traditional preamplifier. Some, however, digitize analog input signals, then convert them back to analog for output to your power amplifier. These A/D and D/A conversions inevitably degrade sound quality.

If you decide that a digital preamplifier is right for you, an important feature is a variable input level on the analog inputs. This is a knob on the front panel accompanied by a meter or LEDs that display the input level, that controls the level feeding the preamplifier's A/D converters. The ability to control the level feeding the A/D converter is crucial: if the level is too low, you'll hear noise and distortion; if too high, the signal will distort on loud peaks.

Audio/Video Controllers and Multichannel Preamplifiers

The increasing popularity of home theater, with its multichannel sound, has enticed many high-end preamp manufacturers to produce models that work in 2-channel stereo systems as well as those incorporating multichannel surround-sound. These products are called A/V (for Audio/Video) preamplifiers or A/V controllers. The latter term is more technically correct, and better describes the product's function.

Although A/V preamplifiers are covered in depth in Chapter 13, a brief introduction here is illustrative. A/V controllers are distinguished by three factors: multichannel sound capability, video switching, and surround decoding. First, an A/V controller will typically have six audio channels instead of two to accommodate the 5.1 channels of audio in the Dolby Digital and DTS surround-sound formats. Second, the A/V model can switch video sources as well as audio ones. Finally, A/V preamplifiers all have some form of surround decoding, such as Dolby Pro Logic, Dolby Digital, DTS, or all three.

A key feature of a high-end A/V controller is the ability to pass analog input signals to the output without converting the signal to digital and then back to analog. This analog bypass feature avoids unnecessary sonic degradation imposed by A/D and D/A conversions.

For those who want multichannel music reproduction without video switching and surround decoding, the multichannel preamplifier is a better choice than an A/V controller. A multichannel preamplifier is simply a conventional preamplifier with six channels rather than two. Although it offers no surround decoding, bass management, or other home-theater related functions, it will likely offer better sound quality than a digital controller, for several reasons. First, the chassis contains no digital circuitry, which creates noise that can get into the analog signal. Second, the designer can focus the entire parts budget on making the product sound good without worrying about including all that other complex circuitry. Very few multichannel preamplifiers are available, since they are only for those who will use their systems exclusively for music listening.

Passive Level Controls:
Are They Right for Your System?

A passive level control replaces a line-stage preamplifier with a simple volume control. Passive level controls have no ability to amplify the signal, only to attenuate (reduce) it. This means they work only with source components that put out enough voltage to drive a power amplifier. Most CD players and digital processors can drive a power amplifier through a passive level control.

On the plus side, passive level controls introduce the fewest electronics into the signal path between the source and power amplifier. A passive level control usually consists of only a continuously variable potentiometer (volume control), or a stepped knob that switches-in one of many discrete resistors. Fig.5-6 shows a high-quality stepped-resistor passive level control.

Fig. 5-6 A stepped-resistor passive level control

Courtesy First Sound

Removing the capacitors, transistors (or vacuum tubes), circuit-board traces, and wiring found inside a line-stage preamplifier reduces the likelihood of degrading the signal passing through the passive level control. I've found passive controls to be extremely transparent, having very little effect on the signal passing through them. Only the best active line-stages have the passive level control's lack of coloration and degradation of the music. In addition, passive level controls are less expensive than active preamplifiers, making them attractive to the purist on a budget.

There are, however, many factors to consider when deciding if a passive level control will work in your system. Because the passive level control cannot amplify or buffer the source signal, the burden of driving the power amplifier and interconnects falls on the source component. I described a preamplifier's buffering function earlier, which is to act as an intermediary between source components and the power amplifier. Because of the active preamplifier's buffering function, source components have an easy time driving the preamplifier. The more difficult job of driving the power amplifier through interconnects falls on the shoulders of the active preamplifier.

Most source components are designed to drive the relatively high input impedance of preamplifiers (usually 47k ohms), not the low input impedance of passive level controls. The source component's output impedance must be added to the passive control's output impedance to find the total output impedance driving the interconnects and power amplifier. This high output impedance can cause high-frequency rolloff, particularly if high-capacitance interconnects run between the passive level control and the power amplifier. (A full explanation of how and why this high-frequency rolloff occurs is included in Appendix B.)

Finally, a passive level control has no buffer to drive the tape output jacks. The source component must therefore drive both the power-amplifier and tape-deck inputs when recording, a condition that can degrade sound quality.

Passive level controls aren't the answer for all systems. They're often limited in functions, have only one or two inputs, and are tricky to match to the rest of your system. But replacing a colored line-stage preamplifier with a passive level control can greatly improve your system's sound. Listen to the passive level control in your system before you buy.

How a Preamplifier Works

A preamplifier consists of several *stages*. Each is an electronic circuit that performs a specific function, and can be pictured as a building block of an entire preamp.

The preamplifier's *input stage* is the first circuit element in the signal path. It acts as a buffer between the preamp's internal circuitry and the components driving it. That is, the input stage presents a high input impedance to source components driving the preamp, and a low output impedance to the next preamplifier stage. Impedance is, broadly speaking, the resistance to current flow. You'd intuitively think that more resistance to electrical current flow (a higher input impedance) in the preamplifier would put greater stress on the source components driving the preamp. The opposite is true: the higher the preamplifier's input impedance, the less current the source component must deliver.

Think of a garden hose connected to a faucet. The water pressure is the voltage from the source component, the hose is the interconnect cable, and your thumb and finger squeezing the hose are equivalent to the preamplifier's input impedance. The harder you squeeze the hose, the greater the resistance (impedance), reducing the amount of water flowing through it. If you let go of the hose altogether (a very low input impedance), the water pressure drops because the water supply is limited. In an audio system, some digital-source components with limited current output will distort (or have soft bass) when asked to drive a low-input-impedance preamplifier. The same digital source components will sound just fine when driving a high-input-impedance preamplifier. The preamplifier's high-impedance input stage is designed to make life easy for the source components driving the preamp.

The next circuit stage provides gain, amplifying the input signal. This is where the preamplifier actually boosts the signal level. (Although the input stage can have some gain.) The last stage is the *output stage*, the circuit block that serves as a buffer between the gain stage and the power amplifier connected to the preamp. The output stage has a high input impedance, low output impedance, and is designed to drive interconnects and a power-amplifier input. These circuit blocks are shown in Fig.5-7. Each of these stages can be made from transistors, vacuum tubes, integrated circuits (operational amplifiers, or *op-amps*), or a combination of these devices.

Fig. 5-7
Preamplifier
block diagram

A preamplifier will also have a source-selection switch for selecting which source component is connected to your power amplifier for listening. This can be a series of relays controlled by electronic circuits, or simply a rotary mechanical switch.

Most preamplifiers have separate miniature output stages to drive the tape output jacks. These output stages are nearly always of lower quality than the main output stage, but their sonic role is less crucial. Such products are said to have "independently buffered tape outputs."

If you plan to drive two power amplifiers from your preamplifier (as in a bi-amplified system), make sure that the preamplifier's output jacks are "independently buffered." This means that each output is driven by its own output stage rather than a single output stage driving both outputs.

A feature missing from many high-end preamplifiers is a headphone jack. This connection lets you plug headphones directly into the preamp and listen to music without turning on your power amplifier. Most of the headphone amplifiers in preamps that do include this feature are of compromised quality. The best way to listen to headphones is through a separate headphone amplifier that accepts the main output from your preamplifier. These products are described in Chapter 12.

The preamplifier's power supply delivers a supply of direct current (DC) to power the preamplifier's circuits. To prevent this DC from appearing at the preamplifier output along with the audio signal, *DC blocking capacitors* are often placed between stages, or at the preamplifier output. Some preamps avoid capacitors in the signal path by using a *DC servo* circuit that also prevents DC from appearing at the output jacks. A preamplifier without capacitors in the audio signal path is said to be *direct-coupled*.

Class-A refers to a type of tube or transistor operation in which the tube or transistor is always biased on, meaning that it always conducts current. A *discrete* preamplifier is one that uses no integrated circuits (op-amps), only separate transistors or vacuum tubes. Discrete preamps are more expensive than op-amp–based designs. Virtually all state-of-the-art preamps are discrete Class-A designs. (Descriptions of Class-A operation are included in Appendix B and in Chapter 6, "Power Amplifiers.")

Balanced and Unbalanced Preamplifiers

As described earlier in this chapter, preamplifiers can have balanced inputs, balanced outputs, or both. Although all balanced preamps have XLR jacks, not all balanced preamplifiers are created equal. Two preamps that have balanced inputs and outputs can be very different in how they treat the signal.

Most preamps accepting a balanced signal immediately convert it to an unbalanced signal, perform the usual preamplifier functions (provide gain and volume adjustment) on the unbalanced signal, then convert the signal back to balanced just before the main output. A preamp with balanced inputs and outputs, but unbalanced internal topology, often adds two active stages to the signal path: a *differential amplifier* at the input and the *phase splitter* at the output. A differential amplifier converts a balanced signal to unbalanced; a phase splitter converts an unbalanced signal to balanced. This kind of preamplifier is shown in block form in Fig.5-8.

The preferred, but much more expensive, method is to keep the signal balanced throughout the preamplifier. This technique requires double the audio circuitry; each portion of the balanced signal is amplified separately. Moreover, very close tolerances between halves of the balanced signal are required. The two signal halves must have identical gain and noise characteristics. Further, the four-element volume control must maintain precise tracking at all positions. Although the fully balanced circuit has more active devices in the signal path, the signal isn't subjected to a differential amplifier or a phase splitter. A fully balanced preamplifier is shown in block form in Fig.5-9.

Fig. 5-8 Some "balanced" pre-amplifiers convert a balanced input to unbalanced, then back to balanced.

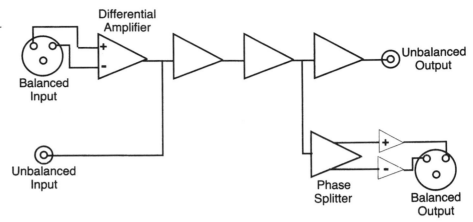

Fig. 5-9 A fully balanced pream-plifier keeps the signal balanced from input to output.

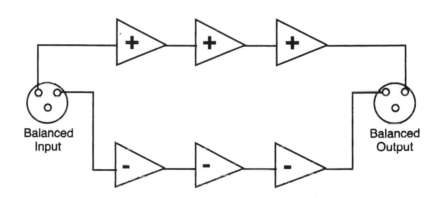

One way to tell if a preamplifier is fully balanced, or if it converts a balanced signal to unbalanced, then back to balanced, is to look at the volume control. If it has two elements (left and right channels), it has unbalanced internal circuitry. If the volume control has four elements (left +, left −, right +, right −), the preamp is fully balanced.

6 Power and Integrated Amplifiers

Introduction

The power amplifier—the last component in the signal chain before the loudspeakers—is the workhorse of a hi-fi system. It takes the low-level signal from the preamplifier and converts it to a powerful signal to drive the loudspeakers. It has a low-level input to receive the signal from the preamplifier, and terminals for connecting loudspeaker cables.

Power amplifiers range from $300 solid-state stereo units to $60,000 monoblocks. Choosing the right one for you begins with narrowing the range of possibilities. If you start by defining your requirements and setting your budget, the vast range of products will be quickly reduced to a more manageable number of contenders.

Because of the power amplifier's unique function, it differs from other components in size, weight, and use. High-quality power amplifiers are usually large and heavy. Moreover, the power amplifier is the component you don't need to touch and adjust. Consequently, power amplifiers are often placed on the floor near the loudspeakers rather than in an equipment rack.

Here are definitions of some of the terms associated with power amplifiers.

Stereo Power Amplifier: A power amplifier with two audio channels (left and right) in one chassis.

Monoblock Power Amplifier: A power amplifier with only one audio channel per chassis. Two monoblocks are required for stereo reproduction.

Multichannel Power Amplifier: An amplifier with, typically, five amplifier channels, for use in a home-theater system.

Watt: A unit of electrical power. Power is the ability to do work; in this case, the ability of the amplifier to make a loudspeaker's diaphragm move.

Power Output: The maximum amount of power the amplifier can deliver to the loudspeaker, measured in watts.

Load: In power-amplifier terminology, a load is the loudspeaker(s) the power amplifier must drive.

Tubed: A tubed power amplifier uses vacuum tubes to amplify the audio signal.

Solid-State: A solid-state power amplifier uses transistors to amplify the audio signal.

Single-Ended Amplifier: A power amplifier in which the output device (a tube or transistor) is operated in such a way that it amplifies the entire musical waveform. Also called *Class-A* amplification. (Compare with "push-pull.")

Push-Pull: A power amplifier in which pairs of output devices (tubes or transistors) alternately "push" and "pull" current through the loudspeaker, with one output device amplifying the positive half of the waveform, another output device amplifying the negative half of the waveform. Also called *Class-B* amplification. (Compare with "single-ended.")

Class A/B: A power amplifier that operates partially in Class A to avoid the crossover distortion that occurs in pure Class B amplifiers.

Hybrid: A power amplifier combining vacuum tubes and solid-state devices. The input and driver stages are usually tubed, the output stage is usually solid-state.

Bridging: Converting a stereo power amplifier into a monoblock power amplifier. Some power amplifiers have a rear-panel bridging switch. Also called "strapping" into mono.

Bi-amping: Driving a loudspeaker's midrange and treble units with one amplifier, the woofer with a second amplifier.

Digital Power Amplifier: An amplifier that takes in a digital, rather than an analog, audio signal. A true digital amplifier amplifies the digital-domain signal and converts it to analog in the same stage.

How to Choose a Power Amplifier

Unlike most of the other components in your system, power amplifiers vary greatly in electrical performance. Consequently, choosing a power amplifier requires careful system matching for electrical compatibility, not just musical compatibility. While any CD player or digital processor will function in a system (even though it may not be musically ideal), some power amplifiers just won't work well with certain loudspeakers on a technical level. Choosing a power amplifier is thus a technical, as well as aesthetic, decision that requires careful attention to system matching. We'll discuss these technical factors throughout this chapter.

Because a power amplifier's cost is often proportional to its output power, read this chapter's "How Much Power Do You Need?" section to select just the right power rating for your needs. Whatever your budget, the power amplifier should consume about 20 to 25% of your total system budget.

The first division of power amplifiers—a stereo unit or a pair of monoblocks—will be decided by your budget. Monoblocks generally *start* at about $2500 per pair. At this price level, a single stereo unit may make more sense; with only one chassis, power cord, and shipping carton, the manufacturer can put more of the manufacturing cost into better parts and performance. I advise against monoblocks if your amplifier budget is less than about $4000. There may be exceptions to this figure, but it nonetheless offers a broad guideline. Many excellent stereo units, for example, cost upward of $6000. A very popular price range for high-quality power amplifiers is $800–$2000, with the $2000 models sometimes offering musical performance close to that of the most expensive amplifiers.

Monoblocks generally perform better than a single stereo unit for several reasons. First, because the two amplifier channels are separate chassis, there is no chance of interaction between channels. Consequently, monoblocks typically have better soundstage performance than stereo units. Second, monoblocks have completely separate power supplies, even down to the power transformers: the left- and right-channel amplifier circuits don't have to share their electrical current source. This gives monoblocks the ability to provide more instantaneous current to the loudspeaker, all other factors being equal. Finally, most manufacturers put their cost-no-object efforts into monoblocks, which are often the flagships of their lines. If you want all-out performance and can afford them, monoblocks are the way to go.

Integrated Amplifiers

At the other end of the scale from monoblocks is the integrated amplifier, in which a preamplifier and a power amplifier are combined in the same chassis. Though the power output from integrated amplifiers is generally lower than that from separate power amplifiers, integrateds are much less expensive, and ideal for budget to moderately priced systems. Integrated amplifiers cost between $300 and $9000.

High-end integrated amplifiers have changed radically in the past few years. Once relegated to low-powered units from European manufacturers, with idiosyncratic operation and non-standard connectors, integrated amplifiers have finally come into their own. Leading high-end manufacturers have realized that an integrated amplifier makes sense for many music lovers. The cost and convenience advantages of an integrated amplifier are compelling: integrateds take up less space, are easier to connect, reduce the number of cables in your system, and can even offer the performance of separate components. Now that high-end manufacturers have taken the integrated amplifier seriously, they're putting their best technology and serious design efforts into their integrateds.

Consequently, many manufacturers have enjoyed booming sales of integrated amps in the $2000–$4000 price range that produce about 50–150Wpc (watts per channel) of power. One such product is shown in Fig.6-1.

Fig. 6-1 Today's integrated amplifiers combine first-rate sound with high power output, making them a good alternative to separates.

Courtesy Ayre Acoustics

Some manufacturers have even included a quality tuner with their integrated amplifier. Not so long ago, the term "high-end stereo receiver" was an oxymoron. Today, however, there's no reason why a receiver designed and built with the dedication given to separate components should offer anything but high-end musical performance.

These newer integrated amplifiers have also overcome one of the limitations of earlier designs: the inability to upgrade just the power amplifier or preamplifier section. Today's integrateds often include preamplifier-out jacks for connecting the integrated to a separate, more powerful amplifier. They also often have power-amplifier input jacks if you want to upgrade the preamplifier section.

When choosing an integrated amplifier, combine the advice in Chapter 5 ("Preamplifiers") with the guidelines in the rest of this chapter. If your budget is under $3000 for amplification, seriously consider one of the new breed of high-end integrated amplifiers rather than separates.

How Much Power Do You Need?

The first question to answer when shopping for a power amplifier or integrated amplifier is how much output power you need. Power output, measured in watts into a specified loudspeaker impedance, varies from about 20Wpc in a very small integrated amplifier to about 1000Wpc. Most high-end power amplifiers put out between 80 and 250Wpc. Single-ended triode amplifiers, described later in this chapter, generally produce between 3Wpc and 20Wpc.

Choosing an appropriate amplifier power-output range for your loudspeakers, listening tastes, room, and budget is essential to getting the best sound for your money. If the amplifier is under-powered for your needs, you'll never hear the system at its full potential. The sound will be constricted, fatiguing, lack dynamics, and the music will have a sense of strain on climaxes. Conversely, if you spend too much of your budget on a bigger amplifier than you need, you may be shortchanging other components. Choosing just the right amplifier power is of paramount importance.

The amount of power needed varies greatly according to loudspeaker sensitivity, loudspeaker impedance, room size, room acoustics, and how loudly you like to play music. Loudspeaker sensitivity is by far the biggest determining factor in choosing an appropriate power output. Loudspeaker sensitivity specifies how high a sound-pressure level (SPL) the loudspeaker will produce when driven by a certain power input. A typical sensitivity specification will read "88dB SPL, 1W/1m." This means that the loudspeaker will produce an SPL of 88 decibels (dB) with one watt of input power when measured at a distance of one meter. Although 88dB is a moderate listening volume, a closer look at how power relates to listening level reveals that we need much more than one watt for music playback.

Each 3dB increase in sound-pressure level requires a doubling of amplifier output power. Thus, our loudspeaker with a sensitivity of 88dB at 1W would produce 91dB with 2W, 94dB with 4W, 97dB with 8W, and so on. For this loudspeaker to produce musical peaks of 109dB, we would need an amplifier with 128W of output power.

Now, say we had a loudspeaker rated at 91dB at 1W/1m—only 3dB more sensitive than the first loudspeaker. We can quickly see that we would need only *half* the amplifier power (64W) to produce the same volume of 109dB SPL. A loudspeaker with a sensitivity of 94dB would need just 32W to produce the same volume. The higher-sensitivity speaker simply converts more of the amplifier's power into sound.

This relationship between amplifier power output and loudspeaker sensitivity was inadvertently illustrated in an unusual demonstration more than 50 years ago. In 1948, loudspeaker pioneer Paul Klipsch conducted a demonstration of live vs. reproduced sound with a symphony orchestra and his Klipschorn loudspeakers. His amplifier power: 5W. The Klipschorns are so sensitive (an astounding 105dB SPL, 1W/1m) that they will produce very high volumes with very little amplifier power. Klipsch was attempting to show that his loudspeakers could closely mimic the tonal quality and loudness of a full symphony orchestra.

The other end of the speaker-sensitivity spectrum was illustrated by a demonstration I attended of an exotic new loudspeaker. During the demo, the music was so quiet that I could barely hear it. I looked at the power amplifiers—300Wpc monsters with large power meters—and was astonished to see that the power meters were nearly constantly pegged at full power. This unusual speaker converted only a minuscule amount of the amplifier's output power into sound.

The importance of loudspeaker sensitivity is also demonstrated by today's 3Wpc single-ended triode amplifiers, which can produce moderately loud listening levels through high-sensitivity speakers. These examples of huge variations in sound-pressure level and amplifier power illustrate how loudspeaker sensitivity greatly affects how big an amplifier you need. Even a small difference in loudspeaker sensitivity—2dB, say—changes your amplifier power requirements.

The dBW Power Rating

We've seen that every doubling of amplifier power yields a volume increase of 3dB. Consequently, there is a 3dB difference between a 10W amplifier and a 20W amplifier, but also between a 500W amplifier and a 1000W amplifier. Although the output power is vastly greater between 500W and 1000W than between 10W and 20W, the difference is still 3dB. That's why we must consider the ratio of output powers, not the number of watts difference, when comparing amplifier power ratings.

Fortunately, there is a way of expressing amplifier power that takes into account this exponential relationship between dB and power, a rating called the *dBW*. The "W" after dB means that 0dB is referenced to 1W of output power. A 10W amplifier has a dBW rating of 10dBW, a 20W amplifier has a dBW rating of 13dBW—twice the power, or the ability to play 3dB louder than a 10W amplifier. A 40W amplifier is rated at 16dBW. One hundred watts equals 20dBW, and a 1000W amplifier is said to have 30dBW of output power. The dBW rating conveys the ratio of amplifier output power referenced to 1W of output power. The relationship between power output (into an 8 ohm load) and dBW is shown in the following table.

Watts	dBW	Watts	dBW	Watts	dBW
1.0	0	10.0	10	100	20
1.25	1	12.5	11	125	21
1.6	2	16	12	160	22
2.0	3	20	13	200	23
2.5	4	25	14	250	24
3.2	5	32	15	320	25
4.0	6	40	16	400	26
5.0	7	50	17	500	27
6.3	8	63	18	630	28
8.0	9	80	19	800	29

Most manufacturers don't include dBW ratings in their amplifiers' specifications. You can, however, perform this conversion yourself with a pocket calculator that has a "log" button. Punch in the number of watts you want to convert to dBW, find the logarithm of that number by pressing the log key, then multiply by 10. This will give you the dBW value when driving an 8 ohm load. To find the dBW rating with a 4 ohm load, subtract 3dB from the result. To calculate for 2 ohms, subtract 6dB from the result.

For example, if an amplifier puts out 150W into 8 ohms, enter "150" into the calculator and press the log key; "2.176" will appear in the display. Then press "x" and "10" to multiply the log by 10, to get the dBW rating of 21.76dBW.

If this same amplifier puts out 225W into 4 ohms, enter "225" into the calculator, press log to get 2.352, then multiply by 10 to get the intermediate result of 23.52dBW. But this is a 4 ohm power rating; subtracting 3 from the result will give us the final dBW rating of 20.52W into 4 ohms.

If you're choosing between 60Wpc and 110Wpc amplifiers, you can calculate the difference in dB between them. Converting 60W (at 8 ohms) into dBW gives us 17.78dBW. Converting 110W (at 8 ohms) into dBW works out to 20.41dBW. The difference is a little less than 3dB. Note that the same dB difference exists between a 600W amplifier and a 1100W amplifier as between a 6W amplifier and an 11W amplifier.

The concept of dBW becomes even more useful when we take a closer look at amplifier output ratings. Most of the power figures we've discussed are with the amplifier driving an 8 ohm load. But most loudspeakers have impedances of less than 8 ohms, and some have impedance dips below 2 ohms. How does our power amplifier behave when asked to drive low-impedance loudspeakers?

Instead of just considering the amplifier's 8 ohm power rating, look at how the power output changes into 4 and 2 ohm loads. An amplifier acting as a perfect *voltage source* will double its power every time the load impedance is cut in half; this amplifier would be capable of driving 100W into 8 ohms, and could deliver 200W into 4 ohms, 400W into 2 ohms, or 800W into 1 ohm. (A more technical discussion of this aspect of amplifier performance appears in Chapter 15.)

Some amplifiers barely increase their output power when driving 4 ohms; others can double it. This means that not all "100Wpc" amplifiers are created equal. One "100Wpc" amplifier might put out 150W into 2 ohms, while another might deliver 350Wpc into 2 ohms. This ability to drive low-impedance loads (specifically, to deliver lots of current) has a large influence on an amplifier's sound and subjective power capability.

This is where our dBW rating again comes into play. When calculating dBW, subtract 3dBW from the 8 ohm dBW rating when the amplifier is driving 4 ohms, and subtract 6dBW when the amplifier is driving 2 ohms. In the example of the two "100Wpc" amplifiers in the preceding paragraph, each is rated at 100Wpc into 8 ohms, or 20dBW. But the first amplifier puts out only 150W into 2 ohms, while the second puts out 350W into 2 ohms. Converting the 2 ohm power ratings into dBW, we see that the first amplifier has a dBW rating of 15.76dBW at 2 ohms, while the second has a dBW rating of 19.44dBW into 2 ohms. Quite a difference—nearly 4dB—between two "100Wpc" amplifiers.

Why Amplifier Output Current Matters

This difference has real-world consequences. The ability to increase output power into low impedances indicates how much current the amplifier can deliver to the loudspeaker. It is current flow through the loudspeakers' voice coils (in dynamic loudspeakers) that creates the electromagnetic force that causes the cones and domes to move, and thus produce sound. If current flow through the voice coil is constrained, so is the music.

In the previous chapter, I described how source components such as a CD player have an easier time driving a preamplifier of high input impedance than one of low input impedance. I likened the situation to a water faucet and hose: the water pressure is voltage, the flow of water through the hose is electrical current, and squeezing the hose forms a resistance (impedance) to the flow. You can extend this analogy to a power amplifier driving a loudspeaker, with the loudspeaker's impedance forming the resistance in the hose. The lower the loudspeaker's impedance, the less the resistance to current flow from the amplifier, and the harder the amplifier must work to deliver current to the loudspeaker. As we'll see in Appendix A, if the impedance is halved (say, from 8 ohms to 4 ohms), the amplifier is asked to deliver double the current to the loudspeaker.

If the amplifier isn't up to the job, the musical result is strain or even distortion on musical peaks, weak bass, loss of dynamics, hardening of timbre, and a collapsing soundstage. In short, we can hear the amplifier give up as it runs out of power. Conversely, amplifiers that can continue increasing their output power as the impedance drops generally have very deep, extended, and powerful bass, virtually unlimited dynamics, a sense of ease and grace during musical peaks, and the ability to maintain correct timbre and soundstaging, even during loud passages. If you have relatively high-impedance loudspeakers with no severe impedance dips, you're much less likely to encounter sonic problems, even with modest power amplifiers; the loudspeaker simply demands less current from the power amplifier.

Amplifiers with high current capability (indicated by their ability to increase output power into low impedances) are often large and expensive. Their current capability comes from massive power transformers, huge power supplies, and lots of output transistors—all expensive items. Fig.6-2 shows such a power amplifier.

Fig. 6-2 Inside a high-current power amplifier

Courtesy Krell Industries

The massive power transformer and filter capacitors seen in the middle of the amplifier can supply large amounts of current to the circuits. The output stage has many output transistors working together for increased current capacity. These transistors are mounted to large *heatsinks* (the fins on the outside of an amplifier) to keep the transistors running relatively cool. Heatsinks transfer heat from the output transistors to the amplifier exterior so that it can be dissipated into the air.

In the "Specifications and Measurements" section on power amplifiers in Chapter 15, we'll look at how to evaluate a power amplifier's ability to deliver current into low-impedance loads. You can also figure out for yourself which amplifiers are good at driving low-impedance speakers by converting their output-power ratings at 8 ohms and 4 ohms into dBW. The less the difference in the dBW ratings into 8 and 4 ohms, the better the amplifier's ability to deliver current.

Keep in mind, however, that not all systems require large power amplifiers. If you have sensitive loudspeakers with a fairly high impedance, the loudspeaker's current demands are vastly lower. Consequently, smaller amplifiers work just fine. As we'll see in the discussion of single-ended triode amplifiers later in this chapter, amplifiers with as little as 3Wpc and very limited ability to deliver current can sound highly musical.

What to Look For when Comparing Power Ratings

When comparing amplifier power ratings, make sure the specified power is continuous or RMS rather than peak. Some manufacturers will claim a power output of 200W, for example, but not specify whether that power output is available only during transient musical events such as drum beats, or if the amplifier can deliver that power continuously into a load. RMS stands for "Root Mean Square," a mathematical calculation expressing the effective, or average, power output. Very few amplifiers are, however, specified by peak power.

Another way manufacturers exaggerate power ratings is by not specifying the *power bandwidth*. This term describes the frequency range over which a power amplifier can deliver its power. A power amplifier delivering 200W at 1kHz is far less powerful than one that can deliver 200W over the full audio bandwidth of 20Hz–20kHz. You'll often see mass-market audio/video receivers with power-output ratings specified only at 1kHz, or from 50Hz to 20kHz. Further, stereo power amplifiers can deliver more power with only one channel driven—look for the words "both channels driven." The maximum power output should also be specified at a certain distortion level.

You can see the potential for misleading power-amplifier output claims. The abuses were so bad at one time that the Federal Trade Commission (FTC) stepped in to regulate power claims—the only example of an audio specification being regulated by a governmental body.

The FTC mandate for power ratings requires that the power rating be continuous (not peak), that the load impedance and bandwidth be specified, and that the Total Harmonic Distortion (THD) be given at full power and measured over the audio bandwidth. You may see a power specification that reads "50Wpc continuous (or RMS) power into 8 ohms, both channels driven, 20Hz–20kHz, with less than 0.1% THD." A power specification including all these conditions is called an "FTC power rating." Some manufacturers no longer adhere to the FTC-mandated power ratings, figuring that the issue has blown over and is no longer enforced. You see fudged power ratings on mass-market audio/video receivers that must now power five loudspeakers rather than two, and in single-ended triode amplifiers that cannot meet the stringent FTC power-output specification requirements.

If you're amplifier-shopping for low-impedance loudspeakers, look at the power-output specifications into 4 ohms. Make sure you see the words "continuous" or "average" in the power rating. See if the bandwidth and distortion are specified. These figures don't tell us what we need to know about the amplifier's musical qualities, but nevertheless indicate good technical performance.

Why Amplifier Power Isn't Everything

We've seen how loudspeaker sensitivity greatly affects how much amplifier power you need, and how power amplifiers with the same 8 ohm power rating can differ radically in their abilities to drive loudspeakers. Now let's look at some other factors influencing how much amplifier power you need.

The first is room size. The bigger the room, the more amplifier power you'll need. A rough guide suggests that quadrupling the room volume requires a doubling of amplifier power to achieve the same sound-pressure level. How acoustically reflective or absorptive your listening room is will also affect the best size of amplifier for your system. If we put the same-sensitivity loudspeakers in two rooms of the same size, one room acoustically dead (absorptive) and the other acoustically live (reflective), we would need roughly double the amplifier power to achieve the same sound-pressure level in the dead room as in the live room.

Finally, how loudly you listen to music greatly affects how much amplifier power you need. Chamber music played softly requires much less amplifier power than rock or orchestral music played loudly. The relationships between loudspeaker sensitivity, room size, room acoustics, and amplifier power are shown in Fig.6-3.

We can see that a low-sensitivity loudspeaker, driven by orchestral music in the large, acoustically dead room of someone who likes high play-back levels, may require hundreds of times the amplifier power needed by someone listening to chamber music at moderate listening levels through high-sensitivity loudspeakers in a small, live room. A 20Wpc amplifier may satisfy the second listener; the first listener may need 750Wpc.

Fig. 6-3 The relationship between loudspeaker sensitivity, room size, room acoustics, and power-amplifier output power (after *High Fidelity*)

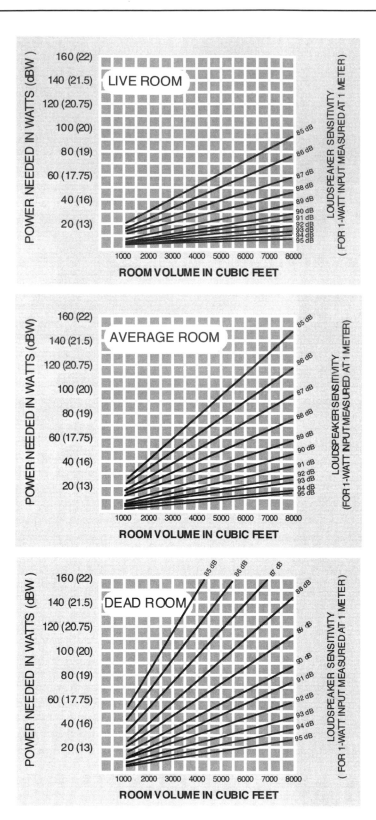

Other Power-Amplifier Considerations

Tubes vs. Transistors

When transistor amplifiers were introduced in the 1960s, it appeared that the days of the vacuum tube were over. Transistors were smaller, lighter, and cheaper than tubes, ran cooler, and produced more output power. If that wasn't enough, transistor amplifiers didn't need an output transformer, a component that added considerably to the amplifier's size, weight, and cost. All the audio manufacturers of the day scrapped their tubed amplifiers in favor of transistor units virtually overnight.

But many music lovers found the sound of these newfangled "solid-state" amplifiers unlistenable. They likened the sound to that of a pocket transistor radio, only louder. Unfortunately, those perceptive audiophiles couldn't buy a new tubed amplifier after the transistor's introduction.

The modern tubed amplifier was created in 1970 by William Zane Johnson of Audio Research Corporation. As did many music lovers, he found the sound of tubed amplifiers more musical. Johnson's demonstration of a tubed amplifier at a 1970 hi-fi show prompted one showgoer to remark, "You've just set the audio industry back 10 years!" But instead of being a setback, Johnson's amplifier began a renaissance in tubed equipment that is still going strong more than 34 years later.

The perennial tubes-vs.-transistors debate arises when you're faced with choosing a power amplifier. Tubed units can offer stunning musical performance, but they have their drawbacks. Here are the advantages and disadvantages of tubed power amplifiers. (For the moment, I'll confine my observations to conventional "push-pull" tubed amplifiers, not the exotic single-ended triode varieties described later in this chapter.)

Tubed power amplifiers are more expensive than their similarly powered solid-state counterparts. The cost of tubes, transformers, and more extensive power supplies all make owning a tubed power amplifier a more expensive proposition than owning a solid-state unit. Moreover, the tubes will need replacing every few years, further adding to the real cost of ownership. A set of sixteen EL34 output tubes, for example, can cost from $200 to $400.

In terms of bass performance, tubed power amplifiers can't compete with good solid-state units. Tubes have less control in the bass, making the presentation less punchy, taut, and extended. Further, tubed power amplifiers often have limited current delivery into low-impedance loads, making them a poor choice for current-hungry loudspeakers. Tubes also require monthly biasing (small adjustments made with a screwdriver) to maintain top performance. Biasing is very easy, but some music lovers would prefer not to have to think about performing routine maintenance on their music-playback systems.

Power-amp tubes can fail suddenly, sometimes in smoke and (momentary) flames. Such dramatic failure is rare, however; I've used tubed amplifiers for nearly all my time as a reviewer and have had two tubes fail in that time, both of them uneventfully.

Finally, there is the possibility of small children or pets burning themselves on hot tubes. Many, but not all, tubed power amplifiers have exposed output tubes. If you have small children, consider a tubed amplifier that is surrounded by a ventilated metal cage.

Given these drawbacks, why would anyone want to own a tubed power amplifier? It's simple: tubes can sound magical. When matched with an appropriate loudspeaker, tubed power amplifiers offer unequaled musicality, in my experience. Even small, moderately priced tubed amplifiers have more than a taste of tube magic.

Many important aspects of music reproduction seem to come naturally to tubed amplifiers. They generally have superb presentation of instrumental timbre, smooth and unfatiguing treble, and spectacular soundstaging. The hard, brittle, edgy midrange and treble presentation of many solid-state amplifiers is contrasted with the purity of timbre and sense of ease conveyed by a good tubed amp. Music has a warmth, ease, and natural musicality when reproduced by many tubed designs. The soundstage has an expansive quality, with a sense of bloom around instrumental images. This isn't to say there aren't good-sounding solid-state power amplifiers, only that tubes seem to more consistently deliver the musical goods. A tubed amplifier's softer bass is often willingly tolerated for its magical midrange, treble, and soundstaging.

Beware, however, of the tubed power amplifier that sounds lush on *every* recording; the amplifier is probably imposing its own sonic signature on the music. Some tubed amplifiers have *euphonic colorations*, or departures from accuracy that are initially pleasing to the ear. Listen for a change in timbre, spatial presentation, or bass quality with different recordings. These characteristics should change with the recording; if they don't, it's likely that the power amplifier is imposing a common sonic signature on the music. Ideally, the power amplifier will reveal exactly what's on the recording without adding any characteristics of its own.

As good as tubed amplifiers can sound, solid-state amplifiers have some decided sonic and technical advantages. For example, tubed units are no match for solid-state amplifiers in bass performance. Transistor power amplifiers have tighter, deeper, and much more solid bass than tubed units. The feeling of bass tautness, kick, extension, and power are all better conveyed by solid-state amplifiers, regardless of how good the tubed amplifier is. Speaking technically, solid-state amplifiers can deliver more current to low-impedance loudspeakers, making them a better choice for such loads.

No one but you can decide if a tubed power amplifier is ideal for your system. I strongly suggest, however, that you audition at least one tubed amplifier before making a purchasing decision. You may get hooked.

Balanced Inputs

If your preamp has balanced outputs, you may want to consider a power amplifier with balanced inputs. Most power amps with balanced inputs also provide unbalanced inputs, allowing you to compare these two connection methods before deciding which one to leave in your system. Some preamplifier/power-amplifier combinations sound better via balanced connection, others via the unbalanced jacks. The best way to discover which method is better is by listening to both. (See Chapter 5 for a discussion of why some preamplifiers may sound better from their unbalanced outputs.) Borrow a pair of interconnects from your dealer so you can make this comparison. If you have a power amplifier with both balanced and unbalanced inputs, but use the unbalanced inputs, be sure you have a shorting plug in the amplifier's balanced input jacks. This is a small U-shaped plug that shorts pin 3 of the balanced input connector to ground, preventing noise from getting into the amplifier.

Bridging

Some stereo power amplifiers can be "bridged" to function as monoblocks. Bridging configures a stereo amplifier to function as a more powerful single-channel amplifier. The amplifier will have a switch on the rear panel to convert the amplifier to bridged operation. Note that two bridged amplifiers are needed for stereo. If you have a stereo amplifier that can be bridged and you want more power, simply buy a second, identical amplifier and bridge the two for more total power. In theory, bridging results in a four-fold increase in output power. That's because bridging doubles the amplifier's maximum output voltage, and, according to Ohm's Law, quadruples the power. In practice, however, bridging roughly doubles an amplifier's 4 ohm power rating, due to the amplifier's current-output limitations.

Bridging changes the amplifier's internal connections so that one channel amplifies the positive half of the waveform and the other channel amplifies the negative half. The loudspeaker is connected as the "bridge" between the two amplifier channels instead of between one channel's output and ground.

Bridging is most beneficial when the power amplifiers are asked to drive low-sensitivity, high-impedance loudspeakers (8 ohms nominal). High-impedance speakers are driven more by voltage than by current. Conversely, low-impedance speakers demand more current from the power amplifier. Bridging doubles the amplifier's maximum output voltage, but quadruples its maximum current output (because two amplifier channels are now driving one loudspeaker). Moreover, connecting a 4 ohm speaker to a bridged power amplifier causes the amplifier to "see" a 2-ohm load, further stressing the amplifier's current capacity. The result can be amplifier overheating, which will either damage the amplifier or cause its protection circuit to activate and shut down the amplifier while music is playing.

Bi-Amping

Any loudspeaker with two sets of input terminals is a candidate for bi-amping. In a bi-amped setup, two power amplifiers are used to drive one loudspeaker. One amplifier drives the woofer, the other drives the midrange and tweeter.

Let's first consider *passive bi-amping*. The preamplifier output is split into two left-channel signals and two right-channel signals. (Many preamps have two stereo output pairs for this purpose.) The left-channel preamp output drives the left-channel inputs on both power amps. The right-channel preamp output drives the right-channel inputs on both power amps. One power amp drives the bass input on both loudspeakers, the other power amp drives the midrange and tweeter input on both loudspeakers. Note that the loudspeaker's crossover still operates; both amplifiers receive and amplify a full-bandwidth signal. This is called passive bi-amping because the frequency division into bass and midrange/treble is performed by passive components (capacitors, resistors, and inductors) in the loudspeaker's crossover.

In *active bi-amping*, rather than allow the loudspeaker's crossover to split the frequency spectrum, an *electronic crossover* between the preamp and power amps does the job. Active bi-amping divides the frequency spectrum *before* the power amplifiers, not after, as in passive bi-amping. The losses and problems inherent in any passive crossover are eliminated by active bi-amping. Moreover, each power amplifier receives only the portion of the frequency band it will amplify. Active bi-amping is more efficient than passive bi-amping, but requires bypassing the loudspeaker crossovers and adding an electronic crossover.

Bi-amping not only increases the total power delivered to the loudspeaker, but allows each amplifier to work over a narrower frequency range. We can thus choose a bass amplifier for its superior bottom-end performance regardless of how it sounds in the mids and treble, and a midrange/treble amplifier without concern for its bass. An ideal combination may include a large solid-state amplifier for the bass and a sweet-sounding tubed amplifier for the top end. The small tubed amplifier is relieved of the burden of driving the bass, allowing it to do what it does best. Bi-amping is one way of getting the best of both the tubed and solid-state worlds.

Another advantage of (active) bi-amping is that the woofer amplifier can be connected directly to the woofer's voice coil rather than through a passive crossover network, particularly the series inductor found in most woofer crossovers. This provides much tighter damping (the ability of the amplifier to control woofer motion) and results in tighter, deeper bass reproduction.

When bi-amping is chosen, the two amplifiers' *gains* (their amounts of amplification) must be exactly matched. If you're using identical amplifiers, the gain will be inherently matched. But with different amplifiers, a gain mismatch will produce too much or too little bass. An amplifier can be *padded down* at the input with an *attenuator* to reduce the input level and match its output to the second amplifier. If you're using an active external crossover, it may include independent output-level controls to balance the levels between the woofer and midrange/tweeter amplifiers.

Bi-amping can be tricky. I don't recommend it for most systems unless you fully understand what's happening, or unless your dealer helps you. One serious drawback is that replacing the speaker's internal crossover with an external one changes the crossover frequencies and characteristics the loudspeaker designer decided were optimum for that loudspeaker's drivers. Many loudspeaker designers don't take kindly to someone second-guessing their crossover characteristics.

A few manufacturers—Linn Products, for example—have designed easy bi-amping upgradeability into their products; bi-amping is just a matter of installing active crossover boards in the company's power amplifiers, adding a second amplifier, and removing the crossovers inside the loudspeaker. In this case, the loudspeaker works optimally with the external crossover.

Incidentally, adding an active subwoofer (one with an integral power amplifier—see Chapter 7) automatically makes your system bi-amped. The subwoofer's internal amplifier drives the low bass, and your main amplifier handles only the upper bass, mids, and treble. Installing an active subwoofer is one way of getting the benefits of bi-amping without changing amplifiers or adding another electronic crossover. Loudspeakers that come with a dedicated woofer amplifier, such as those employing servo-driven woofers are also inherently bi-amplified.

What to Listen For

How can you tell if the power amplifier you're considering will work well with your loudspeakers? Simple: Borrow the amplifier from your dealer for the weekend and listen to it. This is the best way of not only assessing its musical qualities, but determining how well it drives your loudspeakers. In addition, listening to the power amplifier at home will let you hear if the product's sonic signature complements the rest of your system.

The next best choice is if the dealer sells the same loudspeakers you own, and allows you to audition the combination in the store. If neither of these options is practical, consider bringing your loudspeakers into the store for a final audition.

All the sonic and musical characteristics described in Chapter 3 apply to power amplifiers. However, some sonic characteristics are more influenced by the power amplifier than by other components.

The first thing to listen for is whether the amplifier is driving the loudspeakers adequately. The most obvious indicator is bass performance. If the bass is soggy, slow, or lacks punch, the amplifier probably isn't up to the job of driving your loudspeakers. Weak bass is a sure indication that the amplifier is underpowered for a particular pair of speakers. Other telltale signs that the amplifier is running out of current include loss of dynamics, a sense of strain on musical peaks, hardening of timbre, reduced pace and rhythm, and soundstage collapse or congestion. Let's look at each of these individually.

First, play the system at a moderate volume. Select music with a wide dynamic range—either full orchestral music with a loud climax accompanied by bass drum, or music with a powerful rhythmic drive from bass guitar and kickdrum working together. Audiophile recordings typically have much wider dynamic ranges than general-release discs, making them a better source for evaluation. Music that has been highly compressed to play over the radio on a 3" car speaker will tell you less about what the system is doing dynamically.

After you've become used to the sound at a moderate level, increase the volume—you want to push the amplifier to find its limits. Does the bass seem to give out when you turn it up, or does the amplifier keep on delivering? Listen to the dynamic impact of kickdrum on a recording with lots of bottom-end punch. It should maintain its tightness, punch, quickness, and depth at high volume. If it starts to sound soggy, slow, or loses its power, you've gone beyond the amplifier's comfortable operating point. After a while, you can get a feel for when the amplifier gets into trouble. Is the sound strained on peaks, or effortless?

> **NOTE: When performing this experiment, be sure not to overdrive your loudspeakers. Turn down the volume at the first sign of loudspeaker overload (distortion or a popping sound).**

Compare the amplifier's sound at high and low volumes. Listen for brass instruments becoming hard and edgy at high volumes. See if the soundstage degenerates into a confused mess during climaxes. Does the bass drum lose its power and impact? An excellent power amplifier operating near its maximum power capability will preserve the senses of space, depth, and focus, while maintaining liquid instrumental timbre. Moreover, adequate power will produce a sense of ease; lack of power often creates listener fatigue. Music is much more enjoyable through a power amplifier with plenty of reserve power.

All the problems I've just described are largely the result of the amplifier running out of current. Just where this happens is a function of the amplifier's output power, its ability to deliver current into the loudspeaker, the loudspeaker's sensitivity and impedance, the room size, and how loudly you expect your hi-fi system to play. Even when not pushed to its maximum output, a more powerful amplifier will often have a greater sense of ease, grace, and dynamics than a less powerful amplifier.

Assuming that the power amplifier can drive your loudspeakers, let's evaluate its musical characteristics.

First, listen for its overall perspective. Determine if it's forward or laid-back, then decide if the amplifier is too "up-front" or too recessed for your system or tastes. A *forward* perspective seems to put you in Row C of the concert hall; a *laid-back* perspective puts you in Row W. Forwardness gives the impression of presence and immediacy, but can quickly become fatiguing. A presentation that's too laid-back is less exciting and compelling. If the amplifier's overall perspective isn't right, nothing else it does well may matter.

Next, listen for brightness, hardness, treble grain, and treble etch. If you feel a sense of relief when the volume is turned down, you can be pretty sure that the treble is at fault. Listen to midrange timbre, particularly in voice, violin, piano, and flute. Midrange textures should be sweet and liquid, and devoid of grain, hardness, or a glassy edge. Many power amplifiers—particularly inexpensive solid-state units—make the treble dry, forward, and unpleasant. If you hear even a hint of these characteristics in a few hours' listening, rest assured that they will only grow more annoying over time. Many moderately priced amplifiers *don't* add these unmusical characteristics—keep shopping.

Power amplifiers vary greatly in their ability to throw a convincing soundstage. With naturally miked recordings, the soundstage should be deep, transparent, and focused, the loudspeakers and listening room seeming to disappear. Instruments should hang in space within the recorded acoustic. The presentation should provide a transparent, picture-window view into the music. If the sound is flat, veiled, or homogenized, you haven't found the right amplifier.

Bass performance is also largely influenced by the power amplifier. It should sound taut, deep, quick, dynamic, and effortless. The music should be propelled forward, involving your body in its rhythmic drive. Kickdrum should have depth, power, and a feeling of suddenness. The bass guitar and kickdrum should provide a tight, solid, and powerful musical foundation.

The best way to find out which power amplifiers sound good and are well-made is by conferring with a trusted dealer and reading product reviews in reputable high-end magazines. Responsibly written reviews can save you from spending time and trouble on unworthy contenders, and point you toward products that offer promise. Thorough reviews will also include insightful commentary on the amplifier's technical performance. If the amplifier has technical characteristics that make it questionable or unsuitable for a particular type of loudspeaker, the review will reveal this fact. A review's technical section may state that, "Although the XYZ power amplifier sounded terrific with the

Dominator 1 loudspeakers, its high output impedance and limited current delivery make it a poor choice with low-sensitivity loudspeakers (below 86dB/1W/1m), or those with an impedance below 5 ohms." This kind of commentary can point you toward the best amplifiers for your loudspeakers.

In short, read lots of product reviews before drawing up a list of candidates to audition. Restrict candidates to those that fall within your budget, and take the few contenders home for an evening's listen. And don't be in a hurry to buy the first amplifier you audition—listen to several before choosing. Your effort and patience will be rewarded with a more musical amplifier, and one better suited to your system.

A Survey of Amplifier Types

So far I've described mainstream power amplifiers that most audiophiles are likely to buy. But a number of variations on the basic design are a significant force in the amplifier marketplace. These include the single-ended triode amplifier, the single ended solid state amplifier, and switching power amplifiers.

Single-Ended Triode Amplifiers

Perhaps the biggest movement in high-end audio in the 1990s has been the return to the single-ended triode power amplifier. The single-ended triode (SET) amplifier was the first audio amplifier ever developed, dating back to Lee De Forest's patent of the triode vacuum tube in 1907 and his triode amplifier patent of 1912. SET amplifiers typically produce less than 10Wpc.

You heard right: Large numbers of audiophiles are flocking to replace their modern power amplifiers with amplifiers based on 90-year-old technology. Have the past 90 years of amplifier development been a complete waste of time? A surprising number of music lovers and audio designers think so.

The movement back to SET amplifiers began in Japan in the 1970s, specifically with designer Nobu Shishido, who combined SET amplifiers with high-sensitivity horn-loaded loudspeakers. Many who heard SET amplifiers were startled by their goosebump-raising musical immediacy and ability to make the music "jump" out of the loudspeakers. Thus began the rage for SET amplifiers in Japan, which is about 10 years ahead of the SET trend in the United States. You can't open a high-end audio magazine today without seeing lots of ads for very-low-powered single-ended triode amplifiers. The SET enthusiast's mantra is, "If the first watt of amplifier power doesn't sound good, why would you want 199 more of them?"

One of the early audio-amplifier triodes, the Western Electric 300B, was suddenly in such demand that audiophiles were paying as much as $500 for a single tube. This shocking fact prompted Western Electric to start producing the 300B again. If you told Western Electric executives of the 1980s that in 1997 they would put the 300B back into production, they'd have thought you were crazy. (A single-ended triode power amplifier using the 300B output tube is shown in Fig.6-4. The 300B is the bulbous tube in the middle.)

Fig. 6-4 A pair of single-ended monoblock tubed power amplifiers

Courtesy Cary Audio

The triode is the simplest of all vacuum tubes; its glass envelope encloses just three electrical elements rather than the five elements in the more common (and modern) pentode tube. Triodes have much less output power than pentodes, but more benign distortion characteristics. Virtually all modern tubed amplifiers before the SET comeback used pentodes.

In a single-ended triode amplifier, the triode is operated so that it amplifies the entire audio signal. That's what "single-ended" means. Virtually all other power amplifiers are "push-pull," meaning that one tube (or transistor) handles the positive half of the musical waveform and a second tube (or transistor) handles the negative half.

Think of a push-pull amplifier as a two-man saw: one man pushes and the other man alternately pulls the saw. Another way of looking at the way push-pull amplifiers work is a relay race: one tube (or transistor) hands off the signal to the other tube (or transistor), then gets it back, this switching occurring many times a second; in other words, the music signal is split into two parts, then combined at the output. SET proponents believe that because the triode amplifies the entire waveform, SET amplifiers offer the ultimate in sound quality and musicality. Moreover, SET amplifiers have no need for a circuit called a phase splitter, which makes them even simpler. Note that a single-ended tubed amplifier can use more than one output tube; what makes it single-ended is the operation in which the tube or tubes amplify the entire waveform rather than a portion of it. (A more in-depth discussion of single-ended and push-pull operation is included later in this chapter under "How a Power Amplifier Works.")

Push-pull amplifiers suffer from something called *crossover distortion*, which is a discontinuity in the musical waveform in which one tube (or transistor) leaves off and the other tube (or transistor) takes over. A SET never hands off the signal between output devices and thus has no crossover distortion.

In addition, SET circuits are extremely simple and often use very little or no *negative feedback*. Negative feedback is taking some of the amplifier's output signal and feeding it back to the input. Such feedback lowers distortion, but many feel that *any* feedback is detrimental to amplifier musicality.

On the test bench, SET amplifiers have laughably bad technical performance. They typically produce fewer than 10Wpc of output power, and have extremely high distortion—as much as 10% Total Harmonic Distortion (THD) at the amplifier's rated output. Although most SET amplifiers use a single triode output tube, additional triodes can be combined to produce more output power. Some SET amplifiers, however, put out just 3Wpc. In fact, there's a kind of cult around SET amplifiers that strives for lower and lower output power. These SET enthusiasts believe that the lower the output power, the better the sound. One SET designer told a reviewer, in all seriousness, "If you liked my 9W amplifier, wait until you hear my 3W model."

In addition to low output power and high distortion, SET amplifiers have a very high output impedance as amplifiers go: on the order of

1.5–3 ohms. This is contrasted with the 0.1 ohm output impedance of most solid-state amplifiers, and the 0.8 ohms of many push-pull tubed designs. Because a loudspeaker's impedance isn't constant with frequency, the SET amplifier's high output impedance reacts with the loudspeaker's impedance variations to produce changes in frequency response. That is, the SET amplifier will have a different frequency response with every loudspeaker it drives. These variations can range from just 0.1dB with some loudspeakers that have a fairly constant impedance, to as much as 5dB with other loudspeakers. The SET amp's sound will therefore be highly dependent on the loudspeaker with which it is matched.

Despite these technical drawbacks, my listening experience with SET amplifiers suggests that this ancient technology has many musical merits. SET amps have a certain presence and immediacy of musical communication that's hard to describe. It's as though the musicians aren't as far removed from here-and-now reality as they are with push-pull amplifiers. SET amps also have a wonderful liquidity and purity of timbre that is completely devoid of grain, hardness, and other artifacts of push-pull amplifiers. When I listen to SET amplifiers (with the right loudspeakers), it's as though the musicians have come alive and are playing in the listening room for me. There's a directness of musical expression that's impossible to put into words, but is immediately understood by anyone who has listened for themselves. You must hear a SET firsthand to know what the fuss is about; no description can convey how they sound.

When auditioning a SET amplifier, it's easy to be seduced by the midrange. That's because SET amplifiers work best in the midband, and less well at the frequency extremes of bass and treble. If the SET demo is being run for your benefit, be sure to listen to a wide variety of music, not just small-scale music or unaccompanied voice—these will accentuate the SET's strengths and hide its weaknesses.

The importance of matching a SET amplifier to the right loudspeaker cannot be overemphasized. With a low-sensitivity speaker, the SET will produce very little sound, have soft bass, and reproduce almost no dynamic contrast. The ideal loudspeaker for a SET amplifier has high sensitivity (higher than 93dB/1W/1m), high impedance (nominal 8 ohms or higher), and no impedance dips (a minimum impedance of 6 ohms or higher). Such a speaker will produce lots of sound for a small amount of input power, and require very little current. (Remember the example earlier of Paul Klipsch's high-sensitivity speaker that produced concert-hall levels with 5W?) There's been a resurgence in high-sensitivity speakers that has paralleled the popularity of SET amplifiers. Some loudspeakers designed for SET amplifiers have sensitivities of more than 100dB, which enable them to produce satisfying listening levels with 5Wpc. SET amplifiers are often coupled with horn-loaded loudspeakers, which have extremely high sensitivity but, in my experience, introduce unacceptable levels of coloration.

The popularity and unmistakable sound quality of SET amplifiers pose a serious dilemma: how can an amplifier that performs so poorly by every "objective" measure produce such an involving musical experience? How can 90-year-old technology eclipse, in many ways, amplifiers designed in the 21st century? What aren't we measuring in SET amplifiers that would reflect their musical magic? Why do conventional measurements fail so dismally at quantifying what's right in SET amplifiers? Do SET amplifiers sound so good *because* of their high distortion, or *despite* it? As of yet, no one has the answers to these questions.

Single-Ended Solid-State Amplifiers

Single-ended amplifiers aren't confined to those using ancient vacuum-tube technology. Transistors can also be configured to amplify the entire musical waveform. These amplifiers are also called Class-A amplifiers because the mode of operation in which the output device amplifies the entire audio signal is called Class-A. A solid-state, single-ended amplifier is shown in Fig.6-5. Note the large heatsinks required to dissipate the additional heat produced by Class-A operation.

Fig. 6-5 A single-ended solid-state power amplifier

Courtesy Pass Laboratories

Single-ended solid-state amplifiers have better technical performance than single-ended triode amps, with a lower output impedance, more power, and the ability to drive a wider range of loudspeakers. They share many of the benefits of SET amps, particularly the very simple signal path, lack of crossover distortion, and greater linearity. Although single-ended solid-state amplifiers produce less power than their push-pull counterparts, they generally have much more output power than single-ended tubed units. Nonetheless, it's a mistake to equate single-ended solid-state with single-ended tube amplifiers: there are so many other design variables that single-ended solid-state and single-ended tubed amplifiers should be considered completely different animals.

Switching Power Amplifiers

If single-ended triode amplifiers represent a return to fundamental technology, the switching power amplifier may represent the future of audio amplification. Switching amplifiers, also called Class D amplifiers, have been gaining in popularity due to their small size, low weight, high efficiency, and low cost. At the low-end of the audio spectrum, switching amplifiers are becoming ubiquitous in home-theater-in-a-box units and as integral subwoofer amplifiers. A home-theater-in-a-box may need to power six loudspeakers from a DVD player-sized chassis—all for a few hundred dollars. Such a unit can output perhaps 300Wpc (50Wpc x 6), yet run cool enough to be placed in a cabinet. In this application, the advantages of a switching amplifier are undeniable. But are switching amplifiers suitable for high-end systems?

Before tackling that question, let's first look at how a switching amplifier works. In a conventional amplifier (called a *linear amplifier*), the output transistors amplify a continuously variable analog signal—the musical waveform. In a switching amplifier, the continuously variable analog input signal is converted into a series of on and off pulses. These pulses are fed to the output transistors, which turn the transistors fully on or fully off. When the transistors are turned on, they conduct the DC supply voltage to the loudspeaker. When turned off, no voltage is connected to the loudspeaker. The audio information is contained in the durations of these on-off cycles. The train of pulses amplified by the transistors is smoothed by a filter to recover the musical waveform and remove the switching noise. Because the signal amplitude is contained in the width of the pulses, switching amplifiers are also called pulse-width modulation (PWM) amplifiers.

A switching amplifier operates at very high efficiency, thus the low heat dissipation. Because they run cool, switching amplifiers don't need the large heat sinks found in conventional amplifiers, saving space and cost. Another benefit of this high efficiency is the reduced current demands on the power transformer, which can be smaller, lighter, and cheaper.

One major drawback of switching amplifiers is the need for an extremely clean power supply. Remember that the transistors switch the DC supply directly to the loudspeaker. Consequently, any noise or ripple (a small amount of AC on the DC voltage) will appear at the loudspeaker's input terminals. Moreover, the output transistors may not turn on and off at precisely the right time, introducing distortion.

Finally, switching amplifiers generate large amounts of switching noise that must be filtered by large inductors and capacitors at the amplifier output.

Nonetheless, some successful high-end amplifiers employ switching technology. The field is relatively new, and manufacturers are finding ways to get good sound from switching amplifiers. The few high-end switching amplifiers I've heard sounded excellent, suggesting that switching technology may have a future in products other than car stereo and home-theaters-in-a-box.

Digital Power Amplifiers

A related amplifier technology uses a switching output stage, but accepts digital, rather than analog, input signals. These "digital" amplifiers take in the pulse-code modulation (PCM) signal from a CD transport and convert those audio data to a pulse-width modulated signal. This PWM signal drives the output transistors, just as in a switching amplifier. The difference between a switching amplifier and a digital amplifier is that the digital amplifier accepts digital data rather than an analog signal. Fig.6-6 is an example of a digital amplifier.

Fig. 6-6 A true digital power amplifier operates entirely in the digital domain.

Courtesy Tact Audio Inc.

A very promising type of digital amplifier accepts Direct Stream Digital (DSD) data from an SACD player, and uses the DSD bitstream to drive the amplifier's switching output transistors. Direct Stream Digital, explained in Chapter 8, is the encoding format used in SACD. It is a form of pulse-width modulation encoding in which the signal's amplitude is represented by the pulse widths. (The graphic in Chapter 8 showing how Direct Stream Digital's pulses represent an analog waveform is most illustrative.) This PWM signal can feed the amplifier's output transistors directly, with no conversions of any kind. With an SACD transport feeding such an amplifier digitally, the digital data on the disc representing the audio signal are fed directly to the amplifier's output transistors. The digital-to-analog conversion is performed implicitly by the switching output stage.

This technique is a revolutionary departure from the conventional reproduction chain of D/A converter/preamplifier/power amplifier, all linked by interconnects. In addition to combining all these functions in one chassis, the digital power amplifier removes a huge amount of electronics from the signal path, including D/A converter chips, the output stage in the digital processor, all of a preamplifier's circuitry, and nearly all the electronics found in a conventional power amplifier. Also, the digital power amplifier has no need for feedback or the other Band-Aids required of analog amplifiers.

There's one other use of the term "digital amplifier" you should know about. In the mid 1990s, Wadia Digital demonstrated a "digital amplifier" in which the digital-to-analog converter was combined in the same chassis as a conventional power amplifier. This "digital" power amplifier takes in a digital signal from a CD transport, converts the digital signal to analog, then amplifies that analog signal just as a conventional power amplifier would. This amplifier's output stage was linear, and did not use switching technology. The amplifier incorporated a volume control, multiple inputs, and source switching.

How a Power Amplifier Works

It's intuitive to conceptualize a power amplifier as a device that simply makes the input signal bigger. A more accurate visualization is of a device that pulls 120V, 60Hz alternating current (AC) from your wall outlet through the amplifier's power transformer, converts the AC into direct current (DC), stores that energy in large capacitors (the can-shaped objects), and then allows the tiny audio signal at the amplifier input to modulate the stored energy as electrical current that is driven through the loudspeakers by the power amplifier's output transistors or tubes.

This way of thinking about a power amplifier produces the realization that a power amplifier's power supply (the section that converts the AC from the wall outlet to the DC that supplies the output transistors) is actually *in* the audio signal path. The current that ultimately drives the cones in your loudspeakers back and forth comes from the wall outlet via the amplifier's power supply. That's one reason a power amplifier's power supply is so important—and why good power amplifiers tend to have large and heavy power supplies.

At its most basic level, a power amplifier consists of a power supply, an input stage, a driver stage, and an output stage. The input and driver stages prepare the signal for the output stage, which is where transistors or tubes drive electrical current through the loudspeaker. Figs.6-7a and b show a photograph of a power amplifier's circuitry and a power amplifier block diagram. Let's look at each of these sections of the block diagram in more detail.

The Power Supply

The power supply converts 60Hz, 120V AC (Alternating Current) from the wall outlet into the DC the audio circuits need. Power-amplifier power supplies differ greatly from those for other audio components. (A close reading of Appendix B will be helpful in understanding the rest of this explanation.) Power-amplifier supplies must be able to provide large amounts of current, operate at much higher voltages, and have much larger storage capacities. Parts sizes and ratings are thus much higher in a power amplifier than in the power supply of a preamp or CD player.

The first element of the power supply is the power transformer, which *steps down* the 120V AC line voltage to a lower value, perhaps 80V. You can get a pretty good idea of how powerful the amplifier is by the power transformer's size and rating. Transformers are rated in "VA" or "kVA" (x 1000); i.e., voltage (V) multiplied by the maximum current in amperes (A) they can supply. A transformer with a VA rating of 1kVA can deliver 8.34 amperes of current (1000 divided by the AC line voltage of 120V) to the amplifier's circuits (assuming the transformer isn't stepping down the voltage). Because most power transformers step down the voltage to 80V, a 1kVA transformer could deliver 12A.

Note that the amplifier's overall continuous output current for both channels combined can never exceed the power transformer's current rating. The amplifier can, however, deliver short bursts of higher current (such as on musical transients like bass-drum whacks) because of the energy stored in the capacitors—provided the output transistors can handle the current. One very large power amplifier's transformer, with a VA rating of 4.5kVA, weighs 85 of the amplifier's total 147 pounds. A power amplifier of more moderate size may have a power transformer with a rating of 300VA.

This stepped-down AC voltage from the power transformer is then *rectified* (turned into DC) by a *bridge rectifier* and filtered by very large *filter capacitors*. The filter capacitors not only store energy, they smooth the DC by removing any trace of *ripple* (a little bit of AC appearing in the DC supply). The filter capacitors are also called *reservoir* capacitors because they store large amounts of electrical energy. A reservoir of electrical energy is needed because the power supply cannot pull current from the wall outlet fast enough to deliver instantaneous surges of high current to the loudspeakers. The reservoir capacitors act as a temporary storage area between the AC wall outlet and the power-supply output. Some of these capacitors are the size of soda cans, and can store huge amounts of electrical energy. Power-supply reservoir capacitors are typically between 30,000µF (microfarad) and 500,000µF—very large values. Capacitance is the ability to store a charge; the unit of measurement is the Farad, named after Michael Faraday. If you turn off such a power amplifier when music is playing, you'll hear music for a few seconds or nearly a minute. The power to run the amplifier comes from electrons stored in the reservoir capacitors.

This high-energy supply is the power source for the amplifier's output stage; the electrons in the filter capacitors are pulled out by the output transistors and delivered as current flow to the loudspeaker. The small audio signal at the power amplifier input modulates the release of the energy stored in the power supply; this energy release is the amplifier's output signal, which drives the loudspeakers.

The ideal power supply would maintain its voltage no matter how much current the output transistors demanded. In practice, the output supply voltage is *pulled down* when the output transistors suddenly draw current (as happens during a musical peak). This drop in power-supply output voltage is called *droop*. If your lights have ever dimmed momentarily when the refrigerator motor turned on, you've seen the results of power-supply droop. The refrigerator motor draws a large amount of current when it starts, pulling down the voltage available to power the lights. A power supply that resists drooping is called a *stiff* supply.

The fuses on the backs of many power amplifiers are in series with the output stage's power supply. That is, the current drawn from the power supply by the output transistors must flow through the fuse. Because the power-supply voltage is called the voltage *rail*, these fuses are called *rail fuses*. If the output stage draws too much current, the fuse blows. If a fuse blows once, replace it with one of identical rating. *Under no circumstances should you replace a fuse with one of a higher rating*. The fuse is there for a reason: to protect the output stage and the power supply. Defeating the fuse, or replacing a lower-value fuse with a higher-value one, can cause catastrophic damage to the amplifier. Moreover, there's a reason if the fuse blows a second time: something is wrong in the amplifier. Fuses often blow when an output transistor goes bad; have the amplifier serviced by a qualified technician.

An amplifier's power supply also generates lower voltages to power the less power-hungry circuits in the amplifier, such as the input and driver stages (described next).

Input and Driver Stages

The audio input signal driving the power amplifier is first buffered and amplified by the power amplifier's input stage. The input stage has a high input impedance and a low output impedance, making the amplifier easy to drive by the preamplifier. It is here, at the input stage, that the amplifier's input impedance is determined. Specified in ohms, input impedance is the resistance to current flow from the preamplifier's drive signal. An input impedance of 47k ohms is fairly standard for an unbalanced input on an RCA jack.

The input stage is followed by the *driver stage*, the circuit that amplifies the signal and drives the final *output stage*. The driver stage produces a higher-voltage signal that the output transistors need. In Class-A/B amplifiers (explained later in this chapter), the driver stage can act as a phase splitter to create an identical copy of the signal (with polarity inverted) for presentation to the push-pull output stage.

Many amplifiers have *coupling capacitors* between these stages. A coupling capacitor, also called a *DC blocking capacitor*, is a barrier to direct current (DC) but passes the alternating current (AC) audio signal to the next stage. But the fact that these capacitors can degrade the amplifier's musical performance leads some designers to omit them from the signal path. An amplifier without coupling capacitors is called *direct-coupled*. Direct-coupled amplifiers can present a danger: any DC at the input will be amplified and sent to your loudspeakers. Because even small amounts of DC can destroy a loudspeaker, some amplifiers have a *DC servo* to prevent this DC from appearing at the output terminals. A DC servo monitors the DC level and adjusts the circuitry for minimum DC. You can easily measure how much DC appears at a power amplifier's outputs: just put a DC voltmeter across the loudspeaker terminals. Values below 200mV are typical.

Most high-quality power amplifiers use *discrete* circuitry in the input and driver stages. A discrete circuit is made from individual transistors rather than integrated-circuit operational amplifiers (op-amps). Discrete circuits are generally better than op-amp–based designs. *Field Effect Transistors* (FETs) are often used in the input stages of power amplifiers for their intrinsically high input impedance. Their low power capability, however, limits their use to the low-level signals of the input stage.

Nearly all power amplifiers use *feedback*, a technique that takes part of the output signal and returns it to the input. This makes the circuit more linear (the input and output signals have greater similarity) and lowers distortion. Too much feedback, however, results in poor sound. Many power amplifiers are touted as "low-feedback" designs. These amplifiers will probably have higher distortion figures, but may sound better as a result of lower feedback.

Two types of feedback are *local* and *global*. Local feedback is feedback around one stage within an amplifier; global feedback is feedback from the final output stage back to the input stage. Finally, the input and driver stages are almost always run in Class-A, meaning that one transistor amplifies the entire audio signal.

Output Stage

In discussions of power amplifiers, the most common topic is the output stage. The output stage comprises many transistors, usually bipolar types, and, less frequently, MOSFETs, another type of transistor. These transistors are the workhorses of a power amplifier—the current that makes the loudspeaker cones move is driven by the output transistors. Consequently, adding more transistors to the output stage increases the amplifier's output-current capability. More transistors, however, require a bigger power supply. In addition, these output transistors produce lots of heat that must be dissipated by heatsinks, the large black fins protruding from the sides of many power amplifiers.

When the output stage is asked to deliver more power than it is capable of, the top and bottom of the waveform are flattened, or *clipped*. When a power amplifier goes into *clipping*, the output is severely and audibly distorted. If clipping occurs only briefly on a few musical peaks, we may not notice it. An amplifier driven into *hard clipping* will, however, quickly destroy loudspeakers. Loudspeakers can handle surprising amounts of power, provided that the power amplifier driving them isn't itself driven into clipping.

Power-amplifier output stages are often described as being of Class-A or Class-B operation. In Class-B, the most common and economical operation, the output transistors are arranged in *complementary* pairs. A complementary pair consists of one PNP-type transistor and one NPN-type. One transistor handles the signal during the positive-going portion of the signal, the other handles the negative-going signal half. When one is working, the other is resting (and getting some needed cooling). Pure Class-A operation works differently, as we saw in the discussion of single-ended amplifiers. Instead of splitting the signal into positive and negative phases and using a transistor on each signal half, Class-A operation forces the output transistors to handle both positive- and negative-going signal halves. This places much greater demands on the output transistors: they are conducting current all the time instead of half the time. Transistors operating in Class-A are always turned on, instead of half on and half off as in Class-B. In addition, Class-A amplifiers are very inefficient, produce *lots* of heat, require huge heatsinks, have lower power output for their size, and are expensive.

Class-A has many advantages, however. Because the transistors are always conducting, they are more *linear*; i.e., the output signal more closely resembles the input signal. Moreover, Class-A avoids a problem with Class-B amplifiers: crossover distortion. Crossover distortion can occur at the *zero crossing point*, where one transistor turns off and the other turns on. A waveform discontinuity can occur at this transition. Crossover distortion can't occur in Class-A operation because each transistor amplifies the entire audio waveform, not just half of it.

Class-A also has the advantage of keeping the output transistors in thermal stability (a constant temperature). This makes their operating characteristics more uniform, and less subject to changes resulting from the signal characteristics the transistors are amplifying. In other words, if the transistors have just delivered a surge of current to the loudspeakers, they won't behave differently—and thus *sound* different—immediately afterward because they are momentarily hotter.

Most power amplifiers are called Class-A/B power amplifiers because they operate in Class-A at very low power outputs, then switch to Class-B operation at higher power outputs. A 100Wpc amplifier may put out 5W of Class-A power, then switch to Class-B above that level. Even the heftiest Class-A/B amplifiers can put out only about 15% of their rated power in Class-A. A more typical value is about 5%. Although this may not sound like much, an amplifier may be running at just a few watts at low listening levels with high-sensitivity speakers.

Pure Class-A amplifiers are more likely to go by the name "single-ended." A true single-ended, or Class-A, amplifier cannot operate in Class-B mode—it has no phase splitter. Although many manufacturers claim "Class-A" operation, a closer examination reveals they are actually Class-A/B designs operating in Class-A at lower power outputs. Class-A input and driver stages, however, are common. At the low signal levels present in the first stages, Class-A operation is more easily achieved.

How much of an amplifier's output is Class-A is determined by the amount of *bias* applied to the output transistors (or tubes). Bias is a small DC current that partially turns on the transistors when the transistors aren't amplifying. The higher the bias, the more current flows through the transistors, even when no signal is present. The current through a transistor when not amplifying a signal is called *quiescent current*. More bias results in a higher *operating point* and more Class-A output power. In fact, it's possible for a push-pull amplifier to produce a large amount of Class-A power if the transistors are biased high enough. Increasing the bias, however, makes the transistors run hotter. If the heatsinking is inadequate, the transistors will overheat.

Because the quiescent current determines how much Class-A power the amplifier will deliver, we can calculate the point at which the amplifier switches from Class-A to Class-B operation by measuring its quiescent current. First, we measure the voltage across one output transistor's emitter resistor. From that, and using Ohm's law, we calculate the quiescent current flowing through that transistor. We then multiply the quiescent current by the number of output devices to find the total quiescent current. If the amplifier has a fuse on its power-supply output, the total quiescent current can be measured by putting an ammeter (a current meter) in series with the fuse. This is the absolute maximum current that can be delivered to the loudspeaker in Class-A operation. Again, using Ohm's law, the output supply voltage, and quiescent current, we can calculate the maximum power output in Class-A operation into a given load impedance.

Class-A power amplifiers can sound extremely good, with a sweetness and liquidity that set them apart from Class-A/B amps. True Class-A amplifiers are, however, more expensive than similarly powered push-pull amplifiers. They are large for their power ratings, and consume large amounts of power, even when not amplifying music. They draw the same current from the wall at idle as at full power output. Because they also need a long warm-up time to sound their best, Class-A amplifiers can easily double your electric bill. Fortunately, Class-A/B amplifiers offer many of the benefits of full Class-A operation, putting out a significant portion (even 15% is excellent) of their rated output in Class-A.

A unique solution to the problems of Class-A power amplifiers has been devised by designer Dan D'Agostino of Krell Industries. At low power output, less bias is needed to keep the transistors operating in Class-A. As the input signal level increases, more bias is required. "S"-series Krell amplifiers use a technique called "Sustained Plateau Biasing" that changes the bias current according to the input signal level. If the amplifier is driven hard, the bias increases to maintain Class-A operation. When the signal level drops, so does the bias, allowing the output stage to cool. Moreover, with no or very low input signals, the bias is so low the amplifier runs very cool and consumes very little electricity. Front-panel light-emitting diodes (LEDs) indicate the bias level. Incidentally, high-level transient signals—drums, for example—are reproduced in Class-A; the input signal sensor and bias-adjust circuit are fast enough to ramp up the output stage bias before the transient reaches full level at the output stage. The result is full Class-A output operation with less expense, size, and power consumption than conventional Class-A power amplifiers.

Some power amplifiers use MOSFET output devices instead of bipolar transistors. MOSFET stands for Metal Oxide Semiconductor Field Effect Transistor. These devices operate differently: they are turned on (biased) by voltage rather than by current, as are bipolar devices. In this respect, they operate like vacuum tubes. MOSFETs have other technical attributes, and MOSFET amplifiers often have a characteristic sound, particularly a smoothness in the treble. They also exhibit what's been called "MOSFET mist," a tendency to have a less than crystal-clear soundstage and a slightly de-focused treble.

How a Tubed Power Amplifier Works

Though the basic functions of tubed and solid-state power amplifiers are almost identical, instead of using transistors in the input, driver, and output stages, tubed power amplifiers use vacuum tubes. A tubed power amplifier may use one tube in the input stage, another in the driver stage, and perhaps eight in a push-pull configuration in the output stage. Some amplifiers use tubes at the input and driver stages, then use solid-state devices in the output stage. Such amplifiers are called hybrid power amplifiers.

Fig.6-7a shows a tubed power amplifier; Fig.6-7b is a tubed power-amplifier block diagram. The most obvious difference between a tubed power amplifier and a solid-state unit (besides the tubes themselves) is that the tubed amplifier has an *output transformer*. We can clearly see the output transformers (one per channel) at the amplifier's rear, a feature not found in solid-state amplifiers. The output transformer functions as an impedance-matching device between the amplifier's output stage and the loudspeaker. The tubed amplifier's output stage thus "sees" the transformer's high input impedance rather than the loudspeaker's low input

Fig. 6-7a
A stereo tubed
power amplifier

Courtesy Audio Research Corporation

Fig. 6-7b
A tubed power
amplifier block
diagram

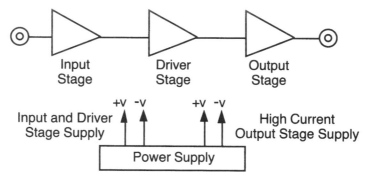

impedance. The transformer also cancels harmonic distortion by mixing the plate currents from both halves of the push-pull output stage. Finally, the output transformer prevents DC from appearing at the amplifier output terminals.

The output transformer must be large enough not to *saturate* at low frequencies. If saturation occurs, the bass becomes soft and "woolly." Some tubed power amplifiers have selectable *taps* on their transformers (see Fig.6-8) for loudspeakers of different impedances. These outputs are additional transformer windings called *secondary windings*, providing the optimum impedance match between the transformer and the loudspeaker.

A few tubed amplifiers have *no* output transformer. They are called *OTL*, for *Output-TransformerLess*. OTLs generally aren't very powerful and don't work well with low-impedance loudspeakers. They are huge, have *lots* of output tubes, and are idiosyncratic in loudspeaker matching. The OTL amps I've heard have mediocre bass and

Fig. 6-8 Some tubed power amplifiers provide different impedance taps from the output transformer.

Courtesy Audio Research Corporation

not much in the way of dynamics, but spectacular soundstaging and beautiful rendering of timbre. OTLs aren't for everyone, but with the right loudspeakers, they can be magical.

Because a tube's operating characteristics change with age, all output tubes need to have their biases adjusted periodically. Bias is a small amount of current (typically between 20mA and 70mA) applied to the tube's grid to turn on the tube. Its transistor counterpart is the bias current we talked about in solid-state output stages. A tubed amplifier will often have test points and trimmer potentiometers, called *trim pots* (tiny variable resistors adjustable with a small screwdriver), readily accessible on the front panel or chassis for bias adjustment.

To set an output tube's bias, put a DC voltmeter probe in the test point, ground the other test lead, and turn the trim pot until the voltage reading matches the manufacturer's bias specification. Bias is especially important in amplifiers having many output tubes; we want the tubes to operate identically. Not only do tubes age differently, but, due to variations in manufacturing, they need different amounts of bias when new. When an output tube approaches the end of its useful life, the bias trim pots may be turned all the way up without reaching the specified bias voltage. When that happens, it's time for a new tube. Bias should be checked about once a month, or whenever changing tubes. (Fig.6-9 shows an amplifier being biased.)

Many tubed amplifiers incorporate a front-panel meter or LED to indicate the bias level. This feature obviates the need for a voltmeter, making owning a tubed amplifier more convenient. In amplifiers with an LED indicator, the LED will illuminate when the bias is set within the correct operating range.

When you buy replacement output tubes, you can specify matched pairs or matched quartets of tubes. These are tubes with matched electrical characteristics for better combined performance. An amplifier with a single push-pull pair per channel will benefit from matched pairs, and an amplifier with four output tubes per channel needs matched quartets. Matched output tubes ensure that each tube operates very similarly, and that one tube isn't working harder than another. An analogy is synchronizing carburetors on a multicylinder motorcycle. Expect to pay a premium for matched tubes.

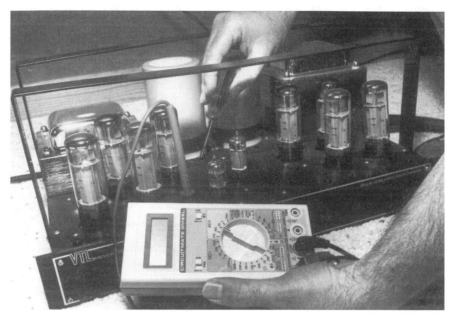

Fig. 6-9 Biasing a tubed power amplifier

A tubed amplifier is often referred to by the type of tube used in its output stage: *triode* or *pentode*. Triode power amplifiers generally sound the best but aren't very powerful, and are much more expensive per watt of output power than other tubed designs. Triode-based amplifiers can be the push-pull variety, or the single-ended type described earlier.

A pentode output tube has five elements, which greatly increases the tube's output power and efficiency. Some tubed amplifiers let you switch between pentode and triode operation from the same output tube. You may choose the purer triode mode for chamber music at low volume, and pentode for louder music that requires more output power. The switchable option also lets you select the best output mode for your loudspeakers. High-sensitivity speakers may work just fine when driven by the amplifier in triode mode; lower-sensitivity models may require the higher output power provided by pentode operation.

Another type of tubed output stage, called *ultra-linear*, was developed in 1951 by David Hafler and Herbert Keroes. Ultra-linear operation is a method of connecting a pentode so that it operates more like a triode. Specifically, some of the plate voltage is returned to the pentode's screen grid. Ultra-linear operation became the dominant circuit topology in tubed amplifiers for decades because it offered the output power of pentodes with the distortion characteristics of triodes.

Some tubed amplifiers, particularly the single-ended variety, let you vary the amount of feedback. You can thus dial in the sound you want, and decide which musical tradeoffs are acceptable. Reducing the amount of feedback often results in purer timbre, but at the expense of bass tautness.

Note that tubed amplifiers don't increase their power outputs as the load impedance drops, as do solid-state units. The output transformer acts as a current source rather than as a voltage source, decreasing the available output voltage when the load impedance drops. This is one reason why tubed amplifiers have less tight and extended bass than solid-state power amplifiers.

Finally, tubed power-amplifier power supplies are different from their solid-state counterparts. The voltage at the output-stage supply rail is many hundreds of volts, not ±60V to ±100V as in a solid-state amplifier's power supplies. Because of this very high voltage, the reservoir capacitors generally store vastly more energy than the reservoir caps in a solid-state amp. This so-called "B+" voltage is very high—the capacitors can deliver lots of current through your body, and can even kill you. Energy storage is measured in Joules, and is a function of the capacitance in Farads (a unit of stored charge) multiplied by the voltage squared. Given the same capacitance (same number of microfarads) but ten times the voltage, power supplies for a tubed amplifier have much greater energy storage than a solid-state amplifier. This factor may account for tube amplifiers' subjectively greater loudness for the same rated power compared to a solid-state amplifier.

Tubed amplifiers must also supply the tube filaments (the part that glows) with a low DC voltage. In low-signal-level tubes, the number beginning the tube's designation (6DJ8, 12AX7, etc.) indicates the filament voltage, usually 6V or 12V. Filaments are also called by their more descriptive name, "heaters."

From a design standpoint, tubed power amplifiers have several inherent advantages. First, they're simple. Comparing the schematics of solid-state and tubed amplifiers reveals many more parts in the transistor design, most of them in the signal path. Fewer parts in the signal path generally results in better sound. When overdriven, tubes *soft-clip*, meaning that the waveform gently rounds off rather than flattening immediately. Moreover, a tubed amplifier in clipping produces primarily second- and third-harmonic distortion, which is fairly benign sonically. A transistor amplifier driven into clipping immediately produces a whole series of very objectionable upper-order odd harmonics (fifth, seventh, ninth). In fact, 10% second-harmonic distortion is less annoying than 0.5% seventh-harmonic distortion.

7 Loudspeakers

Introduction

O f all the components in your audio system, the loudspeaker's job is by far the most difficult. The loudspeaker is expected to reproduce the sound of a pipe organ, the human voice, and a violin through the same electromechanical device—all at the same levels of believability, and all at the same time. The tonal range of virtually every instrument in the orchestra is to be reproduced from a relatively tiny box. This frequency span of 10 octaves represents a sound-wavelength difference of 60 feet in the bass to about half an inch in the treble.

It's no wonder that loudspeaker designers spend their lives battling the laws of physics to produce musical and practical loudspeakers. Unlike other high-end designers who create a variety of products, the loudspeaker designer is singular in focus, dedicated in intent, and deeply committed to the unique blend of science and art that is loudspeaker design.

Although even the best loudspeakers can't convince us that we're hearing live music, they nonetheless are miraculous in what they *can* do. Think about this: a pair of loudspeakers converts two two-dimensional electrical signals into a three-dimensional "soundspace" spread out before the listener. Instruments seem to exist as *objects* in space; we hear the violin here, the brass over there, and the percussion behind the other instruments. A vocalist appears as a palpable, tangible image exactly between the two loudspeakers. The front of the listening room seems to disappear, replaced by the music. It's so easy to close your eyes and be transported into the musical event.

To achieve this experience in your home, however, you must carefully choose the best loudspeakers from among the literally thousands of models on the market. As we'll see, choosing loudspeakers is a challenging job.

How to Choose a Loudspeaker

The world abounds in poor-quality, even dreadful, loudspeakers. What's more, some very bad loudspeakers are expensive, while superlative models may sell for a fraction of an inferior model's price. There is sometimes little relationship between price and musical performance.

This situation offers the loudspeaker shopper both promise and peril. The promise is of finding an excellent loudspeaker for a reasonable price. The peril is of sorting through mediocre models to find the rare gems that offer either high absolute performance, or sound quality far above what their price would indicate.

This is where reviews come in handy. Reviewers who write for audio magazines hear lots of loudspeakers (at dealers, trade shows, and consumer shows), but review only those that sound promising. This weeds out the vast majority of underachievers. Of the loudspeakers that *are* reviewed, some are found to be unacceptably flawed, others are good for the money, while a select few are star overachievers that clearly out-perform their similarly priced rivals.

The place to start loudspeaker shopping, therefore, is in the pages of a reputable magazine with high standards for what constitutes good loudspeaker performance. Be wary of magazines that end every review with a "competent for the money" recommendation. Not all loudspeak-ers are good; therefore, not all reviews should be positive. The tone of the reviews—positive or negative—should reflect the wide variation in performance and value found in the marketplace.

After you've read lots of loudspeaker reviews, make up your short list of products to audition from the *crème de la crème*. There are several criteria to apply in making this short list to ensure that you get the best loudspeaker for your individual needs. As you apply each criterion described, the list of candidate loudspeakers will get shorter and shorter, thus easing your decision-making process. If you find yourself with too few choices at the end of the process, go back and revise your criteria. For example, if you find a loudspeaker that's perfect in all ways but size, you may want to find the extra space in your living room. Similarly, an ideal loudspeaker costing a little more than you planned to spend may suggest a budget revision. As you go through this selection process, remember that the perfect loudspeaker for you is probably out there. Be selective and have high standards. You'll be rewarded by a much higher level of musical performance than you thought you could afford.

1) Size, Appearance, and Integration in the Home

After you've designated a place for your loudspeakers, determine the optimum loudspeaker size for your room—the urban apartment dweller will likely have tighter size constraints than the suburban audiophile. Some listeners will want the loudspeakers to discreetly blend into the room; others will make the hi-fi system the room's center of activity and won't mind large, imposing loudspeakers. When choosing a place for your loudspeakers, keep in mind that their placement is a crucial factor in how your system will sound. (Chapter 4 includes an in-depth treatment of loudspeaker positioning.)

The loudspeaker's appearance is also a factor to consider. An inexpensive, vinyl-covered box would be out of place in an elegantly furnished home. Many high-end loudspeakers are finished in beautiful cabinetry that will complement any decor. This level of finish can, however, add greatly to the loudspeaker's price.

If you don't have room for full-range, floorstanding speakers, consider a separate subwoofer/satellite system. This is a loudspeaker system that puts the bass-reproducing driver in an enclosure you can put nearly anywhere, and the midrange- and treble-reproducing elements in a small, unobtrusive cabinet. You'll still get a full sound, but without the visual domination of your living room that often goes with floorstanding speakers. Moreover, the satellite speakers' small cabinets often help them achieve great soundstaging.

Although the term "bookshelf" is often applied to small speakers, you can't get optimum performance from a speaker mounted in a bookshelf. Small speakers need to be mounted on stands, and placed out in the room. Small loudspeakers mounted on stands, sometimes called *minimonitors*, often provide terrific imaging, great clarity in midband and treble, and can easily "disappear" into the music. On the down side, small loudspeakers used without a subwoofer have restricted dynamics, limited bass extension, and won't play as loudly as their floorstanding counterparts.

2) Match the Loudspeaker to Your Electronics

The loudspeaker should be matched to the rest of your system, both electrically and musically. A loudspeaker that may work well in one system may not be ideal for another system—or another listener.

Let's start with the loudspeaker's electrical characteristics. The power amplifier and loudspeaker should be thought of as an interactive combination; the power amplifier will behave differently when driving different loudspeakers. Consequently, the loudspeaker should be chosen for the amplifier that will drive it.

The first electrical consideration is a loudspeaker's sensitivity—how much sound it will produce for a given amount of amplifier power. Loudspeakers are rated for sensitivity by measuring their sound-pressure level (SPL) from one meter away while they are being fed one watt (1W) of power. For example, a sensitivity specification of "88dB/1W/1m" indicates that this particular loudspeaker will produce a sound-pressure level of 88dB when driven with an input power of 1W, measured at a distance of 1m. High-end loudspeakers vary in sensitivity between 80dB/1W/1m and 106dB/1W/1m.

A loudspeaker's sensitivity is a significant factor in determining how well it will work with a given power-amplifier output wattage. To produce a loud sound (100dB), a loudspeaker rated at 80dB sensitivity would require 100W. A loudspeaker with a sensitivity of 95dB would require only 3W to produce the same sound-pressure level. Each 3dB decrease in sensitivity requires double the amplifier power to produce the same SPL. (This is discussed in greater technical detail in Chapter 6, "Power Amplifiers.")

Another electrical factor to consider is the loudspeaker's *load imped-ance*. This is the electrical resistance the power amp meets when driving the loudspeaker. The lower the loudspeaker's impedance, the more demand is placed on the power amp. If you choose low-impedance loudspeakers, be certain the power amp will drive them adequately. (See Chapter 6 for a full technical discussion of loudspeaker impedance as it relates to amplifier power.)

On a musical level, you should select as sonically neutral a loud-speaker as possible. If you have a bright-sounding CD player or power amp, it's a mistake to buy a loudspeaker that sounds soft or dull in the treble to compensate. Instead, change your CD player or amplifier.

Another mistake is to drive high-quality loudspeakers with poor amplification or source components. The high-quality loudspeakers will resolve much more information than lesser loudspeakers—including imperfections in the electronics and source components. All too many audiophiles drive great loudspeakers with mediocre source components and never realize their loudspeakers' potential. Match the loudspeakers' quality to that of the rest of your system. (Use the guidelines in Chapter 2 to set a loudspeaker budget within the context of the cost of your entire system.)

3) Musical Preferences and Listening Habits

If the perfect loudspeaker existed, it would work equally well for cham-ber music and heavy metal. But because the perfect loudspeaker remains a mythical beast, musical preferences must play a part in choosing a loudspeaker. If you listen mostly to small-scale classical music, choral works, or classical guitar, a minimonitor would probably be your best choice. Conversely, rock listeners need the dynamics, low-frequency extension, and bass power of a large full-range system. Different loud-speakers have strengths and weaknesses in different areas; by matching the loudspeaker to your listening tastes, you'll get the best performance in the areas that matter most to you.

Other Guidelines in Choosing Loudspeakers

In addition to these specific recommendations, there are some general guidelines you should follow in order to get the most loudspeaker for your money.

First, buy from a specialty audio retailer who can properly demon-strate the loudspeaker, advise you on system matching, and tell you the pros and cons of each candidate. Many high-end audio dealers will let you try the loudspeaker in your home with your own electronics and music before you buy.

Take advantage of the dealer's knowledge—and reward him with the sale. It's not only unfair to the dealer to use his or her expensive showroom and knowledgeable salespeople to find out which product to buy, then look for the loudspeaker elsewhere at a lower price; it also prevents you from establishing a mutually beneficial relationship with him or her.

In general, loudspeakers made by companies that make *only* loudspeakers are better than those from companies who also make a full line of electronics. Loudspeaker design may be an afterthought to the electronics manufacturer—something to fill out the line. Conversely, many high-end loudspeaker companies have an almost obsessive dedication to the art of loudspeaker design. Their products' superior performance often reflects this commitment.

Don't buy a loudspeaker based on technical claims. Some products claiming superiority in one aspect of their performance may overlook other, more important aspects. Loudspeaker design requires a balanced approach, not reliance on some new "wonder" technology that may have been invented by the loudspeaker manufacturer's marketing department. Forget about the technical hype and listen to how the loudspeaker reproduces *music*. You'll hear whether or not the loudspeaker is any good.

Don't base your loudspeaker purchases on brand loyalty or longevity. Many well-known and respected names in loudspeaker design of 20 years ago are no longer competitive. Such a company may still produce loudspeakers, but its recent products' inferior performance only throws into relief the extent of the manufacturer's decline. The brands the general public thinks represent the state of the art are actually among the worst-sounding loudspeakers available. These companies were either bought by multinational business conglomerates who didn't care about quality and just wanted to exploit the brand name, or the company has forsaken high performance for mass-market sales. Ironically, the companies with the biggest advertising spreads in the mainstream magazines often offer the lowest-performance loudspeakers.

The general public also believes that the larger the loudspeaker and the more drivers it has, the better it is. Given the same retail price, there is often an *inverse* relationship between size/driver count and sonic performance. A good two-way loudspeaker—one that splits the frequency spectrum into two parts for reproduction by a woofer and a tweeter—with a 6" woofer/midrange and a tweeter in a small cabinet is likely to be vastly better than a similarly priced four-way in a large, floorstanding enclosure. Two high-quality drivers are much better than four mediocre ones. Further, the larger the cabinet, the more difficult and expensive it is to make it free from vibrations that degrade the sound. The four-way speaker's more extensive crossover will require more parts; the two-way can use just a few higher-quality crossover parts. The large loudspeaker will probably be unlistenable; the small two-way may be superbly musical.

If both of these loudspeakers were shown in a catalog and offered at the same price, however, the large, inferior system would outsell the high-quality two-way by at least 10 times. The perceived value of more hardware for the same money is much higher.

The bottom line: You can't tell anything about a loudspeaker until you listen to it. In the next section, we'll examine common problems in loudspeakers and how to choose one that provides the highest level of musical performance.

Finding the Right Loudspeaker—Before You Buy

You've done your homework, read reviews, and narrowed down your list of candidate loudspeakers based on the criteria described earlier—you know what you want. Now it's time to go out and listen. This is a crucial part of shopping for a loudspeaker, and one that should be approached carefully. Rather than buying a pair of speakers on your first visit to a dealer, consider this initial audition to be simply the next step. Don't be in a hurry to buy the first loudspeaker you like. Even if it sounds very good to you, you won't know how good it is until you've auditioned several products.

Audition the loudspeaker with a wide range of familiar recordings *of your own choosing*. Remember that a dealer's strategic selection of music can highlight a loudspeaker's best qualities and conceal its weaknesses—after all, his job is to present his products in the best light. Further, auditioning with only audiophile-quality recordings won't tell you much about how the loudspeaker will perform with the music you'll be playing at home, most of which was likely *not* recorded to high audiophile standards. Still, audiophile recordings are excellent for discovering specific performance aspects of a loudspeaker. The music selected for auditioning should therefore be a combination of your favorite music, and diagnostic recordings chosen to reveal different aspects of the loudspeaker's performance. When listening to your favorite music, forget about specific sonic characteristics and pay attention to how much you're enjoying the sound. Shift into the analytical mode only when playing the diagnostic recordings. Characterize the sound quality according to the sonic criteria described in Chapter 3, and later in this chapter.

Visit the dealer when business is slow so you can spend at least an hour with the loudspeaker. Some loudspeakers are appealing at first, then lose their luster as their flaws begin to emerge over time. The time to lose patience with the speakers is in the dealer's showroom, not a week after you've bought them. And don't try to audition more than two sets of loudspeakers in a single dealer visit. If you must choose between three models, select between the first two on one visit, then return to compare the winner of the first audition with the third contender. You should listen to each candidate as long as you want (within reason) to be sure you're making the right purchasing decision.

Some loudspeakers have different tonal balances at different listening heights. Be sure to audition the loudspeaker at the same listening height as your listening chair at home. A typical listening height is 36", measured from the floor to your ears. Further, some loudspeakers with first-order crossovers sound different if you sit too close to them. When in the showroom, move back and forth a few feet to be certain the loudspeaker will sound the same as it should at your listening distance at home.

Make sure the loudspeakers are driven by electronics and source components of comparable quality to your components. It's easy to become infatuated with a delicious sound in a dealer's showroom, only to be disappointed when you connect the loudspeakers to less good electronics. Ideally, you should drive the loudspeakers under audition with the same level of power amp as you have at home, or as you intend to buy with the loudspeakers.

Of course, the best way to audition loudspeakers is in your own home—you're under no pressure, you can listen for as long as you like, and you can hear how the loudspeaker performs with your electronics and in your listening room. Home audition removes much of the guesswork from choosing a loudspeaker. But because it's impractical to take every contender home, and because many dealers will not allow this, save your home auditioning for only those loudspeakers you are seriously considering.

What to Listen For

There are several common flaws in loudspeaker performance that you should listen for. Though some of these flaws are unavoidable in the lower price ranges, a loudspeaker exhibiting too many of them should be quickly passed over.

Listen for thick, slow, and tubby bass. One of the most annoying characteristics of poor loudspeakers is colored, peaky, and pitchless bass. You should hear distinct pitches in bass notes, not a low-frequency, "one-note" growling under the music. Male speaking voice is a good test for upper-bass colorations; it shouldn't have an excessive or unnatural chesty sound.

Certain bass notes shouldn't sound louder than others. Listen to solo piano with descending or ascending lines played evenly in the instrument's left-hand, or lower, registers. Each note should be even in tone and volume, and clearly articulated. If one note sounds different from the others, it's an indication that the loudspeaker may have a problem at that frequency.

The bottom end should be tight, clean, and "quick." When it comes to bass, quality is more important than quantity. Poor-quality bass is a constant reminder that the music is being artificially reproduced, making it that much harder to hear only the music and not the loudspeakers. The paradigm of what bass should *not* sound like is a "boom truck." Those car stereos are designed for maximum output at a single frequency, not articulate and tuneful bass. Unfortunately, *more* bass is generally an indicator of *worse* bass performance in low- to moderately-priced loudspeakers. A lean, tight, and articulate bass is preferable in the long run to the plodding boominess that characterizes inferior loudspeakers.

Listen to kickdrum and bass guitar working together. You should hear the bass drum's dynamic envelope through the bass guitar. The drum should lock in rhythmically rather than seem to lag slightly behind the bass guitar. A loudspeaker that gets this wrong dilutes rhythmic power, making the rhythm sound sluggish, even slower. But when you listen to a loudspeaker that gets this right, you'll find your foot tapping and hear a more "upbeat" and involving quality to the music.

Midrange coloration is a particularly annoying problem with some loudspeakers. Fortunately, coloration levels are vastly lower in today's loudspeakers than they were even 15 years ago. Still, there are lots of colored loudspeakers out there. These can be identified by their "cupped hands" coloration on vocals, a nasal quality, or an emphasis on certain vowel sounds. A problem a little higher in frequency is manifested as a "clangy" piano sound. A good loudspeaker will present vocals as pure, open, and seeming to exist independently of the loudspeakers. Midrange problems will also make the music sound as though it is coming out of boxes rather than existing in space.

Poor treble performance is characterized by grainy or dirty sound to violins, cymbals, and vocal sibilants (*s* and *sh* sounds). Cymbals should not splash across the soundstage, sounding like bursts of undifferentiated white noise. Instead, the treble should be integrated with the rest of the music and not call attention to itself. The treble shouldn't sound hard and metallic; instead, cymbals should have some delicacy, texture, and pitch. If you find that a pair of speakers is making you aware of the treble as a separate component of the music, keep looking.

Another thing to listen for in loudspeakers is their ability to play loudly without congestion. The sounds of some loudspeakers will be fine at low levels, but will congeal and produce a giant roar when pushed to high volumes. Listen to orchestral music with crescendos—the sound should not collapse and coarsen during loud, complex passages.

Finally, the loudspeakers should "disappear" into the soundstage. A good pair of loudspeakers will unfold the music in space before you, giving no clue that the sound is coming from two boxes placed at opposite sides of the room. Singers should be heard as pinpoint, palpable images directly between the loudspeakers (if that's how they've been recorded). The sonic image of an instrument should not "pull" to one side or another when the instrument moves between registers. The music should sound open and transparent, not thick, murky, or opaque. Overall, the less you're aware of the loudspeakers themselves, the better.

Some loudspeakers with less-than-high-end aspirations have colorations intentionally designed into them. The bass is made to be big and fat, the treble excessively bright to give the illusion of "clarity." Such speakers are usually extremely sensitive, so that they'll play loudly in comparisons made without level matching. These loudspeakers may impress the unwary in a two-minute demonstration, but will become extremely annoying not long after you've brought them home. You're unlikely to find such products in a true high-end audio store.

Finally, the surest sign that a loudspeaker will provide long-term musical satisfaction at home is if, during the audition, you find yourself greatly enjoying the music and not thinking about loudspeakers at all.

The flaws described here are only the most obvious loudspeaker problems; a full description of what to listen for in reproduced music in general is found in Chapter 3.

Loudspeaker Types and How They Work

Many mechanisms for making air move in response to an electrical signal have been tried over the years. Three methods of creating sound work well enough—and are practical enough—to be used in commercially available products. These are the dynamic driver, the ribbon transducer, and the electrostatic panel. A loudspeaker using dynamic drivers is often called a box loudspeaker because the drivers are mounted in a box-like enclosure or cabinet. Ribbon and electrostatic loudspeakers are called planar loudspeakers because they're usually mounted in flat, open panels. The term transducer describes any device that converts energy from one form to another. A loudspeaker is a transducer because it converts electrical energy into sound.

The Dynamic Driver

The most popular loudspeaker technology is without question the dynamic driver. Loudspeakers using dynamic drivers are identifiable by their familiar cones and domes. The dynamic driver's popularity is due to its many advantages: wide dynamic range, high power handling, high sensitivity, relatively simple design, and ruggedness. Dynamic drivers are also called point-source transducers because the sound is produced from a point in space.

Dynamic loudspeaker systems use a combination of different-sized dynamic drivers. The low frequencies are reproduced by a paper or plastic cone *woofer*. High frequencies are generated by a *tweeter*, usually employing a small metal or fabric dome. Some loudspeakers use a third dynamic driver, the *midrange*, to reproduce frequencies in the middle of the audio band.

Despite the very different designs of these drivers, they all operate on the same principle (Fig.7-1).

First, the simplified explanation: Electrical current from the power amplifier flows through the driver's *voice coil*. This current flow sets up a magnetic field around the voice coil that expands and collapses at the same frequency as the audio signal. The voice coil is suspended in a permanent magnetic field generated by magnets in the driver. This permanent magnetic field interacts with the magnetic field generated by current flow through the voice coil, alternately pushing and pulling the voice coil back and forth. Because the voice coil is attached to the driver's cone, this magnetic interaction pulls the cone back and forth, producing sound.

On a more technical level, the voice coil is a length of wire wound around a thin cylinder called the voice-coil former. The former is attached to the diaphragm (a cone or dome). Electrical current from the amplifier flows through the voice coil, which is mounted in a permanent magnetic field whose magnetic lines of flux cross the gap between two permanent magnets. According to the "right-hand rule" of physics, the circular flow of current through the voice-coil windings generates magnetic forces that are directed along the voice coil's axis. The interaction between the fluctuating field of the voice coil and the fixed magnetic field in the gap produces axial forces that move the voice coil back and forth, carrying the diaphragm with it. The faster the audio signal alternates, the faster the diaphragm moves, and the higher the frequency of sound produced. Dynamic drivers are also called *moving-coil* drivers, for obvious reasons.

Other elements of the dynamic driver include a *spider* that suspends the voice coil in place as it moves back and forth. The *basket* is a cast- or stamped-metal structure holding the entire assembly together. (Cast baskets are generally found in higher-quality loudspeakers, stamped baskets in budget models.) A ring of compliant rubber material, called the *surround*, attaches the cone to the basket rim. The surround allows the cone to move back and forth while still attached to the basket. The maximum distance the cone moves back and forth is called its *excursion*.

Common cone materials include paper, paper impregnated with a stiffening agent, a form of plastic such as polypropylene, or exotic materials such as Kevlar. Metal (including titanium) has also been used in woofer cones, as have sandwiched layers of different materials. Designers use these materials to prevent a form of distortion called *breakup*. Breakup occurs when the cone material flexes instead of moving as a perfect piston. Because the cone is driven at a small area at the inside (an area the size of the voice coil), the cone tends to flex, which produces non-linear distortion. Stiff cone materials help prevent breakup. Although all dynamic drivers exhibit breakup at a certain fre-

Fig. 7-1
Dynamic driver
cutaway
(Courtesy Thiel)
and cross section

Aluminum diaphragm for rigidity
and transparent reproduction

Magnesium frame for rigidity
and clearer reproduction

Copper sleeve for low distortion
and exceptional attack

Two magnets with a
total weight of 1.1 Kg
for exceptional bass
control and low stray
magnetic field

Short coil / long gap
motor for very low
levels of distortion

Phase plug for more
uniform response

Surround Cone Dust Cap Voice Coil Former Spider

Basket Assembly Magnet Voice Coil Magnetic Gap Magnet Assembly

quency, the competent loudspeaker designer makes sure that a driver is
never driven by frequencies that would cause breakup. For example, if a
woofer has its first breakup mode at 4kHz, the designer would probably
operate the driver only up to about 2kHz, well away from the breakup
frequency.

The cone should be lightweight as well as stiff. A lighter cone has
less inertia, allowing it to respond faster to transient signals and stop

faster after the drive signal has ceased. Think of a bass-drum whack. A large and heavy cone may not be able to move fast enough to reproduce the sound's attack, diminishing the drum's dynamic impact. Similarly, once the drum whack is over, the heavy cone's mass will want to continue moving. Loudspeaker designers therefore search for cone materials that combine high stiffness with low mass. Many of the advances made in loudspeaker design of the past 15 years have been the result of materials research.

Tweeters work on the same principle, but typically use a 1" dome instead of a cone. Common dome materials include plastic, woven fiber coated with a rubbery material, titanium, aluminum and aluminum alloys, and gold-plated aluminum. Diamond tweeter diaphragms have also been used in extremely expensive loudspeakers. Unlike cone drivers, which are driven at the cone's apex, dome diaphragms are driven at the dome's outer perimeter. Most dome tweeters use Ferrofluid, a liquid cooling agent, to remove heat from the tweeter's small voice coil. The first breakup mode of well-designed modern dome tweeters is above 25kHz, well out of the audible range.

Midrange drivers are smaller versions of the cone woofer. Some, however, use dome diaphragms instead of cones.

Dynamic Compression

When a dynamic driver plays loudly, it must dissipate a tremendous amount of heat from its voice coil. As the voice coil heats up, its electrical resistance increases, reducing the amount of current flow through the voice coil. Because it is current flow through the voice coil that causes the cone to move back and forth, increased voice-coil resistance reduces the amount of sound produced by the driver. In other words, you can keep turning up the volume, but the speaker reaches a point where it won't play any louder.

This phenomenon, called *dynamic compression*, obviously alters musical dynamics. Specifically, loud musical peaks aren't reproduced quite as loudly as they should be. An electroacoustic mechanism is changing the score's dynamic markings; *fff* may be reproduced as *ff*, for example.

Although this distortion of the music's dynamics is a departure from accuracy, dynamic compression introduces a worse form of distortion. The multiple drivers in a three-way dynamic loudspeaker will have different levels at which they begin to compress. If the tweeter exhibits dynamic compression at a lower volume than the midrange and woofer, the sound will be slightly duller on musical peaks. Conversely, if the woofer and midrange compress at a lower level than the tweeter, the sound will grow brighter as it gets louder. In essence, the speaker's tonal balance changes as a function of the music's dynamics. You may not hear this phenomenon directly as a change in tonal balance, but this form of distortion creates an impression of strain on musical peaks that may momentarily draw our attention away from the music. It's just one more cue to the brain that we're not hearing live music.

Loudspeaker designers combat dynamic compression by creating drivers with oversized voice coils, physical structures that naturally cool the voice coil, and through innovative voice-coil wire shape and winding techniques.

There's a related mechanism by which drivers can distort music. When a driver is producing a loud sound, the ends of its voice coil can momentarily leave the magnetic field in which the coil sits. This robs the driver of its ability to faithfully move back and forth in response to the drive signal, again changing the music's dynamics and creating distortion. This problem is addressed by designing drivers with a very short voice coil and a very long magnetic gap. Although a short voice coil is more susceptible to dynamic compression, it doesn't introduce this form of non-linear distortion. Loudspeaker designers must balance these trade-offs.

Finally, a dynamic driver can "bottom out," heard as a popping or cracking sound from the woofer. The popping sound is caused by the voice-coil former (the bobbin around which the voice coil is wound) hitting the back of the magnet structure. If you ever hear this sound, immediately turn down the volume.

Problems with Dynamic Drivers

Of all the components in your system, the loudspeaker is the most likely to develop trouble. The most common problem is a blown driver, usually the tweeter—it simply stops working. Tweeters are often destroyed by too much current flowing through their voice coils. The tweeter can't dissipate the resultant heat quickly enough, and its voice coil is burned open.

Another common cause of speaker failure is the buzzing sound produced by a loose voice coil. Too much current through the voice coil melts the glue holding the coil to the former (the bobbin around which wire is wound to make the coil). This loosens turns of wire, which then rub against the magnet to cause the buzzing sound.

Driver mounting bolts can loosen over time and degrade a loudspeaker's performance by allowing the entire driver to vibrate rather than just its diaphragm. Gently tightening these bolts from time to time—particularly when a loudspeaker is new—can improve its sound. Be careful not to overtighten and strip the bolts.

The Planar Magnetic Transducer

The next popular driver technology is the planar magnetic transducer, also known as a ribbon driver. Although the term "ribbon" and "planar magnetic" are often used interchangeably, a true ribbon driver is actually a sub-class of the planar magnetic driver. Let's look at a true ribbon first.

Instead of using a cone attached to a voice coil suspended in a magnetic field, a ribbon driver uses a strip of material (usually aluminum) as a diaphragm suspended between the north-south poles of two magnets (see Fig.7-2). The ribbon is often pleated for additional strength. The audio signal travels through the electrically conductive ribbon, creating a magnetic field around the ribbon that interacts with the permanent magnetic field. This causes the ribbon to move back and forth, creating sound. In effect, the ribbon functions as both the voice coil and the diaphragm. The ribbon can be thought of as the voice coil stretched out over the ribbon's length.

Fig. 7-2 A true ribbon driver

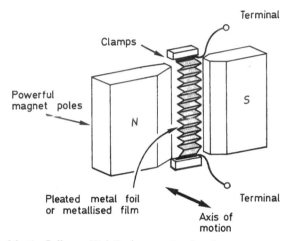

Courtesy Martin Colloms, *High Performance Loudspeakers*

In all other planar magnetic transducers, a flat or slightly curved diaphragm is driven by an electromagnetic conductor. This conductor, which is bonded to the back of the diaphragm, is analogous to a dynamic driver's voice coil, here stretched out in straight-line segments. In most designs, the diaphragm is a sheet of plastic with the electrical conductors bonded to its surface. The flat metal conductor provides the driving force, but it occupies only a portion of the diaphragm area. Such drivers are also called *quasi-ribbon* transducers. Fig.7-3 shows the difference between a true ribbon and a quasi-ribbon driver.

A planar driver is a true ribbon only if the diaphragm is conductive and the audio signal flows directly through the diaphragm, rather than through conductors bonded to a diaphragm, as in quasi-ribbon drivers. (Despite this semantic distinction, I'll use the term "ribbon" throughout the rest of this section, with the understanding that it covers both true ribbons and quasi-ribbon drivers.)

Ribbon drivers like the one in Figs.7-2 and 7-3 are called *line-source* transducers because they produce sound over a line rather than from a point, as does a dynamic loudspeaker. Moreover, a ribbon's radiation

Fig. 7-3
Cross-section
comparison of
true ribbon (left)
and quasi-ribbon
(right) drivers.

Courtesy Magnepan

pattern changes dramatically with frequency. At low frequencies, when
the ribbon's length is short compared to the wavelength of sound, the
ribbon will act as a point source and produce sound in a sphere around
the ribbon—just like a point-source woofer. As the frequency increases
and the wavelength of sound approaches the ribbon's dimensions, the
radiation pattern narrows until it looks more like a cylinder around the
ribbon than a sphere. At very high frequencies, the ribbon radiates horizontally but not vertically. This can be an advantage in the listening
room: the listener hears more direct sound from the loudspeaker and
less reflection from the sidewalls and ceiling. Reduced wall reflections
aid in soundstaging: Pinpoint imaging and the ability to project a concert
hall's acoustic signature are hallmarks of good ribbon loudspeakers.

The main technical advantage of a ribbon over a moving-coil driver
is the ribbon's vastly lower mass. Instead of using a heavy cone, voice
coil, and voice-coil former to move air, the only thing moving in a ribbon
is a very thin strip of aluminum. A ribbon tweeter may have one quarter
the mass and 10 times the radiating area of a dome tweeter's diaphragm.
Low mass is a high design goal: the diaphragm can respond more quickly to transient signals. In addition, a low-mass diaphragm will stop moving immediately after the input signal has ceased. The ribbon starts and
stops faster than a dynamic driver, allowing it to more faithfully reproduce transient musical information.

The ribbon driver is usually mounted in a flat, open-air panel that
radiates sound to the rear as well as to the front. A loudspeaker that
radiates sound to the front and rear is called a *dipole*, which means "two
poles." Fig.7-4 shows the radiation patterns of a point-source loudspeaker (left) and a dipolar loudspeaker.

Fig. 7-4
A point-source loudspeaker (left) radiates sound in one direction; a dipole loud-speaker (right) radiates sound equally to the front and rear.

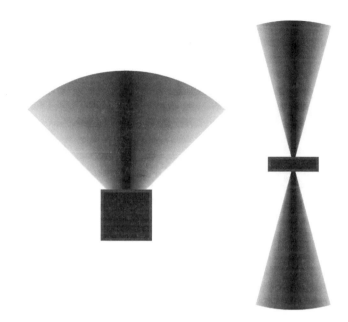

Another great advantage enjoyed by ribbons is the lack of a box or cabinet. As we'll see in the section of this chapter on loudspeaker enclosures, the enclosure can greatly degrade a loudspeaker's performance. Not having to compensate for an enclosure makes it easier for a ribbon loudspeaker to achieve stunning clarity and lifelike musical timbres.

A full-range quasi-ribbon loudspeaker is illustrated in Fig.7-5. The large panel extends the system's bass response: when the average panel dimension approaches half the wavelength, front-to-rear cancellation reduces bass output. Consequently, the larger the panel, the deeper the low-frequency extension.

Ribbon loudspeakers are characterized by a remarkable ability to produce extremely clean and quick transients—such as those of plucked acoustic guitar strings or percussion instruments. The sound seems to start and stop suddenly, just as one hears from live instruments. Ribbons sound vivid and immediate without being etched or excessively bright. In addition, the sound has an openness, clarity, and transparency often unmatched by dynamic drivers. Finally, the ribbon's dipolar nature produces a huge sense of space, air, and soundstage depth (provided this spatial information was captured in the recording). Some argue, however, that this sense of depth is artificially *produced* by ribbon loudspeakers, rather than being a *re*production of the actual recording.

Despite their often stunning sound quality, ribbon drivers have several disadvantages. The first is low sensitivity; it takes lots of amplifier power to drive them. Second, ribbons inherently have a very low impedance, often a fraction of an ohm. Most ribbon drivers therefore have an *impedance matching transformer* in the crossover to present a higher impedance to the power amplifier. Design of the transformer is therefore crucial to prevent it from degrading sound quality.

Fig. 7-5 A full-range dipolar ribbon loud-speaker

Courtesy Magnepan

From a practical standpoint, ribbon-based loudspeakers are more difficult to position in a room. Small variations in placement can greatly change the sound, due primarily to their dipolar radiating pattern. This dipolar pattern requires that the ribbon loudspeakers be placed well away from the rear wall, and that the rear wall be acoustically benign.

Low-profile, ribbon-based loudspeakers with the ribbon top at the same height as the listener's ears will have a radically different treble balance if the listener moves up or down a few inches. That's because ribbon loudspeakers have very narrow vertical dispersion, meaning they radiate very little sound above and below the ribbon at high frequencies. If you sit too high or listen while standing, you'll hear less treble. Some ribbon loudspeakers have a tilt adjustment that allows you to set the correct treble balance for a particular listening height.

Ribbons also have a resonant frequency that, if excited, produces the horrible sound of crinkling aluminum foil. Consequently, the ribbon must be used within strict frequency-band limits. In addition, ribbon drivers are tensioned at the factory for optimum performance. If under too much tension, a ribbon will produce less sound; if under too little tension, a ribbon can produce distortion that sounds like the music is "breaking up." This is most noticeable on piano; the transient leading edges sound "shattered" and distorted. A sudden increase in ambient temperature can cause a ribbon driver to lose some of its tension and introduce the distortion described. If you hear this sound from your ribbon loudspeakers, contact the manufacturer for advice. The solution may be as simple as turning a few tensioning bolts half a turn.

Ribbon drivers don't necessarily have to be long and thin. Variations on ribbon technology have produced drivers having many of the desirable characteristics of ribbons but few of the disadvantages. The superb 1" ribbon tweeter developed by Genesis Technologies is a good example. This device is a layer of Kapton (a plastic-like material) 2.5μm (0.0001") thick with a conductor bonded on the back. The conductor sits in a magnetic field. The diaphragm is of extremely low mass—less mass than the air in front of it—and its point-source radiation pattern allows it to be used like a conventional dome tweeter.

A row of such tweeters may be positioned next to a 4'-tall midrange ribbon to simulate the line-source radiation pattern of the ribbon midrange. In addition to mimicking a line source, a vertical array of tweeters increases dynamic range and lowers distortion because each tweeter need produce only a small amount of sound. With each tweeter barely driven, the system can play very loudly without distortion or strain.

Because the signal-carrying conductors are bonded to the diaphragm, the Genesis tweeter (Fig.7-6) is technically a planar magnetic driver, not a true ribbon. Infinity's EMIT (Electromotive Induction Tweeter) is another example of a planar magnetic driver.

Fig. 7-6 A planar tweeter

Courtesy Genesis Technologies, Inc.

Finally, some loudspeakers use a combination of dynamic and ribbon transducers to take advantage of both technologies. These so-called *hybrid* loudspeakers typically use a dynamic woofer in an enclosure to reproduce bass, and a ribbon midrange/tweeter. The hybrid technique brings the advantages of ribbon drivers to a lower price level (ribbon woofers are big and expensive), and exploits the advantages of each technology while avoiding the drawbacks.

The Electrostatic Driver

Like the ribbon transducer, an electrostatic driver uses a thin membrane to make air move. But that's where the similarities end. While both dynamic and ribbon loudspeakers are electromagnetic transducers—they operate by electrically induced magnetic interaction—the electrostatic loudspeaker operates on the completely different principle of electrostatic interaction.

In the electrostatic driver, a thin moveable membrane—sometimes made of transparent Mylar—is stretched between two static elements called *stators* (Fig.7-7). The membrane is charged to a very high voltage with respect to the stators. The audio signal is applied to the stators, which create electrostatic fields around them that vary in response to the audio signal. The varying electrostatic fields generated around the stators interact with the membrane's fixed electrostatic field, pushing and pulling the membrane to produce sound. One stator pulls the membrane, the other pushes it. This illustration also shows a dynamic woofer as part of a hybrid dynamic/electrostatic system. (A full-range electrostatic loudspeaker is illustrated in Fig.7-8.)

Fig. 7-7
An electrostatic loudspeaker employs two stators separated by a membrane that is pulled back and forth by the stators.

Courtesy MartinLogan

Fig. 7-8
A full-range
electrostatic
loudspeaker

Courtesy MartinLogan

The voltages involved in an electrostatic loudspeaker are very high. The polarizing voltage applied to the diaphragm may be as high as 10,000 volts (10kV). In addition, the audio signal is stepped up from several tens of volts to several thousand volts by a *step-up transformer* inside the electrostatic loudspeaker. These high voltages are necessary to produce the electrostatic fields around the diaphragm and stators.

To prevent arcing—the electrical charge jumping between elements—the stators are often coated with an insulating material. Still, if an electrostatic loudspeaker is overdriven, the electrostatic field strips free electrons from the oxygen in the air, making it *ionized*; this provides a conductive path for the electrical charge. Large diaphragm excursions— i.e., a loud playing level—put the diaphragm closer to the stators and also encourage arcing. Arcing can destroy electrostatic panels by punching small holes in the membrane. Arcing is a greater problem in humid climates than in dry climates because moisture makes the air between the stators more electrically conductive.

Electrostatic panels are often divided into several smaller panels to reduce the effects of diaphragm resonances. Some panels are curved to reduce the *lobing* effect (uneven radiation pattern) at high frequencies.

Lobing occurs when the wavelength of sound is small compared to the diaphragm. Lobing is responsible for electrostatics' uneven high-frequency dispersion pattern, which *Stereophile* magazine founder J. Gordon Holt has dubbed the *vertical venetian-blind effect*, in which the tonal balance changes rapidly and repeatedly as you move your head from side to side.

Electrostatic panels are of even lighter weight than planar magnetic transducers. Unlike the ribbon driver, in which the diaphragm carries the audio signal current, the electrostatic diaphragm need not carry the audio signal. The diaphragm can therefore be very thin, often less than 0.001″. Such a low mass allows the diaphragm to start and stop very quickly, improving transient response. And because the electrostatic panel is driven uniformly over its entire area, the panel is less prone to breakup. Both the electromagnetic planar loudspeaker (a ribbon) and the electrostatic planar loudspeaker enjoy the benefits of limited dispersion, which means less reflected sound arriving at the listening position. Like ribbon loudspeakers, electrostatic loudspeakers also have no enclosure to degrade the sound. Electrostatic loudspeakers also inherently have a dipolar radiation pattern. Because the diaphragm is mounted in an open panel, the electrostatic driver produces as much sound to the rear as to the front. Finally, the electrostatic loudspeaker's huge surface area confers an advantage in reproducing the correct size of instrumental images.

In the debit column, electrostatic loudspeakers must be plugged into an AC outlet to generate the polarizing voltage. Because the electrostatic is naturally a dipolar radiator, room placement is more crucial to achieving good sound. The electrostatic loudspeaker needs to be placed well out into the room and away from the rear wall to realize a fully developed soundstage. Electrostatics also tend to be insensitive, requiring large power amplifiers. The load impedance they present to the amplifier is also more reactive than that of dynamic loudspeakers, further taxing the power amp. (*Reactance* is described later in this chapter.) Nor will they play as loudly as dynamic loudspeakers; electrostatics aren't noted for their dynamic impact, power, or deep bass. Instead, electrostatics excel in transparency, delicacy, transient response, resolution of detail, stunning imaging, and overall musical coherence.

Electrostatic loudspeakers can be augmented with separate dynamic woofers or a subwoofer to extend the low-frequency response and provide some dynamic impact. Other electrostatics achieve the same result in a more convenient package: dynamic woofers in enclosures mated to the electrostatic panels. Some of these designs achieve the best qualities of both the dynamic driver and electrostatic panel. (An example of a hybrid electrostatic/dynamic loudspeaker is illustrated in Fig.7-9.) Audition such hybrid speakers carefully; they sometimes exhibit an audible discontinuity at the transition frequency at which the woofer leaves off and the electrostatic panel takes over. Listen, for example, for a change in a piano's timbre, bloom, projection, and image size as it is played in different registers. Acoustic bass in jazz is also a good test of woofer/panel discontinuity in dynamic/electrostatic hybrid loudspeakers.

One great benefit of full-range ribbons and full-range electrostatics is the absence of a crossover; the diaphragm is driven by the entire audio signal. This prevents any discontinuities in the sound as different frequencies are reproduced by different drivers. In addition, removing the resistors, capacitors, and inductors found in crossovers greatly increases the full-range planar's transparency and harmonic accuracy.

Fig. 7-9 A hybrid electrostatic loudspeaker employs a dynamic woofer mated to an electrostatic midrange/tweeter panel.

Courtesy MartinLogan

Even hybrid planars put the crossover frequency between the dynamic woofer and the planar panel very low (below 800Hz, a frequency nearly an octave above middle A), so there's no discontinuity between drivers through most of the audible spectrum.

Finally, the large diaphragms of electrostatic and ribbon drivers are gently driven over their entire surface areas, rather than forcefully over the relatively small voice-coil area of a dynamic driver. This high force over a small area contributes to the dynamic driver's breakup described earlier, a phenomenon less likely to occur with large planar diaphragms.

The Dipolar Radiation Patterns of Ribbons and Electrostatics

Because planar loudspeakers (ribbons and electrostatics) are mounted in an open frame rather than an enclosed box, they radiate sound equally from the front and back. As we saw earlier, the term dipolar describes this radiation pattern. This is contrasted with point source loudspeakers, whose drivers are mounted on the front of a box. Point-source loudspeakers are usually associated with dynamic drivers, but any type of driver in an enclosed cabinet qualifies as a point-source loudspeaker.

The dipolar radiation patterns of ribbons and electrostatics make using them very different from point-source loudspeakers. Because they launch just as much energy to the rear as they do to the front, positioning a dipole is more crucial, particularly their distance from the rear wall. Dipoles need a significant space behind them to work well. In addition, the rear wall's acoustic properties have a much greater influence over the sound. A few attempts have been made to absorb a ribbon's rear energy inside an enclosure to make placement easier, but these have been largely unsuccessful.

Ribbons and electrostatics also tend to have much narrower radiation patterns than point-source loudspeakers. That is, they disperse less sound to their sides. Consequently, the listener hears much more of the loudspeaker's direct sound and much less sound reflected from the floor, ceiling, and sidewalls. This is particularly true in the midrange and treble, where the radiation pattern becomes cylindrical. The result is often a greatly improved transparency and more natural timbre. (The effects of these reflections are discussed in Chapter 4.) The negative effects of this tendency for planar loudspeakers to "beam" at high frequencies is a disturbing shift in the tonal balance with small motions of the head from side to side—the "vertical venetian-blind effect" described earlier. This tendency can be minimized with a curved diaphragm (seen in the earlier photographs of an electrostatic loudspeaker) or by electrically segmenting the diaphragm.

Bipolar and Omnipolar Loudspeakers

We've seen that a diaphragm mounted in an open panel will naturally radiate sound equally to the front and rear. These front and rear waves are out of phase with each other. That is, as the diaphragm moves forward, it creates a positive pressure wave in front of the diaphragm, and a negative pressure wave (called a rarefaction) behind the diaphragm.

Some loudspeaker designers see the advantages of front- and rear-launched sound, but believe that the front and rear waves should be in phase with each other. Because this is impossible to achieve with a diaphragm mounted in an open panel, these designers employ a second set of dynamic drivers on the rear of the loudspeaker enclosure. This design, called a *bipolar* loudspeaker, has a radiation pattern similar to that of a dipole, but the front and rear waves are now in phase. Other designers add just a rear-firing tweeter, which they contend produces a smoother treble response at the listening position and better reproduces a sense of spaciousness and ambience.

A bipolar loudspeaker produces a radiation pattern slightly different from that of a dipole. The dipole's out-of-phase front and rear waves cancel at the sides of the speaker, narrowing their radiation pattern. A bipolar speaker's in-phase waves don't exhibit this cancellation, and thus have wider dispersion.

Advocates of dipoles and bipoles believe that reflecting sound from the wall behind the speakers increases the sense of musical realism because we hear such reflected sound in live music. In addition, point-source speakers (those firing in one direction) exhibit frequency-response changes off-axis (to the speaker's sides). The sound reflected from the sidewalls has a different spectral balance compared with the direct sound from the loudspeaker. This confuses the ear/brain, and provides yet another clue that the sound isn't real. Because dipole and bipole loudspeakers distribute a more uniform spectral balance around the room, aficionados of such designs believe that they produce a more musically natural sound.

An extension of this idea is the Omnipolar™ loudspeaker created by Mirage Loudspeakers. An Omnipolar loudspeaker (see Fig.7-10) produces a spherical dispersion pattern; that is, it radiates sound in *all* directions. Mirage claims that Omnipolar loudspeakers produce a ratio of direct to reflected sound that more closely matches that of live music. This design produces a large and expansive soundstage, but not "pinpoint" imaging. Mirage contends that tight image focus is never heard in real life, but is an artifact of point-source speakers.

The Omnipolar loudspeaker in Fig.7-10 looks like a bipole, but the proximity of the front- and rear-firing drivers (the narrowness of the baffle) creates the spherical radiation pattern. This model also features a built-in power amplifier to drive the woofers, and side-loading of the woofers to reduce the cabinet's visual profile. The dual woofers also tend to cancel cabinet vibration.

Loudspeaker Enclosures

The enclosure in which a set of drivers is mounted has an enormous effect on the loudspeaker's reproduced sound quality. In fact, the enclosure is as important as the drive units themselves. Designers have many choices in enclosure design, all of which affect the reproduced sound.

Fig. 7-10 An Omnipolar loud-speaker radiates sound in all directions.

Courtesy Mirage Loudspeakers

In addition to the very different enclosure types described in this section, any speaker cabinet will vibrate slightly and change the sound. The ideal enclosure would produce no sound of its own, and not interfere with the sound produced by the drivers. Inevitably, however, some of the energy produced by the drive units puts the enclosure into motion. This enclosure vibration turns the speaker cabinet into a sound source of its own, which colors the music.

One of the factors that makes current high-end loudspeakers so much better than mass-produced products is the extreme lengths to which some manufacturers go to prevent the enclosure from vibrating. Mass-market manufacturers generally skimp on the enclosure because, to the uninformed consumer, it adds very little to the product's perceived value.

Let's look at why a loudspeaker needs an enclosure, and survey the most popular enclosure types.

An enclosure around a woofer is required to prevent the woofer's rear-radiated wave from combining with the woofer's front-radiated wave. When the woofer moves forward, a positive pressure wave is launched at the front, and a rarefaction (negative pressure) wave of equal intensity is launched to the rear. Because low frequencies can refract (bend) around small objects such as a woofer, the rear wave will combine with the front wave and cancel the sound, resulting in reduced bass output. Putting an enclosure around the woofer prevents this cancellation and allows the loudspeaker to generate low frequencies. Although this phenomenon occurs with planar loudspeakers, their large size lowers the frequency at which this cancellation occurs. That's why full-range planar loudspeakers don't go very low in the bass, and are often augmented by a woofer in a traditional enclosure.

In addition to preventing this front-to-back cancellation, the enclosure should also present the optimum environment for the drivers, particularly the woofer. This is called *loading*. Various loading techniques have evolved to optimize the way the woofer operates in the cabinet. The most common techniques are the *infinite baffle* (also called a *sealed* cabinet, or *air suspension* in smaller enclosures), and the *reflex* or *ported* enclosure. Less common loading techniques are the *transmission line*, *Isobarik*, and *finite baffle* designs.

These different loading techniques affect the speaker's bass response. A woofer in an enclosure will go only so low in the bass; as the frequency drops below a certain point, so does the woofer's output. The point at which the woofer's output is down by 3dB is called the *low-frequency cutoff point*. Below this frequency, the woofer produces less and less sound as the signal driving the woofer decreases in frequency—a phenomenon called *rolloff*. Rolloff is why not every speaker can reproduce 20Hz bass. The loading technique chosen by the loudspeaker designer greatly affects the woofer's low-frequency cutoff point and how steeply this rolloff occurs.

Let's look at the advantages and drawbacks of the most popular loading techniques.

Infinite Baffle Loading

The infinite baffle simply seals the enclosure around the driver rear to prevent the two waves from meeting. In theory, such an enclosure approximates a baffle (the surface on which the drivers are mounted) of "infinite" size; in fact, it wraps around the driver. The air inside the sealed enclosure acts as a spring, compressing when the woofer moves in and creating some resistance to woofer motion. This is why infinite baffle loading is also called *air suspension*. All sealed-enclosure speakers have a low-frequency rolloff slope of 12dB per octave; this means that, one octave below the system's resonant frequency, the output will be reduced by 12dB. This rolloff is relatively gradual, meaning you'll still hear some lower bass.

Reflex Loading

I mentioned earlier that a woofer in a box produces just as much sound inside the box as outside. The bass-reflex enclosure exploits this fact, channeling some of this bass energy out of the cabinet and into the listening room. You can instantly spot a reflex-loaded loudspeaker by the hole, or vent, on the front or back of the enclosure. Reflex-loaded loudspeakers are also called *vented* designs.

Reflex loading extends the low-frequency cutoff point by venting some of the energy inside the enclosure to the outside. That is, a reflex-loaded woofer will go lower in the bass than one in a sealed enclosure, other factors being equal. The designer can't, however, just cut a hole in the cabinet. Instead, a duct inside the cabinet delays the woofer's rear-firing wave so that it emerges in-phase with the front-firing wave. The rear wave channeled outside the cabinet by the port thus reinforces, rather than cancels, the front wave. A loading material such as long-hair wool or Fiberglas batting is sometimes put in the duct to smooth any peaks in the sound emerging from the port.

Reflex loading has three main advantages. First, it increases a loudspeaker's maximum acoustic output level—it will play louder. Second, it can make a loudspeaker more sensitive—it needs less amplifier power to achieve the same volume. Third, it can lower a loudspeaker's cutoff frequency—the bass goes deeper. Note that these benefits are not available simultaneously; the acoustic gain provided by reflex loading can be used either to increase a loudspeaker's sensitivity or to extend its cutoff frequency, but not both.

Although a reflex system's low-frequency cutoff point is lower than that of a sealed system (assuming the same woofer and enclosure volume), the reflex system's bass rolls off at a much faster rate. Specifically, a reflex system rolls off at 24dB/octave compared to the sealed enclosure's 12dB/octave rolloff. If all other factors are equal, the reflex-loaded system maintains flat bass response down to a lower frequency, but then the bass output drops off more quickly than it does in a sealed system. A comparison of low frequency cutoff points and rolloff slopes is illustrated in Fig.7-11.

Subjectively, the sealed loudspeaker's higher cutoff frequency and gradual rolloff provide a more satisfying feeling of bass fullness than the reflex system's lower cutoff frequency and steeper rolloff. Some designers have found that a loudspeaker's –10dB point is the most reliable indicator of a loudspeaker's subjective bass fullness and extension because it takes into account not only the low-frequency cutoff point, but also the steepness of the rolloff.

Reflex loading is more often used in small enclosures, which trade low-frequency extension and sensitivity for compactness. It's easier to get more bass from a small reflex enclosure than from a sealed one. However, a small reflex enclosure can still achieve some of the extension and sensitivity of a larger cabinet.

Fig. 7-11
Frequency-
response charac-
teristics of
vented and
sealed enclosures

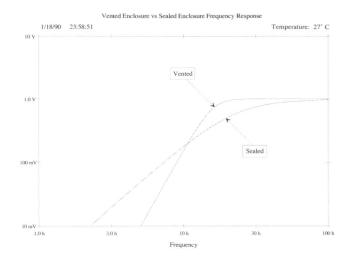

Fig. 7-12
Transient-
response com-
parison between
vented and
sealed enclosures

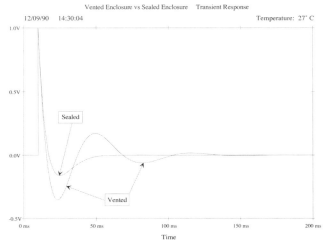

Fig. 7-11 and Fig.7-12 courtesy Avalon Acoustics, Inc.

Some controversy exists over the merits of reflex loading. Some designers believe that reflex systems are fundamentally wrong. Reflex systems in general have gotten a bad name, both because of inherent limitations and poor implementation in certain products. Small, inexpensive loudspeakers are often reflex-loaded to increase their sensitivity.

Ineptly implemented reflex systems tend to be boomy, slow, and poorly defined in the bass. In addition, you can sometimes hear the sound emerging from the port, a phenomenon perfectly (and onomatopoetically) described by the term *chuffing*. Critics also point to the reflex system's poor transient performance compared with a sealed loudspeaker. Specifically, a woofer in a vented enclosure will tend to keep moving after the drive signal has stopped, as shown in Fig.7-12. This difference in transient response can be manifested as sluggish sound in, for example, a kickdrum. A sealed enclosure has better transient response and better bass definition, but at the cost of lower sensitivity and less deep bass extension. Nonetheless, many very-high-quality loudspeakers have been based on ported designs.

Passive Radiators

A variation on the reflex system is the passive radiator, also called an auxiliary bass radiator, or ABR. This is usually a flat diaphragm with no voice coil or magnet structure, that cannot produce sound on its own. Instead, the diaphragm covers what would have been the port in the reflex system, and moves in response to varying air pressure inside the cabinet caused by the woofer's motion. The passive radiator smooths out any response peaks, and eliminates a ported system's wind noise (the "chuffing" mentioned earlier) and port resonances. Fig.7-13 shows a loudspeaker using a passive radiator; it's the flat, oval diaphragm below the woofer. This particular design has exploited the advantages of reflex loading while minimizing the drawbacks.

Fig. 7-13 A passive radiator is an undriven diaphragm that couples bass energy inside the cabinet to the outside.

Courtesy Thiel

Transmission-Line Loading

Another loading technique is the transmission line. In a transmission line, the rear wave from the woofer is channeled through a folded labyrinth or duct—the transmission line—filled with absorbent material such as wool. The end of the transmission line appears at the outside of the enclosure, just as in a reflex system. The acoustic energy traveling down the transmission line is absorbed, with the goal of no acoustic output at the end of the transmission line. In theory, the woofer's rear wave is dissipated in the line. This isn't the case in practice: most transmission lines have some output at the end of the line, causing them to function partially as reflex systems. Because the line must be at least as long as the lowest wavelength to be absorbed, transmission-line enclosures are usually very large. Proponents of transmission lines argue that the springiness of sealed enclosures is not the ideal environment for the woofer. The transmission line removes the spring action of the sealed enclosure without the disadvantages of reflex designs.

Transmission-line loudspeakers have extremely deep extension and the ability to deliver very loud and very clean bass with an effortless quality not heard from other loading designs. They aren't as popular as their sound quality would suggest they should be, mostly because of their large size.

British loudspeaker manufacturer Bowers and Wilkins (B&W) has developed a variation on transmission-line loading the company calls Nautilus. Each driver in a Nautilus system is mounted in a tapered or coiled (thus the Nautilus name) enclosure that absorbs the driver's rear wave. The rear wave cannot interact with the drivers, nor can it form standing waves inside the enclosure. An exploded view of a B&W loud-

Fig. 7-14
B&W's Nautilus technology absorbs the drivers' rear-firing energy via a computer-optimized tapered-tube enclosure.

Courtesy Bowers & Wilkins Loudspeakers

speaker using Nautilus technology is shown in Fig.7-14. Note also the spherical midrange enclosure, which reduces cabinet diffraction. This "boxless" approach to loudspeaker design is an attempt to reduce the enclosure's contribution to the reproduced sound.

Isobarik Loading

A fourth type of loading, used primarily by Linn Products, is called Isobarik (Linn's trade name), or by the more descriptive generic term constant pressure chamber. (See Fig.7-15.) In the Isobarik system, a second woofer is mounted directly behind the first woofer and driven in parallel with it. As the front woofer moves back, so does the second; this maintains a constant pressure inside the chamber separating the two woofers. This technique offers deeper low-frequency extension, higher power handling, greater linearity, and reduced standing-wave reflections inside the enclosure. Isobarik loading reduces sensitivity because the amplifier must drive two woofers, although only one produces acoustic output. Two woofers mounted in an Isobarik configuration can be modeled as a single woofer whose greater mass and compliance deliver useful deep bass in an enclosure half the usual size.

Fig. 7-15
Isobarik loading

Main enclosure

Small linking air volume

Drivers electrically linked in parallel

Courtesy Martin Colloms, *High Performance Loudspeakers*

Energy Multiplied Bandpass

Another dual-driver loading cleverly exploits driver resonance to work to the designer's advantage. The technology, found in subwoofers made by James Loudspeakers, is called Energy Multiplied Bandpass by that company. In the EMB-1000 subwoofer (the first product to use EMB technology), a 10" woofer is hidden inside the cabinet behind the 10" woofer you see at the outside of the cabinet. This internal woofer is driven by the subwoofer's internal amplifier. The internal woofer's acoustic output is acoustically coupled to the passive external woofer to produce sound.

Fig. 7-16 In the Energy Multiplied Bandpass technique, an active, interior woofer is acoustically coupled to an exterior passive woofer.

Courtesy James Loudspeakers

To understand this approach, you need to know that the lower the frequency the woofer is reproducing, the farther the woofer's cone must move. For example, a woofer must move 16 times farther at 25Hz than at 100Hz to produce the same sound-pressure level. Such high excursion creates distortion as the woofer's voice coil moves out of the magnetic gap, making its movement non-linear. In other words, as frequency decreases, distortion increases.

Back to the EMB technique. The external passive woofer is not driven by an electrical signal, but by air compression in the chamber between it and the driven woofer behind it. The passive woofer's resonant frequency is 35Hz, which causes its acoustic output to rise by 12.5dB at that frequency. To maintain flat response, the signal driving the internal woofer is equalized with a 12.5dB dip at 35Hz, which perfectly complements the passive woofer's resonant peak to achieve flat response. Because of this equalization dip in the signal driving the internal woofer, the woofer isn't driven as hard in the low frequencies, lowering its excursion and, with it, distortion. In this system, the driven woofer moves only about one-tenth as far at 35Hz as it would in a conventional system. The passive driver moves much farther than the internal woofer (thus the "multiplying" factor claimed in the technique's name). The result is lower distortion, greater output in the band where bass energy is concentrated, and increased dynamic headroom. Fig.7-16 is a cutaway illustration of this technique.

The Finite Baffle

The only examples of the finite-baffle, or open-panel, loading technique are planar loudspeakers such as the full-range ribbon system illustrated in Fig.7-5. The finite baffle has a rolloff of only 6dB/octave until the driver's free-air resonance frequency, then drops at the rate of 18dB/octave.

System Q

Just as a struck bell produces a certain pitch, a woofer in an enclosure will naturally resonate at some frequency. The nature of that resonance is an important characteristic of the loudspeaker, and one that greatly influences its sound. The term Q, for "quality factor," is a unitless number that expresses how a woofer resonates in an enclosure.

Specifically, a loudspeaker's Q equals the resonant peak's center frequency divided by the peak's bandwidth. A woofer that "rings" (resonates) over a very narrow frequency band is said to have a higher Q than a woofer that resonates less severely over a wider band of frequencies. The steeper the resonance, the higher the Q.

The woofer has its own resonant Q, which is modified by the enclosure's Q. These resonances combine and interact to reach the system Q, which usually falls between 0.7 and 1.5, as shown in Fig.7-17. A Q of less than 1 is considered *overdamped,* while a Q of more than 1 is *underdamped.* You'll sometimes hear a loudspeaker described as having subjectively "underdamped bass," which means the bass is full and warm but lacks tightness. Technically, these terms refer to the system's *anechoic response* (the speaker's response in a reflection-free room), specifically whether the response is up or down at the resonant frequency. A "critically damped" system having a Q of 0.5 provides perfect transient response, with no detectable *overhung.* That is, the woofer stops moving the instant the drive signal stops. The higher the Q, the more the woofer rings.

Fig. 7-17
A comparison of system Qs

Courtesy Martin Colloms, *High Performance Loudspeakers*

Subjectively, an underdamped alignment has lots of bass but lacks tightness, has poor pitch definition, and tends to produce "one-note" bass. An overdamped alignment produces a very tight, clean, but decidedly lean bass response. An overdamped loudspeaker has less bass, but that bass is of higher quality than the bass from an underdamped system. Overdamped speakers tend to satisfy intellectually by resolving more detail in the bass, but often lack the bass weight and power that viscerally involve your whole body in the music. Most loudspeaker designers aim for a Q of about 0.7 to reach a compromise between extended bass response (down only 3dB at resonance) and good transient response (very slight overhang). Some designers maintain that a Q of 0.5 is ideal, and that a higher Q produces bass of poorer quality. Mass-market loudspeakers are virtually always underdamped (high Q) so that the unwary will be impressed by the loudspeaker's big bottom end. An example of absurdly high Q is the "boom truck" that produces a big bass impact but fails to resolve pitch, dynamic nuances, or any semblance of musical detail. That boom you hear is the woofer resonating in its enclosure at a specific frequency—the antithesis of what we want in a high-end loudspeaker.

Powered and Servo-Driven Woofers

Loudspeaker designers are increasingly choosing to include a power amplifier within the loudspeaker to drive the woofer cone. In such designs, the external power amplifier is relieved of the burden of driving the woofer, and the loudspeaker designer has more control over how the woofer behaves. For example, equalization can be applied to extend the bass response.

In the most notable and successful example of a powered-woofer system, the Vandersteen Model 5 and 5A, the bass is rolled off by an external crossover before it reaches the loudspeaker, and a complementary boost restores flat response to the signal driving the woofer. This technique eliminates crossover parts (specifically, the large series inductor) between the internal amplifier and the woofer cone, conferring a significant improvement in the amplifier's ability to control woofer motion, which, in my experience, translates to tighter and better-defined bass. This loudspeaker also employs an 11-band equalizer to minimize room-induced frequency-response variations below 120Hz. As you can see, a loudspeaker employing an integral power amplifier has some decided advantages.

Some designers don't try to juggle these laws of physics to produce the most musically satisfying compromise in bass performance; instead, they take brute-force control of woofer movement with the servo-driven woofer. A servo woofer system consists of a woofer with an accelerometer attached to the voice coil, and a dedicated woofer power amplifier. An accelerometer is a device that converts motion into an electrical signal. The accelerometer sends a signal back to the woofer amplifier, telling the woofer amplifier how the woofer cone is moving. The woofer amplifier compares the drive signal to the cone's motion; any difference is a form of distortion. The woofer amplifier can then change the signal driving the woofer so that the woofer cone behaves optimally.

For example, the inertia in a woofer would cause it to continue moving after a bass-drum whack. The woofer servo amplifier would see the cone moving and instantly stop the cone motion. In fact, if you try to gently press in the cone of a servo-driven woofer with the amplifier connected without playing music, you'll find that the cone doesn't move. Because there's no drive signal, the servo amplifier knows the cone shouldn't be moving and locks it in place.

A servo-driven woofer doesn't follow the same rules as a woofer in an enclosure with no servo drive. Instead of rolling off in the bass below the woofer's resonant frequency, a servo-driven woofer can have flat response down to very low frequencies. The woofer's natural rolloff is counteracted by equalization in the servo amplifier that forces the woofer to keep going lower and lower in frequency. The servo amplifier simply pumps more and more current through the woofer's voice coil as the frequency gets lower, which increases the woofer's back-and forth excursion to produce more sound at low frequencies. The lower the frequency, the farther the woofer cone must move back and forth to maintain the same volume.

This puts enormous stress on both the woofer and the servo amplifier. The woofer's voice coil must be able to handle the large amount of current flow, and the woofer cone is susceptible to flexing because it is driven over an area the size of the voice coil—the outside area of the cone may not move exactly in step with the area near the voice coil.

Servo systems therefore must be designed to withstand such rigors. Servo amplifiers are often large and powerful, with huge power transformers and many output transistors. The woofer cone may be made of a trilaminate material that sandwiches a damping compound between two metal diaphragms. This structure ensures that the cone moves as a perfect piston, even when driven hard. Oversized voice coils provide high power handling, and the woofer's structure accommodates high excursion.

A loudspeaker using servo-driven woofers may use many woofers operating together. An array of woofers reduces the contribution each must make to the sound, reducing the demands placed on individual woofers. Not every woofer in such an array will have an accelerometer; one accelerometer may serve four woofers, the servo amplifier assuming that the other three woofers are behaving identically.

Servo-driven woofers are characterized by an unparalleled sense of slam and impact in the bottom end. There's a feeling of suddenness to bass transients that sounds closer to live music. Moreover, the bass stops just as quickly, with no overhang, slowness, or blurring of the music's dynamic structure. Kickdrum has a crispness and punch rather than sounding like a dull thud. I also find that servo-driven woofers have superb rendering of pitch and precise articulation of each note. Servo-driven woofers can also produce deep bass from a small enclosure.

Servo-driven woofer systems are uncommon because they are more expensive than "cones-in-a-box" loudspeakers, and require specialized expertise to get them to work properly. Keep in mind that any loudspeaker system that uses a dedicated woofer amplifier and a separate amplifier to drive the midrange and tweeter enjoys all the advantages conferred by bi-amping, such as greater ability to play loudly without strain.

Enclosure Resonances

A casual acquaintance once tried to impress me with how great his brother's hi-fi system was by describing how water in a glass placed on top of the loudspeaker would splash out when the system played loudly. This person held the mistaken impression that the ability to make the water fly from the glass was an indicator of the system's power and quality.

Ironically, his description told me immediately that this loudspeaker system was of poor quality. That's because low-quality loudspeaker systems have thin, vibration-prone cabinets that color the sound. The more a loudspeaker cabinet vibrates, the worse it is. Any speaker system that will splash water out of a glass *must* sound dreadful. We're about to see why.

When excited by the sound from the driver (primarily the woofer), the enclosure resonates at its natural resonant frequencies. Some of the woofer's back-and-forth motion is imparted to the cabinet. This causes the enclosure panels to move back and forth, producing sound. The enclosure thus becomes an acoustic source: we hear music not only from the drivers, but also from the enclosure.

Enclosure vibrations produce sound over a narrow band of frequencies centered on the panel's resonant frequency. The loudspeaker has greater acoustical output at that frequency. Consequently, cabinet resonances change the timbres of instruments and voices. With a recording of double-bass or piano, you can easily hear cabinet resonances as changes in timbre at certain notes. Some musical instruments exhibit a similar phenomenon, producing "wolf tones."

Enclosure resonances not only color the sound spectrally (changing instrumental timbre), they smear the time relationships in music. The enclosure stores energy and releases that energy slowly over time. When the next note is sounded, the cabinet is still producing energy from the previous note. Loudspeakers with severe cabinet resonances produce smeared, blurred bass instead of a taut, quick, clean, and articulate foundation for the music. Enclosure vibration also affects the midrange by reducing clarity and smearing transient information.

The acoustic output of a vibrating surface such as a loudspeaker enclosure panel is a function of the excursion of the panel and the panel's surface area. Because loudspeaker cabinet panels are relatively large, it doesn't take much back-and-forth motion to produce sound. A large panel excited enough that you can feel it vibrating when you play music will color the sound of that loudspeaker. That's why smaller loudspeakers often sound better than similarly priced but larger loudspeakers; it's much harder (and more expensive) to keep a large cabinet from vibrating.

Cabinet vibration is why the same loudspeaker sounds different when placed on different stands, or with different coupling materials between the speaker and stand. Cones, isolation feet, and other such accessories all cause the speaker cabinet to have a different resonant signature. I noted with interest a paper presented at an Audio Engineering Society convention that explored how much cabinet resonance was audible. Before the researchers could begin the experiment, however, they discovered that the material on which the loudspeaker was resting had an enormous effect on how the cabinet vibrated. For consistency in the experiment, they hung each speaker under test in a rope harness.

Enclosure resonances can be measured and displayed in a way that lets you intuitively see how bad the resonances are, and at what frequency they occur. (This technique is discussed in Chapter 15 under loudspeaker measurements.) An easier way of judging an enclosure's inertness is the "knuckle-rap" test. Simply knock on the enclosure and listen to the resulting sound. An enclosure relatively free of resonances will produce a dull thud; a poorly damped enclosure will generate a hollow, ringing tone. You can also drive the loudspeaker with a swept sinewave (a special test signal found on some test CDs consisting of a pure tone that gradually and continuously increases in frequency) with your hand on the enclosure. When the test signal's frequency momentarily matches the enclosure's resonant frequency, the enclosure will vibrate and you will hear a change in the tone's sound. The less the enclosure vibrates and the fewer the frequencies that cause the enclosure to vibrate, the better.

Designers reduce enclosure resonance by constructing cabinets from thick, vibration-resistant material. Generally, the thicker the material, the better. Most loudspeakers use 3⁄4" Medium Density Fiberboard (MDF). MDF 1" thick is better; some manufacturers use 3⁄4" on the side panels and top, and 1" or 2" MDF for the front baffle, which is more prone to vibration. Exotic materials and construction techniques are also used to combat cabinet resonances. These include making the front baffle from Corian (a synthetic material used in kitchen countertops), or molding a baffle from a mixture of concrete and special polymers. One such baffle weighed more than 100 pounds but was absolutely inert.

Cross-braces inside the enclosure reduce the area of unsupported panels and make the cabinet more rigid. Some braces are called "figure-

8" braces because their four large holes form a figure-8 pattern. These braces are strategically placed for maximum effectiveness. (A heavily braced enclosure is illustrated in Fig.7-18.)

Fig. 7-18 Braces inside the loud-speaker enclosure reduce cabinet vibration and improve the sound.

Courtesy Thiel

The modern trend toward building inert loudspeaker enclosures was started by Wilson Audio in 1986 with the WATT loudspeaker. This small two-way loudspeaker employed lead panels fitted in hollowed-out sections of the cabinet walls. Today's WATT is made from a combination of materials Dave Wilson calls "X" material and "M" material. These materials were developed by Wilson Audio in conjunction with the materials-technology laboratory at Brigham Young University. The goal was to develop a loud-speaker-cabinet material with the ideal properties of low resonance, quick decay of those resonances, and structural rigidity. After experimenting with and measuring 165 different materials, Wilson settled on what he calls X and M materials, both of which are resin-based ceramics. X material contains no wood products, is machined like metal, and according to Wilson, has much better resonance and damping characteristics compared to the medium-density fiberboard (MDF) typically used in loudspeaker cabinets. The top-of-the-line X material has the rigidity of steel and is very heavy—a 3"-thick sheet measuring 2' x 2' weighs 250 pounds. M material is slightly less dense, contains 3% wood products, and is used in less critical applications as well as in midrange enclosures where its properties make it ideal for mounting midrange drivers. (Fig. 7-19 shows a Wilson cabinet under construction. The darker colored panels are made from X material.)

While on a tour of the Wilson factory, I saw dozens of cumulative-spectral decay plots (a measurement that shows the frequency and dura-

Fig. 7-19 A loud-
speaker cabinet
employing differ-
ent exotic materi-
als under con-
struction

Courtesy Wilson Audio Specialties

tion of resonances) for different materials, and M and X were orders of
magnitude better than MDF. Dave Wilson has the luxury of asking the
factory to make identical loudspeakers except for the cabinet material,
and after listening to hundreds of different combinations, can identify
some cabinet materials by their sonic signature.

M and X materials are reportedly as much as fifteen times more
expensive than MDF. Moreover, they take much longer to cut because
they machine more like steel than wood—one side panel for the X-2 loudspeaker takes eight hours to machine. Because the material is so hard, the
cutter must move slowly and be withdrawn periodically to cool.

Much of the improvement in loudspeaker systems over the past 15
years can be attributed to a greater understanding of the importance of
reducing cabinet vibration.

Enclosure Shapes

The enclosure can also degrade a loudspeaker's performance by
creating diffraction from the cabinet edges, grill frame, and even the drivers' mounting bolts. Diffraction is a re-radiation of energy when the
sound encounters a discontinuity in the cabinet, such as at the enclosure
edge. (Diffraction is illustrated conceptually in Fig.7-20) Diffracted energy combines with the direct sound to produce ripples (i.e., colorations)
in the frequency response. Rounded baffles, recessed drivers and mounting bolts, and low-profile grille frames all help to reduce diffraction. The
midrange enclosure shown earlier in Fig.7-14 (B&W's Nautilus technology) is an example of diffraction reduction taken to an extreme.

Some loudspeaker enclosures are tilted back to align the drivers in
time. This tilt aligns the acoustic centers of all the drivers so that their

outputs arrive at the listener at the same time (see Fig.7-21). Fig.7-13, shown earlier, illustrates a time-aligned cabinet, as well as the diffraction-reducing techniques described in the previous paragraph. Although many loudspeaker manufacturers use the words "time-aligned," the term is a trademark owned by loudspeaker designer Ed Long.

Fig. 7-20 Diffraction causes re-radiation of the sound from cabinet edges.

Fig. 7-21 A sloped baffle causes the sound from each driver to reach the listener simultaneously.

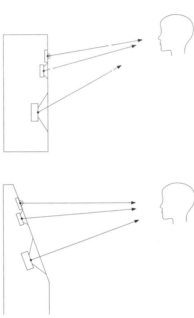

Courtesy Thiel

Crossovers

A loudspeaker crossover is an electronic circuit inside the loudspeaker that separates the frequency spectrum into different ranges and sends each frequency range to the appropriate drive unit: bass to the woofer, midband frequencies to the midrange, and treble to the tweeter (in a three-way loudspeaker). Fig.7-22 illustrates this process.

A crossover is made up of capacitors, inductors, and resistors. These elements selectively filter the full-bandwidth signal driving the loud-

Fig. 7-22 A comparison of crossover slopes

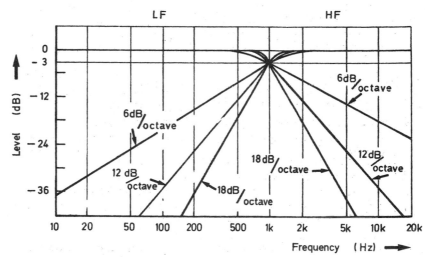

Courtesy Martin Colloms, *High Performance Loudspeakers*

speaker, creating the appropriate filter characteristics for the particular drivers used in the loudspeaker. A crossover is usually mounted on the loudspeaker's inside rear panel.

A crossover is described by its *cutoff frequency* and *slope*. The cutoff frequency is the frequency at which the transition from one drive unit to the next occurs—between the woofer and midrange, for example. The crossover's slope refers to the rolloff's steepness. A slope's steepness describes how rapidly the response is attenuated above or below the cutoff frequency. For example, a *first-order crossover* has a slope of 6dB/octave, meaning that the signal to the drive unit is halved (a reduction of 6dB) one octave above the cutoff frequency. If the woofer crossover circuit produces a cutoff frequency of 1kHz, the signal will be rolled off (attenuated, or reduced in level) by 6dB one octave higher, at 2kHz. In other words, the woofer will receive energy at 2kHz, but that energy will be reduced in level by 6dB. A first-order filter producing a 6dB/octave slope is the slowest and most gentle rolloff used.

The next-steeper filter is the *second-order crossover*, which produces a rolloff of 12dB/octave. Using the preceding example, a woofer crossed over at 1kHz would still receive energy at 2kHz, but that energy would be reduced by 12dB (one quarter the amplitude) at 2kHz. A *third-order crossover* has a slope of 18dB/octave, and a *fourth-order crossover* produces the very steep slope of 24dB/octave. Using the previous example, the fourth-order filter would still pass 2kHz to the woofer, but the amplitude would be down by 24dB (1/16th the amplitude). Fig.7-22 compares crossover slopes.

Typical crossover points for a two-way loudspeaker are between 1kHz and 2.5kHz. A three-way system may have crossover frequencies of 800Hz and 3kHz. The woofer reproduces frequencies up to 800Hz, the midrange driver handles the band between 800Hz and 3kHz, and the tweeter reproduces frequencies above 3kHz.

Note that the actual *acoustic* crossover slope—the drive unit's acoustical output—may be different from the *electrical* slope produced by the crossover. If a drive unit is operated close to its own rolloff frequency, this inherent rolloff is added to the electrical rolloff. For example, a woofer rolling off naturally at 1kHz at 6dB/octave will produce an acoustic rolloff of 12dB/octave when crossed over at 1kHz with an electrical 6dB/octave crossover.

The crossover slope is a major design decision. A shallow first-order slope produces the least phase error in the crossover region between the two drive units. The two drive units operate in-phase at both the cross-over point and outside the crossover region. That is, the sounds produced by the various drivers are in step with each other in time. A fourth-order filter, by contrast, can cause a phase lag between drivers; the individual drivers' output don't occur at exactly the same time. Loudspeakers with second-order crossovers usually have their tweeters wired in inverse polarity to correct for the crossover's phase lag and provide correct acoustic polarity.

Simple first-order crossovers have inherently better time behavior than more complex crossovers. First-order crossovers, however, produce considerable overlap between drive units. There is a relatively wide band over which both the woofer and the midrange driver produce the same frequency, and over which the midrange and tweeter overlap. This can cause dips in the frequency response if the listener's ears aren't exactly the same distance from each drive unit. The outputs of the two drivers can combine, causing destructive interference and irregular amplitude response. The listener should also sit farther away from a loudspeaker with first-order crossovers to give the sounds from the individual drive units more time to integrate.

In addition, first-order crossovers can allow the tweeter to be overdriven by midrange frequencies in the octaves below the nominal cutoff frequency. A tweeter's excursion quadruples with each halving of frequency, moving four times farther at 1kHz than at 2kHz, given the same drive level. At 500Hz its motion quadruples again, if it isn't rolled off by the tweeter's fundamental resonance. Although a 6dB/octave crossover slope halves the drive signal with each halving of frequency, that's not enough to offset the tweeter's natural quadrupling of excursion as the frequency is halved. The result can be reduced power handling by the system as the drivers are driven to their excursion limits at a lower sound-pressure level. A tweeter driven by excessive midband energy can also introduce distortion, which is manifested as a hard and metallic sound. Proponents of high-order crossovers suggest that any phase advantages of first-order slopes are more than offset by the unwanted overlap between drivers, and the concomitant potential for driver overload. A fourth-order crossover provides a sharper delineation between the frequency ranges of each pair of drivers.

A factor in choosing crossover points is the individual drivers' *directivity* —their dispersion of sound with frequency. As the frequency a driver is producing increases, the dispersion pattern becomes narrower. In other words, bass is omnidirectional and high frequencies tend to beam. Driver size and crossover points are chosen so that there is no discontinuity in directivity between drivers. This is why you don't see a 10" woofer mated to a 1" tweeter—the discontinuity between the two drivers' dispersion patterns would be audible.

Some loudspeakers can be connected to a power amp with two runs of loudspeaker cable, a technique called *bi-wiring*. A loudspeaker with provision for bi-wiring has separate high-pass (tweeter) and low-pass (woofer) crossover sections, along with two pairs of input terminals. You should always take advantage of this feature by running two pairs of loudspeaker cables: Bi-wiring can significantly improve a loudspeaker's sound. (Bi-wiring is discussed in more detail in Chapter 11.)

Crossovers vary greatly in the quality of parts used. Budget loudspeakers will likely use *iron-core* inductors rather than the preferable *air-core* types. Air-core inductors are larger and more expensive than iron-core coils, but are immune to a phenomenon called saturation, which introduces distortion. Similarly, lower-cost loudspeakers use *electrolytic* capacitors rather than the more expensive *plastic-film* types. Electrolytic capacitors are sometimes *bypassed* with small-value *polypropylene* or other similar high-quality capacitors. Bypassing is putting a smaller-value, higher-quality capacitor in parallel with the larger-value capacitor. Some of the sonic virtues of high-quality capacitors are retained, accompanied by the cost and size advantages of an electrolytic capacitor. Finally, some loudspeakers are wired internally with high-end cable rather than generic cable.

The Crossoverless Coaxial Driver

Thiel Audio recently introduced a unique driver that combines a dome tweeter within a midrange cone in the same drive unit. Although such "coaxial" loudspeakers aren't new, Thiel's innovation is that the driver requires no electrical crossover. The tweeter's physical mounting serves as a mechanical crossover, keeping midrange frequencies out of the tweeter. Getting rid of the tweeter crossover confers significant advantages in sound quality, and the coaxial alignment perfectly time-aligns the two drivers.

Jim Thiel had long considered such a driver, but doubted that it would work. One Saturday he cobbled one together just to see how much more work would be needed to make it practical—or even if it could work at all. To his surprise, the device worked nearly perfectly. This driver is now used throughout the Thiel loudspeaker line.

Digital Loudspeakers

The capacitors, inductors, and resistors that make up a loudspeaker crossover are far from perfect. Not only do they exhibit variations in value that affect performance, these components split up the frequency spectrum in a relatively crude way. As mentioned, higher-order crossovers produce better division of the frequency spectrum, but their phase response suffers. Moreover, a significant amount of amplifier power is wasted in the crossover.

The widespread availability of digital audio sources provides an opportunity to remove traditional crossovers from the signal path. If we can divide the frequency spectrum digitally—that is, by performing mathematical computations on the audio signal—we can create just about any crossover characteristics we want, with none of the problems of capacitors, inductors, and resistors.

These "digital loudspeakers" accept a digital input signal and implement the crossover in the digital domain with *digital signal-processing* (*DSP*) chips. Instead of subjecting the audio signal to resistors, capacitors, and inductors, DSP crossovers separate the frequency spectrum by performing mathematical processing on the digital audio data. DSP crossovers can have perfect time behavior, any slope and frequency the designer wants without regard for component limitations or tolerances, and employ equalization to the individual drive units.

Fig.7-23 is a side view of a combination pictorial/block diagram of a digital loudspeaker. The speaker accepts a digital input signal from a CD transport, DVD-Audio player, or other digital source. DSP chips inside the speaker split the frequency spectrum into bass, midrange, and treble. These chips can also equalize and delay signals to produce nearly perfect acoustic behavior at the drive units' output. Each of the three digital signals (bass, midrange, treble) is then converted into an analog signal with a digital-to-analog converter (DAC). The DAC output feeds a power amplifier specially designed to power the particular drive unit used in the digital loudspeaker. This aspect of a digital loudspeaker confers a large advantage: the power amplifiers are designed to drive a known load. The power amplifiers amplify an analog signal, just like a conventional power amp, then drive conventional cone loudspeakers. Fig.7-24 shows the electronics board of a commercially available digital loudspeaker.

Digital loudspeakers offer the designer the ability to equalize the signal driving the woofer to achieve deeper bass extension for a given enclosure volume than is possible in a conventional loudspeaker. Earlier in this chapter we saw how a woofer in an enclosure begins rolling off just below its resonant frequency, with the resonant frequency and rolloff slope determined by the loading. In a digital loudspeaker, the signal driving the woofer can be boosted to compensate for this rolloff, extending the low-frequency response. It is possible to achieve amazingly deep bass extension from a moderately sized enclosure with this technique.

Fig. 7-23 A digital loud-speaker incorporates separate digital-to-analog converters and power amplifiers for each driver.

In addition to employing virtually perfect crossovers, digital loud-speakers also simplify your system. You need only a digital source and a pair of loudspeakers for a complete music system. This eliminates monoblock power amplifiers on the floor and long runs of garden-hose speaker cable. Moreover, the digital nature of the system provides for remote control of the loudspeaker. You can adjust the tonal balance, correct for different listening heights, and even delay one loudspeaker if your room doesn't permit symmetrical speaker placement. The digital speaker will also have a volume readout, which makes setting the correct playback level for different music more convenient. When considering the price of digital loudspeakers, keep in mind that you don't need to buy an outboard digital-to-analog converter or power amplifiers.

A digital loudspeaker also "knows" the sound-pressure level the loudspeaker is producing and can add a continuously variable loudness compensation. You may have seen the "loudness" button on some audio products, which engages a circuit that boosts bass and treble at low volumes to compensate for the ear's reduced sensitivity to bass and treble at low volume. (See Appendix A for a complete explanation.) Although loudness compensation is, in theory, a good idea, loudness controls are eschewed by audiophiles because they are crude and are effective at only one precise volume setting. A digital loudspeaker, by contrast, can apply exactly the right amount of loudness compensation at any volume setting. The correct amount of bass and treble boost for a given sound-pressure level is precisely known from decades of psychoacoustic research.

Fig. 7-24 The electronics board inside a digital loudspeaker.

Courtesy Meridian Audio

Another advantage of a loudspeaker under DSP control is the ability to protect the drivers from damage; the DSP knows the driver's limitations and can impose a maximum excursion limit.

Digital loudspeakers were pioneered by Meridian Audio, which has been producing them since 1993. Meridian's first models accepted the 44.1kHz, 16-bit datastream from a CD transport, but newer models have been upgraded to accept high-resolution digital audio with sampling rates up to 192kHz and word lengths up to 24 bits.

Subwoofers

A *subwoofer* is a loudspeaker that produces low frequencies that augment and extend the bass output of a full-range loudspeaker system. The term "subwoofer" is grossly misused to describe any low-frequency driver system enclosed in a separate cabinet. But "subwoofer" actually means "below the woofer," and should be reserved for those products that extend bass response to below 20Hz. A low-frequency driver in an enclosure extending to 40Hz and used with small satellite speakers is more properly called a woofer.

You'll also see full-range speakers with a built-in "subwoofer" powered by its own amplifier. Most of these products actually employ woofers that are simply driven by an integral power amplifier. Such a design relieves your main amplifier of the burden of driving the woofer, but requires that the loudspeakers be plugged into an AC outlet.

Subwoofers come in two varieties: *passive* and *active*. A passive subwoofer is just a woofer or woofers in an enclosure that must be driven by an external amplifier. In one variation of the passive subwoofer, the same stereo amplifier driving the main loudspeakers also powers the subwoofer. In this least desirable method of connecting a subwoofer, the full-range output from a power amp is input to the subwoofer, and a crossover in the subwoofer removes low frequencies from the signal and outputs the filtered signal to the main loudspeakers. This technique puts an additional crossover in the signal path to filter speaker-level signals.

A better way of driving the subwoofer is with an *electronic crossover* and separate power amp. This method separates the bass from the signal driving the main loudspeakers at line level, which is much less harmful to the signal than speaker-level filtering. Moreover, adding a separate power amp for the subwoofer greatly increases the system's dynamic range and frees the main loudspeaker amplifier from the burden of driving the subwoofer. Adding a line-level crossover and power amp turns the passive subwoofer into an active subwoofer, and also makes the system bi-amplified.

A self-contained active subwoofer combines a subwoofer with a line-level crossover and power amp in one cabinet, eliminating the need for separate boxes and amplifiers. Such a subwoofer has line-level inputs (which are fed from the preamplifier), line-level outputs (which drive the power amp), and a volume control for the subwoofer level. The line-level output is filtered to roll off low-frequency energy to the main loud-speakers. This crossover frequency is often adjustable on subwoofers to allow you to select the frequency that provides the best integration with the main loudspeakers (more on this later).

Adding an actively powered subwoofer to your system can greatly increase its dynamic range, bass extension, midrange clarity, and ability to play louder without strain. The additional amplifier power and low-frequency driver allow the system to reproduce musical peaks at higher levels. Moreover, removing low frequencies from the signal driving the main loudspeakers lets the main loudspeakers play louder because they don't have to reproduce low frequencies. The midrange often becomes clearer because the woofer cone isn't furiously moving back and forth trying to reproduce low bass.

Now for the bad news. More often than not, subwoofers degrade a playback system's musical performance. Either the subwoofer is poorly engineered (many are), set up incorrectly, or, as is increasingly common, designed for reproducing explosions in a home-theater system, not resolving musical subtleties.

Let's first look at the theoretical problems of subwoofers. First, most subwoofers—passive or active—add electronics to the signal path. The active subwoofer's internal crossover may not be of the highest quality. Even well-executed crossovers can still degrade the purity of very-high-quality source components, preamplifiers, and power amps. This drawback can be avoided by running the main loudspeakers full-range (no rolloff), but you lose the dynamic advantages and additional midrange clarity con-ferred by keeping low frequencies out of the main loudspeakers.

Second, the subwoofer's bass quality may be poor. The subwoofer may move lots of air and provide deep extension, but a poorly designed subwoofer often adds a booming thumpiness to the low end. Rather than increasing your ability to hear what's going on in the bass, a subwoofer often obscures musical information.

Third, a subwoofer can fail to integrate musically with the main loudspeakers. Very low frequencies reproduced by the subwoofer can sound different from the midbass produced by the main loudspeakers. The result is an extremely distracting discontinuity in the musical fabric. This discontinuity is manifested as a change in the sound of acoustic bass in different registers. Ascending and descending bass lines should flow past the crossover point with no perceptible change in timbre or dynamics.

Another factor that can make integrating a subwoofer difficult is matching a slow and heavy subwoofer to taut, lean, articulate main loud-speakers. Put another way, the sound from an underdamped subwoofer won't integrate very well with that from an overdamped loudspeaker.

Fourth, subwoofers often trade tight control, pitch resolution, and lack of overhang for greater sensitivity or deeper extension. This is par-ticularly true of subwoofers designed for home theater. Consequently, many subwoofers sound bloated, slow, and lacking in detail.

Finally, a subwoofer can fill the listening room with lots of low-frequency energy, exciting room-resonance modes that may not have been that bothersome without the subwoofer. Placement is therefore crucial—you can't just put a subwoofer anywhere and expect musical results. This problem of room-mode excitation can be ameliorated by two subwoofers; they excite different room modes, substantially smoothing out the room's low-frequency response.

All of these problems are exacerbated by most people's tendency to set subwoofer levels way too high. The reasoning is that if you pay good money for something, you want to hear what it does. But if you're *aware* of the subwoofer's presence, either its level is set too high, it isn't positioned correctly, or the subwoofer has been poorly designed. The highest compliment one can pay a subwoofer is that its contribution can't be heard directly. It should blend seamlessly into the musical fabric, not call attention to itself.

It's a rare subwoofer that doesn't degrade the signal driving the main loudspeakers, integrates well with main loudspeakers, has tight and controlled bass, and can improve a playback system. You should therefore approach the purchase of a subwoofer with great caution. I can think of only a few true subwoofers worth owning. Further, most well-engineered, full-range loudspeakers go deep enough in the bass for most listeners. Very little program material requires 16Hz extension; most analog recordings have very little energy below about 30Hz.

Subwoofer Technical Overview

Designers of subwoofers face the same low-frequency loading choices that designers of full-range loudspeakers do. The woofer or woofers can be loaded into an infinite baffle (sealed box), reflex enclosure (ported), or a transmission line. Transmission-line subwoofers are rare because of the large cabinet required for such a design. Instead, the sealed-box and reflex are the most popular. Some subwoofers use servo drive (explained earlier in this chapter on pages 226–228).

The simplest subwoofer is a single driver—usually a 10″ or 12″ unit—in a reflex enclosure. The choice of a reflex design keeps the cabinet at a moderate size and maintains reasonable sensitivity. A larger enclosure extends the subwoofer's bass response, but is more expensive to manufacture, particularly if the enclosure is properly constructed (i.e., well-braced).

The sealed-box subwoofer is less common due to its inherently higher cutoff frequency. A sealed subwoofer would have to be enormous to achieve sub-20Hz extension; most sealed-box units are actually woofers, not subwoofers. They trade extension for higher-quality bass: better control, faster transient response, and excellent pitch definition, for example.

Some small sealed subwoofers can, however, achieve sub-20Hz extension because the signal driving them has been equalized to produce flat response. The equalization applies a boost to the low bass that counteracts the woofer's natural rolloff, producing flat response far below the woofer's natural cutoff frequency. Equalization puts enormous stress on the woofer cone because it forces the woofer to handle a large amount of power and have high excursion at very low frequencies. Consequently, a woofer designed for use in an equalized system will have a large magnet and huge voice coil. If an equalized subwoofer uses a separate, rather than integral, power amplifier and equalization circuit, be aware that the amplifier will work correctly only with the subwoofer for which it was designed. Similarly, a subwoofer designed to be driven by an equalized signal will work correctly only when driven by its matching amplifier.

Some subwoofers are mounted in *bandpass* enclosures that limit the system's bandwidth with both electrical and acoustical filtering. In a bandpass enclosure (see Fig.7-25), the woofer drives a chamber that is vented through a port or slot. The woofer is often loaded in a smaller, rear chamber. This version is called a *second-order* bandpass alignment. Porting the smaller chamber results in a *fourth-order* alignment, producing steeper filter slopes. Advantages of bandpass enclosures include greater low-frequency extension, lower distortion, greater sensitivity, and higher power handling.

Fig. 7-25
A bandpass
enclosure

Subwoofers usually offer a choice of crossover frequencies, typically 80Hz, 120Hz, and 180Hz. A higher crossover frequency would be selected for a minimonitor than for a full-range loudspeaker. Generally, the lower the crossover frequency, the better; the main loudspeaker's bass is probably of higher quality than the subwoofer's, and a low crossover frequency moves any crossover discontinuity lower in frequency, where it will be less audible. In addition, a low crossover frequency ensures that you won't be able to locate the sound source of the low bass. A subwoofer reproducing frequencies above 100Hz can be "localized" — i.e., the location of the source of the bass can be detected—which is musically distracting. A crossover frequency that is too low will, however, burden small loudspeakers with excessive bass and reduce the system's power handling and maximum listening level.

Another variable in subwoofer crossovers is the slope. Most use second-order (12dB/octave) or higher filters. Ideally, the crossover frequency and slope would be tailored to the particular loudspeaker used with the subwoofer. But because the subwoofer manufacturer doesn't know which loudspeakers will be used with the subwoofer, these parameters are compromised for good performance with a variety of loudspeakers.

Some subwoofers have a "delay" control that lets you time-align the subwoofer's wavefront with that of the main loudspeakers. You can accomplish the same thing by moving the subwoofer forward or backward in relation to the main loudspeakers—a much less practical approach than the delay control.

If the subwoofer has a delay control, there's a simple trick for aligning the subwoofer with the main loudspeakers. Drive the system with a pure tone at exactly the crossover frequency. Many test CDs include a full range of test tones. Driving the system with a pure tone at the crossover frequency causes the main loudspeakers and the subwoofer to reproduce the same signal. Now invert the polarity of the main loudspeakers relative to the subwoofer by reversing the red and black leads going to *both* loudspeakers. Sit in the listening chair and have an assistant slowly vary the delay control until you hear the *least* bass. Return the loudspeaker leads to their former (correct) polarity. The delay control is now set optimally. Here's why: When the main loudspeakers' and subwoofer's wavefronts are 180° out of phase with each other, the greatest cancellation (the least sound heard) will occur. That's because as the subwoofer's cone moves outward, the main speakers' cones are moving in, canceling each other. When the loudspeaker leads are returned to the correct position (removing the 180° phase shift), the subwoofer and loudspeaker outputs are maximally in-phase. Any time lag between the main speakers and subwoofer has been eliminated.

When positioning a subwoofer, follow the guidelines on loudspeaker placement outlined in Chapter 4. If the subwoofer is between the loudspeakers, it should be located behind them to avoid interfering with the soundstage created by the main loudspeakers.

Loudspeaker Stands

Small loudspeakers should be mounted on stands for best performance. In fact, the stands' quality can greatly affect the reproduced sound. Flimsy, lightweight stands should be avoided in favor of solid, rigid models. The stands should include spikes on their bottoms to better couple the stand and loudspeaker to the floor. Some loudspeaker stands can be filled with sand or lead shot for mass loading, making them more inert and less prone to vibration. A great loudspeaker on a poor stand will suffer significantly degraded performance. Plan to spend several hundred dollars on stands. When comparing a floorstanding loudspeaker to one requiring stand-mounting, include the cost of the stands in your budgeting.

The interface between loudspeaker and stand also deserves attention. Spikes, cones, and other isolation devices (see Chapter 12) can allow the loudspeaker to perform at its best. In a series of experiments attempting to quantify the effects of different materials installed between stand and loudspeaker, an accelerometer was attached to the loudspeaker's side panel and its vibration measured with the different interface materials. The loudspeaker's resonant "signature" was changed considerably with the stand, and again with the material or device between the stand and loudspeaker. Most effective was a small ball of Bostik Blue-Tak placed at each corner of the speaker stand. This very effective yet inexpensive interface is a sticky, gum-like material available at hardware stores. Best of all, a lifetime supply costs about $2.

When setting up speaker stands, be sure that each of the stands' three or four spikes contacts the floor, and that the stand can't rock back and forth. You can also improve the coupling of the speaker to the stand, and the stand to the floor, by putting a heavy object on top of the speaker. Commercial products, made from lead shot in a canvas bag, are available for this purpose. The bags also help damp enclosure resonances.

8 Digital Source Components

Introduction

Digital source components are any products or combinations of products that play music from a digital medium. A digital front-end can be as simple as a CD player or as complex as a separate CD transport and multi-box digital processor. Other digital source components include SACD players, DVD machines (which also play CDs), DVD machines with DVD-Audio capability, and universal players that support all disc formats. Whatever the configuration, your system's digital front-end is a vital link in the audio reproduction chain, and the source you'll probably spend the most time listening to.

The digital front-end reads information from a digital medium such as a 120mm optical disc and converts that information (which has been stored digitally, i.e., as binary "ones" and "zeros") into an analog signal to drive the rest of your playback system. The digital front-end must not only retrieve the digital data representing the music, but also convert it to analog form. This is a very exacting process. Consequently, the musical differences between digital components can be significant.

When the compact disc was introduced in 1982, many music lovers found its sound inferior to the "crude" technology of vinyl records. CD's marketing slogan, "Perfect Sound Forever," seemed like a cruel joke. But despite the fundamental limitations of CD, its sound quality has steadily improved to the point where it now can be musical and enjoyable.

Nonetheless, CD's days are numbered. The CD format is slowly being replaced by two new formats that deliver high-resolution digital audio to consumers, with significantly better sound quality. One of these formats, DVD-Audio, is an extension of the immensely popular DVD format that has effectively replaced VHS tape as a movie carrier. The second high-resolution format replacing CD is Super Audio Compact

Disc (SACD), invented by Sony and Philips, the two companies that brought us CD.

CD's hegemony as a digital-music carrier has also been challenged by MP3-based machines, at least in the mass market. The Apple iPod is a good example; this handheld device can store hundreds of hours of music on its internal hard-disk drive. Although MP3 may be compelling for its low data-storage requirements (which confer small size, portability, and the ability to share files via the Internet), its inferior sound disqualifies it as a source component for a high-end audio system. I would use an iPod as a portable music carrier, but would never consider putting it at the front end of my hi-fi system.

We'll look at each of these formats in detail. First, let's survey the range of components that make up a digital front-end.

CD Player: A CD player is a self-contained component that plays CDs. The CD player's analog line-level output feeds a line-level input on your preamplifier. Every CD player includes, in the same chassis, a transport mechanism (which spins and reads the CD) and a digital-to-analog converter (or DAC).

Super Audio Compact Disc Player: An SACD player is a self-contained component that will play conventional CDs as well as Super Audio Compact Discs.

DVD-Audio Player: A DVD-Audio machine plays DVD-Audio discs, CDs, and DVD-Video.

Universal Disc Player: A machine that plays all 120mm disc formats, including CD, SACD, DVD-Video, DVD-Audio, CD-R/RW, DVD-R/RW, MP3, Video CD, and Super Video CD.

Digital Audio Server: A device that stores digital audio on hard-disk drives, and organizes a music collection for immediate access.

Digital-to-Analog Converter: Also called a "digital processor" or "D/A converter" or "DAC," the digital-to-analog converter is a component that receives digital audio data and converts it to an analog signal. The digital processor has a digital input and analog output, the latter feeding one of your preamplifier's line-level inputs.

CD Transport: The CD transport reads the digitally encoded information from a CD and sends it to the D/A converter for conversion to analog. Unlike a CD player, a transport has no D/A converter built into it. CD transports are becoming increasingly rare; the recent trend has been toward multifunction players such as CD/DVD/SACD that also provide a digital output.

Digital Output: A jack on all CD, DVD, and SACD players that provides access to the digital datastream. A digital output allows a player to send digital data to a separate digital processor or digital controller (see Chapter 13 for an explanation of digital controllers).

S/PDIF Interface: S/PDIF stands for "Sony/Philips Digital Interface Format," after the two companies that invented the compact disc. The S/PDIF interface is a standard format for transmitting digital audio, primarily between a CD transport or DVD player and digital processor. The S/PDIF signal can be transmitted via a variety of interface types, such as optical or coaxial (described in detail later in this chapter). All consumer digital audio products—transports, digital processors, and digital recorders—use the S/PDIF interface. A professional version of S/PDIF, called AES/EBU (Audio Engineering Society/European Broadcast Union), is sometimes included in consumer digital audio products.

How to Choose a Digital Source

Since its introduction in 1982, CD playback technology has advanced more rapidly than any other field of audio. The sound quality of the first CD players was a far cry from the musical performance available from today's high-end CD players, or even today's budget machines. The musical and technical performance of current state-of-the-art transports and digital processors was unthinkable to the designers of first-generation CD players.

As much as CD sound has improved, technological advances have rendered it virtually obsolete. The primary technological advance is in the storage capacity of optical discs; today's CD-size discs can store 25 times more information than can a CD. This additional data capacity can be used to store more information about the musical signal, resulting in better sound quality, as well as opening the possibility for multichannel music.

This rapidly changing technology can make choosing a digital front-end more difficult than selecting other components. Should you make a significant financial investment in CD-playback equipment to enjoy the best of today's technology, or begin investing in one of the high-resolution formats? As compelling as the new formats are, there simply isn't nearly as wide a selection of music titles available, meaning that high-quality CD playback is a requirement for a high-end audio system. Still, though CD will be with us for a long time to come (many of us have huge collections), its days are numbered.

Although the digital source is an important factor in the system's overall sound quality, digital components continually improve in musical performance. The audiophile is thus faced with the choice of spending a significant amount of money on playback components that are likely to be bettered in a year (and at a lower price), or spend very little now and wait until the products have more fully evolved. Of all the components that make up a high-end system, the digital front-end is the most likely to be left behind by technology's inexorable progress.

What to Listen For

Perhaps more than any other components, digital sources come in the most "flavors." That is, their sonic and musical characteristics vary greatly between brands and models. This variability has its drawbacks ("Which one is *right*?"), but also offers the music lover the chance to select one that best complements her playback system's characteristics and suits her musical tastes. The different types of musical presentations heard in CD players, SACD machines, DVD-A players, transports, and digital processors tend to reflect their designers' musical priorities. If the designer's parts budget—or skill—is limited, certain areas of musical reproduction will be poorer than others. The trick is to find the processor that, *in the context of your system*, excels in the areas you find most important musically.

Selecting a digital source specifically tailored for the rest of your playback system can sometimes ameliorate some of the playback system's shortcomings. For example, don't choose a bright-sounding digital processor for a system that is already on the bright side of reality. Instead, you may want to select a processor whose main attribute is a smooth, unfatiguing treble. Each digital product has its particular strengths and weaknesses. Only by careful auditioning—preferably in your own system—can you choose the product best for you.

To illustrate this, I've invented two hypothetical listeners—each with different systems and tastes—and two hypothetical digital processors. I've used a digital processor in the example, but CD transports, CD players, SACD, or DVD-A machines could be easily substituted. Although the following discussion could apply to all audio components, it is particularly true of digital components. Not only are there wide variations in sonic characteristics between processors, but a poor-sounding digital processor at the front-end of a superb system will ruin the overall performance.

Listener A likes classical music, particularly early music, Baroque, and choral performances. She rarely listens to full-scale orchestral works, and never plays rock, jazz, or pop. Her system uses inexpensive solid-state electronics and somewhat bright loudspeakers; the combination gives her a detailed, forward, and somewhat aggressive treble.

Listener B wouldn't know a cello from a clarinet, preferring instead electric blues, rock, and pop. He likes to feel the power of a kickdrum and bass guitar working together to drive the rhythm. His system is a little soft in the treble, and not as dynamic as he'd like.

Now, let's look at the sonic differences between two inexpensive and similarly priced digital processors and see how each would—or wouldn't—fit in the two systems.

Processor #1 has terrific bass: tight, deep, driving, and rhythmically exciting. Unfortunately, its treble is a little etched, grainy, and overly prominent. Processor #2's best characteristics are its sweet, silky-smooth treble. The processor has a complete lack of hardness, grain, etch, and fatigue. Its weakness, however, is a soft bass and limited dynamics. It doesn't have a driving punch and dynamic impact on drums compared to Processor #1.

I think you can guess which processor would be best for each system and listener. Processor #1 would only exacerbate the brightness Listener A's system already has. Moreover, the additional grain would be more objectionable on violins and voices. Processor #2, however, would tend to soften the treble presentation in Listener A's system, providing much-needed relief from its relentless treble. Moreover, the sonic qualities of Processor #1—dynamics and tight bass—are less important musically to Listener A.

Conversely, Listener B would be better off with Processor #1. Not only would Processor #1's better dynamics and tighter bass better serve the kind of music Listener B prefers, but his system could use a little more sparkle in the treble and punch in the bass.

Which processor is "better"? Ask Listener A after she's auditioned both products in her system; she'll think Processor #2 is greatly superior, and wonder how anyone could like Processor #1. But Listener B will find her choice lacking rhythmic power, treble detail, and dynamic impact. To him, there's no comparison: Processor #1 is the better product.

Though exaggerated for clarity, this example shows how personal taste, musical preference, and system matching can greatly influence which digital products are best for you. The only way to make the right purchasing decision is to *audition the products for yourself*. Use product reviews in magazines to narrow your choice of what to audition. Read reviewers' descriptions of a particular product and see if the type of sonic presentation described is what you're looking for. But don't buy a product solely on the basis of a product review—a reviewer's system and musical tastes may be very different from yours. You could be Listener A and be reading a review written by someone with Listener B's system and tastes.

Use reviews as guides in pointing you to products you might want to audition yourself, not as absolute truth. You're going to spend many hours with your decision, so listen carefully before you buy—it's well worth the investment in time. Moreover, the more products you evaluate and the more careful your listening, the sharper your listening skills will become.

It's important to realize that the specific sonic signatures described in the example are much more pronounced at lower price levels. Two "perfect" digital processors would sound identical. At the very highest levels of digital playback, the sonic tradeoffs are much less acute—the best products have very few shortcomings, making them ideal for all types of music.

Still, a significant factor in how good any processor or CD player sounds is the designer's technical skill and musical sensitivity. Given the same parts, two designers of different talents will produce two very dif-ferent-sounding products. Consequently, it's possible to find skillfully designed but inexpensive products that outperform more expensive products from less talented designers.

Higher-priced products are not necessarily better. Don't get stuck in a specific budget and audition products only within a narrow price range. If an inexpensive product has received a rave review from a reviewer you've grown to trust, and the sonic description matches your taste, audition it—you could save yourself a lot of money. If you decide not to buy the product, at least you've added to your listening database, and can compare your impressions with those of the reviewer.

In addition to determining which digital products let you enjoy music more, there are specific sonic attributes you should listen for that contribute to a good-sounding digital front-end. How high a priority you place on each of these characteristics is a matter of personal taste.

In the following sections, I've outlined the musical and sonic qualities I look for in digital playback.

The first quality I listen for in characterizing how a digital component sounds is its overall perspective. Is it laid-back, smooth, and unaggressive? Or is it forward, bright, and "in my face"? Does the product make me want to "lean into" the music and "open my ears" wider to hear the music's subtlety? Or do my ears tense up and try to shut out some of the sound? Am I relaxed or agitated?

A digital product's overall perspective is a fundamental characteristic that defines that product's ability to provide long-term musical satisfaction. If you feel assaulted by the music, you'll tend to listen less often and for shorter sessions. If the product's fundamental musical perspective is flawed, it doesn't matter what else it does right.

Key words in product reviews that describe an easy-to-listen-to digital product include *ease, smooth, laid-back, sweet, polite,* and *unaggressive.* Descriptions of *bright, vivid, etched, forward, aggressive, analytical, immediate,* and *incisive* all point toward the opposite type of presentation.

There is a fundamental conflict between these extremes of presentation. Processors that are smooth, laid-back, and polite may not actively offend, but they often lack detail and resolution. An absence of aggressiveness is often achieved at the expense of obscuring low-level musical information. This missing musical information could be the inner detail in an instrument's timbre that makes the instrument sound more lifelike. It could be the sharp transient attack of percussion instruments; a slight rounding of the attack gives the impression of smoothness but doesn't accurately convey the sound's dynamic structure. Consequently, very smooth-sounding digital products often have lower resolution than more forward ones.

The other extreme is the digital product that is "ruthlessly revealing" of the music's every detail. Rather than smoothing transients, these products hype them. In a side-by-side comparison, a ruthlessly revealing product will appear to present much more detail and musical information. It will sound more upbeat and exciting, and will appeal to some listeners. Such a presentation, however, quickly becomes fatiguing. The listener feels a sense of relief when the music is turned down—or off. The worst thing a product can do is make you want to turn down the volume, or stop listening altogether.

This conflict between lacking detail and over-emphasizing it can be resolved by buying a higher-quality (and often correspondingly higher-priced) processor. I've found a few models that can present all the music, yet are completely unaggressive and un-fatiguing. This is a rare virtue, and one that I find musically important. The digital front-end must walk a fine line between resolving real musical information and sounding etched and analytical.

Digital reproduction also has a tendency to homogenize individual instruments within the soundstage. This tendency to blur the distinctions between individual instruments occurs on two levels: the instruments' unique timbral signatures and specific locations within the soundstage.

On the first level, digital products can overlay music with a common synthetic character that diffuses the unique textures of different instruments and buries the subtle tonal differences between them—the music sounds as if it is being played by one big instrument rather than many individual ones. Instead of separate and distinct objects (instruments and voices) hanging in three-dimensional space, the listener hears a synthetic continuum of sound. There is a "sameness" to instrumental textures that prevents their individual characteristics from being heard.

The second way in which digital playback can diffuse the separateness of individual instruments is by presenting images as flat "cardboard cutouts" pasted on top of each other. The instruments aren't surrounded by an envelope of air and space, the soundstage is flat and congested, and you can't clearly hear where one image ends and the next begins. Good digital playback should present a collection of individual images hanging in three-dimensional space, with the unique tonal colors of each instrument intact and a sense of space and air between the instrumental images. This is easy for analog to accomplish, but quite difficult for digital. A recording with excellent portrayal of timbre and space will help you identify which digital products preserve these characteristics.

Another important quality in digital playback is soundstage transparency. This is the impression that the space in which the music is presented is crystal-clear, open, and transparent. (The opposite of this is thick, congested, and opaque.) Soundstage transparency is analogous to looking at a city skyline on a perfectly clear day: Just as smog or haze will reduce the buildings' immediacy, vibrancy, and visible detail, so too will soundstage opacity detract from the musical presentation.

I've focused on these aspects of the sonic presentation for evaluating digital products because they are the most common flaws in digitally reproduced music. You should also listen for other aspects—treble grain, rhythm, dynamics—described in Chapter 3.

Beyond these specifics, a good question to ask yourself is, "How long can I listen without wanting to turn the music down—or off?"

Conversely, the desire—or even compulsion—to bring out CD after CD is the sign of a good digital front-end. Some components just won't let you turn off your system; others make you want to do something else.

This ability to musically engage the listener is the essence of high-end audio. It should be the highest criterion when judging digital front-ends.

State-of-the-Art CD Playback: Dedicated CD Players and Separate Transports and Processors

If you want the very best in CD playback, you'll probably choose a high-end CD player or separate CD transport and digital processor rather than listen to the CD-player section of a DVD-A, SACD, or universal player. If your budget is less than about $5000 the dedicated CD player will probably give you better performance for your money than a separate transport and processor. The reason is two-fold: 1) By combining the transport and processor in one chassis, with one power supply, one front panel, one shipping carton, and one AC cord, the manufacturer can put more of the manufacturing budget into better sound; and 2) A CD player has no need of a sonically degrading digital interface (cable) between its transport and processor, which means that it might have better sound. (The interface's detrimental effect on musical performance is described later in this chapter.) In addition, the soft economic climate in the first few years of the millennium has driven manufacturers to focus on building good-sounding CD players that sell for under $3000. Consequently, there are many excellent models from which to choose.

A CD player also makes your life much simpler than owning separates. Rather than requiring two chassis in your rack, two power cords, and a digital interconnect, the CD player lets you focus on the music rather than on the equipment.

Many excellent CD players are available for under $1000, including some legitimate "high-end" machines that sell for as little as $300. This is, however, the lower limit of true high-end CD players. Below this level you enter the realm of mass-market products designed for maximum features and minimum manufacturing cost, not musical performance. You should also avoid multi-disc players; most manufacturers cut corners in sound quality to cover the extra expense of the disc-changing mechanism. The single-disc player will provide better sound quality for the same price, and also better ultimate fidelity—single-disc transport mechanisms can be made better than carousel-type changers. If, however, you're set on a changer, consider using it as a transport to feed a high-quality outboard D/A converter. A few CD changers can be called high-end, but they are rare.

If you opt for a CD player, look for one that has a coaxial digital output on an RCA jack. This will let you use the CD player as a transport if you upgrade to a separate digital processor in the future. Notice that I said a *coaxial* digital output on an RCA jack. Nearly all recently made mass-market CD players use a much inferior optical connector called *TosLink.* If you drive an outboard digital processor with TosLink, you won't be getting the sound you paid for. Insist on a CD player with a coaxial digital output. That way, you can be assured of a clear upgrade path in the future.

Until recently I would have recommended without qualification that those with more ambitious digital budgets consider separate transports and digital processors. Indeed, until just a few years ago, separates were essential to realizing first-rate sound quality, offering several advantages over one-box CD players. First, they allow you to upgrade the transport and the processor independently. Second, putting the sensitive D/A conversion electronics in a separate chassis from the mechanical transport lowers the chance of polluting the analog signal with digital noise. Third, the cutting-edge design work took place in separates, not CD players.

Those arguments, however, are less compelling in light of what's been happening in CD-player design recently. Designers are now applying the same level of parts and design quality to CD players once reserved for separates. These premium parts and techniques include large and well-regulated power supplies, high-quality DAC (digital-to-analog converter) chips, and the designer's best analog circuits. Moreover, many innovative design techniques are starting to appear first in CD players. The CD player is no longer automatically the entry-level product in the digital manufacturer's line, instead it's become worthy of the manufacturer's best efforts.

As for the assertion that transport noise can get into a one-box CD player's analog stage and degrade the sound, designers have recently found ways of better isolating its transport and D/A-conversion sections. While a one-box unit will never have the signal isolation of two-chassis separates, the CD player more than makes up for its reduced isolation with one large advantage it holds over separates: reduced jitter.

Jitter describes timing inaccuracies in the digital-to-analog conversion process that degrade sound quality. A "clock" in the digital processor controls *when* the digital samples that represent the music are converted to analog. If this clock isn't perfectly precise, sound quality is degraded. Specifically, the treble gets harder, the soundstage shrinks, and the music takes on a somewhat synthetic character.

Think of the bass drum in a marching band as a D/A-converter clock, and of the band members as the digital samples representing the music. Each row of musicians is one audio sample. On each drum beat, the musicians take one step forward in unison. Now consider what would happen if the drummer started to get sloppy, leaving too much time between some beats and not enough time between others. Without a precise timing reference, the distance between each row of musicians would no longer be uniform.

In digital audio reproduction, each clock pulse triggers the conversion of a digital sample to analog form. If these clock pulses aren't perfectly uniform—the very definition of jitter—we hear the timing imprecision as reduced musicality. Jitter causes the samples representing the music to be put back together with slightly staggered spacing, creating distortion in the audio waveform. Just as the marching-band musicians can't step together if the drummer isn't perfectly precise, digital audio samples can't be correctly reconstructed into music if the clock is jittered. To give you an idea of how precise the clock must be, timing errors of as little as 10 picoseconds (0.00000000001 second)—about the time it takes light to travel a tenth of an inch—are nonetheless audible. (A more technical explanation of clock jitter appears in Appendix C.)

One of the main sources of jitter is the digital interface that connects a CD transport to a digital processor. Because the interface carries the digital audio data and a clock in the same cable, jitter can be introduced. By eliminating the interface, CD players have potentially lower jitter than separates.

Today's CD players also offer more features, such as volume control (so that they can drive a power amplifier directly) and digital inputs (for decoding other digital sources). Some CD players even include line-level inputs and source switching, obviating the need for a separate preamplifier.

For the few manufacturers who have overcome the jitter problem (using techniques described later in this chapter), the state of the art in digital replay is still largely the domain of separates. With greater physical separation of the transport mechanism and digital-to-analog conversion electronics, separates still have an advantage over CD players. Moreover, the separates designer has more space in which to work, space that can contain more extensive power supplies and optimum layout of the internal components.

If you do decide on separates, you must allocate your digital front-end budget to a transport, processor, and digital interconnect. A good strategy for top-quality digital playback is to use an SACD, DVD-A, or universal player for playback of high-resolution formats, feeding the player's analog outputs to your preamp, but when playing conventional CDs, use the high-res machine as a CD transport only, feeding its digital output to an external digital processor. (I use the term "CD transport" in the following discussion to refer to any digital source component—SACD, DVD-A, universal player, or dedicated CD-only transport—that recovers information from a CD and outputs a digital datastream.) In the past you'd probably have gotten the best CD performance from a dedicated CD-only transport, but that situation is changing as high-resolution players get better.

When shopping for a digital front-end, remember that technical performance is secondary to sound quality. Manufacturers will often tout their products on the basis of some technical innovation, or because it uses the latest parts. Although interesting, such descriptions don't tell you how the product *sounds*. Many technical factors influence a component's musical performance; which parts it uses are only some of these. Don't buy a product just because it uses a particular DAC or digital filter—many digital processors with excellent parts pedigrees just don't measure up in the listening room. Listen to the product and decide for yourself if it sounds good. Just as you wouldn't consider buying an amplifier based on how little THD it has, so you shouldn't choose a digital component because it features parts used successfully in highly regarded products.

Another claim you should consider with suspicion is a processor's clock-jitter specification. Some manufacturers make unverifiable jitter claims, sometimes even picking a jitter number out of the air. Not only are there no standards for jitter specifications, but jitter is very difficult to measure—conditions that led to the current confusion in the marketplace. When shopping for digital components, forget the marketing hype—just listen.

Why 44.1kHz Sampling and 16-bit Quantization Aren't Enough

As explained in Appendix C, the Nyquist Theorem tells us that the sampling frequency must be at least twice as high as the highest audio frequency we want to encode. CD's 44.1kHz was chosen because 44.1kHz is slightly higher than twice 20kHz, the highest frequency humans can reportedly hear. (But why such an odd number? Early digital recorders were based on video formats such as ¾" U-Matic tape, and 44.1kHz sampling happened to fit mathematically with the 30 frame-per-second rate of black and white video. The sampling frequency of 44.056kHz, used in Sony's F1 format, relates mathematically to color video's frame rate of 29.97fps.)

So if humans can hear only up to 20kHz, and CD's sampling rate of 44.1kHz perfectly preserve a 20kHz sine wave, why does 96kHz sampling sound more open and transparent, and deliver greater transient detail?

When high sampling rates became available in professional recorders in the mid-to-late 1990s, a debate raged over whether the sonic improvements were attributable to the preservation and reproduction of information higher in frequency than 20kHz, or some other factor. That "other factor" turned out to be the relaxation in digital-filter requirements for higher sampling rates.

The digital filter in a CD player or digital processor removes all energy above half the sampling frequency. Unfortunately, digital filters introduce distortion in the time domain by smearing transients. Think of a snare drum that starts and stops very suddenly. Digital filters take some of that sudden energy and spread it out over time. Oddly, this *energy-smearing* occurs not just *after* the transient musical signal, but *before* it as well. Such distortion is also called *ringing* because the filter "rings" like a bell when "struck" by the music signal. The steeper the filter, the longer the time period before and after the signal the energy is smeared. In addition, steep filters introduce phase shift and amplitude-response ripples in the passband. The result is loss of definition, detail, and transparency, along with a collapse of the sense of space. (The range of frequencies passed by the digital filter is called the *passband*. The frequency range stopped by the digital filter is called the *stopband*. The frequency range between the passband and the stopband is called the *transition band*.)

The problems caused by steep digital filters right next to the audio passband are exacerbated by the sometimes low quality of the filter. It's possible to design filters that reduce these problems by employing greater mathematical precision, but they are too costly to implement except in the most expensive products. And because high-end companies are often reliant on mass-market semiconductor manufacturers for their digital filters, even expensive digital components don't always include high-performance digital filters.

The steeper (more rapid) the filter's rolloff, the greater the ringing and energy-smear. Digital filters used in decoding 44.1kHz audio are steep indeed; they must pass the entire audioband up to 20kHz, yet attenuate the signal by a whopping 120dB at 22.05kHz (half the sampling frequency). For comparison, analog filters used in loudspeaker crossovers are much more gradual, attenuating the signal by about 12dB over a full octave.

A filter designed for a 96kHz-sampled system, however, can begin attenuating at a much higher frequency, and have a far gentler slope. The stopband for such a filter begins at 48kHz; the transition band is much wider; and the frequency at which the filter begins attenuating can be moved higher, away from the audio passband. The result is less distortion (amplitude-response ripple, phase shift, and energy-smearing) within the audio passband, and thus improved sound quality. For an academic treatise on this subject, see "A Suggested Explanation for (some of) the Audible Differences Between High-Sample Rate and Conventional Sample Rate Audio Material" by Mike Story of Data Conversion Systems (dCS) at www. dcsltd.co.uk/papers.htm.

Although the relaxation of digital filter requirements is certainly a factor in 96kHz's improved sound quality, some respected researchers also suggest that even though we can't hear sine waves above 20kHz, we can nevertheless perceive the greater steepness—that is, speed—of transient musical information that an ultra-wideband digital audio system provides. The wider the bandwidth of a system, the faster the events (sudden changes in amplitude) it can preserve.

Consider a subwoofer, a very low-bandwidth device, reproducing the sound of a triangle. The subwoofer removes only the very-fast-changing components of the signal (the steep transient of the attack), but reproduces the rest of the signal. Similarly, a 20kHz-bandwidth audio system filters out the steepest transients of musical signals, perhaps introducing a kind of distortion. Some believe that the steeper transients allowed by a wide-bandwidth digital audio system improve the sense of space because the ear/brain uses transient information in localizing sound sources.

Although the causes of the superior sound quality delivered by increasing the sampling rate are debatable, the benefits of the increase in word length from 16 to 18, 20, and even 24 bits are not in dispute. As I mentioned earlier, word length is the number of bits used to encode the audio signal's amplitude at each sample. Assigning a number—called a word—to represent the audio signal's amplitude is called *quantization*. The word length determines the system's resolution, dynamic range, distortion, and signal-to-noise ratio. We also call the word length *resolution*, as in the phrase "20-bit resolution." The greater the number of bits per word, the higher the resolution.

Think of a digital clock with only two digits; we could discern only between the hours, with no resolution of minutes. If we add a third digit, we can know the time with ten-minute precision (an error of plus or minus five minutes). Adding a fourth digit allows us to know the time with one-minute accuracy. A fifth digit to indicate tens of seconds further increases the clock's precision. Similarly, the more bits in a digital-audio word, the finer the precision with which we can encode the audio signal's amplitude.

The CD format uses 16-bit quantization, which provides 98dB of dynamic range. Although this number may sound high in theory, it's not enough in practice. Consider an engineer setting the recording levels for a symphony recording. He must adjust the signal driving the analog-to-digital converter so that at the end of the fourth movement when everyone is playing full-bore, the levels never exceed full-scale digital—the maximum amplitude that can be encoded. At full-scale, all 16 bits are used. Now think about a quiet flute passage in the slow movement; the low signal level is encoded with perhaps four or five bits, which offers very low resolution. And if the recording engineer leaves 6dB of "headroom" to account for unexpectedly loud peaks, he's effectively throwing away one full bit of resolution.

Thus the resolution of a digital audio signal isn't defined by the maximum number of bits available, but by the number of bits being used at any given moment. The lower the signal level, the lower the precision with which the signal is encoded.

The advent of 20- and 24-bit digital audio not only expands the dynamic range, but also increases the resolution of low-level detail. This low-level detail can be fine nuances of an instrument's timbre, which enhance the sense of realism. It can also be subtle spatial cues such as discrete acoustic reflections and reverberation decay, which the ear interprets as a more convincing soundstage.

Longer word lengths also contribute to better sound because the post-processing common in the recording or mastering studio (mixing, equalization, signal processing) is performed with much greater mathematical precision. Moreover, noise added by these processes is spread out over a wider bandwidth, which makes the noise less audible.

The combination of higher sampling rate and longer word length results in greatly improved sound quality. Note, however, that true 20-bit resolution in a digital audio system represents the absolute state-of-the-art. Very few of us have heard real 20-bit resolution, never mind 24-bit. Although DVD-Audio can store 24 bits of information, and some digital-to-analog converters have 24 "rungs" in their resistor ladders, those last four bits do not have sufficient precision to encode musical information. This is a limitation of the analog-to-digital and digital-to-analog converters. The last four bits in a 24-bit digital-to-analog converter are sometimes cynically referred to as "marketing bits" because consumers assume that 24 bits are better than 20.

High-Resolution Digital Audio: SACD and DVD-Audio

The compact disc format is limited in musical performance by its sampling rate of 44.1kHz and 16-bit quantization. When an audio signal is converted to digital for release on CD, the analog-to-digital converter "samples" (looks at) the audio waveform 44,100 times each second, in a process called *sampling*. The converter assigns a number to each sample; this number represents the waveform's amplitude at the sample point, a process called *quantization*. The CD format uses 16-bit quantization, meaning that each sample's amplitude is represented by a 16-bit binary (ones and zeros) number.

Sampling and quantization are the cornerstones of digital audio; sampling preserves the time information in an audio signal, quantization preserves the amplitude information. The faster the sampling rate, the wider the range of audio frequencies that can be preserved. The more bits in the quantization "word," the greater the dynamic range, the lower the noise, and the greater the resolution. These fundamentals of digital audio are described in much greater detail (with graphics) in Appendix C.

When the compact disc was developed in the late 1970s, 44.1kHz sampling and 16-bit quantization were chosen to achieve 74 minutes of playing time on a 120mm disc. The D/A converters of the day were limited to 14-bit resolution. Some argued at the time that a sampling rate of 32kHz with 14-bit quantization were sufficient for CD, but fortunately, the standard was established at 44.1kHz and 16 bits. These specifications are, however, not sufficient to encode all the musical information humans can hear. Nonetheless, the compact disc has been a massive commercial success, with more than one billion players sold.

Technological advances have greatly expanded the storage capacity of the 120mm optical disc. In 1995, Sony and Philips, inventors of the CD, proposed Multi-Media CD, which could store about four times the data of a conventional CD. Simultaneously, Toshiba and Time-Warner proposed Super Density (SD) disc, based on similar technology. These new discs could hold a full-length movie with digital surround sound, or a huge amount of computer data. But the two formats were incompatible.

The stage was set for a format war between the competing proposals. Fortunately, the two sides reached an agreement on a single format that came to be known as *DVD,* and which embodied aspects of each camp's proposal. Though a DVD is the same size as a CD, it has in its maximum configuration 25 times the storage capacity.

If we don't care about video, we can exploit DVD's huge storage capacity to encode digital audio with much higher resolution than was possible on CD. The recording industry's three major trade associations formed a group called the International Steering Committee to explore this possibility, and to standardize a new high-quality digital-audio carrier. The three trade associations were the Recording Industry Association of America (RIAA), the Recording Industry Association of Japan (RIAJ), and Europe's International Federation of Phonographic Industry (IFPI).

The International Steering Committee issued 15 requirements for the new format, including improved sound quality, multichannel sound, and some form of copy protection. Another ISC requirement was that the new disc be backward-compatible with existing CD players (i.e., the disc must play in CD players as well as in high-resolution players). This last provision makes possible a single inventory of music titles for record labels and retailers—retailers needn't stock two versions of the same title. The technical details for the new format were to be decided by a group of hardware representatives, called Working Group 4 (WG4).

Unfortunately, the WG4 immediately became politicized, with each member representing his or her company's economic interests, not the interests of high-quality music or even consumers. For example, the consortium that holds many of the patents on DVD wanted the new disc to be based on DVD technology. That way, they would receive royalties on every DVD sold. Sony and Philips argued that the new carrier should be an extension of the compact disc—a technology they developed and on which they would continue to receive royalties. (Although Sony and Philips also hold several key DVD patents.)

To give you an idea of how economic considerations take precedence over what should be engineering decisions, consider why 96kHz sampling is proposed by the DVD proponents. It would be much easier for everyone—and better-sounding for the music lover—if the sampling rate were 88.2kHz, exactly double the CD's sampling rate. Professional recorders would operate at 88.2kHz, with these master recordings converted to 44.1kHz for most consumers who don't have high-resolution players. Converting 88.2kHz to 44.1kHz is very simple, and the filtering involved only moderately degrades sound quality. A 44.1kHz version is necessary because most consumers will listen to conventional CD with 44.1kHz sampling for many years. But conversion from 96kHz to 44.1kHz involves enormous (and expensive) mathematical processing that audibly degrades the sound. In fact, the calculations are so intensive that 96kHz must first be converted to 48kHz in one step, then from 48kHz to 44.1kHz in a second step.

So why would anyone propose 96kHz sampling? Because the DVD-Video proponents wanted to distinguish DVD from CD, and chose sampling frequencies of 48kHz and 96kHz for the new video format. It's shameful that millions of music listeners may listen to needlessly degraded sound quality because corporate suits, not engineers, ultimately determine a format's specifications.

Through Working Group 4, Sony and Philips proposed a new disc, called the *Super Audio CD (SACD)*, that met the ISC's requirements, but their offer was rejected by other committee members who had business interests in seeing DVD as the next audio carrier. Super Audio CD provides 74 minutes of high-quality digital audio in 2-channel and 6-channel modes. SACD also offers the possibility (but not the requirement) of a "hybrid" disc containing two layers on the same disc for backward compatibility with CD. One layer contains conventional 16-bit/44.1kHz audio and the second layer holds the high resolution multichannel version. After more months of wrangling with no resolution in sight, Sony and Philips announced that they would introduce the Super Audio CD format on their own, without the consensus of WG4.

About the same time, audiophile record labels began releasing high-resolution music recordings by taking advantage of a provision of the DVD-Video specification that allows the disc to hold two channels of audio sampled at 96kHz with 24-bit quantization. This format, called Digital Audio Disc (DAD), was a stopgap measure until the full DVD-Audio specification could be agreed upon and finalized. This format is now essentially dead, although those who bought DAD discs can still play them in DVD players.

That DVD-A specification was finalized in 2001, and record companies began releasing titles in the format.

Note that DVD-A and SACD are not compatible with each other, although "universal" players will play CD, DVD-Audio, SACD, and other 120mm disc formats such as CD-R/RW, DVD-R/RW, MP3, Video CD and Super Video CD. (More on universal players later.)

From a marketing perspective, a new audio format is a much tougher sell to the general public than was CD. The average Joe instantly saw the advantages of a wear-free 120mm disc over his aging 12" LP collection. CD was an easy sale because it represented a wholesale improvement in convenience, and promised superior sound quality (a promise which CD did not always live up to). A high-resolution audio format is a different matter. To the average consumer, who thinks CDs are the ultimate in fidelity, a new audio format may be considered superfluous. That's one of the reasons both SACD and DVD-Audio include multichannel audio. Surround sound is easier to demonstrate and sell than higher-quality 2-channel audio.

With that history, let's look at the two formats that are replacing the compact disc.

Super Audio Compact Disc (SACD)

Sony and Philips, co-inventors of the CD, officially launched SACD in September of 1999 with the SCD-1, a $5000 "statement" product designed to showcase the format's potential. The SCD-1 was a 2-channel machine; later models featured multichannel SACD play-back. Since the launch, SACD player prices have steadily declined to the point that many machines are priced below $200. Sony has also helped the format gain a foothold by including SACD playback in its entire DVD-player line (Sony has the number one market-share in DVD players), and even in its inexpensive "home-theater-in-a-box" units sold at warehouse chains. Some of the low-priced SACD players sound surprisingly good, making it an easy decision to try SACD for yourself in your own system. Further, universal players that play every possible 120mm disc are increasingly common, providing another avenue to SACD. Note that these players offer six analog outputs, which are connected to a 6-channel analog input (six separate RCA jacks) on a controller or multichannel preamplifier. These outputs can be seen in Fig.8-1, the rear panel of a multichannel SACD player.

Fig. 8-1 A multi-channel SACD player provides six analog outputs in addition to the conventional stereo output. High-resolution, multichannel digital output is provided on the i.LINK (FireWire) connector.

Sony SCD-999ES

The first few SACD titles were from Sony Music and a few audio-phile labels; as of early 2004, more than 1500 SACD titles are available from 120 different labels. Sony's strategy has been to drive the hardware side of the format by making compelling software available with releases of titles aimed at the demographic most likely to be "early adopters" of the SACD format. These titles have included many reissues, such as the Rolling Stones, Sting, and Bob Dylan catalogs, and Pink Floyd's *Dark Side of the Moon*.

Hybrid SACD

A key element of SACD is backward compatibility with the world's more than 1 billion CD players. The advantages of backward compatibility are manifold: single inventory for record companies and music retailers and the ability to play the same disc in a home SACD player and a CD-based car stereo. Moreover, consumers needn't make a conscious decision to stop buying music in one format (CD) and start buying into a new format. The transition from CD to SACD can be gradual and painless, particularly since SACDs don't cost any more than CDs. Indeed, some consumers buying a hybrid SACD may be unaware that the disc is not a conventional CD. The hybrid SACD re-release of the Rolling Stones catalog in 2003 did not include on the packaging any clue that the discs were hybrid SACD. This strategy avoided the possibility of the discs being relegated to the "new formats" or "audiophile" sections of record stores, or of confusing consumers.

A hybrid SACD looks just like a conventional CD, but contains two layers of information rather than one. The lower layer contains 16-bit/44.1kHz information that can be read by any CD player. The upper layer contains high-resolution digital audio information (called HD, for High Density; see Fig.8-2).

Fig.8-3 shows the SACD's physical structure. It is, in essence, a CD with an additional layer of information-carrying pits embedded in its playing surface. This second, higher-density layer is semi-transparent to the 780-nanometer wavelength of CD laser light, but reflective to the shorter 650-nanometer wavelength of the SACD player's laser. The CD player's laser focuses all the way through the disc; the SACD player's laser focuses halfway through the disc to the HD layer. A switch on SACD players allows the user to switch between layers, and to compare the CD and high-resolution layers. The CD-quality layer is sometimes called the Red Book layer, after the color of the cover of the official specification describing the compact disc.

More information is contained in the second layer because the information-carrying pits are about half the size of a CD's pits, are spaced closer together, and the information is recovered with a shorter wavelength playback laser. Fig.8-4 shows the difference in pit size between the two layers.

This high-density layer contains a 2-channel mix and, at the artist's discretion, a 6-channel version of the music, along with the potential for text, graphics, and limited video information. You can select between

Fig. 8-2 A Super Audio CD contains a high-density layer and a conventional CD layer on the same disc.

CD Layer: fully reflective

0.6mm

HD Layer: reflective for 650 nm, transparent for 780 nm

0.6mm

HD Pick up
λ = 650 nm
NA = 0.6
focused on
HD layer

CD Pick up
λ = 750 nm
NA = 0.45
focused on
CD layer

Courtesy Sony Corporation

Fig. 8-3 Super Audio CD physical structure

Standard Reflective Layer

Substrate

High-Density Layer

Substrate

Laser Pickup

Courtesy Sony Corporation

Fig. 8-4 The information-carrying pits on an SACD are about half the size of those on a CD.

Courtesy Sony Corporation

stereo and multichannel playback from the same disc, depending on your tastes and the number of channels in your system.

SACD also contains strong anti-copy and anti-piracy provisions, issues that are dear to the hearts of record-company executives. First, a digital code is embedded in the disc that allows the SACD player to read the disc. If this code, which is difficult to find and duplicate, is missing, the player simply ejects the disc immediately after it is inserted. Second, the SACD can carry an image faintly visible to the naked eye, similar to a watermark on paper. The image is created by slightly varying the width of the information-carrying pits, which changes the diffraction pattern given off by the disc. If the disc is pirated (as occurs on a massive, government-sanctioned scale in some parts of the world), this image disappears. Pirated discs are thus instantly recognizable.

Direct Stream Digital (DSD) Encoding on SACD

Sony and Philips developed for SACD an entirely different method of digitally representing music, called *Direct Stream Digital* (DSD). Instead of sampling the musical waveform at a relatively slow 44,100 times per second and assigning a 16-bit binary number to represent the amplitude at sample time (the parameters of CD), DSD samples the musical waveform at a lightning-fast 2.8224 *million* times per second. Each "sample" is, however, only one bit. If the waveform's amplitude is increasing, a binary "one" is recorded. If the waveform's amplitude is decreasing, a binary "zero" is recorded. An audio signal at full-scale positive is represented by all ones; a signal at full-scale negative is represented by all zeros. The zero point is represented by alternating ones and zeros, as shown in Fig.8-5. The musical information is contained in the width of the pulses, which is why this type of encoding is sometimes called Pulse Width Modulation (PWM). The data rate of DSD is exactly four times that of 16-bit/44.1kHz encoding (44,100 x 16 x 4 = 2,822,400 bits per second).

Fig. 8-5 The DSD bitstream is a train of single-bit pulses.

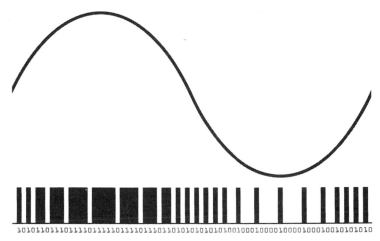

10101101110111110111110111101101010101010101001000100001000010001001010101010

Courtesy Sony Corporation

Interestingly, the pulse train generated by DSD encoding "looks" remarkably analog-like. That is, you can look at the pulse train and get an idea of what the analog waveform looked like. Moreover, converting this pulse train to analog can be as simple as putting the pulses through an analog low-pass filter.

In practice, the DSD-encoded signal is too noisy to convert directly to analog. Because this noise is distributed over a very wide bandwidth, a technique called *noise shaping* shifts the noise away from the audioband and up to a higher frequency, where it is inaudible. Although the amount of noise in the signal remains constant, the noise in the audioband is radically reduced. Fig.8-6 shows how noise shaping shifts noise away from the audioband.

Fig. 8-6 Noise shaping shifts noise away from the audioband.

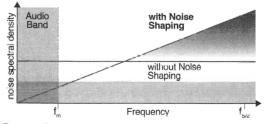

(Courtesy Sony Corporation

DSD can record frequencies of up to 100kHz, far higher than the 20kHz of conventional 44.1kHz-sampled digital audio. In addition, the signal-to-noise ratio (the difference between the loudest sound that can be recorded and the system's noise level) is a whopping 120dB. This is contrasted with the 98dB signal-to-noise ratio of 16-bit quantization. Note, however, that DSD cannot achieve 120dB signal-to-noise ratio across the full 100kHz bandwidth, only over the audioband of 20kHz. That's because the noise shaping described earlier reduces the signal-to-noise ratio above the audioband. One of the benefits of DSD is the elimination of complex filters from the signal path. Conventional digital audio coding requires so-called decimation and oversampling filters, which introduce noise and errors. DSD is a much more direct method of storing music digitally.

Moreover, the DSD pulse train can be converted to 16-bit/44.1kHz form with fairly simple processing. The same DSD master tape can be the source for both the high-resolution and standard-resolution layers on an SACD. Interestingly, many of the sonic benefits of DSD are apparent in the 16-bit/44.1kHz signal. I've heard comparisons of music recorded on DSD then downconverted to 16-bit/44.1kHz, and the same music originally recorded at 16-bit/44.1kHz. The DSD/downconverted version sounded significantly better than the conventionally coded disc.

Before being recorded on an SACD master disc, the DSD bitstream is compressed so it takes up less space on the disc. Unlike "lossy" compression systems that throw away portions of the signal considered to be "inaudible," the compression system used in SACD ensures perfect bit-for-bit accuracy with the source data by more efficiently coding the audio data. For example, a string of eight consecutive 0s may be coded as 8x0. (In practice, the compression system is vastly more complex.) This compression system is what allows SACD to carry both 2-channel and 6-channel representations of the music on the high-resolution layer.

A drawback of DSD is that all professional recording, mixing, mastering, and signal-processing equipment is based on pulse-code modulation digital audio, not the 1-bit representation of DSD. As a result, many SACD titles have been recorded direct to two-track (or multitrack) DSD, with no mixing or processing after the recording. This approach maintains the greatest sonic purity and is the preferred process for audiophile labels, but isn't practical for the entire music industry. Sony has worked to provide recording and mastering engineers with DSD-based tools, but access to those tools is still limited.

DSD encoding provides the intriguing possibility of converting the pulse-width modulated bitstream directly to analog in a switching amplifier. Rather than convert the DSD bitstream to analog, and then amplify it conventionally, the DSD bitstream can be fed to a switching amplifier, with the pulses turning on and off the amplifier's output transistors. An SACD player's DSD output is fed directly into the amplifier, with the amplifier's output stage functioning as the digital-to-analog converter. (Switching amplifiers are explained in Chapter 6.)

DSD Sound Quality

I've listened to DSD extensively under ideal conditions, both in demonstrations and in my own reference system. For my first demonstration, early in DSD's development, a pair of Wilson Audio Specialties WATT/Puppies, driven by Cello electronics, was installed in the control room of Sony Music Studios in New York. The setup was optimized for a single listening seat. As a four-piece acoustic jazz band (including

Randy Brecker on trumpet) played live in the adjacent studio, I could sit in the sweet spot and switch between the live microphone feed, the DSD-processed signal, and a 20-bit/48kHz analog-to-digital and digital-to-analog converter chain. Levels were matched every hour to within 0.1dB. Having a live microphone feed for reference is an extremely powerful tool for assessing the sonic effects of the encoding system.

The sound of DSD was most impressive. The music had a lack of hardness and glare through the midrange and treble that sounded much closer to the live microphone feed. I heard a sense of ease, accompanied by fine resolution of detail. In addition, DSD better preserved the sense of depth, space between instrumental images, and overall soundstage size. I've also heard a number of SACD players in my reference system, and overall am greatly impressed with its sound quality. You can easily compare SACD to CD with a hybrid disc by simply switching between the two layers using the player's remote control. It takes perhaps 30 seconds to switch because the player must switch lasers and read the other layer's table of contents before it will play. DSD is, in my view, a significant advance in sound quality over 16-bit/44.1kHz compact disc.

There's an important caveat to be aware of when evaluating SACD (or DVD-Audio): some titles have been remastered in the new format from 44.1kHz, 16-bit master tapes. This means the SACD or DVD-A release will contain no more information than the CD version; the 44.1kHz, 16-bit master is the limiting factor in the disc's fidelity. The remastered disc can, however, sound better than the original CD because post-processing is performed at a higher sampling frequency (and the errors introduced are distributed over a wider bandwidth), and the filtering performed in the player can be more gentle. Nonetheless, the best way to judge SACD is to choose titles originally recorded in DSD, and to evaluate the DVD-A format using recordings originally made at high sampling frequencies and long word lengths.

DVD-Audio

The DVD format has been a massive commercial success, rapidly replacing VHS as the preferred movie-delivery format. As mentioned earlier in this chapter, DVD's huge data capacity (nearly 18 gigabytes in its maximum form, 25 times that of CD) makes it possible to store high-resolution audio—the DVD-Audio format. Specifically, the DVD-A specification calls for a disc that can contain 6-channel music along with a 2-channel mix on the same disc, and with sampling rates as high as 192kHz and word lengths of up to 24 bits. You can think of a DVD disc as a "bit bucket" that can hold a wide variety of sampling frequencies, word lengths, playing times, and number of channels.

Specifically, DVD-A supports sampling rates of 44.1kHz, 48kHz, 88.2kHz, 96kHz, 176.4kHz, and 192kHz, with word lengths between 16 and 24 bits, in one-bit increments. The disc can contain a 2-channel mix, a multichannel mix (any number of channels up to six), or both. The highest sampling frequencies of 176.4kHz and 192kHz are available only for 2-channel discs, not multichannel ones. That's because these high-sampling rates have a very high data rate (number of bits per second) that exceeds the maximum data rate that can be read from the disc. (DVD's maximum data-transfer rate is 9.6 million bits per second.)

Record producers can choose from these sampling frequencies and resolutions (number of bits per sample), keeping in mind that faster sampling and higher resolutions shorten the disc's playing time. To save disc space, producers can elect to include only a multichannel mix, and allow the DVD player to "downmix" a 2-channel version on the fly. Codes inserted in the bitstream (called "Smart Content") tell the player how to perform the downmix conversion.

Even DVD-A's storage capacity and maximum transfer rate are not high enough to deliver multichannel audio with high resolution on all channels. To overcome this limitation, DVD-A employs a lossless coding system developed by Meridian Audio called Meridian Lossless Packing (MLP). Unlike "lossy" compression systems such as MP3 or Dolby Digital that remove information and reduce fidelity, MLP is a perfectly lossless process, producing identical bit-for-bit data on playback with no sonic degradation.

Without MLP, a single-layer, single-sided DVD-A could hold up to 65 minutes of 5-channel audio with a sampling rate of 96kHz and 20-bit resolution. 6-channel audio with 96kHz sampling frequency and 24-bit resolution isn't possible because the data rate exceeds DVD-A's maximum transfer rate of 9.6Mbs.

MLP eliminates this bottleneck by reducing the number of bits needed to represent the audio signal, expanding the possibilities for playing time, sampling frequency, and resolution. The chart in Fig.8-7 shows the

Fig. 8-7 The relationship between sampling frequency, word length, playing time, and number of channels for a single-layer DVD-A disc with MLP encoding

Courtesy Meridian Audio

relationship between sampling frequency, resolution, and playing time. Note that these figures are for a single-layer, single-sided DVD with MLP (more than 90% of DVD-A releases use MLP). As mentioned earlier, a DVD can have two information layers per disc side; a double-sided, dual-layer disc thus contains four information layers. Such a disc is called "DVD-18" because it stores nearly 18GB of data. It's interesting to note that a single-sided, single-layer DVD-A can store two hours of audio at 96kHz with 24-bit resolution.

By reducing the number of bits needed to represent the audio signal, MLP also frees up room on the disc for "added content" such as a "slide show" of still pictures, "browsable" pictures, text, video, Web links, MP3 samples, and PDF files.

In addition to a multichannel mix and an optional 2-channel mix on the disc, DVD-Audio carries a Dolby Digital-encoded surround track to make the disc compatible with all DVD players, not just those with DVD-A capability. The data rate from the multichannel Dolby Digital track is either 384,000 or 448,000 bits per second—a tiny fraction of even CD's data rate of 705,600 bits per second *per channel*. Ironically, most listeners's first experience with DVD-A will be via the sonically compromised Dolby Digital track, which is inferior to CD.

Note that DVD-A is *not* backward-compatible with CD, although it has been reported that a hybrid disc that will also play on CD players is under development.

DVD-Audio Sound Quality

DVD-Audio, when reproduced through a high-end player, sounds quite a bit better than CD, and different from SACD. DVD-A is characterized by extremely wide dynamics, a smoother treble than CD, greater resolution (particularly of low-level detail), and a more convincing soundstage.

DVD-A's greater resolution of detail results in a more natural rendering of instrumental timbres, which can sound comparatively coarse and lacking in refinement when reproduced on CD. The music is more nuanced, with a liquidity and smoothness closer to the sound of real instruments.

Soundstaging has always been a challenge for CD—44.1kHz, 16-bit digital audio simply can't compete with analog in the ability to throw a huge, three-dimensional soundstage with a sense of air between instruments. DVD-A greatly narrows that gap by providing (on some recordings) a magnificent feeling of depth and layering. Where CD often presents a flat canvas, DVD-A renders a large and well-defined sense of space, as well as the impression of bloom around instrumental outlines.

Also by comparison with CD, DVD-A has a much cleaner, smoother, and more analog-like treble. The treble hardness and glare so often heard on CD is replaced in DVD-A by a greater sense of delicacy, refinement, and ease. It is much easier to listen for long periods of time to DVD-A without fatigue.

Finally, DVD-A simply presents much more musical information to the listener, making it easier to forget the playback system and become immersed in the musical expression.

Bass Management in SACD and DVD-A Players

The term *bass management* describes a system in which bass is filtered out of some channels and directed to a subwoofer, if the system employs one. Bass management is necessary in multichannel audio systems, and is found in most SACD and DVD-A players, as well as in multichannel controllers.

To see why we need bass management, consider a recording containing full-bandwidth information (low bass as well as midrange and treble) in every channel. A good example is a recording of popular music in which the bass guitar and kick drum are at least partially positioned in the center channel. Most multichannel loudspeaker arrays employ large, floorstanding loudspeakers in the left and right positions, and smaller speakers in the center and rear positions. Low frequencies from the bass guitar and kick drum would overload the small center speaker, introducing distortion or damaging the speaker. Bass management selectively filters bass from certain channels you specify according to the kind of loudspeakers in your system. That low bass can be directed to a subwoofer, if your system includes one.

If you've set up a home-theater receiver or controller and selected LARGE or SMALL from the menu for each of your speakers, you've worked with bass management. The SMALL setting simply engages a high-pass (low-cut) filter on that channel, preventing low bass from reaching the speaker. A typical cutoff frequency is 80Hz.

Ideally, bass management would be performed in the multichannel controller or preamplifier the player drives, and the connection between them would be digital. But because of copy-protection issues (more on this later), DVD-A and SACD players are connected to a controller or multichannel preamplifier via the analog outputs. The player manufacturers can't assume the multichannel preamplifier has bass management, so they include it in the player.

Bass management in the DVD-A format is performed via on-screen menus. SACD players typically have a selection of common loudspeaker configurations from which to choose; you simple engage one from the player's front panel with no need for a video display. For example, setting #1 may be ideal for a system with large left and right speakers, small center and surround speakers, and a subwoofer.

The bass-management set-up controls are sometimes accompanied by a variable delay to each channel. You set the amount of delay according to how far you sit from each loudspeaker so that the sound from each speaker reaches you simultaneously. For example, if you sit 12′ from the left and right speakers, but only 6′ from the rear speakers, six milliseconds (6ms) of delay to the rear speakers result in coincident arrival of front sounds with those from the rear.

Universal Players

The spectre of a "format war" between SACD and DVD-Audio is rendered moot by the emergence of the "universal" disc player. A universal player accepts any 120mm disc—regardless of the format—and outputs music and pictures. True universal players support the following formats: CD, DVD-Audio, SACD, CD-R/RW, DVD-R/RW, MP3, Video CD, and Super Video CD.

In the real world, consumers don't really care that much about the format; they just want to play music. The universal player eliminates concerns about format incompatibility and allows the user to simply put the disc in the player and hear music. The first universal players have, however, tended to exhibit compromised sound quality compared with stand-alone DVD-A and SACD players.

Choosing Between CD, SACD, DVD-A, and Universal Players

Despite the proliferation of DVD-A and SACD players, many of us will continue to listen to our large CD libraries for a long time. CD remains an important music source for the audiophile, particularly considering the limited music catalogs in the new formats.

SACD, DVD, and universal players all include CD playback. Very few SACD and DVD players (and even fewer universal machines), however, deliver the level of performance available from the best dedicated CD players and separate transports and digital processors. If you are on a budget, want the simplicity of a single digital source component in your rack, or have an audio system that also functions as a home theater, a DVD player with either SACD or DVD-A capability will suit your needs. For those with more ambitious systems, a separate CD-based digital front-end, combined with a separate SACD or DVD-A player, may be more appropriate.

When buying a new digital source, you'll be confronted with the question of whether to buy a high-end dedicated CD player, an SACD machine, a DVD player with DVD-A capability, a universal player, or a separate disc transport and outboard digital processor. You may even opt for a combination of these components that best suits your needs.

Perhaps your most important decision is whether to buy into SACD, DVD-A, both, or neither. In the past, when two formats competed in the marketplace, one format "won" and the other "lost," with consumers who bought into the losing format finding themselves stuck with virtually worthless hardware and limited software with no possibility of enjoying a steady stream of new music releases. The consumer-electronics industry's history is littered with failed formats.

Fortunately, that "either/or" scenario is unlikely to come to pass with regard to SACD and DVD-Audio. As of this writing (2004), it appears that both formats will co-exist, for several reasons. One compelling reason is that universal players blur the distinction between formats; the consumer buys any 120mm disc, puts in in his universal player, and he hears music. Secondly, SACD will continue to grow because the music industry has embraced the format, with producers and artists increasingly turning to SACD as the preferred format for their releases. Sony also has a long history of never giving up on its format. Sony has made a massive investment in SACD, and will continue its strong support of the format. And because it has the number one market share in DVD players, Sony can include SACD playback in its machines and get large numbers of SACD players into consumers' homes. It is unlikely that Sony will ever produce a DVD player with DVD-A capability.

DVD-A will achieve massive market penetration purely by dint of being part of the DVD standard; every DVD player will include DVD-A capability. Consumers buying a DVD player for its video capabilities will eventually end up buying into the DVD-A format by default.

More music is available in the SACD format, although that situation could quickly change if several major record companies begin supporting DVD-A in earnest. Whether the mass-market consumer will invest in a new DVD-A music library is another question.

Regardless of the high-res format you select, CD playback quality will remain important since CD will probably be your primary source for many years until a large and diverse music library becomes available in the new formats. This becomes a tricky issue because the CD performance of SACD and DVD-A players ranges from poor to very good. In some machines, CD quality is an afterthought. In others, the manufacturer realizes the importance of high-performance 44.1kHz, 16-bit playback, and gives equal attention to both high-resolution and standard-resolution performance. As always, the best way to begin shopping is to read reviews in a reputable magazine and then *listen to the player yourself.* Spend plenty of time with CDs, not just the high-resolution formats. And don't judge the player's CD performance by comparing CD to SACD or DVD-A on the same player. Instead, try to compare the player's CD sound to a dedicated CD-only machine that has a good reputation.

One approach to the problem of getting high-quality CD playback while you decide on a new format is to buy a high-end dedicated CD player along with an inexpensive SACD or DVD-A machine. There are some surprisingly good-sounding SACD and DVD-A players available for less than $300. This strategy gives you the best of both worlds: high-end CD performance and the ability to sample the new formats without a significant financial investment. After you've made up your mind about the new formats, you can then add a true high-end SACD or DVD-A player to your system. You also have the benefit of improving technology, lower prices, and greater selection of music before you commit heavily to one format or another. Yet another approach is to buy a universal player and forget about formats and just enjoy the widest selection of music possible.

Open Architecture: Customizing and Future-Proofing Your Digital Purchase

Some manufacturers of digital playback equipment have the foresight to make their products adaptable to changing technology. If you plan to buy an expensive digital component, look for one that can be upgraded to accept high-resolution digital audio, such as 96kHz sampling with 24-bit resolution.

One sign of an upgradeable digital component is an open architecture in which the machine's main components are modular. Instead of putting all the circuitry on one board, the modular product splits up the electronics into key sub-sections, allowing relatively easy replacement of certain parts. Modular construction lets you keep the power supply, chassis, analog output stage, and other components that aren't affected by changing technology.

Let's take a look at one product, the Meridian 800, that exemplifies the possibilities provided by open-architecture. The 800 plays DVD-Video, DVD-Audio, and CD. As you can see in Fig.8-8, the 800 is built like a personal computer, with a motherboard into which a variety of cards can be inserted.

Fig. 8-8 A modular product can be updated as technology progresses, and expanded to incorporate new functions.

Courtesy Meridian Audio

These cards contain sub-systems that can be updated as technology advances. The 800's modular construction not only allows the product to be upgraded, but also to be customized according to your needs. For example, if you want only 2-channel playback of DVD-Audio, you need only a 2-channel analog-output board. If you connect the 800 to Meridian's digital controller or digital loudspeakers, you need only a digital output card, and are not forced to pay for digital-to-analog converters you'll never use. Another benefit of this approach is the possibility of expanding the product's capabilities. For example, the Meridian 861 (the companion controller that shares the same architecture as the 800) can be fitted with a room-correction card that measures the response of your loudspeakers and room, and then corrects these response variations in the digital domain. Purchasers of the first 861 probably had no idea their unit could one day perform room correction.

Although manufacturers can't predict the future, they can design their products for maximum adaptability to changing technology. If you're about to invest in high-end CD playback, find out the manufacturer's intentions for upgrading the product.

Digital-Audio Servers

An entirely new product category called the *digital-audio server* made its introduction in 2002. This digital-audio recording device employs large hard-disk drives to store hundreds of hours of music, usually recorded from CD. Transferring your CD library to a single computer-based device confers many advantages, including instant access to any piece of music without searching through CDs; no need to open a CD and insert it into a player; no CD-storage problems or clutter; and the ability to create custom music playlists by genre or group. You could, for example, tell the server to play two hours of a particular artist, or six hours of classic jazz, or three hours of chamber music. The digital-audio server opens up new possibilities for the way in which we access our music.

Audio can be stored on the server's hard drives uncompressed (consuming about 10.5MB per stereo minute), or with a compression scheme that increases a given drive's storage capacity at the expense of sound quality. Some servers have fixed hard-drive capacity, with no provision for expansion if you need more storage space. Others allow you to add additional drives as your music collection grows. A few also provide the option of removable drives so that you can back-up your music. This requires copying the data from one drive to another, removing one of the drives, and putting it away in case of a drive crash. Others simply store the audio data on two separate drives. As anyone who's used a personal computer knows, the hard-disk drive is the least reliable component, and prone to sudden and catastrophic failure. If this happens to the drives in your server, you'll need to re-record (and re-classify) all your CDs, unless you have a server with the removable backup option. If you choose to commit your music library to a digital-audio server, I strongly recommend keeping the original CDs in case of a drive crash. You'll probably want to keep the CDs anyway for a car stereo or other mobile application.

Gracenote CDDB System

Because CDs don't contain artist names or song titles (information called metadata), users of digital-audio servers or those who play CDs on their computers (or portable MP3 players, if you're so inclined) must either enter this information manually, or live with the uninformative "Disc 4, Track 3" data in the player's display. This limitation was overcome by the Gracenote Music Management System, part of the Gracenote CDDB music-recognition service. If you've ever played a CD on a computer and seen the artist name or song title, you've used the Gracenote system.

Gracenote CDDB is licensed to consumer electronics manufacturers, and enables them to display the artist, album, and track listing information in the player's display. Gracenote is used by more than 60 million desktop computers, and is found in virtually all Internet-based music devices. Gracenote's database contains more than two million albums as of early 2004. Users can update or add to this database by connecting to Gracenote's Web site. Any Gracenote-enabled device will automatically generate a list of titles and artists of your music selections. The system recognizes more than 28 million pieces of music, and provides metadata in 60 languages. The system also assigns a genre to each musical selection (e.g., jazz, classical, rock), making it easy to organize custom playlists.

The system recognizes music in one of two ways. The first is by reading a CD's table of contents (TOC), a chunk of data recorded at the inside diameter of every CD. When you put a CD in a player and it first spins up, then shows the number of tracks and disc duration, the player has read the TOC. The TOC data pattern is unique for each title. Second, Gracenote has developed a technique for analyzing the actual music (in a variety of formats, including MP3 and WAV files).

There is no charge to end-users of the Gracenote service; the company receives its revenue from licensing the technology to consumer-electronics manufacturers.

Upsampling

In the late 1990s, someone experimented with inserting a professional sample-rate converter between a CD transport and a digital processor.

The sample-rate converter increased the transport's 44.1kHz output to 88.2kHz, where it was decoded by a digital processor capable of receiving and decoding 88.2kHz. This so-called *upsampling* resulted in improved sound quality from CD, at least with the transport and processor involved in the experiment. Consequently, a new component category was born, with several manufacturers jumping in to offer stand-alone sample-rate converter boxes, and others developing CD players and digital processors with integral upsampling.

But how is upsampling different from oversampling, the technique employed in digital filters in which the baseband 44.1kHz signal is increased to some higher value, typically 352.8kHz in an 8x oversampling system? (Oversampling digital filters are explained later in this chapter.) This question has created some controversy. Technically, upsampling and oversampling are identical. The term "upsampling" is used when the process is performed outside the digital processor; "oversampling" describes the same process when performed by circuits integral to the digital processor. The sonic improvements heard by many listeners can be partially attributed to superior filtering (a better-sounding filtering algorithm coupled with greater mathematical precision) in the outboard upsampler compared with the digital processor's integral digital filter.

There are, however, inherent advantages to upsampling. Among them are the opportunity to increase the word length from 16 bits to 20 or 24 bits. Although no new information is contained in these additional bits, any digital signal processing after the upsampler is less likely to degrade the signal. In addition, increased word length leads to lower jitter in the digital interface, as well as the opportunity to apply noise shaping. Moreover, subsequent digital-to-analog converters operate at the higher rate (88.2kHz, for example) so that the signal is not subjected to cascaded filters with cutoff frequencies just above the original baseband audio bandwidth.

Upsampling can, however, also degrade performance. Ideally, *integer upsampling* should be employed, in which the output sampling frequency is an integer multiple of the input sampling frequency, such as 44.1kHz upsampled to 88.2kHz (2x) or 176.4kHz (4x). Non-integer upsampling converts, for example, 44.1kHz to 96kHz, a process that doesn't necessarily retain all the original sample points—that is, upsampling changes the values of the samples representing the audio signal. Non-integer upsampling is also far more mathematically complex, which has the potential of introducing errors in the signal. Note that there is no practical improvement in 96kHz signals over 88.2kHz signals.

Sample-Rate Conversion

A related subject is sample-rate conversion performed in some digital recorders. Although sample-rate conversion changes the sampling frequency, it is not to be confused with upsampling, where the goal is to improve sound quality.

Digital recorders that operate at a fixed sampling rate must lock-on to the digital signals driving them and record that signal at the particular recorder's "native" sampling frequency. Even with a source and recorder that both operate at the same nominal sampling frequency, there may be a small discrepancy between the input's and recorder's sample rates due to a slight difference in their clock frequencies. Conversely, there can be quite large differences in sampling frequencies, as when feeding 44.1kHz into a recorder that operates at 48kHz.

To accommodate these variations in the sampling frequency fed to a fixed-frequency recorder, some manufacturers employ an *asynchronous sample-rate converter* chip at the recorder's input that takes in an infinitely variable range of sample frequencies (within the limits of the chip) and outputs a fixed sample rate to the recorder's electronics. The term "asynchronous" means the input and output frequencies can run independently of each other and need not be related or locked together; the input frequency can be varied and the output frequency will remain the same. This chip is in the signal path at all times, even if you input, for example, a 44.1kHz signal to a recorder operating at 44.1kHz. The sample-rate converter chip is essentially an oversampling digital filter that interpolates new samples. This means the output data are not identical to the input data, even when the input and output sampling frequencies are identical. The result is degraded sound quality, which can be heard in recordings made from a CD player to a CD-R machine that employs an asynchronous sample-rate converter. The CD R machine doesn't make an identical bit for bit copy (a *clone*, in digital parlance) of the source data.

The Digital Transport

The CD transport can be thought of as a CD player without a digital-to-analog converter. Instead of generating an analog audio signal as does a CD player, the transport outputs a digital datastream that must be converted to analog by another component, the digital processor. A transport-and-processor combination is essentially a CD player in two boxes. Fig.8-9 shows the three digital front-end connection methods: a CD player, a transport/digital processor combination, and a CD player used as a transport.

As mentioned earlier, I use the term CD transport to describe any product that reads information from a CD and outputs a digital datastream that can be converted to analog by an external digital processor. That product can be a dedicated CD-only transport,

Fig. 8-9 A digital front-end can be a CD, SACD, or DVD-Audio player (top), a transport and digital processor (center), or a CD player driving a digital processor (bottom).

CD/SACD/DVD-A PLAYER

TRANSPORT AND DIGITAL PROCESSOR

CD/SACD/DVD-A PLAYER USED AS TRANSPORT

SACD, DVD-A, or universal disc player. Moreover, many CD players have digital output jacks that enable them to function as transports. In such cases a digital interconnect cable runs from the CD player's digital output jack to a digital processor's digital input, bypassing the CD player's analog circuits and outputs. This connection method, shown in Fig.8-9, merely replaces the CD player's digital-to-analog converter with the (sometimes) higher-quality D/A in a separate unit. Many audiophiles upgrade their digital front-ends by adding separate digital processors to their existing CD, DVD-A, or SACD players.

Transports have a variety of output connections. The four main types are coaxial (RCA jack), TosLink optical, AES/EBU (XLR connector), and AT&T ST-Type glass-fiber optical. (These interfaces are described in detail later in this chapter under "The Digital Interface.") Virtually all high-end transports at least have coaxial output, and some offer all four types. A transport will often include coaxial output as standard, and offer AES/EBU or ST-Type optical as an option. These output options usually cost between $200 and $400 each. To use ST-Type glass-fiber or AES/EBU output, however, your processor must accept these interfaces. If you are buying new products today, you can ignore the ST-Type glass-fiber interface; it has virtually disappeared from modern products.

The best way to audition a transport is to listen to several models in your price range, using the same processor that you'll be driving with the transport. This will allow you to get the best musical match, since how the transport sounds is affected by the digital processor the transport is driving. That's because all digital processors respond differently to *transport jitter*. Transport jitter is caused by timing variations in the digital datastream output from the transport. This datastream jitter is either passed along to the digital processor's clock (where it degrades the sound), or is rejected by the digital processor and thus is less sonically detrimental. Consequently, transports make much more of an audible difference with some processors than with others. If you choose a digital processor that's relatively immune to transport jitter, you can spend less on a CD transport and still get great sound.

The interface between transport and processor will also affect the sound. There are noticeable sonic differences not only between types of interface (coaxial, ST-Type optical, AES/EBU, and TosLink), but among cables in the same interface family. Indeed, two coaxial cables may sound almost as different as two transports. A top-end coaxial digital interconnect costs about $200, but you can get a 75-ohm video cable from your local RadioShack for about $5. Whichever cable you choose, be sure to get one designed for digital (not analog) data transfer. I demonstrated the importance of this advice for myself, using a unique jitter-analysis instrument, by measuring the jitter introduced by a variety of digital interconnects. Those designed for analog audio had the highest jitter, and those made specifically for digital data transfer had the lowest. The $5 RadioShack video cable's jitter was almost as low as that of the $200 high-end digital interconnects—and it sounded nearly as good, too.

Incidentally, evaluating digital transports and digital interconnects is much easier than comparing other components because the levels are automatically and precisely matched. All transports and interconnects will produce the same listening volume when driving the same processor—the transport or interconnect doesn't change the ones and zeros in the digital code.

Sonic differences between digital transports are almost certainly solely the result of jitter in their S/PDIF outputs. Recovering the correct ones and zeros from the disc is relatively straightforward; the digital output from a transport is an identical copy, bit for bit, of the source data. The timing of those bits, however, can greatly affect playback quality. Fortunately, today's digital processors have better jitter rejection than products made during the 1990s, and are less affected by transport and interface jitter.

When evaluating digital transports, listen for the same artifacts we talked about in judging digital front-ends in general. Transports vary greatly in their low-frequency dynamics, treble smoothness, overall perspective, and soundstaging. Choose one that complements your processor and playback system.

Because one company—Philips of Holland—supplies most of the transport mechanisms to high-end audio manufacturers, CD transports tend to have very similar features and functions. Many even share the same remote control. Virtually all transports have track-skip forward and back, audible search, and a time display. Other features include index search, index readout, and a variety of time-display options. This last feature allows you to switch the display between elapsed time of the track, elapsed time of the disc, remaining track time, and remaining disc time. This feature is useful when making cassette tapes for your car stereo. Transports vary more widely in their ease of use. Some have small buttons bunched together, making it hard to find the one you want. Others have large, clearly marked buttons. Although ergonomics take second place to sound quality, consider a transport's ease of use when deciding whether or not to buy it.

Another factor to consider is the transport's loading method. Some are top-loading, in which a lid or top opens to accept the disc. The second method is drawer-loading, with a drawer that recesses into the front panel. A top-loading transport usually requires the top shelf of an equipment rack, while a drawer-loading unit can fit on a lower shelf.

The Digital Processor

Digital processors convert the S/PDIF digital output from a transport or other digital source to an analog signal that is fed to your preamplifier. They range in price from $200 to $20,000, but many good-sounding units can be had for under $1000. The most basic processor has one digital input on an RCA jack and one pair of unbalanced analog outputs. More complex processors have multiple digital inputs, digital outputs, balanced analog outputs, polarity-inversion switching, and sometimes even a volume control.

Digital Processor Features

Let's take a closer look at the features and options available on digital processors.

HDCD Decoding: Many processors can decode CDs recorded using the High Definition Compatible Digital (HDCD) process. HDCD is explained later in this chapter.

DSD Decoding: Some digital processors can accept the DSD bitstream from an SACD player with a high-resolution digital output and convert the DSD signal to analog. The interface format is FireWire (IEEE1394), explained later in this chapter.

High-Resolution PCM Decoding: These processors can accept and decode high-resolution PCM bitstreams (96kHz, 24-bit, for example) and convert those signals to analog.

Multiple Digital Inputs: An essential feature if you have more than one digital source. Multiple digital inputs let you change digital sources with a push of a front-panel button instead of rerouting digital interconnects. An LED often accompanies the input selector switch to indicate which input the processor has locked to.

Various Input Types: Most processors offer different types of input connections. Virtually all processors include coaxial input on an RCA jack; some offer ST-Type glass-fiber optical, AES/EBU, and TosLink optical. ST-Type optical and AES/EBU are often options that add between $200 and $400 each to the processor's price. To use these input options, you must have a source (CD transport or high-res player) with the same output options. For example, if you want to use the AES/EBU interface, both the transport and processor must be fitted with AES/EBU jacks.

Balanced Outputs: Balanced outputs come standard on many processors, but are sometimes an option that adds between $200 and $1000 to the price. Balanced outputs allow you to run balanced lines between your digital processor and preamp. Note that a preamp with balanced inputs is required to use this option. (See the section on balanced outputs later in this chapter for a description of different methods of creating a balanced signal.)

Digital Output: This feature allows you to send the digital signal to a digital recording device such as a MiniDisc recorder. Some processors allow you to record from one digital source while listening to another. A digital output is an important feature if you own a digital recording device—without it, you'll need to unplug the digital signal going into your digital processor and run it to the digital recorder every time you want to record through the recorder's digital input. A transport with multiple digital outputs will also drive a digital processor and digital recorder simultaneously.

Polarity Inversion Switch: This front-panel switch inverts the *absolute polarity* of the signal to match its original polarity. To find correct absolute polarity, simply throw the switch back and forth to find the position that sounds the best (if there is an audible difference). A polarity-inversion switch is often marked "180°" to indicate polarity reversal.

Volume Control: For those who listen only to CD (no tuner, tape deck, or turntable), the processor with a volume control is ideal. This feature allows you to do without a preamplifier and drive a power amplifier directly. This saves money—on both the preamp and an additional pair of interconnects—and has the potential to sound better because fewer electronic components are in the signal path. Because a disc player (CD, SACD, DVD-A) or digital processor with a volume control won't accept other input signals, this approach is recommended only for those who listen to just a single digital source. Note, however, that some processors performing digital-domain volume control can degrade the sound.

Line-stage Preamplifier: Some CD players and digital processors incorporate a line-stage preamplifier that allows you to switch sources, control the volume, and perform other preamplifier functions.

If you want the most sound for the money, avoid processors with features you won't use (balanced outputs, multiple digital inputs, digital outputs). Some excellent products have only a coaxial input and unbalanced analog output. You should, however, choose a processor to accommodate your system as it grows. If you plan to get a balanced-input preamplifier, spend the money now for a balanced-output processor. Before you do, however, take a close look at how the balanced signal is created, a topic covered below.

Balanced Outputs: Why They're Not All Created Equal

Balanced output has become a popular feature in digital processors. A balanced-output processor can drive a balanced-input preamplifier, often with better sound quality than is possible with unbalanced operation.

As explained in Chapter 11, a balanced signal is carried on three conductors: a ground wire and two signal-carrying conductors. The two signals are identical but opposite in polarity. That is, they are mirror images of each other. When one is swinging positive, the other is swinging negative. One of the phases of a balanced signal is called the "+" phase, the other the "−" phase.

Designers can use one of two very different techniques to create this balanced signal. The easiest way is to simply put a *phase splitter* in the digital processor's analog output stage. A phase splitter is an electronic circuit that generates a second signal of opposite polarity to the input signal. These two signals are then connected to an XLR jack on the processor's rear panel. This technique, shown in block form in Fig.8-10, is the inexpensive and easy way to create a balanced signal.

Some processors, however, use a much more elaborate scheme. Rather than create the balanced signal in the analog domain with an additional active device (the phase splitter), these processors create a balanced signal in the digital domain *before* digital-to-analog conversion. The left and right audio-channel digital datastreams are split into a balanced signal (left +, left –, right +, right –), which is processed and converted to analog separately. This technique requires nearly double the circuitry, with four DACs and four sets of analog output electronics. A digitally balanced DAC is shown in block form in Fig.8-11.

This method is a lot more expensive than a simple phase splitter in the analog stage, but has many advantages. When the balanced signal is eventually summed (in the preamplifier or power amplifier), any noise or distortion common to both channels will be rejected. This phenomenon, called *common-mode rejection*, is described in Chapter 11, "Cables and Interconnects." Any artifacts or spurious signals introduced by the

Fig. 8-10 A balanced output can be created simply by adding a phase splitter to the analog output stage.

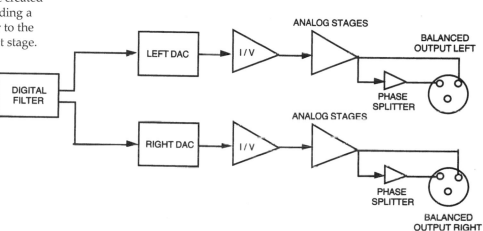

Fig. 8-11 A truly balanced processor splits the signal before the DACs.

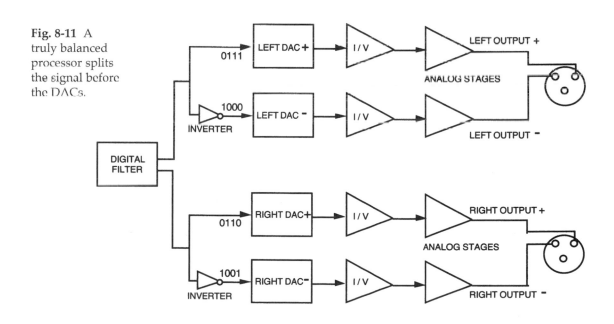

Fig. 8-12 A comparison of two methods of deriving unbalanced outputs from a balanced processor.

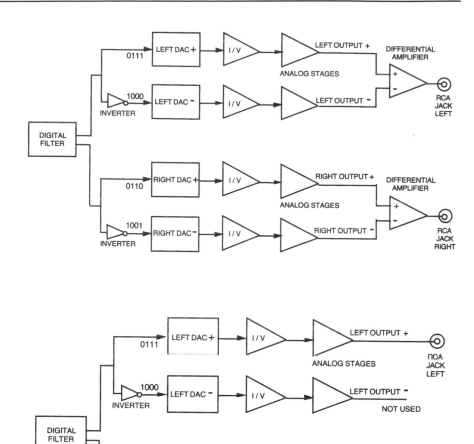

DACs will thus cancel. Moreover, balanced DACs yield a 3dB increase in signal-to-noise ratio. Finally, a fully balanced DAC doesn't add another active device (the phase splitter) to the signal path.

A final consideration with fully balanced DACs is how the unbalanced signal is derived. Some products merely connect half the balanced circuit (the left- and right-channel + signals) to the left and right rear-panel RCA jacks. Others sum the + and − signals with a *differential amplifier* (a circuit that converts a balanced signal to an unbalanced one) to drive the unbalanced RCA output jacks. The latter approach provides the benefits of balanced DACs even for those users who don't use the balanced XLR outputs. Conversely, taking half the balanced signal at the unbalanced output obviates the advantages of fully balanced DACs when using the unbalanced outputs. A comparison of these two techniques is shown in Fig.8-12.

The S/PDIF Digital Interface

The S/PDIF interface is a method of transmitting digital audio from one component to another. For example, a digital transport's S/PDIF output is carried down a digital interconnect to the S/PDIF input on a digital processor. As described earlier, transports and processors come fitted with a variety of connection methods—AES/EBU, coaxial, TosLink, or ST-Type optical. All are based on the S/PDIF (Sony/Philips Digital Interface Format) interface standard. Note that all transmit the same S/PDIF signal, but in different ways.

Digital Interconnects

Digital interfaces can be divided into two categories: electrical and optical. In an electrical interconnect, electrons carry the signal down copper or silver wire. An optical interface transmits light down a plastic or glass tube.

Fig.8-13 shows the four common interconnect types: coaxial, TosLink, ST-Type optical, and AES/EBU. Coaxial and AES/EBU are both electrical; ST-Type and TosLink are optical.

The most common type of connection, *coaxial*, is carried on an RCA cable. This is the electrical connection found on virtually all CD transports, most good CD players, and other consumer digital audio products such as digital preamplifiers, room-correction systems, and digital recorders. A variation on the coaxial connection is the BNC cable, which is used in only a few products. Though BNC is better than RCA—mechanically, electrically, and sonically—it never caught on.

TosLink is the low-cost optical interface promoted by mass-market audio manufacturers as an alternative to coaxial connection. TosLink, a trademarked name of the Toshiba Corporation, is more properly called "EIAJ Optical," after the Electronics Industries Association of Japan. The major electronics companies had two good reasons for trying to convert the world to TosLink. First, TosLink jacks and cables are cheaper to make than coaxial jacks and cables. Second, TosLink connection makes it easier for the components to meet FCC (Federal Communications Commission) requirements for radiated noise. An electrical signal traveling down copper (such as the S/PDIF signal in a coax connection) throws off RF (radio frequency) noise that could interfere with radio and television transmission. The FCC will simply ban products that don't meet its criteria for radiated noise. Because TosLink sends the signal as light down glass or plastic fiber, it produces no radiated noise.

The *ST-Type optical* interface, developed by AT&T for telecommunications, was popular in the mid-1990s, but is rarely found on contemporary products. ST-Type connection transmits the optical signal down glass fiber instead of TosLink's plastic light path (some higher-

Fig. 8-13 The
four digital inter-
face types

Coaxial (RCA)

TosLink

ST-Type Optical

AES/EBU
Courtesy AudioQuest

qualityTosLink cables also use glass). ST's locking bayonet connector
ensures a good junction between the cable and optical transmitter and
receiver. Although ST-Type is generally considered a very good-sounding interface, it is no longer common on high-end products.

A few years ago, ST-Type optical was, in my view, the best-sounding interface. The reason is not because of ST's inherent superiority, but
because few designers achieved a good implementation of the coaxial
and AES/EBU interfaces. An electrical interface not only required careful
design, but was subject to quality variability. Conversely, a designer
using ST simply bought an ST transmitter or receiver kit, which was
already engineered and worked perfectly out of the box. There were no
variables in how well ST worked or sounded.

Now that designers have more experience in designing electrical
interfaces, they tend to sound better and are more consistently good.
Consequently, ST has fallen out of favor in recent years.

The interface of choice is now the *AES/EBU* interface, which is carried on a balanced line terminated with three-pin XLR connectors. Of the
three conductors in a balanced signal, one is ground, one is the digital
signal, and the third is the digital signal inverted. AES/EBU benefits
from all the advantages of balanced lines (described in Chapter 11), and
is transmitted at 5V, compared to S/PDIF's 0.5V.

Virtually all transports and processors have RCA jacks, and most
include TosLink for compatibility. AES/EBU is usually found on only the

more expensive components, or offered as an option on mid-priced digital equipment. The ST-Type option can add between $200 and $400 to the product's price. Note that both the transport and processor must have the same interface. This increases ST's cost to between $400 and $800 if it is included on both the transport and processor. As of this writing, only a few manufacturers offer the ST-Type optical interface.

TosLink is by far the worst interface, mechanically (the physical connection between cable and jack), electrically (it has the lowest bandwidth), and sonically. TosLink connection tends to blur the separation between individual instrumental images, adds a layer of grunge over instrumental textures, softens the bass, and doesn't have the same sense of black silence between notes. Better results can be achieved with a high-end glass-fiber TosLink cable, but my advice is to forget about TosLink unless you have a laserdisc player equipped only with TosLink output.

Some digital front-ends will benefit from an optical interface because there is no ground connection between the transport and processor, as exists with an electrical interconnect. Sonically degrading high-frequency noise on a transport's ground can contaminate the digital processor's ground through an electrical connection. Because an optical interface transmits the signal without an electrical connection, there is no chance for coupling ground noise between the two components.

In theory, the electrical interfaces will work best because they have the widest bandwidth. The transmission of digital data from a source to a digital processor should be over the widest possible bandwidth link for low jitter. TosLink has a bandwidth of 6MHz (6,000,000Hz), ST-Type optical is between 50MHz and 150MHz, and electrical interfaces have a potential 500MHz bandwidth (if implemented correctly).

The best way to choose an interface is by listening to the various types. When comparing electrical and optical interfaces, be sure to disconnect the electrical interface from the processor when listening to the optical interface. The advantage of keeping the transport ground isolated from the processor ground is lost if the electrical cable is still connected between the transport and processor, even though it may not be active.

A primary reason for poor-sounding transports and interfaces in electrical connections is an impedance mismatch between the transport's output impedance, the cable's characteristic impedance, and/or the digital processor's input impedance. An impedance mismatch causes reflections of the signal in the cable, introducing jitter in the datastream. The impedance specification is 75 ohms (±5%) for S/PDIF and 110 ohms (±20%) for AES/EBU. Manufacturers of digital products should strictly adhere to these impedance standards, although many do not.

Finally, it should be noted that improvements in digital processors have largely reduced the sonic differences between interface types, and between specific models of interface cables. Today's digital processors are much better at rejecting jitter, and some even employ technologies to completely isolate interface jitter from the processor's clock. Keep in mind that the greater the differences you hear between interfaces, the worse the digital processor is at rejecting jitter.

Jitter in the S/PDIF Interface

Jitter refers to timing errors in the clock that controls *when* the CD's digital samples are converted into music. Musicians say that "The right note at the wrong time is the wrong note," and this perfectly describes the jitter problem in digital audio reproduction. If the digital samples are converted into an analog signal (music) with a jittered clock, distortion is introduced. Specifically, the treble takes on a hardness manifested as cymbals that sound like bursts of noise, screechy and metallic violins, and leading-edge piano transients that sound brittle and "glassy." The bass becomes less taut and loses dynamic impact. Jitter also truncates the sense of space, shrinking the soundstage and making images within it poorly defined. The transparent sense of air between you and the performers seems clouded.

The main source of jitter in digital audio playback is the digital interface that connects a CD transport to a digital processor. Get rid of the digital interface—as naturally happens in a one-box CD player—and you eliminate the most significant source of jitter. That's the reason one-box CD players have a major sonic advantage over separates, everything else being equal.

Despite the elegance of having left- and right-channel audio data and a clock carried in the same digital channel, some sonic compromises are inherent in the S/PDIF format. The digital processor's input receiver "recovers" the clock from the S/PDIF datastream, generating a new clock that becomes the timing reference for the digital processor. Virtually all input receivers pass interface jitter to the clock that controls the DAC timing. As explained earlier in this chapter, and in greater detail in Appendix C ("Digital Audio Basics"), jitter at the DAC can introduce audible problems.

This interface-induced jitter isn't random in nature; it is directly correlated with the audio signal being transmitted. In other words, the clock is modulated by the music carried by the interface. The recovered clock is jittered at exactly the same frequency as the audio signal traveling down the interface. Using a jitter-analysis instrument, it's possible to *listen* to only the jitter component of the S/PDIF signal. Just from hearing the jitter, you can readily discern the piece of music being transmitted. This audio-correlated jitter ends up at the DAC's word clock, where it degrades the processor's sound quality.

Jitter-Reduction Devices

Jitter-reduction devices, launched in 1993, constituted a previously unheard-of component category. The jitter-reduction device is inserted in the digital signal path between a digital transport (or any other digital source) and a digital processor. In theory, the jitter-reduction device takes in a jittered S/PDIF digital signal and outputs a less jittered digital signal.

Sound quality will be degraded when the jitter-reduction device's output jitter is higher than the transport's jitter. Jitter-reduction devices can improve high-jitter transports, but can degrade low-jitter transports. These devices should therefore be auditioned in your own system before you buy one. Further, many jitter-reduction devices claim some low level of output jitter ("less than 50ps," for example), but the manufacturer has no way of verifying such claims. Never buy a jitter-reduction device on the basis of a specification; instead, listen to it in your own system.

Moreover, most jitter-reduction boxes have a serious flaw: they may reduce incoming jitter, but they then must output that low-jitter signal via an S/PDIF interface, which introduces jitter all over again.

Some jitter-reduction boxes add *dither* (a small amount of noise) to the signal to improve sound quality. Dither keeps the lower bits of the DAC from ever becoming static, which is claimed to make the sound more analog-like.

Another breed of jitter-reduction device claims to enhance resolution by increasing the 16-bit word length of CD to 20 bits. Digital Signal Processing (DSP) chips in the device attempt to figure out what the lower bits would have been had the music originally been recorded with higher resolution. For these devices to be of any benefit, the digital processor they feed must be capable of processing 20 bits of data. Older digital filter chips (the ubiquitous NPC 5813 and 5803, for examples) pass only 16-bit data. If you feed such a processor 20-bit data from a resolution-enhancement device, the processor will truncate (cut off) the lower four bits of the 20-bit words, introducing audible harmonic distortion.

Jitter-reduction devices were popular in the early 1990s, but have fallen out of favor as digital-to-analog converters have become less sensitive to jitter. In fact, jitter-reduction devices can be rendered superfluous by high-quality internal clocking in the digital-to-analog converter. Some digital processors employ an internal data buffer that stores a small amount of digital-audio data, and then clocks those data out from the buffer to the actual digital-to-analog converter chips with a high precision clock. A digital processor with a buffer should be completely immune to interface jitter and variations in digital cables.

Finally, keep in mind that jitter-reduction devices have no effect on a recording made through them. Because recorders store audio data and not a clock signal, the concept of jitter is irrelevant when talking about storage media. Jitter matters only at the clock that controls the digital-to-analog conversion process.

Custom Digital Interfaces

As digital front-ends become more and more sophisticated, designers are finding that the limiting factor in sound quality is interface jitter.

Consequently, several custom interface technologies have been developed to reduce interface jitter.

One solution is to send the clock signal separately from the audio data on a second cable. This technique avoids the problem of signal-correlated jitter, but the clock must still travel down a cable and be recovered to become the timing reference for the digital processor. A better method is to put the master clock in the digital processor, send the clock separately to the transport, and force the transport to "slave" to the digital processor. The crucial D/A clock is located right next to the DACs and is unaffected by external variables. With no need to recover a clock and no interface through which the clock must pass, sound quality is improved.

High-end digital processors using a separate clock line also have a conventional input receiver to recover the clock. This makes them compatible with transports lacking a clock input (or output). It is therefore possible to compare the standard clock-recovery technique with using a separate clock line just by disconnecting the separate clock cable. In listening tests, I've found this additional link greatly improves sound quality. Moreover, processors and transports having a separate clock signal should be immune to sonic differences between interfaces (coax, ST-Type, TosLink, AES/EBU) and different cables within an interface family.

Despite the sonic benefits, using a second clock line between a transport and processor has been adopted by very few manufacturers. This is because there is no standard format for the clock signal, making the feature useful only on transport/processor pairs from the same company. With few transport manufacturers offering a clock input—and a lack of standardization among those who do—most digital processor manufacturers simply don't include a separate clock line on their products.

Some manufacturers have recently started using newer, more sophisticated input receivers that provide low jitter without a separate clock line.

An innovative method of reducing interface jitter was developed by Spectral Audio for their SDR-2000 processor and SDR-3000 CD transport. Called Spectralink, the interface doesn't send a clock signal from processor to transport in the conventional sense, but instead uses a proprietary analog-like control signal to synchronize the transport with the processor. Auditioning the Spectral pair through both the Spectralink and conventional interfaces suggests that Spectralink offers a significant improvement in sound quality. Unfortunately, this technique is confined to Spectral products.

Another way to eliminate interface-induced jitter is simply to buy a CD player. Because a one-box CD player doesn't need to transmit audio data and a clock, it doesn't need the S/PDIF interface. With no interface, there is no interface-induced clock jitter. CD players thus have an inherent advantage over separate processors and transports.

As previously mentioned, some digital processors can reject jitter by employing a data buffer and high-precision clock, rendering moot the question of interface jitter.

Copy Protection, High-Resolution Digital Interfaces, and Watermarking

Record companies are terrified by the prospect of consumers having access to high-resolution digital bitstreams, since those bitstreams can be copied and distributed without sonic degradation. Consequently, DVD-A and SACD players generally do not provide high-resolution digital outputs, forcing listeners to use the player's analog outputs. Although DVD-A and SACD players include digital outputs, the signal has been downsampled to 44.1kHz with 16-bit resolution, rendering the output signal identical to that of a CD player's output, regardless of the disc type being played.

The industry needs to settle on a single high-resolution, multichannel digital interface that works across all equipment brands. Until that happens, consumers are stuck with using the analog outputs of SACD and DVD-A players.

Some players, however, employ a proprietary high-resolution digital output that allows the company's DVD-A or SACD player to connect digitally with the company's other products. An example is the Meridian High-Resolution (MHR) Smart Link, which features proprietary encryption to prevent illegal copying of the datastream. Meridian's DVD-A players and controllers output high-resolution, multichannel digital audio on the MHR Smart Link, which can be received and decoded by Meridian's other products, notably its digital loudspeakers. The MHR interface also carries information about the disc content, such as whether the disc is stereo or multichannel, and the audio encoding format (DVD-Audio, Dolby Digital, DTS, etc.). This information allows the MHR-equipped controller to automatically invoke the correct decoding and DSP modes.

Some Sony SACD players offer high-resolution, multichannel digital output on an optical i.LINK connector, which can connect to some of Sony's other products, as well as outboard high-end digital-to-analog converters featuring i.LINK input. This high-resolution digital output is copy protected by Digital Transmission Content Protection (DTCP), described below.

Another way content providers can protect their music is by *watermarking*, the insertion of control and identification data in the musical signal that can prevent copying, as well as identify the specific source of the data. Watermarking was originally used to authenticate documents; the wet paper slurry was pressed into a mold and allowed to dry, creating an impression on the paper. Digital watermarking works the same way; the content's owner embeds the watermark in the form of digital data that appears in the music signal as noise. The data pattern is unique for each disc, meaning that if the data are re-transmitted or copied, the source of that illegal transmission can be identified. The watermark is a forensic tool for tracing the pirated copies to the infringer. The watermark can also control whether the content can be copied, and at what resolution. Watermarking can also be used in automated royalty calculation for radio airplay. Radio stations pay license fees on the music they play; a computer identifies the watermark and tallies the royalties owed. The watermark cannot be hacked or removed, and it survives any transmission format or media because it is an integral part of the musical waveform.

This last statement has profound implications for the audiophile—the last thing we want in our music is noise added to the signal. Although the promoters of watermarking claim that their technologies are "inaudible," and "transparent," some critical listeners who have heard the various schemes report that watermarking can in fact be heard. Very few audiophiles have heard watermarking comparisons under ideal conditions; the reports I'm aware of were made by recording engineers listening to their own material over reference-quality playback systems.

Watermarking is a key ingredient of the Secure Digital Music Initiative (SDMI), a proposal created by a consortium of music-industry and electronics-company representatives to develop a technique of preventing unauthorized duplication of music.

FireWire (IEEE1394) and Digital Transmission Content Protection (DTCP)

To meet the challenge of creating a digital interface that can transmit high-resolution, multichannel audio data, yet protects copyright holders from unauthorized duplication, a consortium of five companies, dubbed "5C", developed a scheme called *Digital Transmission Content Protection* (DTCP). The term 5C refers to the five companies who contributed to the standard: Hitachi, Intel, Panasonic, Sony, and Toshiba.

DTCP allows content providers to specify the manner in which their content can be recorded by consumers. Specifically, four scenarios are possible:

1. **Copy-Never**—no copies allowed
2. **Copy-One-Generation**—one copy allowed
3. **Copy No-More**—prevents making copies of copies
4. **Copy Freely**—no restrictions on copying

This control over copying is realized via special codes embedded in the digital audio datastream carried on a FireWire cable. Also known as i.LINK (a Sony tradename) or its official name, IEEE1394 (the Institute of Electrical and Electronics Engineers codified the standard on January 3, 1994, hence the name), FireWire is a bi-directional interface that can carry digital audio, digital video, computer data, and control signals on one cable. In Sony's SACD players equipped with a high-resolution digital output, the interface carries only audio data and the control signals needed for copy protection. FireWire is bi-directional—an essential element of Digital Transmission Content Protection. Specifically, DTCP establishes two-way communication between components with a challenge and response. When a device has been authenticated as authorized to record the digital datastream, the decryption key is downloaded into the receiving device. Content that has been encoded Copy-Never will send the decryption key only to decoding devices such as digital-to-analog converters, not digital recorders. This authentication and key exchange, which occurs in just 30 milliseconds, is invisible (and inaudible) to the user.

In fact, the entire DTCP system works behind the scenes. If you're not trying to record the high-resolution digital bitstream, you won't even know 5C is being used. DTCP simply secures the content of the FireWire digital bus between components. The only time you'll be aware of DTCP is if you attempt to record material restricted by the content provider.

DTCP also works with video signals, not just high-resolution digital audio. The system was developed with input from the Motion Picture Association of America (MPAA), Recording Institute Association of America (RIAA), the Consumer Electronics Manufacturers Association (CEMA), and groups representing computer companies. The system has already been accepted and standardized by the Society of Cable Television Engineers for OpenCable Home Digital Network Interface.

High Definition Compatible Digital (HDCD)

The fundamental problem with CD sound is that the amount of digital data representing the music isn't nearly enough to correctly encode all the musical information we can hear. As explained earlier in this chapter, the CD's sampling frequency of 44.1kHz isn't fast enough, and 16 bits per sample are too few. The challenge, then, is to put more information about the musical signal through the compact disc's 44.1kHz, 16-bit pipeline.

But how can you pack more information into a pipeline that's already filled to capacity? High Definition Compatible Digital (HDCD) uses some ingenious techniques to accomplish just that. The result is musical and technical performance that exceeds the limits of conventional 44.1kHz, 16-bit digital audio. The process was invented by Keith Johnson and Michael Pflaumer, who, with Michael Ritter, formed Pacific Microsonics Inc. to develop and market HDCD. In 2000, Pacific Microsonics was acquired by Microsoft, which has a keen interest in the art of transmitting more information in fewer bits. Despite the increasing availability of music in SACD or DVD-A (technologies which obviate the need for HDCD), many discs are encoded with HDCD, players with HDCD decoding are still available, and HDCD offers, in my view, a significant improvement in CD performance.

Recordings encoded with HDCD can be decoded and played back on any CD player, with some improvement in fidelity. But if your CD player is equipped with an HDCD decoder, HDCD recordings can be reproduced with much better sound quality than is possible with conventional CDs. Here's how it works.

The HDCD encoder takes in an analog audio signal (either from analog tape or a live microphone feed) and converts it to digital with a very fast sampling rate (176.4kHz) and 20-bit resolution. The amount of data generated is far too great to store on CD, so the HDCD encoder analyzes the high-resolution signal to determine what *musically significant* information will be lost when that signal is converted into a 44.1kHz, 16-bit signal for storage on CD. The encoder then outputs a 44.1kHz, 16-bit digital audio signal, but with a control code hidden in the 16th bit. This hidden and inaudible control code tells the HDCD decoder in the CD player to perform certain processes on the audio signal to restore some of the information present in the original high-resolution digital signal. (Note that you don't give up one bit of resolution with an HDCD recording; the control code is present only 3–5% of the time.)

The small amount of information in the control code can produce large changes in the audio signal when decoded. That's because the control code is a kind of shorthand that the decoder recognizes. Here's an analogy: Say we want to transmit Beethoven's Ninth Symphony from one place to another. Rather than transmit the entire symphony, we instead send just a few bits that tell another device to output Beethoven's Ninth Symphony. That's how HDCD works: instead of transmitting the musical information that would normally be lost in conventional coding, the control code transmits instructions to the decoder telling how to restore that information. Because so much of HDCD's "intelligence" is in the decoder, a few bits in the control code accomplish the work of many.

Although HDCD uses many techniques to improve sound quality, let's look at the way in which HDCD overcomes the limitations of the CD's 20kHz bandwidth.

While it's true that humans can hear pure tones only up to 20kHz (if you're 16 years old; at age 40 you're lucky to hear 15kHz), that doesn't mean there's no perceptible *musical* information above 20kHz. Very high frequencies imply a steep attack; the ear/brain can reportedly detect the difference in steepness of a signal with a bandwidth of 20kHz and one of 40kHz, according to HDCD's inventors.

The bandwidth of an audio system implies how quickly it can respond to musical signals. Earlier in this chapter I described a subwoofer, a low-bandwidth device, trying to reproduce the attack of a triangle. The woofer simply can't move fast enough to accurately reproduce the steep transient of the triangle's waveform.

That's exactly what happens when we record music with a bandwidth of only 20kHz. The 20kHz-bandwidth digital audio system simply can't encode the parts of the music that quickly change in intensity. The musical result is a closing-in of the sound and a reduced ability to pinpoint the positions of instruments. Experiments have shown that the ear/brain combination uses that steep transient information as directional cues. Moreover, limiting the speed of musical signals changes their timbre. For example, the component of an oboe's sound that includes the tiny "clicks" of the reeds moving disappear. We don't hear this as distortion, but as a dilution of realism. This is one reason that a live oboe has a vitality and presence we don't hear from a recording of an oboe. Because the CD's bandwidth isn't wide enough, instrumental timbres are changed, along with their directional cues.

Remember that hidden control code buried in the 16th bit of an HDCD-encoded recording? Part of that control code tells the decoder in your CD player that a particular signal had its transient attack slowed; the decoder then restores the signal's original transient steepness. This is how HDCD can reproduce signals whose speed implies a bandwidth greater than 20kHz within the limitations of the CD's 44.1kHz sampling frequency.

This is just one of the many techniques HDCD uses to squeeze more music through the 44.1kHz, 16-bit pipeline. Similar techniques address the dynamic-range limitations of 16-bit coding. The system is extremely sophisticated in practice, and reflects a decade of research into human hearing, recording, electronic design, and digital signal processing.

The first HDCD-compatible products used the Pacific Microsonics PMD100 HDCD decoder, which incorporated an 8x-oversampling digital filter that is integral to HDCD decoding. This filter also operates on conventionally encoded discs, which makes all recordings sound better, not just HDCD-encoded ones. That's because its integral digital filter operates with a higher mathematical precision than previous filters, and employs some tricks to improve sound quality. Today, HDCD decoding is more likely to be incorporated into a digital-signal processing chip that performs many other functions.

HDCD is used primarily at the mastering stage of the recording chain. After an album has been recorded and mixed, the producer and artist take the final tape to a mastering studio to generate the digital master tape from which CDs are made. The mastering engineer, artist, and producer decide if they want to use the HDCD process. (For a list of titles, see www.hdcd.com.)

Microsoft sells professional HDCD encoders and licenses HDCD decoding to other companies. For example, Motorola, Analog Devices, and Sanyo manufacture audio-processing chips that include HDCD decoding, and pay Microsoft a royalty on every chip sold. This licensing agreement is similar to that used by Dolby Laboratories in licensing its ubiquitous Dolby B noise-reduction circuit and Dolby Digital decoding technology.

In my view, HDCD is a significant advancement in digital audio sound quality. I've had the opportunity to compare an original analog master tape with an HDCD-encoded/decoded version, along with conventional 44.1kHz, 16-bit coding. I've also heard comparisons of a live microphone feed (and the instrument in the hall) against state-of-the-art analog tape and HDCD. My experience suggests that HDCD improves sound quality in these ways: with a finer resolution of detail, more accurate rendering of timbre, smoother and less synthetic treble, wider dynamic contrast, clearer articulation of loud and complex passages, bigger soundstage, tighter image focus, more front-to-back layering, more bloom around instrumental outlines, and a greater projection of quiet instruments in the presence of louder instruments.

Digital Recording Formats: CD Recordable, MiniDisc, and MP3

Many music lovers like to make their own digital recordings at home. Home recording allows you to make custom compilation recordings for portable use, or to archive LPs or other sources to a digital format.

Three formats are available to the home recordist: CD Recordable and its variants (CD-R, CD-RW), MiniDisc (MD), and MP3. Since the first edition of this book, the Digital Compact Cassette (DCC) promoted by Philips has become defunct. DCC suffered from being a tape-based format in an increasingly optical world: it was slow, clunky, and didn't represent a significant advance over the compact cassette, which it was targeted to replace.

Let's look at the pros and cons of recordable CD, MiniDisc, and MP3 to the home recordist.

Compact Disc Recordable and Compact Disc Re-Writable

The Compact Disc Recordable (CD-R) format allows the user to record her own compact disc and play that disc on nearly any conventional CD player. The advantage of CD-R is compatibility with the huge base of CD players around the world. The big drawback to CD-R is that the disc can be recorded only once. If you make a mistake in recording, or want to record something else on the disc, you're stuck. As CD-R has taken off for storing computer data, the price of blank discs has dropped significantly, although blank CD-R discs for music recording are still more expensive than blank CD-R data discs.

As its name suggests, the CD Re-Writable (CD-RW) format allows the disc to be recorded multiple times. Re-writable discs are more expensive than CD-R blanks, and may not play in all CD players.

MiniDisc

The MiniDisc (MD) is a recordable/erasable optical disc format designed by Sony to replace the analog cassette. It uses a 2.5" optical disc encased in a plastic caddy, much like a smaller version of a 3.5" computer diskette (also designed by Sony). MD is extremely portable, easy to use, and, like CD, has instant track access. It also has a shock-resistant memory buffer that prevents the player from skipping even when it's vigorously shaken.

In addition to being re-recordable and allowing instant random access to any track, MD has other useful features. For example, if you accidentally record a few seconds of a track you don't want, you can identify that section and the MD player will always skip the errant sound. Say you want to replace two four-minute tracks that are recorded on separate areas of the disc with one seven-minute track. No problem. MD will record the seven-minute track in separate sections where the two four-minute tracks were, yet play back the seven-minute track seamlessly. What's more, you'll never hear the left-over minute of the old track.

Because MD doesn't always record the digital audio data linearly, you can add a track in the middle of a disc you've already recorded. The MD doesn't care where the audio data are; adding a track in the middle of a disc is simply a matter of encoding on the disc instructions as to which sections of the disc the MD player should play, and in what order. All this occurs automatically and transparently to the consumer. This flexibility in recording and editing is unprecedented, and a great benefit in real-world use.

Although a big hit in Japan, MD didn't catch on in the US at its initial launch in 1993. Consumers were confused: if I have CD, why do I need MiniDisc? The MD advertising campaign didn't clearly convey that CD was for home use, MD for portable applications. Moreover, the high price of the first players ($500–$700) and blank discs ($15 for 60 minutes), coupled with the scarcity of pre-recorded discs, discouraged MD's target market, the Walkman user.

Sony has recently re-introduced MD in the US, this time with more success. The players are much less expensive (under $100), 74-minute blank discs are now available for less than $2, and more pre-recorded titles are available. Consequently, MD sales in 2003 hit 2.6 million players in 2003. However, with the recent and precipitous drop in the price of memory, solid-state players with no moving parts will increasingly challenge MD in portable applications.

MD's 74-minute storage capacity is achieved by reducing the number of bits representing the music. While 16-bit/44.1kHz digital audio consumes 705,600 bits per second per channel, MD consumes just 128,000. A circuit in all MD recorders called ATRAC (Adaptive Transform Acoustic Coding) analyzes the music signal and encodes only the information deemed to be audible. Such "perceptual coders" or "data reduction" systems reduce fidelity, but sound better than the numbers would indicate. (For comparison, Dolby Digital uses a data rate of 384,000 or 448,000 bits per second for six channels, or an average of 64,000 bits per second per channel—half that of MD's ATRAC.) One aspect of perceptual coders is that the encoding technology can be improved without changing the decoders. That means that ATRAC can continue to improve, with those sonic improvements realizable on every MD player ever sold. Indeed, the latest generation of ATRAC sounds considerably better than the first, although the sound quality is still a step below that of CD.

MDs come in two varieties: pre-recorded plastic discs that cannot be recorded on again, and recordable *magneto-optical* discs. Pre-recorded discs store information in pit and land structures just like a CD. Blank magneto-optical (MO) discs use a combination of optical and magnetic techniques to provide digital recording.

In MO technology, magnetic particles are arranged vertically on the disc, like trees in a forest. A laser focused on the spinning disc briefly heats the magnetic particles so that they become more easily magnetized. A magnetic head in the MD recorder changes the magnetic north/south orientation of the particles, storing the binary ones and zeros that represent the music. MD discs can be re-recorded up to one million times with no loss of integrity.

MP3

MP3, which began as an academic research project at Germany's Franhoffer Institute into coding an audio signal with very few bits, has overturned the music-industry model of selling music in packaged media (CD, LP, cassette) to consumers. When coupled with the Internet, MP3 allows consumers to efficiently transmit music between computers. This so-called "file sharing" has cut into record-company revenues, changed the way people listen to music (particularly youngsters), closed down many record retailers, and forced the music industry to develop a new distribution model.

MP3 may be acceptable to some in portable applications, but it is by no means a high-performance format. It uses about one-tenth the data rate of CD, resulting in substantially inferior sound quality.

This low data-rate, however, allows music to be stored in players that have no moving parts; instead, audio data are stored in solid-state memory. The solid-state memory can be integral and permanent in the player, or on tiny removable cards.

Helpful Digital Recording Hints

Here are a few pointers that will help you get the best sound from home digital recordings. First, if you have the option of connecting the source to the digital recorder via analog cables or digital interconnect, always choose the digital connection. For example, you can take the analog output from a CD player and feed it into a DAT machine's analog input; or you can connect the CD player's digital output to the DAT machine's digital input. By choosing the digital connection, you don't subject the signal to unnecessary A/D and D/A conversions. The result is better sound.

When recording through the analog inputs, you'll need to adjust the recording level using the recorder's meters. (With a digital-to-digital connection, you can't adjust the levels.) If the level is set too low (the meters don't approach their full scale on musical peaks), you'll lose resolution and add noise to the recording. If the levels are set too high, the musical peaks will overload, which in digital produces an unpleasant "crunching" sound. Ideally, the loudest peak of your source music should just reach full scale on your recorder's meters. Set the recorder's levels by playing the loudest passage. Some CD players have a feature that scans the disc for the loudest peak just for this purpose.

If you're recording from an analog source and want the highest possible fidelity, consider buying a separate high-end or professional A/D converter. The converters built into CDR, DAT, and MD machines are usually decent, but not superlative. You may also consider renting a high-quality ADC from a professional audio rental firm for a few weeks if you plan to archive your LP collection to a digital format. High-quality ADCs also have much more accurate meters, allowing you to more precisely set the recording level.

Finally, be aware that home digital recording products may include a copy-protection system called *Serial Copy Management System* (*SCMS*). SCMS (some say it's pronounced "scams") lets you make a digital-to-digital copy from an original source, but not a second-generation copy. For example, you can record from a CD onto a DAT machine equipped with SCMS, but not from that DAT to another DAT.

How a Digital Processor Works

For the technically minded, the rest of this chapter delves into the inner workings of the compact disc, CD transports, the S/PDIF interface, and digital processors. You don't need to know this information to enjoy music in your home, but I've included it for those who want to understand what goes on inside those sculpted metal boxes in their equipment racks. If you like, simply skip ahead to the beginning of the next chapter.

Fig.8-14 shows a block diagram of a digital processor along with a photograph illustrating how those blocks are implemented in an actual product. The main components are a power supply, input receiver, digital filter, digital-to-analog conversion stage, current-to-voltage converter, and analog output stage.

The *input receiver* takes the S/PDIF signal from a digital source and converts the serial datastream into raw digital audio data. It also generates a clock signal based on the clock embedded in the datastream (this is discussed in more detail later in this chapter). A *Phase Locked Loop* (*PLL*) compares the input signal frequency (the clock) with a reference frequency (usually generated by a crystal oscillator) and creates a new clock locked to the incoming datastream's clock. This so-called "recovered" clock becomes the master clock for the processor. The input receiver is a significant source of clock jitter and can have a large effect on how the processor sounds. Recent attempts to minimize jitter created by the input receiver include dual PLLs and custom low-jitter modules.

Before we move to the next step in digital-to-analog conversion, let's look at what happens when we convert a digital signal to analog. The discrete samples that represent the analog signal don't form a smooth and continuous waveform; they instead create a stairstep waveform. The energy in the stairstep waveform's sharp edges appears as images of the signal centered at multiples of the sampling frequency (Fig.8-15). These images must be removed by an analog low-pass filter.

In the first Sony players, these images were removed and the stairstep waveform smoothed by a brickwall analog filter (the top drawing in Fig.8-15). This filter was extremely steep, and close to the audioband, resulting in phase shift, ripple, and other audible artifacts.

Philips, co-inventor of the CD with Sony, took a different approach. Its first CD players used an *oversampling* digital filter that increased the sampling frequency by four times by interpolating three new samples for each audio sample. This raised the sampling frequency to 176.4kHz (44.1 x 4), which pushed the first image to 176.4kHz, where it could be filtered by a much gentler and better-sounding analog filter well away from the audioband (lower drawing in Fig.8-15).

Today's digital products typically use an 8x oversampling digital filter, which interpolates seven new values for each existing sample, bringing the sampling frequency to 352.8kHz (8 x 44.1kHz). Again, the spurious images at multiples of the sampling frequency still appear, but are now shifted well away from the audioband. Contrary to some beliefs, oversampling's sonic benefits are not the result of adding new information between the existing samples, nor from "smoothing out" the waveform with more samples. Moreover, oversampling doesn't increase the audio bandwidth; an 8x-oversampling CD player still has a bandwidth of 20kHz. The sonic advantage is achieved by replacing the brickwall filter with a gentler analog output filter.

In addition to increasing the effective sampling rate, oversampling digital filters increase the output word length from 16 bits to (typically) 20 bits. Note that no new information is generated by the filter when outputting longer words. Instead, the longer words reduce errors resulting from the filter's internal calculations. The audio data being filtered may temporarily have very long word lengths—perhaps 30 bits—that need to be reduced before being output from the filter. Because simply truncating (cutting off) all but the 16 needed bits results in audible distortion, some filters use redithering techniques to reduce round-off errors. These techniques attempt only to compensate for errors introduced in the filter; they cannot improve incoming data.

Fig. 8-14 Signal flow in a digital processor

Courtesy Sonic Frontiers, Inc.

Fig. 8-15 Spurious images are created at multiples of the sampling frequency (top). An oversampling digital filter shifts the first image to a higher frequency that is more easily filtered (bottom).

Courtesy Ken Pohlmann, *Principles of Digital Audio*

Custom Digital Filters

Manufacturers of CD players and digital processors have two choices: buy an "off-the-shelf" filter chip that performs eight-times (8x) oversampling, or create a custom filter from general-purpose Digital Signal Processing (DSP) chips. The custom filter designer must write the software that controls the DSP chips, an expensive and time-consuming task. Consequently, custom filters are quite a bit more expensive, but allow the CD-player designer greater creative control over the product's sound. In addition, custom digital filters can run faster than the 8x oversampling of chip filters. A custom filter can be made to run at 16x, 32x, and even 64x oversampling.

Proponents of this approach—notably Krell, Theta, and Wadia—believe their custom filtering software is better than that found in conventional integrated circuit chips. Specifically, most custom digital filters are optimized for time-domain performance rather than frequency-domain performance. The Wadia processors, for example, have superb time-domain behavior: near-perfect reconstruction of squarewaves and no pre- or post-echo in the impulse response. This excellent time-domain performance is sometimes achieved at the price of a steep rolloff in the audioband; the Wadia filter exhibits a nearly 3dB rolloff at 20kHz. The Meitner Intelligent Digital Audio Translator (IDAT) uses a combination of filters to achieve ideal time- and frequency-domain behavior.

Digital-to-Analog Conversion

After digital filtering, the oversampled data are input to the *digital-to-analog converter* or *DAC*. The DAC converts digital data at its input to an analog output signal. The most common type of DAC is the "ladder," or "R/2R" DAC. Both names describe the same operating principle. Ladder DACs have "rungs" of resistors, each rung corresponding to one bit in the digital code. A 16-bit DAC will thus have 16 resistor rungs, which allow 65,536 (2^{16}) possible input codes. The input data act as switches on the rungs; a binary "1" closes the switch at that particular bit and allows current to flow through the resistor, while a binary "0" opens the switch and no current flows. The DAC's output current is thus determined by the digital input code. (An R/2R resistor-ladder DAC is shown in Fig.8-16.)

Each rung has an effective resistor value half that of the adjacent rung; the resistor determines how much "weight" the bit has by determining how much current flows through the "switch." The *LSB* (Least Significant Bit) has the lowest weight, the *MSB* (Most Significant Bit) has the highest. Each bit upward from the LSB should produce an exact doubling of current, in the progression 1, 2, 4, 8, 16, 32, 64, 128, 256, and so

Fig. 8-16 An R/2R resistor-ladder digital-to-analog converter

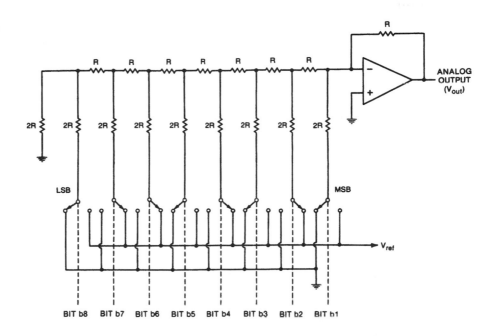

Courtesy Ken Pohlmann, *Principles of Digital Audio*

on, up to 524,288 in a 20-bit DAC. The LSB has a value of 1, the MSB a value of 524,288 (in a 20-bit DAC). When the MSB value of 524,288 is combined with the 19 lower bits, a 20-bit DAC can accommodate up to 1,048,576 input codes.

The precision of these resistor values is crucial: Any deviation from a doubling of resistance causes that bit to have more or less value than it should. These *bit-weighting errors* result in poor *linearity*. That is, the analog output level doesn't track the digital input code. A perfectly linear DAC will produce an analog output at exactly the same level as the digital input. For example, if the DAC is driven by the code representing a –90dB dithered sinewave, the analog output should be exactly 90dB below full scale. A non-linear DAC would produce an output level of perhaps –93dB or –86dB. Linearity errors generally occur at low signal levels.

Another factor that influences DAC linearity is the value of the MSB. The MSB should be equal in value to all the other bits combined, plus one; when this transition occurs, the 19 LSBs switch from all ones to all zeros, and the MSB toggles from zero to one. It's similar to the situation when a car's odometer changes from 99,999 miles to 100,000 miles. Ideally, this single quantization step should be identical in amplitude to every other quantization step. Returning to the odometer analogy, the distance driven to make the odometer rollover should be one mile, just as every other mile registered. Unfortunately, making the MSB have exactly the value of the 19 LSBs plus one is difficult. Consequently, the

MSB's value can be *trimmed* by an external potentiometer located on the circuit board next to the DAC. After the digital processor has been assembled, a technician measures the processor's low-level linearity and adjusts the *MSB trimmer* for least linearity error. The MSB value is adjusted so that it is exactly one quantization step above the 19 LSBs.

If the MSB is misadjusted or goes out of calibration over time and with temperature variations, a distortion called *zero-crossing distortion* results. Because the MSB represents half the signal amplitude, the MSB transition occurs at the point the waveform crosses the zero threshold. Any discontinuity produces a distortion of the waveform at the zero crossing point. This is absolutely the worst place for distortion: small-amplitude signals—such as reverberation decay—move around the zero-crossing point. Moreover, the zero-crossing distortion is very large in relation to the low signal amplitude. Consequently, zero-crossing distortion can cause significant corruption of low-level waveforms.

Newer DACs don't need MSB trimming: they are either factory-calibrated to have no MSB error, or they shift the zero-crossing transition to a large-signal amplitude, where an MSB error is less significant. Both of these techniques ensure good linearity without trimming, and these DACs are not subject to misadjustment or going out of calibration over time. The UltraAnalog family of DACs, found in many excellent processors built in the 1990s, is an example of converters that have been precision-calibrated at the factory and need no MSB trimmer. This is accomplished by measuring the quantization step amplitudes, then hand-soldering the appropriate precision resistors on the ladder rungs so that the resistor values are perfectly matched. This procedure is performed on each DAC. Conversely, the Burr-Brown PCM63, PCM1702, and PCM1704 DACs shift the MSB transition away from the zero crossing.

Some DAC chips come in different grades, sorted according to their linearity or distortion. The classic Philips TDA1541, for example, was available in three grades: "R" for "relaxed," "S" for "standard," and "S1"—the so-called "Crown" version. The Burr-Brown PCM63 is available in three grades, with the "PK" designation being the highest quality. Although all the DACs of a given part number are made the same way, manufacturing tolerances produce variations within a production run.

One-bit DACs

Some older CD players and digital processors use so-called *1-bit* DACs. These are more correctly called *noise shaping* DACs, *Delta-Sigma* DACs, or *oversampling* DACs. These converters are also known by their trade names: Bitstream (Philips), MASH (Matsushita's process, developed by Nippon Telephone and Telegraph), and PEM (Pulse Edge Modulation, developed by JVC). All of these converters work on the same principle: instead of using a resistor ladder with different bit weightings to convert a binary code into analog, 1-bit DACs operate in only two states: zero and one. The

1-bit code is a series of varying-length pulses with a single amplitude. The pulse width determines the analog output voltage. This is why 1-bit coding is also called *pulse-width modulation*. Except in SACD players, all manufacturers now incorporate multi-bit DACs in their products.

The single-bit code is of a high enough frequency (typically between 64x and 256x oversampling) that the audio signal can be reconstructed from these two logic states with a switched-capacitor network. Consequently, 1-bit DACs don't require the amplitude precision of ladder DACs. Oversampling DACs trade resolution in amplitude for resolution in time. They have inherently good linearity without the need of an MSB trimmer (they have no MSB to trim). Nor do oversampling DACs require a current-to-voltage converter.

Because oversampling DACs operate at such high frequencies, noise shaping can be used to shift quantization noise from the audio band to just above the audioband.

Many 1-bit DACs incorporate an analog output stage and analog filter in addition to an integral digital filter. Consequently, a single 1-bit DAC can take the place of a digital filter, dual-ladder DACs, dual current-to-voltage converters, dual MSB trimmers, and two analog output stages. This makes 1-bit technology much cheaper to implement than multi-bit ladder DACs.

My listening experience suggests, however, that digital processors based on multi-bit DACs sound better than those using 1-bit technology. Processors employing 1-bit DACs tend to lack bass tautness, dynamics, and pace. They may have a smooth and transparent presentation, but often don't have the rhythmic intensity and "slam" of multi-bit designs. There are, however, some excellent-sounding 1-bit–based digital processors on the market.

Analog Stages

The DAC's output is a series of currents at varying levels. This current output must be converted into a voltage that can be amplified by the processor's analog output stage. This is the next step after the DAC, called *current-to-voltage conversion*, or *I/V conversion* (I is the electronic symbol for current, V the symbol for voltage). The I/V converter takes the DAC's current output and converts it to a voltage. Virtually all digital processors use an *op-amp* (operational amplifier, an integrated circuit that takes the place of a circuit using separate transistors) for I/V conversion. In addition to being easier and cheaper to implement, an op-amp is generally faster than a discrete (separate transistor) I/V stage. This is because the circuitry is on a single silicon chip rather than spread out in discrete components on a circuit board.

After I/V conversion, the analog voltage is put through an analog output stage. This circuit has several functions. First, it can provide gain to bring the final output level to the CD standard of 2V RMS (with a full-scale input signal). Second, the output stage incorporates an output filter to remove high-frequency noise above the audioband. This filter is often a gentle first-order type. The output filter can be an elaborate active circuit, or as simple as a capacitor put across the analog output jacks. Finally, the output stage acts as a buffer between the I/V converter and the final analog output. The output stage generally has a low output impedance and is designed to drive cables and a preamplifier. The analog output stage can be a single active gain stage, or several intermediate stages followed by an output driver stage. A direct-coupled output stage has no capacitors in the signal path to block direct current (DC) from getting into the audio signal. Most direct-coupled output stages use a *DC servo* to prevent DC from appearing on the analog output jacks. A DC servo is a circuit that monitors the DC level at the amplifier's output and makes adjustments to reduce the amount of DC.

The processor's de-emphasis circuit is often built into the analog output stage. *De-emphasis* is a treble-rolloff circuit that restores flat response to discs that have had their treble boosted (emphasized) during recording or mastering. Very few discs—about 2%—have been emphasized. Emphasized discs carry a flag in the subcode within the digital datastream that triggers the processor's de-emphasis circuit. On some processors, a front-panel LED identifies emphasized discs.

The de-emphasis circuit can be an active stage built around an op-amp or discrete circuit, or simply an RC network (resistor and capacitor) connected to ground. Because of component tolerances (a capacitor's actual value varies from its specified value, for example), de-emphasis circuits don't always produce a perfectly flat response. Nearly all digital filters perform de-emphasis in the digital domain. This eliminates the need for an analog de-emphasis circuit, and ensures that no de-emphasis errors can occur. But because an analog de-emphasis circuit appears after the DAC, it can attenuate DAC noise and help the processor achieve a lower noise floor.

Digital vs. Analog Volume Control

The volume control in digital processors (or CD players) can be implemented in the analog or the digital domain. That is, the analog audio signal can be put through a standard volume-control knob as is found on a preamplifier, or the volume can be adjusted by performing mathematical operations on the digital data representing the music. Before deciding on a digital processor with volume control, you should know the tradeoffs inherent in each approach.

An analog volume control can slightly degrade the signal—no volume control is perfectly transparent—and can introduce small channel-balance errors at certain volume settings. For example, when the volume is turned very low, the left channel may be half a dB louder than the right. This situation could reverse as the volume is turned up.

A digital volume control has its own problems. Each 6dB reduction in volume from the maximum setting throws away one bit of resolution. A low volume setting (say, 30dB of attenuation) is equivalent to discarding five bits. If you had true 20-bit resolution in your D/A converter, you'd be listening to 15-bit audio instead of 20-bit. The lower the volume setting, the greater the loss in resolution.

Digital volume control is actually easier and cheaper to implement than analog volume control. Most digital filters have a volume control built-in; the designer need only send a control code to the filter chip to adjust the volume. An analog control requires a potentiometer (the volume control itself), another hole in the chassis, and wiring between the circuit board and potentiometer.

How a CD Transport Works

A CD transport has four main sections: the transport mechanism, the servo systems, the decoding electronics, and the output driver stage. The transport mechanism spins the CD, reads the CD's pits with a laser, and outputs a signal to the decoding electronics. The decoding circuits, usually on one integrated circuit chip, demodulate the datastream, perform error correction, and convert the data into a form that can be transmitted from the transport to a digital processor. The servo systems maintain correct disc speed (the rotational servo), keep the laser on the spiral track of pits (tracking servo), and maintain laser focus on the spinning disc (focus servo). The output stage is a digital line driver sometimes including a small transformer called a *pulse transformer*—to drive the cable and digital processor input.

Let's look at each of these subsystems in more detail.

The compact disc and laser pickup mechanism constitute a remarkable feat of engineering. The CD has a spiral track of alternating pits and land, recorded from the inside of the disc to the outside. *Pits* are indentations in the disc surface; *land* is the disc surface itself. The space between adjacent tracks of pits is 1.6µm (micrometer), or 1.6 millionths of a meter. The pits vary in length from 0.8µm to 2.8µm, and are 0.56µm wide. To put these numbers into perspective, a human hair has a diameter of about 75µm. If each pit on a CD were the size of a grain of rice, the CD itself would be the size of a baseball diamond. Fig.8-17 shows a CD surface photographed by a scanning electron microscope.

DVD and Super Audio CD achieve greater data density with smaller pits and a shorter-wavelength laser beam. The pits on a DVD, and on an SACD's high-density layer, are about half the size of CD pits, and the tracks are more closely spaced (Fig.8-4 earlier). Nonetheless, the operating principle is identical.

Fig. 8-17 A CD surface has a spiral track of "pits" embedded in the "land."

Courtesy Disc Manufacturing, Inc.

The laser beam is reflected from the CD's surface to a photodetector, a device that converts light into an electrical signal. When the beam strikes either land or pit bottom, it is reflected to the photodetector at full strength. This condition represents binary "zero." But when the laser beam strikes a land-to-pit or pit-to-land transition, part of the beam is reflected from the land and part is reflected from the pit bottom. Because the pit depth is one quarter the wavelength of the laser light, the beam portion reflected from the pit bottom is 180° out of phase with the beam reflected from the land, as shown in Fig.8-18. The two beam portions—now out of phase with each other—cancel each other, reducing the output from the photodetector. This reduced output, caused by a pit-to-land or land-to-pit transition, represents binary "1."

Fig. 8-18 A pit-to-land or land-to-pit transition produces a 180° phase reversal in part of the reflected beam, reducing the beam's intensity.

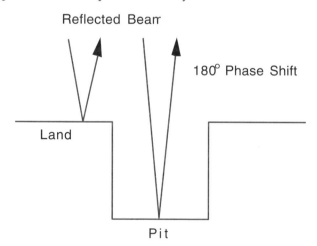

The pits thus produce a reflected beam of varying intensity, which produces a varying voltage at the photodetector output. The output signal is a series of sinewaves, the peaks representing land or pit bottom, and the zero-crossing transitions representing the pit edges. Because the pits and lands have nine discrete lengths, the recovered signal is composed of nine discrete-frequency sinewaves. The recovered signal, called an "eye pattern" or "RF" signal, is shown in Fig.8-19. Although the RF signal looks like an analog signal, the digital data are encoded in the zero-crossing transitions. The shortest pit or land length represents the digital data 1001; the ones are the pit edges and the zeros are the pit bottoms or land. The longest pit length represents the digital data 100000000001. The shortest pit produces a frequency (in the RF signal) of 720kHz, and the longest pit produces a frequency of 196kHz.

Fig. 8-19 A signal reflected from the disc is composed of nine discrete-frequency sinewaves.

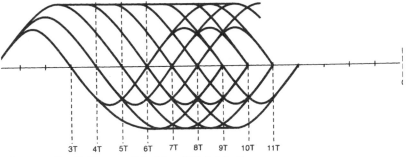

3T   4T   5T   6T   7T   8T   9T   10T   11T

Courtesy Ken Pohlmann, *Principles of Digital Audio*

The data read from the disc don't directly represent digital audio data. Instead, a coding method is used to increase the disc's storage density and provide a clock signal within the data. The coding method is called *Eight-to-Fourteen Modulation*, or *EFM*. EFM coding takes a block of 8 bits and assigns it a unique 14-bit word. These 14-bit words are joined together by three "merging" bits to form the data pattern recorded on the CD. EFM coding inserts a minimum of two zeros between successive ones (remember, the shortest pits represent the data 1001), and a maximum of ten zeros between ones. The result is a pit-and-land pattern of nine discrete lengths. Fig.8-20 shows the relationship between the original data, EFM-coded data, and pit structure. SACD and DVD use a modified version of this encoding system that achieves slightly greater packing efficiency.

Although it is counterintuitive to think that increasing the number of bits by EFM coding stores data more efficiently, that's exactly what it does. Moreover, the specific pattern of ones and zeros creates a clock signal at the data rate read from the disc: 4.3218 million bits per second. Of these, only 1.41 million bits are audio data. The rest are error-correction, subcode, and the result of EFM coding. EFM coding also inherently makes the signal self-clocking.

Subcode is non-audio data recorded on the CD. It contains track time, track number, whether the CD has been recorded with pre-emphasis, and other such "housekeeping" information. When the de-emphasis circuit in your CD player or digital processor is activated, it has been triggered by a bit in the subcode. The track and time information displayed on your CD player is also recovered from the subcode.

The EFM signal is input to the decoding electronics, which convert the 14-bit words back into the original 8-bit data. These chips also perform error-correction and strip out the subcode. (A general description

Fig. 8-20 The relationship between original data, EFM-coded data, pit structure, and the RF signal.

Courtesy Ken Pohlmann, *Principles of Digital Audio*

of error-correction is included in Appendix C.) The *Cross Interleaved Reed-Solomon Code* (CIRC) error-correcting system used in the CD has two levels, called "C1" and "C2." The first decoder (C1) corrects as many errors as it can before sending the data to the C2 decoder. The C2 decoder de-interleaves the data (puts it back in its original order), thereby converting a long-burst error into many shorter errors, which are more easily corrected.

The rotational servo uses an *elastic buffer* between the disc motor and the decoding electronics. Data are fed into the buffer at one end and clocked out at the other end. When the buffer is more than half full, a signal tells the rotational motor to slow down, decreasing the rate at which data are read from the disc. When the buffer is less than half full, the motor speed is increased to fill up the buffer faster. This servo mechanism always keeps the buffer half full. Data can be read in at an irregular speed, but are clocked out at a precise rate.

The focus servo system maintains the laser's objective lens at a precise distance from the spinning disc. The tracking servo keeps the laser centered on one track of the spinning disc.

A transport's output stage takes the S/PDIF signal from the S/PDIF encoder circuit and presents it to the final output jack. The job of driving the interface cable and digital-processor input falls on the output stage. Some transports have a reclocking circuit at the output stage to reduce jitter in the datastream. The output stage determines the transport's output impedance, which should be 75 ohms. Most transports use a pulse transformer at the output to couple the S/PDIF signal to the outside world.

How the S/PDIF Interface Works

Those with a technical bent may want a closer look at the S/PDIF datastream. The S/PDIF signal contains audio data for both audio channels, as well as a synchronization signal called a *clock*. This clock is recovered in the digital processor, locking the transport and processor to the same timing reference. The "Lock" light or sampling-frequency indicator on the front panel of many digital processors indicates that the clock has been recovered and the two components are locked together, i.e., their clocks are synchronized.

S/PDIF and AES/EBU use a type of coding called "bi-phase mark," a form of self-clocking code. Fig.8-21 shows how the audio data and clock signal are combined to produce the S/PDIF datastream. Each audio data bit is represented by a two-cell doublet, each of which begins and ends with a transition. These doublets are clearly visible in the signal of Fig.8-21. A data bit "1" produces a transition within the doublet. A data bit "0" generates a doublet with no transition within the doublet. Thus, audio data and a clock signal are combined into a single data-stream.

Fig. 8-21 The S/PDIF datastream uses "biphase mark" coding.

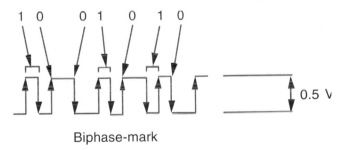

Biphase-mark

The S/PDIF datastream carries not just audio data, but house-keeping information as well, including some of the CD's subcode. This includes the sampling frequency, whether the data has been pre-emphasized, and whether the signal is professional AES/EBU or consumer S/PDIF. The subcode data also includes all the track number and timing information displayed on a CD player or transport.

Audio and subcode data are combined to form 32-bit *subframes,* shown in Fig.8-22. Each subframe begins with a *preamble,* a 4-bit pattern that violates the rules of bi-phase mark coding. The preamble acts as a synchronization signal to indicate the beginning of a new subframe. The preamble is followed by 4 bits of auxiliary data, then 20 bits of audio data. If 16-bit data are being transmitted, the four additional bits are not used (coded as all zeros). The 4-bit auxiliary data area can be used for audio, bringing the total audio word-length capacity to 24 bits. Four additional bits (audio sample validity, user bit data, audio channel status, and subframe parity) complete the subframe.

Fig. 8-22
S/PDIF subframe
structure

Courtesy Ken Pohlmann, *Principles of Digital Audio*

Left and right audio-channel subframes are identified by slightly different preambles. They are interleaved, making a single bitstream from both audio channels. Subframes are combined to form blocks, each of which is 192 bits long. A sampling rate of 44.1kHz has an overall bit rate of 2.8224 million bits per second.

9 Turntables, Tonearms, and Cartridges: The LP Playback System

Introduction

The long-playing (LP) record playback system is a combination of a turntable, tonearm, and phono cartridge that converts the mechanical information encoded on vinyl records into an electrical signal that can be amplified by the rest of your playback system. The turntable spins the record, the tonearm holds the cartridge in place, and the cartridge converts the wiggles in the record's groove into an electrical signal. Each of these elements, and how they interact with each other, plays a pivotal role in getting good sound from your system.

The LP record playback system has been the mainstay of the audio and music industries since the early years of this century. If you wanted recorded music, you bought records. The advent of the compact disc has, however, severely restricted the availability of LPs. As the world abandons LPs in favor of the more convenient digital formats, the audiophile is left with difficult choices about how much to invest in the competing LP and digital playback hardware.

This quandary—LP vs. CD, SACD, or DVD-Audio—emerges from the fact that even today's state-of-the-art CD playback doesn't approach the sound quality offered by a good LP playback system. At the very highest level of music reproduction, there's not even a debate: LP is musically superior to CD.

I must qualify that last statement: a high-quality, properly set-up LP playback system, playing a record in good condition, will sound better than any CD. If, however, the record is played on a low-quality or poorly set-up system, the CD will usually offer higher sonic performance. The general public's perception that CD is vastly superior to LP (remember the "Perfect Sound Forever" marketing campaign for CD?) is perpetuated because very few listeners have heard high-quality LP playback. When done right, LP playback has an openness, transparency, dynamic expression, and musicality not matched by CD. There's just a fundamental musical rightness to a pure analog source (one that has never been digitized) that seems to better convey the music's expression.

This isn't to say that LPs are perfect. They suffer from a variety of distortions such as mistracking, ticks and pops, speed instability, surface noise, cartridge frequency-response variations, inner-groove distortion, wear, and susceptibility to damage. But for many listeners, these problems are less musically objectionable than the distortion imposed by digitally encoding and decoding an audio signal. Some listeners can hear past the LP's flaws and enjoy the medium's overall musicality. Other listeners can't stand the ritual of handling and cleaning records—not to mention keeping the turntable properly adjusted—and think CD is just fine. I think of it this way: LP's distortions are apparent, but separate from the music; digital's distortions are woven into the music's fabric. Consequently, analog's distortions are easier to ignore. If you're inclined to think CD is without fault, and you've never heard a properly played LP, give yourself a treat and visit a specialty audio dealer with a high-end turntable. Listen to what vinyl can do before you write off the possibility of owning a high-quality turntable.

There's been a surprising resurgence in LP playback since the late 1990s, reflected by increasing turntable sales and more new vinyl releases than at any time since the late 1980s. Audiophiles with existing record collections are taking advantage of the improved performance of today's components by upgrading their LP front ends, and young music lovers are discovering the pleasures of vinyl for the first time. Record companies are responding with more new LP releases and reissues. In fact, sales of LP records in 2003 exceeded sales of SACD and DVD-Audio discs combined.

LP's popularity as the medium of choice is threatened by these high-resolution digital formats. The relative sonic merits of each format—LP, SACD, DVD-A is open to debate, but until the high-resolution digital formats have a large catalog of titles behind them, many of us will continue enjoying our record collections.

System Hierarchy: Why the LP Front End Is So Important

My suggestion later in this chapter that some audiophiles spend as much as 40% of their total system budget on an LP front end may strike some as excessive. After all, how much effect can the cartridge, tonearm—and especially the turntable—have on the reproduced sound compared to the contribution of amplifiers and loudspeakers?

The answer is that the components at the front of the playback chain should be of at least as good a quality as those at the end of the chain (loudspeakers). The LP playback system's job is to extract as much musical information from the LP grooves as possible, and with the greatest fidelity to the signal cut into the LP. *Any musical information not recovered at the front end of the playback system cannot be restored later in the chain.* It doesn't do any good to have superlative electronics and loudspeakers if you're feeding them a poor-quality, low-resolution signal from an inadequate LP front end. If the music isn't there at the start, it won't be there at the end.

The importance of the turntable was first brought to the world's attention by Ivor Tiefenbrun of Linn in the early 1970s. He sold his turntable by walking into audio dealerships unannounced with the turntable under his arm, and asking the store owner to listen with him to the best system in the store with the store's turntable. Then they listened to the store's least expensive system hooked up to the Linn LP12 turntable. When the store owners heard their most modest system outperform their most expensive system, many became convinced of the turntable's importance. (When asked by the store owner "But how can I sell this to my customers?" Tiefenbrun responded "The same way I just sold it to you.") It took years of these kinds of demonstrations to convince the audio community that the turntable was a significant variable in a system's sound quality. Today, no debate exists over the turntable's importance in achieving good sound. (To date, more than 120,000 Linn LP12s have been sold worldwide.)

How to Choose an LP Playback System

Because there are many more variables to account for in LP playback, how much of your audio budget you should spend on this part of your system is a more complicated decision than setting a budget for, say, a power amplifier.

Let's look at two hypothetical audiophiles, one of whom should spend much more on a turntable, tonearm, and cartridge than the other audiophile.

Our first audiophile has a huge record collection that represents a lifetime of collecting music. Her record collection is a treasure trove of intimately known music that she plays daily. Conversely, she has very few CDs, buying them only when her favorite music isn't available on vinyl. She much prefers the sound of LPs, and doesn't mind the greater effort required by LPs: record and stylus cleaning, turning over the record, lack of random access.

The second audiophile's record assortment represents a small percentage of his music collection—most of his favorite music is on CD. His

LP listening time is a fraction of the time spent listening to CD. He likes the convenience of CD, and can happily live with the sound of his excellent digital processor and CD transport.

The first audiophile should commit a significant portion of her overall system budget to a top-notch LP front end—perhaps 40%. The second will want to spend much less—say, 10 to 15%—and put the savings into the components he spends more time listening to.

If you're more like the first audiophile and are about to upgrade your turntable, I suggest you stretch your budget and get a really top-notch turntable, tonearm, and cartridge. Here's why: Superlative turntables won't be around forever. Although the early part of this century has seen a resurgence of interest in vinyl playback, the market will some day dwindle (particularly if SACD or DVD-Audio achieve mass-market acceptance). Consequently, fewer and fewer manufacturers will offer high-end turntables. If you buy a turntable good enough to keep you going for a few years with the idea of upgrading later, your upgrade options may be severely limited. By buying an excellent system now, you can probably keep it for the rest of your life. The turntable you buy now may be the last turntable you'll ever need. Make it a good one.

Further, today's turntables, tonearms, and cartridges are at the pinnacle of technical and musical achievement. They are vastly superior to the products of even the middle 1900s, and provide you with a means of hearing your LP collection with a quality you may not have thought possible. It's ironic that LP playback hardware's great progress has coincided with the mass-market shift away from LP.

There's another way of getting a superb analog front end: Buy a used one from someone who's abandoned LPs in favor of CDs. (While you're at it, you can also pick up the owner's record collection.)

A decent entry-level turntable with integral tonearm runs about $300, with an appropriate cartridge adding from $30 to $150 to the price. A mid-level turntable and arm costs $800 to $1500; the cartridge price range for this level of turntable is from $200 to $700.

There are roughly two quality and price levels above the $2000 mark. The first is occupied by a wide selection of turntables and arms costing between $3000 and $6000. At this price, you can achieve very nearly state-of-the-art performance. Plan to spend at least $1000 for a phono cartridge appropriate for these turntables.

The very highest price level is established by turntables costing between $10,000 and $20,000. A topflight phono cartridge can add as much as $5000 to the price. These systems are characterized by extraordinary and elaborate construction techniques such as vacuum hold-down systems to keep the record in intimate contact with the platter, massive vibration-resistant bases, an exceptional vibration isolation system, lots of high-precision machining, and a high-gloss finish. Although many of these turntables are sonically superlative, some turntables in the $8000 to $12,000 range are equal (or even superior) to the costliest units in construction quality, finish elegance, reliability, and sonic performance.

Once you've decided on an LP front-end budget, allocate a percentage of that budget to the turntable, tonearm, and cartridge. Many lower-priced turntables come with an arm—or an arm and cartridge—already fitted and included in the price. At the other end of the scale, the megabuck turntables also include a tonearm. In the middle range, you should expect to spend about 50% of your budget on the turntable, 25% on a tonearm, and 25% on a cartridge. These aren't hard figures, but an approximation of how your LP front-end budget should be allocated. As usual, a local audio retailer with whom you've established a relationship is your best source of advice on assembling the best LP playback system for your budget.

An item of utmost importance in achieving good sound from your records is a good turntable stand or equipment rack, particularly if the turntable has a less than adequate suspension. (Turntable suspensions are described later in this chapter.) I cannot overstate how vital a solid, vibration-resistant stand is in getting the most from your analog front end. Save some of your budget for a solid equipment rack or you're wasting your money on a good turntable, arm, and cartridge. (The very best turntables have extraordinary mechanical systems to isolate the turntable from vibration, and thus don't benefit as much from a solid stand. These turntables are rare, and occupy the upper end of the price range.)

The importance of a good rack was underscored for me recently while I was reviewing a turntable isolation system. I moved the turntable (a model that lacked a suspension) from its usual place on a 350-pound sand-filled and spiked turntable stand (the Merrill Stable Table) to a generic wooden "stereo rack" to test the effectiveness of the turntable isolation system. The difference was like night and day—and far greater than you'd expect. I'll talk more about turntable stands later in this chapter, under "LP System Setup," and also in Chapter 12.

I'll also go into some detail about how turntables, tonearms, and cartridges are built, and what to look for when choosing each element of the LP front end. You can use this information to assemble your own turntable system, or just brush up on the subject so you can talk confidently with the dealer who puts together your LP playback system. Whichever route you choose, you'll still want to listen and evaluate the turntable system's sonic merits.

What to Listen For

Judging the sonic and musical performance of an LP playback system is more difficult than evaluating any other component. If you want to audition a phono cartridge, for example, you cannot do so without also hearing the turntable, tonearm, and how the cartridge interacts with the rest of the LP playback system. The same situation applies to each of the elements that make up an analog front end; you can never hear them in isolation. Further, how those three components are set up greatly affects the overall performance. Other variables include the turntable stand, where it's located in the room, the phono preamp, and the load the pre-amp presents to the cartridge. Nonetheless, each turntable, tonearm, and cartridge has its own sonic signature. The better products have less of a sonic signature than lower-quality ones; i.e., they more closely approach sonic neutrality.

A high-quality LP front end is characterized by a lack of rumble (or low-frequency noise), greatly reduced record-surface noise, and the impression that the music emerges from a black background. Low-quality LP front ends tend to add a layer of sonic grunge below the music that imposes a grayish opacity on the sound. When you switch to a high-quality front end, it's like washing a grimy film off of a picture window—the view suddenly becomes more transparent, vivid, and alive.

Even if the LP front end doesn't have any obvious rumble, it can still add this layer of low-level noise to the music. The noise not only adds a murkiness to the sound, it also obscures low-level musical detail. A better turntable and tonearm strip away this film and let you hear much deeper into the music. It can be difficult to identify this layer of noise unless you've heard the same music reproduced on a top-notch front end. Once you've heard a good LP playback system, however, the difference is startling. To use a visual analogy, hearing your records on a good analog front end for the first time is like looking at the stars on a cloudless, moonless night in the country after living in the city all your life. A wealth of subtle musical detail is revealed, and with it, a much greater involvement in the music.

Another important characteristic you'll hear on a superlative system is the impression that the music is made up of individual instruments existing in space. Each instrument will occupy a specific point in space, and be surrounded by a halo of air that keeps it separate from the other instruments. The music sounds as if it is made up of individual elements rather than sounding homogenized, blurred, congested, and confused. There's a special realness, life, and immediacy to records played on a high-quality turntable system.

A related aspect is soundstage transparency—the impression that the musical presentation is crystal-clear rather than slightly opaque. A transparent soundstage lets you hear deep into the concert hall, with instruments toward the rear maintaining their clarity and immediacy, yet still sounding far back in the stage. The ability to "see" deep into the soundstage provides a feeling of a vast expanse of space before you in which the instruments can exist (if, of course, the recording engineers have captured these qualities in the first place). Reverberation decay hangs in space longer, further conveying the impression of space and depth.

Conversely, a lower-quality LP front end will tend to obscure sounds emanating from the stage rear, making them sound undifferentiated and lacking life. The presentation is clouded by an opaque haze that dulls the music's sense of immediacy, prevents you from hearing low-level detail, and tends to shrink your sense of the hall's size. The differences between superb and mediocre LP reproduction are much like those described Chapter 1's Grand Canyon analogy.

Other important musical qualities greatly affected by the LP front end are dynamic contrast and transient speed. A top-notch LP replay system has a much wider dynamic expression than a mediocre one; the difference between loud and soft is greater. In addition to having wider dynamic range, musical transients have an increased sense of suddenness, zip, and sharpness of attack. The attack of an acoustic guitar string, for example, is quick, sharp, and vivid. Many mediocre turntables and arms slow these transient signals, making them sound synthetic and lifeless. A good LP front end will also have a coherence that makes the transients sound as if they are all lined up in time with each other. The result is more powerful rhythmic expression.

Just as we want the LP front end to portray the steep attack of a note, we want the note to decay with equal rapidity. A first-rate LP front end is characterized by its ability to clearly articulate each note with a sense of silence between the notes, rather than blurring them together. A good test for an LP front end's transient characteristics is intricate percussion music. Any blurring of the music's dynamic structure—attack and decay—will be immediately obvious as a smearing of the sound, lack of immediacy, and the impression that you're hearing a replica of the instruments rather than the instruments themselves. Hearing live, unamplified musical instruments periodically really sharpens your hearing acuity for judging reproduced sound.

All turntables, tonearms, and cartridges influence the sound's overall perspective and tonal balance. Even high-quality components can have distinctive sonic signatures. Careful matching is therefore required between the turntable, arm, and cartridge to achieve a musical result. Matching a bright, forward cartridge to an arm with the same characteristics, and mounting both on a somewhat aggressive-sounding turntable, could be a recipe for unmusical sound. Those same individual components may, however, be eminently musical when in a mix of components that tend to complement each other.

The very best turntables, tonearms, and cartridges are more sonically neutral than lesser products. System matching is therefore less critical as you go up in quality. State-of-the-art turntables and tonearms tend to be so neutral that you can put together nearly any combination and get superlative sound.

You should listen for two other aspects of turntable performance: *speed accuracy* and *speed stability*. Speed accuracy is how close the turntable's speed is compared to 33-1/3 rpm. You need to worry about speed accuracy only if you have absolute pitch (the ability to identify a pitch in isolation). Speed instability, however, is easily audible by any-one, and is particularly annoying. Speed stability is how smoothly the platter rotates. Poor speed stability causes *wow and flutter*. Wow is a very slow speed variation that shifts the pitch slowly up and down and is most audible on solo piano with sustained notes. Flutter is a rapid speed fluctuation that almost sounds like tremolo. Together, wow and flutter make the sound unstable and blurred rather than solidly anchored. A good turntable with no obvious flutter can still suffer from speed insta-bility. Instead of hearing flutter overtly, you may hear a reduction in timbrel accuracy—an oboe, for example, will sound less like an oboe and more like an undifferentiated tone.

Technical Aspects of Choosing an LP Front End

Matching a turntable, tonearm, and cartridge involves some technical decisions, not just aesthetic choices about which combinations sound the most musical.

First, the tonearm must be able to fit the turntable's arm-mounting area. Many turntables have an *arm-mounting board* on which the ton-earm is fastened. The arm-mounting board must be at least as big as the arm's base, and be able to securely hold the arm. Any looseness here will seriously degrade the sound. When mounted to the arm-board, the tonearm's cartridge end should be positioned within a range that allows the cartridge to be positioned at exactly the correct distance from the tonearm's pivot point, a parameter called *overhang*. Overhang can be set using the turntable manufacturer's template, or a third-party alignment protractor.

The turntable's suspension should be stiff enough to support the tonearm's weight. If the tonearm is too heavy for the turntable's suspen-sion, the turntable won't be level. Turntable manufacturers will specify a range of tonearm weights appropriate for their turntables.

Next, the tonearm's *effective mass* must be matched to the cartridge's *compliance*. Let's define these terms before examining how they interact.

An arm's effective mass isn't the tonearm's weight, but the mass of the moving parts, and where along the tonearm's length that mass is dis-tributed. Any body has a certain amount of inertia: a body at rest tends to stay at rest, and a body in motion tends to stay in motion. The amount of a body's inertia is its mass. If this body is rotated, however, the amount of its inertia in the rotational direction is called its *moment of inertia*. The effective mass of a rotating or pivoting object is the amount of mass that object would have if all of its mass were located at its "cen-ter of mass."

For example, adding one gram to the armtube near the pivot point would increase only slightly the effective mass; adding that same gram to the cartridge end of the armtube would greatly increase the effective mass. If you imagine pushing down on the counterweight side of the tonearm to lift the cartridge end of the arm, you can see how that one gram would require more force to lift when it is far away from the pivot point.

Less than 10 grams of effective mass is considered low mass, 11 to 20 grams is considered mid-mass, and more than 20 grams is high mass.

A cartridge's compliance describes how stiffly or loosely the suspension holds the *cantilever*. The cantilever is the thin tube that emerges from the cartridge *body* and holds the *stylus*. If the cantilever is easily moved, the cartridge is *high-compliance*. If the cantilever is stiffly mounted, the cartridge is said to have *low compliance*.

Compliance is expressed as a number indicating how far the cantilever moves when a force is applied. Specifically, a force of 10^{-6} dynes is applied, and the cantilever's movement in millionths of a centimeter is the cartridge's compliance. For example, a low-compliance cartridge (a stiff suspension) may move only ten millionths of a centimeter; we say the cartridge has a compliance of 10. Because this method of expressing compliance is standardized, the reference to millionths of a centimeter is dropped, leaving only the value 10. Moderately compliant cartridges have compliances of 12 to 20, and high-compliance cartridges are of any value above 20.

A cartridge's compliance and the tonearm's effective mass form a resonant system. That is, the combination will vibrate much more easily at a particular frequency than at other frequencies. When a bell is struck, it rings at the bell's resonant frequency. Similarly, a tonearm and cartridge will resonate when put into motion. Energy is imparted to the tonearm and cartridge by record warp, turntable rumble, the turntable's resonance, record eccentricity (the center hole isn't exactly centered), and footfalls (the vibrations of someone's footsteps transmitted from the floor to the turntable). These energy sources are all of very low frequencies, perhaps below 8Hz. Higher in frequency, the tonearm and cartridge can be set in motion by the musical signal in the grooves, with the lowest frequency being about 20Hz. Although we can't avoid resonance in the tonearm and cartridge, we can adjust it so that their resonant frequency falls *above* the very low frequency of rumble and record warp, but *below* the lowest musical pitch recorded in the record grooves. By matching the arm's effective mass to the cartridge's compliance, we can tune the resonant frequency to fall between the sources of vibration. Fig.9-1 shows the resonant frequencies of different values of arm mass and cartridge compliance.

Preventing the tonearm and cartridge from resonating is of utmost importance. The audio signal is generated in the phono cartridge by the motion of the cantilever relative to the cartridge. If the arm and cartridge are vibrating even slightly, that vibration is converted into an electrical signal by the cartridge. Because the cartridge can't distinguish between groove modulation (the musical information) and tonearm resonance,

Fig. 9-1 The relationship between a tonearm's effective mass, cartridge compliance, and resonant frequency

After Merrill

distortion is mixed in with the music. Tonearm resonance distorts the music's tonal balance, colors instrumental timbre, changes the music's dynamic structure (the way notes start and stop), and destroys the sense of space and imaging on the recording.

The Turntable

It's easy to think of the turntable as having a minor role in a playback system's sound quality. After all, the turntable only spins the record and holds the tonearm; how much sonic influence could it have?

The answer is surprising: a high-quality turntable is absolutely essential to getting the best performance from the rest of your system. A good turntable presents a solid, vibration-free platform for the record and tonearm, allowing the cartridge to recover the maximum amount of information in the grooves while minimizing interference with the audio signal.

The turntable is composed of a base, platter, platter bearing, plinth, drive system, and often a sub-chassis. The *base* is the turntable's main structure; it holds all the components, and is usually finished in black or natural wood. The *platter* is the heavy disc that supports the record; it rests on the *bearing assembly*. The *plinth* is the top of the turntable beneath the platter. The *drive system* conveys the motor's rotation to the platter. Some turntables have a *sub-chassis* suspended within the base on which the platter and tonearm are mounted. Every turntable will also have an *armboard* for mounting a tonearm. Many turntables have no base or plinth, instead suspending the sub-chassis in open air.

Let's look at how each of these components is assembled into the modern turntable.

The Base and Plinth

A turntable's base and plinth play important roles in sound quality. The base must be a rigid, vibration-resistant structure on which the other turntable components can be mounted. If the base is flimsy, it will vibrate and transmit that vibration to the platter and tonearm, thus degrading the sound.

A turntable system can be set vibrating by four forces: 1) acoustic energy impinging on the turntable (called *feedback*); 2) structure-borne vibration traveling through the turntable stand (primarily when the stand is located on a suspended floor); 3) the turntable's mechanical systems, such as the platter bearing and motor vibration; and 4) the motion imparted to the tonearm by groove modulations.

This vibration creates relative motion between the stylus and the cartridge. Because the cartridge can't distinguish between groove modulation and turntable resonance, this vibration is converted to an electrical signal and amplified by your system. This is why turntable designers go to elaborate measures to prevent vibration.

Let's first take the case of acoustic energy impinging on the turntable. If the base and plinth aren't rigid, they're more likely to be set in motion by sound striking the turntable. In extreme cases, the loudspeakers and turntable create an *acoustic feedback loop* in which sound from the loudspeakers is converted into an electrical signal in the cartridge through vibration, which is amplified by the loudspeakers, which causes even more feedback to be produced by the cartridge, and so forth. This acoustic feedback can muddy the music, or even make it impossible to play records at a moderately high playback level. You can hear this phenomenon by putting the stylus on the lead-in groove without the record spinning, then gradually turning up the volume. You'll start to hear a howling sound as the acoustic feedback loop grows strong enough to feed on itself, and a "runaway" condition develops in which the sound keeps getting louder. If you try this, keep your hand on the volume control and be ready to turn down the volume as soon as you hear the howl—if you don't turn down the volume *immediately*, the system could be damaged. The more vibration-resistant the turntable, the less severe this phenomenon. You might try this with and without the turntable's dustcover in place. A turntable's dustcover can catch acoustic energy and feed it into the base and plinth, degrading the sound. Other dustcovers protect the turntable from vibration.

Turntable bases and plinths are designed to resist vibration by making them very massive (so it's hard to put them in motion), and by *damping* any vibrations that do exist. Inert materials such as Medium Density Fiberboard (MDF) and Fountainhead are often used in turntable bases. Very-high-quality turntables are made from machined acrylic. Vibration damping is achieved with layers of material applied to or within the base so that the vibration stops rather than being allowed to ring. An example of vibration damping is putting a wet rag on a steel plate before striking the plate. Instead of hearing the plate ring, you hear a dull thud—the vibrational energy is dissipated more quickly. In practice, damping materials are often exotic compounds (one turntable uses the same sound-deadening material that lines a submarine's hull). One technique, called *constrained-layer damping*, puts layers of soft damping material between layers of harder materials to more effectively dissipate vibrational energy. When vibration encounters a discontinuity in the material, shear forces between layers produce *shear strain*, which causes frictional losses. The mechanical energy is converted into a minute amount of heat. In another technique lead inserts are distributed throughout the base and platter.

The armboard should have vibration resistance and damping properties similar to those of the base. Some armboards of acrylic and lead weigh up to six pounds.

Another theory of turntable design suggests that the *less* massive the base and plinth, the better. This belief argues that a very rigid, low-mass base is ideal because there's less mass to resonate. This theory, used in only a few turntable models, has been discredited by proponents of high-mass turntables.

So much for the problem of acoustic energy putting the turntable in motion. Now let's look at how turntable design addresses the problems of structure-borne vibration. Vibration entering the turntable through the stand or rack can be greatly reduced by mechanically isolating the turntable's key components (platter, armboard, and tonearm/cartridge) with a suspension system—the sprung turntable.

Sprung and Unsprung Turntables

Most turntables are *sprung*, meaning that the platter and armboard are mounted on a sub-chassis that floats within the base on springs. The terms *suspended* and *floating* describe the same construction.

Sprung turntables can be one of three designs. In one method, the sub-chassis sits on springs attached to the base bottom. In the second method, the sub-chassis hangs down from the plinth on springs. (Fig.9-2 shows the latter of these two techniques.) The third technique dispenses with the base entirely and hangs the sub-chassis in open air on pillars (Fig.9-3). The turntable is suspended on the four pillars at each corner of the turntable.

Fig. 9-2 The sub-chassis can be hung from the plinth.

Courtesy Audio Advisor, Inc. and SOTA Industries

Fig. 9-3 The sub-chassis can also be mounted in open air, with no base.

Courtesy Basis Audio, Inc.

Whichever technique is used, the goal of all sprung designs is to isolate the platter and tonearm from external vibration. Any vibration picked up by the supports on which the turntable rests won't be transferred as effectively to the platter and tonearm. The primary sources of structure borne vibration are passing trucks, footfalls, air conditioners, and motors attached to the building. Structure-borne vibration is much less of a problem in a single-family home with a concrete floor than in an apartment building or frame house with suspended floors.

The suspension on which the sub-chassis is mounted is carefully tuned to a very low frequency. The vertical resonant frequency of the suspension can also be tuned to a slightly different frequency than the horizontal resonant frequency. In addition, the suspension can be immersed in a viscous fluid to damp any remaining vibration. An advantage of viscous damping over mechanical damping such as foam or Sorbothane (a rubberlike material) is that the viscous fluid doesn't compress, retaining its damping properties under all conditions. (The turntable shown in Fig.9-3 uses this technique.)

You can judge a suspension's effectiveness by putting the stylus on a stationary record and tapping on the stand on which the turntable is mounted. The volume should be turned up to what would be a moderate listening level if the record were spinning. You should start by gently tapping the stand, then gradually increasing the force. The less sound you hear from the loudspeakers, the more effective the turntable's suspension. With the best models, you can even hit the stand as hard as you like with a hammer and hear no sound from the loudspeakers; the suspension completely isolates the platter and tonearm from the hammer blow. In less effective designs, a small tap on the stand can be heard through the loudspeakers.

A small minority of turntable designers believe, however, that the springs used in suspended turntables can resonate and actually introduce vibration into the platter and arm. They believe the answer is the *unsprung* turntable, in which the platter and tonearm are mounted directly to the base. If the base is made rigid and non-resonant enough, they argue, the platter and arm won't vibrate—and you don't have to worry about springs resonating. Unsprung turntables sometimes use constrained-layer damping in the base to dissipate mechanical energy before it reaches the platter and tonearm. Constrained-layer damping, however, is more effective at high frequencies than at low frequencies. A prime example of an unsprung design is the very popular Well Tempered Turntable.

The Platter and Bearing Assembly

The platter not only provides a support for the record, it also plays two other important roles: as a flywheel, to smooth the rotation; and as a "sink," to draw vibration from the record. Many platters are very heavy (up to 30 pounds), with most of their mass concentrated toward the outside edge to increase their moment of inertia. This high mass also counters bearing friction and stylus drag. Irregular (non-linear) bearing friction can create rapid irregularities in the platter's speed, which frequency-modulates the recovered audio signal. Massive platters greatly reduce the audible effects of bearing friction.

Most platters are made of a single substance such as acrylic, stamped metal (in the cheaper turntables), or cast and machined aluminum (in better turntables), or exotic materials such as ceramic compounds. The platter sometimes has a hollowed-out ring around the outer edge that is filled with a heavy material to increase the platter's mass, or is loaded with a damping substance to make the platter more inert and resistant to vibration.

These techniques also attempt to make the platter act as a "sink" for record vibration. When the record is clamped to the platter, any record vibration will be transferred to the platter. The platter's material and geometry are thus important design considerations: The platter should have no resonant peaks within the audioband. Some platters use constrained-layer damping and combinations of different materials to provide the ideal sink for record vibration.

I recently heard the difference that a layer of damping material applied to a platter can make to sound quality. The Well Tempered Turntable was recently upgraded to include a platter with a layer of highly effective damping material put into a recess machined into the platter's underside. With the two platters side by side, I auditioned each and heard an enormous improvement. My review of the damped platter in *Stereophile* read, in part: "Seconds into the first record, I was stunned by the difference the Black Damped Platter made. It was like listening to a different turntable! . . . First, there was a huge increase in dynamic contrast. The music seemed to jump out of the loudspeakers with an effortless, unfettered quality. . . .Transients seemed to "line up" together instead of being smeared slightly over time." Other characteristics I heard from just adding a layer of damping material to the platter included tighter and better-defined bass, deeper low-frequency extension, a more transparent soundstage, and greater resolution of fine detail.

Because the platter spins on a stationary object (the rest of the turntable), there must be a bearing surface between the two. With one technique, the bearing is mounted at the end of a shaft to which the platter is attached (Fig.9-4). This shaft—often made of stainless steel—extends down a hollow column in the base. The shaft has some form of bearing on the end, either a chrome-hardened steel ball, tungsten-carbide, Zirconium, ceramic, or even a very hard jewel such as sapphire. The bearing often sits in a well of lubricant.

Fig. 9-4 A platter bearing at the bottom of the shaft

Solid Machined Acrylic — Threaded for Reflex Clamp

Six Pound Lead Ring — Stainless Steel Spindle Ground and Polished — Aluminum Housing — Delrin Bushing — Chrome Hardened Ball — Tungsten Carbide

Courtesy Audio Advisor, Inc. and VPI Industries

A second technique puts the bearing surface on top of a stationary shaft, with the bearing surface between the platter and shaft (Fig.9-5).

Fig. 9-5 A platter bearing at the top of the shaft

Courtesy Audio Advisor, Inc. and SOTA Industries

Whichever technique is used, the bearing must provide smooth and quiet rotation of the platter. Any noise or vibration created by the bearing will be transmitted directly to the platter. Turntable bearings are machined to very close tolerances, and are often highly polished to achieve a smooth surface.

A bearing that suffers none of the traditional mechanical problems is the *air bearing*. The platter rides on a cushion of air rather than on a mechanical bearing. A pump forces compressed air into a very tiny gap between the platter and an adjacent surface. This air pressure pushes the platter up slightly so that the platter literally floats on air. Air-bearing turntables are, however, very expensive and can be difficult to set up.

Platter Mats, Record Clamps, and Vacuum Hold-Down Systems

Platter mats are designed to minimize record vibration, and then to absorb what vibration remains. Designers of soft mats suggest that an absorbent felt mat works better in drawing vibration away from the record. Designers of hard mats contend that a stiffer mat material better couples the record to the platter. Finally, some turntable manufacturers discourage using any mat at all, believing that their platter design provides the best sink for record vibration.

Record clamps couple the record to the platter so that the record isn't allowed to vibrate freely. The platter acts as a vibration sink, draining vibration from the record. By more intimately coupling the record to the platter, the record clamp improves the sound.

Record clamps come in three varieties. First, the clamp can simply be a heavy weight put over the spindle. The clamp's weight squeezes the record between clamp and platter. Other clamps have a screw mechanism that threads down onto the spindle. The third type is the "reflex" clamp, in which a locking mechanism pushes the clamp down onto the record. Which type works best should be decided by your listening, the turntable manufacturer's recommendations, or your local dealer's suggestion. Note that very heavy clamps can put a strain on some sprung turntables, compressing the springs (or expanding them if the sub-chassis is hung from the plinth). Some form of record clamping is, however, a must for any high-end turntable.

Another technique for coupling the record to the platter is the *vacuum hold-down system*. An external pump creates a vacuum that is transferred by tubes to the platter. The vacuum holds the record tightly to the platter surface so that vibration is drained away from the record. A vacuum hold-down also makes the record more flat, even if it is mildly warped. Vacuum pumps can be noisy, however, and benefit from some form of acoustic isolation from the listening room. Bright Star Audio makes a small acoustic isolation chamber, called "The Padded Cell" (their motto: "Every audiophile needs a padded cell"), for isolating vacuum hold-down and air-bearing pumps. (A vacuum hold-down system is shown in Fig.9-6.)

Fig. 9-6
A vacuum hold-down system

Courtesy Basis Audio, Inc.

The Drive System

A turntable's drive system transfers the motor's rotation to the platter. Virtually all high-end turntables currently made are belt-driven; the platter is spun by a rubber belt or silk thread stretched around the motor pulley and outer rim of the platter (Fig.9-7).

Mass-market mid-fi turntables are usually *direct-drive*; i.e., the motor is connected directly to the platter. The motor's spindle is often the spindle over which you place the record. Direct drive was sold to the public as superior to belt drive—there are no belts to stretch and wear, and a direct-drive motor can be electronically controlled to maintain precise

Fig. 9-7 A belt-drive turntable showing the drive motor, belt, and platter.

Courtesy VPI Industries

speed and have low wow and flutter. Indeed, the wow and flutter specifications of a direct-drive turntable are generally better than those of a belt-drive turntable. Direct-drives often have an electronic speed control and sometimes a *Phase Locked Loop* (PLL) servo mechanism to assure perfect speed stability. In a servo system, the platter's speed is sensed and a signal is fed back to the motor, which responds to keep the platter turning at a precisely constant speed. Direct-drive turntables also have high-torque motors, allowing them to come up to speed instantly.

But, without question, belt-drive turntables sound far better than direct-drive units. Rather than directly coupling the motor's vibration to the platter as in direct-drive, the drive belt acts as a buffer to decouple the platter from the motor. Motor noise is isolated from the platter, resulting in quieter operation than is possible from a direct-drive turntable. Belt drive also makes it easier to suspend the platter and drive system on a sub-chassis.

No elaborate speed controls are used on belt-drive turntables; the motor just sits there spinning at a fairly high speed (as fast as 1000rpm). This high-speed rotation is coupled to the large platter with a small pulley, resulting in 33-1/3 rpm rotation of the platter. Belt-drive motors are usually *AC-synchronous*, meaning that their rotational speed is determined by the frequency of the AC voltage driving them. But because the AC line is subject to noise and fluctuation, the platter's speed can be very slightly affected by dirty AC power. Although this speed variation is minute, it doesn't take much to destroy the music's pitch definition, timbre, and image stability. Consequently, some manufacturers synthesize their own 50Hz or 60Hz AC sinewave with an outboard drive unit. This device creates a pure, stable sinewave with a precision oscillator, then amplifies it to 120V to drive the turntable's AC synchronous motor. The Linn Lingo power supply for the Linn LP12 turntable is the most notable example of this technique. Some AC-synchronous motors run on voltages lower than 120V.

The drive motor can be a source of turntable vibration. As the motor spins, it produces vibration that can be transferred to the other components in the turntable, producing a low-frequency rumble. Even if you don't hear rumble directly, motor vibration can still degrade the sound. The motor assemblies of some turntables are completely separate from the base and encased in damping material. Other designs mount the motor to the sub-chassis, and isolate its vibration from the other turntable components.

The Tonearm

The tonearm's job is to hold the cartridge over the record and keep the stylus in the groove. We want the tonearm to be an immovable support for the cartridge, yet also be light enough to follow the inward path of the groove, track the up-and-down motions of record warps, and follow any record eccentricity caused by an offset center hole—all without causing undue wear on the delicate grooves themselves. As we'll see, this is a challenging job.

Tonearms come in two varieties: *pivoted* and *tangential-tracking*. A pivoted tonearm allows the cartridge end of the arm to traverse the record in an arc while maintaining a fixed pivot point. A tangential tonearm (also called a *linear tracking* tonearm) moves the entire tonearm and bearing in relation to the record.

Let's look at the pivoted tonearm first; its fundamental limitations will explain the reason for the tangential tonearm's existence.

The ideal tonearm would allow the cartridge to maintain the same angular relationship with the record groove as the record-cutting stylus had with that groove. LP cutting lathes are all tangential-tracking—the cutting head moves in a straight line across the lacquer master. But in a pivoted tonearm, the cartridge end swings in an arc over the record, causing the playback stylus to turn slightly in relation to the groove. The stylus/groove relationship is constantly changing with a pivoted tonearm. The result is *tracking error*, defined as a difference in the stylus/groove relationship between the cutting stylus and the playback stylus.

Tracking error is minimized by putting a bend in the tonearm, called the *offset*. Offset can be a sudden angle at the end of the tonearm, or a gradual bend that gives the armtube a J or S shape. The offset angle in modern tonearms is 25°, which provides the least tracking error. Note that adding an offset to the tonearm doesn't eliminate tracking error. Instead, the offset produces a small tracking error toward the outside of the record, which gradually decreases until the cartridge reaches a midpoint in the record. At this midpoint, the playback stylus and cutting stylus share the same geometric relationship with the groove, and the tracking error is zero. As the arm continues its arc toward the record's center, the tracking error gradually increases again.

The tonearm offset needed to reduce tracking error introduces a problem in pivoted arms called *skating*. Skating is a force that pulls the tonearm toward the center of the record. The result is a force acting on the stylus that must be compensated for by applying an equal but opposite force on the cartridge. This compensation, called *anti-skating*, counteracts the skating force caused by tonearm offset. Anti-skating allows the stylus to maintain equal contact pressure with both sides of the groove, and prevents the cartridge's cantilever from being displaced from its center position in the cartridge. Anti-skating can be generated by springs, weights with pulleys, or mechanical linkages. (I'll talk about anti-skating adjustment later in this chapter under "LP Playback System Setup.")

On a more technical level, skating is caused solely by the friction between the groove and stylus. Frictional force always acts in the direction of the attempted motion; the frictional force of the record pulling the stylus is in the tangential direction of the record groove. This force vector doesn't pass through the tonearm pivot. As with any vector quantity, this force can be resolved into two component forces at right angles to each other. Because one of the component forces is in-line with the pivot, the second (and much smaller) force is at a right angle to the primary force, causing the arm to skate inward.

As you can see, the problems of pivoted tonearms—tracking error and skating—don't exist with tangential-tracking arms. Since the entire arm moves across the record, the stylus/groove relationship is identical to that of the LP cutting lathe at any record radius. And because the arm has no offset, no skating force is generated. Tangential-tracking arms have another advantage: Because they're generally very short, tangential-tracking arms can have lower vertical mass than pivoted arms. Tangential-tracking arms, however, have *higher* horizontal mass. Because they don't pivot, the effective horizontal mass of a tangential arm is the arm's actual mass, which is higher than the effective horizontal mass of a pivoted arm. Tangential arm design is a compromise between too-low vertical mass and too-high horizontal mass.

Tangential tracking is also much more complex, and consequently more expensive to execute well. The entire arm must be moved along a track tangential to the record—a difficult engineering challenge. In mid-fi tangential-tracking turntables, the arm is driven by a servo motor whose motion may not exactly match the record's *pitch* (spacing between record grooves), forcing the stylus first against one side of the groove, then the other. Although the servo system attempts to correct for this error, servo systems by their very nature work only *after* an error has occurred.

The solution in high-end tangential-tracking arms is the *air bearing*, in which the arm rides on a cushion of air surrounding a tube. The only force moving the tonearm is the gentle force of the stylus. Owing to the air bearing, the friction between the arm and the tube on which it is mounted is practically zero. (The turntable in Fig.9-3 is fitted with a tangential-tracking, air-bearing tonearm.)

Tangential-tracking arms are more difficult to correctly set up, require periodic adjustment, and have air pumps that can be audible if not properly isolated from the listening area. Proponents of pivoted tonearms argue that the inherent geometric advantages of tangential arms are far outweighed by concerns over the tangential arm's rigidity and resonance damping. They suggest that the distortion produced by tracking error isn't a significant source of sonic degradation.

Let's take a closer look at the pivoted tonearm, by far the most popular type of arm. Its major components are, from back to front, the counterweight, bearing, armtube, and headshell. (These elements are shown from left to right in the photograph of Fig.9-8.) The *counterweight* counteracts the weight of the armtube and cartridge; its weight and position determine the downward force of the stylus in the groove. The *bearing* provides a pivot point for the arm, in both the vertical and horizontal planes. The *armtube* extends the cartridge position away from the pivot point to an optimum position over the record. The *headshell* is attached to the end of the armtube and provides a platform for mounting the cartridge to the armtube. The small, flat disc near the bearing in Fig.9-8 sets the anti-skating compensation.

Fig. 9-8 A high-quality pivoted tonearm

Courtesy Linn Products

A tonearm's bearing is an important aspect of its design. The bearing should provide very low friction and not impede the arm's movement. If the bearing is sticky, the stylus will be forced against the groove wall, causing distortion and record wear. Loosening the bearings reduces friction, but can cause the bearings to "chatter" as the tonearm is rattled by the motion of the stylus in the groove, or by other sources of tonearm vibration. Remember, any movement of the tonearm in relation to the stylus in the groove is interpreted by the cartridge as a groove modulation, and is converted into an electrical signal that appears at the cartridge output along with the musical signal. Tightening the bearings decreases chatter but also increases friction. Tonearm designers must balance these tradeoffs.

The most common type of tonearm bearing is the *gimbal*, in which a set of rings attached to bearings allows the arm to move in any direction. Gyroscopes are sometimes mounted in gimbal bearings. Another bearing type, called the *unipivot*, has recently come back into favor, partially from its exemplary use in the Graham tonearm. A unipivot bearing is similar to a ball within a cup, allowing motion in any direction. The unipivot is the simplest design, and offers the lowest friction of any bearing (except an air bearing). Gimbal and unipivot bearings are lubricated internally, and some are immersed in a silicon fluid to damp resonances.

An innovative approach to tonearm bearings is the Well Tempered Tonearm. The tonearm is attached to a vertical post and horizontal paddle suspended in a cup of silicon by monofilament line. In essence, the WTA has no bearing; the arm moves in a fluid with no hard connection between the arm and the rest of the turntable.

A tonearm's armtube is designed to be rigid, low in mass, resistant to vibration, and have the ability to damp any resonances that do occur. Armtubes are often made of exotic materials to combine rigidity with low mass (carbon fiber is a popular armtube material). Armtubes can be filled with damping material to kill resonances, and one particular arm (the Graham) is even made of concentric tubes separated by damping material to form a constrained-layer-damping design. The goal is to make the arm inert and less likely to ring and transmit vibration to the cartridge. A well-damped armtube correlates with an improved retrieval of low-level musical detail.

A tonearm's effective mass (defined earlier in this chapter) is carefully chosen to strike a balance between the ability to hold the cartridge as its stylus is moved from side to side (where high mass is desired), and the ability to follow record warps (where low mass is desired). When a massive tonearm encounters a record warp, it will increase the downward force of the stylus on the "uphill" side of the warp, then tend to reduce the downward force of the stylus on the "downhill" side. In some cases, the stylus can even fly out of the groove. Although this phenomenon occurs with all tonearms, it is magnified by high effective tonearm mass.

A tonearm's *effective length* is the distance from the pivot point to the stylus tip. Most tonearms measure between 210 and 230 millimeters of effective length. (The effective length is shorter than the actual length due to the tonearm's offset.) The technical definition of *overhang* is the distance the stylus extends past the spindle. In general parlance, "overhang" means where the stylus falls in relation to the pivot point. Overhang can be adjusted by moving the cartridge forward or backward in the headshell. Some tonearms have adjustable-length armtubes for setting overhang. These alignment procedures are described later in this chapter.

The Phono Cartridge

The phono cartridge has the job of converting the modulations of the record groove into an electrical signal. Because the cartridge changes one form of energy into another (mechanical into electrical), the cartridge is called a *transducer*. There's one other transducer in your system—the loudspeakers at the other end of the playback chain.

A phono cartridge consists of the cartridge body, stylus, cantilever, and generator system. The *body* is the housing that surrounds the cartridge, and comprises the entire surface area. The stylus is a diamond point attached to the cantilever (the tiny shaft that extends from the bottom of the cartridge body). The stylus is moved back and forth and up and down by modulations in the record groove. This modulation is transferred by the cantilever to the *generator system*, the part of the cartridge where motion is converted into an electrical signal.

Moving-Magnet and Moving-Coil Cartridges

Cartridges are classified by their principle of operation: moving-magnet or moving-coil. In a *moving-magnet* cartridge, tiny magnets attached to the cantilever move in relation to stationary coils in the cartridge body. The movement of the magnetic field through the coils induces a voltage (the audio signal) across the coils. (This phenomenon is explained in detail in Appendix B.) Less common variations on the moving-magnet cartridge are the *induced magnet* and *moving-iron* types. (Fig.9-9 shows the essential elements of a moving-magnet cartridge.)

Fig. 9-9 Moving-magnet cartridge construction

Courtesy Audio-Technica U.S., Inc.

A *moving-coil* cartridge works on exactly the same physical principles, but the magnets are stationary and the coils move. A moving-coil cartridge generally has much less moving mass than a moving-magnet cartridge. Consequently, a moving-coil cartridge can generally track better than a moving-magnet type, and also have better transient response. With less mass to put into motion (and less mass to continue moving after the motivating force has stopped), moving-coil cartridges can better follow transient signals in the record. Because of their construction, moving-coil cartridges generally don't have user-replaceable styli; you must return the cartridge to the manufacturer.

Cartridge output voltage varies greatly between moving-magnet and moving-coil operation. A moving-magnet's output ranges from 2mV (two thousandths of a volt) to about 8mV; a moving-coil cartridge's output is typically between 0.15mV and 2.5mV. Although moving-coil cartridges generally have lower output voltage than moving-magnet types, some so-called "high-output" moving-coils have higher output voltage than some moving-magnet cartridges. A cartridge's output voltage is specified when the stylus is subjected to a recorded lateral groove velocity of 5cm per second RMS at 1kHz.

This wide range of cartridge output voltage requires that the phono preamplifier's gain be matched to the cartridge's output voltage. The lower the cartridge output voltage, the higher the gain needed to bring the phono signal to line level. (A full discussion of matching cartridge output voltage to phono-stage gain is included in Chapter 5.)

A moving-coil's output voltage is determined largely by the number of turns of wire on the coil: The greater the number of turns, the higher the output voltage. More turns means less gain is needed in the phono preamp, but most designers use the minimum number of turns possible to keep the moving mass low.

The method of generating the audio signal, whether moving-magnet or moving-coil, affects how sensitive the cartridge is to the effects of preamplifier "loading." The cartridge output "sees" an electrical load of the preamplifier's input impedance and capacitance, and the tonearm cable's capacitance. The load impedance is in parallel with the capacitance.

The frequency response of a moving-magnet cartridge is greatly influenced by the amount of capacitance in the tonearm cable and preamplifier input. A moving-magnet cartridge terminated with the correct impedance (47k ohms), but with too much capacitance, can have frequency-response errors in the upper midrange and treble of 5dB. Most cartridge manufacturers specify the ideal load impedance and capacitance for their cartridges. A typical load for a moving-magnet cartridge is 47k ohms in parallel with 200-400pF (picofarads) of capacitance. Moving-coil cartridges are nearly immune to capacitance loading effects.

Stylus Shapes and Cantilever Materials

Styli (the plural of *stylus*) come in a variety of shapes, the simplest and least expensive of which is the *conical* or *spherical* tip. The conical stylus is a tiny piece of diamond polished into a cone shape. Because the stylus tip must be smaller than the record groove, the radius of a conical stylus tip is about 15μm, or about 0.0006".

The conical stylus, however, cannot perfectly track the groove's modulations because its shape is different from that of the cutting stylus used to make the record. As shown in Fig.9-10, the conical stylus contacts different points on the groove wall compared to the cutting stylus, causing distortion. In a related problem, called *pinch effect*, the stylus is pushed up out of the groove. Although the cutting stylus created a groove of equal width, the conical playback stylus may see a narrower groove because it touches different places on the left and right groove walls in relation to the cutting stylus. Pinch effect is most likely to occur where there are large high-frequency groove modulations.

Fig. 9-10
Comparison of conical and elliptical styli in relation to the cutting stylus

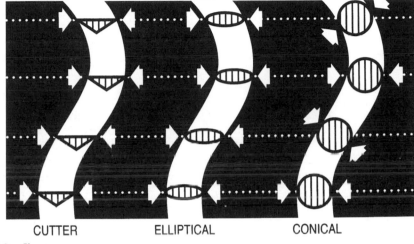

CUTTER   ELLIPTICAL   CONICAL

After Shure

The solution to these two related problems is the elliptical stylus. Instead of using a rounded tip to track the groove modulations, an elliptical stylus has an oval cross section, with two flattish faces. Because this shape more closely approximates the shape of the cutting stylus, it results in lower tracking distortion and eliminates the pinch effect. An elliptical stylus can also track high-frequency modulations better, and distributes its force over a wider area to reduce record wear. (Fig.9-10 compares the stylus/groove relationships of cutting, conical, and elliptical styli.)

A third type of stylus takes the elliptical shape one step further by making the tip even narrower. These stylus shapes are called *Shibata*, *line-contact*, *fine-line*, *van den Hul*, and *hyperelliptical*. A cartridge with any of these stylus shapes requires more precise alignment and setup than conical or standard elliptical types.

A variation of the elliptical stylus is the *microridge*, which has a tiny groove cut into each edge. As the stylus wears, the microridge stylus maintains the same shape, and thus its relationship to the record groove.

Keeping your stylus clean is of paramount importance: The stylus should be cleaned before every record side. A speck of dust or dirt is like a boulder attached to the stylus, grinding away at the groove walls. An appreciation of the enormous pressure a stylus imposes on the groove further highlights the need for a clean stylus. For example, a tracking force of 1.4 grams applied to a typical stylus contact area (0.2×10^{-6}") results in a pressure of nearly four tons per square inch. This pressure is enough to momentarily melt the outer layer of the groove wall. It's easy to see how stylus motion through the groove is much smoother with a clean stylus, and produces much less record wear. A clean stylus sounds better, too.

A stylus should be cleaned with a back-to-front motion so that the brush follows the record's motion. Some manufacturers recommend that no cleaning fluid be used; others suggest that a fluid is essential to removing accumulated dirt. There is also debate over the best type of brush. Some have short, stiff bristles, while other cleaners resemble nail-polish brushes. Your best bet is to follow the cartridge manufacturer's cleaning instructions. And don't clean the stylus with the tonearm locked in place; you could apply too much force and damage the stylus.

With good maintenance, a stylus should last for about 1000 hours of use. It's a good idea to have the stylus examined microscopically after about 500 hours, then again at 800 hours to check for irregular wear that could damage records.

Because the cantilever transfers stylus motion to the generator, its construction is extremely important. Cantilevers are designed to be very light, rigid, and non-resonant. The lower the cantilever mass, the better the cartridge's trackability, all other factors being equal. To obtain stiffness with low mass, exotic materials are often used in cantilever design, including boron, diamond, beryllium, titanium, ceramic, ruby, and sapphire. Cantilevers are often hollow to reduce their mass, and are sometimes filled with a resonance-damping material.

The cantilever is mounted in a *compliance* inside the cartridge body at the end opposite to that which bears the stylus. The compliance allows the cantilever to move, yet keeps it in position. Because this compliance is stiff when the cartridge is new, it takes many hours of use for the cartridge to break-in and sound its best. It isn't unusual for a cartridge to continue to sound better after 100 hours of use. (Cartridge compliance is described earlier in this chapter under "Technical Aspects of Choosing an LP Front End.")

Some audiophiles remove the cartridge body to run the cartridge "naked." The body can be a source of resonance, and adds a fair amount of effective mass to the tonearm. Removing a cartridge body should be attempted only if you are very skilled in working with tiny precision devices, and then only if you're willing to risk destroying your cartridge.

LP Playback System Setup

Correctly playing back a record is a delicate art. It takes patience, skill, a keen ear, a delicate touch, an appreciation for the forces involved—and a high-quality LP front end. Doug Sax, co-founder of Sheffield Lab and the pioneer of the modern direct-to-disc recording, has said, "Probably the easiest thing in the world is to play an LP record incorrectly."

What prompted Sax's observation is the great variability in setup possible with a turntable, tonearm, and cartridge. When you add to the equation how the phono preamp loads the cartridge, the turntable stand, and its placement in the room, you have the potential for not getting all the music out of the record grooves.

But this situation also offers the promise of improving the sound of your LP front end without spending any more money. By just setting up the system correctly, you can realize far better sound from a modest turntable than from a poorly set-up front end costing thousands more. Great musical rewards await those willing to tweak their LP front ends.

The best sources of advice for LP system setup are the manufacturers of the components in the LP playback system, and your dealer. The dealer will have undoubtedly set up many turntable/tonearm/ cartridge combinations like yours, and will have the techniques down pat. A good dealer will set up your system when you buy a product from him.

Nonetheless, you should know the procedure for getting the best sound from your LP front end. This will let you converse with the dealer from a position of knowledge, and also allow you to set up your system if you just change cartridges or move your turntable from one location to another.

The first rule of LP system setup is to put the turntable on a good platform. I can't emphasize this enough; a flimsy rack, or one prone to resonating, will seriously degrade the sound of your system. The less good the turntable's suspension, the more important the rack. The very best turntables (those having superlative isolation from structure-borne vibration) are affected very little by the stand. With all but the very best turntables, you won't hear your system at its best without a solid, non-resonant support structure for your turntable. Many stands and racks are made specifically for turntables. Invest in one.

The most massive racks can, however, put too much stress on a suspended wood floor. In addition, footfalls and other vibrations can be transmitted right through the rack and to the turntable if the turntable has inadequate suspension. If you live in a building with a shaky floor, you have several options. The first is to use a turntable shelf that mounts to the wall instead of to the floor. The second option is to locate the rack directly above the point in your room where the floor joists meet the foundation. The third alternative, which can be used in conjunction with the second option, is to support the joists with house jacks. Put a concrete block on the ground below the floor joists, put the house jack between the concrete block and the joist, and raise the jack to meet the joist. Continue raising the jack about half a turn past where contact is made between the jack and the joist. Don't try to move the joist; all you want to do is provide a stable support. Finally, you can further increase the turntable's isolation from vibration by using a commercially available product such as the Marigo Turntable Isolation System. Such products decouple the turntable from the stand. Finally, the best solution is to buy a turntable with a superior suspension system.

Once you've got a good rack, where you place it in the room can have a large effect on the sound. Here's why: When the air in a room is excited by sound from the loudspeakers, the pressure isn't evenly distributed throughout the room. Instead, there are pockets of high and low pressure. You can demonstrate this by playing an organ recording and walking around the room; you'll hear the sound get louder and softer. Moreover, the pressure tends to build up along walls and in corners. If the turntable is in an area of high pressure, it will be more prone to resonate from the acoustic energy impinging on it. Conversely, a turntable located in a room "null" won't be as affected by sound from the loudspeakers striking it. You can avoid the worst turntable placements by following a few simple rules. First, don't put the turntable in a corner where bass tends to build up. Second, keep the turntable away from the wall, if possible. An extra 8" or 12" can make a difference.

With the turntable on your stand, make sure that the turntable is level by using a pair of small round bubble levels and adjusting the turntable's feet. If you have a sprung turntable, make sure the tonearm cable doesn't impede the motion of the sub-chassis.

I'll assume you've followed the manufacturer's directions for installing the tonearm and are ready to mount the cartridge. After you've attached the four tiny tonearm cable clips to the cartridge pins, mount the cartridge to the headshell with minimal torque on the bolts — we'll be adjusting the cartridge position in the headshell later.

Move the counterweight forward or backward until the arm floats, evenly balanced, then move it slightly forward to apply some tracking force. Use a *stylus pressure gauge* (also called a *vertical tracking force gauge*) to set the tracking force to the cartridge manufacturer's tracking-force specification. (Some tonearms include built-in calibrated tracking-force gauges.)

The next step roughly sets the *vertical tracking angle* (VTA), also called the stylus *rake angle*. Adjusting the VTA changes the angle at which the stylus enters the groove. Ideally, the VTA of the playback stylus should match the VTA of the cutting stylus. Most cartridges work best when the cartridge body is exactly parallel with the record surface (Fig.9-11a). VTA is adjusted by moving the tonearm rear up or down at the pivot point. Negative VTA is when the cartridge rear is *below* the level of the cartridge front (Fig.9-11b). Positive VTA is when the cartridge rear is *above* the level of the cartridge front (9-11c). Follow the car-

Figs. 9-11 a, b, c
Vertical Tracking
Angle (VTA)
adjustments

a) Neutral VTA   b) Negative VTA   c) Positive VTA

tridge manufacturer's suggestions for rough setting of VTA. (We'll fine-tune the VTA later.)

If the tonearm manufacturer provides a protractor, place it on the spindle and make sure the stylus reaches the indicated point on the protractor. If necessary, move the cartridge body forward or backward in the headshell. This is called the *overhang* adjustment.

The protractor will have an alignment grid on it for setting the correct angle of the cartridge in the headshell relative to the tonearm. Getting this adjustment right minimizes tracking error.

Azimuth describes the cantilever's perpendicular relationship to the record groove. A cantilever with perfectly aligned azimuth will form a right angle with the record (Fig.9-12b). Notice that I said the *cantilever's*—not the *cartridge's*—relationship to the groove. Many cantilevers are slightly skewed in their mountings, making it impossible to get perfect azimuth alignment by looking at the cartridge body alone. Instead, you can put the stylus tip on a small mirror and look for a perfectly straight line through the cantilever and its reflection. If there's a bend in the reflection at the mirror, the azimuth is wrong. Some tonearms are designed to allow for ease of azimuth adjustment; those that aren't require you to insert tiny shims between headshell and cartridge. Azimuth alignment is vital to correct left-right channel balance, and consequently to soundstaging and imaging. Azimuth can also be checked with a dual-trace oscilloscope and a test record. With each channel feeding one input of the 'scope, play a test record with a pure tone. Perfect azimuth alignment will produce identical amplitudes from both 'scope channels.

Recheck the cartridge alignment and overhang with the protractor; when these are correct, gently tighten the cartridge mounting bolts. The

Fig. 9-12
Azimuth is the
perpendicular
relationship of
the cantilever to
the record.

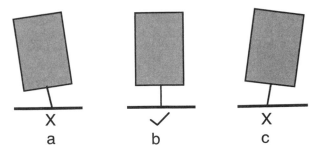

X   ✓   X
a   b   c

tightness of the bolts should strike a balance between making the cartridge tight in the headshell and distorting the cartridge body. Don't overtighten them.

Following the tonearm manufacturer's instructions, set the anti-skating force. If you don't have the instructions, and the tonearm doesn't have a calibrated anti-skating scale, you can set the anti-skating with a grooveless record (test pressings always have one grooveless side), or a sheet of Mylar cut into the shape of a record with a spindle hole. Put the stylus about halfway between the spindle and the outer edge, and spin the grooveless record or Mylar sheet. Adjust the anti-skating so that the arm moves very slowly toward the outside of the record. If the anti-skating is set incorrectly, mistracking on loud passages will occur more in one channel than in the other. Too much anti-skating will cause the left channel to distort first; too little will make the right channel distort first.

Another trick for setting the anti-skating force is to sum the left and right channels into mono, and invert the phase of one channel. When playing a record, the anti-skate will be properly set when the least sound is heard from the loudspeakers. Correct anti-skating adjustment will produce equal output from both channels; when one channel is inverted, the greatest cancellation will occur (the least sound heard) when the output levels are most closely matched. To make an inverting cable, buy a Y adapter with two female jacks and one male. Cut off one lead and reverse the shield and center conductor to invert the phase. The turntable output drives the two female jacks, and the single output feeds one phono input on the preamplifier. This method works very well, and costs about $3 for the Y adapter.

The next step is to fine-tune the VTA by listening. Mark on the tonearm rear the position that produces a parallel line between the cartridge bottom and the record. Raise the tonearm rear a few millimeters, then listen. Lower the tonearm rear a few millimeters below the parallel line and listen again. Find the position that provides the smoothest tonal balance and best imaging. Use several records for setting VTA, not just one or two.

There are many more ways to improve the sound of your LP front end. You can replace the stock tonearm cable with a high-end one; place isolation feet under the turntable; put contact enhancer on the cartridge pins; or put damping material on the tonearm tube, cartridge, finger lift, and counterweights. Damping material should be applied with care; it may upset the careful balance and resonance tuning designed into the turntable and tonearm.

There's another way of getting the best performance from your analog front-end: hire a local turntable set-up expert. Such experts often work in high-end retail stores; others are independent but can be recommended by your dealer. Watching him fine-tune your 'table can also be a great learning experience.

10 FM Tuners and Digital Audio Radio

Introduction

Atuner is a source component that receives radio transmissions from the air and converts them into a line-level audio signal that feeds an input on a preamplifier. The tuner has an antenna input (or inputs) and usually one pair of unbalanced line-level outputs.

Compared with other source components, the tuner plays a different role in a high-end system. On one hand, FM is a lower-quality source than LP and CD, and doesn't let your system live up to its full sonic potential. On the other hand, a tuner is an unending source of free music, and an invaluable way of being exposed to new musical forms and artists you might not have otherwise heard. How important a tuner is in your listening life is greatly influenced by the musical programming of stations in your area, how far away you live from transmitters, the care (or lack of care) taken by the station in achieving good sound, and the quality of your tuner.

The limiting factor in broadcast sound quality is often the radio station, not the FM transmission format or even the tuner. FM broadcasts of live concerts by radio stations that care about sound, and received by a good tuner, can be spectacular. I haven't any firsthand experience, but the live broadcasts by WGBH in Boston of the Boston Symphony Orchestra reportedly sounded superb.

Further, it's possible to set up a closed-circuit FM broadcast in a listening room using the highest-quality source components, then receive that broadcast signal with a tuner under evaluation. The source signal can thus be compared directly with the closed-circuit FM transmission. Listening tests and demonstrations of this technique reveal that FM is capable of extremely high sound quality.

How to Choose a Tuner

Choosing a tuner for your system is a little different from choosing other components. When auditioning other components, we're primarily concerned with their sound quality, not their technical performance. If, for example, a preamplifier under audition sounds good, we don't need to worry much about its technical performance—if it sounds good, it's probably working well.

Tuners, on the other hand, exhibit great variability in their technical performance. We're interested not only in aspects of a tuner's sound— tonal balance, soundstaging, portrayal of timbre, etc.—but also in more basic characteristics such as the ability to pick up weak or distant stations, reject adjacent stations, provide a noise-free audio signal, and stay tuned to a station without drifting. A tuner's performance in these areas can be accurately characterized by measurement; this makes tuner specifications much more meaningful than those of other audio components. There is a direct correlation between a tuner's specifications and its sonic performance. You'll still need to listen to the tuner before you buy, but you can often separate poorer-performing models from better units by looking at the specification sheets. And unlike most audio products, in which the highest-performance units have the fewest features, the best high-end tuners have more features, front-panel controls, and displays than the lower-end products.

How much of your audio budget you should allocate to a tuner varies greatly with the individual. Some listeners just want a tuner for background music and National Public Radio, not for serious music listening. If this describes you, or if you listen to FM only occasionally, you may consider a tuner from a mid-fi company. The performance will be acceptable (if you choose wisely), and you can put more of your budget into components that matter more to you musically and sonically.

Those listeners who want the best possible technical and musical performance from FM will opt for a tuner designed and made by a high-end company. Several companies have dedicated themselves exclusively to the design and manufacture of tuners: their products are often superb, but expensive. Without the economies of scale provided by a factory making an entire line of audio products, the dedicated tuner company must charge more for its products. It can, however, focus its talents and engineering expertise on making the best tuner possible. If you want the highest performance and are willing to pay for it, seek out companies that have established reputations for making superlative tuners.

The price range for a good tuner from a mass-market manufacturer is between $400 and $1000. Some of the higher-end models from mass-market companies offer excellent performance. The price range from $750 to $1200 is very competitive, with many superb units to choose from. The very best tuners cost as much as $12,000.

Although we'll discuss tuner specifications in detail later in this chapter, I'll briefly describe here the primary differences between mediocre and excellent tuners.

Good tuners are characterized by their *sensitivity*, or ability to pull in weak stations. The greater a tuner's sensitivity, the better it can pick up weak or distant stations. This aspect of a tuner's performance is more important in suburban or rural areas that are far from radio transmitters.

A tuner characteristic of greater importance to the city dweller is *adjacent-channel selectivity*—the ability to pick up one station without interference from the station next to it on the dial. The *alternate-channel selectivity* specification defines a tuner's ability to reject a strong station two channels away from the desired channel. When stations are packed closely together, as they are in cities, adjacent-channel and alternate-channel selectivity are more important than sensitivity.

Equally important to all listeners is the tuner's signal-to-noise ratio, a measure of the difference in dB between background noise and the maximum signal strength. A tuner with a poor signal-to-noise ratio will overlay the music with an annoying background hiss.

In short, a poor tuner will have trouble receiving weak stations, may lack the ability to select one station when that station is adjacent to another station, have high background noise, and be overloaded by nearby FM transmitters or other radio signal sources (taxi dispatchers, for example).

Tuners can be roughly divided into two categories: analog tuning and digital tuning (the latter is more correctly called *frequency-synthesized* tuning). If the tuner has a dial and pointer moved with a flywheel knob, it uses analog tuning. Frequency-synthesized tuners move in discrete jumps; from, say, 88.1MHz to 88.3MHz. A frequency synthesized tuner will lock on to the station and can't be mistuned (unless the tuner is misaligned). (Note that the presence of a digital station readout doesn't mean that the tuner is synthesized, only that the display is digital.) Synthesized tuners provide features such as *seek*—to move to the next station—and the ability to store many stations in a preset memory, recalled at the touch of a button. Another common feature of synthesized tuners is *scan*, which stops briefly at each station until you find a station you want and tell it to stop. *Memory scan* samples only the stations preset in the tuner's station.

Although it would appear that synthesized tuners have a big advantage over analog tuners, the very best tuners are all analog. Analog tuners have lower noise, and also allow fine-tuning to find the center of a station. Synthesized tuners jump in discrete steps of at least 25kHz, precluding the precise degree of fine-tuning possible with an infinitely variable analog tuner.

Better tuners have a feature called *selectable IF bandwidth* that adjusts the bandwidth in the tuner's intermediate frequency (IF) stage for best sound quality and minimum interference from adjacent stations. When in the "wide" mode, the audio quality improves at the expense of lower selectivity (less adjacent-channel rejection) and lower sensitivity. Specifically, a wide IF bandwidth provides the lowest distortion and the best high-frequency audio response. The high-frequency audio response of some tuners isn't affected by IF bandwidth, but all tuners have better imaging with wider IF bandwidths: phase shift in the IF filter may compromise stereo separation (and add distortion) at high frequencies. Wide bandwidth is used when no strong adjacent stations are present; narrow bandwidth is selected when the dial is crowded near the desired station. The best tuners have three selectable IF bandwidth settings.

Nearly every tuner has a *signal-strength meter* to indicate the strength of the received signal. The meter, usually a row of Light Emitting Diodes (LEDs), is helpful in positioning an antenna for best reception. The most sophisticated tuners have an oscilloscope display that provides a means of perfectly locating the center of a station. This expensive feature is found only on analog tuners.

Another useful tuner feature, used in conjunction with the signal-strength meter, is a *multipath indicator*. Multipath occurs when the broadcast signal reaches the tuner's antenna directly, in addition to reflections of that same signal off objects such as buildings. The slight delay between the two signals causes loss of audio-channel separation and increased distortion. In a car stereo, multipath distortion is sometimes called "picket-fencing": the signal swells and fades as the car travels quickly in and out of multipath reflections. A tuner's multipath indicator allows you to rotate your antenna for least multipath. A signal-strength meter alone doesn't discriminate between a clean signal and a signal with multipath, making a multipath indicator a very useful feature.

The high-end tuner shown in Fig.10-1 has a multipath indicator (the meter on the left side of the front panel). The middle meter shows center tuning (how closely to the station's center frequency the tuner is set). The right-hand meter indicates signal strength.

Nearly all tuners have a *local/distant* switch. When in the Local position, the tuner simply attenuates the antenna's signal level before it gets to the tuner's input circuit, and prevents the tuner from being overloaded by strong stations.

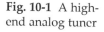

Fig. 10-1 A high-end analog tuner

Courtesy Magnum Dynalab

A tuner's *muting* function mutes the audio output when the signal received by the tuner drops below some defined level. Muting prevents a blast of noise through your system when the tuner is between stations, or on a very weak station. A tuner's muting can be turned off (if the tuner has a muting on/off switch) to receive very weak stations.

The *mono/stereo* button found on most tuners allows you to reduce noise from weak stations by making the signal mono instead of stereo. The complete loss of left/right stereo separation is more than offset by the significant reduction in noise.

Many tuners have a *high-blend* circuit that automatically switches the signal to mono when the signal strength falls below a certain level. The difference between high-blend and the mono/stereo switch just described is that the high-blend circuit puts only the treble into mono, leaving the rest of the spectrum in stereo. This gets rid of most of the noise, but maintains stereo separation through most of the midrange and bass.

Some tuners have a switch marked "MPX" that invokes a 19kHz filter to remove the 19kHz pilot tone from the broadcast signal. This feature is necessary when recording on a cassette deck: the 19kHz pilot tone can interfere with the cassette deck's Dolby noise-reduction tracking. Some cassette decks have a switchable 19kHz filter (also marked "MPX") in case your tuner lacks this feature.

Finally, all good tuners have a 75 ohm coaxial antenna input as well as the more commonly used 300 ohm flat lead input. The coaxial input should be used for best signal transmission between the antenna and tuner.

What to Listen For

If the tuner has high technical performance standards—particularly sensitivity and selectivity—we can then characterize the tuner's musical performance using the listening techniques described in Chapter 3.

In addition to the usual sonic checklist, tuners should be auditioned with an ear to certain qualities unique to tuners. Many tuners overlay the music with a whitish haze that makes listening fatiguing. This sound isn't perceived as noise, but as a fuzz that rides over the music. It sounds as though the channel isn't perfectly tuned, even though it's tuned in as well as the tuner allows.

Better tuners have a more extended and open treble. Lower-quality units tend to sound closed-in, lacking air, and even rolled-off in the treble. This characteristic can obscure low-level detail and make the music bland.

The music's dynamic contrast is also greatly affected by the tuner's audio quality. Some tuners squash dynamics to a point where the sound is lifeless and flat. Others have a much wider variation between loud and soft. Note, however, that most radio stations compress the music's dynamic range before the transmitter to achieve a higher average signal level, making the station seem louder and "stick out" when someone is scanning the dial. The best stations—primarily classical music stations— leave the dynamic range intact. When evaluating a tuner's dynamic range, be sure to use a variety of stations, particularly high-quality classical ones.

A mediocre tuner can compress soundstage depth to the point where the music is a flat, sterile canvas, not a huge, spacious panorama. The music becomes congested, thick, cold, and uninviting. The best tuners can present a deep, spacious soundstage, with real depth and precise imaging.

Many of the negative sonic qualities I've described aren't inherent in the FM format; an excellent radio station broadcasting to a high-end tuner is capable of outstanding musical performance.

When evaluating tuners, keep in mind that a tuner is only as good as the signal supplied to it from the antenna. A high-quality antenna is essential to getting the best technical and musical performance from your tuner. If you're auditioning a tuner at a dealer's showroom or a friend's house, remember that the antenna's quality is a significant variable. Depending on your antenna, you may get better or worse performance than you expect. Further, the very tiny voltages transmitted down the antenna lead, through the connections, and to the tuner input require tight, clean connections. A loose-fitting jack, or some corrosion on the terminals, can greatly degrade a tuner's performance.

Tuner Specifications and Measurements

The earlier part of this chapter described some of a tuner's fundamental specifications and how they relate to choosing a tuner. In this next section, we'll take a closer look at what constitutes good and poor tuner performance.

Sensitivity, or the ability to receive weak or distant stations, is defined technically as the radio frequency (RF) signal strength required to produce an audio signal output with a specified signal-to-noise ratio: the lower the sensitivity specification, the better (less signal required for good reception). Sensitivity is expressed as a voltage across the antenna in microvolts (μV), or as signal power in dBf (decibels referenced to one femtowatt, 10^{-15}W, or one trillionth of a watt). Two methods of expressing the signal strength across the antenna exist because of the differences between the two antenna impedances (300 ohms and 75 ohms). For example, 30dBf represents 18μV across 75 ohms, but only 9μV across 75 ohms. If you compare dBf specifications, you don't need to worry about this difference. But when looking at microvolts, be certain that the impedance is specified. If one tuner's sensitivity is specified across the 75 ohm input, and the other across a 300 ohm input, simply double the 75 ohm figure and the two specifications will be directly comparable.

Tuner sensitivity is more precisely defined by specifying the voltage across the antenna required to produce an audio signal with a specified signal-to-noise ratio, usually 50dB. This specification is called the 50dB *quieting sensitivity*. A less stringent specification, called *usable sensitivity*, is the voltage required to achieve a 30dB signal-to-noise ratio—which is barely listenable. When comparing tuner specifications, be sure that the manufacturer specifies the 50dB quieting-sensitivity figure.

Sensitivity is different for mono and stereo reception: Mono requires less RF signal strength to achieve a specified quieting sensitivity. In fact, a tuner may require more than double the signal strength to achieve the same quieting sensitivity in stereo than in mono.

The very best tuners have a sensitivity (for 50dB quieting) of 30dBf (stereo) and 10dBf (mono). Usable sensitivity (for 30dB quieting) figures for an excellent tuner are 10dBf (stereo) and 8dBf (mono). Lower-sensitivity tuners may have a 50dB quieting specification of 40dBf (stereo) and 20dBf (mono). The lower the number, the better the tuner.

With alternate-channel selectivity, however, the higher the number, the better. This specification indicates how well the tuner can reject strong stations near the desired station. Technically, alternate selectivity is the ratio (in dB) of the signal strength needed to produce a reference output level on the wanted channel to the signal strength needed to produce an audio output level 30dB below the reference level from a station two channels away. The higher the selectivity, the greater the tuner's ability to reject unwanted adjacent or alternate stations. Selectivity may be the most important tuner specification, particularly in areas with a crowded FM dial.

Selectivity is often specified with both narrow and wide IF bandwidths. The narrower bandwidth improves the selectivity figures, but decreases audio quality. The best tuners have an alternate-channel selectivity of 100dB in narrow mode, and an adjacent-channel selectivity of 40dB (also in narrow mode). In wide mode, a tuner's alternate-channel selectivity may be reduced to 30dB. Lower-quality tuners may have an alternate-channel selectivity specification of 40dB. These tuners generally don't have selectable IF bandwidth.

When a tuner receives two stations at the same frequency, the tuner must suppress the weaker one and capture the stronger one. *Capture ratio* is the difference in dB between the strengths of the two stations needed before the tuner can lock to the stronger station and reject the weaker one. The lower the capture ratio, the better; the stronger station doesn't have to be that much stronger for the tuner to reject the weaker one. Although it is relatively uncommon to receive two stations at the same frequency, a good capture ratio helps in preventing multipath distortion; the weaker reflected signal is more easily rejected. A capture ratio of 1dB is excellent, 1.5dB is average, and 2dB is poor. This specification, along with adjacent-channel selectivity, is of paramount importance to the city dweller who receives strong multipath reflections from buildings. Capture ratio has a high degree of correlation with sound quality, particularly for those listeners who can't put up a directional antenna to minimize multipath. Multipath interference often produces severe amplitude modulation of the FM carrier, an aberration that multiplex stereo decoders are particularly sensitive to.

A tuner's signal-to-noise ratio specifies the level of background noise, usually in both mono and stereo. Signal-to-noise must be specified with a given input signal, usually a very high 65dBf. Some manufacturers specify signal-to-noise ratio at 85dBf, which yields a better number than 65dBf. With a roof antenna located ten miles from a transmitter, many signals may be in the 65dBf range, and the strongest signals may exceed 85dBf. When comparing specifications, be certain that the signal-to-noise ratio is specified with the same signal strength. A good signal-to-noise specification is 90dB (mono) and 80dB (stereo) with a 65dBf signal. The higher the signal-to-noise ratio, the quieter the tuner (all other factors being equal).

Stereo separation is the degree of isolation, measured in dB, between the left and right audio channels. Greater separation correlates with increased spaciousness to the sound. Stereo separation is measured at 1kHz with a 50dB quieting input, and the IF bandwidth adjustment in the wide position (if the tuner has selectable IF bandwidth). A tuner designer can hype a separation specification by tailoring the tuner for wide separation at 1kHz at the expense of the rest of the audio band. It is more difficult to achieve wide separation consistently over the band. This requires excellent phase linearity in the IF stage, or careful phase-compensation of the feed to the multiplex decoder. The IHF/EIA standards for tuner measurements include separation figures up to a frequency of 6kHz. The separation at 6kHz is a more reliable indicator of a tuner's stereo separation than the 1kHz specification. Unfortunately, not all tuner manufacturers adhere to the IHF/EIA measurement standards. Tuners range from about 40dB of stereo separation, to 70dB in the best models (both are specified at 1kHz).

Digital Audio Radio Service: XM Satellite Radio and Sirius Satellite Radio

The decades-long tradition of broadcasting analog radio signals over the air has been overthrown by the distribution of digitally encoded audio programs. The new technology, known generically as Digital Audio

Radio Service, delivers digitally encoded audio via a cable-TV hookup, satellite, or over the air along with a conventional AM or FM broadcast. One such system, Digital Music Express (DMX), has been in operation since the early 1990s. The service provides continuous, commercial-free music through an existing cable-TV channel. The user buys the "tuner" (cost: about $200) and pays a monthly fee for the service.

Digital Audio Radio Service didn't become a significant force, however, until the launch in 2001 of two competing systems, XM Satellite Radio and Sirius Satellite Radio. Both services offer about 100 commercial-free channels of music and news, sports, talk, and other programming (XM offers 70 music channels, 30 non-music channels; Sirius delivers 60 music channels and 40 non-music channels). XM charges $9.95 per month, Sirius $12.95. "Premium" channels are available for an additional fee.

The big attraction of XM and Sirius, aside from a wide selection of commercial-free music, is the ability to receive this programming anywhere in the country with no static, fading, or the other problems associated with analog broadcasting. When installed in a car, XM and Sirius provide clear reception no matter where you are—no more searching for new stations as you travel out of range of one broadcast antenna. In urban areas where reception could be blocked by buildings, ground-based repeater stations retransmit the signal. XM and Sirius are offered as standard equipment on many new automobiles, with the first three months of service usually provided free.

The competing systems work the same way: original programming is beamed from broadcast centers to satellites in geo-stationary orbit, which reflect the signal back to earth. Both operate on the so-called "S-band" of radio frequencies, allocated to XM and Sirius by the FCC in 1997 for a period of eight years. To receive the XM or Sirius signal, you'll need a small antenna and a receiver. The receiver, whether in a car, home, or portable unit, appears to the user to function as the familiar FM radio. To receive XM or Sirius in your existing car stereo or home FM tuner, you'll need an adapter to retransmit the XM or Sirius signal as FM to a conventional analog tuner.

A variety of home, portable, and car receivers are available. Fig.10-2 shows an XM portable unit (left photo) that works in the car, as a stand-along portable radio, or that will dock in a "boombox"(right photo in Fig.10-2) to provide larger speakers and more amplifier power. Fig.10-3 is a Sirius home receiver (manufactured by Kenwood), which features a digital output jack (S/PDIF) for connection to your audio system.

These systems provide reasonably high-quality audio without the problems inherent in FM or AM transmission. The sound quality is less good than that of the compact disc, a result of perceptual coding. Perceptual coding reduces the number of bits needed to encode an audio signal by ignoring information in the music judged to be inaudible. Despite the small reduction in fidelity introduced by perceptual coding, XM and Sirius can sound better than conventional AM and FM broadcasting in many ways.

Fig. 10-2 An XM Satellite Radio receiver and its docking "boombox"

Courtesy XM Satellite Radio

Fig. 10-3 A Sirius Satellite Radio home receiver

Courtesy Kenwood Corporation

Radio Data System (RDS)

A new broadcast technology, called Radio Data System (RDS), combines digital data with the FM radio broadcast. This data is picked up by a tuner and decoded into text that can be displayed on the tuner's front-panel display. This data can include the radio station's call letters, song name, or other limited information. In some RDS-equipped products, a video-output jack can be connected to a video monitor to display the data. RDS is also known as "Smart Radio." A tuner incorporating RDS, with its front-panel alpha-numeric display, is shown in Fig.10-4.

Fig. 10-4 Tuners equipped with RDS include an alpha-numeric display.

Courtesy Denon Electronics

11 Cables and Interconnects

Introduction

Loudspeaker cables and line-level interconnects are an important but often overlooked link in the music playback chain. The right choice of loudspeaker cables and interconnects can bring out the best performance from your system. Conversely, poor cables and interconnects—or those not suited to your system—will never let your system achieve its full musical potential. Knowing how to buy cables will provide the best possible performance at the least cost.

In this chapter we'll look at all aspects of loudspeaker cables and interconnects. We'll cover balanced and unbalanced lines, bi-wiring, matching cables to your system, and how to get the most cable for your money. Moreover, we'll see why the most expensive cables and interconnects aren't always the best.

But first, let's start with an overview of cable and interconnect terms.

Cable: Often used to describe any wire in an audio system, "cable" more properly refers to the conductors between a power amplifier and a loudspeaker. Loudspeaker cables carry a high-current signal from the power amplifier to the loudspeaker.

Interconnect: Interconnects are the conductors that connect line-level signals in an audio system. The connection between source components (turntable, CD player, tuner, tape deck) and the preamplifier, and between the preamplifier and power amplifier, are made by interconnects.

Unbalanced Interconnect: An unbalanced interconnect has two conductors and is usually terminated with RCA plugs. Also called a *single-ended* interconnect.

Balanced Interconnect: A balanced interconnect has three conductors instead of two, and is terminated with 3-pin *XLR* connectors. Balanced interconnects are used only between components having balanced inputs and outputs.

Digital Interconnect: A single interconnect that carries a stereo digital audio signal, usually from a CD transport or other digital source to a digital processor.

Bi-wiring: Bi-wiring is a method of connecting a power amplifier to a loudspeaker with two runs of cable instead of one.

RCA Plug and Jack: RCA plugs and jacks are the most common connection termination for unbalanced signals. Virtually all audio equipment has RCA jacks to accept the RCA plugs on unbalanced interconnects. RCA jacks are mounted on the audio component's chassis; RCA plugs are the termination of unbalanced interconnects.

XLR Plug and Jack: XLR plugs are three-pin connectors terminating a balanced interconnect. XLR jacks are chassis-mounted connectors that accept XLR plugs.

Binding Post: Binding posts are terminations on power amplifiers and loudspeakers that provide connection points for loudspeaker cables.

Five-way Binding Post: A type of binding post that can accept bare wire, spade lugs, or banana plugs. Five-way posts are found on most power amplifiers and loudspeakers.

Spade Lug: A flat, pronged termination for loudspeaker cables. Spade lugs fit around power-amplifier and loudspeaker binding posts. The most popular kind of loudspeaker cable termination.

Banana Plug and Jack: Banana plugs are sometimes found on loudspeaker cables in place of spade lugs. Banana plugs will fit into five-way binding posts or banana jacks. Many European products use banana jacks on power amplifiers for loudspeaker connection.

AWG: American Wire Gauge: a measure of conductor thickness, usually in loudspeaker cables. The lower the AWG number, the thicker the wire. Lamp cord has an AWG of 18, usually referred to as "18 gauge."

Some of these cables, interconnects, and terminations are shown in Fig.11-1.

Fig. 11-1 From left to right: balanced interconnects terminated with XLR connectors, unbalanced interconnects terminated with RCA plugs, a spade lug, and a banana plug

Courtesy AudioQuest

How to Choose Cables and Interconnects

Ideally, every component in the system—including cables and interconnects—should be absolutely neutral and impose no sonic signature on the music. As this is never the case, we are forced to select cables and interconnects with colorations that counteract the rest of the system's colorations.

For example, if your system is a little on the bright and analytical side, mellow-sounding interconnects and cables can take the edge off the treble and let you enjoy the music more. If the bass is overpowering and fat, lean- and tight-sounding interconnects and cables can firm up and lean out the bass. A system lacking palpability and presence in the midrange can benefit from a forward-sounding cable.

Selecting cables and interconnects for their musical compatibility should be viewed as the final touch to your system. A furniture maker who has been using saws, planers, and rasps will finish his work with steel wool or very fine sandpaper. Treat cables and interconnects the same way—as the last tweak to nudge your system in the right direction, not as a Band-Aid for poorly chosen components.

Cables and interconnects won't correct fundamental musical or electrical incompatibilities. For example, if you have a high-output-impedance power amplifier driving current-hungry loudspeakers, the bass will probably be soft and the dynamics constricted. Loudspeaker cables won't fix this problem. You might be able to ameliorate the soft bass with the right cable, but it's far better to fix the problem at the source—a better amplifier/loudspeaker match.

Good cables merely allow the system's components to perform at their highest level; they won't make a poor system or bad component match sound good. Start with a high-quality, well-chosen system and select cables and interconnects that allow that system to achieve its highest musical performance. Remember, a cable or interconnect can't actually effect an absolute improvement in the sound; the good ones merely do less harm.

A typical hi-fi system will need one pair of loudspeaker cables (two pairs for bi-wiring), one long pair of interconnects between the preamplifier and power amplifier, and several short interconnect pairs for connections between source components (such as a turntable or CD player) and the preamplifier.

If the power amplifier is located near the loudspeakers, the loudspeaker cables will be short and the interconnects between the preamplifier and power amplifier will be long. Conversely, if the power amplifier is near the source components and preamplifier, the interconnects will be short and the loudspeaker cables long. There is no consensus among the experts about which method is preferable, but I use long interconnects and short loudspeaker cables. Ideally, interconnects *and* loudspeaker cables should be short, but that often isn't practical.

Once you've got a feel for how your system is—or will be—configured, make a list of the interconnects and cables you'll need, and their lengths. Keep all lengths as short as possible, but allow some flexibility for moving loudspeakers, putting your preamp in a different space in the rack, or other possible changes. Although we want to keep the cables and interconnects short for the best sound, there's nothing worse than having interconnects 6" too short. After you've found the minimum length, add half a meter for flexibility.

Interconnects are often made in standard lengths of 1, 1.5, and 2 meters. These are long enough for source-to-preamplifier connections, but too short for many preamplifier-to-power-amplifier runs. These long runs are usually custom-made to a specific length. Similarly, loudspeaker cables are typically supplied in 8' or 10' pairs, but custom lengths are readily available. It's best to have the cable manufacturer terminate the cables (put spade lugs or banana plugs on loudspeaker cables, and RCA or XLR plugs on interconnects) rather than trying to do it yourself.

Concentrate your cable budget on the cables that matter most. The priority should be given to the sources you listen to most. For example, you may not care as much about the sound of your cassette deck or tuner as you do your CD player. Consequently, you should spend more on interconnects between the CD player and preamplifier than between the tape deck and preamp. And because all your sources are connected to the power amplifier through the interconnect between the preamplifier and power amplifier, this link must be given a high priority. But any component—even a cassette deck—will benefit from good interconnects.

Should all your interconnects and loudspeaker cables be made by the same manufacturer? Or is it better to mix and match brands? There are two schools of thought on this issue. The first holds that an entire system with one brand of cable and interconnect is the best route. If one interconnect works well in your system, use it throughout. This argument also suggests that the cable designer made his interconnects and loudspeaker cables to work together to achieve the best possible sound.

The second school of thought holds that different brands are best. Because each cable or interconnect affects the sound in a certain way, using the same interconnect and cable throughout the system will only reinforce the cable's sonic signature. By using cables and interconnects from different manufacturers, the characteristic sonic signature of a cable won't be superimposed on the music by every interconnect.

This second theory has an analog in the recording world. Engineers will record through one brand of recording console, then mix the record through a different brand of console. They don't want to hear the console's sound in the final product, so they don't subject the signal to the same sonic signature twice.

My experience suggests that the only way to determine the best cable or interconnect for your system is to experiment and listen. In some cases, the best results will be achieved with all the interconnects and cables made by the same manufacturer. In others, a mix of different interconnects will work best. It's impossible to predict which cables will sound best in your system.

Most dealers will let you take home several cables at once to try in your system. Take advantage of these offers. Some mail-order companies will send you many cables to try: you keep the ones you want to buy—if any—and return the others. Compare inexpensive cables with expensive ones—sometimes manufacturers have superb cables that sell for a fraction of the price of their top-of-the-line products.

If you're starting a system from scratch, selecting cables is more difficult than replacing one length in your system. Because different combinations of cables will produce different results, the possibilities are greatly increased. Moreover, you don't have a baseline reference against which to judge how good or bad a cable is. In this situation, the best way of getting the ideal cables for your system is your dealer's advice. Try the cables and interconnects he suggests, along with two other brands or models for comparison.

How Much Should You Spend on Cables and Interconnects?

At the top end of the scale, cable and interconnect pricing bears little relationship to the cost of designing and manufacturing the product. Unlike other audio products, whose retail prices are largely determined by the parts cost (the retail price is typically four to six times the cost of raw parts), cables and interconnects are sometimes priced according to what the market will bear. This trend began when one company set its prices vastly higher than everyone else's—and saw its sales skyrocket as a result. Other manufacturers then raised *their* prices so they wouldn't be perceived as being of lower quality. Although some very expensive cables and interconnects are worth the money, many cables are ridiculously overpriced.

The budget-conscious audiophile can, however, take advantage of this phenomenon. Very often, a cable manufacturer's lower-priced products are very nearly as good as its most expensive models. The company prices their top-line products to foster the impression of being "high-end," yet relies on its lower-priced models for the bulk of its sales. When shopping for loudspeaker cables and interconnects, listen to a manufacturer's lower line in your system—even if you have a large cable budget. You may be pleasantly surprised.

Because every system is different, it's impossible to be specific about what percentage of your overall system investment you should spend on cables and interconnects. Spending 5% of your system's cost on cables and interconnects would be an absolute minimum, with about 15% a maximum figure. If you choose the right cables and interconnects, they can be an excellent value. But poor cables on good components will give you poor sound and thus constitute false economy.

Again, I must stress that high cost doesn't guarantee that the cable is good or that it will work well in your system. Don't automatically assume that an expensive cable is better than a low-priced one. Listen to a wide variety of price levels and brands. Your efforts will often be rewarded with exactly the right cable for your system at a reasonable price.

What to Listen For

Cables must be evaluated in the playback system in which they will be used. Not only is the sound of a cable partially system-dependent, but the sonic characteristics of a specific cable will work better musically in some systems than in others. Personal auditioning is the *only* way to evaluate cables and interconnects. Never be swayed by technical jargon about why one cable is better than another. Much of this is pure marketing hype, with little or no relevance to how the cable will perform musically in your system. Trust your ears.

Fortunately, evaluating cables and interconnects is relatively simple; the levels are automatically matched between cables, and you don't have to be concerned about absolute-polarity reversal. One pitfall, however, is that cables and interconnects need time to break in before they sound their best. Before break-in, a cable often sounds bright, hard, fatiguing, congested, and lacking in soundstage depth. These characteristics often disappear after several hours' use, with days or weeks of use required for full break-in. You can't be sure, however, if the cable is inherently bright- and hard-sounding, or if it just needs breaking-in. Note that break-in wears off over time. Even if a cable has had significant use, after a long period of not being used it may not sound its best until you've put music through it for a few days.

With those cautions in mind, you're ready to evaluate cables and interconnects. Listen to the first interconnect for 15 minutes to half an hour, then replace it with the next candidate. One way of choosing between them is merely to ask yourself which interconnect allows you to enjoy the music more. You don't need to analyze what you're hearing; just pick the interconnect that makes you feel better.

The other method is to scrutinize what you're hearing from each interconnect and catalog the strengths and weaknesses. You'll often hear trade-offs between interconnects: one may have smoother treble and finer resolution than another, but less soundstage focus and transparency. Another common trade-off is between smoothness and resolution of detail: The smooth cable may lose some musical information, but the high-resolution cable can sound analytical and bright. Again, careful auditioning in your own system is the only way to select the right cables and interconnects. Keep in mind, however, that a better cable can sometimes reveal flaws in the rest of your system.

Cables and interconnects can add some annoying distortions to the music. I've listed the most common sonic problems of cables and interconnects. (A full description of these terms is included in Chapter 3.)

Grainy and hashy treble: Many cables overlay the treble with a coarse texture. The sound is rough rather than smooth and liquid.

Bright and metallic treble: Cymbals sound like bursts of white noise rather than a brass-like shimmer. They also tend to splash across the soundstage rather than sounding like compact images. Sibilants (s and sh sounds on vocals) are emphasized, making the treble sound spitty. It's a bad sign if you suddenly notice more sibilance. The opposite condition is a dark and closed-in treble. The cable should sound open, airy, and extended in the treble without sounding overly bright, etched, or analytical.

Hard textures and lack of liquidity: Listen for a glassy glare on solo piano in the upper registers. Similarly, massed voices can sound glazed and hard rather than liquid and richly textured.

Listening fatigue: A poor cable will quickly cause listening fatigue. The symptoms of listening fatigue are headache, a feeling of relief when the music is turned down or stopped, the need to do something other than listen to music, and the feeling that your ears are tightening up. This last condition is absolutely the worst thing any audio component can do. Good cables (in a good system) will let you listen at higher levels for longer periods of time. If a cable or interconnect causes listening fatigue, avoid it no matter what its other attributes.

Lack of space and depth: Using a recording with lots of natural depth and ambiance, listen for how the cable affects soundstage depth and the sense of instruments hanging in three-dimensional space. Poor cables can also make the soundstage less transparent.

Low resolution: Some cables and interconnects sound smooth, but they obscure the music's fine detail. Listen for low-level information and an instrument's inner detail. The opposite of smoothness is a cable that's "ruthlessly revealing" of every detail in the music, but in an unnatural way. Musical detail should be audible, but not hyped or exaggerated. The cable or interconnect should strike a balance between resolution of information and a sense of ease and smoothness.

Mushy bass or poor pitch definition: A poor-quality cable or interconnect can make the bass slow, mushy, and lacking in pitch definition. With such a cable, the bottom end is soggy and fat rather than taut and articulate. Low-frequency pitches are obscured, making the bass sound like a roar instead of being composed of individual notes.

Constricted dynamics: Listen for the cable or interconnect's ability to portray the music's dynamic structure, on both small and large scales. For example, a guitar string's transient attack should be quick, with a dynamic edge. On a larger scale, orchestral climaxes should be powerful and have a sense of physical impact (if the rest of your system can portray this aspect of music).

I must reiterate that putting a highly colored cable or interconnect in your system to correct a problem in another component (a dark-sounding cable on a bright loudspeaker) isn't the best solution. Instead, use the money you would have spent on new cables toward better loudspeakers—*then* go cable shopping. Cables and interconnects shouldn't be Band-Aids; instead, cables should be the finishing touch to let the rest of your components perform at their highest level.

Binding Posts and Cable Terminations

Binding posts vary hugely in quality, from the tiny spring-loaded, push-in terminal strips on cheap loudspeakers to massive, custom-made, machined brass posts plated with exotic metals. Poor binding posts not only degrade the sound, they also break easily. When shopping for power amplifiers and loudspeakers, take a close look at binding-post quality.

The most popular type is the five-way binding post. It accepts spade lugs, banana plugs, or bare wire. Some five-ways are nickel-plated;

higher-quality ones are plated with gold and won't tarnish. Five-way binding posts should be tightened with a 1/2" nut driver, not a socket and ratchet or wrench that could easily overtighten the nut. The connection should be tight, but not to the point of stripping the post or causing it to turn in the chassis. When tightening a five-way binding post, watch the inside ring or collar next to the chassis; if it begins to turn, you've overtightened the post and are in danger of damaging the power amplifier or loudspeaker.

Custom posts of heavy-duty machined metal are more robust than five-way posts—they can accept more torque without stripping or coming loose in the chassis. Custom posts are often found on the most expensive equipment. The amplifier rear panel shown in Chapter 6 (Fig.6-8) uses high-quality custom posts.

Some binding posts have such a large center post that spade lugs won't fit around them. These posts have large holes in the center for accepting large bare wires or banana jacks. Although these posts are expensive and appear to be of high quality, they're inconvenient to use. If your equipment has this sort of post, the best solution is to terminate your loudspeaker cables with oversized spade lugs. Most spade lugs have a distance between the prongs of 1/4" to 3/16"; oversized spades have prongs 5/16" apart—enough of a difference to fit the large-holed posts.

If you have a choice of bare wire, banana plug, or spade lug on loudspeaker cable terminations, go with the spade lug. It forms the best contact with a binding post and is the most standard form of connection. Many European products provide only banana jacks, forcing you to use sonically inferior banana-plug terminations.

You should be aware that any termination slightly degrades the sound of your system. Consequently, some audiophiles have gone to the trouble of removing all plugs, jacks, spade lugs, and binding posts from their systems and hard-wiring everything together. This is an extreme measure and makes switching equipment difficult or impossible. Hard-wiring is an option, but not one that should be undertaken without considerable deliberation and technical expertise.

Bi-Wired Loudspeaker Cables

Bi-wiring is running two lengths of cable between the power amplifier and loudspeaker. This technique usually produces much better sound quality than conventional single-wiring. Most high-end loudspeakers have two pairs of binding posts for bi-wiring, with one pair connected to the crossover's tweeter circuit and the other pair connected to the woofer circuit. The jumpers connecting the two pairs of binding posts fitted at the factory must be removed for bi-wiring.

In a bi-wired system, the power amplifier "sees" a higher impedance on the tweeter cable at low frequencies, and a lower impedance at high frequencies. The opposite is true in the woofer-half of the bi-wired pair. This causes the signal to be split up, with high frequencies traveling mostly in the pair driving the loudspeaker's tweeter circuit and low frequencies conducted by the pair connected to the loudspeaker's woofer circuit. This frequency splitting reportedly reduces magnetic interactions in the cable, resulting in better sound. The large magnetic fields set up around the conductors by low-frequency energy can't affect the transfer of treble energy. No one knows exactly how or why bi-wiring works, but on nearly all loudspeakers with bi-wiring provision, it makes a big improvement in the sound. Whatever your cable budget, you should bi-wire if your loudspeaker has bi-wired inputs, even if it means buying two runs of less expensive cables.

You can bi-wire your loudspeakers with two identical single-wire runs, or with a specially prepared bi-wire set. A bi-wire set has one pair (positive and negative) of terminations at the amplifier end of the cable, and two pairs at the loudspeaker end of the cable. This makes it easier to hook up, and probably offers slightly better sound quality.

Loudspeakers can also be connected with a *single bi-wire* set in which a single cable with multiple internal conductors has two pairs of terminations on one end and a single pair of terminations at the other end. Although this approach is much less expensive than two runs of cable, you lose the benefit of magnetically isolating the low- and high-frequency conductors from each other. A bi-wired set and single bi-wire set are shown in Fig.11-2.

Fig. 11-2
Loudspeakers can be connected with a single bi-wire connection (top), or with two separate runs of cable (bottom).

Courtesy AudioQuest

Most bi-wired sets use identical cables for the high- and low-frequency legs. Mixing cables, however, can have several advantages. By using a cable with good bass on the low-frequency pair, and a more expensive but sweeter-sounding cable on the high-frequency pair, you can get better performance for a lower cost. Use a less expensive cable on the bass and put more money into the high-frequency cable. If you've already got two pairs of cable the same length, the higher-quality cable usually sounds better on the high-frequency side of the bi-wired pair. If you use different cables for bi-wiring, they should be made by the same manufacturer and have similar physical construction. If the cables in a bi-wired set have different capacitances or inductances, those capacitances and inductances change the loudspeaker's crossover characteristics.

Balanced and Unbalanced Lines

Line-level interconnects come in two varieties: balanced and unbalanced. A balanced interconnect is recognizable by its three-pin XLR connector. An unbalanced interconnect is usually terminated with an RCA plug. Balanced and unbalanced lines are shown in the photograph at the beginning of this chapter.

Why do we use two incompatible systems for connecting equipment? At one time, all consumer audio hardware had unbalanced inputs and outputs, and all professional gear was balanced. In fact, balanced inputs are often called "professional inputs" to differentiate them from "consumer" unbalanced jacks. Balanced connection was considered both unnecessary and too expensive for home playback systems.

The emergence of high-end audio changed that thinking. Instead of using the least expensive connection method, high end product designers started using higher-quality balanced lines and terminations in consumer gear. The better the equipment, the more likely that it has at least some balanced connections in addition to unbalanced jacks. Moreover, more and more manufacturers are offering balanced connections on their equipment. This is why we have two standards—balanced and unbalanced. The technical and sonic advantages of balanced connection, once the exclusive domain of audio professionals, are becoming increasingly available for home playback systems.

But what exactly is a balanced line, and how is it different from a standard RCA cable and jack?

In an unbalanced line, the audio signal appears across the center pin of the RCA jack and the shield, or ground wire. Some unbalanced interconnects have two signal conductors and a shield, with the shield not used as a signal conductor. If this unbalanced interconnect happens to be close to fluctuating magnetic fields—an AC power cord, for example—the magnetic field will induce a noise signal in the interconnect that is heard as hum and noise reproduced through the playback system's loudspeakers.

In a professional application, this hum, buzz, and noise is unacceptable, leading to the development of an interconnection method that is immune to noise interference: the balanced line. A balanced line has three conductors: two carrying signal, and one ground. The two signals in a balanced line are identical, but 180° out of phase with each other. When the signal in one of the conductors is at peak positive, the signal in the other conductor is at peak negative (see Fig.11-3). The third conductor is signal ground. Some balanced interconnects use three conductors plus a shield.

Fig. 11-3 Signal voltages applied to an unbalanced and a balanced line

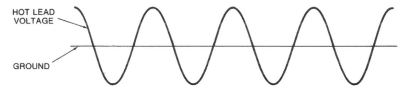

(A) Unbalanced line (using two conductors)

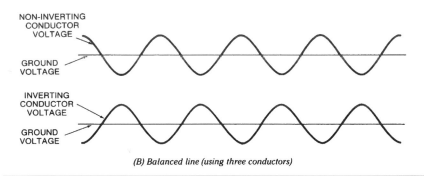

(B) Balanced line (using three conductors)

Fig. 11-4 When the two signals carried by the balanced line are input to a differential amplifier, noise common to both conductors is rejected (bottom).

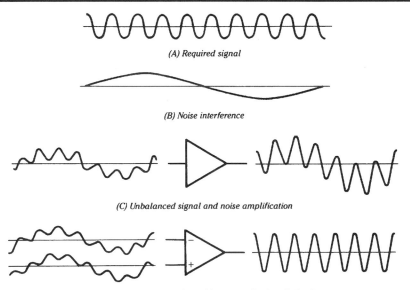

(A) Required signal

(B) Noise interference

(C) Unbalanced signal and noise amplification

(D) Balanced line—signal amplification and noise elimination

Figs. 11-3 and 11-4 copied with permission from *Audio Technology Fundamentals* by Alan A. Cohen

When the two identical but opposite polarity signals carried on the balanced line are input to a *differential amplifier* in the component receiving the signal, noise picked up by the interconnect is rejected. Here's why: a differential amplifier amplifies only the *difference* between the two signals (see Fig.11-4). If noise is introduced into the line, the noise will be common to both conductors and the differential amplifier will reject the noise. This phenomenon of rejecting noise signals common to both conductors in a balanced line is called *common-mode rejection*. Differential inputs are specified according to how well they reject signals common to both conductors, a measurement called *Common-Mode Rejection Ratio*, or *CMRR*. Note that a balanced line won't make a noisy signal clean; it just prevents additional noise from being introduced in the interconnect. If the noise is common to both halves of the balanced line, however, common-mode rejection will eliminate the noise.

In professional applications, a transformer sometimes serves the same function as the differential amplifier, passing only the difference between the two signal conductors and rejecting signals common to both conductors. Consumer audio equipment uses differential amplifiers, not transformers, but the concept is identical.

In a balanced line terminated with XLR connectors, pin 1 is always signal ground. There is, however, no universal convention for which of the two signal conductors carries the non-inverted signal and which carries the inverted signal. The non-inverted conductor is often called the "hot" conductor, with the inverted conductor designated "cold." After decades of no clear standard, the Audio Engineering Society recently adopted the North American tradition of having pin 2 carry the non-inverted ("hot") signal, pin 3 the inverted ("cold") signal.

How the balanced line is wired (pin 2 or pin 3 "hot") can determine if your playback system is inverting or non-inverting of absolute polarity (see the section on absolute polarity in Appendix A). If your system is non-inverting—that is, a positive-going signal on the LP or CD produces a positive-going signal at the loudspeakers—substituting a pin 3 "hot" balanced input power amplifier for a pin 2 "hot" power amplifier will make your system inverting. When switching balanced components— digital processors, preamps, or power amplifiers—you should know if the new component's XLR jacks are wired the same—either pin 2 or pin 3 "hot"—as the existing component. You can also change your system's absolute polarity by rewiring the balanced interconnect to swap the wires going to pins 2 and 3. It's far better, however, to simply reverse absolute polarity by switching red for black and black for red on both your loudspeaker cables if you want to change your system's absolute polarity. The freak interconnect with pins 2 and 3 switched at one end may wind up in another system or application where you don't want the polarity switched.

Quite apart from the advantage of noise cancellation in a balanced line, a balanced connection often sounds better than an unbalanced line. A system connected by balanced interconnects can, however, also often sound less good than one connected with unbalanced lines. Say you have a digital processor that takes an unbalanced signal from the digital-to-analog converter chip and converts it to a balanced signal so that the processor manufacturer can tout the product as having "balanced outputs" (see the section on balanced digital processors in Chapter 8). Inside the digital processor, the unbalanced signal is converted to a balanced signal by a *phase splitter*, a circuit that takes a signal of one polarity and turns it into two signals of opposite polarity. Phase splitting subjects the unbalanced signal to an additional active (transistor- or op-amp–based) stage and puts more circuitry in the signal path.

The balanced digital processor output is then input to a balanced-input preamplifier. Because all but the very best balanced preamplifiers convert a balanced input signal to an unbalanced signal for the preamplifier's internal gain stages, the preamplifier's input converts this balanced signal to an unbalanced signal—adding yet another active stage to the signal path. After the unbalanced signal is amplified within the preamplifier, it is converted back to balanced with another phase splitter.

The preamplifier's balanced output is then sent from the preamplifier output to the power amplifier's balanced input where it's—that's right—converted to unbalanced with yet another active stage. The result of these unbalanced/balanced/unbalanced/balanced/unbalanced conversions is additional electronics in the signal path—just what we don't want. This is why you can't assume that balanced components sound inherently better than unbalanced ones. Magazine reviews of audio components should include musical and technical comparisons of the product's balanced and unbalanced modes.

Some products, however, are truly balanced and don't rely on phase splitters and unbalancing amplifiers. For example, a digital processor may create a balanced signal in the digital domain (at no sonic penalty but, indeed, a sonic gain) and convert that balanced signal to analog with four digital-to-analog converters and analog output stages (left channel + and –, right channel + and –). Similarly, some preamplifiers are truly balanced and have double the circuitry to operate on the non-inverting and inverting signals separately. You can tell a truly balanced preamplifier by the number of elements in the volume control. A preamplifier that operates on an unbalanced signal internally will have two volume-control elements: one for the left channel, one for the right. A fully balanced preamplifier will have four elements: ± left channel and ± right channel. The signal thus stays balanced from before the DACs inside the digital processor all the way to the final stages in the power amplifier.

As in all things audio, the proof is in the listening. When shopping for a component, listen to it in both balanced and unbalanced modes. Let your ears decide if the component works best in your system when connected via the balanced or unbalanced lines.

Digital Interconnects

A digital interconnect carries two channels of digitally encoded audio down a single interconnect, usually between a CD transport and outboard digital processor. A full discussion of digital interconnect methods, cables, and terminations is included in Chapter 8.

Cable and Interconnect Construction

Cables and interconnects are composed of three main elements: the signal conductors, the dielectric, and the terminations. The *conductors* carry the audio signal; the *dielectric* is an insulating material between and around the conductors; and the *terminations* provide connection to audio equipment. These elements are formed into a physical structure called the cable's *geometry*. Each of these elements—particularly geometry—can affect the cable's sonic characteristics.

Conductors

Conductors are usually made of copper or silver wire. In high-end cables, the copper's purity is important. Copper is sometimes specified as containing some percentage of "pure" copper, with the rest impurities. For example, a certain copper may be 99.997% pure, meaning it has three-thousandths of one percent impurities. These impurities are usually iron, sulfur, antimony, aluminum, and arsenic. Higher-purity copper—99.99997% pure—is called "six nines" copper. Many believe that the purer the copper, the better the sound. Some copper is referred to as *OFC*, or *Oxygen-Free Copper*. This is copper from which the oxygen molecules have been removed. It is more proper to call this "oxygen-reduced" copper because it is impossible to remove all the oxygen. In practice, OFC has about 50ppm (parts per million) of oxygen compared to 250ppm of oxygen for normal copper. Reducing the oxygen content retards the formation of copper oxides in the conductor, which can interrupt the copper's physical structure and degrade sound quality.

Another term associated with copper is *LC*, or *Linear Crystal*, which describes the copper's structure. Drawn copper has a grain structure that can be thought of as tiny discontinuities in the copper. The signal can be adversely affected by traversing these grains; the grain boundary can act as a tiny circuit, with capacitance, inductance, and a diode effect. Standard copper has about 1500 grains per foot; LC copper has about 70 grains per foot. Fig.11-5 shows the grain structure in copper having 400 grains per foot. Note that the copper isn't isotropic; it looks decidedly different in one direction than the other. All copper made into thin wires exhibits a chevron structure, shown in the photograph of Fig.11-5. This chevron structure may explain why some cables sound different when reversed.

Fig. 11-5 Copper in cables and interconnects has a grain structure.

Courtesy AudioQuest

Conductors are made by casting a thick rod, then drawing the copper into a smaller gauge. Another technique—which is rare and expensive—is called "as-cast." This method casts the copper into the final size without the need for drawing.

The highest-quality technique for drawing copper is called "Ohno Continuous Casting" or *OCC*. OCC copper has one grain in about 700 feet—far less than even LC copper. The audio signal travels through a continuous conductor instead of traversing grain boundaries. Because OCC is a process that can be performed on any purity of copper, not all OCC copper is equal.

The other primary—but less prevalent—conductor material is silver. Silver cables and interconnects are obviously much more expensive to manufacture than copper ones, but silver has some advantages. Although silver's conductivity is only slightly higher than that of copper, silver oxides are less of a problem for audio signals than are copper oxides. Silver conductors are made using the same drawing techniques used in making copper conductors.

The Dielectric

The dielectric is the material surrounding the conductors, and is what gives cables and interconnects some of their bulk. The dielectric material has a large effect on the cable's sound; comparisons of identical conductors and geometry, but with different dielectric materials, demonstrate the dielectric's importance.

Dielectric materials absorb energy, a phenomenon called *dielectric absorption*. A capacitor works in the same way: a dielectric material between two charged plates stores energy. But in a cable, dielectric absorption can degrade the signal. The energy absorbed by the dielectric is released back into the cable slightly delayed in time—an undesirable condition.

Dielectric materials are chosen to minimize dielectric absorption. Less expensive cables and interconnects use plastic or PVC for the dielectric. Better cables use polyethylene; the best cables are made with polypropylene or even Teflon dielectric. One manufacturer has developed a fibrous material that is mostly air (the best dielectric of all, except for a vacuum) to insulate the conductors within a cable. Other manufacturers inject air in the dielectric to create a foam with high air content. Just as different dielectric materials in capacitors sound different, so too do dielectrics in cables and interconnects.

Terminations

The terminations at the ends of cables and interconnects are part of the transmission path. High-quality terminations are essential to a good-sounding cable. We want a large surface contact between the cable's plug and the component's jack, and high contact pressure between them. RCA plugs will sometimes have a slit in the center pin to improve contact with the jack. This slit is effective only if the slit end of the plug is large enough to be compressed by insertion in the jack. Most high-quality RCA plugs are copper with some brass mixed in to add rigidity. This alloy is plated with nickel, then flashed with gold to prevent oxidation. On some plugs, gold is plated directly to the brass. Other materials for RCA plugs and plating include silver and rhodium.

RCA plugs and loudspeaker cable terminations are soldered or welded to the conductors. Most manufacturers use solder with some silver content. Although solder is a poor conductor, the spade lugs are often crimped to the cable first, forming a "cold" weld that makes a gas-tight seal. In the best welding technique, *resistance welding*, a large current is pulsed through the point where the conductor meets the plug. The resistance causes a small spot to heat, melting the two metals. The melted metals merge into an alloy at the contact point, ensuring good signal transfer. With both welding and soldering, a *strain relief* inside the plug isolates the electrical contact from physical stress.

Geometry

How all of these elements are arranged constitutes the cable's geometry. Some designers maintain that geometry is the most important factor in cable design—even more important than the conductor material and type.

An example of how a cable's physical structure can affect its performance: simply twisting a pair of conductors around each other instead of running them side by side. Twisting the conductors greatly reduces capacitance and inductance in the cable. Think of the physical structure of two conductors running in parallel, and compare that to the schematic symbol for a capacitor, which is two parallel lines.

This is the grossest example; there are many fine points to cable design. I'll describe some of them here, with the understanding that I'm presenting certain opinions on cable construction, not endorsing a particular method.

Most designers agree that *skin effect*, and interaction between strands, are the greatest sources of sonic degradation in cables. In a cable with high skin effect, more high-frequency signal flows along the conductor's surface, less through the conductor's center. This occurs in both solid-core and stranded conductors (Fig.11-6). Skin effect changes the cable's characteristics at different depths, causing different frequency ranges of the audio signal to be affected by the cable differently. The musical consequences of skin effect include loss of detail, reduced top-octave air, and truncated soundstage depth.

Fig. 11-6 Skin effect causes more of the audio signal to travel on the outside of the conductor.

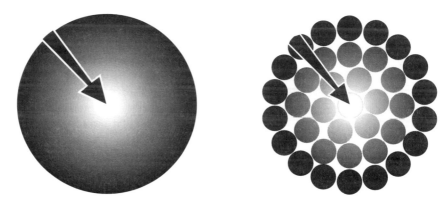

Courtesy AudioQuest

A technique for battling skin effect is *litz* construction, which simply means that each strand in a bundle is coated with an insulating material to prevent it from electrically contacting the strands around it. Each small strand within a litz arrangement will have virtually identical electrical properties. Litz strands push skin-effect problems out of the audible range. Because litz strands are so small, many of them bundled together in a random arrangement are required to achieve a sufficient gauge to keep the resistance low.

A problem with stranded cable (if it isn't of litz construction) is a tendency for the signal to jump from strand to strand if the cable is twisted. One strand may be at the outside at a point in the cable, then be on the inside farther down the cable. Because of skin effect, the signal tends to stay toward the outside of the conductor, causing it to traverse strands. Each strand interface acts like a small circuit, with capacitance and a diode effect, much like the grain structure within copper.

Individual strands within a conductor bundle can also interact magnetically. Whenever current flows down a conductor, a magnetic field is set up around that conductor. If the current is an alternating-current audio signal, the magnetic field will fluctuate identically. This alternating magnetic field can induce a signal in adjacent conductors (see

Appendix B), and degrade the sound. Some cable geometries reduce magnetic interaction between strands by arranging them around a center dielectric, which keeps them farther apart.

These are just a few of the techniques used by cable designers to make better-sounding cables.

Terminated Cables and Interconnects

Some cables and interconnects are not merely pieces of wire, but contain electronic components. These cables are identified by "boxes" on one or both cable ends housing the resistors, inductors, and capacitors that form an electrical "network." Pioneered by Music Interface Technologies (MIT), these products are often called *terminated* cables (Fig.11-7).

Fig. 11-7
Terminated cables and inter-connects are identified by "boxes" on the cables.

Courtesy Music Interface Technologies (MIT)

According to MIT, some of the audio signal's voltage is stored in the cable's capacitance, and some of the signal's current is stored in the cable's inductance. The amount of energy stored in the cable varies with frequency, which is manifested as tonal and dynamic emphases at those frequencies. Moreover, the energy stored in the cable is released over time, rather than being delivered to the loudspeaker along with the rest of the signal. This frequency-dependent, non-linear energy storage distorts the size and shape of the soundstage, according to MIT.

Terminated cables are designed to prevent such energy storage, and to deliver all the signal to the loudspeaker with the correct phase (timing) relationship. MIT claims that terminated cables are essential to realizing correct bass weight, smooth tonal balance, and a full-sized soundstage with precise image focus.

Because terminated cables form a low-pass filter (i.e., they don't start filtering until about 1MHz, well above the audioband), they are useful for connecting very-wide-bandwidth electronics. The Spectral brand of electronics, for example, has bandwidths as high as 3MHz—not because the designer wants to pass those frequencies, but to make the circuits behave better in the audioband. Terminated cables filter those very high frequencies, ensuring that loudspeakers are never fed energy in the megahertz range, and making the system more stable.

Battery Bias in Cables and Interconnects

Anyone who has listened to loudspeaker cables and line-level interconnects will have discovered that cables and interconnects start to sound better (smoother treble, greater ease, less grain, more dimensional soundstage) after they've been in the system for a few days. This phenomenon is often called "break-in." It's easy to understand "break-in" of loudspeakers and phono cartridges (the rubber surround in loudspeaker drivers and the rubber compliance in cartridges relaxes with use), but why would putting audio signals down a conductor cause that conductor's sound to change?

The answer is that the cable's dielectric "forms" to the charged state created by current flowing through the conductor. The same phenomenon occurs in capacitors, and is one reason why electronics sound better when left on for a few days. After a cable or capacitor "forms," it returns to its uncharged state slowly. This means that cables that have been "broken-in" will slowly return to their original state when the system is not in use. The process is not fully understood, but extensive listening experience confirms this cycle.

Rather than rely on the audio signal to "form" the cable's dielectric, the cable designer can apply a relatively high DC voltage across the dielectric when the cable is made, in essence "breaking-in" the cable more effectively than could an audio signal, and keeping the cable in that state indefinitely.

That is the theory behind a new breed of cable that is supplied with a battery attached. AudioQuest, which has applied for a patent on the idea, calls the technique Dielectric-Bias System (DBS). A wire connected to a 24V battery's positive terminal runs down the cable's length, and is not connected to the cable or to the battery's negative terminal. The battery's negative terminal is connected to a shield around the conductors. Because there is no path for current between the battery's positive and negative terminals, the battery experiences no current drain and will last for years. An interconnect employing this technology is shown in Fig.11-8.

Fig. 11-8 An interconnect employing the Dielectric-Bias System

DBS Anode

\+

DBS Cathode

Courtesy AudioQuest

Keep in mind that the battery system is completely outside the audio signal path, and doesn't interact with the audio signal.

A related technique was employed by Richard Vandersteen in his Model 5 loudspeaker. The Model 5 uses an integral powered woofer and an external crossover to roll off bass driving the loudspeaker. Vandersteen included a battery-bias system across the capacitors in this crossover which kept the capacitors biased at a relatively high voltage. This DC shifts the audio signal away from the zero-crossing point, improving sound quality. This technique is different from AudioQuest's Dielectric-Bias System in that the audio signal is combined with the battery's DC voltage.

Cable and Interconnect Specifications

There's a lot of hype and just plain misinformation about cables and interconnects. Manufacturers sometimes feel the need to invent technical reasons for why their cables sound better than the competition's. In reality, cable design is largely a black art, with good designs emerging from trial and error (and careful listening). Although certain conductors, dielectrics, and geometries have specific sonic signatures, successful cable designs just can't be described in technical terms. This is why cables should never be chosen on the basis of technical descriptions and specifications.

Nonetheless, some cable and interconnect specifications should be considered in some circumstances. The three relevant specifications are *resistance*, *inductance*, and *capacitance*. (These terms are explained in detail in Appendix B.)

A cable or interconnect's resistance, more properly called *DC series resistance*, is a measure of how much it opposes the flow of current through it. The unit of resistance is the *Ohm*. The lower the number of ohms, the lower the cable or interconnect's resistance to current flow. In practice, cable resistance is measured in tenths of ohms. Resistance isn't usually a factor in interconnect performance (except in some of the new non-metallic types), but can affect some loudspeaker cables—particularly thin ones—because of their higher current-carrying requirements.

The sounds of interconnects and loudspeaker cables can be affected by inductance. It is generally thought that the lower the inductance, the better, particularly in loudspeaker cables. Some power amplifiers, however, need to see some inductance to keep them stable; many have an output inductor connected to the loudspeaker binding post (inside the chassis). When considering how much inductance the power amplifier sees, you must add the cable inductance to the loudspeaker's inductance.

Capacitance is an important characteristic of interconnects, particularly when long runs are used, or if the source component has a high output impedance. Interconnect capacitance is specified in picofarads (pF) per foot. What's important isn't the interconnect's intrinsic capacitance, but the total capacitance attached to the source component. For example, 5' of 500pF-per-foot interconnect has the same capacitance as 50' of 50pF-per-foot interconnect. High interconnect capacitance can cause treble rolloff and restricted dynamics. (A full technical discussion of interconnect capacitance is included in Appendix B.)

Cables in the Power Amplifier/Loudspeaker Interface

The interface between a power amplifier and a loudspeaker through a cable is a critical point in a playback system. Unlike interconnects, which carry low-level signals, loudspeaker cables carry much higher voltages and currents. Loudspeaker cables thus react more with the components they are connected to.

Damping factor is an amplifier's ability to control the woofer's motion after the drive signal has ceased. For example, if you drive a loudspeaker with a bass-drum whack, the woofer's inertia and resonance in the enclosure will cause it to continue moving after the signal has died away. This is a form of distortion that alters the music signal's dynamic envelope. Fortunately, the power amplifier can control the motion; the degree of this control, or damping factor, is expressed as a simple number.

Damping factor is related to the amplifier's output impedance. The lower the output impedance, the higher the damping factor. When you connect a power amplifier and loudspeaker with cable, the cable's resistance decreases the amplifier's effective damping factor. For example, an amplifier's damping factor of 100 may be reduced to 40 by 20' of moderately resistive loudspeaker cable. The result is reduced tightness and control in the bass. Loudspeaker cables should therefore have low resistance and be as short as possible.

Getting the Best Sound from Cables and Interconnects

One of the most important issues is cable dressing—the way cables are positioned in your system. In an attempt to make their systems look tidy, some audiophiles bundle all the cables together with tie-wraps. But grouping AC cords, interconnects, and digital cables right next to each other can degrade your system's musical performance.

To understand why, consider how a moving-magnet phono cartridge works. The tiny magnets, suspended between coils of wire, are moved back and forth by the modulations in the record groove. The relative motion between the magnetic field and the coils induces (creates) electrical current flow through the coils. When this electrical current flow is amplified and converted into sound by the loudspeakers, we hear it as music.

The same sort of magnetic field around a cable in your rack can induce an unwanted signal in an adjacent cable. Audio signals flowing through a conductor create a magnetic field around that conductor. This magnetic field expands and collapses around the conductor at the same frequency as the audio signal. The magnetic field's expansion and collapse provide the relative motion between the magnetic field and a nearby conductor, inducing an electrical signal in any conductor within that field. This means that AC power cords, which carry 60Hz from the wall to your components, will induce a 60Hz noise in any cable that happens to be nearby. Similarly, a digital interconnect from a CD transport to a digital processor will radiate high-frequency noise (in the megahertz range) into analog interconnects, and even into AC cords. Although you don't hear this contamination as audible noise, it overlays the music with a grainy patina.

That's why the first rule of system setup is to keep AC cords away from interconnects and loudspeaker cables. If they must meet, AC cords and signal conductors (interconnects and speaker cables) should cross at right angles, not run parallel to each other. Crossing cables at right angles minimizes the amount of induced noise.

A simple trick for further reducing interaction between cables is to place 1"-square blocks of Styrofoam between AC cords, interconnects, or speaker cables where they cross. Use the blocks at every cable junction to separate interconnects, speaker cables, and AC cords from each other.

Putting Styrofoam blocks between interconnects at the back of your rack is more of a challenge than laying out cables on the floor. A little glue on the interconnect or power cord will hold the lightweight Styrofoam, provided you're not constantly moving interconnects. Rubber bands can also hold the blocks in place.

Even a small physical separation has a large effect. The "inverse square law" states that the strength of a magnetic field diminishes in proportion to the square of the distance. Consequently, you don't need large distances between cables to isolate them from one another.

Next, avoid stacking two components on one rack shelf. The components will be better isolated from each other electrically, and get better ventilation, when each is given its own shelf. Also pay attention to the positioning of components within the rack. Don't put phono preamplifiers near digital sources (CD players, transports, digital processors), or close to a power amplifier. You can also avoid running a digital interconnect next to analog interconnects by thoughtful component positioning. Take special care with the interconnects that run from your turntable to your preamplifier's phono input; they carry extremely tiny signals that are easily contaminated by radiated noise.

Here are several other tricks to help you keep interconnects and cables from degrading your system's sound:

1) Because all wire degrades the signal passing through it, the less wire you have in your system, the better. Keep interconnects and loudspeaker cables short.

2) Keep left and right loudspeaker cables, and left and right interconnects, the same length.

3) If you have excess cable or interconnect, don't wind it into a neat loop behind the loudspeaker or equipment rack. This will make the cable more inductive and change its characteristics. Instead, drape the cable so it crosses other loops at right angles.

4) Periodically disconnect all interconnects and loudspeaker cables for cleaning. Oxide builds up on jacks and plugs, interfering with the electrical transfer. Use a contact cleaner (available at most high-end stores). It works. In fact, switching interconnects sometimes cleans the jacks, making the system sound better even though the interconnect may not be intrinsically better.

5) When connecting and disconnecting RCA plugs, always grip the plug, never the cable. Remember to push the tab when disconnecting XLR plugs.

6) Ensure tight connection of all RCA plugs, and particularly spade lugs on power amplifiers and loudspeakers. Get lots of contact surface area between the spade lug and post, then tighten down the binding posts.

7) Avoid sharp bends in cables and interconnects.

8) High contact pressure is more important than a large contact area when connecting loudspeaker cables. A tight connection—enough to slightly distort a thin spade lug—is ideal.

12   High-End Audio Accessories

T he vast array and wide availability of audio accessories bears wit-
ness to audiophiles' need to "tweak" their systems to squeeze out
that last little bit of musical performance. Accessories can not only
make your system sound better, they're fun to try. It's quite rewarding
to discover some simple trick or product that elevates your system's
sound at little cost. This chapter surveys available accessories, describes
what they do, and explains how they work.

How to Choose Accessories

Some of the accessories described in this chapter can make your system
sound better than you thought it could—and at a modest cost. Other
accessories can not only fail to improve the sound, but can actually
degrade your system's musical performance. To make matters even
more complicated, many accessories are completely worthless and are
nothing more than "snake oil" sold by less-than-honest promoters.
Finally, the effectiveness of an accessory can vary from system to system.

Fortunately, there's a simple and effective way of deciding which
accessories are worth the money and which aren't: *listen to the accessory
in your system before you buy*. Most dealers will let you either borrow
the accessory overnight, or return it for a refund if you don't hear an
improvement. If you hear an improvement that seems commensurate
with the product's asking price, buy it. If you don't, return the product.
It's that simple. And if the accessory is inexpensive but not returnable,
you can try it at minimal cost. Some CD treatments cost only a few
dollars; if they don't work, it hasn't cost you much.

But by all means try some of the devices described in this chapter.
They can often make the difference between merely good and superlative sonic performance.

Stands and Racks

The most important accessory for any audio system is the equipment rack. A good rack presents your components in an attractive way, makes your system functional and easy to use, and, most important, helps achieve the best sound possible from your system. If your system includes a turntable, a high-quality rack is absolutely essential to realizing the LP front end's musical potential.

Apart from providing convenient housing for your equipment, the rack's main job is isolating the equipment from vibration. There is no question that vibrations degrade the sonic performances of preamplifiers, digital processors, CD transports, and particularly turntables. This vibration is generated by transformers in power supplies, motors in turntables and CD transports, and from acoustic energy impinging on the electronics.

Vibration affects electronic products through a phenomenon called *microphony*. A microphonic component emits a small electrical signal when vibrated; in other words, it acts as a microphone, converting mechanical energy into electrical energy. This electrical energy pollutes the audio signal, resulting in degraded musical performance.

Tubed products are particularly susceptible to vibration. In fact, you can shout into a tubed preamplifier and hear your voice come out of the loudspeakers. The preamplifier converts the acoustic energy of your voice into an electrical signal. When the tubed component is vibrated by the sound from the loudspeakers, noise is added to the music.

The sound qualities of digital products are also degraded by vibration, but through a different mechanism. The crystal oscillators in many transports and digital processors change their frequencies slightly when vibrated. Although this frequency shift is slight, even small timing variations can wreak havoc in digital audio systems. Some manufacturers of digital products go to extreme lengths to ensure accurate and stable crystal frequencies, and build some form of vibration isolation around the oscillators.

The LP playback system is the most sensitive to vibration; the vibrational energy is transmitted to the tonearm and cartridge, adding sonic garbage to the tiny signal recovered from the record groove. This vibration comes from the turntable motor, from resonances in the tonearm, and from acoustic energy impinging on the turntable, arm, and cartridge. Clearly, isolating your system from vibration is essential to realizing the best musical performance.

A good equipment rack fights vibration with rigidity, mass, and careful design. The massive, inert structure of a high-quality rack is much less likely to vibrate when in the presence of sound pressure generated by the loudspeakers. Moreover, the equipment rack can absorb, or damp, the vibration created by power transformers and motors. Many equipment racks have built-in vibration-damping mechanisms in their shelves.

The ultimate in vibration control is the *pneumatic rack* that floats the rack shelves on a cushion of air. An air bladder in the rack is filled from a bicycle-tire pump, which isolates the components in the rack from vibration. *Pneumatic platforms* are devices that hold a single component; the component sits on the platform, and the platform rests on a shelf in the equipment rack. One pneumatic platform that works particularly well for audio was actually designed to isolate a scanning electron microscope from vibration. If you want to experiment with pneumatic isolation without spending much money, try putting a bicycle inner tube underneath a component and pumping it half full of air. It's surprising how much of an improvement pneumatic isolation can render in a high-quality music system.

When choosing an equipment rack, look for a thick steel frame (14-gauge steel is excellent), welded construction, the ability to be filled with sand, vibration-damping shelves (Medium Density Fiberboard, or MDF, for example), bracing posts around the shelves, and floor spikes. Spikes between the rack and a floor act as a mechanical diode, draining vibrational energy from the rack and providing the best coupling between the rack and floor. For a spiked rack to be effective, the floor must be sturdy and flat so that the rack doesn't rock. The heights of most spikes are adjustable; you can level the rack and get good contact between the floor and all four (or three) spikes. Rack spikes are usually much heavier duty, with more rounded points than loudspeaker spikes. Note, however, that both types of spike will damage wood floors. Some racks are supplied with small plates to hold the spikes, preventing floor damage.

Not all good racks will have each of these features, but most will have at least some of them. The ability to fill the rack's posts with sand or lead shot is especially important. Sand is an excellent vibration-absorbing material, and it adds mass to the rack. It's also cheap.

The preceding discussion of high-mass racks, floor spikes, and intimate coupling between components, the rack, and the floor is only one school of thought. The second theory holds that audio components should be *decoupled* from the support surfaces and the floor with light-weight racks and compliant feet. Vibration in the rack and components is thus damped rather than transmitted to the floor. Generally, mass coupling works better for heavy components, and decoupling for light-weight components. The best way to determine which method is best for your system is to try both before you buy, or ask your dealer's advice.

Before installing a heavy rack—particularly one to be filled with sand—make sure the floor structure can support the weight. Suspended wood floors may need additional bracing. Bracing also makes the floor more solid and less prone to vibrating. A concrete slab is the ideal foundation for an equipment rack; you don't have to worry about the weight, and it provides a solid surface for the rack. You should set up the rack exactly where you want it before filling it with sand.

These features—sand-filled, spikes, vibration-absorbing shelves, thick steel construction, and bracing—are found together in the most elaborate and expensive racks. Many racks without all of these features still provide good performance. Avoid racks with large, unsupported shelves, flimsy construction, low mass, and poor vibrational damping. And don't even consider the generic "stereo stands" sold in furniture and department stores. Get a rack specially designed for high-performance audio systems. A rack offering the ultimate in vibration isolation and damping is shown in Fig.12-1. The elaborate rack shown in the photograph is fitted with optional vibration-absorbing blocks that fit below and on top of components, forming a massive structure for maximum vibration isolation.

Consider a good equipment rack an essential part of your hi-fi system; it will help your system achieve its full musical potential.

Fig. 12-1
A braced and
damped
equipment rack

Courtesy Bright Star Audio

Accessories to Isolate and Control Vibration: Spikes, Feet, and Cones

Vibration-isolation accessories have the same goals as the specialized audio equipment rack: reduced vibration in the audio component.

Isolation devices can be used on their own or in conjunction with an equipment rack.

The field of vibration-control accessories for audio systems was established with a product called Tiptoes, shown in Fig.12-2. Invented by Steve McCormack of The Mod Squad, Tiptoes are machined aluminum cones with sharp points. When used point-side down to support pieces of audio equipment, they act as mechanical diodes to remove mechanical energy from the components. When first introduced, Tiptoes were greeted with scorn—until their effects were heard. Today, Tiptoes and similar products are universally recognized as making an important contribution to high-quality music reproduction.

Fig. 12-2
Tiptoes—the original vibration treatment device

Courtesy McCormack Audio

A different approach to vibration control is supporting the component with compliant feet, or mounting the component on a compliant platform. These devices are made of a rubber-like material (usually Sorbothane) chosen for its excellent damping characteristics. Compliant feet isolate the audio product from external vibration by absorbing the energy before it can get into the product. These devices are also excellent for stacking one component atop another. The feet provide airspace for ventilation, and reduce potential magnetic interaction between components.

The most effective place for Tiptoes or other vibration-control devices is underneath tubed power amplifiers, particularly if the amplifiers are placed near loudspeakers. The acoustic energy from the loudspeakers impinges on the tubes, which convert that energy into an electrical signal that degrades sound quality. These devices also provide a small airspace between the floor and amplifier, increasing ventilation around the amplifier.

One designer of extremely high-quality turntables—who is also a physicist and mechanical engineer—considers vibration control so important that he has had a local tombstone maker cut huge slabs of granite on which to support his equipment.

You probably won't go to that extreme, but you should certainly try some of the available vibration-control devices.

AC Power Conditioners

An AC power conditioner plugs into the wall outlet and provides multiple AC outlets for plugging in your audio equipment. But before we talk about what a power conditioner does, let's look at the AC power line and its relationship to an audio system.

The AC power from the wall outlet is a 60Hz, 120VRMS sinewave that powers the audio system (see Appendix B for more detail on the power line). All your components are connected via the power line. In fact, your audio components are connected to every other electrical device in your house, and to every home and factory also using the power grid.

Power equipment on the AC line generates noise that travels back into the line where it enters your audio components. The FCC regulates the amount of noise that can be put back into the power line by appliances and industrial products. This noise is called *electromagnetic interference*, or *EMI*. Light dimmers, refrigerators, and other household appliances put high-frequency junk in the AC line. Vacuum cleaners and electrical power tools are a major source of power-line noise because the fibers in the motors' brushes are continually making and breaking contact. The line is also polluted by AM radio stations; power lines act as antennae, superimposing the AM signal over the 60Hz line.

Another source of EMI is your audio system. CD players, digital processors, CD transports, and any component using a microprocessor (some preamps, for example) put noise on the power line through their line cords. This noise then gets into preamps and source components to degrade their musical performance. In addition to putting noise in the AC line, audio components with digital circuits pollute other components by radiating *radio frequency* noise, or *RF*, through the air. Digital circuits work with clock pulses and electronic switches that operate in the AM radio frequency range; their operation radiates this RF noise, which is picked up by other components.

In addition to introducing noise in the AC line through the power cord and radiating it into the air, components also transmit noise to other components through the AC ground line. The AC ground connects all the chassis of an audio system. If you've got a noisy ground on one component, you've got a noisy ground on all your components. For example, digital noise in a CD player's ground can get into your pream-plifier, with the AC power line acting as a conduit for this noise. Noise can also get in the ground by leakage through electrolytic capacitors in power supplies.

All of these problems can be controlled with a well-designed AC power-line conditioner. First, nearly all conditioners filter the incoming AC line to remove the high-frequency garbage generated by factories, neighbors, and your own appliances. The filters allow the 60Hz AC to pass, but remove noise from the line. Second, some filters isolate the components from each other with small isolation transformers on some of the conditioner's AC outlets. These transformers break the physical connection between components, preventing noise from traveling from one component to another. The isolated outputs are often marked "digi-tal" for plugging in digital components, preventing a digital processor from polluting the AC supplying the preamplifier, for example. Third, a good line conditioner will reduce the amount of noise coupled to signal ground. Finally, AC line conditioners can protect components from volt-age spikes, lightning strikes, and surges in the power-supply voltage. Not all conditioners perform every function listed here; conditioners vary in their design principles, with some addressing one problem but not another.

Cleaning up the power line for source components and preamplifiers is a different job from conditioning AC power for power amplifiers. Power amplifiers have very different AC requirements and thus must be treated differently. The description earlier of what a good line conditioner should do applies to source components and preamplifiers that draw very little current. Power amplifiers, however, draw enormous amounts of current from the wall. When the power amplifier delivers a significant amount of current to the loudspeaker—for a bass-drum whack, for exam-ple—the amplifier's power-supply reservoir capacitors are drained to supply the current. The amplifier then draws a huge amount of instanta-neous current from the wall outlet to replenish its filter capacitors. The amount of current pulled from the wall can be so great that the AC wave-form distorts under the amplifier's current draw; the waveform's tops and bottoms are clipped off under the load. Any isolation transformer or conditioning device in the AC path could limit the amplifier's ability to draw current, and thus degrade the amplifier's performance. Power-line filters that remove high-frequency noise can benefit a power amplifier, but transformers in series with the AC supply should be avoided. These AC line conditioners that work with power amplifiers operate in parallel with the amplifier. That is, they drain noise to ground without putting any electrical components directly between the amplifier and the wall outlet.

Some audiophiles have separate, dedicated AC lines for their power amplifiers. This reduces the chance of distortion of the AC line caused by power-amplifier current draw from affecting the preamplifier and source components. Dedicated lines are often wired with "hospital grade" AC outlets. These are orange in color, and are of higher quality and are more mechanically secure than standard household outlets. Running dedicated lines to your listening room can have a dramatic sonic effect. You can also improve AC power by providing a separate, isolated ground for the listening room's AC outlets. An electrician disconnects the grounds from the listening room's AC outlets, runs a wire from the ground outside your house, then pounds a copper ground rod into the earth and attaches the wire. Your audio equipment is no longer connected to the house ground.

Because the AC line voltage varies according to the time of day and the load on the line, one may expect a line conditioner to regulate the voltage and provide a constant 120VAC to your system. Regulation, however, doesn't improve the sound of an audio system, and can actually degrade it if the input voltage moves around the threshold at which a separate transformer tap kicks in. Moreover, most high-end audio equipment is designed to work within the tolerances of the AC line supplied by the electric company. This is why power conditioners for computers that incorporate line regulation shouldn't be used for audio systems.

When choosing a line conditioner, make sure its power capability exceeds the power consumption of the components you'll be plugging into it. Also look for the UL (Underwriters Laboratories) or CSA (Canadian Standards Association) seal of approval, indicating that the power conditioner meets certain safety requirements. Choose a conditioner with a sufficient number of outlets for your present and anticipated needs. As with all accessories, try the power conditioner in your system before you buy. Expect to pay a minimum of $250 for a conditioner with just a few outlets, to several thousand dollars for a state-of-the-art system. Many excellent conditioners cost less than $500.

Another type of power-line conditioning device removes noise in the AC line simply by being plugged into a wall outlet. Instead of plugging your equipment into this type of AC conditioner, the device merely plugs into the wall near your hi-fi system. These products act as noise filters in parallel with the AC line powering your system. In theory, any junk on the line is shunted by the filter.

The most radical approach to AC line conditioning is to create an entirely new 60Hz sinewave by amplifying the output from a small 60Hz oscillator. This technique, used in PS Audio's PowerPlant products (Fig.12-3), is essentially a power amplifier. The PowerPlant converts the incoming 60Hz, 120V to DC; a low-level oscillator generates a clean 60Hz sinewave, which is amplified to 120V. As you can imagine, the output power is limited, making the PowerPlant best suited to front-end components rather than power amplifiers. Different models are available depending on your power needs; they range from 300W to 1200W. The PowerPlant is large, heavy, runs hot, and—unlike a power amplifier whose output depends on the audio signal's

Fig. 12-3 PS Audio's PowerPlant is a radical approach to AC power conditioning.

Courtesy PS Audio

amplitude—consumes just as much power when your audio system is running as when it is idle. Because the PowerPlant creates a new sinewave from a variable internal oscillator, you have the opportunity to run your audio equipment at a higher AC-line frequency. A front-panel adjustment lets you increase the frequency (shown in a display) and listen to the difference in sound. Most equipment sounds better when fed a frequency higher than 60Hz.

A power-line conditioner can't make poor audio components sound good; instead, it merely provides the optimum AC environment for those components so that they may realize their full potentials. The sonic benefits of a good line conditioner include a "blacker" background, with less low-level grunge and noise. The music seems to emerge from a perfectly quiet and black space, rather than a grayish background. The treble often becomes sweeter, less grainy, and more extended. Soundstaging often improves, with greater transparency, tighter image focus, and a newfound soundstage depth. Midrange textures become more liquid, and the presentation has an ease and musicality not heard without the conditioner.

If you haven't tried a power-line conditioner, you may not have heard your system at its best.

AC Power Cords

At first glance, it may seem that the several short pieces of wire carrying AC to the components in your audio system—the AC power cords—couldn't affect the sound of the system. But specialty audio power cords have become very popular recently as more and more listeners discover their benefits.

The AC cord is an integral part of the AC delivery system. The noise problems described earlier can be reduced with careful AC cord design. Magnetic interaction and coupling between the conductors is reduced with dedicated audio power cords, resulting in better transfer of AC to the components. This magnetic interaction, addressed in interconnects and loudspeaker cables, affects AC transmission to a greater degree because of the high current flow in an AC cord.

Specialty AC cords also have superior construction, sometimes with Teflon dielectric, silver-plated wire, and high-quality plugs. Some also have an RF (radio frequency) noise suppressor built into the cord. Good AC cords cost between $100 and $200. Again, try them in your system before buying.

CD Treatments

A wide variety of devices are available that claim to improve CD sound quality. These run the gamut from rubber rings that fit around a CD to oils applied to a CD's surface. Some CD treatments make a worthwhile improvement to the sound; others are of dubious value.

The main category of CD tweaks is the damping device. This can take the form of a rubber ring stretched around the CD's edge, a flat adhesive ring stuck to the outer perimeter of the CD, or a mat that covers the entire label side of the CD. The theory is, the less disc vibration, the better the sound. One idea holds that a more stable CD results in less servo activity on the part of the transport's electromechanical systems, which maintains focus, tracking, and rotational speed. This means less current demand on the power supply.

Be careful about applying rings that cannot be removed. If they degrade the sound—as some may—you're stuck. In addition, some transports simply won't play discs that are a different size or shape. If you want to experiment with CD rings, use the removable kind. Rings generally cost between $1 and $3 each. Try a few: if they don't make an audible improvement, you're out only a few dollars.

CD mats can improve sound quality, but also stress the CD player's or transport's motor system; the rotational motor was designed to spin the mass of a CD, not a CD and a heavy mat. Some transport manufacturers have devised lightweight magnetic clamps that hold the CD firmly in place, yet add very little mass.

The second main category of CD treatments are those intended to improve the CD system's optical performance. These include liquids applied to the CD surface, and colored paint around the disc edge. How these potions work is a mystery, but some of them do improve the sound. Again, you must be careful about what you apply to a CD surface: some chemicals can attack the CD's polycarbonate substrate and ruin the disc. Further, wiping the liquid off the disc can create scratches that may cause mistracking on playback.

Finally, CD lens cleaners are available to remove dust and dirt from a player's lens. They are the size of a CD, with tiny brushes that wipe the lens as the disc spins. Lens cleaners cost about $20.

Portable Audio

Being an audiophile shouldn't prevent you from enjoying music at any time and place, even if the sound quality is less than superlative. A personal portable audio system, such as an Apple iPOD and quality headphones, can create a private musical sanctuary during the rigors of travel, exercise, or when you don't want your music to disturb others. Moreover, it's possible to achieve much higher sonic performance from a portable system than is commonly realized.

The three main formats for portable audio are CD, MiniDisc, and MP3. CD is popular because just about everyone has a CD player at home, and thus an instant portable music library. MiniDisc, covered in Chapter 8, was a huge hit in Japan and is still gaining popularity in North America. MP3 players are favored for their extremely small size, light weight, and low cost. MP3 players, however, offer the lowest sound quality.

MP3 players employ either solid-state flash memory to store the audio data or tiny hard-disk drives. Solid-state players have the advantage of no moving parts, but typically have lower storage capacity than hard-disk drive units. Some players accept tiny memory cards, such as the SD format used in digital cameras.

Apple's iPOD has revolutionized portable audio. The hard-disk-based iPOD can store MP3 files, uncompressed WAV files (which offer the same sound quality as CD), or Apple's own AAC file format used in it's iTunes Internet-download music service.

Whatever format you choose, I recommend replacing the headphones that come with a portable player. Selecting high-quality headphones is the first and most significant step toward achieving good portable sound.

Headphones and Headphone Amplifiers

Headphones are essential for portable listening, but can also be used at home when you don't want to disturb family members. Headphones vary not only in sound quality, but in comfort; it's a mistake to buy headphones that you want to take off after just a short time. A significant factor in long-term comfort is the headphones' weight; the lighter models, of course, enjoy an advantage.

Some very-lightweight headphones sound excellent and are comfortable, but don't provide much isolation from outside sounds. If you plan on listening in a noisy environment, choose *closed-ear* headphones over the *open-ear* variety. In addition to keeping outside sounds out, closed-ear 'phones keep your music in, and are less likely to disturb others.

High-quality headphones range in price from about $59 to as much as $2000 for electrostatic "earspeakers." The sound quality of the best under-$100 units is surprisingly good. Superlative models are available for about $500. The better-quality headphones provide a smoother tonal balance, greater resolution of detail, and a more open and transparent sound. It's worth shopping for headphones; just as with loudspeakers, less expensive models often outperform more costly units.

A recent trend has been toward the "ear bud" style, in which two small transducers fit inside your ears. Ear buds are much less bulky and obtrusive than traditional headphones, and are more easily portable. Although ear buds are commonly supplied with low-quality MP3 players, high-quality units are available that deliver superb sound. The Shure E5c, for example, uses two separate transducers, one for reproducing bass and one for reproducing midrange and treble. A small in-line crossover splits up the frequency spectrum. A small isolating seal blocks outside sounds. This particular model is so sensitive (needs very little power to achieve a high volume) that it is supplied with an optional attenuator to prevent overload.

Most headphones use tiny dynamic drivers, which operate on the same principle as dynamic drivers in loudspeakers. Electrostatic headphones, which are very expensive but offer state-of-the-art performance, operate on the same principle as electrostatic loudspeakers (see Chapter 7).

Most listeners have never heard headphones at their full potential. That's because the headphone jack on the front of some components outputs a severely compromised signal. The headphone amplifier is usually an afterthought considered unworthy of serious design effort or expense. After all, how many consumers make purchasing decisions based on the quality of the headphone amplifier?

Audiophiles wanting a better headphone-listening experience can choose an aftermarket headphone amplifier. This small device, which works for portable or home use, takes in a line-level signal from a portable CD or MD player and amplifies it enough to drive headphones. Most headphone amplifiers operate on both AC and battery power.

The headphone amplifier is a miniature power amplifier that provides perhaps half a watt of output. The amplifier should be able to drive low impedances and deliver current to the headphones, be stable into reactive loads, and be built with audiophile-quality components. High-quality headphone amplifiers have a discrete output stage (made from separate transistors) rather than an operational amplifier chip, and are fed from power supplies designed with high-end techniques and circuits. They also incorporate audiophile-quality volume controls.

One problem with listening to conventional stereo recordings on headphones is that the left ear hears only the left-channel signal, and the right ear only the right-channel signal. In loudspeaker listening you hear some of the left-channel signal in the right ear, and vice versa. The slight arrival-time difference between the two ears allows the brain to locate the sound source in front of the listener. Without this information, the brain becomes confused and localizes the sound in the center of the head. This "in-the-head" imaging is unnatural and disconcerting.

A circuit found in some headphone amplifiers, the HeadRoom Image Processor, electronically simulates the delay you hear when listening to loudspeakers. A portion of the left channel is delayed and mixed with the right channel, and vice versa. This technique tricks your brain into thinking the sound source is in front of you rather than inside your head. The result is a more natural and enjoyable listening experience.

The HeadRoom Image Processor circuit is available in HeadRoom headphone amplifiers, as well as products from a few other companies that have licensed the technology. HeadRoom didn't invent the technique—the fundamental research into this phenomenon was done in the 1960s—but does provide a high-end implementation of it with modern circuitry. (The HeadRoom web site, www.headphones.com, is filled with excellent information on high-end portable audio systems.)

Another way to get great headphone sound at home is to drive the 'phones with a single-ended tubed amplifier. Some SET amplifiers drive the headphone output not with a cheap op-amp, but with the amplifier's tubed circuitry. These low-powered amplifiers make ideal headphone drivers, and can produce superlative sound. The high impedances of many headphones, along with their low current draw, make them the perfect load for SET amplifiers. Check with the manufacturer to find out if the headphone jack is driven by the same tubed circuitry that powers the loudspeakers.

Binaural Recordings

Binaural recording is a special recording technique that can provide stunning three-dimensional sound when reproduced through headphones. Binaural recordings are made by inserting the recording microphones in a dummy head's "ears," then placing the head in a concert hall or other acoustic space. When played back through headphones, such recordings create an extremely realistic sense of being in a three-dimensional acoustic space.

Several classic binaural demonstrations highlight the ability of binaural recordings to provide pinpoint imaging in a 360° sphere around your head. One recording simulates the sounds of getting a haircut. With the headphones on, the listener hears the precise location and distance of the scissors moving around the head. In another, the sound of an insect flying in a circle around the listener is eerie enough, but then the insect appears to fly right up to your ear. It's not unusual to see listeners jump or turn around when experiencing binaural recording for the first time.

Although these gimmick recordings show off the technique's capabilities, binaural recording can be used seriously to capture and reproduce the original soundfield of a musical event. Binaural recording provides perfectly natural and realistic surround sound from two channels, with no need for decoders or multiple speaker arrays.

To understand why, it helps to know a little about human hearing. Sound striking a person's torso, head, and outer ear is modified by those structures. For example, sound arriving from the rear has less treble content than sound arriving from the front. Moreover, the outer ear's shape creates reflections that combine with the sound directly striking the eardrum. As described in Chapter 4, combining direct and reflected sound creates comb filtering, or a series of notches in the frequency response.   The brain analyzes the nature of the comb filtering (specifically, which frequencies are attenuated) to help determine the location of the sound source. This modification of the impinging sound is technically called the *Head-Related Transfer Function* (HRTF).

Such spatial cues don't exist when music is recorded with microphones sitting in open space, but are imprinted on a recording picked up by tiny microphones inserted in the ear "canals" of a dummy head. When the recording is played back through headphones, your brain receives these cues and is more easily fooled into thinking it is actually in the original three-dimensional soundfield.

Binaural recording is analogous to the old 3-D stereopticon photographs. These were photos taken of the same subject with two cameras whose lenses were 2.5" apart—the same as the average distance between the pupils of the human eyes. When the left image is presented to the left eye only, and the right image to the right eye, the brain combines the two images, interpreting the slight difference in their perspectives as three-dimensional depth and solidity. In fact, the term "stereo" comes from the Greek word for "solid."

Headphone listening to binaural recordings ensures that the left ear hears only the left-channel information as picked up by the dummy head's left microphone, and the right ear hears only what the head's right microphone picked up. A binaural recording will still sound fine on loudspeakers, but you must wear headphones to achieve the dramatic surround-sound effect. For a catalog of binaural recordings, call The Binaural Source at (800) 934-0442, or visit www.binaural.com.

Cassette Decks

If you like to record your own analog cassettes at home, buy a cassette deck of high enough quality to preserve the good sound of your CD player or turntable source. A good mass-market cassette deck can make remarkably good recordings when fed a clean signal from high-end electronics. Friends for whom I've made sampler tapes are surprised at the improvement in quality over their own or prerecorded tapes.

The first rule is to buy a single-well tape deck, not the dual-well machines that have become so popular recently. A single, high-quality mechanism and electronics is preferable to two sets of cheaper components. Moreover, manufacturers don't put serious design effort into dual-well decks.

If you have a sizable budget, a cassette deck with three heads will produce far better sound quality than a two-head deck. In the latter, one head is the erase head, with the second head serving as a record head during recording and as a playback head when playing tapes. A three-head machine uses separate heads for erase, record, and playback. The physics of magnetic-tape recording dictate that the tiny magnetic gap in the record head should be wide, the gap in the playback head narrow. A head designed to perform both duties is inherently compromised—the gap width is somewhere between the ideal dimensions for recording and playback. But with separate heads for recording and playback, each can be optimized for its specific job. Three-head decks are characterized by a more extended treble and greater clarity.

Three-head decks have another advantage: you can listen to the tape off the playback head a split-second after it's been recorded. This feature, call *off-tape monitoring*, allows you to check the tape quality as it's being recorded. If anything goes wrong, you'll know it immediately. In addition, off-tape monitoring allows you to fine-tune the recording parameters to achieve a better recording. For example, some decks have a knob that lets you manually fine-tune the amount of bias. With a three-head deck, you can switch back and forth while making a test recording between "source" (the signal coming into the deck) and "tape" (the signal coming off the tape) while adjusting the bias. By turning the bias-adjustment knob until the two signals sound closest in quality (particularly the amount of treble), you can more accurately set the correct amount of bias.

Some decks have an automatic bias-adjustment feature that sets the correct amount of bias for the brand of tape you're using. Bias is a very-high-frequency signal (above 100kHz) added to the music before recording that makes magnetic tape recording more *linear* (i.e., the output signal more closely resembles the input signal). Too much bias causes the upper treble to be erased; too little bias increases distortion, making the tape sound hard and bright. In a deck with automatic bias adjust, the deck makes a test recording and calibrates the bias level for each tape.

Auto bias-adjust is often accompanied by automatic calibration of the *Dolby level*. Dolby noise reduction is a two-step process for reducing tape hiss. Calibrating the Dolby level ensures that the two Dolby noise-reduction steps, called encode and decode, are perfectly complementary. Correct setting of the Dolby level provides noise reduction without treble loss.

Dolby noise reduction revolutionized the compact cassette by turning a low-quality dictation medium into the world's most popular music-delivery format. Dolby noise reduction works by boosting low-level, high-frequency signals during recording, then attenuating those signals during playback. When high frequencies are attenuated on playback, tape hiss is attenuated as well. This action is gentle enough that Dolby-encoded tapes can be played back without Dolby decoding and still sound acceptable, if a little bright. This form of Dolby, called *Dolby B*, reduces tape hiss by about 10dB. Dolby B is also used on the audio channels of VHS tapes.

A more powerful version of Dolby noise reduction, called *Dolby C*, doubles Dolby B's noise reduction to 20dB in the treble, but at the expense of not sounding right unless played back with Dolby C decoding. If you plan to play your recordings on a player with Dolby C noise reduction, use Dolby C when recording. If you're unsure of the playback deck, stick with Dolby B.

The most advanced form of consumer Dolby noise reduction is called *Dolby S*. Based on the very effective professional Dolby SR (Spectral Recording) system, Dolby S achieves even quieter recordings by splitting the audio spectrum into separate bands and operating on those bands separately. The result is a 24dB increase in signal-to-noise ratio in the treble, and a 10dB increase in the low frequencies. Dolby S is found only on the best cassette decks.

Finally, you may see some high-quality decks with the *Dolby HX Pro* logo on the front panel. Dolby HX Pro isn't a noise-reduction system, but a technique of improving recording quality. I mentioned earlier that different tapes require different amounts of bias to perform optimally. But even on a single tape, the optimum amount of bias constantly changes with the music's spectral content; more treble in the music requires less bias. That's because treble energy in the music acts as bias, momentarily over-biasing the tape on cymbal crashes, for example. Dolby HX (for Headroom eXtension) Pro monitors the amount of treble in the music and continually adjusts the bias to maintain the optimum bias sent to the record head. The technique is so successful that, today, virtually all mass-produced cassettes are made with Dolby HX Pro. It's also a worthwhile feature on your home deck. Note that a cassette recorded with HX Pro doesn't need decoding, and will sound better on any cassette deck, even the cheapest. In addition, HX Pro is used in conjunction with one of the Dolby noise-reduction systems for the best performance.

Using high-quality tape is essential to making good-sounding recordings. Tapes are categorized according to the amount of bias they need, and are generally labeled *high bias* or *normal bias*. This difference in bias is large (much larger than the bias change effected by a bias fine-tune knob), and usually set by a switch on the cassette deck's front panel. Premium tapes are generally high-bias, and offer extended treble response. Some cassette decks can roughly set the correct bias automatically by sensing the type of tape in the machine from the tabs on the cassette's top edge. Without this feature, you'll need to set the deck's front-panel bias switch to the correct position for the type of tape.

A switch that often accompanies the bias switch is marked *Equalization*. This engages one of several treble-cut circuits that restore flat response. Different tapes require different playback equalization. Remember that bias is applicable only during recording, and equalization only during playback.

Setting the recording level is a trade-off between noise, distortion, and treble response. A low recording level results in low distortion and extended treble. Unfortunately, a low recording level also decreases the signal-to-noise ratio, meaning you'll hear more tape hiss. Increasing the recording level reduces hiss, but increases distortion and causes the treble to be attenuated.

High-resolution meters are vital to setting the correct recording level. Old-fashioned analog meters are the best. If the deck you're considering has LED metering (a row of tiny lights), make sure that the meter display has plenty of LEDs; the greater the number of LEDs, the more precise the metering.

Another factor that greatly influences the treble response is a mechanical head-alignment parameter called *azimuth*; i.e., how perpendicular the tape is to the head. A difference in azimuth between the record head in your home deck and the playback head in your portable machine or car deck will cause treble rolloff, making the music sound dull. If you want the highest fidelity, the azimuth can be aligned by a service technician. Both decks should be aligned for optimum performance.

When all the possible advantages are available and correctly employed—three-head deck, Dolby S, HX Pro, correct azimuth alignment, premium tape—the analog cassette format is capable of outstanding sound quality.

Other Accessories

Cable Enhancers

A cable enhancer is a device that reportedly breaks-in line-level interconnects and loudspeaker cables faster and more completely than running music through the cables. Both ends of the interconnect or cable are connected to the enhancer, which puts out a high-level signal to produce current flow through the cable. Cable enhancers cost about $200. Many dealers, however, will break in your new cables on an enhancer at no charge.

RF Filters

An RF filter is a device that fits around cables and AC cords and prevents high-frequency noise from passing through the cable to the audio component connected by the cable. The filter is, in essence, a "choke" that turns the cable or power cord into a low-pass filter. RF filters can be put around interconnects at the preamp side to prevent RF from getting into the preamp, around interconnects at the power amplifier, or around AC cords. They cost about $25 per pair, are easy to install and remove, and can be an inexpensive improvement to your system. RadioShack sells a $5.50 snap-together ferrite core that will fit around cables (part number 273-105).

Contact Cleaners

Contact cleaners remove the residue and oxidation that builds up on RCA plugs and jacks, interconnect terminations, and loudspeaker and power-amplifier terminals. The fluid comes in a small bottle and is usually supplied with pipe cleaners for applying the liquid. Some cleaners come in spray form, but the contacts should still be rubbed to remove oxidation.

Start by cleaning all the RCA and XLR jacks on your equipment and cables. Treat the outer ring as well as the unseen junction inside the jack that contacts the RCA plug's center pin. Pay special attention to phono jacks and plugs; connectors that carry the tiny phono signals to your preamplifier are the most sensitive to degradation from dirt and oxidation. Next, clean the binding posts on loudspeakers and power amplifiers, as well as the spade lugs on speaker cables. Be sure not to touch any cleaned surface with your fingers—body oils will trap contaminants. You may also consider cleaning the pins on phono cartridges and the tonearm's cartridge sleeve connectors.

Periodic cleaning of all electrical contacts in a system can keep your system sounding its best. Once every two months is a good interval. Make sure, however, that the contact cleaner doesn't leave a residue that could attract dust and end up degrading the connection. Expect to pay about $15 for a bottle of cleaner, which should provide about ten to twenty complete system cleanings.

A related product is the contact enhancer, a fluid applied to electrical contacts in your system. Contact enhancers promote better conductivity between a plug and jack, improving the sound. Contact enhancers work especially well on phono-cartridge pins.

Record-Cleaning Machines

As vinyl records become more scarce, preserving the sound on your LPs becomes even more important. The best way to keep your LPs sounding good and lasting longer is to clean them with a record-cleaning machine. Unlike a brush that removes only some of the dirt, or redistributes it to other parts of the record, a record-cleaning machine uses a motor-driven vacuum to extract dirt and grime from the record grooves. Although some record brushes can help remove dirt, none are nearly as effective as a cleaning machine.

A record cleaned with a vacuum cleaner will have far fewer ticks and pops, and also have a cleaner, more open midrange. Removing the junk in the grooves allows the cartridge to extract more musical information from the record. A clean record will also last much longer than a dirty one; the stylus won't constantly be grinding dirt into the groove walls.

Record-cleaning machines vary in price according to their level of automation. Some machines, like the Record Doctor II by Nitty Gritty, require you to apply the cleaning fluid to the record surface, turn the record over (so the fluid side faces the vacuum slot), and spin the record yourself. Semi-automatic machines spin the record with a motor, but still require manual application of the cleaning fluid and turning over the record. Fully automatic machines apply the fluid, spin the record, and even clean both sides of the record at the same time.

Expect to pay about $200 for a bare-bones cleaner, and up to $2500 for a state-of-the-art automatic system.

Cartridge Demagnetizers

Cartridge demagnetizers are often referred to generically as "flux-busters," after the Sumiko Fluxbuster, the first commercially available demagnetizer. Demagnetizers are about the size of a cassette box and cost less than $100. They generally have two RCA jacks that you connect to your turntable's RCA outputs with a pair of interconnects. When the demagnetizer's power switch is engaged, the demagnetizer puts out a high-frequency signal that slowly diminishes in intensity, removing unwanted residual magnetism in the phono cartridge.

Moving-coil phono cartridges need demagnetizing because the core around which the coils are wound gradually becomes magnetized by the powerful permanent magnets surrounding the coils. Air-cored moving-coil cartridges are not susceptible to accumulated residual magnetism and don't need demagnetizing.

Moving-magnet cartridges build up magnetism on the pole pieces, degrading sonic performance. Note that you must remove the stylus from a moving-magnet cartridge before demagnetizing. Otherwise, the demagnetizer will demagnetize the magnets, reducing the cartridge's output level. If you accidentally demagnetize the magnets, replace the stylus: the stylus assembly contains new magnets.

Cartridges should be demagnetized after each 50 hours of playing time. Note that demagnetizers designed to bulk-erase tapes or degauss televisions should not be used to demagnetize cartridges.

Stylus Cleaners

Cleaning your stylus before every record is essential not only to good sound, but to preserving record life. A dirty stylus will grind junk into the groove walls where it cannot be removed, even by a record-cleaning machine. Stylus cleaners resemble nail polish, with a brush in a bottle of cleaning fluid. The Discwasher brush, by contrast, has short, stiff bristles on which a fluid is applied. Whichever brush you use, the stylus should be cleaned with a gentle stroke from the back of the cartridge to the front. A stylus-cleaning kit sells for about $15.

Other LP accessories—stylus pressure gauges, damping devices, record clamps, and alignment protractors—are covered in Chapter 9.

Tube Dampers

Tube dampers are devices that fit over vacuum tubes to make them less microphonic. The damper is made from a rubber-like material—often Sorbothane—that damps a tube's vibration and improves sound quality. Some dampers are also claimed to extend tube life by acting as heatsinks, radiating heat away from the tube. Tube dampers cost between $4 and $25 each.

AC Polarity Testers and AC "Cheater" Plugs

The AC plug's orientation in the wall socket can affect a component's sound quality. Most audio components have three-pronged plugs, with the rounded lower pin connected to the component's chassis. This ground lead ultimately ends up at a copper rod buried in the ground outside the electrical service panel. If, for some reason, the AC voltage touches a component's chassis, the chassis will short that voltage to ground, blowing the breaker fuse and protecting anyone who may touch the chassis. The two other conductors are connected to the component's power transformer, which tends to leak some current to ground. The amount of current leaked depends on the orientation of the AC plug. One direction may produce a lower chassis voltage than the other. The system will sound best with the plug oriented in the direction producing the lower chassis voltage.

Determining which way the AC plug should go can be determined with an AC polarity tester. Just put the polarity tester near the chassis of the component and read the tester's meter. Reverse the AC plug and see if the voltage is lower. Repeat this process on each component until the entire system has been connected for best AC polarity. You can do the same thing with a voltmeter, but the polarity meter avoids direct contact with the AC line. A polarity meter costs less than $30.

Reversing a three-pronged AC plug can be accomplished by adding a "cheater" plug (available at any hardware store) that allows the plug to be inserted upside down. The cheater plug's ground wire (which replaces the rounded pin) must be connected to the screw holding the AC wall cover in place to maintain the safety aspect of a grounded plug and receptacle. If the ground wire isn't attached, the cheater plug "lifts" the ground connection. When this happens, the component is grounded only through the interconnects connecting the ungrounded component to another component that is grounded at the wall. For example, the ground can be lifted on a preamplifier provided the power amplifier is grounded to the wall and the two are linked by interconnects. Ground lifting is sometimes required to eliminate hum and noise in the system created by *ground loops*. A ground loop occurs when there are two paths to ground of unequal resistance. A slight voltage difference is thus created that causes a small current to flow in the ground conductors, producing a hum.Lifting the ground at one component breaks the ground loop and removes the hum.

Note that the safety feature of a grounded system is defeated if one component is plugged into a cheater plug and not connected to a grounded component through the interconnects. Further, lifting the ground on all the components is extremely dangerous; if for some reason a high voltage appears on the chassis, you'll have no way of knowing it and could receive a lethal shock. But if the component is properly grounded, the chassis will cause a breaker fuse in your AC wall panel to blow, preventing electric shock.

Ground Isolators

A ground isolator may be needed when a cable TV connection is made to a component audio system, or in a system that includes a tuner for cable-delivered digital radio. The cable TV ground is likely to be different from your audio system's ground, producing hum and buzz when the signal from the digital radio tuner is connected to your preamp. A ground isolator keeps the two grounds separate.

Vibration Absorbers for Loudspeakers

Several products are said to reduce a loudspeaker's cabinet vibrations and improve sound quality. One device that I've found particularly effective is a cloth bag of small but very heavy damping beads—the finished product looks like a bean bag. When put on top of the loudspeaker, the bags absorb vibration, and are especially effective on small, lightweight, stand-mounted loudspeakers. The weight also helps couple the loudspeaker to the stand, and the stand to the floor.

Other vibration-control devices address the problem with small discs that reportedly absorb vibration through some internal mechanism, or are made of solid wood. The discs are placed on components, loud-speakers, listening-room walls, or equipment racks. These products tend to be quite expensive, however, and reports of their effectiveness are mixed.

Voodoo Accessories and the Lunatic Fringe

In any pursuit are those who abandon reason, and high-end audio has its share of nonsensical, even bizarre accessories. Most of these products are completely worthless.

Examples include an alligator clip attached to the loudspeaker cable that prevents the loudspeaker's "gravitational influence" from affecting the audio signal. Another claims to "energize" the electrons in an audio system with a combination of lithium salts and cobra venom.

We must be careful, however, in branding certain products as fraud-ulent. Many accessory products whose value is now without question—AC power conditioners and Tiptoes, for examples—were once dismissed as worthless by those who had never listened to their effects. In the early days of CD, it was assumed that all CD transports and digital intercon-nects sounded the same because they all produced the same stream of binary ones and zeros. It was only after much critical listening and closer scientific scrutiny that other mechanisms for creating differences in the sounds of transports and digital interconnects (primarily timing varia-tions called "jitter") were discovered. It is undisputed today that trans-port and digital-interconnect jitter affects sound quality. We must listen and trust our ears, and not rely solely on pure theories, no matter how elegant or well-argued.

The bottom line with any accessory, as with any audio component, should sound familiar by now: listen before you buy. If the device makes an audible improvement, buy it—regardless of whether or not there's a scientific explanation.

13 Audio for Home Theater

Introduction

The massive growth of home theater over the past decade has had a profound effect on high-end audio. On one hand, home theater—the combination of high-quality audio and video presentation in the home—has opened new markets to high-end companies and new possibilities for the music enthusiast. On the other hand, combining a music-reproduction system with a video display and multichannel surround-sound all too often compromises the system's musical performance. As audiophiles, we go to great lengths to achieve the highest possible sound quality and get closer to the music. Any compromise of that pursuit is anathema to the goals and spirit of high-performance audio.

Yet the application of high-end products to movie watching can create an enormously compelling experience. Film is as important an art form as music; just as good technical quality in music reproduction brings us closer to the musician's expression, home theater done right conveys to us more of the filmmaker's art. Moreover, the emergence of multichannel music formats (Super Audio CD and DVD-Audio) has fueled a push toward more than two loudspeakers in the listening room—loudspeakers that can reproduce film soundtracks as well as multichannel music programs.

I explored this conflict between high-end audio and home theater in the following short essay, first published as "From the Editor" in Issue 140 of *The Absolute Sound*.

Now I know why I hate home theater," said a colleague to me after a series of home-theater demonstrations at a Consumer Electronics Show. The fellow journalist, a dedicated 2-channel music enthusiast, voiced a familiar refrain in high-end audio circles—namely, that music is a pure art form and home theater is merely glorified television at best, and an abomination at worst. At the time (1992), I had to agree; the demonstration consisted of subjecting a group of audio writers to a series of the loudest and most violent five-minute clips from the loudest and most violent movies at ear-splitting levels. The manufacturer was trying to impress us, but succeeded only in perpetuating the myth that home theater and high-quality music reproduction are antithetically opposed.

I say "myth" because since that demonstration ten years ago, I've come to believe that the antipathy between music and home theater is a false dichotomy. High-end audio equipment is about getting closer to the artistic expression of composers and musicians. Home theater is (or should be) about getting closer to the artistic expression of filmmakers. The greater the technical quality of the presentation, the more deeply we can experience the artists' intent—whether musical or cinematic. So what went wrong with this picture?

The home-theater industry has, unfortunately, given those of us in the high end many reasons to abhor its intrusion into music reproduction: gimmicky surround-sound modes; amusical, pant-rattling subwoofer bass; excessive volume levels; and an aesthetic that values impact over nuance. But an entire concept—the pursuit of high-quality film reproduction in the home—cannot be dismissed solely because of the excesses of those who appeal to the lowest common denominator. Rather than viewing home theater as a bastardization of audio, I've come to the belief that home theater, when done right, is an *expansion* of the high-end ethic, and one that forges an entirely new path for creating an immensely rewarding connection between artist and audience.

This expansion has been made possible by the entry of true high-end audio companies into the home-theater arena. These companies, driven by high-end ideals, create products that are faithful to the source, eschew gimmicks, and don't sacrifice musical performance for explosions and sound effects.

Moreover, home theater has been a boon to high-end audio in several ways. First, the exploding market for home-theater equipment has kept many traditional 2-channel companies prosperous. This allows them to stay in business, and continue to offer 2-channel and well as multichannel products. Second, home theater causes many who once had a "stereo" with loudspeakers in opposite corners of a room to set up the loudspeakers correctly and, for the first time, consider the spatial aspects of reproduced music. Third, a decent-quality home theater that's well setup can inadvertently become a vehicle for rediscovering the joys of music. I recently recommended the Paradigm Atom multichannel loudspeaker system to an "average joe" friend ($1106 complete). I ran into him a few weeks later, and the first thing he said to me was that he and his wife now spend much more time listening to music, and that they are happily rediscovering their music collection. Multiply this scenario by millions, factor in upward mobility, and you have a recipe not only for a robust high-end audio industry, but more importantly, the return of music to a prominent place in daily life.

§

With that introduction, let's look at the nuts and bolts of high-quality audio for home theater. Note that this chapter cannot cover the field in the same detail as other topics throughout this book, and I've avoided describing the video aspects of home theater. For an in-depth treatment of home theater, including video displays, see my *Home Theater for Everyone*, also available from Acapella Publishing (800) 848-5099.

Overview of Home-Theater Systems

Home theater is made possible by multichannel surround sound. Instead of two speakers in front of you as in a stereo system, home theater surrounds you with five, six, or even seven. Three speakers are placed in the front of the room, with two, three, or four *surround* speakers located to the rear or sides of the listening/viewing position. Surround sound is what provides the sense of envelopment, of being in the action, that makes the home-theater experience so engrossing.

Multichannel surround sound is encoded on DVDs, some satellite transmissions, and over-the-air high-definition television (HDTV) broadcasts in the Dolby Digital format. This format, introduced in 1997 to replace Dolby Surround (and its decoding variant, Dolby Pro Logic), encodes six discrete audio channels in a single digital bitstream. The six channels are called *left, center, right, left surround, right surround,* and *low-frequency effects* (LFE), and correspond to loudspeakers arrayed in the pattern shown in Fig.13-1. The LFE channel carries only high-impact, low-bass information (below 100Hz), and can be reproduced by any of

Fig. 13-1 A home-theater loudspeaker array uses three front loudspeakers, two surround loudspeakers, and a subwoofer.

Courtesy Digital Theater Systems (DTS), illustration by Patrick Beard

the loudspeakers, or by a separate subwoofer. Typically, the LFE channel drives a subwoofer. With five full-bandwidth channels plus the 100Hz LFE channel, we call Dolby Digital a *5.1-channel* format. The ".1" in 5.1-channel sound is the LFE channel. The competing Digital Theater Systems (DTS) surround-sound format, found on some DVDs as an option, also delivers 5.1 discrete audio channels to your home-theater system.

More recently, Dolby Laboratories and DTS have introduced surround-sound formats that provide additional surround channels. Specifically, *Dolby Digital EX* encodes a third surround channel in the existing left and right surround channels in the Dolby Digital signal. This additional surround channel, called *surround back*, is decoded on playback, and the signal drives a loudspeaker (or two loudspeakers) located directly behind the listener. Dolby Digital EX allows filmmakers to more precisely position and pan (move) sounds around the room. For example, the sound of an object moving directly overhead from the front of the room to the back tends to become smeared; the sounds starts in the front speakers, then splits along the sidewalls as it moves toward the rear of the room. By adding a third surround channel directly behind the listener, these "flyovers" can be made more realistic. Note that an EX-encoded soundtrack is compatible with all Dolby Digital playback equipment because the addition of the surround-back channel is encoded into a conventional 5.1-channel Dolby Digital signal.

DTS' equivalent format is called *DTS ES*. You'll also see it called *DTS ES Matrix*, because the additional surround channel is matrix-encoded into the existing left and right surround channels. DTS also offers *DTS ES Discrete*, in which the surround-back channel is a discrete channel in the ES Discrete bitstream. DTS ES Discrete is a true 6.1-channel format. The advantage of a discrete format is complete separation between channels. Matrix surround systems have limited channel separation.

The job of decoding the Dolby Digital or DTS bitstream into separate audio channels, and then converting those digital data to analog signals, falls to the home-theater *controller*, also known as a *surround-sound processor*. In addition to performing surround-sound decoding (Dolby Digital, DTS, Pro Logic, etc.), the controller receives audio and video signals from the source components (DSS, DVD, tuner, CD, SACD, DVD-A) and selects which one is decoded and amplified by your home-theater audio system and sent to your video monitor for display. The controller also performs digital signal processing, adjusts the overall volume, and fine-tunes the levels for individual channels. The controller's output is six line-level signals: the left, center, right, left surround, right surround, and subwoofer channels. Controllers that support Dolby Digital EX and DTS ES have eight line-level outputs rather than six.

These six or eight separate outputs are fed to a 5- or 7-channel power amplifier (plus an optional subwoofer), where they are amplified to a level sufficient to drive the home theater's loudspeaker system. A home-theater power amplifier can have five, six, or seven amplifier channels in a single chassis. Alternately, some power amplifiers have three channels, others have two, and some are available as monoblocks: one amplifier channel per chassis. A 3-channel power amplifier allows you to use your existing 2-channel stereo power amplifier on the surround channels and the 3-channel amplifier on the front three loudspeakers, for example. Most subwoofers have built-in power amplifiers to drive their woofer cones.

An audio/video receiver (AVR) incorporates, in one chassis, an A/V controller and multichannel power amplifier. AVRs are less expensive than separate controllers and power amplifiers. If you are installing a second system dedicated to home theater, the AVR is a good option. If you are adding home-theater capability to an existing 2-channel music system, or building a dual-purpose system from scratch, a separate controller and power amplifier is the better route.

A conventional stereo system provides two audio channels, left and right, which are reproduced by the left and right loudspeakers. When correctly set up, two channels of information driving two loudspeakers produce a soundfield in front of the listener that seems to exist between and around the two loudspeakers.

A home-theater system provides multiple channels, each channel feeding a loudspeaker located in front of, alongside, and/or behind the listening/viewing position. Specifically, a home-theater system has three *front* loudspeakers located across the front of the room, and two, three, or four *surround loudspeakers* behind or to the side of the listening position. Two of the front three loudspeakers flank the video monitor; the third is positioned above or below the video monitor. The front loudspeakers are called *left*, *center*, and *right*.

The left and right loudspeakers reproduce mostly music and sound effects. The center loudspeaker's main job is reproducing dialogue, and anchoring onscreen sound effects on the television screen. Having three loudspeakers across the front of the room helps the sound's location to more closely match the location of the sound source in the picture. For example, in a properly set-up home-theater system, if a car crosses from the left side of the picture to the right, you hear the sound of the car move from the left loudspeaker, through the center loudspeaker, and then to the right loudspeaker. The sound source appears to follow the image on the screen.

The surround loudspeakers have a different job. They're generally smaller than the front loudspeakers, and handle much less energy. Consequently, they can be mounted unobtrusively on or inside a wall. Surround speakers mostly reproduce "atmospheric" or ambient sounds, creating a diffuse aural atmosphere around the listener. In a jungle scene, for example, the surround loudspeakers would re-create sounds such as chirping birds, falling raindrops, and blowing wind; in a city scene, the viewer would be surrounded by traffic sounds. The surround loudspeakers' contribution is subtle, but vitally important to the overall experience. Correctly set-up surround loudspeakers should not be able to be heard directly, but should instead envelop the viewer/listener in a diffuse soundfield.

Let's look at each of these components of a home-theater system in more detail.

Home-Theater Controllers

No product better exemplifies the fundamental shift in home-entertainment technology than the controller. The controller is an entirely new product category that combines many diverse functions in a single chassis. To understand what a controller is and does is to understand the technologies that are transforming the way we reproduce sound in our homes.

A modern controller, shown in Fig.13-2, replaces as many as four separate components in your music and home-theater system: the source-switching functions of a preamplifier, a surround-sound decoder, six (or eight) channels of digital-to-analog conversion, and an electronic crossover to split up the frequency spectrum. Moreover, the rapidly increasing computing power of today's controllers points to a future in which they will incorporate even more functions and capabilities, such as digital-signal processing for loudspeaker and room correction. While power amplifiers and loudspeakers change relatively little over time, the controller represents a radical new path to the future by seamlessly merging a diverse array of sophisticated processing and controls to provide nearly transparent interoperability to the user.

Specifically, a controller performs these functions:

1) receives video and audio signals from various source components (PVR, VCR, DSS, DVD) and selects which are sent to the video monitor and home-theater audio system (this function is called "source switching");

2) performs surround decoding, whether Dolby Pro Logic, Pro Logic II, Pro Logic IIx, Dolby Digital, DTS, Dolby Digital EX, or DTS-ES;

3) controls playback volume;

4) makes adjustments in system setup, such as the individual channel levels;

5) directs bass to the appropriate loudspeakers or subwoofers (called bass management); and

6) performs THX processing (if so equipped).

A controller has multiple audio and video inputs to accept signals from your source components. It then performs surround decoding to create a multichannel signal for output to the separate power ampli-

Fig. 13-2 A modern high-end digital controller

Courtesy Classé Audio

fiers. Controllers with Dolby Digital decoding have six line-level outputs, those with Dolby Digital EX and DTS-ES have eight line-level outputs. As mentioned earlier, one of these outputs is marked LFE (Low-Frequency Effects), the ".1" channel in 5.1-channel sound that carries additional bass signals for high-impact, very low bass sounds, such as explosions. The LFE output is connected to a powered subwoofer. Bass from other channels can be selectively added to form the subwoofer drive signal. For example, if you have small front speakers, you can direct the front-channel bass to the subwoofer along with the LFE channel.

The controller is the master control center of your home-theater system. When you first set up a controller, its onscreen display will guide you through selecting such things as whether or not you're using a subwoofer, if your surround loudspeakers are large or small, and calibrating individual channel levels and delay times. You will also control the system on a day-to-day basis through the controller's front panel and remote control. This includes source selection, volume adjustment, and the setting of individual channel levels (described later in this chapter).

THX Certification of Controllers

Some controllers are THX-certified, meaning that they incorporate certain types of signal processing to better translate film sound into a home environment and meet a set of specific technical criteria established by Lucasfilm to better translate the theater experience into the home. THX processing in a controller includes re-equalization, surround decorrelation, and timbre matching. *Re-equalization* removes excessive brightness from film soundtracks for home-theater playback. *Surround decorrelation* improves the sense of spaciousness from the surround channels by introducing slight differences between the two surround signals. *Timbre matching* compensates for the fact that the ear doesn't hear the same tonal balance of sounds in all directions. The THX timbre-matching circuit ensures that sounds from the front and rear have the same timbre (tonal balance). To keep their products' prices low, some manufacturers of budget controllers license only the THX re-equalization circuit from Lucasfilm. Such controllers cannot, however, be billed as "THX-certified."

A THX-certified controller will also include a *crossover* circuit to separate the bass from the rest of the audio spectrum when a subwoofer is connected to the system. The crossover keeps bass out of the front-channel signals, and filters mid and high frequencies from the subwoofer output. A THX crossover has a specified *cutoff frequency* of 80Hz. (The cutoff frequency is the frequency below which bass is sent to the subwoofer output and above which higher frequencies are sent to the front-channel outputs.)

How to Choose a Controller

Controllers range from entry-level units costing about $1500 to state-of-the-art models that will set you back as much as $20,000. This wide price range reflects the significant differences between controllers in their features, connectivity, future expandability, and sonic performance.

When choosing a controller, first make sure the controller has enough inputs for your system, provides your preferred surround-format decoding (Dolby Digital EX and DTS-ES, for example), offers a friendly user interface, has THX processing and certification (if desired), is well-built, and has good sound quality.

Inputs, Outputs, and Source Switching

Let's start with the controller's most basic function: selecting the source you listen to or watch. The controller accepts audio or A/V (audio and video) signals from all your source components and lets you select which source signal is sent to the power amplifiers and video monitor. A basic controller will offer two analog-audio inputs (for a tuner and CD player, for example) and perhaps four audio/video (A/V) inputs. In addition to the main outputs that drive your TV and power amplifiers, two record outputs are often provided, to drive two VCRs or a VCR and an analog tape recorder.

When choosing a controller, make sure its array of inputs matches or exceeds the number of source components in your system. Your system is likely to expand in the future, so look for a controller with at least one more input than you need right now.

All controllers have inputs for digital audio signals as well as for analog. These inputs receive the digital-audio output of a DVD player, DSS receiver, or CD transport. The signals carried on these digital connections include Dolby Digital, DTS, Dolby Surround, and 2-channel PCM (Pulse Code Modulation) signals, such as from a CD transport.

As more DVD players and video monitors incorporate component-video inputs and outputs, controllers are now offering component-video switching. That is, the controller may have two component-video inputs and one component-video output, allowing you to select which component-video source is displayed on your video monitor. If your controller lacks this feature, you'll need to run the component-video output from your DVD player directly to the component-video input of your video monitor. Some video-switching circuits don't have a wide enough bandwidth to pass HDTV signals without removing high-frequency information. Because fine picture detail is contained in high-frequencies, controllers without sufficient video bandwidth can make an HD picture look soft. Note that this problem is avoided by connecting source components directly to the video display, bypassing the controller. Unlike receivers, with their RCA jacks for inputs and outputs, higher-end controllers sometimes have balanced inputs and outputs. A balanced cable, described in Chapter 11, is found only on higher-end separates. An RCA cable, also called an unbalanced or single-ended cable, carries the signal on one conductor plus a ground conductor. A balanced cable carries the signal on two conductors, plus a ground. Balanced cables are used in professional audio, and have some advantages over unbalanced cables. Controllers with balanced inputs and outputs will usually offer both balanced and unbalanced connection jacks to ensure compatibility with a wide range of power amplifiers and source components. To use a controller's balanced inputs, your source components must also have balanced output jacks. And a controller's balanced output jacks work only with a power amplifier with balanced input jacks. If your source components or power amplifier lack balanced jacks, you can still connect them through the unbalanced (RCA) connections.

Analog Bypass Modes

For the music lover shopping for a controller that will also serve as a 2-channel preamplifier for his system, one of the most significant considerations is its performance with 2-channel analog sources (especially if you have an extensive vinyl collection) and signals from an SACD or DVD-Audio player. In that case, you'll want a controller that has an *analog bypass mode*. Without an analog bypass mode, the analog signal will be converted to digital and back to analog as it passes through the controller. Digital conversion is far from sonically transparent, so the sound will suffer.

There are two catches to look out for regarding the bypass mode. First, the controller must have an analog volume control. Most modern controllers adjust the volume digitally in their DSP (digital signal processing) chips, which usually don't sound as good as an old-fashioned volume knob. Second, whenever you engage bass management, even a controller with a bypass mode will convert the analog signal to digital because bass management is performed by the DSP chips. If you have a subwoofer with satellite speakers and use the controller's crossover to divide the frequency spectrum, the bypass mode won't remove the A/D and D/A conversions from the signal path. This is a serious limitation for music lovers who demand the ultimate in sound quality.

One novel approach used by a few manufacturers is to split the incoming analog signal and filter bass from the left and right outputs with an analog filter. This signal, which has never been digitized, drives the left and right channels. The other half of the split signal is digitized and processed through the controller's bass management, which derives a subwoofer signal. It's not pure analog bypass because the signal driving the subwoofer has been digitized, but bass frequencies are less prone to sonic degradation by digital conversions.

If you've found a controller that meets your home-theater needs but lacks an analog bypass mode, you can still enjoy uncompromised music performance by adding an analog preamplifier to your system. Your analog source components connect to the analog preamplifier, as do the left and right outputs from the controller. In essence, the preamplifier is inserted in the signal path between the controller and left- and right-channel power amplifiers. When you play movies through the controller, the analog preamp acts as if it's not there, and has no effect on the signal. Some preamps have a feature (called something like "cinema pass-through") that sets their gain (volume) at a predetermined level when you play movies, so that you don't have to adjust the preamp's volume control to achieve correct volume from the left and right loudspeakers in relation to the other loudspeakers.

Digital Signal Processing (DSP) and Surround Decoding Formats

The availability of powerful Digital Signal Processing (DSP) chips has revolutionized controllers in the past few years. DSP chips are the heart and brain of the controller, performing surround-sound decoding, signal processing (equalization, crossovers), and THX post-processing (if the controller is THX-certified). Today's advanced controllers boast the computing power of a late-1980s mainframe computer.

The first job of the DSP chip is decoding, that is, converting a stream of digital data into separate digital signals that can be converted to analog audio. All controllers today decode the three major surround-sound formats: Dolby Digital, DTS, and Dolby Surround. Dolby Digital is the mandatory surround-sound format for DVD (DTS is optional), and has been chosen as the surround-sound format for high-definition television (HDTV).

Even inexpensive A/V receivers sport DSP chips, although generally they have less computing power than those in high-end controllers. Consequently, high-end controllers offer better implementations of surround-sound decoding, more flexible features, and higher sound quality. (More powerful DSP chips allow greater precision in the mathematical computations performed on the audio signal.)

A DSP chip is a number cruncher that operates on specific instructions (the software) controlling it. When decoding a Dolby Digital source, for example, the software tells the DSP how to decode Dolby Digital. When decoding DTS, the same DSP operates under the instructions for decoding the DTS bitstream. A DSP chip is only as good as the software it is running. That's why some high-end companies write all their own software in-house rather than rely on stock software that performs a given task. As DSP chips grow increasingly more powerful and less expensive, controller capabilities increase proportionately.

In mid-2001, Dolby Laboratories made available a more sophisticated version of Pro Logic decoding, called Pro Logic II. The idea behind Pro Logic II was to create from 2-channel sources a listening experience similar to that of a discrete 5.1-channel digital format. And with more consumers having 5.1-channel playback available to them for reproducing music sources, Pro Logic II attempts to deliver multichannel sound from 2-channel recordings, even those that have not been surround-encoded.

Found on most A/V receivers and controllers made after early 2002, Pro Logic II offers improved performance over its predecessor in several areas. First, Pro Logic II delivers full-bandwidth stereo surround channels rather than the bandwidth-limited monaural surround channel of conventional Pro Logic decoding. This attribute provides a more enveloping soundfield, greater precision in the placement and pans (movements) of sounds behind the listener, and more natural timbre of sounds reproduced by the surround channels. In this respect, Pro Logic II emulates the experience of listening to a 5.1-channel discrete digital source.

Pro Logic II also uses more sophisticated "steering" circuits that monitor the level in each channel and selectively apply attenuation (reduction in level) to prevent sounds in one channel from leaking into another channel. Pro Logic IIx, announced in late 2003, creates 7.1-channel playback from 2-channel and 5.1-channel sources.

Digital Theater Systems has developed a suite of surround-decoding formats that either enhance the DTS experience or provide decoding of non-DTS sources such as conventional stereo.

DTS Neo:6 Music and *Neo:6 Cinema* are decoding algorithms that convert stereo or Dolby–Surround encoded 2-channel sources into multichannel surround sound. Neo:6 Music leaves the front left and right channel signals unprocessed for the purest reproduction, and extracts center and surround-channel signals from the 2-channel source. DTS recommends this mode for all 2-channel sources, such as CD and FM broadcasts.

Neo:6 Cinema is similar to Dolby Pro Logic II decoding, and can be used with Dolby Surround-encoded sources. Neo:6 Cinema has a much larger effect on the signal, rearranging the signal distribution among the front three channels. Both Neo:6 Music and Neo:6 Cinema create a 7.1-channel signal from 2-channel sources.

These new decoding algorithms are a boon to those, like me, who greatly enjoy musical performances on DVD. When a DVD gives me the choice of listening to the Dolby Digital or 2-channel Surround-encoded linear pulse-code modulation (LPCM) mix, I always opt for the 2-channel mix. Although I lose all the advantages of Dolby Digital (complete channel separation, for example), I hear smoother treble, less grainy instrumental and vocal textures, and a greater sense of space. That's because Dolby Digital uses 384,000 bits per second (or 448,000 bits per second) to encode all 5.1 channels; the linear PCM track uses 1.536 million bits per second to encode just two channels. When using Pro Logic II and DTS Neo:6 to decode these two channels, however, I hear the superior spatial resolution of Dolby Digital with the more natural timbres of the linear PCM track.

The Future-Proof Controller: Software Upgrades and Modular Construction

Because of this software control, some controllers can be updated simply by downloading new software into the machine. As new technologies arrive or refinements in existing systems are discovered, you simply install new instructions for the DSP chips. Such "software-based" controllers can be thought of as general-purpose DSP devices that happen to be running the software for Dolby Digital, DTS, and Dolby Pro Logic decoding.

New software can add capabilities such as Pro Logic IIx decoding (by changing the DSP code), refining the user interface (by updating the operating system), or configuring the unit to accept formats not available when the product was designed (by changing the input-receiver software). Updating software in this way reduces the likelihood of needing expensive hardware changes.

Another method of heading off controller obsolescence is "modular" construction. Rather than build all the electronics onto a single circuit board inside the controller's chassis, the modular controller is built more like a computer. The modular controller's slotted motherboard accepts plug-in boards that perform specific functions.

The modular controller is a basic platform that can be customized to fit your particular system, expanded as your system grows, or configured to be compatible with future technology. Rather than scrap your controller and start over when technology inevitably marches on, the modular controller is simply reconfigured by plugging in a new board. Modular controllers are also more reliant on software than on hardware. The benefit is that your system never becomes obsolete, and will probably cost less in the long term. The only disadvantage to modular controllers is their higher initial cost.

Bass-Management Flexibility

An important controller function performed within the DSP chips is bass management, the subsystem that lets you selectively direct bass information in the soundtrack to the main loudspeakers or to the subwoofer. Bass management allows a controller to work correctly with a wide variety of speaker systems. For example, if you have five small loudspeakers and a subwoofer, you tell the controller to filter bass from each of the five channels and to direct it, in sum, to the subwoofer. With a Dolby Digital or DTS movie, the bass from the left, center, right, and surround channels is mixed with the LFE channel to drive the subwoofer. The controller's "subwoofer" output is the LFE channel selectively mixed with bass from any of the other channels. The bass management in most controllers lets you direct the full frequency range to the left and right channels (including the LFE channel), but filter bass from the center and surround channels.

A feature of the most advanced controllers is their ability to specify the crossover frequency and slopes between the subwoofer and main speakers. The crossover is implemented in the digital domain with DSP. That is, the audio spectrum is divided by performing mathematical computations on the ones and zeros representing the audio signal. Splitting the frequency spectrum into bass and treble in the controller is a vastly better approach than subjecting the analog audio signal to the capacitors, resistors, and inductors found in the crossovers built into subwoofers.

The most sophisticated controllers let you specify the crossover frequency (40Hz, 80Hz, 120Hz, for examples), as well as the crossover slope or phase characteristics. The greater the flexibility in specifying crossover frequency, slope, and phase, the greater the likelihood that you can seamlessly integrate the subwoofer with the main speakers. (Crossover slope and phase are described in Chapter 7.)

Keeping low bass out of smaller loudspeakers confers large advantages in the speakers' power handling, dynamic range, midrange clarity, and sense of ease. When the woofer doesn't have to move back and forth a long distance trying to reproduce low bass, the midrange sounds cleaner and the speaker can reproduce loud peaks without distortion.

High-Resolution Digital Audio Decoding and 6-Channel Analog Input

Many controllers today feature the ability to accept digital input signals with word lengths of up to 24 bits and a sampling frequency of 96kHz. This allows them to decode high-resolution digital audio output from those few DVD players that can output 24/96 digital signals. Although DVD-Audio players have no trouble reading and decoding high-resolution digital audio, their digital outputs are downconverted to 44.1kHz. That's because manufacturers are sensitive to the music industry's concern about providing consumers access to a recordable, high-resolution digital bitstream that can produce near-perfect copies of the professional master. The industry needs a universal, high-resolution, multichannel, copy-protected digital interface.

Until that happens, a more useful feature for taking advantage of the high-resolution multichannel formats (DVD-Audio and Super Audio CD, or SACD) is a 6-channel analog input on the controller. Until the digital-interface issue is resolved (which may take a long time because it is inextricably linked to the copy-protection problem), DVD-Audio and SACD players will have six analog outputs for reproducing multichannel music discs. Unless your controller has a discrete 6-channel analog input, you won't be able to play high-resolution multichannel music through your system. The 6-channel analog input approach has its drawbacks: You're paying for six DACs in the DVD-A or SACD player and for six DACs in the controller. It would obviously be better and more cost-effective if multichannel DVD-A or SACD were provided to the controller in a single digital datastream. Until then, the most important thing to look for is that the analog bypass is available for the DVD-A and SACD signals. Adding extra layers of conversion will only degrade the sound. The issue becomes more complicated when you add bass management to the mix, since bass management is usually done in the digital domain.

Digital-to-Analog Conversion

Built into every 5.1-channel controller are six digital-to-analog converters (DACs) and six analog output stages. Controllers with Dolby Digital EX and DTS-ES capability have eight DACs and eight analog output stages. The DACs convert the digital data for each channel into analog signals. The quality of these DACs and the subsequent analog output stage (which drives the power amplifier through interconnects) is crucial to realizing good sound quality. DACs vary greatly in their sound, and a poor-sounding DAC (or a poor implementation of a good one) can ruin an otherwise excellent controller. More expensive controllers use higher-quality parts and design techniques, including metal-film resistors, polystyrene capacitors, four-layer circuit boards, and exotic circuit-board material. Also look for analog stages made from discrete transistors instead of inexpensive operational-amplifier (or op-amp) chips. Some high-end companies now have considerable expertise in designing cutting-edge digital converters, expertise they can apply to building multichannel digital controllers.

Don't be swayed by marketing hype that touts DACs as "24-bit." Although the DAC may have 24 resistor "rungs" on its "ladder," that doesn't mean it has 24-bit resolution. The last four bits often contain only noise, not real information.

7.1-Channel Playback from 5.1-Channel Sources

Some home-theater receivers and controllers provide 7.1-channel play-back from 5.1-channel sources such as Dolby Digital and DTS. These products have eight channels (seven channels plus a subwoofer) rather than the six channels of most Dolby Digital- and DTS-equipped products. The two additional channels drive two extra speakers placed behind the listener, augmenting the two surround speakers at the sides of the listening location. The eight speakers in a 7.1-channel system are front left, center, and right, surround left and right, surround back (x 2), and a subwoofer.

Making effective use of the additional surround speakers requires sophisticated signal processing in the controller. Controllers with THX Ultra2 processing incorporate a circuit that creates a 7.1-channel signal from any source, allowing you to use your entire 7.1-channel loudspeak-er system on all source material, not just on those movies that have been THX EX or DTS-ES encoded. Dolby's Pro Logic IIx will also generate from 5.1-channel sources a 7.1-channel signal that can drive the eight loudspeakers in some home-theater systems.

Multichannel Power Amplifiers

The power amplifier is the workhorse of your home-theater system. It takes in line-level signals from the output of your controller and amplifies them to powerful signals that will drive your home-theater loudspeaker system. A power amplifier has line-level inputs to receive signals from the controller, and terminals for connecting loudspeaker cables. The power amplifier is the last component in the signal path before the loudspeakers.

A separate multichannel power amplifier can offer higher output power than the power amplifiers found in A/V receivers. The most pow-erful receivers can have outputs of 140 watts per channel; separate power amplifiers offer as much as 350Wpc.

A power amplifier is described by the number of amplifier channels in its chassis. The most common home-theater power amplifiers have five channels for powering the left, center, right, surround left, and sur-round right loudspeakers (Fig.13-3). The next most common number of channels is three. A 3-channel amplifier can power the front three loud-speakers, leaving a 2-channel amplifier to handle the two surround loud-speakers. If you already have a stereo (2-channel) amplifier, you can update your system for home theater by adding a 3-channel home-the-ater amplifier. Alternatively, a 3-channel amplifier can power the center and two surround channels, leaving your stereo amplifier to drive the left and right loudspeakers. As the Dolby Digital EX and DTS-ES formats become more popular, power amplifiers with seven channels are becom-

Fig. 13-3 Inside a
high-end multi-
channel power
amplifier

Courtesy Plinius

ing increasingly available. Note that if you upgrade your controller to a
7.1-channel unit, you can augment your 5-channel power amplifier with
a stereo amplifier to power the surround-back speakers.

Some home-theater power amplifiers, called monoblocks, drive only
one amplifier channel per chassis. The monoblock approach lets you
upgrade more easily by buying power for only as many channels as you
need. Monoblocks have the potential of better sonic performance, but
also cost more than the same number of amplifier channels in a multichannel power amplifier.

How to Choose a Home-Theater Power Amplifier

High-quality multichannel power amplifiers are big, heavy, and can be
expensive. The more output power provided by the amplifier, the bigger, heavier, and more expensive it will be.

Most home-theater enthusiasts listen at moderate levels to loudspeakers of average sensitivity (85–88dB) in rooms of average size

(3000–4500 cubic feet) with average furnishings (carpet, some drapes), and so will need a minimum of about 70W for each of the five, six, or seven channels.

Some multichannel power amplifiers feature a single large power transformer to supply all five, six, or seven channels. Others provide smaller, separate transformers for each channel. There is no consensus as to which approach is better. The argument for a single large transformer goes like this: For 2-channel music sources, the amplifier benefits from the extra power-supply capacity provided by a huge transformer. Moreover, even when multichannel sources are played, the rear channels don't work as hard as the front, allowing some of their power-supply capacity to be delivered where it's needed. The opposing point of view holds that separate smaller transformers completely isolate the channels from each other and eliminate interaction between channels. For example, a loud explosion in the film soundtrack reproduced by the center channel can pull power from the transformer needed for the musical score that is being reproduced by the left and right channels.

Note that driving five, six, or even seven loudspeakers places extraordinary current demands on the amplifier. There's a way to reduce the strain placed on multichannel amplifiers: use high-sensitivity loudspeakers. Remember that every 3dB increase in sensitivity is equivalent to doubling amplifier power.

More specific information on power amplifiers may be found in Chapter 6. The discussion of sound quality, build quality, and matching to loudspeaker sensitivity applies equally well to multichannel amplifiers as it does to 2-channel amplifiers.

Loudspeakers for Home Theater

A home-theater loudspeaker system will perform double-duty, reproducing 2-channel music sources through the front left and right speakers, and film soundtracks through all five, six, or seven loudspeakers (plus an optional subwoofer). Home-theater loudspeakers can be evaluated using the criteria described in Chapters 3 and 7, with one difference: film soundtracks present somewhat different challenges to a loudspeaker system than music. Specifically, film soundtracks are generally more dynamic than most music, and have much more low-frequency energy. Consequently, great home-theater sound requires loudspeakers that not only meet our criteria for good music reproduction, but also have a wide dynamic range and the ability to handle loud and complex signals without sounding smeared or confused. (A home-theater loudspeaker package is shown in Fig.13-4.)

Fig. 13-4 A multi-channel loud-speaker array with subwoofer

Courtesy Krell Industries

The Center-Channel Speaker

Though the center-channel loudspeaker carries a large part of the film soundtrack—nearly all the dialogue, many effects, and some of the music—only recently have center-channel speakers been elevated from afterthoughts to recognition that they are the anchor of the entire home-theater loudspeaker system.

The center speaker is usually mounted horizontally on top of the video monitor. It can also be placed beneath the video monitor or mounted inside a wall above the video display, or, if you're using a front-projection system, behind an "acoustically transparent" screen.

Because a stereo system uses only two loudspeakers—left and right—across the front, you may be wondering why you need a third loudspeaker between them for home theater. The center-channel loudspeaker provides many advantages in a home-theater system. First, it anchors dialogue and other sounds directly associated with action on the screen in the center of the sonic presentation. When we see characters speaking, we want the sound to appear to come from their visual images. Similarly, when sounds are panned (moved from one location to another) across the front, we want the sound to move seamlessly from one side to another. For example, if the image of a car travels from the left side of the screen to the right, the sounds of the car's engine and tires should travel with it, precisely tracking the car's movement. Without a center speaker, we may hear a gap in the middle as the car sounds jump from the left loudspeaker to the right. The center speaker makes sure on-screen sounds come from the screen.

A 2-channel stereo system is, however, capable of producing a sonic image directly between the two speakers. This so-called "phantom" center image is created by the brain when the same signal is present in both ears. A sound source directly in front of us in real life produces soundwaves that strike both ears simultaneously. The brain interprets these cues to determine that the sound source is directly in front of us. Similarly, two speakers reproducing the same sound send the same signal to both ears, fooling the brain into thinking the sound is directly in front of us.

For two loudspeakers to create this phantom center image, they must be precisely set up, and the listener must sit exactly the same distance from each of them—if you sit off to the right, the center image will pull to the right. In addition, creating a phantom center image from two loudspeakers may be a learned skill; some listeners may never hear a phantom center image. There's also evidence that the work the brain must perform to conjure up this phantom center image is distracting and fatiguing.

These problems are overcome by putting a center-channel speaker between the left and right speakers. Dialogue and onscreen sounds are firmly anchored on the screen for all listeners, not just those sitting in the middle. With three speakers across the front, someone sitting way off at the left end of the couch can still hear dialogue coming from the area of the screen—not just from the left loudspeaker. The center speaker also prevents the entire front soundfield from collapsing into the speaker closest to where you're sitting. Moreover, the center speaker provides a tangible sound source directly in front of you; your brain doesn't have to work to create a phantom image between the left and right speakers. Finally, the center speaker reduces the burden on the left and right loudspeakers. With three speakers reproducing sound, each can be driven at a lower level for cleaner sound.

Adding a Center Speaker to Your System

Although you can add a different brand of center speaker to your existing left and right speakers, you're better off with three matched speakers across the front of your home theater. Speakers all sound different from one another. No matter how good the quality of a speaker, it will have some coloration, or variations from accuracy, in its sound. I mentioned earlier that you want to hear a seamless movement of sounds across the front soundfield. If the center speaker has a different sound from the left and right speakers, you'll never achieve a smooth and continuous soundfield across the front—when sound sources move from one side to another through the center speaker, the sound's character will abruptly change.

The solution is to buy three matched front-channel speakers. Their identical tonal characteristics will not only provide smooth panning of sounds, but also produce a more stable and coherent soundfield across ·

the front of the room. If you already have high-quality left and right loudspeakers that you want to keep, buy a center-channel speaker made by the manufacturer of the left and right loudspeakers. They probably won't be as well-matched as a three-piece system, but the added center speaker is much more likely to sound similar to your existing left and right speakers. Separate center speakers sometimes use the same drivers (the raw speaker cones themselves) and other parts as the stereo speakers from the same manufacturer.

For state-of-the-art home theater, the three front loudspeakers should be identical. Although most home-theater enthusiasts will use a smaller center speaker that will fit on top of a television set and doesn't reproduce much bass, more ambitious systems use large, full-range center speakers. These speakers are hard to position, and are generally used only with front-projector systems; the center speaker can be placed behind a perforated projection screen, just as in a movie theater.

Left and Right Speakers

The left and right loudspeakers carry the majority of the film's musical score and many of the effects. And if you aren't using a subwoofer, nearly all the bass will be reproduced by the left and right speakers. Consequently, left and right speakers are often the largest speakers in a home-theater system.

Left and right speakers can also be small units that sit on speaker stands or on an entertainment cabinet. If that's the case, the small speakers must be used with a subwoofer to reproduce bass. The small left and right speakers reproduce the midrange and treble frequencies, and the subwoofer handles all the bass. Such a system, called a *subwoofer/satellite system*, is ideal if your available space is limited, or if you want the left and right loudspeakers to better blend into your decor. Satellite speakers can be small and unobtrusive, and the subwoofer can be tucked out of the way. If you build the three front speakers into a wall in a custom installation, they will most likely be satellites. All THX-certified loudspeaker systems use a subwoofer.

Surround Speakers

The surround loudspeakers are completely different in design and function from left, center, and right speakers. Their job is to re-create a diffuse atmosphere of sound effects to envelop us in a subtle sonic environment that puts us *in* the action happening on the screen. Unlike front and center speakers that anchor the sound onscreen, surround speakers should "disappear" into a diffuse "wash" of sound all around us.

A good example of how surround speakers create an atmosphere comes from the film *Round Midnight*. Toward the beginning of the movie the character François is outside a Paris jazz club in a driving rainstorm, listening to Dexter Gordon's character playing inside. The scene cuts between the intimate sound of the jazz club and the rainy Paris street. Inside the club, the sound is direct and immediate to reflect the camera's perspective of just a few feet from the musical group. When the scene cuts to the street, we are surrounded by the expansive sound of rain, cars driving by, people talking as they walk past—in other words, all the ambiance and atmosphere of a rainy night in Paris. This envelopment is largely created by the surround speakers. We don't want to hear the rain and street sounds coming from two locations behind us, but to be surrounded by the sounds, as we'd hear them in real life. The surround speakers perform this subtle, yet vital role in home theater.

Surround speakers envelop us by their design and placement in the home-theater room. They are best located to the side or rear of the listening position, and several feet above ear level. Because they don't have to reproduce bass, surround speakers can be small and unobtrusive, and are often mounted on or inside a wall.

Dipolar and Bipolar Surround Speakers

Most of the surround speakers' ability to wrap us in sound comes from their *dipolar* design. Dipolar simply means that they produce sound to the front and rear equally. While front speakers have one set of drivers that project sound forward, dipolar surround speakers have two sets of drivers, mounted front and back. This arrangement produces a directional pattern that fires to the front and back of the room (see Chapter 7). Because the surround speakers are positioned to the sides and fire to the front and back of the room, we hear no direct sound from them. The listener sits in the surround speakers' "null"—the point where they don't directly project sound. Instead of hearing direct sound from the surround speakers, we hear their sound after it's been reflected, or bounced off the room's walls and furnishings. The surround speakers' dipolar directional pattern makes their sound diffuse and harder to localize. You shouldn't be able to tell where a properly set-up surround speaker is just by listening. (This dipolar radiation pattern is shown in Fig.7-4 on page 208.)

You may see surround speakers called either *dipolar* or *bipolar*. Although both produce sound equally from the front and rear, the bipolar speaker produces sound from the rear that is in-phase with the front sound. A dipolar produces sound from the rear that is out-of-phase with the front sound. In-phase means that the front and rear waves have the same polarity: when the front-firing woofer moves forward to create a positive pressure wave, the rear-firing woofer also moves forward. The opposite is true in a dipole: when the front-firing woofer moves forward, the rear-firing woofer moves backward. In a dipole, the front and back waves are identical, but have the opposite polarity. Both bipolar and dipolar achieve the objective of enveloping the viewer/listener in the film's aural ambiance, but the dipolar type is preferred because it creates a greater "null," or reduction in sound, at the side of the speaker that faces the listener.

A true dipolar or bipolar surround speaker can't be flush-mounted inside a wall. Instead, it must be mounted *on* the wall so it can radiate sound toward the front and rear of the room. Some surround speakers approximate a dipolar radiation pattern by mounting small drivers on an angled baffle. Although not true dipoles, these flush-mounted surround speakers accomplish the goal of creating a diffuse ambiance *and* fit unobtrusively in your living room.

Surround speakers are also helped in their job by the surround decorrelation circuit found in all THX receivers and controllers. Because the surround channel in Dolby Pro Logic is monophonic (the same signal feeds both surround loudspeakers), we experience the unwanted effect of localizing the surround speaker's sound at the listening position rather than perceiving a diffuse soundfield. THX surround decorrelation slightly changes the signal fed to the left and right surround speakers to provide a greater sense of envelopment.

The amount of sound produced by the surround speakers is adjustable through the receiver's or controller's remote control. Their volume level should be set so that you never hear them directly; but if you turned them off, the soundfield would collapse toward the front. All too often, consumers set surround speaker levels too high; their thinking seems to be that if they *bought* speakers, they should be able to *hear* them.

Surround-Back Speakers for Dolby Digital EX and DTS-ES

As described earlier, the Dolby Digital EX and DTS-ES formats add one or two additional surround speakers behind the listener. THX recommends that two speakers be used, and that their radiation patterns be dipolar. According to Lucasfilm, the surround channels are best reproduced by four identical dipolar speakers. The two surround speakers remain at their normal position (normal for 5.1-channel reproduction), which is 110°, or slightly behind the listener on the side walls. The surround back speakers are located at 150° as shown in Fig.13-5.

The two surround back speakers should be arranged so that their facing sides are in-phase with each other. That is, the side of the dipole that would face the back of the room if mounted on a sidewall should face toward the room's centerline when the speaker is mounted on the rear wall. This arrangement keeps the drivers of two surround back speakers that face each other in-phase, contributing to their ability to create an image between them directly behind the listening position.

Fig. 13-5 The surround loudspeakers should be positioned at 110° and the surround back loudspeakers at 150°.

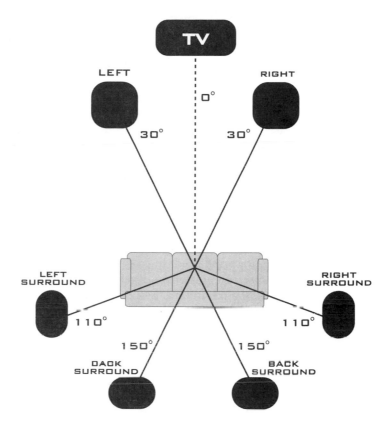

Subwoofers

A subwoofer is a speaker that reproduces only low bass. Subwoofers are usually squarish or rectangular cabinets that can be positioned nearly anywhere in the home-theater room. A good subwoofer adds quite a bit of impact and visceral thrill to the home-theater experience.

Most subwoofers for home-theater use are *powered* or *active* sub woofers. These terms describe a subwoofer with a built-in power amplifier that drives its large woofer cone. The powered subwoofer takes a line-level output from the jack marked SUBWOOFER OUT on your A/V receiver or controller, and converts that electrical signal into sound. Because powered subwoofers have built-in amplifiers, they must be plugged into an AC wall outlet. (See Chapter 7 for more on subwoofers.)

Setting up a Home Theater

How a home-theater system is setup and calibrated has an enormous influence on the quality of the sound you hear. Just as with 2-channel music system, ideal loudspeaker placement and careful attention to detail will reward you with superior performance. The acoustic principles described in Chapter 4 apply equally well to a multichannel audio system.

Basic Setup

The first step in setting up your system is deciding where to install it. More than likely, the room where you watch television will become the home-theater room. But this room may have been arranged for casual TV watching, not for experiencing the full impact of what a home-theater system can deliver. Now is the time to rethink the room's layout and consider making the home-theater system the room's central focus.

The home-theater room should be arranged with the video monitor and front loudspeakers at one end, the couch or viewing chairs at the other. Ideally, the couch will be positioned partway into the room and not against the back wall. This location is better acoustically (excessive bass build-up occurs near the back wall), and allows the surround speakers to better do their job of enveloping you in the film's soundtrack. Of course, the setup should provide room for the left and right speakers on either side of the video monitor.

The optimum viewing distance between you and the video monitor is determined by the video monitor's size. The smaller the monitor, the closer you should sit to maintain the maximum image area in your field of view. Sitting too close to a large monitor, particularly a rear-projection set, exposes the line structure inherent in a video presentation. If you are watching high-definition programming on an HD set, you can sit much closer without seeing the line structure. The best viewing distance offers the largest possible picture without making that picture look grainy. A good rule of thumb is to sit three-to-four picture *heights* away from the screen. You should also try to sit no more than 15° off to the side of the video monitor. Plasma panels, with their wider field of view, maintain a good picture even when they are watched from an extreme angle.

Once you've decided on where the couch and video monitor will be positioned, you'll need to determine the best place for your equipment. A simple home-theater system will have a VCR or hard-disk digital video recorder, A/V receiver, satellite receiver, and DVD player. These components can be easily accommodated in a TV stand or rack.

Acoustical Treatment

Before we get to the specifics of loudspeaker placement, here are a few guidelines on how to make your home-theater room sound better. First, if you have a bare tile or wood floor between you and the front three speakers, covering the floor with a rug is probably the single most important thing you can do to improve your room's acoustics. The rug absorbs unwanted acoustic reflections from the floor, which improves dialogue intelligibility and adds to a sense of clarity. Similarly, absorbing the acoustic reflections from the side walls between you and the left and right speakers also helps you get better sound. Bookcases and hanging rugs are both effective in absorbing or diffusing side-wall reflections. Generally, the front of the room should be acoustically absorptive, with drapes, carpets, and hanging rugs.

Conversely, the back of the room should be more acoustically reflective. Bare walls behind the listening/viewing position tend to reflect sound and add to the feeling of spaciousness generated by the surround speakers. The sounds produced by a movie theater's array of surround speakers all reach your ears at different times, increasing the feeling of envelopment. But because a home-theater system uses just two surround speakers, we must help them achieve their goal by providing reflective surfaces near them.

Ideally, the lower portion of the room's front end should be acoustically absorptive, the upper portion acoustically reflective. This situation absorbs unwanted wall reflections from the three front speakers, but lets the dipole surround speakers positioned on the sidewall just below the ceiling create a bigger sense of envelopment by reflecting sound off the front walls as well as the rear walls.

Speaker Placement

Where speakers are located in your room has a huge influence on the quality of sound you will achieve. Correct speaker placement can make the difference between good and spectacular performance from the same equipment. If you follow a few simple speaker-placement techniques, you'll be well on your way toward getting the best sound from your system. Correct speaker placement is the single most important factor in achieving good sound.

Surround Speaker Placement

Let's start with the most difficult of a home-theater system's six speakers: the two surround speakers. As I said earlier, the surround speakers are usually dipolar. That is, they produce sound equally to the front and the rear of the speaker cabinet. Dipoles produce a "null," or area of no sound, at the cabinet sides. Here's a simple rule for positioning dipolar surround speakers no matter what the installation: point the surround speakers' null at the listening position. Never point the surround speakers directly at the listening position.

Ideally, the surround speakers would be located on the side walls directly to the side of the listening position and at least two feet above the listeners' heads when seated. Dipolar surround speakers should never be located in front of the listening position, where they could be heard directly; the surround speakers' sound should be reflected around the room before reaching the listener. This helps to mimic the sound of a movie theater's surround array with just two speakers, and to create the envelopment that's so important to the home-theater experience.

Keep in mind that reflections from the front speakers are bad; reflections from the rear speakers are good. Well-positioned surround speakers make a tremendous difference in the quality of the home-theater experience by re-creating the sense of ambience and space we hear in a movie theater.

Surround-Back Speaker Placement for Dolby Digital EX and DTS-ES

According to THX, soundtracks encoded in the Dolby Digital EX format are best reproduced through four dipolar surround speakers located at 110° and 150°, as shown in Fig.13-5 earlier. This placement provides the greatest sense of envelopment, along with the most continuous soundfield behind the listener. The two surround-back speakers should be positioned so that the speakers facing the room's centerline are in-phase with each other. This produces a central image between the two surround-back speakers.

If you're using a single surround-back speaker, position it directly behind the listener at 180°.

Center Speaker Placement

Correct positioning of the center speaker results in better dialogue intelligibility, smoother movement of onscreen sounds, and a more spacious soundstage. As just mentioned, reflections from the front speakers that reach the listener work against good sound. This is particularly true of the center speaker, which carries the all-important dialogue. Because most center-channel speakers are mounted on top of a direct-view TV or rear projector—both of which are highly reflective—there's the potential for unwanted reflections from the video monitor.

To reduce reflections from the center speaker, align its front edge absolutely flush with the front of the video monitor so that they form as contiguous a surface as possible. This positioning reduces a phenomenon called *diffraction*, which is the re-radiation of sound when the soundwaves encounter a discontinuity. (Specifically, diffraction introduces variations in the speaker's frequency response.) Think of waves rippling in a pond: If you put a stick in the water, the waves will strike the stick and be re-radiated around it. The same thing happens when the sound from the center speaker encounters the "stick" of the video monitor: the monitor re-radiates that sound toward the listener, making the overall sound less accurate. That's why making the center speaker flush with the front of the video monitor is so important.

High-end loudspeaker manufacturers carefully design their enclosures to reduce diffraction. You'll notice that high-quality loudspeakers have smooth surfaces around the speaker cones. Some have rounded fronts and even the mounting bolts securing the individual drivers within the speaker are recessed to reduce diffraction from the speaker cabinet.

You should also tilt the center speaker down toward the listening position if it is mounted on a large rear-projection set, or on a direct-view TV positioned on a tall stand. If the center speaker is located below the video monitor, point it up toward the listeners. Direct the center speaker's sound toward the height of the listeners' ears when seated. Finally, be sure the center speaker is less than 2' different in height from the left and right speakers, measured from each speaker's tweeters.

Left and Right Speaker Placement

The left and right speakers should be pulled slightly in front of the video monitor, and not be in a straight line with it (as some owner's manuals erroneously advise). Positioning the left and right speakers so that they form a gentle arc with the center speaker has two advantages. First, acoustic reflections from the video monitor are reduced. Second, the left, right, and center speakers are now all the same distance from the listener. The sounds from each of the three front speakers will reach the listener at the same time. If the front three speakers were lined up, we would hear the center speaker slightly ahead of the left and right speakers, which tends to make sounds bunch together in the center and reduces the soundstage's left-to-right width

If you're using large, full-range left and right speakers, putting the speakers near the front and side walls will increase the amount of bass you hear. The walls reinforce bass to produce a weightier sound. This can be a good or a bad thing, depending on the speakers and your room. Speakers that have lots of bass already will probably sound boomy and unnatural if put too close to the front wall. Pulling them out into the room often produces a huge improvement in bass definition (the bass no longer sounds like a continuous blur) and midrange clarity. The unnatural boominess of a speaker too close to a wall makes the midrange sound thick, and lacking in openness and clarity. If you're using small left and right speakers with a separate subwoofer, the left and right speaker placement in relation to the front wall is less important.

How far apart the left and right speakers are positioned is also important to achieving a natural and spacious sound. If the left and right speakers are too close to the video monitor, you'll never get a sense of large space at the front of the room. If too far apart, onscreen sounds are reproduced too far away from their apparent sources on the screen. It can be subconsciously confusing and distracting to hear a sound come from a location different from the visual location of the sound source. A good rule of thumb is to position the left and right speakers so that they form a 60° angle when seen from the listening/viewing location (Fig.13-5).

Left and right speakers can be positioned so that they point straight ahead, or are angled in (called *toe-in*) toward the listening position. No toe-in (speakers pointing straight ahead) produces a wider and more spacious soundstage, but at the expense of precise localization of sounds. Too much toe-in creates a more tightly focused sound but a smaller sense of overall soundstage size. Toe-in has the advantage of directing more sound at the listener and less sound toward the side walls. Reflection of sound from the side walls is the single worst problem in getting good sound from your speakers.

Some speakers are meant to be toed-in; that position provides their flattest (most accurate) frequency response. Others achieve their best performance with no toe-in. If you toe-in speakers designed for no toe-in, the sound will be too bright. Consult your owner's manual or your dealer for guidance. You can also experiment by playing the same section of a movie soundtrack or a piece of music with varying degrees of speaker toe-in to determine which position sounds best.

Calibrating a Home Theater

Once your system is connected, you'll need to configure it for your particular room and speaker system. This is done through a series of menus or graphical icons generated by the A/V receiver or A/V controller and appearing on your video monitor. You use the receiver's remote control to make selections from the onscreen display. Every A/V receiver or controller includes instructions for setting up your system; the following section explains why you make certain selections, and in what circumstances.

When you turn on your system for the first time, don't be alarmed if you don't hear any sound when you expect to. (This usually happens when I first set up a product for review.) Don't turn up the volume to a high level and then start pushing buttons—when you push the right button, the sound will blast you out, possibly damaging your speakers, your amplifier or receiver, and/or your hearing. Turn the volume to a low level and make sure the correct source is selected. Check to make sure the MUTE and TAPE MONITOR buttons *aren't* pressed. The lack of sound is probably due to one of these three incorrect settings.

Bass Management

First, you must tell the A/V receiver or controller what kind of loud-speakers you have so it can direct bass appropriately. Most of today's controllers ask you whether each of the speakers is LARGE or SMALL. By selecting SMALL for the left and right speakers, you're telling the receiver to keep low-bass signals out of those speakers. This configuration is used when you have a subwoofer connected to the system to reproduce low bass instead of the left and right speakers. You'll also need to answer YES when asked if the system includes a subwoofer. The bass-management option labeled "THX" in THX-certified products automatically sets all speakers to SMALL and engages the subwoofer.

If you full-range left and right speakers and no subwoofer, answer LARGE in the setup menu when asked if the left and right speakers are LARGE or SMALL. The LARGE setting directs bass to the left and right speakers.

The setup menu will also ask if the surround speakers are LARGE or SMALL. Nearly every installation will use the small setting. Only if you have full-range, floorstanding speakers should you answer LARGE.

Setting Individual Channel Levels

Next you'll need to individually set the loudness of each of the five channels (six if you're using a subwoofer), or seven channels in a system equipped with Dolby Digital EX decoding. In addition to providing an overall volume control, all A/V receivers provide adjustment of the individual channel volumes. This process begins by turning on the "test signal," a noise-like sound generated by the A/V receiver. (Dolby licensing requires that the receiver or controller incorporate this noise generator.) The noise is produced by each speaker in turn. Ideally, the noise signal's volume should be the same for each speaker when you're sitting at the listening/viewing position. If it isn't, you can adjust the volume of each speaker independently using the receiver's remote control. Individually adjusting the channels lets you compensate for different loudspeaker sensitivities, listening-room acoustics, and loudspeaker placements.

Although setting the individual channel levels by ear will get your system in the ballpark, a more precise calibration can be achieved by using a Sound Pressure Level (SPL) meter. Available from RadioShack for about $30, an SPL meter lets you accurately calibrate your home-theater system. RadioShack offers digital and analog SPL meters; buy the easier-to-read analog type (catalog #33-2050). Switch the meter to the C-WEIGHTED position, SLOW RESPONSE, and set the knob to 70. Turn on the test noise on your A/V receiver and set each channel's volume until the meter's display reads 5. This indicates that the noise is being reproduced at a level of 75dB. Repeat this procedure for each channel.

A powered subwoofer usually has a knob on its back panel for setting loudness. When you set the subwoofer's level, the meter will be hard to read because the indicator will be jumping around (it's reading a low frequency). Stare at the meter for a few minutes as it jumps to get an idea of where the average level is.

These settings will get you very close to the optimum volume for each channel, but you should use your ear and some well-recorded film soundtracks in making the final adjustment. If you find that dialogue is hard to hear, a 2dB boost in the center-channel level will help bring it out (although the soundstage will be focused more in the center than spread out across the front of the room). If the bass is thumpy and boomy, turn down the subwoofer. Don't be afraid to adjust the volume of the subwoofer, center channel, or surround speakers—each movie soundtrack is mixed differently. You may find yourself slightly adjusting the surround- and center-channel levels at the beginning of each movie.

Although your ears should be the final judge when setting the individual channel levels, calibrating your system first with the SPL meter (or by ear with the test noise) will at least get you started from the right place. The most common mistakes in setting channel levels are a subwoofer level set too high and too much volume from the surround speakers. The bass shouldn't dominate the overall sound, but instead serve as the foundation for music and effects. Many listeners think the more bass you hear, the more "impressive" the sound. In reality, a constantly droning bass is fatiguing, and robs the soundtrack of impact and surprise when the filmmakers *want* you to hear bass. Low frequencies are used as punctuation in a film soundtrack; by keeping the subwoofer level appropriate, you'll achieve a more accurate and satisfying sound than if the subwoofer is constantly droning away. Though it's understandable that you paid for this big box in your living room and you want to hear what it does, try to avoid the temptation to set the subwoofer level too high.

Similarly, listeners who have never had surround speakers in their homes think they should be aware of the surround speakers at all times. In truth, film soundtracks don't always contain signals in the surround channels; long stretches of the movie may have *nothing* in the surrounds. But even when a signal is driving the surround speakers, you should barely notice their presence. Remember, the surround channels provide a subtle ambience and envelopment. If you're consciously aware of the surround speakers because they're set too loud, the illusion they're supposed to be creating is diminished. Just as it's a temptation to set a subwoofer's level too high, don't turn up the surround speakers to the point where you hear them. Note that you won't hear *any* sound from the surround speakers unless the source program has been Dolby-encoded.

Adding Home Theater without Compromising Music Performance

As Editor-in-Chief of *The Absolute Sound* and *The Perfect Vision* magazines, my job involves evaluating cutting-edge, state-of-the-art 2-channel audio products as well as high-performance home-theater components. Clearly, the performance of my 2-channel system cannot be compromised by the presence of home-theater products. Here's what I've done to integrate home theater into my music-playback system, along with some tips for adding home theater to your music system.

First, my video display is a front-projection system with a retractable, motorized screen. The projector is at the back of the room, and when I listen to music, the screen is rolled up into a small enclosure. With the screen in the lowered position, soundstage depth is compromised, as is the precision of image placement. If you use a front projector, a motorized screen's ability to retract for music listening is a big benefit. If you must use a fixed screen, drapes that can be drawn across the screen when you play music are effective at preventing the screen from reflecting sound.

Those who use a direct-view television or rear-projector big-screen are faced with the challenge of having a large, acoustically reflective object near the loudspeakers. As described in Chapter 4, absorbing acoustic reflections at the loudspeaker-end of the room is of paramount importance. To minimize the television's degradation of the sound, move the television back as far as possible, and bring the left and right loudspeakers forward. You can get an idea of how much the television is degrading stereo imaging by throwing a blanket over the TV to absorb its reflections. If you hear a big improvement with the blanket, consider keeping the blanket on hand for critical musical listening.

As mentioned earlier, an analog-bypass mode on a controller is absolutely essential if you want to listen to analog sources with the highest possible fidelity. This feature passes analog input signals through the controller without converting the signal to digital and then back to analog. Keep in mind, however, that even the very best multichannel controllers fall short of the performance standards set by high-end 2-channel preamplifiers, even in analog-bypass mode.

If you want uncompromised musical performance, you'll need a controller and a separate preamplifier. The preamplifier should have a "theater pass-through" mode that sets one of the inputs at unity gain (the output signal's amplitude is the same as the input signal). The left and right outputs from your controller drive this unity-gain input, and the preamplifier is connected to the power amplifier in the usual way. When watching movies, it's as though your preamp isn't there. When listening to music, it's as though your controller isn't there. With this technique, shown in Fig.13-6, your analog sources never go through the

Fig. 13-6 A pre-amplifier with a "theater pass-through" mode avoids passing music signals through a digital controller.

TURNTABLE   TUNER   DIGITAL CONTROLLER

LEFT & RIGHT

CENTER,
SURROUND LEFT,
SURROUND RIGHT

2-CHANNEL
PREAMPLIFIER

MULTICHANNEL
POWER
AMPLIFIER

controller. If you choose this option, you don't need a controller with analog bypass, except on the multichannel input.

If you're adding home theater to your music system and are happy with your power amplifier, you should choose a 3-channel amplifier to drive the center and two surround loudspeakers, or a 5-channel amplifier if you want a 7.1-channel system employing two surround back speakers for Dolby Digital EX or DTS ES decoding. If you're starting from scratch, or have been thinking about upgrading your amplifier, consider a multichannel amplifier; some of today's multichannel amplifiers are fully the equal of high-end 2-channel models.

Some subwoofers have separate PROCESSOR and LINE inputs. The PROCESSOR input (a single jack) accepts the LFE output from a controller; the LINE input is stereo, and is connected to a second output from your preamplifier. When watching movies, set the subwoofer's input switch to PROCESSOR. When listening to music, set the sub's input switch to LINE. This assumes, of course, that you prefer listening to music with the subwoofer engaged. Unless you have small loudspeakers, you'll probably leave the subwoofer off for music listening by leaving the switch set to PROCESSOR.

14 Multichannel Audio

Introduction

Since the commercialization of the stereo LP in 1958, music has been delivered to consumers through two channels: left and right. Storing an acoustic event in two information channels was considered a compromise by early audio researchers (the literature suggests some considered three channels a minimum), but no consumer format could hold more than two channels. The LP groove has only two sides, and multichannel tape machines were impractical for home playback.

The industry attempted to bring multichannel playback to the masses in the 1970s with Quadraphonic. As we all know, Quad was a commercial flop. The idea of a multichannel consumer-audio format died with Quad until the late 1990s, when a new generation of high-capacity 120mm optical discs (SACD and DVD-Audio) was developed that could easily accommodate multichannel audio.

Before we look at these new multichannel formats, discuss their merits, and talk about how to get multichannel audio in your home, let's take a brief look back on the history of multichannel audio.

A Short History of Multichannel Audio

Stereo audio recording and reproduction was invented by a young British engineer named Alan Dower Blumlein. At the age of 26, Blumlein was hired by the Columbia Gramophone company to develop a record-cutting system that didn't infringe on the patents held by Bell Telephone Laboratories. Although the cutting system he devised was monophonic,

Blumlein was nonetheless thinking about a new technique that would capture audio signals with greater spatial fidelity. Blumlein was aware of the mechanisms by which humans localize sound sources (phase and amplitude differences—see Appendix A), and was working in the background on a 2-channel recording and reproduction chain that would allow spatial positioning of sounds.

By early 1931, at the age of 29, Blumlein had conceptualized and built a system he called "Binaural Sound"—what we today call stereo. In that year he filed his landmark patent "Improvements in and relating to Sound-transmission, Sound-recording and Sound-reproducing Systems" (patent number 394,325, filed December 14, 1931) which described in great detail a new microphone technique, a "shuffler" circuit, and record-cutting system that made stereophonic sound possible. Blumlein described it this way:

The invention relates to the transmission, recording and reproduction of sound, being particularly directed to systems for recording and reproducing speech, music and other sound effects especially when associated with picture effects as in talking motion pictures. The fundamental object of the invention is to provide a sound recording and reproduction system whereby a true direction- al impression may be conveyed to a listener, thus improving the illusion that the sound is coming from the artist or other sound source as presented to the eyes.

Blumlein employed two bi-directional (also called figure-of-eight microphones because their directional-sensitivity pattern looks like a fig- ure-of-eight) crossed at 90°, with the two positive-lobe axes pointed at the center of the musical group. When their signals are reproduced through two loudspeakers, the listener can localize sound between the two loudspeakers. (This explanation is simplified to remain within the scope of this book. For a detailed analysis, see John Eargle's *The Microphone Handbook.*)

Blumlein also invented other so-called "coincident" microphone techniques (M-S, X-Y) that are still used today, although only the crossed figure-of-eight technique is named after him. (Incidentally, you can hear "Blumlein" miking on many titles released by Water Lily Acoustics, notably *A Meeting by the River.*)

Although Blumlein and his colleagues made many convincing recordings and films (Blumlein himself walking across a stage while counting, a train leaving a station, for examples), none of his contempo- raries realized the significance of this work. The world would have to wait 27 years for the first commercial realization of stereo—the long-play record in 1958—long after Blumlein's patent had expired. (Alan Blumlein was killed in a Royal Air Force plane crash in 1942 while work- ing on radar research.)

About the same time, the Bell Telephone Laboratory was furiously researching all aspects of sound recording and transmission. In 1932 Harvey Fletcher of Bell Labs made a 2-channel recording with conductor

Leopold Stokowski. Despite the obvious advantages of two channels over one, stereo recording and reproduction lay dormant until the late 1950s—on both sides of the Atlantic. Soon thereafter, of course, it became the standard for all recorded music.

The stereo record-cutting system developed by Blumlein, in which each channel is cut into one side of a 90° groove (the "45/45" system), appeared to limit the number of playback channels to two. In the 1970s, however, engineers developed several different techniques for encoding four audio channels within the two walls of a record groove. Although competing systems were developed, the technique was generally called Quadraphonic. The two major Quad formats are SQ (developed by CBS, later bought by Sony) and CD-4 (developed by JVC). SQ is a matrix system in which the rear channels were matrix-encoded in the front channels. SQ suffered from extremely limited channel separation (as low as 3dB before logic steering became prevalent). CD-4 (Compatible Discrete 4) combined the front and rear channels in one signal, and recorded a difference signal between 30kHz and 50kHz. This high-frequency carrier was demodulated to obtain four discrete channels from a two-walled LP groove. CD-4 required a special phono cartridge and precise turntable setup. (Other proposed Quad systems such as QS and UMX were never fully realized in the marketplace.)

Quad was a musical and commercial disaster, primarily because the market was presented with competing systems and the demonstrations were laughably bad. In an attempt to show off Quad's 4-channel sound, Quad recordings often put the listener in the middle of a musical group, with instruments coming from all directions. Moreover, the theory behind Quad was fundamentally flawed, as was repeatedly pointed out at the time by British audio genius Michael Gerzon. For one thing, Quad called for two loudspeaker pairs spaced at 90 ° (roughly one speaker in each room corner), which is too far apart to produce phantom images between the loudspeakers. The general public never cottoned to this gimmickry and Quad quickly died. (There are, however, Quad aficionados who still debate the relative merits of SQ and CD-4.)

Although CD is a 2-channel medium (it has a provision for four discrete, lower-quality channels, but that capability was never used), it is possible to encode multichannel music on CD. Digital Theater Systems (DTS) has released a small number of multichannel titles encoded with its "perceptual coding" technique that reduces the number of bits required to represent the audio signal. The result is some loss of fidelity (CD's bit-rate of 1.41 million bits per second for two channels must be spread over six channels), but a gain in the number of channels. Such discs must be played in a DTS-compatible player. Titles were also released in the Dolby Digital format, with the best examples coming from the classical label Delos. These formats were, however, a stopgap measure until a true multichannel music carrier became a reality.

The advent of high-capacity digital audio discs—SACD and DVD-Audio—again offers the possibility of playing back music recorded with more than two channels of information. These new formats obviate the serious technical compromises inherent in both SQ and CD-4 Quadraphonic, and don't require a reduction in sound quality and lower bit-rates to achieve multichannel capability. Consequently, we're entering another age in which the general public will again be asked to embrace multichannel audio.

Multichannel music is appearing on the scene today for several reasons. First, we now have the technology to deliver up to six channels without the compromises inherent in earlier multichannel systems. Second, home theater has greatly increased the number of homes with a multichannel loudspeaker array (more than 40 million as of this writing). Third, the music industry is looking for a way of selling its music libraries again and of reducing the incidence of illegal "file sharing" (which is not practical with multichannel audio). Finally, the consumer-electronics industry would like to sell you all new electronics and six loudspeakers rather than two.

And there's another important reason why multichannel audio is being marketed now: it's a way of further differentiating the new music carriers (SACD and DVD-A) from the CD. When the CD was introduced, its small size, random track access, portability, and freedom from wear made it an easy sell to the general public. CD was very different from LP. But it's hard to sell the mass market on the superior sound of SACD and DVD-Audio when most consumers consider CD the pinnacle of audio perfection. Improved sound quality is, unfortunately, not a sufficient motivator for people to adopt an entirely new format. Putting the listener in the middle of a band, with instruments all around him, is a much more dramatic demonstration of the difference between CD and the new multichannel formats. Simply put, multichannel sharply differentiates SACD and DVD-A from CD.

Do We Want Multichannel Music Playback?

But just because we *can* play back multiple channels in the home, should we? Is multichannel audio a significant advance in sound quality, or a marketing gimmick foisted upon us? This issue is perhaps the most polarizing of any current controversy among audiophiles. The majority of audiophiles consider 2-channel music reproduction sacrosanct, and not something to be tampered with. Surround-sound for music is associated with surround-sound for film, in which explosions and special effects are presented all around the listener—fine for movies but justifiably abhorrent to the purist music lover. Moreover, 2-channel listening can be immensely satisfying, so why bother with surround sound? Multichannel audio is viewed by many audiophiles as a fad, not a legitimate means of advancing the goal of recreating the original musical event in our homes with the greatest possible fidelity. On the other hand, some of the most ardent and dedicated audiophiles have championed multichannel as the most significant advance in audio since stereo.

In my view, multichannel audio is a quantum leap forward in advancing the music-listening experience—*with a properly set-up system playing recordings made with musical sensitivity*. There's no question in my mind that multichannel audio can greatly increase the spatial realism of reproduced music and deliver a more involving experience. The catch is that the system must be properly configured, and that the recording use the technology in a musically appropriate way rather than as an "effects" gimmick.

Multichannel overcomes a fundamental limitation of stereo, which is that it tries to create a 360° soundfield from two loudspeakers spaced 60° apart. Let's explore this idea with a thought experiment. Suppose we are in a concert hall enclosed in an acoustically isolated shell. If we cut two holes in the front of the shell facing the stage, we'll hear mostly direct sound from the instruments. If we cut additional holes in the back of the shell, reflections from the back of the concert hall can enter the shell and create a soundfield in the shell that is closer to that in the concert hall. How could anyone argue that putting more than two holes in the shell is a step backward? Reverberation and reflections arrive at our ears in the concert hall from behind us; why shouldn't they in the home?

I've attended many demonstrations of multichannel sound; I'll tell you about two of them that exemplify the problems and promise of multichannel music reproduction.

In one demonstration, the sound from the speakers behind the listening position was played as loudly as the sound from the front speakers. I heard a blasting trumpet just behind my left ear, and an electric guitar behind my right ear. Most of the rest of the band was reproduced by the front channels, giving the impression not of hearing a musical group performing in front of me, but of being surrounded by the musicians. Not only was this unnatural and musically distracting, but hearing loud sounds suddenly blare out from behind me caused me to turn my head toward the sound source. Human beings have a survival instinct that makes them turn around when they hear a sharp sound behind them. Putting the listener in an instinctive state of defensive readiness is not conducive to musical involvement. Moreover, hundreds of years of Western musical tradition call for the performers on a stage and an audience in front of those performers. (Some compositions call for instruments behind the audience, but those are the rare exception.) To top it off, the overall sound was far too loud. All of this added up to a most unpleasant experience.

Now consider a second demonstration of surround sound I attended. For the original recording, five microphones had been placed in a large concert hall, three across the front and two in the rear. The five microphone signals were recorded in Sony's DSD format (the encoding format of SACD), and then reproduced in the demonstration through five loudspeakers arranged similarly to the microphone placement. The re-creation of the original acoustic space was breathtaking; instead of hearing reverberation come from the front channels along with the instrumental images, the warmth of the hall was reproduced from behind me. More precisely, I wasn't aware of sound sources behind me, only of being inside a large acoustic space. Only ambience and hall reflections were reproduced by the rear channels, and at a *very* low level. Moreover, the front of the soundstage was more spacious, and the impression of air between instrumental images was greater than I've heard from any 2-channel playback. The soundstage didn't stop at the loudspeaker boundaries; it instead gently enveloped me, just as in live music. This microphone array, along with the multichannel delivery path, captured the spatial aspects of musicians in a hall with far greater realism than is possible from two channels.

The promoters of the first demonstration wanted to hit people over the head with the fact that they could place instruments behind the listener. They had absolutely no regard for whether the technology was being used in a musically appropriate way. In the second demonstration, surround-sound technology increased the realism and provided a more satisfying experience than was possible with two channels. Unfortunately, the first example is the rule, the second the exception. Those who conducted the first demonstration apparently believe that most listeners are not sophisticated enough to discern and appreciate subtlety. It's demonstrations like the first one that will further polarize the audio community over the validity of multichannel audio.

This comparison makes the point that surround sound is neither a miracle technology nor the evil that many 2-channel "purists" consider it to be. Provided that it is used tastefully, multichannel audio has the potential of elevating the music-listening experience to a new level. If you have an antipathy toward multichannel audio, be sure your opposition is based on your own listening experience rather than on dogma or prejudice.

I'd like to tell you about another experience I've had with multi-channel audio. Peter McGrath, one of the world's finest classical-music recording engineers, visited my listening room with his 4-channel Nagra D digital recorder and some 4-channel master tapes he'd made. Listening in multichannel mode first (for more than two hours), I was never conscious of sound originating from behind me. Rather, I felt enveloped in a large acoustic space. Halfway through a piece, we switched to stereo, and the magic disappeared. The soundstage collapsed into the front channels, depth was reduced, and I suddenly had the feeling of hearing the music through a window in front of me rather than the illusion of being inside the concert hall. Had I heard the 2-channel recording first, I would have thought it excellent. But after hearing reverberation and hall ambience reproduced from behind me—the same place it originates in live orchestral music—there was no going back.

During this listening session, I had another epiphany. Peter suggested that I walk around the listening room while the music was playing. Standing between the front speakers and facing the listening room's rear, I had the distinct impression of standing on a stage. The direct sound of instruments was to my left and right, and I heard reflections and reverberation in front of me coming from the rear speakers, just as one would when standing on a concert-hall stage. Standing between the rear speakers and facing forward, I heard more sound from the rear channels, which created the impression of being in the back of the concert hall. I could move forward a few steps and hear the spatial perspective change, exactly as one would hear in a hall, as the ratio of direct to reverberant sound changed. The movements were, of course, exaggerated; a few steps in my listening room were equivalent to moving several dozen feet in a hall.

I then stood on the right sidewall facing out into the room, with the front speakers to my right and the rear speakers to my left. Again, the impression of standing in that location in the concert hall—performers on the right, hall reverberation on the left—was eerily palpable.

This loudspeaker array created four separate but connected sound-stages: the conventional left/right; between the front and rear left loudspeakers; between the front and rear right loudspeakers; and between the two rear loudspeakers. These soundstages are much easier to hear when moving around the room as I did; when facing forward, precise imaging between front and rear loudspeakers was diminished because the sounds arrive from the side rather than from the front, which the brain processes differently from two front-arriving sounds.

This experience suggests that multichannel audio, done right, creates a more accurate, realistic, and compelling document of the original acoustic event. That the illusion survived my walking around the room says to me that the process is fundamentally valid. By contrast, the imaging we hear from 2-channel stereo is fragile; move your head sideways by a foot—or even a few inches—and the illusion can collapse.

Unfortunately, very few recording engineers currently view multichannel audio as an opportunity to better recreate the spatial aspects of live music. Rather, they see it as a new tool for fundamentally changing the listening experience. For example, AIX Records founder Mark Waldrep, a highly respected recording engineer and musicologist (he holds a Ph.D. in the subject), believes that multichannel audio is a means of escaping from the musical straightjacket that is 2-channel stereo. His recordings are often made with the musicians in a circle around the microphones. The rear channels contain just as much information as the front channels—even with a string quartet recording. In my interview with him in Issue 134 of *The Absolute Sound*, Waldrep articulated his approach: "For me, it's an active choice to *not* create an archival document of a space where musicians are performing, and instead try to enhance or energize that performance with the technology we can bring to the equation." Waldrep's approach may be musically valid at some level—he knows far more about music than I ever will—yet I find such recordings disconcerting. (All AIX titles, which are superbly recorded at 96kHz with 24-bit resolution, contain both multichannel and 2-channel mixes, as well as "stage" and "audience" spatial perspectives—enough choices to satisfy any listener's sensibilities.)

At an Audio Engineering Society convention, I attended a workshop that explored how multichannel music should be recorded and mixed. The panel was a "who's who" of contemporary popular-music engineers. Each panelist took a turn presenting his views on how to use the additional channels. There was absolutely no consensus among the panelists; everyone had a different approach. One engineer believed in placing the lead vocal *only* in the center channel. Someone else stated that the vocal should be mainly reproduced by the left and right channels, with slight augmentation by the center channel. Yet another advocated putting the vocal in the center channel with slight augmentation in the left and right channels. And the discussion hadn't yet considered the rear channels.

(You can judge for yourself the appropriateness of "hard" placement of the lead vocal in the center channel with James Taylor's *Hourglass* SACD. Simply switch between the multichannel and 2-channel mixes. The multichannel mix puts Taylor's voice only in the center channel. The 2-channel mix puts his vocal equally in the left and right channels, which we hear as a phantom image between the two loudspeakers. In my experience with this recording, the hard placement of the vocal in the center channel kills the sense of depth and air around Taylor's voice.)

At any rate when it's used judiciously—however much experimentation that may require—multichannel audio can be a legitimate vehicle for musical expression, freeing the artist from the constraint of positioning sounds solely in front of the listener. In addition to this (potential) expansion of a musical aesthetic, multichannel audio can increase the listener's ability to hear deeper into the music. Psychoacoustic research has shown that humans can absorb more aural information when that information arrives from different locations. That is, a sound arriving from behind the listener is more intelligible than the same sound arriving from the front along with other sounds. We can better differentiate individual sounds, and thus more easily explore their musical meanings, when those sounds arrive from different locations around us.

This phenomenon was graphically demonstrated at a Consumer Electronics Show a few years ago. Tomlinson Holman, inventor of THX (THX stands for "Tomlinson Holman's eXperiment"), set up and conducted the most unusual demonstration I've ever attended. Ushers with flashlights guided groups of showgoers to seats in a huge and nearly pitch-black room. The lack of light deprived us of any clue as to what we were about to hear—and prevented any prejudicial conclusions. Without any announcement describing what the demo was all about, the music began. The piece, an instrumental performed on synthesizer, was densely layered, yet perfectly intelligible on first listening. Each of the many parts seemed to originate from a different point in space surrounding me. There were no discrete sound sources, only a seemingly continuous soundfield. I could easily shift my attention from one musical line to another. In fact, the unique sonic presentation encouraged—perhaps "compelled" is a more appropriate word—such an exploration of the music. It was an unforgettable experience.

After the demonstration, Holman turned on the lights and explained what we had just heard—a 10.4-channel audio system playing a piece composed and performed by Herbie Hancock that had been recorded in 10.4 discrete channels (ten full-range channels and four subwoofer channels). Hancock used this wide sonic palette to expand his musical expression. My enthusiasm for what I'd just heard was tempered by the fact that a 10.4-channel audio system is never likely to become a commercial reality. Still, Holman proved his points: multichannel audio opens up new musical horizons, and more channels are better than fewer channels. (Holman's company, TMH Audio, develops and builds innovative products for the recording, film sound, and music industries.)

An unfortunate side effect of the home-theater boom is that multichannel music formats and playback systems have been dictated by the movie industry rather than developed from first-principles for the highest possible musical fidelity. Today's multichannel loudspeaker layout, channel configurations, and use of a single subwoofer all trace their origins to the film-sound industry. For example, a center loudspeaker is required in movie theaters because of the very wide placement of the left and right speakers. Dialogue must seem to originate on-screen; in fact, the center channel in movie sound is called the "dialogue channel." For music reproduction, we may want a center loudspeaker, but not a center channel driving it. (This is explained later in the discussion of Trifield processing.)

A fundamental problem of judging multichannel audio is the scarcity of good set-ups and demonstrations. Most multichannel loudspeaker arrays at high-end audio dealers are optimized for home-theater playback, not music listening. After all, home-theater is a booming industry, while multichannel audio is not.

Ironically, the best demonstrations of multichannel audio's capabilities may be in the car. Specifically, Acura's 2004 TL sport sedan is the first automobile to include DVD-Audio capability and discrete multichannel playback. The system was voiced by multiple-Grammy-winning recording engineer Elliot Scheiner, who used his own recordings and mixes to tune the system's sound. Apart from the DVD-A and multichannel capability, the TL's audio system is superb, which makes it a good test bed for the new format.

The big advantage of a car stereo is that the loudspeaker placement, listener position, and acoustic environment are all known. There's no chance for a botched demonstration because of less-than-ideal loudspeaker placement, or other variables. Of course, a car audio system, no matter how good, won't approach the quality of a true high-end system set up in a room. Nonetheless, the TL's discrete multichannel audio system and overall high quality offer the general public a good representation of multichannel audio's potential.

How to Get Multichannel Audio in Your Home

If you decide to make the multichannel plunge, you can follow one of four paths:

1) Build a system optimized for 2-channel music playback and home-theater reproduction, and accept compromised multichannel music performance.

2) Build a system optimized for 2-channel and multichannel music playback, and accept compromised home-theater sound.

3) Build a system optimized for 2-channel and multichannel audio without any capability for reproducing film soundtracks.

4) Build a system that does it all—that's equally adept at both 2-channel and multichannel music as well as home-theater soundtrack reproduction.

This first approach is the most common, which is why it's difficult to hear state-of-the-art multichannel audio demonstrations. Such a system employs sidewall-mounted dipolar loudspeakers, which are ideal for film-soundtrack reproduction but not for multichannel music. As described in Chapter 13, dipolar surround speakers mounted on the sidewalls better create a sense of envelopment and diffusion in the surround soundfield. They "smear" the rear-channel information by their directional pattern; the listener hears their sound only after the sound has been reflected around the room (this phenomenon is described in more detail in Chapter 13). Although this smearing may be appropriate for the atmospheric sounds in a film soundtrack (a rainstorm, jungle scene, or cityscape, for examples), when applied to a multichannel music mix this smearing is a distortion of the musical presentation created by the recording engineer. Multichannel music is recorded and mixed with uni-polar loudspeakers, and should be played back with an identical loudspeaker array. You will never hear imaging between dipolar surround loudspeakers.

The second option—optimize your system for multichannel music at the expense of compromised film-soundtrack performance—simply involves using uni-polar, rather than dipolar, surround loudspeakers. These need to be positioned behind the listener rather than on the sidewalls, as would dipolar models. When listening to multichannel music, you'll hear a better representation of what the recording engineer intended, but film soundtracks won't sound quite as spacious or enveloping. The atmospheric sounds in the surround channels will appear to originate from two points in space (the left and right surround speakers) rather than enveloping you in a diffuse wash of sound. Nonetheless, many listeners find uni-polar surround loudspeakers perfectly acceptable—even preferable—for film-soundtrack reproduction.

Both these options require a home-theater controller (described in Chapter 13), which will function as a surround-sound decoder for film soundtracks and be the source selector and volume control for multichannel music. The six analog outputs from a DVD-A or SACD player feed the controller's multichannel analog input. The digital outputs from your other sources (satellite, DVD player) feed the controller's digital inputs.

Which brings us to the third option of dismissing film-soundtrack reproduction entirely. If you never intend to use your system for movie watching, you'll obviously choose uni-polar surround loudspeakers. Although you won't necessarily need a home-theater controller, you will need a way of selecting sources (one of which will be multichannel) and controlling the volume. The solution for this system is the multichannel preamp. This new breed of product includes no provisions for surround-sound decoding, bass management, or other home-theater requirements. Rather, it is simply a preamplifier with six channels rather than two. Fig.14-1 shows an example of a multichannel preamplifier. Note the two sets of balanced and unbalanced multichannel inputs on the lower left.

Fig. 14-1 A multichannel preamplifier— rather than a digital controller— provides the highest audio quality in multichannel music reproduction.

Courtesy Audio Research Corporation

Finally, if you want the ultimate performance for both multichannel music and movies, you'll install two sets of surround speakers, one dipolar on the sidewalls and one uni-polar toward the rear. You'll need two separate 2-channel power amplifiers, one to drive the dipoles and one to drive the uni-poles. A pair of "Y" adapters on the controller's surround-channel outputs splits the signals so that the surround signal can drive two amplifiers. You select which surround loudspeakers are engaged by which power amplifier you turn on. This method is a bit cumbersome, but does solve the music/movie dilemma.

All these approaches require a multichannel source such as a DVD-Audio or SACD player. These machines are described in detail in Chapter 8.

Loudspeaker Types and Placement

The home-theater paradigm calls for five (or seven) loudspeakers and a single subwoofer. The subwoofer is driven by the Low-Frequency Effects (LFE) channel in a Dolby Digital soundtrack and selectively, bass from any of the other channels. In fact, many home-theater systems employ small satellite loudspeakers and a single subwoofer that reproduces all the bass in the system. Even if your home-theater loudspeaker system has full-range left and right loudspeakers, chances are that the center loudspeaker will be the small, horizontally-mounted variety.

This arrangement is, however, not ideal for multichannel music reproduction. The best loudspeaker configuration for multichannel music is five identical full-range loudspeakers in the locations shown in Fig.14-2 (shown earlier as Fig.4-12 but reproduced here for convenience). No subwoofer is required. Of course, if your system also functions as a home theater, you can have a subwoofer that is engaged only for film-soundtrack reproduction, not music playback. The loudspeakers should be equidistant from the listener. This array creates four separate but connected soundstages: between the left and right loudspeakers; between the surround loudspeakers, between the front left and rear left loudspeakers; and between the front right and rear right loudspeakers.

Fig. 14-2
Loudspeaker placement for multichannel music reproduction

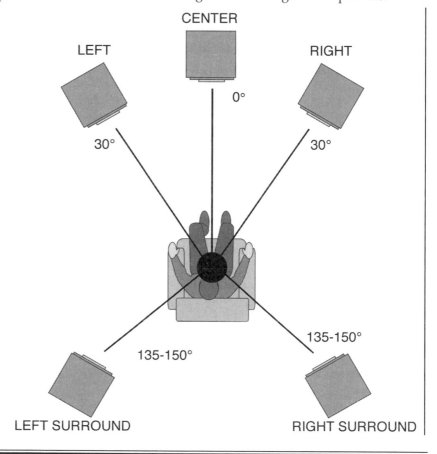

Chesky Records objected to the film-sound industry dictating multichannel music playback standards, so the company developed its own channel configuration and loudspeaker array and made some recordings for playback on what it considered its ideal system. That system, called Chesky 6.0, uses the loudspeaker array shown in Fig.14-3.

Demonstrations of this technique have sounded exceptionally good. Unfortunately, it's unlikely that this excellent approach will become a standard.

Fig. 14-3
Loudspeaker placement in the Chesky 6.0 technique

Courtesy Chesky Records

Bass Management

Bass management is a subsystem within a multichannel source machine (DVD-Audio, SACD player) or digital controller that allows you to selectively distribute bass information among your loudspeaker array. For example, if you have full-range left and right loudspeakers, but small center and surround loudspeakers, bass management keeps bass out of the small center and surround speakers and directs that bass to a subwoofer (if the system uses one). Bass management is essential in a multichannel loudspeaker system because not all systems use full-range loudspeakers.

Although bass management is provided in both multichannel players and controllers, you need set up only one device to perform bass management. Note that if you choose a system with a multichannel preamp rather than a digital controller, you'll need to set up bass management in the player.

Calibration

Just as it's vital to 2-channel playback that the left and right loudspeakers produce identical sound-pressure levels, the loudspeakers in a multichannel audio system need to be precisely calibrated so they produce the same level at the listening position. Adjusting the individual channel levels compensates for differences in loudspeaker sensitivity, placement, distance from the listener, and the effects of room acoustics.

All digital controllers are equipped with a pink-noise generator that can be programmed to cycle around all the channels. Pink noise is a hissing-like sound. You'll need to use this test signal in conjunction with a sound-pressure level (SPL) meter; setting the levels by ear is not accurate enough. Available from RadioShack for about $230, an SPL meter lets you accurately calibrate your multichannel audio system. RadioShack offers digital and analog SPL meters; buy the easier-to-read analog type (catalog #33-2050). Switch the meter to the C-WEIGHTED position, SLOW RESPONSE, and set the knob to 70. Position the SPL meter where your head would be in the listening seat, and point the meter toward the ceiling. (This ensures that the meter doesn't favor any one channel.) Turn on your controller's test noise and set each channel's volume until the meter's display reads 5. This indicates that the noise is being reproduced at a level of 75dB. Repeat this procedure for each channel. You may need to repeat this cycle over all the channels a few times to get the levels precisely matched.

After calibration, the controller's volume display will accurately show the level relative to 0dB. A typical listening level may be read as "–10dB" in the display. This may be confusing; why is 0dB the reference level? As explained in Appendix A, decibels express a difference, or ratio, between two values rather than an absolute value. At the 0dB volume setting, the system should produce a peak sound-pressure level of 105dB. This calibration standard comes from film sound, where the maximum sound-pressure level of the loudest peaks is 105dB. All other volume settings are referenced to this maximum value. With the system properly calibrated and the controller set to 0dB, the sound-pressure level in your listening room should be the same as on the film-sound mixing stage.

If the surround channels are too high in level, you'll hear too much ambience and reverberation and not enough direct sound. Set the rear channels too low in level and you won't experience the full surround effect. It's a little like changing rows in a concert hall; the farther from the stage you sit, the lower the ratio of direct to reflected sound. Unfortunately, multichannel music discs in which the surround channels contain reverberant information vary greatly in the amount of signal in the surround channels. This means that one calibration is not ideal for all discs. It's best to start with the precise meter-derived calibration, and adjust slightly from there to suit the recording.

You'll also need to set the controller's individual channel delays so that the sound from each loudspeaker arrives at the listening position at the same time. The controller's set-up menu will ask you for the distance between each loudspeaker and the listening seat. The controller then calculates the amount of delay to apply to each channel. If the center channel has too little delay, soundstage width will be constricted, with instruments tending to bunch up in the middle. The middle of the soundstage will seem more forward than the sides. Conversely, too much center-channel delay will increase the sense of depth, but at the expense of presence and tonal fidelity.

Multichannel Playback from 2-Channel Sources

The proliferation of multichannel loudspeaker arrays, combined with the scarcity of multichannel recordings, has led to the creation of decoding algorithms that generate 5- or 7-channel playback from unencoded stereo program material. Consumers who paid for those center and surround loudspeakers want to hear them working all the time, not just when watching movies. Aside from that cynical view, unencoded stereo programs often contain ambience information that is sufficiently decorrelated with the direct component of the signal that this ambience can be extracted and reproduced by rear loudspeakers to "unlock" the recording's spaciousness—sometimes with stunning effect.

Among these processes are Dolby Pro Logic II, Pro Logic IIx, DTS Neo:6, Logic 7, and Music Logic. All create signals to drive the center and surround loudspeakers from 2-channel sources. These decoding circuits are standard in virtually all digital controllers, except Logic 7 which is available only in products made by Harman International (Harman Kardon, Lexicon, JBL, for examples). Another example is EARS, developed by NAD Electronics. EARS is relatively gentle, feeding in-phase information common to the left and right channel to the center loudspeaker, and extracting ambience that feeds the rear loudspeakers. The effectiveness of these systems varies greatly with the recording; some sound worse with processing, others sound the same (if there is very little uncorrelated ambient information), and a few sound spectacular—almost like a discrete multichannel recording.

These decoding algorithms all attempt to extract ambience *present in the recording* and deliver that ambience to the rear loudspeakers. These techniques are not to be confused with the digital-signal-processing (DSP) modes on home-theater receivers and controllers with labels such as "Concert Hall," "Jazz Club," or "Stadium." Rather than extract ambience from the original program, these DSP modes synthesize reverberation and add it to the music. Attempts have been made to measure the acoustic properties of concert halls and other venues and encode that acoustic signature in DSP algorithms that can be overlaid on the musical signal. All these schemes are nothing more than marketing gimmicks; many consumers choose audio/video receivers based on the number and variety of these surround modes. (One audio/video receiver I know of offers 499 possible surround-mode variations.) Needless to say, such manipulation is antithetical to high-end values, and should be avoided. (Some would argue that even ambience recovery techniques that only extract information already in the recording are antithetical to high-end values.)

I've found the most effective and musically appropriate algorithm for playing back 2-channel sources over more than two loudspeakers to be Trifield, a process found in products made by Meridian Audio. According to Meridian, "Trifield extracts the mono and surround components of the original recording. It then calculates the signals for the front left, center, and right speakers, using the phase and amplitude differences between the three front channels, to redistribute the sounds on a frequency-dependent basis. This gives a significant improvement over traditional stereo, which converts the differences between the microphone signals into amplitude differences in the speaker signals. Trifield is recommended for well-made recordings and stereo television broadcasts that are not Dolby Surround encoded."

Trifield, which is derived from Ambisonics (described later in this chapter), is actually two algorithms. The listener has the choice of frontal stereo only or the addition of extracted ambience in the rear channels. Meridian controllers allow you to select side or rear surround loudspeakers, or both. The extracted ambience signal is extremely subtle; the listener is never consciously aware of sound sources behind or to the side. Rather, the extracted ambience seems to make the front soundstage more spacious, open, and detached from the loudspeakers. A "width" control allows you to widen the soundstage. A wider soundstage is possible without the "hole in the middle" imaging because the center loudspeaker anchors the soundstage center.

In my experience, listening in Trifield fills in the center of the soundstage, presents a wider sweet spot, and creates more stable images between the loudspeakers. Moreover, the imaging doesn't shift with small head movements, as it often does when listening to two loudspeakers (the so-called "head-in-the-vice" syndrome).

Here's an interesting story about Trifield: During a visit to my listening room by an electronics designer who was a "2-channel purist" (someone who believes music should be reproduced by just two loudspeakers), I performed an experiment. We listened to music for about an hour, but unbeknownst to him, I had Trifield engaged. Part of the way through a piece of music, I switched to 2-channel stereo and he was instantly and visibly let down by this sudden change. He heard a reduction in sound quality, but had no idea what could have caused it—until I gave away the secret. Trifield is subtle in that it's not an obvious "effect," but profound in its ability to solidify the soundstage.

It's important to keep in mind that there's nothing sacrosanct about using two loudspeakers to reproduce music. Early researchers considered two channels a compromise dictated by practicality and the technology of the day. Further, the term "stereo" doesn't mean 2-channel reproduction. Rather, it comes from the Greek word for "solid" because two channels can create apparently solid images between the loudspeakers.

Ambisonics

The solution to how best to capture a soundfield, and to reproduce that soundfield through more than two loudspeakers, has been solved for more than 30 years. It's called Ambisonics. Invented by Michael Gerzon, Ambisonics is a simple expansion of Alan Blumlein's idea, adding an omnidirectional microphone to the crossed figure-of-eight microphones that constitute a Blumlein pair. This setup captures all the information (in the horizontal plane) present in the original soundfield. When reproduced by four or more loudspeakers (the more loudspeakers the better), Ambisonics reconstructs the original acoustic soundfield. This isn't merely a marketing claim; there's a solid body of mathematics that shows that Ambisonics indeed encodes and reconstructs every aspect of the soundfield.

An additional figure-of-eight microphone can be added to capture the height information as well. In Ambisonic recording, the monaural sound pressure is called the "W" component, the left-right velocity component is called "Y," the front-back component is called "X," and the optional up-down (height) component is called "Z."

The W, X, and Y signals are called the "B-Format" and are obviously not compatible with 2-channel distribution media. The signals can, however, be combined to produce stereo (and mono) compatibility. This encoding method, called UHJ, matrix encodes the three (or four with the Z channel) signals for mono, stereo, and multichannel compatibility. UHJ-encoded material is decoded on playback by an Ambisonic decoder in a digital controller.

Ambisonic recordings are made without regard for the number of loudspeakers through which the program will be reproduced. The special microphone samples the soundfield and encodes all the necessary information about that soundfield. On playback, the Ambisonic decoder generates the appropriate output signals based on the number of loudspeakers in the system. Because the multichannel audio is hierarchically represented, it can be played back through as few or as many loudspeakers as your room can accommodate. The B-Format representation is completely independent of the loudspeaker array; the Ambisonic decoder will correctly map the soundfield to the number of loudspeakers.

Many hundreds of Ambisonic recordings have been made in the past 30 years, notably by the classical label Nimbus, which uses the technique exclusively. Nimbus is releasing an extensive series of Ambisonic recordings on DVD-Audio during 2004. Even if the signal will never be decoded, Ambisonics has many advantages for 2-channel recording and reproduction. (Nimbus at one time owned the Ambisonics trademarks, but sold them to Meridian Audio.)

The advent of high-capacity, multichannel digital-audio discs such as DVD-A provides an opportunity to deliver to the listener the full Ambisonics experience. The Meridian Lossless Packing (MLP) technology used in the DVD-Audio format (explained in Chapter 8) can encode the hierarchical Ambisonics information and flag that data so it can be reproduced by a 5.1-channel loudspeaker system, even if the playback system doesn't include an Ambisonic decoder. A hierarchically-encoded multichannel signal is not tied to any particular number of loudspeaker feeds; rather it is a method of storing and transmitting multichannel audio to fit into a wide variety of loudspeaker configurations. The hierarchical signal is "scalable" to the number of loudspeakers through which the signal will be reproduced, thus making a multichannel signal perfectly compatible with any number of playback channels (including mono).

Ambisonics was developed long before any standards were in place that specified the number of loudspeakers in homes. However, today's ubiquity of 5.1-channel playback systems presents an opportunity to deliver Ambisonics without a decoder in the playback chain. With the number of loudspeakers known in advance, the Ambisonic signal can be "pre-decoded" for playback on a 5.1-channel loudspeaker array. No decoder is required, although it isn't possible to use more than five loudspeakers with this so-called "G-Format." In addition, height information in the G-Format can't be reconstructed without a decoder. If the system does employ an Ambisonic decoder, that decoder can be programmed to generate the appropriate number of signals to feed the loudspeaker system. This decoding is automatically engaged by the datastream flag, making the process completely transparent to the user.

The ideal loudspeaker placement for Ambisonic playback is four loudspeakers in a rectangle; five loudspeakers in a regular pentagon; or six loudspeakers in a regular hexagon. As mentioned earlier, the greater the number of loudspeakers, the more faithful the reconstruction of the original soundfield that was sampled by the microphone array.

There's no question that Ambisonics is by far the most musically appropriate multichannel recording technology. It reconstructs the soundfield in a way that the ubiquitous 5.1-channel systems can't approach, producing a much more believable sense of space, more precise image placement, and a much larger listening area than the typically small, sharply limited "sweet spot."

So why didn't Ambisonics catch on? First, Ambisonics came to market just as Quad was dying. Ambisonics was lumped in with Quad's failures, and record companies and electronics manufacturers wanted to put that failure behind them. Ambisonics was also seen, mistakenly, as just another competing Quad format. Moreover, no major record labels had any interest in Ambisonics because all had already associated themselves with one of the existing Quad formats. Ambisonics was also seen as an audiophile technique suitable only for capturing classical music in a concert hall with natural ambience, and not appropriate for studio records (although Alan Parsons' Ambisonic-encoded *Stereotomy* destroyed that argument). Finally, Ambisonics was doomed by a complete marketing failure, the result of the patents being turned over to a

British government agency whose job was to promote and market British inventions. The agency was ill-equipped to promote Ambisonics and negotiate licensing agreements with hardware manufacturers.

Still, Ambisonic titles are readily available today, and Meridian Audio incorporates Ambisonic decoders in all its digital controllers. The provision in the DVD-Audio format for including Ambisonics hierarchical data may breathe new life into the technology. Just as it took 28 years for Alan Blumlein's invention of stereo to become a widespread commercial reality, Ambisonics may one day become the dominant multichannel music format.

More information on Ambisonics, including a comprehensive list of titles and decoding hardware, can be found at ambisonics.net.

15 Specifications and Measurements

An audio component's technical specifications and measured performance can tell us much about the component. Understanding what the specifications mean, and interpreting laboratory-test results is useful—though not essential—to the audiophile. Specifications and measurements have their place in audio, but they are not the beginning and ending of the story. Rather, they are just one facet of a multidimensional puzzle.

What specifications and measurements cannot tell us is how the product communicates musical expression. To discover that, we must listen. The primacy of the listening experience is expressed in Appendix D, a newly revised and updated version of my Audio Engineering Society paper "The Role of Critical Listening in Evaluating Audio Equipment Quality," first presented at the 1991 New York AES convention.

Although understanding this chapter is not essential to enjoying high-quality music reproduction in your home, I've included an explanation of specifications and measurements for each component category for those interested readers, and to make this book complete.

Preamplifier Specifications and Measurements

An important preamplifier specification is a line-stage's gain, or the amount of amplification the preamp provides. Gain is expressed either in decibels (dB), or as a number representing the ratio between the input and output voltages.

The preamp's gain is important to consider in relation to the output voltage of source components. If you have a very-high-output CD player or digital processor feeding a high-gain preamplifier, you'll barely crack open the volume control before you get loud listening levels. This has several disadvantages. First, it makes setting a "just right" volume difficult: The volume control is rendered so insensitive by such high outputs that even small adjustments make large differences in listening level. Second, volume controls are often less well matched between channels at the low end of their range. This means that one channel becomes louder than the other when the volume control is turned down. The effect is the same as if you'd turned a balance control off-center. This difference can be as much as 3dB—enough to shift the image to one side. A digital processor putting out, say, 5V RMS at full scale and driving a line-stage preamp with 25dB of gain would produce this problem.

High gain can be an advantage when using a line-stage preamplifier with an external phono stage. Many phono stages have just enough gain of their own to feed a line-stage, but no more. The line-stage therefore requires a fair amount of gain.

Line-stage gain varies between 5dB and 25dB. The 5dB figure is very low—perhaps too low for some outboard phono stages, and even for tuners and tape decks. This will be especially true if the power amplifier has low gain or the system has insensitive loudspeakers, and could require using the volume control near the maximum setting. For most CD sources, about 10dB of gain is ideal.

As described earlier, phono-stage gain should be matched to your phono cartridge. Moving-magnet cartridges need about 35dB of gain, while moving-coil types require up to 60dB. If the phono preamp has less than adequate gain, a line-stage preamp with high gain can further amplify the phono signal for adequate listening levels.

A preamplifier's gain can be expressed indirectly as *input sensitivity*. This is the voltage required to produce some reference level (usually 0.5V) at the preamplifier output with the volume turned all the way up. A preamplifier with an input sensitivity of 0.05V has a gain of 10 (which can also be expressed as 20dB, because 20dB represents a 10-to-1 voltage ratio).

A preamplifier's *input impedance* specification describes the electrical resistance to current flow "seen" by the source component (such as a CD player) driving the preamp. Most preamps have input impedances between 10,000 and 50,000 ohms (10–50k ohms). The preamp's input impedance is the *load* the source component drives. As described earlier, the higher the input impedance, the easier it is for the source to drive. As the input impedance increases, however, current flow though the interconnects and preamplifier input stage decreases. Some designers believe moderate rather than very high input impedance results in the best sonic performance. If the preamplifier's input impedance is too low, it can *load down* the source component, resulting in poor technical and sonic performance.

A preamplifier is also specified according to its *output impedance*. Output impedance is best thought of as a resistor inside the preamplifier that couples its output stage to the rear-panel jacks. Output impedance describes the preamplifier's ability to deliver current into a load (the power amplifier). A preamplifier's output impedance is much lower than its input impedance; where input impedance may be 50k ohms or more, output impedance may be less than a thousandth of that value.

By having a high input impedance and a low output impedance, the preamplifier acts as a buffer between the source components and the power amplifier. The sources drive a high input impedance—which is very easy for them—and the preamp takes on the burden of driving the interconnects and power amplifier. The preamplifier's low output impedance makes it ideal for this job. (The advantages of low output impedance are discussed in more detail in the section on passive level controls earlier in this chapter.)

A preamplifier's *input overload* specification refers to the maximum input voltage the preamp can accept without distorting (with distortion defined as 1% Total Harmonic Distortion, or THD). The higher the input overload figure, the better. A full-function preamplifier will have two input overload specifications: one for the line-level inputs (typically more than 10V RMS), and one for the phono inputs (typically several hundred millivolts).

Maximum output level is the maximum output voltage the preamplifier can swing from its output stage. Maximum output level is often as much as 50V—far higher than any audio signal. Because most power amplifiers have an *input sensitivity* (the input voltage required to produce maximum power output) of under 1.5V, virtually any preamp has enough output voltage to drive any power amplifier.

Signal to noise ratio, or *S/N ratio*, is a measurement of how quiet the preamplifier is. It expresses in decibels the ratio between a signal level of 0.5V output and the residual noise floor. The higher the signal-to-noise ratio, the quieter the preamp. Because the ear isn't equally sensitive to noise at all frequencies, a *weighting curve* is sometimes applied to the noise spectrum to more closely approximate the noise's audibility. (Weighting curves are described in more detail in Appendix A.) A signal-to-noise ratio of 90dB unweighted (no weighting curve applied) is good; higher signal-to-noise ratios are common when "A"-weighted (some of the noise is removed from the measurement to approximate the audibility of the noise). A preamp with lots of 60Hz hum in the audio signal (caused by AC from the wall getting into the audio signal path) will exhibit a very large increase in S/N ratio (as much as 25dB) when "A"-weighted. If the preamplifier's S/N ratio is referenced to 1V output instead of 0.5V, subtract 6dB from the S/N to find the equivalent 0.5V figure.

Preamps rarely have frequency-response errors; virtually all modern preamps have flat response from below 20Hz to above 50kHz. Phono stages, however, often have errors in their RIAA response, producing the equivalents of frequency-response errors. These errors are caused primarily by capacitor tolerances in the RIAA circuit. An example of a preamp with RIAA errors is shown in Fig.15-1a. The solid line is the left channel, the dotted line is the right channel. A phono preamplifier with no RIAA errors would produce a perfectly flat line. The rolloff in the upper midrange and treble seen in Fig.15-1a will make this phono stage sound dark, closed-in, and lacking immediacy. A phono preamp with more accurate RIAA equalization is shown in Fig.15-1b.

Fig. 15-1a & b Examples of poor (left) and typical (right) RIAA accuracy (Courtesy *Stereophile*)

A preamplifier's *Total Harmonic Distortion* (THD) is often measured and expressed as THD+N (Total Harmonic Distortion Plus Noise). This name reflects the technique that measures the sum of harmonic distortion and noise. Here's how THD+N is measured: The preamp under test is driven by a swept sinewave signal, a band-reject filter removes the test signal, and whatever is left (distortion and noise) is plotted as a function of frequency. Note that very-low-distortion preamps can have a higher THD+N figure than their intrinsic harmonic distortion; the noise, rather than distortion, dominates the measurement.

The THD+N vs. frequency plot of a typical preamplifier is shown in Fig.15–2. The vertical scale is THD+N in percent. The upper pair of traces is measured through the phono inputs, the lower pair through the line inputs. The apparently higher distortion through the phono inputs is undoubtedly caused by its higher noise level, not increased distortion.

Fig. 15-2 A typical preamplifier THD+N measurement

Courtesy *Stereophile*

Interchannel crosstalk, also called *channel separation*, is a measure of how much the signal in one channel leaks into the other channel. The higher the channel separation number, the better, with 100dB being excellent and 50dB being on the poor side. A crosstalk specification should include the measurement frequency; crosstalk usually increases as frequency rises. Crosstalk will generally increase at the rate of 6dB per octave, due to capacitive coupling between channels.

When expressing this phenomenon as *crosstalk*, the *lower* the specified crosstalk, the better; this figure indicates how much signal has leaked into the other channel. Conversely, when expressing *channel separation*, the *higher* the figure, the better; the number indicates the degree of isolation between channels. Both terms, however, describe the same phenomenon.

Fig.15-3a shows mediocre crosstalk performance; Fig.15-3b shows excellent crosstalk performance. The measurement is made by driving one channel of the preamplifier with a swept sinewave at a reference output level (the 0dB reference on the graph's vertical scale), then plotting the undriven channel's output signal as a function of frequency. The measurement is repeated with the channels switched, and both traces are combined on the same graph. In the example of poor crosstalk performance, the crosstalk in the undriven left channel was 60dB below that of the driven right channel at 1kHz. In Fig.15-3b, the signal in the undriven channel was down by 100dB at 1kHz.

Fig. 15-3a & b Examples of poor (left) and excellent (right) crosstalk (Courtesy *Stereophile*)

Channel balance is a measure of how closely in level the two channels are matched. Some preamplifiers have slightly more gain in one channel than the other, creating a channel imbalance. Volume controls can also introduce channel imbalance, particularly at the low end (counterclockwise) of their range. Channel balance is often measured at three volume-control positions, and should be within 0.2dB at all volume settings. Large channel imbalances can cause the center image to shift to one side. Tubed preamps sharing a single dual tube for left and right channels are particularly susceptible to channel imbalances; the two elements within the tube may have slightly different gains. Fortunately, the problem can be corrected simply by changing the tube to one with matched gain.

Preamplifier specifications should be used to ensure electrical compatibility with other components, not as indicators of sound quality. Many superb-sounding preamps measure poorly, and some preamps that look great on paper disappoint in the listening room. Let your ears—not the specification sheet—be your guide in choosing a preamplifier.

Power Amplifier Specifications and Measurements

Power amplifiers share many specifications (signal-to-noise ratio, crosstalk, etc.) with other components, yet have some unique specifications and measurements.

Power amplifiers typically have input impedances of between 20 and 150k ohms, with 47k ohms being a standard for unbalanced inputs. This is a high enough value to ensure that the power amplifier's input stage won't *load down* the preamplifier's output and put a strain on the preamplifier's output stage.

A power amplifier's *output impedance* is usually a very low value—between 0.05 and 0.5 ohms for solid-state amplifiers. Tubed power amplifiers have a higher output impedance—about 0.5 ohms to as high as 2 ohms. Single-ended tubed amplifiers can have output impedances as high as 3 ohms. Think of output impedance as a resistor in series with the output transistors (or output transformer in a tubed amplifier) connected to the load. Low output impedance is a desirable design goal; when the power amplifier's output impedance becomes a significant fraction of the loudspeaker's input impedance, the loudspeaker and amplifier interact. The result can be peaks and dips in the amplifier's frequency response caused by the loudspeaker's impedance change with frequency. This is a serious consideration when contemplating a single-ended tubed amplifier; the amplifier will have a different tonal balance when driving different loudspeakers. A high output impedance is also characterized by soft bass, lack of bass extension and dynamics, and less bass control. A power amplifier with a high output impedance is less able to control woofer motion. Output impedance is related to an amplifier's *damping factor*—its ability to control cone motion in the loudspeaker. The higher the damping factor, the better. Note that damping factor is specified at the amplifier's output terminals; resistance in loudspeaker cables can dramatically decrease the effective damping factor, particularly in long cable runs.

Gain refers to the ratio between the input and output voltages. Gain can be specified as the ratio between the voltages, or as a figure in decibels (dB). Typical gain is about 26dB, or a ratio of 20:1 (i.e., an input voltage of 1V will produce 20V at the output). *Input sensitivity* is the input voltage required to drive the amplifier to clipping. A typical value is between 0.775V and 2V, with about 1.2V being standard. If the power amplifier has a very high input sensitivity (less than 0.5V), the preamplifier's volume control will be extremely insensitive—you'll get plenty of volume with the knob barely turned up. Conversely, a low-output preamp driving a low-sensitivity power amplifier (2V, say) will require the preamp's volume control to be turned up very high to get adequate volume.

We've talked a lot about maximum output power; now let's see how it's measured. With a dummy load (a huge power resistor) connected to the amplifier's output, the power amplifier is driven with a gradually increasing voltage. Distortion in the output is monitored and plotted as a function of output power. When the amplifier clips, the distortion shoots up instantaneously. The clipping point, defined as 1% THD, is the amplifier's maximum output power. This test is performed with the amplifier driving loads of 8, 4, and 2 ohms. The results are combined and plotted on a single graph (Fig.15-4a). The farther to the right the "knee" (bend) in the distortion trace, the higher the output power at clipping. Note that some plots of THD vs. output power have only two traces, at 8 and 4 ohms. These amplifiers cannot be tested into 2 ohms at full output power: the power-supply fuses blow, or the amplifier simply shuts down.

By combining the three traces on one graph, we can quickly assess the amplifier's ability to increase its output power into low impedances. The greater the distance between the curves' knees, the greater the amplifier's ability to drive current into low-impedance loads. Fig.15-4b shows the measurement of an amplifier with very little ability to deliver current into a 4 ohm load: It produced 15.6dBW at 8 ohms, but only 12.5dBW at 4 ohms.

Figs. 15-4 a and b The power output vs. THD curves show an amplifier's maximum output power, and how well it can increase its power into low-impedance loads. (Courtesy *Stereophile*)

By contrast, Fig.15-4a shows an amplifier behaving as a virtually perfect voltage source, maintaining its voltage and doubling its current output each time the load impedance is halved. This graph, the result of an actual measurement, reveals exemplary—and extraordinary—performance. The performance would have been even better had the AC line voltage not drooped under the heavy load, decreasing the raw power available to the amplifier—the amplifier pulled so much current out of the wall that the AC line voltage dropped from 118V to 106V. This amplifier put out 325W into 8 ohms (25.1dBW), 635W into 4 ohms (25dBW), 1066W into 2 ohms (24.3dBW), and 1548W into 1 ohm (22.9dBW). Moreover, it was perfectly stable driving this tremendous amount of current into such a low impedance.

These methods are used for most tubed and solid-state push-pull amplifiers. Single-ended tubed amplifiers produce so much distortion that a different criterion must be used to determine the clipping point.

Rather than using 1% THD as the point at which we say the amplifier has run out of power, 10% THD is often called the clipping point of a single-ended amplifier. That's because a single-ended tubed amplifier may produce 2 or 3% THD when operated at just a few watts of output power.

Another way to look at a power amplifier's output capability is the *power-bandwidth* test, which determines the widest bandwidth over which the amplifier can maintain full output power. The amplifier is driven to just below clipping, and the output power is plotted against frequency.

How much peak power an amplifier can deliver on transient signals (musical peaks) above its continuous power rating is called its *dynamic headroom*, expressed in dB. A power amplifier rated at 100Wpc (RMS) that can deliver 200Wpc for brief periods (measured in milliseconds) without severe distortion is said to have 3dB of dynamic headroom. You may remember from earlier in the chapter that doubling the power represents an increase in volume of 3dB. An amplifier's dynamic-headroom specification says a lot about its subjective ability to play loudly.

In addition to plotting THD against output level to find the clipping point, a power amplifier's distortion can be measured at low signal levels and plotted as a function of frequency. Fig.15-5 is such a graph. The lower trace is THD+N (THD plus Noise) measured at 1W into 8 ohms. The next higher trace is at 2W into 4 ohms, and the upper trace (highest distortion) is with 4W driving a 2 ohm load. The lower the distortion and noise, the better, with less than 0.2% constituting good performance.

Fig. 15-5 THD vs. frequency measurements show how the amplifier's distortion changes into low-impedance loads.

Courtesy *Stereophile*

Although knowing how much *total* distortion a power amplifier generates is important, an examination of the harmonic-distortion *spectrum* is more instructive. We want to know *which* harmonics are present; some harmonic products are much more audible and annoying than others. As stated earlier in the discussion of tubed power amplifiers, 10% second-harmonic distortion is less musically objectionable than 0.5% seventh-harmonic distortion. We thus need to characterize the distortion spectrum rather than use a single THD figure.

To do this, the power amplifier is driven at two-thirds rated power with a 50Hz sinewave, and a *Fast Fourier Transform* (FFT) is performed on the output signal. The FFT captures the amplifier's output signal and transforms it into its constituent parts. (Specifically, the FFT can convert a time-domain signal into the frequency domain.) An FFT produces a plot showing energy vs. frequency, shown in Fig.15-6a. We can see that this particular amplifier generates an entire series of harmonic-distortion products. The distortion spectra of Fig.15-6b, however, show a much lower level of distortion products.

Figs. 15-6a and b An FFT of an amplifier's output shows the amplifier's individual harmonic-distortion components. (Courtesy *Stereophile*)

Although harmonic distortion has been touted as the definitive performance parameter of power amplifiers and receivers, this specification in itself isn't that significant a criterion in the evaluation of power amplifiers. Many amplifiers with 3% distortion sound just fine, while others with 0.01% sound awful. As described in Chapter 1, THD can be reduced by increasing the amount of negative feedback in the amplifier. Unfortunately, negative feedback introduces other problems that make the amplifier sound worse. Although it's interesting to know how much harmonic distortion an amplifier produces and the spectral distribution of those distortion products, I wouldn't let THD figures influence my purchasing decision.

Intermodulation Distortion (IMD) is distortion that occurs when two signals of different frequencies are amplified simultaneously—something that happens all the time in music. IMD creates *sum-and-difference* signals related to the frequencies being amplified. For example, if we drive a power amplifier with 10kHz and 1kHz sinewaves, the amplifier produces an output signal containing the original test tones at 10kHz and 1kHz, but also *intermodulation products* at 11kHz (the *sum* of the two signals) and at 9kHz (the *difference* between the two signals). Though the 9kHz and 11kHz sum-and-difference IMD products are usually the highest in amplitude, IMD creates an infinite series of distortion products.

Intermodulation distortion is expressed as a percentage of the IMD products in relation to the test-signal amplitude, with typical values falling between 0.01% and 0.2%. IMD test signals are often 60Hz and 7kHz combined at equal amplitude, or with the higher-frequency tone at one-quarter the amplitude (–12.04dB), or 19kHz and 20kHz at equal amplitude. To test with the latter signals, the amplifier is driven at two-thirds rated power and an FFT is performed on the amplifier's output. We look for the 1kHz difference signal (20kHz minus 19kHz); the lower its amplitude, the better. This 1kHz intermodulation product is usually between 55dB down (55dB below the test signal amplitude) and 75dB down. We also sometimes see a family of sideband signals around the test tones.

Some of these measurements are unique to power amplifiers. Other, more universal measurements include those of frequency response, crosstalk, and signal-to-noise ratio. Except for single-ended amplifiers, however, it's rare for a modern amplifier to depart from flat frequency response. Note that the sonic characteristics of "bright," "extended," "forward," etc. are not functions of the amplifier's frequency response.

Finally, a power amplifier is said to be *inverting* if it reverses absolute polarity between its input and output. A *non-inverting* amplifier maintains the same polarity between input and output. In an inverting amplifier, the positive- and negative-going parts of the wave are flipped over: positive at the input becomes negative at the output. This can slightly improve some recordings and degrade others. Because most gain stages invert absolute polarity, an inverting amplifier usually has an odd number of gain stages, while a non-inverting amplifier has an even number; one isn't necessarily better than the other. (See "Absolute Polarity" in Appendix A.)

Loudspeaker Specifications and Measurements

There is more correlation between a loudspeaker's measured performance and its sound quality than there is with any other component in an audio system. A loudspeaker that measures as having a treble rolloff will likely sound dull; a loudspeaker with a measured rising top end will likely sound bright and forward. Having said that, however, I must stress that you can't judge a loudspeaker's performance by reading its specifications or measurements. Although good measured performance is valued, the loudspeaker's musical abilities in the listening room are what count. To find that out, we must listen.

Following is an explanation of each of the measurements found in some loudspeaker reviews or manufacturers' specification sheets.

Impedance is the electrical resistance the loudspeaker presents to the power amp. As described in detail in Appendix B, a loudspeaker's impedance is a combination of its simple DC resistance, inductive reactance, and capacitive reactance. The higher the impedance, the easier it is for the amplifier to drive. A low-impedance loudspeaker requires the amplifier to drive more current through the loudspeaker, which puts more stress on the amplifier.

Even though a loudspeaker's impedance may be specified as "6 ohms," the actual impedance almost always varies with frequency. Fig.15-7a shows an impedance curve (solid line) for a loudspeaker of rather low impedance. The impedance dips to less than 4 ohms (the "40.0m" horizontal division) through the bass and most of the midrange. The impedance minima is just over 1 ohm at 30Hz—an extremely low value.

Figs. 15-7a and b A loudspeaker's impedance magnitude (solid line) and phase angle (dotted line) indicate how easy or difficult it is for a power amplifier to drive. (Courtesy *Stereophile*)

The dotted trace in the impedance plot shows the loudspeaker's *phase angle*, which indicates how inductive or capacitive the loudspeaker looks to the amplifier. If the loudspeaker presented a pure resistance (no capacitance or inductance), the phase-angle plot would be a straight line. The farther away from the center line, the more reactive the loudspeaker is at that frequency. (Phase angle is discussed in detail in Appendix B.)

A combination of high reactance and low impedance is especially difficult for a power amp to drive. The severe phase-angle swings seen in Fig.15-7a, coupled with its low impedance, will be more demanding of the power amplifier. This doesn't mean that the loudspeaker won't work, only that it will work better with a power amp that can deliver a substantial amount of current into low-impedance loads. For example, a power amp that nearly doubles its power into a 4 ohm load compared to an 8 ohm load would be a better choice than one that barely increases its power into 4 ohms.

A much easier load to drive is illustrated in Fig.15-7b. The impedance is much higher over a wider band, and the phase-angle swings are less severe. The impedance never dips below 6 ohms, and is well above that figure over wide bands. This loudspeaker will demand much less current from the power amplifier.

A loudspeaker's impedance magnitude and phase angle must be considered in relation to its sensitivity. A loudspeaker with a high sensitivity is much less demanding of a power amp than one with a low sensitivity, regardless of the loudspeaker's impedance. The combination of low sensitivity, low impedance, and severe phase angle requires an amplifier of the highest quality to achieve musically acceptable results.

Sensitivity can be expressed as a sound-pressure level with 1 watt input measured 1 meter away. A loudspeaker's sensitivity may be expressed as 88dB/1W/1m. High sensitivity is generally considered any value above 90dB/1W/1m, while low sensitivity is a value below 85dB/1W/1m.

Note that sensitivity can also be expressed with a drive signal of 2.83V, which corresponds to 1W into an 8 ohm load. Loudspeaker manufacturers can cheat on sensitivity figures by using the 2.83V figure into a 4 ohm loudspeaker, which increases the loudspeaker's sensitivity rating by 3dB. The loudspeaker isn't 3dB more sensitive, it's just drawing twice as much current from the power amp at the same 2.83V. If you see the 2.83V figure, make sure the impedance is 8 ohms.

Note that the term *efficiency* is often used incorrectly in place of *sensitivity*. Technically, efficiency is the percentage of electrical power converted by the loudspeaker into acoustical power.

Measuring a loudspeaker's impedance and phase angle can be done electrically on a test bench. Measuring a loudspeaker's acoustical characteristics, however, requires putting a microphone in front of the loudspeaker and driving the loudspeaker with test signals. Consequently, the measured response will be not the loudspeaker's intrinsic characteristics, but the loudspeaker's response as modified by the room in which the measurements are taken. As we know, a loudspeaker's performance is greatly dependent on the room in which it is used. We could end up measuring more of the room's characteristics than the loudspeaker's.

One way of solving this problem is to measure the loudspeaker in an *anechoic chamber*—a room whose surfaces are covered with highly absorbent material. This material absorbs virtually all the sound energy striking it, reflecting no energy back into the room. In fact, the term *anechoic* literally means "no echo." Consequently, the measurement microphone "sees" only the loudspeaker's response.

Anechoic chambers are expensive to build and consume lots of real estate. Engineers have therefore developed methods of measuring loudspeakers in a normal room to exclude the room's influence from the measured results. One of these techniques, invented by Richard Heyser, is called *time-delay spectrometry* (TDS). In TDS measurements, the loudspeaker under test is driven by a swept sinewave. The signal picked up by the measurement microphone is filtered by a narrow filter that allows only a narrow range of frequencies to pass. The frequency the filter allows to pass tracks the swept sinewave driving the loudspeaker, but is delayed in time by a few milliseconds (ms). The filter's delay is exactly the amount of time it takes for sound from the loudspeaker to reach the measurement microphone. The sound reaching the measurement microphone is the loudspeaker's direct acoustic output, followed a few milliseconds later by room reflections; or, the same sound after it has been reflected/bounced off of the room's walls, floor, and ceiling.

This is where the swept bandpass filter comes in. The filter tracks the sinewave stimulus so that when a reflection reaches the microphone, the filter has already moved past the reflection's frequency and rejects it. The result is the loudspeaker's intrinsic response, unmodified by the room.

A second, more popular technique is implemented in a personal-computer–based hardware and software package called the Maximum Length Sequence System Analyzer (MLSSA). The loudspeaker under test is driven by a stimulus containing a specific pattern of noise sequences. The measurement microphone a few feet in front of the loudspeaker picks up this signal, which is compared to the noise-sequence pattern stored in memory. From the way the loudspeaker alters this sequence, the system computes the loudspeaker's impulse response. The period between the impulse and the first reflection is free from reflections and is indistinguishable from an anechoic measurement. The impulse response is then "windowed" to remove the information from the first reflection onward, leaving only the anechoic window.

The impulse response, which is a time-domain signal, is transformed into the frequency domain using Fourier analysis. Fourier analysis is a mathematical technique of converting an impulse response (a time-domain signal) into a frequency response (a frequency-domain signal), or vice versa. The term *Fast Fourier Transform (FFT)* describes this conversion from one domain to another.

From the loudspeaker's impulse response we can derive the system's frequency response. The result is the loudspeaker's response minus the room's contribution. Note, however, that the anechoic window's length determines the low-frequency resolution of the measurement. The longer the anechoic portion of the impulse response that is transformed into the frequency domain, the lower the frequency that can be accurately measured. When we measure loudspeakers with this technique, the loudspeaker is placed on a tall stand so that it is halfway between the floor and ceiling, maximizing the anechoic window. The room should therefore also be as large as possible.

Despite these techniques, the low-frequency resolution of MLSSA measurements isn't satisfactory unless you have a huge room (a long anechoic window). To better measure a loudspeaker's low-frequency performance, a measurement microphone is placed so that it nearly touches the woofer cone. At this position, the room's contribution is negligible. This separately measured *nearfield* woofer response is appended to the MLSSA-derived response to provide an accurate wideband measurement.

With that background, let's go through a set of measurements that you might find in a typical loudspeaker review and examine what they mean.

A loudspeaker's impulse response reveals its time behavior, including how *time-coherent* the loudspeaker system is, how much the drivers exhibit *ringing*, and whether the drivers are connected in the same polarity. I described time coherence in the section on crossovers; a time-coherent loudspeaker has no phase lag between drivers. That is, they all move in step in response to the input signal. In a loudspeaker that isn't time-coherent, the output from the individual drivers is slightly staggered in time. Ringing is driver motion after the input signal has stopped.

Fig.15-8a is the impulse response of a loudspeaker that has poor time coherence. Notice the negative-going spike (the tweeter's output), which indicates that the tweeter's output occurs before the other drivers' outputs, and that it is connected in the opposite polarity. The impulse response in Fig.15-8b is much more coherent; all the drivers respond to the impulse in an identical manner. Ideally, the impulse response should have a fast rise-time (indicated by the steepness of the impulse) and minimal driver ringing after the impulse has stopped. (Ringing can be seen as squiggles after the impulse.)

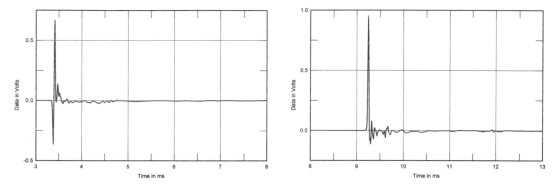

Figs. 15-8a and b A poor impulse response (left) and an excellent impulse response (right). (Courtesy *Stereophile)*

Another way of looking at a loudspeaker's time behavior is the *step response,* or how the loudspeaker behaves when presented with direct current (DC). Derived from the impulse response, the step response plots the loudspeaker's output vs. time. Fig.15-9a is the step response of the same loudspeaker whose impulse response we saw in Fig15-8a. The lag between the tweeter (the negative-going spike) and the other drivers is apparent, as well as a slow *risetime* (the time it takes for the loudspeaker to reach full amplitude in response to the input signal). For con-

Figs. 15-9a and b A poor step response (left) and an excellent step response (right). (Courtesy *Stereophile*

trast, Fig.15-9b is a virtually perfect step response. The drivers are time-coherent, and the risetime is extremely fast (the step is a straight vertical line). This step response was derived from the impulse response in Fig.15-8b.

Fig.15-10 is a loudspeaker's overall frequency response as measured over a 30° horizontal window. This simply means that the frequency response was measured at various angles from the loudspeaker's front baffle and averaged to produce the curve. Averaging the response gives a better representation of the listener's subjective response to the loudspeaker; some of that side energy will reach the listener after being reflected from the listening room's sidewalls. This particular loudspeaker has some excess treble energy between 5kHz and 15kHz, which may make it sound tizzy in the treble. Notice how the response drops rapidly above 15kHz. The broad dip between 500Hz and 5kHz may give the loudspeaker a distant, rather than present, perspective. The rising bass indicates that the low-frequency alignment may be underdamped, giving the bass a generous but fat quality. In short, these deviations from a flat line indicate colorations in the loudspeaker.

Fig. 15-10
Frequency response averaged over a 30° horizontal window

Courtesy *Stereophile*

Fig.15-11 is a loudspeaker's "horizontal family" of response curves. These show how a loudspeaker's response changes as the measurement microphone is moved around the loudspeaker. The frequency-response measurement just described is an average of these individual curves.

The trace representing the frequency response directly in front of the loudspeaker (on-axis) has been normalized to be a straight line so that the other curves show only the *difference* from the on-axis response. The horizontal family shows the loudspeaker's dispersion, or how it radiates acoustical energy into the room as a function of frequency. This particular loudspeaker shows a typical treble rolloff as the microphone is moved to the sides of the cabinet, but also excess treble energy on-axis.

Fig.15-11
A horizontal
response family

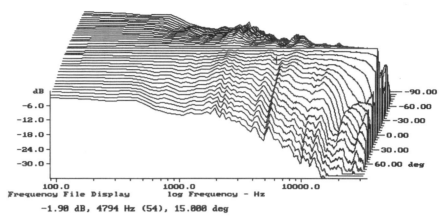

Courtesy *Stereophile*

These curves suggest that this loudspeaker should be listened to without toe-in; the excess treble on-axis will be reduced if the listener sits slightly off-axis (no toe-in). A loudspeaker that exhibits radical changes in off-axis response can sound colored, even though the on-axis response may be fairly flat.

The next measurement (Fig.15-12) shows how the loudspeaker's response changes with listening height. Again, the flat line has been normalized so that only the differences from vertical on-axis response are shown. The on-axis point is usually the tweeter axis, or a typical listening axis (the text accompanying the measurement will usually indicate which). As you can see, the frequency response changes radically with listening height. The loudspeaker has severe peaks and dips in the response (caused by interference effects) above and below the optimum listening axis. This means the loudspeaker will sound very different

Fig. 15-12 A vertical response family

Courtesy *Stereophile*

depending on listening height. This example is extreme; most loud-speakers don't exhibit such radical response changes along the vertical axis. All loudspeakers, however, evince some change in tonal balance at different listening axes. This measured response underscores the impor-tance of listening height when auditioning a loudspeaker.

The ideal loudspeaker would stop generating acoustical energy as soon as the input signal stopped. In practice, some acoustical energy, however small the amount, is always stored in the drivers and enclo-sure. This energy is radiated over time, like a bell ringing. To look at a loudspeaker's response over time, its frequency response is plotted in discrete slices of time. As described previously, the frequency response is derived from the impulse response using the Fast Fourier Transform. By moving the window in the impulse response on which the FFT is per-formed, the loudspeaker's frequency response can be derived at different points in time. Specifically, the FFT-derived frequency response is calcu-lated perhaps 100 times over 4 milliseconds (ms) to create the plots of Figs.15-13a and b. This graph is properly called a *cumulative spectral-decay* plot, but is more commonly called a *waterfall* plot because of its similarity to cascades of falling water. It shows how the loudspeaker's output changes over time and with frequency. The topmost curve is the loudspeaker's frequency response at time zero. The next lower line is the frequency response 40 microseconds (40μs) later. The next lower line is 40μs after that, and so forth.

By plotting the response over time, we can easily see cabinet reso-nances, driver ringing, driver breakup, and other problems. A driver res-onance is seen as a vertical ridge in the plot; the loudspeaker continues to radiate energy at the ridge's frequency long after the impulse has stopped. The perfect loudspeaker would produce a flat line at the top, and instantly decay to no energy output.

Examples of poor and excellent performance on the cumulative spec-tral-decay test are illustrated in Figs.15-13a and b. In Fig.15-13a we can see a ridge at 3729Hz, indicating that the loudspeaker continues to pro-duce acoustic energy at this frequency for 2ms after the drive signal has ceased—a long time in loudspeaker terms. By contrast, Fig.15-13b shows exemplary behavior: the acoustic output drops very quickly (the white

Figs. 15-13a and b Poor (left) and excellent (right) cumulative spectral-decays. (Courtesy *Stereophile*)

space between the top few traces and the lower traces), and almost no ridges are apparent. The one minor resonance at 2963Hz is minuscule compared to the resonances seen in Fig.15-13a, which will be audible as a change in timbre when this frequency is excited by the music.

The same technique can be used to examine the behavior of loudspeaker cabinets. An accelerometer is attached to the loudspeaker, which is driven by the MLS signal. The accelerometer output is drawn in a waterfall plot, which shows the frequency and amplitude of cabinet vibrations. For example, Fig.15-14 shows an enclosure with a severe resonance at 187Hz, seen as the narrow ridge at that frequency. This loudspeaker stores, then slowly releases, energy at 187Hz. This will undoubtedly color the bass when the loudspeaker is excited by music with energy at this frequency.

Fig. 15-14
Cumulative spectral-decay of an accelerometer output attached to a loudspeaker cabinet

Courtesy *Stereophile*

Those readers wanting to delve deeper into loudspeaker design are directed to Martin Colloms's definitive reference book on the subject, *High Performance Loudspeakers* (Halsted Press, ISBN 0-470-21721-9).

Digital Specifications and Measurements

Many tests and measurements exist to quantify a digital processor's technical performance, but few—if any—measurements tell us how the processor sounds. Nonetheless, good technical performance indicates that the processor is well-engineered, and is more likely to have good sonic performance as well.

Let's start with a digital processor's maximum output level. (I'll use the term "digital processor," although I'm also referring to CD players— the measurements are the same.) The standard analog output voltage is 2VRMS, with units varying between 1.75V and a whopping 7.2V. Most CD players and processors put out between 2.2V and 3.5V. Note that this value is the highest RMS output voltage possible from the player, measured by playing a full-scale, 1kHz sinewave.

Knowledge of a processor's output level is useful in several ways. First, a processor of very high output wouldn't be ideal for driving a preamplifier that had lots of gain. Although it is unlikely that the processor would overload the preamplifier's input, you would end up using the preamp's volume control at the very low end of its range. Most volume controls exhibit their greatest channel imbalances (i.e., one channel is louder than the other) when turned down. In addition, setting a "just right" volume is more difficult with high-output processors and high-gain line-stage preamplifiers; the volume control becomes overly touchy to small movements. This is particularly true of preamps with detent level steps instead of a continuously variable volume control. A high output level is an asset when driving a passive level control, but a drawback with a high-gain line-stage preamplifier.

Another important measurement to consider when determining if a particular processor or CD player is a good candidate for a passive level control is output impedance. If a passive level control is used between a digital processor and power amplifier, the burden of driving the cables and power amplifier falls on the digital processor's output stage. If the processor has a high output impedance, dynamics can become compressed and the bass may get mushy. In extreme cases, a processor with a very high output impedance can even become current-limited and flatten the waveform peaks if it is asked to drive a low-input-impedance preamplifier. Processors with the highest output impedances have an impedance of nearly 2k ohms at 20kHz and 1.5k ohms at 1kHz. This high output impedance causes the processor's output stage to clip when asked to drive impedances of less than about 15k ohms.

Further, the output impedance of the passive level control itself must be added to the equation. The passive control's output impedance (which varies depending on which resistor is switched in, or the position of the potentiometer) must be *added* to the driving component's source impedance to find the total source impedance driving the power amplifier.

Digital-processor output impedances vary from less than 1 ohm to 5.6k ohms (the highest value I've measured in a product). Generally, if the output impedance is less than a few hundred ohms, the processor should have no trouble driving a passive level control. Between 50 and 500 ohms is a typical value.

Bottom line: Don't drive a low-input-impedance power amplifier (less than about 20k ohms) with a passive level control, with a high-output-impedance (greater than about 800 ohms) digital processor through long, high-capacitance interconnects. These aren't hard-and-fast numbers but general guidelines. Appendix B includes a full analysis of what can happen with a passive level control and high-output-impedance sources.

The next measurement, frequency response, doesn't reveal a processor's overall tonal balance as it often does with loudspeakers, but is included in specifications and measurements for the sake of completeness. Most processors are down a few tenths of a dB at 20kHz, the result of rolloff in the digital filter.

More revealing, however, is a CD player's or processor's *de-emphasis error*. As previously described, some CDs have had their trebles boosted (emphasized) during recording, and carry a flag that tells the CD player to switch in its de-emphasis circuit to restore flat response. These de-emphasis circuits are often inaccurate (due to resistor and capacitor tolerances), producing frequency-response irregularities when the player is decoding emphasized discs. De-emphasis error should be less than ±0.1dB across the band. De-emphasis errors can cause tonal-balance irregularities (tizzy upper treble, for example) when playing pre-emphasized CDs. De-emphasis errors of 0.2dB over an octave of bandwidth are audible. Poor and good de-emphasis accuracy is shown in Figs.15-15a and b. Both of these measurements were made on digital processors using analog de-emphasis circuits; processors with digital-domain de-emphasis have no errors. The positive error in Fig.15-15a will make the processor sound bright when playing pre-emphasized CDs.

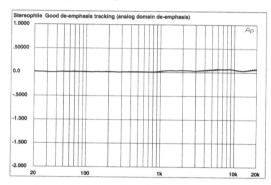

Figs. 15-15a and b De-emphasis errors (left) and accurate de-emphasis tracking (right) (Courtesy *Stereophile*)

Interchannel crosstalk, also called *channel separation*, is a measurement of how well the left and right channels are isolated from one another. Ideally, when a digital processor is fed a right-channel signal, that signal should not appear in the left channel, and vice versa. The lower the crosstalk (or, put another way, the greater the channel separation), the better. Many processors (and other products) have decreasing channel separation as frequency increases, a result of capacitive coupling between channels. Typical CD players and digital processors have about 90dB of channel separation at 1kHz, this decreasing to about 70dB at 20kHz. Although there is no correlation between low crosstalk and soundstage width (an intuitive link), high channel separation indicates good overall engineering. Mediocre and good crosstalk performance are shown in Figs.15-16a and b. At 1kHz, the processor shown in Fig.15-16a has 67dB of channel separation, compared with the 112dB of channel separation at 1kHz measured in the processor shown in Fig.15-16b.

A very revealing test of a processor's ability to re-create low-level signals looks at the processor's output vs. frequency (*spectral analysis*) when the processor under test is driven with the digital code representing a –90dB, dithered 1kHz sinewave. A spectral analysis plots energy

Figs. 15-16a and b Poor (left) and good (right) crosstalk performance (Courtesy *Stereophile*)

level vs. frequency. Peaks in the trace at 60Hz, 120Hz, 180Hz, and related frequencies indicate that power-supply noise is getting into the audio circuitry. A spectral analysis can also hint at how well the unit's DACs (digital-to-analog converters) are performing; the signal should peak at the –90dB horizontal division, and the left and right traces should overlap. This indicates that the DACs are linear and have similar performance between channels. The spectral analysis also shows the process sor's noise level, and reveals if there is any spurious energy in the audioband. Figs.15-17a and b, respectively, show poor and good performance on this test. In the poor-performing processor, we can see power-supply noise in the audio signal at 60Hz and harmonics of 60Hz, linearity error (the traces don't peak at the –90dB horizontal division), no overlap of the traces (indicating that the DACs are not well matched between channels), and a higher overall noise level. The performance shown in Fig.15 17b is exemplary.

Figs. 15-17a and b Poor (left) and good (right) performance on the spectral analysis test (Courtesy *Stereophile*)

The same type of spectral analysis, but with the processor driven by "digital silence" (all zeros), is also performed and plotted to 200kHz. This test can reveal the presence of spurious junk in or above the audioband, and DAC artifacts such as idle tones (seen as a peak in the trace). Ideally, the trace should be a smooth line sloping gently upward, with no peaks at the power-line frequencies and no spikes in the audioband.

The effects of noise shaping in 1-bit–type converters can also be seen in this measurement. As described earlier in this chapter, noise shaping is a technique that pushes noise from the audioband into the ultrasonic band. Fig.15-18 shows the effects of noise shaping as revealed by this wideband, 1/3-octave spectral analysis: the noise floor rises sharply above 10kHz. We can also see some peaks in the left-channel trace (the solid line) at 18kHz and 25kHz that may be DAC artifacts.

Fig. 15-18 A wideband spectral analysis reveals the effects of noise shaping in 1-bit converters.

Courtesy *Stereophile*

Low-level linearity was touted a few years back as the definitive measurement in digital processors. While good linearity is a high engineering goal, it doesn't guarantee good sound.

Understanding linearity is easy: it's how well the processor's analog output level tracks the digital input level. If we put in the code representing a –88dBFS signal, for example, the analog output of the test tone should be exactly –88dB (88dB below full scale). Any difference between digital input level and analog output level is linearity error. Linearity error occurs in all DACs, and is compensated for in many processors with an MSB (Most Significant Bit) trimmer, installed at the factory.

Linearity error is expressed as the dB difference between the digital input level and the analog output level at a specific digital level (with any gain error normalized out of the measurement). For example, we can say that a particular converter has a 3dB positive error at –90dBFS. This means that when the processor is driven by the digital code representing a –90dBFS signal, the processor's analog output is actually –87dB, or 3dB higher than the digital input level. Note that the digital input level refers to the signal levels represented by the value of the ones and zeros in the binary code, not the input voltage to the processor's digital input, which remains constant.

A comparison of mediocre and excellent linearity is shown in Fig.15-19. A perfect processor would produce a ruler-flat line, with no deviation above or below the zero horizontal division. The linearity measurement in Fig.15-19b comes very close to this ideal. Conversely, the measurement in Fig.15-19a has a 2.6dB negative error in the right channel (dotted trace) and a 4dB negative error in the left channel (solid trace) at a signal level of –90dB.

Figs. 15-19a and b Mediocre (left) and excellent (right) linearity (Courtesy *Stereophile*)

If the linearity trace dips below the center line, this indicates a negative linearity error. If it rises above the center line, the processor has a positive linearity error (the analog output is higher than it should be). The digital input level is read across the bottom, with the highest level at the graph's right-hand side. Some processors with excellent low-level linearity appear to have a positive error at very low signal levels (–115dB). This is actually noise swamping the DAC's output. The practical lower limit of measuring linearity is about –112dBFS (in quiet processors). Linearity is determined by the DAC (digital-to-analog converter) chip inside the processor.

A digital processor test, called "noise modulation," looks at how a digital processor's noise floor shifts, or modulates, with changing input level. Not only does the noise floor shift, but the noise floor's spectral balance can be very different at different input levels.

In the noise-modulation test, the processor is driven by the code representing a 41Hz sinewave at –60dBFS. The processor's output is high-pass–filtered to remove the test signal, and the residual noise is plotted vs. frequency. Ten samples are taken at each data point, and the average of those samples is plotted. The low-frequency test signal exercises the DAC, and the resulting noise is measured and plotted. The test is repeated at four additional levels (–70dB, –80dB, –90dB, –100dB), and the plots are combined on a single graph. This makes comparing noise-floor levels and spectral balance between input levels easier.

In a perfect processor the five traces would overlap, indicating that there was no change in the noise level or spectral content as a function of signal level. All processors, however, exhibit some difference between the traces. The tighter the traces, the better. Any time one trace crosses another, the noise floor's spectral balance has shifted. The amount of this shift can be calculated by looking at the difference between traces, using the horizontal-division scale on the far-left side of the graph. Examples of poor and good noise-modulation performance are shown in Figs.15-20a and b.

Figs. 15-20 a and b Poor (left) and excellent (right) performance on the noise-modulation test (Courtesy *Stereophile*)

Another test is the FFT-derived spectral analysis of the processor's output when decoding a full-scale mix of 19kHz and 20kHz. This test reveals intermodulation components such as the 1kHz difference tone (20kHz minus 19kHz), and interactions between the sampling frequency (44.1kHz) and the test signals.

As with the spectral analysis we saw earlier of the –90dB, 1kHz sinewave, this spectral analysis also plots energy against frequency. But this technique does it a little differently. In an FFT-derived spectral analysis, the processor's output is captured in the time domain, creating a waveform which is then transformed into the frequency domain using the Fast Fourier Transform (FFT).

The result of this technique is shown in Figs.15-21a and b, the FFT-derived spectral analysis of two processors' outputs when decoding this unusual test signal. Ideally, there should be no spikes in the noise floor; Fig.15-21b shows exemplary performance on this test. Note the greater number of spikes in Fig.15-21a. The higher the spikes' amplitude and the

Figs. 15-21a and b Some processors produce high intermodulation distortion (left); others generate very little IMD (right). (Courtesy *Stereophile*)

greater their number, the worse the intermodulation distortion performance. The trace in Fig.15-21b reveals a 1kHz difference component, but very few other intermodulation products.

Digital processors run into problems when converting very-low-level signals to analog. One way to examine a DAC's behavior on small signals is to capture its analog output waveform when reproducing a –90dB, undithered 1kHz sinewave. This test signal produces three quantization steps: 0, +1, and –1. The three levels should be of equal amplitude, and the signal should be symmetrical around the center horizontal division. A poor-quality reproduction of this signal is shown in Fig.15-22a, a high-quality one in Fig.15-22b. Note the absence of noise in Fig.15-22b, and the three clearly defined quantization steps. By contrast, Fig.15-22a is so noisy it's difficult to make out the wave's shape.

Figs. 15-22a and b Comparison of a noisy and poorly shaped 1kHz –90dB undithered sinewave (left), and nearly perfect reproduction (right). (Courtesy *Stereophile*)

A processor's reproduction of a 1kHz, full-scale squarewave (not shown) reveals its time-domain behavior. Most measurements show the overshoot and ringing typical of the digital filters used in most processors and CD players. The digital filter determines the waveform shape; the time distortion occurs in the digital filter. Some digital processors with custom DSP-based filters don't suffer from this type of distortion.

The amount of DC at the digital processor's analog outputs is measured and noted. The lower the DC level, the better. DC may cause a thump through the system when the preamplifier's input selector is switched to select the processor's output. If the preamplifier and power amplifier are both direct-coupled (no DC blocking capacitors in the signal path) and use no DC servo correction, the DC from the processor could be amplified and appear at the loudspeaker terminals—not a good condition. Low DC—less than, say, 20mV—is therefore desirable.

The measurements section of a digital product review will often mention that the processor is *polarity-inverting* or *non-inverting*. A non-inverting processor's analog output will be of the same absolute polarity as the digital data on the CD. Most processors don't invert polarity, but if one does, that's no reason for concern. Without knowing the absolute polarity of the recording and the rest of your system, it's a fifty-fifty chance that the absolute polarity will be wrong. Knowing that a processor inverts absolute polarity is useful when comparing processors: all processors under audition should maintain the same polarity for the listening comparisons to be valid.

Measuring a digital processor's *word-clock jitter* (inaccuracy in the crucial timing signal) was first made possible in 1992 by an instrument called the LIM Detector, developed by Ed Meitner of Museatex. LIM stands for Logic Induced Modulation. Although other designers have looked at word-clock jitter, the LIM Detector was the first commercially available jitter-analysis tool. When used with an FFT machine and an RMS-reading voltmeter, the LIM detector provides the digital processor's overall RMS jitter level (over a specified bandwidth) and a spectral analysis of that jitter.

To use the LIM Detector, the word-clock pin on the DAC is found, and a probe is connected between the word clock and the LIM Detector. The LIM Detector output is only the jitter component of that word clock. A wide range of word-clock frequencies is accommodated. The LIM Detector output is fed to the input of an FFT analyzer, which displays the jitter's spectral content. The analyzer's RMS reading meter displays an overall RMS voltage, which is converted to jitter in picoseconds (ps). We thus end up with a number indicating the overall amount of jitter on the digital processor's word clock, and FFTs showing the jitter's spectral distribution.

The FFT of Fig.15-23a shows a jitter spectrum in which the jitter is periodic; that is, the jitter energy is concentrated at specific frequencies, seen as spikes in the plot. Where you see a spike, it means the digital processor's word clock is being jittered at that frequency. Note that the spikes occur at 1kHz and multiples of 1kHz; the test tone driving the digital processor is a 1kHz sinewave. As described earlier in this chapter, jitter is often correlated with the audio signal—something we can readily see in Fig.15-23a. The RMS jitter level, measured over a 400Hz–20kHz bandwidth, is 350ps.

For contrast, Fig.15-23b is the jitter spectrum of a very-low-jitter digital processor. Not only is the overall RMS level lower (less than 80ps), but the jitter spectrum is nearly free from signal-correlated jitter.

Figs. 15-23a and b High word-clock jitter in a digital processor (left), and low jitter with few periodic jitter components (right). (Courtesy *Stereophile*)

In short, the lower the trace on the FFT, and the smoother the line (lack of spikes), the better the processor's jitter performance.

There are few measurements available that even attempt to characterize a transport's performance. One of them, however, can be made by anyone, and gauges how well the transport's tracking and error-correction systems work. All you need is the Pierre Verany *Digital Test* CD (Pierre Verany PV.788031/788032). Disc 2 of this two-CD set contains a section in which the spiral track of pits is interrupted by blank areas (no pits). This simulates data dropouts caused by poor-quality CDs, dirt, scratches, or other media contamination. A continuous tone is recorded on the tracks. The blank areas gradually increase in length, and each increase is represented by a different track number. The higher the track number in this series, the longer the dropout. By listening for when the test tone is interrupted and noting the track number, the dropout length the player can track and correct can be determined. The higher the track number the transport will play flawlessly, the better. Most transports will play up to track 33. Skip-free reproduction of track 37 or higher is excellent.

A recently devised method of characterizing transport quality measures the amount of jitter in the transport's output signal. The test instrument, developed by the now defunct UltraAnalog corporation, takes a transport's S/PDIF or AES/EBU signal and separates the jitter component from the data. The jitter signal is then plotted as a function of frequency so that we can examine the jitter's spectral content. The best transports have about 30 picoseconds (ps) of broadband jitter, the worst about 500ps. Fig.15-24a shows high transport jitter; Fig.15-24b shows low transport jitter. The three traces are made with different test signals: the solid trace is with the transport outputting a full-scale, 1kHz sinewave; the heavy dotted trace is with a –90dB 1kHz tone; and the light trace is measured with a signal of all zeros output from the transport. The peaks in the trace at 1kHz indicate that transport jitter is correlated with the audio signal. The peak at 7.35kHz in Fig.15-24b is the CD's 7.35kHz subcode data rate.

Figs. 15-24 a and b Comparison of high jitter in the S/PDIF signal (right) and low jitter (left). (Courtesy *Stereophile*)

Finally, good bench performance from a digital processor or transport doesn't guarantee high sound quality. There is no way to predict a component's musical character from looking at its test results.

Appendix A: Sound and Hearing

Introduction: What is Sound?

Sound is a series of physical disturbances in a medium such as air. When an object vibrates, it sends out a series of waves that propagate through the air. These waves are composed of fluctuations in air pressure above and below the normal atmospheric pressure of 14.7 pounds per square inch. When a loudspeaker cone moves forward, for example, it compresses the air in front of it, creating an area in which the air molecules are denser than normal atmospheric pressure. This portion of the sound wave is called a *compression*.

When the loudspeaker cone moves backward, it creates an area in front of it in which the air molecules are less dense than atmospheric pressure. This portion of the sound wave is called a *rarefaction*. Sound is made up of a series of alternating compressions and rarefactions moving through the air.

Sound waves are transmitted through the air by passing on the moving molecules' momentum to adjacent molecules. The original compressed molecules return to their original positions because of the elastic properties of air. The air molecules don't move very far; instead, their "bumping into each other" is what transmits sound energy.

When these compressions and rarefactions strike our eardrums, we perceive the phenomenon as sound. The greater the change in air pressure above and below normal atmospheric pressure, the greater the *amplitude* of the sound.

Because most objects vibrate with a periodic back-and-forth motion, or oscillation, most sound waves (and nearly all musical sounds) have a periodic repetition. The sound wave is a replica of the object's motion. Consequently, sound waves have a regular, periodic pattern of compressions and rarefactions.

This periodic pattern is illustrated in Fig.A-1. The loudspeaker at one end of the tube of air is driven by a periodic signal, such as that made by the cyclic back-and-forth motion of a tuning fork. Fig.A-1 (b) shows the movement of the loudspeaker diaphragm as a function of time. When the cone moves forward, a compression is created; when it moves backward, a rarefaction is formed. This pattern moves down the tube at 1130 feet per second, the speed of sound. The resulting pattern of pressure change, shown in Fig.A-1 (c), is called a *sinewave*, the most basic periodic repetition. Fig.A-1 (c) shows the instantaneous pressure distribution over the tube's length. Fig.A-1 (d) represents the change in atmospheric pressure as a function of time at some point along the tube.

Fig. A-1 The relationship between a loud-speaker moving back and forth, pressure distrib-ution in a tube, wavelength, and period

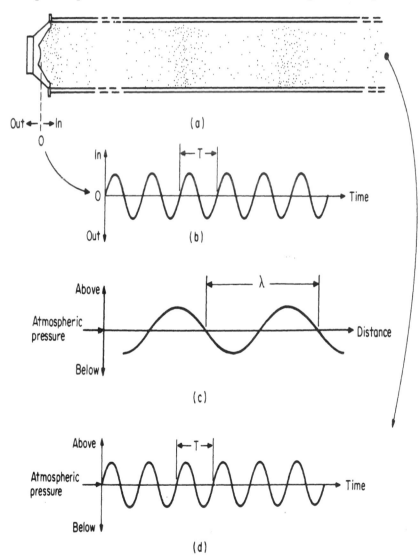

Courtesy *Audio Engineering Handbook*, K. Benson, McGraw-Hill, Inc., 1988

Another way of relating periodic motion to a sinewave is to imagine a tuning fork with a pen attached to it, with the pen touching a moving strip of paper. As the paper moves under the pen, the tuning fork's oscillations trace a sinewave on the paper.

Period and Frequency

The time it takes to complete one cycle of a sinewave (indicated by the "T" in A-1 (b)) is called its *period*. The *frequency* of a sinewave is the number of periods per second. A sound's frequency largely determines the sound's *pitch*, our subjective impression of frequency.

The unit for expressing frequency is the *Hertz*, abbreviated *Hz*. This unit of measurement is named after Heinrich Hertz, the German physicist who established that light and heat are electromagnetic radiations. The use of the unit Hz is relatively recent; the older unit of frequency was the more descriptive *cycles per second*, or *cps*.

Frequency is the reciprocal of time, expressed in the equation $F = 1/T$, where F is the frequency in Hz and T is the wave's period in seconds. For example, a sinewave with a period of 0.01 seconds (one one-hundredth of a second) has a frequency of 100 cycles per second, or 100 Hertz (100Hz). Because each period occupies one one-hundredth of a second, there are one hundred periods in a second, or 100Hz.

A sinewave with a period of 0.001 seconds (one one-thousandth of a second, or one millisecond) has a frequency of 1000Hz. The shorter the period, the higher the frequency.

Wavelength

If a wave's period is the *time* it takes to complete one cycle, a wave's *wavelength* is the *distance* between successive cycles. Wavelength, represented by the Greek letter lambda (λ), is shown in Fig.A-1 (c).

A sound's wavelength in air is directly related to frequency: the shorter the wavelength, the higher the frequency. To calculate wavelength, we simply divide the wave's frequency into the speed of sound in air. The formula is $\lambda = V/F$, where λ is the wavelength in feet, V is the speed of sound in feet per second, and F is the frequency in Hz. A sinewave with a frequency of 100Hz has a wavelength of 11.3' (1130 divided by 100). At a very high audio frequency of 10,000Hz (10kHz), the wavelength is about an inch.

Notice that a sound's wavelength is dependent on the speed of sound in the medium. For most applications, the speed of sound in air (1130 feet per second) is all we're concerned about. Because sound travels about five times faster in water than in air, the wavelengths of sounds transmitted through water are five times longer.

Phase

The term *phase* describes the fraction of a period that has elapsed in a sinewave. Phase is expressed in degrees, with one complete cycle of a sinewave represented by 360° (see Fig.A-2). Although phase can be measured from any arbitrary point along the sinewave, 0° is usually where the wave begins its positive-going zero crossing.

Fig. A-2
The phase of a wave is its time relationship to a reference point.

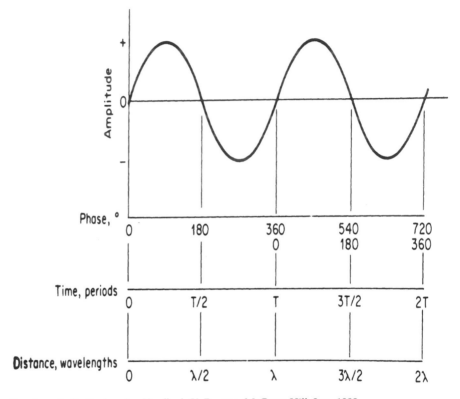

Courtesy *Audio Engineering Handbook*, K. Benson, McGraw-Hill, Inc., 1988

The term *phase shift* describes a time displacement of the sinewave relative to a fixed point. For example, if the sinewave in Fig.A-2 were delayed by half its period, we would say it experienced a 180° phase shift (because one cycle is 360°, half a period is 180°).

Phase can also describe the time relationship between two or more sinewaves. If one wave is delayed by half a period in relation to a second wave, we say the second wave lags the first wave by 180°. If one wave is delayed by one whole period (360°) in relation to another wave, it as though the phase shift never occurred—the wave is returned to its original phase relationship with the first wave. This is analogous to a clock's second hand returning to the same location every minute.

Phase shift has important consequences when waves are combined. If two waves of equal frequency and the same phase are superimposed, their combination will create a wave of greater amplitude. Specifically, two waves of equal amplitude, equal frequency, and the same phase will yield an increase of 6 decibels (dB) when combined. (Decibels are explained later in this appendix.) These waves are said to *reinforce* each other. If, however, one of these waves is phase-shifted by 180°, the two waves will *cancel* each other and produce no signal. When one wave is at peak positive, the wave shifted by 180° is at peak negative, producing the cancellation.

This is exactly what happens in a hi-fi system if *one* loudspeaker is connected with the loudspeaker cables reversed (the red amplifier terminal is connected to the loudspeaker's black terminal, and the black amplifier terminal is connected to the loudspeaker's red terminal). Reversing the leads to one loudspeaker "flips" that signal over, making positive into negative and negative into positive. This is similar to a phase shift of 180°. Now, when one woofer cone pushes forward to create a compression, the second loudspeaker's woofer pulls back to make a rarefaction. When the compressions and rarefactions are combined, they cancel; the compression from one loudspeaker "fills in" the rarefaction from the second loudspeaker, and less sound is heard. Because the two waves don't perfectly coincide, they don't completely cancel, but they do greatly reduce the acoustic output in the bass. If these two signals were combined electrically, however, complete cancellation would occur. Note that if you reverse the red and black leads on *both* loudspeakers, there is no phase shift between the left and right signals, and thus no cancellation occurs.

Absolute Polarity

Some audio products (primarily preamplifiers and digital processors) have switches marked "polarity," "phase," or "180°." These invert the polarities of *both* audio channels. The switch "flips" the signals over, making positive into negative and negative into positive. The switch inverts the stereo signal's *absolute polarity*.

Absolute polarity shouldn't be confused with *phase* reversal *between* channels (described earlier). In that case, there was a 180° phase shift in one channel with respect to the other—with severe audible consequences.

Absolute polarity, however, describes a polarity reversal of *both* channels. If musical waveforms were completely symmetrical—that is, identical in the positive- and negative-going halves—absolute polarity would make no difference. You could flip the signal upside-down and never be able to detect the difference, either by listening or by measuring.

But most musical signals aren't perfectly symmetrical, and are degraded if reproduced with inverted absolute polarity. When a recording is played back with correct absolute polarity, a compression from the musical instrument or voice at the original acoustic event causes a compression from the loudspeaker; a rarefaction from the instrument causes a rarefaction from the loudspeaker. Conversely, playing a recording with inverted polarity results in a compression from the instrument or voice to be reproduced as a rarefaction from the loudspeaker.

It may seem obvious and intuitive that all recordings and playback systems should maintain correct absolute polarity, but that isn't the case. An audio signal undergoes many reversals of absolute polarity during the recording and reproduction chain—reversals that no one keeps track of. Some recordings have correct absolute polarity and others don't—there's about a 50-50 chance that it's right. Similarly, some playback systems invert absolute polarity and others don't. The only thing that matters is that the sum total of all the polarity reversals results in correct polarity at the loudspeaker output. If a recording with inverted absolute polarity is played on a system that inverts absolute polarity, the result is correct polarity at the loudspeaker end of the playback chain.

The only way to ensure correct absolute polarity for each recording is by throwing the polarity switch and listening for which position sounds more natural. You can mark your records and CDs as to their polarity, and put the polarity switch in the appropriate position for each recording. Reversing the red and black leads on the cables going to *both* loudspeaker will also invert absolute polarity.

Note that it doesn't do any good to have a non-inverting playback system: roughly half your records and CDs will be reproduced with incorrect polarity whether your system is inverting or not. Moreover, many recordings have no single correct polarity; the disc often contains a mix of inverted and non-inverted tracks. Finally, music recorded with multi-track techniques often contains a mix of inverted and non-inverted signals in the same piece of music, making moot the entire issue of absolute polarity.

Some listeners report radical degradation of the sound when absolute polarity is reversed; others never notice the difference. The audibility of absolute polarity is highly variable, depending on the listener's polarity sensitivity, the instruments on the recording (some instruments produce a less symmetrical wave shape than others), whether or not the recording has a mix of inverted and non-inverted signals (from different microphones), and the phase coherence of the loudspeakers. Loudspeakers with poor time-domain performance can obscure the difference between correct and incorrect polarity.

There's an entire book devoted to absolute polarity. *The Wood Effect*, by R.C. Johnsen, is available from The Modern Audio Association, 23 Stillings Street, Boston, MA 02210.

Complex Waves

Real sounds and musical signals are made up not of sinewaves, but of *complex waves*. Complex waves are many sinewaves of different frequencies superimposed on one another. A vibrating object will produce a *fundamental* frequency (its lowest frequency) overlaid with *overtones* or *harmonics* that are mathematically related to the fundamental frequency. For example, a guitar string vibrating at 440Hz (middle A) will also vibrate at multiples of 440Hz. The second harmonic has a frequency of 880Hz, the third harmonic is at 1320Hz, the fourth at 1760Hz, and so forth.

It is the presence of these harmonics that give an instrument its *timbre* or tonal color. If a piano and a violin both play middle A, both instruments produce the same fundamental frequency of 440Hz. They sound very different because they have different *harmonic structures*: the violin produces stronger harmonics that extend higher in frequency than the piano's.

Harmonics can be *even-order* or *odd-order*. Even-order harmonics are the second, fourth, sixth, eighth, and so on. Odd-order harmonics are the third, fifth, seventh, ninth, etc.

The phase relationships of these harmonics and the fundamental have a great influence on the resulting complex wave. The top of Fig.A-3 is a complex wave composed of a fundamental, a third harmonic, and a fifth harmonic, all shown below the fundamental. Just by changing the phase relationship between the fundamental and its harmonics, we get a very different-looking complex wave (top of Fig.A-4). In this case, the fundamental was shifted by 90° (one quarter of a period) in relation to the third and fifth harmonics.

Fig. A-3
A complex wave is composed of multiple sinewaves.

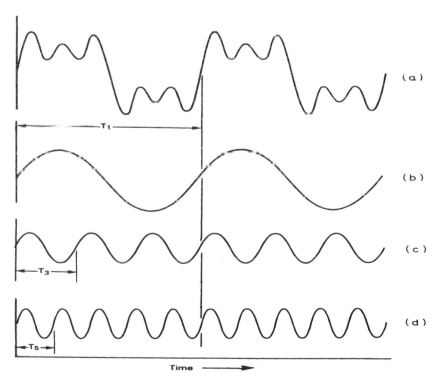

Courtesy *Audio Engineering Handbook*, K. Benson, McGraw-Hill, Inc., 1988

Fig. A-4 Changing the phase relationship between the constituent sinewaves greatly changes the complex wave's shape.

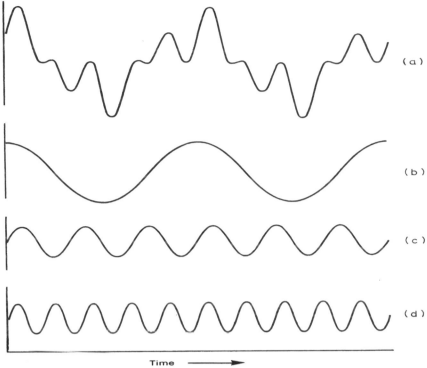

Courtesy *Audio Engineering Handbook*, K. Benson, McGraw-Hill, Inc., 1988

A *squarewave* is a sinewave with the addition of the entire series of *odd-order harmonics*. The shape of the complex wave in Fig.A-3 looks somewhat like a squarewave, even though only the third and fifth harmonics are present. If we added seventh harmonic the wave would look even more like a squarewave.

Comb Filtering

A waveform can also be altered if it is combined with a slightly delayed version of itself. This situation occurs when a loudspeaker is placed near a sidewall of a listening room: the listener receives the direct sound from the loudspeaker, and a reflection from the sidewall. The additional distance the reflected sound travels causes the delay. When these two sounds combine and interact, they reinforce at some frequencies and cancel at others. This phenomenon, called *comb filtering*, is a sequence of peaks and notches—hence its similarity to a comb—in the frequency response caused by constructive and destructive interference between the direct and reflected sounds. Chapter 4 includes a detailed description of comb filtering's effects on reproduced sound.

Absorption, Reflection, and Diffusion

When sound strikes a surface, it is absorbed, reflected, or diffused by that surface—or some combination of all three. A soft surface such as carpet or drapes absorbs energy because sound can enter its porous surface to be dissipated within the material's fibers. In this mechanism, sound energy is converted into a minute amount of heat within the absorbing material.

Reflective surfaces are hard and don't allow sound to penetrate the surface; nearly all the energy is reflected back toward the source. Sound is reflected at the same angle at which it strikes; i.e., "the angle of incidence equals the angle of reflection." Light and other electromagnetic waves behave similarly. Commercially available diffusers are shown on pages 86 and 97.

Diffusion is a scattering of sound. A diffuser converts a sound traveling in one direction into many lower-amplitude sounds moving in many directions. An irregularly shaped surface tends to diffuse sound, provided that the irregular structures are similar in size to the wavelength of sound striking them. A convex surface acts as a diffuser, but a concave surface does the opposite, concentrating sound into a point.

Diffraction

Diffraction is the bending of sound waves around an object and the re-radiation of energy through an opening. Diffraction makes it possible to hear sounds around corners and behind walls, or through a small opening in an obstruction.

The way sound behaves when it encounters an obstruction, or an opening in an obstruction, changes according to the obstruction's or opening's size in relation to the sound's wavelength. For example, low frequencies encountering an obstruction such as a large wall will bend around that wall, while high frequencies will not. If the obstruction is small compared to the impinging wavelength, it is almost as though the obstruction isn't there; sound just bends around it. The same-sized obstruction would, however, be a barrier to high frequencies.

Diffraction is easily demonstrated by standing behind your loudspeakers; you'll hear bass but no treble. This is because low frequencies can diffract around the loudspeaker cabinet, but mid and high frequencies cannot. The loudspeaker cabinet is small compared to the bass wavelengths, but large in relation to midrange and treble wavelengths.

This phenomenon is shown in Fig.A-5. The following excerpt is the caption accompanying Fig.A-5, reprinted from the McGraw-Hill *Audio Engineering Handbook* by K. Benson, with permission:

Stylized illustration of the diffraction of sound waves passing through openings and around obstacles. The sound waves are depicted by their wave-

fronts. The distance between successive wavefronts is the wavelength. The sound waves approaching the barriers are shown as plane waves, as is approximately the case when the source of sound is far away. (a) The wavelength is large compared with the size of the opening and the obstacle. The sound radiates from the small opening as a spherical wave, dispersing equally in all directions and displaying no shadowing behind the small obstacle. (b) The wavelength is small compared with the size of the opening and the obstacle. The plane wave continues through the opening with only slight spreading, and there is a substantial shadow zone behind the obstacle. Although it is not shown, some of the sound would also be reflected back toward the source.

Fig. A-5 How sound behaves when it encounters an obstacle or opening depends on the obstacle's or opening's size in relation to the wavelength of sound.

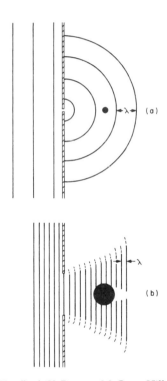

Courtesy *Audio Engineering Handbook*, K. Benson, McGraw-Hill, Inc., 1988

Diffraction can cause problems in loudspeaker performance: When sound from the drivers reaches the cabinet edge, the energy is re-radiated. This makes it appear acoustically as though the sound is coming from more than one source (the driver and the cabinet edges). Because this energy re-radiated from the cabinet edges is delayed in relation to the driver's output (it travels slightly farther), the two signals combine to produce peaks and dips in the loudspeaker's frequency response due to constructive and destructive interference (similar to the comb-filtering effects described earlier). Diffraction can be reduced in loudspeakers by rounded baffles, recessed driver mounting bolts, low-profile grille frames, and absorbent material around the drivers. Diffraction is one reason why loudspeakers sound better with their grilles removed.

The Decibel (dB)

An understanding of the decibel is essential to understanding many aspects of sound and audio. Decibel notation is a convenient way of expressing very large numbers, and also corresponds closely with our perception of sound. A figure in decibels can describe the magnitude of voltages, electrical powers, acoustic powers, and sound pressure levels.

The decibel doesn't express an absolute value, but a *ratio* between *two* values. When we say that one CD player has 2.5dB higher output voltage than another, we are expressing the *difference* in output voltages *between* the players. In the case of our CD players, the decibel notation expresses the *ratio* of their respective output voltages. Any time a decibel notation is used, it must be accompanied by a reference level either to another level, as with the two CD players, or against a standard reference.

This is where the dB notation's suffix comes into play. The letters after the number of dB (80dB SPL, or –20dBFS, for examples) denote the reference level to which the expressed value is referenced. If we say a certain *sound pressure level* (SPL) is 80dB SPL, "SPL" tells us that the sound pressure is referenced to 0dB SPL, the threshold of hearing. By saying "80dB SPL," we mean that the sound is 80dB greater in magnitude than the threshold of hearing. Note that 0dB SPL isn't absolute silence, but the softest sound an average person can hear in a very quiet environment.

The decibel scale is logarithmic, meaning that as the number of dB increases arithmetically, the value that number expresses increases exponentially. For example, each doubling of sound pressure level represents an increase of 6dB, as shown in Table 1.

Sound or electrical power ratio	Decibels	Sound pressure, voltage, or current ratio	Decibels
1	0	1	0
2	3.0	2	6.0
3	4.8	3	9.5
4	6.0	4	12.0
5	7.0	5	14.0
6	7.8	6	15.6
7	8.5	7	16.9
8	9.0	8	18.1
9	9.5	9	19.1
10	10.0	10	20.0
100	20.0	100	40.0
1,000	30.0	1,000	60.0
10,000	40.0	10,000	80.0
100,000	50.0	100,000	100.0
1,000,000	60.0	1,000,000	120.0

Let's say you were in a very quiet room and measured the sound of a fly buzzing at 40dB SPL. We can see in Table 1 that 40dB represents a pressure ratio of 100; the sound of the buzzing fly produces a pressure 100 times greater than a sound at 0dB SPL, the threshold of hearing. The threshold of hearing, represented by the reference level of 0dB SPL, has been established as a pressure of 0.0002 dynes per square centimeter (dynes/cm^2). A dyne is a unit of force. The letters "SPL" after the decibel notation tell us that 0.0002 dynes/cm^2 is the reference level. Knowing this, we can calculate that the sound a buzzing fly produces is a pressure 100 times that of the pressure at 0dB SPL, or 0.02 dynes/cm^2 (100 x 0.0002).

Two flies would produce a sound pressure level of 46dB—double the pressure, and an increase of 6dB over the 40dB one fly produces. Because 40dB represents a pressure of 0.02 dynes/cm^2, 46dB represents a pressure of 0.04 dynes/cm^2. (For the purposes of this illustration, we'll assume the flies produce the same sound pressure, and that their sounds are perfectly in-phase with each other. In reality, the phase relationship between the two sounds will be random, producing a sound *power* increase of 3dB.)

Now consider another example: Let's say that a jet taking off produces an SPL of 120dB. Looking at Table 1, we see that 120dB represents a ratio of 1,000,000—in other words, the jet creates a pressure on our eardrums a million times greater than the pressure at the threshold of hearing. Multiplying 1,000,000 by the reference pressure (0.0002 dynes/cm^2), we know that the jet creates a pressure of 200 dynes/cm^2 (0.0002 x 1,000,000).

If we add a second jet taking off, we know that the number of dB SPL will increase from 120dB to 126dB, and also that the pressure will double from 200 dynes/cm^2 to 400 dynes/cm^2. (Again, we'll assume for illustrative purposes that the jets produce equal loudness and are in-phase.)

Obviously, the sound of the second jet taking off is much greater than that of the second fly. But both increased the sound pressure level by the same *ratio*: 6dB. The same 6dB increase represented an increase of only 0.02 dynes/cm^2 in the case of the buzzing fly, but a whopping 200 dynes/cm^2 with the jet.

This logarithmic nature of the decibel makes handing very large numbers easier. These very large numbers are needed to express the vast range of sound pressure levels we can accommodate, from the threshold of hearing to the threshold of pain. The threshold of pain, 140dB SPL, is a pressure on your eardrum of 2000 dynes/cm^2, or ten million times the pressure at the threshold of hearing. Rather than saying that the threshold of pain is 10,000,000 times louder than the threshold of hearing, it's easier to represent this value as 140dB.

Moreover, this exponential increase parallels our subjective impression of loudness. If we asked a person listening to music at 60dB SPL to turn up the volume until it was "twice as loud," the person would increase the volume by about ten dB. If the person were listening at 100dB SPL and was asked to turn up the volume until it was twice as loud, he would also increase the volume by 10dB. As we can extrapolate from the fly and jet examples, the increase in pressure from 60dB to 70dB is far less than the pressure increase from 100dB to 110dB. Both increases, however, produce similar subjective increases in loudness.

This phenomenon is analogous to the way we perceive pitch: We hear each doubling of frequency as an octave, yet each ascending octave spans a frequency difference twice that of the next lower octave. The octave span between 20Hz and 40Hz is perceived as the same musical interval as the octave between 10kHz and 20kHz, although the latter is a much larger change in frequency.

We can calculate the number of dB between two values with the following formula: *NdB = 20 log P1/Pr* where *NdB* = the number of dB, *P1* is the measured pressure, and *Pr* is the reference pressure. Expressing this formula verbally, we say, "The number of dB equals twenty times the logarithm of the ratio between the two pressures (or voltages, or currents)." This formula works for voltage, electrical current, or sound pressure level. Just as a doubling in SPL is represented by an increase of 6dB, a doubling of voltage is represented by an increase of 6dB.

Using this formula, we can calculate the difference in dB between two CD players having different output voltages. We'll say CD player A puts out 3.6V when playing a full-scale, 1kHz test tone, and CD player B puts out 2.8V with the same test signal. How much difference in dB is there between the two players?

We first find the ratio between the two voltages by dividing 3.6 by 2.8. The ratio is 1.2857. By pressing the "log" key on a calculator with 1.2857 in the display, we get the logarithm of the ratio (0.0109). Then we multiply the result by 20, giving us the answer in dB. CD player A's output voltage is 2.18dB higher than that of CD player B.

Calculating power ratios is slightly different. With acoustic or electrical power, an increase of 3dB represents a doubling of power. This is given by the following formula: *NdB = 10 log P1/Pr* where *P1* is the measured power and *Pr* is the reference power. If we want to find the difference in power output in dB between two amplifiers, we multiply the logarithm of the ratio of the two values by 10, not by 20 as in voltage, current, and sound pressure.

Let's say one power amplifier has a maximum output power of 138W, and another has a maximum output power of 276W. What is the decibel difference between them? First find the ratio between the two powers by dividing 276 by 138. The answer is 2. Find the logarithm of 2 (0.301) and multiply by 10. The answer is that the second amplifier has 3dB more output power than the first amplifier. Note that a doubling of power yields an increase of 3dB.

Frequency, Loudness, and Equal Loudness Contours

So far, we've looked at only the purely physical properties of sound and how it behaves. But sound is meaningless without our perception of it. *Psychoacoustics* is the study of the interaction between the physical properties of sound and our perceptions of those physical properties.

Humans can perceive a frequency range of sound from about 16Hz to 18kHz. The commonly cited range of 20Hz–20kHz is less accurate but easier to remember and express. In reality, most people can hear tones below 20Hz, but few can hear above 18kHz. Teenagers and young to middle-aged women can hear above 18kHz, but that sensitivity decreases with age. It has been proved that women have a greater ability to hear high frequencies than men, and that they retain this ability longer. Although we can't hear sinewaves higher than 20kHz, we *can* hear the effects of limiting the frequency response to 20kHz. The wider the audio system's bandwidth, the faster it can follow steep transient signals. An audio bandwidth of 20kHz isn't wide enough to accurately follow rapid dynamic changes in the music.

This frequency range is wider than it first appears; the frequency span is huge when considering the wavelength of sound. A 16Hz tone has a wavelength of more than 70'; an 18kHz tone has a wavelength of about 3/4".

One of our most fundamental auditory perceptions is *loudness*, the term that describes the magnitude of an auditory event. Loudness is a *perception* that is influenced by factors other than the physical amplitude of sound. In fact, we perceive loudness very differently depending on the sound's frequency. This was first established by two researchers, Fletcher and Munson, who produced a set of curves called the *equal-loudness contours*, also known as *Fletcher-Munson curves*.

The equal-loudness contours (Fig.A-6) show how much difference in sound pressure level is required to make all frequencies have the same perceived loudness as the 1kHz reference tone. The numbers running down the middle above each curve are *phons*, a measure of loudness. At the reference frequency of 1kHz, phons are equal to dB.

For example, at a very quiet level of 30 phons (30dB SPL at 1kHz), a bass tone of 50Hz would have to be reproduced at 60dB SPL to be perceived as having the same loudness as the 30dB SPL 1kHz tone. In other words, our ears are less sensitive at the bass and treble frequency extremes than in the midrange.

This large disparity in sensitivity with frequency is more acute at low sound pressure levels, shown by the steep slope of the curves at the graph bottom, and by the gradual flattening of the curves toward the graph top. As the SPL increases, our ears become nearly equally sensitive at all frequencies. At 110 phons (110dB at 1kHz), a 50Hz tone would need to be reproduced at 120dB to be perceived as being

Fig. A-6
The perception of loudness is affected by a sound's frequency and volume.

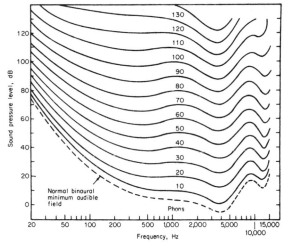

Courtesy *Audio Engineering Handbook*, K. Benson, McGraw-Hill, Inc., 1988

of equal loudness to the 1kHz tone—quite a difference from the 30 phon example.

Everyone has heard this effect; when you turn up the volume on your hi-fi, you hear more bass and treble. The bass seems to extend lower in frequency, and there's more of it. Conversely, if you turn down the volume to where it's barely audible, you hear only midrange sounds. The "Loudness" button on mid-fi receivers boosts the bass and treble to compensate for the ears' reduced sensitivity to bass and treble at low volume.

Weighting Filters

SPL measurements, and measurements of noise in audio equipment, often invoke a *weighting filter* to remove some bass and treble from the reading. Weighting filters attempt to simulate our reduced sensitivity to bass and treble and produce a measurement that more accurately reflects

Fig A-7
Weighting curves applied to SPL or noise measurements approximate the ear's varying sensitivity with frequency.

Courtesy *Audio Engineering Handbook*, K. Benson, McGraw-Hill, Inc., 1988

the perceived sound or noise level. Fig.A-7 shows the three weighting curves used in SPL and noise measurements.

A signal-to-noise specification for a preamplifier, for example, may read "85dB, `A' weighted." This means the noise was filtered with the curve with the characteristics of curve "A" in Fig.A-7 *before* the preamplifier's noise level was measured. Consequently, applying the weighting curve makes the signal-to-noise ratio appear higher. Similarly, a weighting curve applied to an SPL measurement makes the measured SPL seem lower than the physical magnitude of the sound.

The Dynamic Nature of Music

So far we've talked about sound only in the context of steady, continuous tones. But music is dynamic, constantly changing in level, and is composed of impulsive sounds as well as steady ones. A basic understanding of this dynamic quality is important to learning about music reproduction.

We can divide a dynamic sound into three components: *attack*, *internal dynamics*, and *decay* (see Fig.A-8). These three aspects of a sound are called the sound's *envelope*. Attack is the way in which a sound begins. The attack can be sudden (a snare drum, for example) or gradual (the build-up of an organ note in a large room). Decay is the way a sound ends. Internal dynamics are the main portion of the sound between the attack and decay. The envelopes shown in Fig.A-8 could be for a snare drum (left figure) or an organ (right). The snare drum has a very sudden attack; it takes very little time for the sound to reach its highest volume. It also has a very short duration and a rapid decay. By contrast, the organ has a very slow attack, taking a longer time to reach

Fig. A-8 Musical sounds are composed of an attack, internal dynamics, and decay.

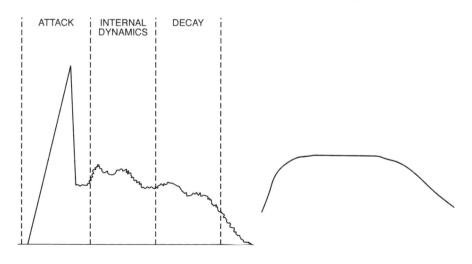

ATTACK | INTERNAL DYNAMICS | DECAY

its full amplitude. The internal dynamics are very long, and define the note's sound. Similarly, the decay is slow and gradual.

A sound characterized by sudden attack and rapid decay is a *transient* signal. *Transient response* refers to an audio component's or system's ability to reproduce the steep attack of transient signals. This type of signal has a high *peak-to-average ratio*, meaning that the peaks are much higher in level than the average level. Conversely, the organ has no peaks, so it has a very low peak-to-average ratio. A sound's peak-to-average ratio greatly influences the perceived volume; the ear tends to integrate the sound so that peaks add very little to the overall perceived volume.

Another way of expressing the dynamics of a musical signal is the term *dynamic range*—the difference between the loudest and softest sounds. Technically, a piece of audio equipment's dynamic range is the difference in dB between the device's noise floor and its maximum undistorted signal level. Subjectively, dynamic range is the contrast between a piece of music's quietest and loudest passages.

Localization

Localization is our ability to identify the spatial position of a sound. This ability to localize sounds derives in part from the fact that we have two ears, and that sounds arriving at each ear differ slightly from one another. The brain uses these differences (and other cues) to construct a three-dimensional representation of where a sound source is located.

The most basic mechanism for localizing a sound source is attenuation of high frequencies by the head. Low frequencies can diffract around the head more easily than high frequencies, causing one ear to receive a signal with a gradual attenuation of the midrange and treble. The brain interprets this high-frequency rolloff at one ear as a cue that the sound originates closer to the other ear.

At low frequencies (below about 700Hz), there is virtually no amplitude difference between the left and right ears for a sound emanating from one side. The sound diffracts around the head and the treble-rolloff localization cue doesn't exist. At these low frequencies, a second mechanism takes over in which the phase difference between the left and right ears is analyzed. Because low frequencies have long wavelengths compared to the size of the head, one ear receives a slightly different phase of the sound wave. This information is another cue as to the location of a sound source.

The head, upper body, and outer ear (called the *pinna*) also modify the acoustic signals before they reach the ear. The pinna's unusual shape reflects sounds from its structures into the ear. These reflections combine with sounds directly striking the eardrum, causing comb-filter effects.

The brain processes the resultant cancellations and reinforcements to determine a sound source's direction. This mechanism is described further in the Chapter 12 section called "Binaural Recording."

The Listening Environment Diagnostic Recording (LEDR) on the first Chesky Test CD (Chesky JD37) is a synthesized percussion sound that appears in one loudspeaker, then slowly moves across to the other loudspeaker. Another LEDR test moves the image from the loudspeaker up to a plane above the loudspeaker. The third LEDR test moves the image in an arc from one loudspeaker to the other. These special signals, used to evaluate a listening room, were created by simulating the frequency and amplitude cues imposed by the pinna. By creating notches in the signal's spectrum at precisely calculated frequencies, the signal simulates the effect of a sound source's movement.

You can conduct a simple experiment to demonstrate the pinna's effect on localization. Close your eyes and have a friend jingle keys about four feet away from you, either at head level, waist level, or knee level. Point to where the sound is coming from. Now repeat the experiment with your hands folding your outer ears forward. This eliminates the pinna cues that aid in localization, making it much more difficult to tell where the sound of the keys is originating.

Other Psychoacoustic Phenomena

An interesting phenomenon occurs when we hear a direct sound and a delayed version of that sound (as we would hear an echo). If the echo occurs within about 30ms (milliseconds) of the first sound, the echo isn't perceived as a discrete sound, but instead slightly modifies the sound's timbre. This first 30ms is called the *fusion zone*, and the phenomenon is called the *Haas Effect*.

Similarly, when exposed to a direct and a delayed sound that originate from different directions, we hear the sound as coming from the direction of the first sound. The ear ignores the second sound. Dolby Surround decoding exploits this phenomenon to increase the apparent channel separation between front and rear channels.

Masking is a psychoacoustic phenomenon that renders one sound inaudible when accompanied by a louder sound. Our inability to hear a conversation in the presence of loud amplified music is an example of masking; the music masks the conversation. Similarly, we hear tape hiss or record-surface noise only during quiet passages, not during most of the music. Masking is particularly effective when the masking sound has a similar frequency to the masked component. This kind of masking is called *simultaneous masking*.

Masking also occurs when two sounds are close together in time, an effect called *temporal masking*. The ear/brain tends to hear only the louder of the two sounds—oddly, within a limited time window, it doesn't matter if the louder sound occurred slightly earlier or slightly later than the softer sound. Although it seems logically impossible that a later sound could mask an earlier sound, this occurs because it takes time for the auditory system to process the signal and send it to the brain. When confronted by a louder sound slightly later in time, the louder sound takes precedence.

This appendix is meant only as a cursory survey of the basics of sound and hearing for the interested audiophile; the subject can be studied in great depth. For those interested in learning more about sound and hearing, I recommend the superb introduction to the subject by Dr. Floyd Toole in *Audio Engineering Handbook*, published by McGraw-Hill, ISBN 0-07-004777-4. Further references are included in Dr. Toole's chapters.

Appendix B: Audio and Electronics Basics

A knowledge of electronics and audio technology isn't necessary to choosing and enjoying a high-end music system. You can just select a system, set it up, and not worry about what's going on inside those mysterious black boxes.

Some audiophiles, however, want at least a basic understanding of how audio products work. They have an inherent fascination with audio equipment and want to broaden their knowledge of high-end audio to include a basic conception of electronics and audio circuits. This Appendix is by no means a comprehensive treatment of the subject—that could fill many books. Instead, it provides an overview of audio technology for the interested audiophile.

Moreover, it bridges the gap between the technical descriptions of products published in some high-end audio magazines and the reader who feels intimidated by all the technical jargon. So next time you read that a particular power amplifier has a transformer with dual secondary windings, three full-wave bridge rectifiers, a discrete, direct-coupled JFET Class-A input and driver stage, with a push-pull output stage that switches to Class B operation at 20W RMS, you'll know what it means.

But before we get to all that, let's take a look at the basic vocabulary of electronics and audio technology.

Voltage, Current, Resistance, and Power

The most basic elements of electronics are voltage, current, and resistance. Let's look first at voltage.

A *voltage* exists between two points when one point has an excess of electrons in relation to the other point. A battery is a good example: the negative terminal has an excess of electrons in relation to the positive terminal. When this happens, we say the battery is *charged*.

Voltage is also called *potential difference*, because it has the *potential* to do work and because voltage is always the *difference* in the electrical charges between two points. This is why we say a voltage exists *across* two points, such as a pair of loudspeaker terminals (when driven by an amplifier), or the positive and negative terminals of a battery. One point is more negative (an excess of electrons) than the other point. The *volt* is the unit of measurement that expresses just how great the difference in electrons between two points is. Another way of thinking of voltage is as electrical pressure, like the pressure in a water faucet.

When an electrical *conductor* such as a wire connects two points that have a voltage across them, *current* flows. Current is the electron charge moving through the conductor. The electrons travel through the conductor from the negative charge to the positive charge. If we put a wire across a battery's terminals, current will flow until both terminals have the same number of electrons; the potential difference no longer exists and the battery is discharged, or "dead." Current from a battery is called *direct current*, or *DC*, because the voltage pushing the electrons produces a steady, non-fluctuating electron flow.

If voltage is analogous to water pressure in a faucet, current flow is analogous to water moving through a hose (the conductor). Just as water in the hose is pushed by the pressure of the water behind it, current flows through a conductor pushed by voltage. Current is measured in *amperes*, or *amps* for short.

Resistance is opposition to current flow. If our hose had a kink in it, the flow of water would be reduced. Similarly, an electrical resistance opposes current flow, reducing the number of electrons flowing through the conductor. The higher the resistance, the less the current flow in the conductor (given the same voltage). The unit of electrical resistance is the *ohm*.

Ohm's Law

With that introduction, let's look at a simple circuit involving voltage, current, and resistance. Fig.B-1 is a schematic diagram and pictorial representation of a battery connected to a resistor by a conductor. The dashed arrow shows the direction of current flow *through* the resistor, and the two solid arrows point to the voltage *across* the resistor. The voltage source supplies electrons that flow through the conductor and resistor, returning to the positive battery terminal. The current flow will be maintained as long as the voltage exists across the battery.

The amount of current flow is determined by two things: the resistor's resistance value and the battery's voltage. More resistance will decrease current flow. Conversely, a higher voltage will increase current flow. This relationship is expressed by *Ohm's law*, which states that one volt of charge across one ohm of resistance will push one ampere of current. Mathematically, Ohm's law is $E = I \times R$. E is *electromotive force* (another term for voltage), I is current (for "intensity" of electron flow), and R is resistance. If we know any two values, we can calculate the third using Ohm's law. For example, if we know the voltage and current and want to find the resistance, the formula is $R = E/I$. If we want to find the current from the voltage and resistance, we use $I = E/R$.

Fig. B-1 A simple series circuit. Electrons from the negative battery terminal flow through the resistor to the positive battery terminal.

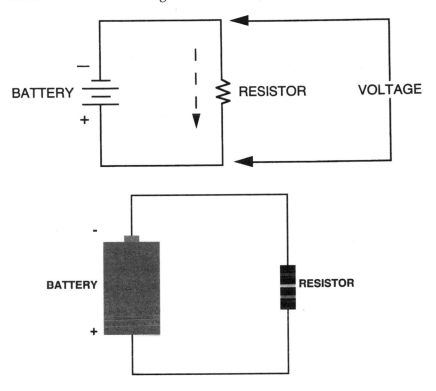

Let's put some units on our schematic diagram (Fig.B-2). We'll say the voltage is 10V and the resistance is 100 ohms. How much current flows through the resistor? Using $I = E/R$, we divide 10 by 100, getting 0.1 ampere, also expressed as 100 milliamps (100mA). If the resistance is doubled, the current is halved. Similarly, doubling the voltage doubles the current flow. This relationship between voltage, current, and resistance is perfectly linear.

Fig. B-2 With an applied voltage of 10V and a resistance of 100 ohms, the current flow through the resistor is 0.1 ampere (100mA).

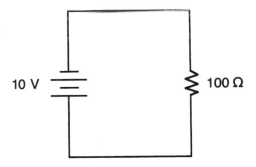

There's another factor here that particularly concerns us in audio— *power*. Power is an expression of the amount of work done by the voltage and current, measured in watts. Power is the product of voltage and current, expressed by Ohm's law as $P = I \times E$ (power equals the current times the voltage). Power is dissipated as heat in the resistor. A resistor is also called the *load*. Going back to our schematic of Fig.B-2, we can calculate the power dissipated by the resistor. We know that the voltage across the resistor is 10V, and the current through the resistor is 0.1A. Multiplying the voltage by the current tells us that the power dissipated by the resistor is 1 watt (10 x 0.1). Again, the relationship between power, voltage, current, and resistance is linear.

A power amplifier's output power is a product of its output voltage and current. It describes how much *voltage* the amplifier can develop *across* the load (the loudspeaker input), and how much *current* it can drive *through* the load. Current flow through voice coils in the loudspeaker's drive units makes the cones move back and forth, producing sound.

A perfect amplifier would double its power as the load resistance is halved: it would maintain its voltage and double its current. We know from Ohm's law that if the voltage is kept the same and the current is doubled, the power will double. Such an amplifier is called a *perfect voltage source*. Most amplifiers, however, can't maintain the same voltage across a low-impedance load as they can across a higher impedance, thus the power available to drive a low-impedance loudspeaker is reduced. Amplifiers can also run out of current, again limiting the power delivered to the load.

Series and Parallel Circuits

So far we've discussed a type of circuit called a *series* circuit. In a series circuit, there is only one path through which current can flow. A *parallel* circuit provides multiple paths for current flow. If we add another resistor to our series circuit, we've turned it into a parallel circuit (Fig.B-3). Some of the current flows through the first resistor, some through the second resistor.

Fig. B-3 A parallel circuit provides more than one path for current.

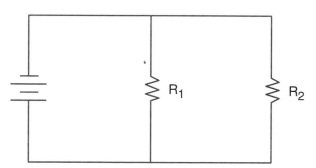

Let's look at series and parallel circuits from the standpoint of a power amplifier driving loudspeakers. An amplifier driving a single loudspeaker is shown in Fig.B-4. The amplifier and loudspeaker form a series circuit; there is only one path for current. If we want to add another loudspeaker to this amplifier channel, we can do it two ways. The first is to put the second loudspeaker in series with the first one (Fig.B-5). The same current flows through both loudspeakers. In a series circuit, the individual resistances are added to find the total resistance. If each loudspeaker presents a resistance of 8 ohms, the total load the amplifier must drive is 16 ohms.

Fig. B-4 An amplifier driving a loudspeaker is a series circuit.

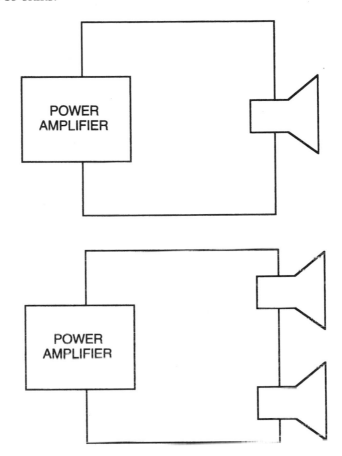

Fig. B-5 Two loudspeakers in series

Another way to connect the second loudspeaker is to wire it in parallel with the first one (Fig.B-6). We've now provided more than one path for current; some current flows through loudspeaker 1, some through loudspeaker 2. Unlike a series circuit, in which the resistances are added to find the total resistance, adding a parallel resistance *lowers* the total resistance (R_T). In the case of our two 8-ohm loudspeakers in parallel, the total resistance the amplifier must drive is 4 ohms. When two equal resistances are in parallel, the total resistance is half that of one resistance. The total resistance (R_T) in a parallel circuit can also be found with the formula $1/R_T = 1/R_1 + 1/R_2 + 1/R_3$, etc.

Parallel circuits differ from series circuits in that the voltage across each branch of a parallel circuit is the same as the applied voltage. If we put ten resistors of different resistance values in parallel and apply a source voltage of 20V, that 20V will appear across all ten resistors. However, the current flow will be different through each resistor. It's the current that changes in parallel circuits, not the voltage.

Fig. B-6 Two loudspeakers in parallel

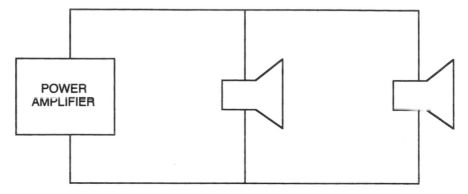

Conversely, in a series circuit, the current remains the same while the voltage across each resistor is different. As current flows through each resistor in series, some of the applied voltage is dropped across each resistor. The amount of that voltage drop is determined by the resistor's resistance value. The sum of the voltage drops across each resistor equals the applied voltage.

Let's work through examples of series and parallel circuits using Ohm's law. We'll build two circuits with identical components, one of them a series circuit and the other a parallel circuit. Fig.B-7 is a series circuit with three resistors.

Fig. B-7 Current flow is the same in all parts of a series circuit.

To find out how much current flows through this circuit, and how much voltage exists across each resistor, we first find the circuit's total resistance. In a series circuit, the total resistance is the sum of the individual resistances. By adding R_1, R_2, and R_3, we know that $R_T = 60$ ohms. Because we know the applied voltage (12V), we use Ohm's law to find the current, specifically $I = E/R$ (current equals voltage divided by the resistance). By dividing the applied voltage by the total resistance, we know that the current flowing through this circuit is 0.2 amperes, or

200mA (200 milliamps). And because current flow is the same in all parts of a series circuit, 200mA flows through all three resistors.

As just mentioned, current flow through the resistors produces a voltage drop across each resistor. To find the individual voltage drops, we turn again to Ohm's law. Using the formula $E = I \times R$ (voltage equals current multiplied by the resistance), we can calculate the voltage drops. We know that R_1 is 10 ohms, and that the current flowing through it is 0.2A. The voltage drop across R_1 is therefore 2V. Similarly, the voltage drop across R_2 is the current multiplied by the resistance (0.2 x 20), or 4V. Repeating the process for R_3 tells us that 6V is dropped across the third resistor. This illustrates that current flow is the same in all parts of a series circuit, but that the voltage across each resistor changes. Also, the sum of the voltage drops equals the applied voltage.

Fig.B-8 shows the same applied voltage and resistors of the same value, but connected in parallel. In this case, the voltage across the three resistors remains the same, but the current flow through each is different. Using the formula $1/R_T = 1/R_1 + 1/R_2 + 1/R_3$, we see that this circuit's total resistance is 5.45 ohms. The current flow through R_1 will be 12V/10 ohms, or 1.2A. The current through R_2 is 12V/20 ohms, or 0.6A. The current through R_3 is 12V/30 ohms, or 0.4A.

Fig. B 8 In a parallel circuit, the voltage across each resistor is the same, but the current through each resistor changes.

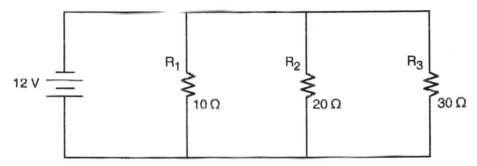

Note that, at each resistor in the parallel circuit, the voltage stayed the same while the amount of current flow was different—the opposite of the series circuit.

Alternating Current (AC)

So far we've talked only about circuits using direct current (DC). Another type of current, called *alternating current*, or *AC*, is the basis for all audio circuits. An audio signal is an example of an AC voltage. An AC voltage reverses polarity, producing current that reverses direction. The principles of DC circuits and Ohm's law described earlier still apply, but AC circuits use additional elements we'll discuss later.

Let's use the AC power line from a wall outlet as an example of AC voltage and current. The 120 volts from the wall socket appear across the socket's two vertical slots. The voltage's polarity (which slot is positive, which negative) reverses itself at the rate of 60 times per second, or 60 Hertz (*Hz*). If we looked at this 120V, 60Hz voltage we'd see the waveform in Fig.B-9.

Fig. B-9 The 120V, 60Hz AC from a wall socket is a sinewave.

Starting at the left side of Fig.B-9, the voltage increases until it reaches its positive peak, then decreases to the zero crossing line (no voltage). The voltage then increases again, but in the opposite polarity. After reaching its negative peak, it decreases again. This represents one complete cycle of a sinewave, sixty of which occur every second. The reversing-polarity voltage causes current to reverse direction in whatever conductor is attached to it—usually an AC power cord and power transformer.

An audio signal is also an AC signal, but unlike our simple 60Hz sinewave, an audio signal is a *complex* AC voltage because it's composed of many frequencies. The AC audio signal is an electrical analog of the sound-pressure wave that created the original audio event. Just as a sound wave is composed of compressions and rarefactions, the audio signal is composed of positive and negative polarity phases.

AC voltage can be expressed in two ways: *peak-to-peak* (p-p) and *root mean square* (RMS). In a p-p expression, the voltage between the waveform peaks is measured. The more commonly used RMS value specifies the voltage at roughly 70% of the peak voltage. RMS better describes the "effective" voltage, or the ability of the voltage to do work. The 120V AC power line has a peak value of 170V, but an RMS value of 120V. Whenever you see an audio signal expressed as a voltage—a preamplifier output level, for example—it is virtually always an RMS value.

Manufacturers of power amplifiers sometimes exploit this difference between peak and RMS to overstate a product's power output. An amplifier can deliver more power on peaks than continuously. Chapter 6 ("Power Amplifiers") has a more complete discussion of power-amplifier output ratings.

Electromagnetic Induction, Inductance, and Capacitance

We've learned how voltage is equivalent to electrical pressure, current is the flow of electrons "pushed" by the voltage, and resistance is the opposition to current flow. Now let's look at three more electrical properties very important in audio: electromagnetic induction, inductance, and capacitance.

Electromagnetic induction is the relationship between moving electrons and magnetism; moving electrons produce a magnetic field, and a moving magnetic field causes electrons to flow through a conductor. Many audio devices, from phono cartridges to loudspeakers, rely on electromagnetic induction to work.

Let's first look at how a moving magnetic field causes electrons to flow. If you have a conductor, a magnetic field, and relative motion between them, a current (electron flow) will be *induced* in the conductor. For example, if we move a magnet upward through a coil of wire (the conductor), a voltage will be induced across that wire. A pointer on a voltmeter across that coil will swing in one direction when the magnet is moved. When the magnet stops moving, the pointer will return to its original position—no more voltage is being induced across the coil. Now, if we move the magnet in the opposite direction, a voltage will also be induced, but of opposite polarity to that of the voltage induced by moving the magnet up. The voltmeter pointer will now swing to the opposite side of the meter while the magnet is moving. When the magnet stops moving, the pointer will return to its center zero position.

This is exactly how a phono cartridge works. In a moving-coil cartridge, the coils (left and right audio channels) are attached to the cantilever; the cantilever is moved back and forth by the stylus as the stylus follows the modulations in the record groove. The coils sit in a fixed magnetic field. As the coil moves back and forth, a voltage is induced across the coil—the audio signal. The coil cuts through *magnetic lines of flux* surrounding the magnets, inducing a voltage across the coil. The faster the coil cuts these magnetic lines of flux, the higher the induced voltage. The more turns on the coil, the more lines of flux are cut, and the higher the induced voltage. High-output moving-coil cartridges have more turns on their windings than low-output moving-coils. A moving-magnet cartridge works on exactly the same principle, but with the roles reversed: the magnets move and the coils are fixed.

There's another interesting phenomenon of electromagnetic induction: electrons flowing through a conductor create a magnetic field around that conductor. A conductor connected across a battery's terminals will be surrounded by a magnetic field. If we make current flow in the opposite direction by reversing the battery terminals, the north-south magnetic field will also reverse polarity. The magnetic field's density can be increased by coiling the wire to concentrate the magnetic lines of flux, creating a device called an *inductor*, which creates a property called *inductance*. Inductance is measured in henrys (the unit of inductance) and is represented by the letter *L*. (The schematic symbol for an inductor is shown in Fig.B-10).

A loudspeaker works on this principle. When current flows through a loudspeaker's voice coil, a magnetic field is set up around that coil.

This magnetic field reacts with the fixed magnetic field generated by the magnets surrounding the voice coil. One polarity of the signal-generated magnetic field makes the loudspeaker cone move forward; the opposite polarity makes it move backward. When we apply an AC audio signal to the loudspeaker, AC current flow through the voice coil causes a reversing magnetic field to be set up around the voice coil, making the voice coil move back and forth, and, with it, the loudspeaker's cone.

Fig. B-10 The schematic symbol for an inductor.

Let's look more closely at what happens when alternating current flows through a coil of wire (an inductor). The AC current flow creates a magnetic field around the coil that expands, collapses, expands in the opposite polarity, and collapses again. The constantly changing magnetic field follows the AC sinewave voltage applied across the coil. (At DC, there is no expanding and collapsing magnetic field, and thus no induced voltage and no opposition to current flow—the inductor looks electrically just like a simple piece of wire.)

We've just satisfied the requirements for electromagnetic induction: a conductor, a magnetic field, and relative motion between them. The relative motion results from the expanding and contracting magnetic field. This fluctuating magnetic field causes magnetic lines of flux to move through the coil, inducing a voltage across that coil.

This induced voltage opposes the applied voltage, reducing current flow. The higher the alternating current frequency, the greater the induced voltage and the greater the opposition to the applied voltage. At a very low frequency, say 5Hz, the magnetic field expands and collapses very slowly, inducing only a very low voltage across the coil to oppose the drive signal. Conversely, at very high frequencies, the rapidly expanding and collapsing magnetic field induces a much higher voltage across the coil to oppose the drive signal.

This opposition to AC current flow in a coil is called *inductive reactance*. The term *reactance* describes how the coil *reacts* to the applied voltage: the higher the frequency of the applied voltage, the greater the opposition to current flow (the higher the reactance). An inductor can be thought of as a frequency-dependent resistor. The higher the frequency, the more it resists current flow.

Inductive reactance is represented by the term X_L. Inductive reactance is proportional to frequency, expressed in the formula $X_L = 2\pi fL$, where f is frequency in Hertz and L is inductance in henrys. For example, a 2-millihenry (2mH) inductor has an inductive reactance of 125.7

ohms at 10kHz. At 20kHz, the inductor's reactance is 251.3 ohms. The higher the frequency, the greater the reactance to the applied voltage.

A power transformer dramatically illustrates how inductive reactance reduces AC current flow. A power transformer consists of two coils of wire placed next to each other, with one coil connected to a 120V AC power line. The DC resistance of that coil is probably about an ohm. If we put 120V DC across one ohm of resistance, Ohm's law tells us that a huge amount of current will flow (120A), which would instantly burn up the transformer. But because that applied voltage is AC, the coil's inductive reactance opposes current flow and prevents the transformer coil from burning. At the 60Hz AC line frequency, the transformer looks like an impedance higher than one ohm.

Another reactive element is called *capacitance*, represented by the letter C and shown schematically in Fig.B-11. Just as inductance produces a reactance to an AC signal, capacitance also reacts to AC. While an inductor becomes more reactive at *high* frequencies, the capacitor becomes more reactive at *low* frequencies. The capacitor acts as a resistor that increases its resistance as frequency decreases, exactly the opposite of an inductor. A few paragraphs ago we saw that inductive reactance could be calculated with the formula $X_L = 2\pi fl$. To calculate capacitive reactance (X_C), we use the formula $X_C = 1/2\pi fC$. Note that capacitive reactance is a reciprocal function; as frequency increases, capacitive reactance decreases. The unit of capacitance is the *farad*.

Fig. B-11 The schematic symbol for a capacitor

Filters

We can exploit inductive and capacitive reactance to perform specialized functions in audio circuits. In a two-way loudspeaker, for example, we want only low frequencies to reach the woofer and only high frequencies to reach the tweeter. Consequently, we may design a circuit that looks something like Fig.B-12.

At low frequencies, the capacitor's high reactance opposes current flow. As the frequency increases, the reactance decreases and the capacitor begins to let current flow to the tweeter. At the highest frequencies, the capacitor virtually disappears electrically, allowing maximum current flow. The tweeter is thus protected from low frequencies while high frequencies are allowed to pass. Conversely, the inductor in series with the woofer has a very high reactance at high frequencies, and virtually no reactance at low frequencies.

Fig. B-12
Inductors and capacitors filter the audio signal, as in this loudspeaker crossover.

The capacitor forms a *high-pass filter* and the inductor is a *low-pass filter*. We've just created a simple loudspeaker crossover. (Practical loudspeaker crossovers are more complex.)

A single capacitor or inductor is called a *first-order filter*, producing a *rolloff* of 6dB per octave. Because inductive reactance doubles as the frequency is doubled, the passed voltage is halved when the signal frequency is increased by one octave. Similarly, capacitive reactance is doubled as the frequency is halved by one octave. Because a halving of voltage represents a decrease of 6dB, first-order filters have a rolloff of 6dB per octave. Another term for rolloff is *slope*. First-order filters are also called *single-pole* filters.

Steeper rolloffs can be realized with more inductors and capacitors. *Second-order filters* have a rolloff of 12dB per octave, *third-order filters* roll off at 18dB/octave, and *fourth-order filters* exhibit a 24dB/octave rolloff. Virtually all loudspeaker crossovers have slopes between first-order and fourth-order. These rolloffs are shown in Fig.7-22 on page 233 in Chapter 7.

In another combination of a capacitor and an inductor, a *bandpass* filter is created. The bandpass filter will roll off frequencies on either side of the *passband*. A three-way loudspeaker crossover will have a high-pass filter on the tweeter, a low-pass filter on the woofer, and a bandpass filter on the midrange driver.

A filter's *cutoff frequency* is the frequency at which the amplitude is reduced by 3dB. Similarly, the *bandwidth* of an audio device or filter is the frequency span between the –3dB points. All the filters described here are called *passive filters* because they aren't built around an amplifier. Filters that use amplifying devices are called *active filters*.

Capacitors are also used to block direct current, yet pass alternating current. As we'll see later in this chapter, many audio circuits mix DC with the AC audio signal. Putting a capacitor in series with the signal blocks the unwanted DC component and allows the desired AC audio signal to pass. The capacitor looks like an infinitely high resistance at DC, but a low-value resistor to AC signals.

Capacitors can also store a voltage. In fact, the definition of capacitance is the ability to store a charge. If we put a battery across a capacitor, electrons flow from the battery's negative terminal to the capacitor's plate. The voltage source redistributes electrons from one plate of the capacitor to the other. The applied voltage stays across the capacitor even after the battery is removed.

This stored charge can be lethal. A power amplifier with large power-supply capacitors can kill you even if the amplifier hasn't been plugged in for years. Even small capacitors can give you a shock. The storage ability of capacitors can be demonstrated by turning off your power amplifier while it is reproducing music. It takes several seconds for the music to fade after the amplifier's power source has been removed. The amplifier is running off the charge stored in its capacitors.

Impedance

Impedance is the opposition to current flow in an AC circuit, specified in ohms and represented by the symbol Z. Impedance is to an AC signal what resistance is to DC. If we're dealing with DC, opposition to current flow is resistance. If the voltage is AC, opposition to current flow is impedance. Because loudspeakers are driven by AC signals, they have an impedance, not a resistance.

Impedance differs from resistance in that impedance implies that the load is not a simple resistance, but a combination of resistance, inductive reactance, and capacitive reactance.

An audio playback chain is a series of impedances. Every component with an input presents an impedance to the signal driving it. The impedance a component presents to the drive signal is called its *input impedance* (also called *load impedance*). A digital processor's analog output drives the preamplifier's input impedance, the preamplifier drives the power amplifier's input impedance, and the power amplifier drives the loudspeaker's impedance. Impedance can be thought of as the load through which the component must force current.

Components in an audio chain also have an *output impedance*, or *source impedance*. If you think of a component—a CD player, for example—as an audio signal generator, its output impedance is like a resistance in series with that signal generator.

Generally, audio products have output impedances of between a few tens of ohms and a few hundred ohms. Input impedances, however, are very high, usually between 10,000 ohms (10k ohms) and 1,000,000 ohms (one Megohm, or one million ohms). A product with a 1M ohm impedance will draw less current through it than one with a 10k ohms input impedance. The higher the input impedance, the easier it is for the source component to drive; the input impedance is less of a load on the source component.

Let's combine our knowledge of Ohm's law, capacitance, and impedance to examine the interaction between a preamplifier and a power amplifier through a long run of interconnect. Fig.B-13 shows this circuit pictorially and schematically. Because all cables and interconnects have some inherent capacitance, we can represent the interconnect capacitance by the symbol for a capacitor between the signal conductor and ground. The preamp's output impedance is represented by the resistor in series with the signal generator. The power amplifier's input impedance is represented by the resistor inside the power amplifier outline.

Fig. D-13
A preamplifier-to-power-amplifier connection shown pictorially and schematically. The interconnect's capacitance is shown as the capacitor in parallel with the power amplifier's input.

Let's say that the preamp has a very low output impedance, the power amplifier has a high input impedance, and the cable capacitance is low. All these are ideal conditions. The power amplifier's high input impedance means very little current will flow, causing very little voltage drop across the preamplifier's output impedance. Because the cable's capacitance is low, its reactance will remain high up to a very high frequency. Everything works just fine.

But if the preamplifier has a high output impedance and the cable is excessively capacitive, we run into problems. At low frequencies, the cable capacitance has no effect: its capacitive reactance is extremely high. In fact, it's almost as if the capacitor weren't there. But as frequency rises and the capacitive reactance drops, the capacitor looks like a resistor connected to ground. The higher the frequency, the lower the value of the "resistor" connected between the signal and ground. Consequently, as the signal frequency increases, more and more of the drive signal is dropped across the source impedance and less and less across the load (the power amplifier's input). We've just created a low-pass filter. The

result is high-frequency rolloff across the power amplifier's input terminals. The capacitor provides high frequencies with an easier path to
ground than does the amplifier's input circuit.

Moreover, the greater current flow caused by the power amplifier's
low input impedance and the cable capacitance causes the preamplifier's
output stage to work harder, perhaps even becoming *current-limited*. This
condition occurs when the source can no longer supply the current
through the load, resulting in a clipped waveform.

The result of an impedance mismatch and high interconnect capacitance between a preamplifier and power amplifier is a rolled-off treble,
lack of air and extension, mushy bass, and loss of dynamics.

We can calculate the –3dB rolloff point for our low-pass filter using
the formula $F = 1/2\pi\, RC$. F is the –3dB point, R is the power amplifier's
input impedance in parallel with the source impedance, and C is the
interconnect capacitance in farads. Interconnect capacitance is measured
in picofarads (10^{-12} farads) per foot, with less than 100pF per foot considered low capacitance.

This example illustrates what can happen with an impedance mismatch between components, particularly if the cable is capacitive. Source
components should have an output impedance of less than a few hundred ohms, preferably a few tens of ohms. Input impedances should be
at least 47k ohms (a standard value).

Loudspeaker Phase Angle

Another application of our knowledge of impedance, capacitance, and inductance is understanding the concept of *phase angle* in a loudspeaker's impedance.
Phase angle describes how reactive a load is compared to the load's resistance.

A loudspeaker impedance measurement includes the impedance
magnitude plotted in ohms, but also a separate plot of how reactive the
loudspeaker is to the drive signal as a function of frequency. This reactance is caused by the inductors and capacitors in the loudspeaker's
crossover. Fig.B-14 is a loudspeaker's impedance magnitude and phase-
angle plot. If we performed this measurement on a resistor (which
exhibits no inductive or capacitive reactance), we would see straight
lines on the impedance-magnitude and phase-angle traces (the latter is
dotted). A pure resistor has no phase angle. But because the loudspeaker
is reactive, its phase angle and impedance change with frequency.

Phase angle is introduced because capacitive reactance causes voltage to lag slightly behind the current flow in time. In an inductor, the
opposite occurs: current lags voltage. Capacitive reactance creates a
phase angle of –90°, while inductive reactance creates a phase angle of
+90°. When capacitive and inductive reactance are combined, the phase
angle may be anywhere between +90° or –90°. When the dotted line on a
phase angle plot is above the 0° center line, the loudspeaker is primarily
inductive. When the dotted line dips below the 0° center line, the loud-

speaker is primarily capacitive. The less severe the phase-angle swings (deviations from a flat line), the less reactive the loudspeaker and the easier it is for the amplifier to drive. A phase-angle trace that stays near the 0° center line makes the loudspeaker look more like a simple resistor to the power amplifier.

Fig. B-14 A loudspeaker's impedance magnitude and phase angle

Courtesy *Stereophile*

Capacitor Types

Capacitors are crucial elements in audio circuit design and manufacture. They are used everywhere in audio products, and can significantly influence the product's sound. Capacitors vary greatly in their physical and electrical properties; some are better than others for use in audio circuits. There are also huge price differences between good and poor capacitors.

Capacitors are formed of two plates separated by an insulator called the *dielectric*. The dielectric can be air, Mylar, ceramic, paper, polystyrene, polypropylene, foil, Teflon, tantalum, or other materials. Capacitors are referred to by their dielectric material: we may say a particular preamplifier uses Teflon capacitors throughout. The best audio capacitors are Teflon, polystyrene, and polypropylene.

One type of capacitor found in power supplies is the *electrolytic* capacitor. These are usually large metal cans that have very high capacitance values. Electrolytics work well in power supplies, but are poor choices for capacitors in the signal path. One manufacturer even gets rid of all electrolytics from the power supply, using much more expensive polypropylene caps instead.

Anatomy of an Audio Product

With this basic knowledge of electronics, let's see how these principles are applied in audio products.

The Power Supply

Every audio component that plugs into a wall outlet contains a power supply. The power supply converts 120V, 60Hz AC power from the wall outlet into the lower DC voltages needed by audio circuits. This is a critical job in high-end audio: the power supply has a large influence on the product's sound quality. Often, the power supply accounts for much of a component's size, weight, and cost. The general thinking in high-end product design is to have extremely simple audio circuits and extremely elaborate power supplies. We want a pure and simple path for the audio signal to follow, and a very clean and stable DC supply.

The first component in the power supply is the *power transformer*. This device *steps down* the 120V AC powerline to a lower AC voltage, perhaps ±30V (we'll see how it does this in a minute). The transformer's schematic symbol is an accurate representation of its construction: it consists of two coils of wire placed next to each other (Fig.B-15).

Fig. B-15
The schematic symbol for a transformer represents its physical structure.

A little earlier we learned that whenever current flows through a conductor, a magnetic field is set up around that conductor. We also learned that whenever we have a conductor, a magnetic field, and relative motion between the two, a voltage is induced. Both principles are in operation in a transformer. When the 60Hz AC flows through the transformer's first coil, called the *primary winding*, an expanding and collapsing magnetic field is set up around this coil. This expanding and collapsing field created around the primary winding induces a voltage across the second coil, called the *secondary winding*. The 60Hz AC signal thus appears across the secondary winding, even though there is no physical connection between this winding and the AC wall outlet.

The voltage induced across the secondary is determined by the *turns ratio* between the primary and secondary. By changing the turns ratio, any value of output voltage can be obtained. Some transformers have multiple secondary windings to supply different circuits. The transformer thus converts 120V, 60Hz AC to a lower 60Hz AC voltage or voltages. The transformer also *isolates* the component from the power line.

Transformers are rated by power capacity, called a *VA* rating (Volt/Amperes). A transformer rated at 1kVA (1000VA), for example, can deliver 100V at 10A (assuming a 1:1 turns ratio). Transformers in low-signal components (preamps, CD players) are typically rated at a few tens of VA, while the largest power-amplifier transformers may reach a whopping 5kVA. Such a transformer may weigh more than 100 pounds.

Many audio products use *toroidal* transformers instead of the more conventional *laminated* type. A toroidal transformer is doughnut-shaped to concentrate its magnetic field in a tighter configuration. Toroidals are more expensive than laminated types, but are more efficient and radiate less noise into the surrounding circuitry. Just as the magnetic field surrounding the primary winding induces a voltage across the secondary winding, audio circuitry near the transformer can pick up 60Hz *hum*. Toroidal transformers reduce this risk.

The stepped-down voltage from the transformer's secondary winding is still AC, but we need DC to supply the audio circuits. The next element in the power supply is the *rectifier*, a device that turns AC into DC. Rectifiers are made from diodes, the most basic *semiconductor* element. A diode allows current to flow in one direction but not the other. Fig.B-16 shows the effect of putting a single diode on a transformer's output. The diode allows one polarity to pass, but blocks the 60Hz sinewave's other half. (Which half it passes—positive or negative—is determined by the diode's direction.) In effect, the diode removes one polarity of the signal. Because the resultant voltage never changes polarity, it is, technically, direct current. This method, called *half-wave rectification*, isn't very efficient. But by putting four diodes together, we can make a *full-wave bridge rectifier* (Fig.B-17). In effect, the other sinewave polarity is "flipped over." The full-wave rectifier produces smoother DC and delivers more power to the supply.

The rectifier output is DC (it never changes polarity), but still has AC *ripple* riding on it. Ripple consists of vestiges of the AC signal superimposed on the DC; the DC shifts up and down at 120Hz. Note that a full-wave rectifier produces ripple at 120Hz, not 60Hz, because the negative phase of the sinewave is "flipped over" (shown earlier in Fig.B-17). Ripple is reduced by adding *filter capacitors*, whose storage function smooths the AC ripple riding on the DC voltage. In fact, filter capacitors are also called *smoothing* capacitors.

The filtered output is now DC with much less ripple, but it still isn't ready to supply our audio circuits. Any changes in the input line voltage will affect the DC voltages supplying the audio circuits—an unacceptable condition. The job of making this DC more stable and at the correct voltage falls on the *voltage regulator*. A voltage regulator maintains a constant output voltage regardless of changes to its input voltage. The voltage regulator's input is DC that may have some ripple and be subject to fluctuation and drift; the regulator's output is a pure, stable, and unwavering DC source. Voltage regulators are fed a voltage slightly higher than the desired output voltage; they can thus maintain a stable output voltage even if the input voltage changes slightly. A typical 12V regulator (the output voltage) may have an input voltage of 15V. This 12V is now good enough to become the power-supply *rail* for the audio circuits. Voltage regulators usually have heatsinks attached to them; the difference between input and output voltage is dissipated as heat.

Fig. B-16 A half-wave rectifier passes only one phase of the AC powerline.

(A) Transformer feeding a half-wave rectifier

Fig. B-17 A full-wave rectifier "flips over" one polarity of the AC powerline.

(C) Transformer feeding a bridge rectifier

Copied with permission from *Audio Technology Fundamentals* by Alan A. Cohen

All these elements—power transformer, rectifier, filter capacitors, and a voltage regulator—are shown schematically in Fig.B-18, and pictorially in Fig.B-19.

The power supply will often produce several DC voltages of different polarities (positive and negative) to supply different parts of the circuit. At the very minimum, a digital processor will need +5V to the digital circuits and ±12V to the analog stage. Most processors have at least four *regulation stages*, with some having up to 15 separately regulated supply voltages. Multiple regulation stages help *isolate* circuits from each other. Different audio circuits can interact with each other through a common regulation stage, degrading performance. For example, if a CD player's tracking-servo power supply also fed the analog output stage, the supply voltage would *droop* when the tracking servo demanded current, affecting the analog circuit's performance. Designers agree: the more regulation stages, the better.

Fig. B-18 A simple power-supply schematic

Fig. B-19 The power supply shown pictorially

Copied with permission from *Audio Technology Fundamentals* by Alan A. Cohen

Most regulators are integrated circuits (see Fig.B-19). Conversely, some regulation stages are called *discrete* because they use separate transistors, resistors, and capacitors to form the regulator. Discrete regulation is much more expensive to implement, but is generally considered to produce better-sounding products than those using IC regulation. Some very elaborate products use *cascaded* regulation, in which the output of one regulator supplies the input to the second regulator. This ensures a purer, more stable DC supply. The ultimate power supply uses many cascaded discrete regulation stages.

The regulated DC voltages are often *bypassed* with very-low-value (0.01μF) high-quality capacitors. The capacitor is placed physically next to the supplied circuit, and electrically between the power-supply rail and ground. The capacitor provides a path to ground for noise or power-supply-rail disturbances.

Other techniques that contribute to good power-supply performance are high values of filter capacitance, with some of the capacitors located next to the audio circuits they supply. A large transformer is also a plus, even though the VA rating may already exceed the circuits' current requirements. Most designers agree that the bigger the transformer, the better. Separate transformers are also an advantage, further isolating individual circuit elements from each other.

Power supplies are a critical element in the music reproduction chain. Although mediocre supplies will still make the product work, the very finest components are distinguished by elaborate and expensive power supplies. Much of what you pay for in high-quality audio products is in the power supply.

Now let's look at some circuits that the power supply feeds—transistor and tube amplifiers.

Amplifier Circuits

Amplifier circuits are the basic building blocks of preamps, power amps, phono stages, and CD players. If you understand a simple, one-transistor amplifier, you'll have a good grasp of how all amplifiers work.

A transistor is a solid-state semiconductor that has three elements: the *base, emitter,* and *collector.* It can be thought of as a sandwich of these three layers, shown schematically in Figs.B-20a and b. The transistor converts a small signal at the base to a large signal at the collector. If you think of a hose with water flowing through it, the water source is the emitter, and the base is a kink in the hose that opens and closes to allow more or less water to flow.

Figs. B-20 a and b
A transistor's
schematic symbol
(NPN and PNP
types)

(A) NPN transistor   *(B) PNP transistor*

Copied with permission from *Audio Technology Fundamentals* by Alan A. Cohen

Let's see how this works by looking at the single-stage transistor amplifier shown in Fig.B-21. The DC power supply is connected to the collector at the top of the figure. The emitter is negative with respect to the collector. Because a voltage exists between the emitter and collector, current wants to flow up through the transistor. The base can prevent or permit current flow, depending on the base voltage. The base is like a control valve that can turn current flow on and off. When the transistor is *turned on* by a tiny base current, a large current flows from the emitter, through the base, and into the collector. When the transistor is *turned off* by a lower base current, no current flows from the emitter to the collector.

Fig. B-21 A simple
one-transistor
amplifier

Copied with permission from *Audio Technology Fundamentals* by Alan A. Cohen

If we put an audio signal on the base, current flow from the emitter to the collector will be controlled by that audio signal. When the audio signal is of higher amplitude, the transistor will be more turned on, allowing more current to flow from the emitter to the collector. A low-amplitude audio signal will allow less current to flow through the transistor. A tiny base current thus controls a large current through the emitter and collector. This is how a transistor amplifies an audio signal.

The amount of amplification provided by a transistor is called *gain*, expressed either as the ratio between the input and output voltages, or in decibels (dB). A gain of 10 means that the output signal has ten times the voltage of the input signal; a 1kHz sinewave with an amplitude of 10mV applied to the base will produce a 1kHz sinewave at the collector with an amplitude of 100mV.

In practice, the transistor is partially turned on all the time. A small base current, called the *bias current*, is always present. Bias is essential to making the transistor work. Bias makes the transistor conduct *quiescent current* through the emitter and collector. Quiescent current is the current that flows through the transistor's collector when no input signal is applied to the base. The amount of bias current is carefully selected so that the transistor operates in its linear operating region (Fig.B-22). Bias allows the transistor to amplify both positive and negative phases of the audio signal; because the supply voltage is positive and the emitter is connected to ground, the transistor can never produce a negative voltage at the collector. By making the transistor conduct all the time with bias, the zero crossing point is some voltage between ground and the supply voltage (determined by the values of the emitter and collector resistors). When the input signal swings negative, the output voltage is simply "less positive" than this zero crossing voltage.

Fig. B-22 Bias makes the transistor operate in its linear region.

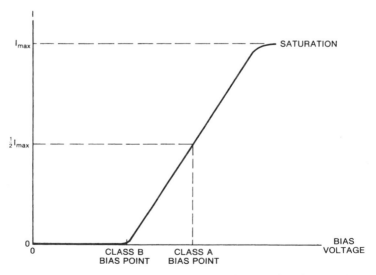

Copied with permission from *Audio Technology Fundamentals* by Alan A. Cohen

As explained in the section on series circuits, two resistances in series will produce a voltage drop across the resistors. This is what happens in a transistor circuit: current flow through the collector and emitter resistors form a *voltage divider*, producing a DC voltage at the collector. When we apply an AC audio signal on top of the bias current, the transistor becomes more and less turned on, amplifying the base current. The signal at the collector is thus a DC voltage with the audio signal riding on it. The final output is an amplified replica of the signal input to the base. In the configuration shown here, called a *common-emitter* amplifier, the output signal is 180° out of phase with the input signal.

Note that the large signal at the output is simply the DC power supply converted to an AC audio signal by the transistor. This is an important point for audio products: the power supply is effectively in the audio signal path. It's easy to conceptualize the power-supply rails as a static DC supply outside the audio signal path. But because the audio signal appears at the collector, and the power supply is also connected to the collector, anything that happens to the power supply—noise, high output impedance, fluctuations—also happens to the audio signal. This is why high-end amplifiers have such elaborate power supplies.

In Fig.B-21, R_1 is the load resistor, R_2 is the emitter resistor that stabilizes the transistor's operation, R_3 and R_4 create a voltage divider that applies the correct bias to the base, and C_3 is a bypass capacitor. C_1 and C_2 are *coupling capacitors*, which block DC from getting into the transistor (C_1) and the next amplification stage (C_2). Because capacitors in the signal path are generally not a good thing, some designers prefer to remove them. An amplifier circuit without coupling capacitors is called *direct-coupled*. If no coupling capacitors are used, DC can be prevented from reaching the amplifier's output with an active device called a *DC servo*.

A technique for decreasing distortion in amplifiers is called *negative feedback*, or just *feedback*. A portion of the amplifier's output signal is returned to the input, reducing distortion. When the feedback *loop* is around a single or several gain stages, the feedback is called *local*. When the feedback is taken from the amplifier's final output and returned to the input stage, the feedback is called *global*. Excessive feedback produces lower distortion figures, but often makes the amplifier sound worse. High-end amplifier designers try to use as little feedback as possible.

Going back to Fig.B-21, we can see that the transistor amplifies the entire audio signal; consequently, it's always turned on—i.e., always conducting current. Because the transistor is always turned on, this amplifier operates in *Class-A* mode. Class-A simply means that the transistor amplifies the entire audio signal and is always turned on.

Although it may seem intuitive that transistors would work this way, virtually all power-amplifier output stages use a more efficient technique called *Class-A/B*. Class-A/B operation produces less heat and is more efficient than Class-A, making Class-A/B stages more economical in circuits that must handle lots of current.

In Class A/B, transistors are arranged in *complementary pairs*. One half of the complementary pair is an *NPN* transistor, the other half is a *PNP* transistor. The NPN/PNP designation refers to the transistor's internal structure, which determines the voltage polarities needed to operate the transistor. In a complementary pair, an NPN transistor is connected to a PNP transistor (Fig.B-23). The "top" transistor will handle the positive half of the audio signal, and the bottom transistor will amplify the negative portion of the signal. When the top transistor is conducting, the bottom transistor is turned off, and vice versa. This technique keeps the transistors turned off half the time, producing less heat and reducing stress on the transistors.

Fig. B-23 A complementary output pair of transistors driven by a Class-A driver stage

Copied with permission from *Audio Technology Fundamentals* by Alan A. Cohen

The signal driving a complementary pair is processed by a *phase splitter* before the transistor bases. A phase splitter duplicates the audio signal so that the positive phase drives the NPN transistor of the complementary pair, and the negative phase drives the PNP half of the pair.

A Class-A/B amplifier is also called a "push-pull" output stage because one transistor "pulls" current while the other transistor "pushes." Current flow is indicated by the directions of the arrows in Fig.B-23.

A true push-pull amplifier actually operates in pure Class-B, but virtually all power amplifiers operate in Class-A up to a few watts, then switch to Class-B operation, hence the "Class-A/B" designation. At low signal levels, both halves of the complementary pair always conduct, meaning that the output stage is operating in Class-A. The power output level at which the amplifier switches into Class-B is determined by the bias current applied to the output transistor bases. More bias current turns the transistors on harder, allowing them to handle both phases of the audio signal up to a higher power output. There's a limit to how much power the amplifier will deliver in Class-A; the designer just can't keep increasing the bias current. Maximum Class-A power output is determined by how much current the transistors can handle, how well heat is removed from the transistors, and how much current the power supply can deliver. Pure Class-A amplifiers are huge, very heavy (due to their massive power transformers), generate lots of heat, and are very expensive in terms of "dollars per watt."

Class-A operation produces less distortion than Class-A/B, and generally sounds better. A kind of distortion in Class-B amplifiers called *crossover distortion* can produce a waveform discontinuity at the zero crossing point where one transistor turns off and the other turns on. The two halves of the complementary pair aren't biased identically, producing crossover distortion. This condition can't occur in Class-A amplifiers. Class-A output stages have other another big advantage: the transistors are always at the same temperature regardless of the signal they are amplifying, making the output stage more stable and linear. (Chapter 6 contains a discussion of amplifier output stages and their musical qualities.)

The NPN and PNP transistors described previously are called *bipolar* devices because current flows through both polarities (P and N) of semiconductor material. Another type of transistor, called the *Junction Field Effect Transistor* (JFET), is often used in small-signal applications. The JFET is called a *unipolar* device because current can flow in only one direction. A JFET, shown schematically in Fig.B-24, has a *gate*, a *source*, and a *drain*, which correspond to the base, emitter, and collector in our NPN and PNP transistors. JFETs are often used in amplifier input stages for their high input impedance. JFETs are also turned on (biased) by voltage rather than by current, as are bipolar transistors. JFETs are found only in small signal circuits. In addition, JFETs are also used as electronic switches.

Fig. B-24 A JFET's gate, source, and drain correspond to the bipolar transistor's base, emitter, and collector.

Another type of field-effect transistor is called the MOSFET (MOS stands for Metal Oxide Semiconductor). MOSFETs are sometimes used in power-amplifier output stages.

Amplifier Distortion

All the amplifier circuits we've talked about produce distortion—their output signals aren't exact replicas of their input signals. Instead, the signals are changed in certain ways. In *harmonic distortion*, harmonics of the input signal appear in the output. For example, if a 100Hz sine-wave is input to the amplifier, the output will be a 100Hz sinewave, but with the harmonics of 100Hz (the second harmonic at 200Hz, third harmonic at 300Hz, fourth at 400Hz, etc.) added to the signal.

Harmonic distortion is expressed as a percentage of the output signal. The term *Total Harmonic Distortion*, or *THD*, is an expression of the percentage of all the harmonic components combined. For example, if the amplifier puts out 10V and the harmonic distortion products are 10mV, the amplifier has 0.1% THD. Although THD is a common amplifier specification, a more instructive analysis of harmonic distortion involves examining *which* harmonics are produced by the amplifier. Second- and third-harmonic distortion components aren't nearly as objectionable as upper-order harmonic distortion components such as the fifth, seventh, and ninth. In fact, 10% second-harmonic distortion is less musically objectionable than 0.5% seventh-harmonic. We can quickly see that a single THD figure tells us very little about the audibility of an amplifier's distortion. All amplifiers produce different harmonic distortion spectra—one possible reason why they sound different.

Another distortion in amplifiers is called *intermodulation distortion*, or *IMD*. When a signal of two frequencies is input to an amplifier, the amplifier will output the two frequencies, plus the *sum* and *difference* of those frequencies. For example, if we drive an amplifier with a mix of 100Hz and 10kHz, the amplifier's output will be 100Hz and 10kHz, *plus* 9.9kHz (the *difference* between 100Hz and 10kHz) and 10.1kHz (the *sum* of 100Hz and 10kHz). In fact, intermodulation distortion produces an infinite number of intermodulation products. Like harmonic distortion, intermodulation distortion is expressed as a percentage of the output signal.

Amplifiers can also distort the audio waveform's transient character, a distortion called *slew-rate limiting*. If the steepness of the input signal's attack is faster than the amplifier's ability to respond, slew-rate limiting will occur. An amplifier's slew rate, measured in volts per microsecond (V/μs), describes how much voltage the amplifier can swing in a specified time period (1μs). If the amplifier can swing 20V/μs and the input signal has transient signals that swing faster than 20V/μs, the amplifier will distort the music's dynamic structure. Slew rate is often referred to as an amplifier's "speed."

Vacuum Tube Amplifiers

Vacuum tube amplifiers are very similar in operation to transistor amplifiers, but are generally much simpler. The three elements in a tube are the *control grid, cathode,* and *plate,* shown schematically in Fig.B-25. These correspond to the base, emitter, and collector of the bipolar transistor. The cathode emits electrons, the plate collects them, and the control grid controls how many electrons flow through the tube from cathode to plate. This most basic form of tube is called a *triode.*

Fig. B-25 The three elements of a vacuum tube are the grid, cathode, and plate.

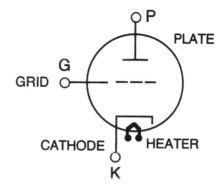

One more element is needed to make the tube work: the *filament,* or *heater.* The heater is the part of the tube that glows, heating the cathode to a high temperature. When the cathode is heated, electrons are given off, a phenomenon called *thermionic emission.* These electrons "boiling" on the cathode surface want to flow through the vacuum to the positively charged plate, but the grid is in the way. The voltage applied to the grid determines how many electrons jump from the cathode to the plate. The grid is a mesh of wire that produces an electric field that controls the flow of electrons, yet doesn't impede them on their way to the plate. By applying an audio signal to the grid, we can control a large current flow though the tube.

In some vacuum tubes the cathode is heated directly rather than indirectly by a separate heater. These so-called direct-heated tubes are sometimes used in single-ended triode amplifiers.

In addition to amplifying audio signals, triodes are also used as *output buffer* amplifiers in a configuration called a *cathode follower.* The cathode follower has a voltage gain of less than one (meaning it provides no amplification), but has other attributes, such as a high input impedance and low output impedance. In tubed digital processors and preamplifiers, cathode followers are often the last stage before the output jacks.

Another tube type, called a *pentode,* is often used in amplifier output stages. A pentode is essentially a triode with two additional elements, called the *screen grid* and the *suppressor grid.* Both of these elements are between the control grid and plate. When connected to a voltage, the two additional grids affect the electric field within the tube, and provide much higher voltage gain than is possible with a triode. While triode voltage gain may be between 10 and 50, pentodes can provide voltage gains of up to 500. Most low-level tubed circuits—such as preamplifier input, gain, and output stages, and power-amplifier input and driver stages—use triodes for their better sound. Pentode stages are usually reserved for tubed output stages where high amplification is needed. Some tubed power amplifiers use triode output stages, but their power output is relatively low. However, they sound extremely good.

Tubed amplifiers usually have much higher power-supply voltages than do transistor amplifiers. While the collector-supply voltage in a transistor amplifier may be 15–100V, tube plate voltages can run as high as 800V. The plate voltage is often called the "B+" supply. Further, tubed amplifiers need a high current supply—usually 6V or 12V—for the tubes' heaters. (See Chapter 6 for more discussion of tubed power amplifiers.)

Operational Amplifiers

An *operational amplifier*, or *op-amp*, is an integrated circuit capable of amplifying audio signals. The op-amp replaces many transistors, capacitors, and resistors with a tiny plastic or metal package. Very few external components are needed to build an audio circuit based on op-amps—just supply them with a DC power supply, a *feedback resistor*, and an input signal, and they work. A typical op-amp circuit for audio signal amplification is shown in Fig.B-26.

Fig. B-26 A simple op-amp circuit

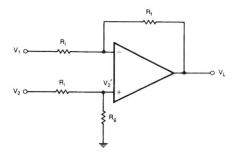

Copied with permission from *Audio Technology Fundamentals* by Alan A. Cohen

In theory, op-amps are ideal for audio circuits: they have very high input impedance, very low output impedance, and can provide high gain over a wide bandwidth. They are much easier and cheaper to implement than *discrete* circuits made of transistors, capacitors, and resistors. Unfortunately, most of them don't sound as good as discrete circuits. The very best audio components use discrete circuitry, while budget and moderately priced products usually use op-amps. Some products employing op-amps have sounded superb, however.

An op-amp has two inputs, one output, and pins for the DC power supply. The op-amp is typically supplied with ±12V DC from the power supply. It has two input terminals, marked + and –, called the *non-invert-*

ing input and the *inverting input*, respectively. A signal input to the non-inverting input will produce an output signal of the same polarity as the input signal. Conversely, an input signal at the inverting input will produce an output signal of opposite polarity to the input signal. Op-amps can thus function as inverting or non-inverting amplifiers. The value of the feedback resistor determines the op-amp's gain.

Op-amps can be used as voltage amplifiers, active filters, or output buffer amplifiers. (They also have thousands of uses not applicable to audio circuits.)

The op-amp's two inputs make it ideal for circuits that need a *differential input*. A differential signal, also called a *balanced* signal, is composed of two signals of opposite polarity. These two signals are 180° out of phase with each other; when one is at peak positive, the other is at peak negative. (Balanced signals are explained in detail in Chapter 11.) When fed signals at both inputs, the op-amp will amplify and pass only the *difference* between those two signals. The two out-of-phase signals will be amplified and combined into one signal at the op-amp's output, but any noise, distortion, or spurious junk common to both polarities will be not be amplified by the op-amp. The phenomenon by which a differential amplifier rejects signals common to both channels is called *common-mode rejection*; the op-amp's ability to reject signals common to both channels is called its *common-mode rejection ratio*, or *CMRR*.

The op-amp driven with a differential signal naturally converts a balanced signal to an unbalanced signal. Many audio components with balanced inputs have a differential amplifier at the input, which converts the balanced signal to a single-ended (unbalanced) signal that the component then amplifies.

Digital Electronics

Digital electronics are becoming increasingly important in audio recording and reproduction. Not only CD players and digital processors use digital electronics: more and more control and switching functions in preamps and power amps are being handled by digital circuits.

Simply, digital circuits operate in one of two states: on or off. The "On" state is represented by a voltage (such as +5V), and "Off" is represented by no voltage (also called *ground*). The terms *high* and *low*, or *one* and *zero*, also describe the two conditions in digital circuits. Unlike an analog signal that has a continuously varying amplitude, digital signals are a train of high and low pulses. Digital circuits are also called *binary* circuits to describe the two-state nature of a digital signal.

In digital signals, information is represented as a series of high and low states. Each state carries one piece of information, or *bit*. (Appendix C explains how binary coding can represent numbers, which in turn can represent an audio signal. Binary coding can store virtually any sort of information; this book's text and graphics were stored as binary code.)

The building blocks of digital electronics are called *logic gates*. A logic gate has more than one input, but only one output. Logic gates are made with tiny transistors that are either fully turned on or fully turned off. Simple logic gates can make basic decisions. For example, an *OR gate* will produce a high output if either input #1 *or* input #2 is high. A two-input *AND gate* will produce a high output if input #1 *and* input #2 are high. Digital electronics use many other types of logic gates.

Logic gates can be arrayed to perform nearly any mathematical task. In practice, many hundreds of thousands of gates are needed to make digital circuits. These gates are combined into *integrated circuits*, or ICs. Several hundred thousand gates can be put on a single IC.

In the next appendix, we'll see how an audio signal can be stored in digital form.

Appendix C: Digital Audio Basics

Introduction

Throughout the history of recorded sound, the goal has been to capture an acoustic event by storing a mechanical or magnetic representation of the original acoustic waveform. The modulations in an LP groove, for example, are an analog of the acoustic wave that was originally heard as music. The more alike the groove modulations and the acoustic waveform, the higher the fidelity. Tiny changes in the shape of that squiggly line—inevitably introduced in record cutting, pressing, and playback—produce an almost infinite variability in sound quality.

The advent of digital audio has fundamentally changed the way audio is encoded, stored, and played back. Rather than attempting to preserve the acoustic waveform directly, digital audio converts that waveform into a numerical representation. The numbers representing the waveform are stored and later converted back into an analog signal. Because those discrete numbers can be stored and recovered more precisely than the infinitely variable analog signal, digital audio has the potential to exceed the musical performance of analog media.

I say "potential" because, in many respects, digital audio has yet to sound better than the best analog formats. Virtually anyone who's listened to a live microphone feed, then the same signal played back both from analog tape and after encoding into digital form, will attest that the analog tape produces a truer representation of the music. Similarly, a comparison of a properly played LP and the CD of the same music reveals musical virtues in the analog representation not heard from the digital medium.

This isn't to say that analog is without flaw; rather, it suggests that the distortions generated by digital audio are less sonically benign than those from analog media.

Fortunately, this state of affairs is only temporary; digital audio has taken a large step forward with the commercial availability of high-resolution formats, such as DVD-Audio and Super Audio CD. Only in the last decade did we discover that building digital audio products is a far more exacting process than theory suggests. Although some audiophiles shun digital, it's shortsighted to summarily reject all digital audio based on the crude sound provided by the technologies of digital's first decades. The future promises much more than that.

With that background, let's take a look at how music can be converted into numbers and back into music again.

Binary Number System

All digital audio systems—and digital electronics in general—use the *binary* number system. "Binary" means "two," reflecting the two possible values in the binary, or base 2, number system: 0 and 1. A binary number of these two values strung together can represent any quantity we want, as can the ten values of the decimal system we're so familiar with.

When we count in decimal and reach the highest digit (nine), the ones place is reset to zero and the sum is carried to the next column, producing the number 10. This number is a code that represents a 1 in the tens column and a 0 in the 1s column—one ten, no ones. The position of a digit indicates the weight given that digit.

Just as there is no single digit greater than nine in decimal notation, there is no single digit greater than 1 in binary notation. Consequently, when we count in binary, we reset and carry with every count. For example, the number 01 in binary represents the decimal number 1. If we add the binary numbers 01 and 01, we reset the ones column and carry to the next column, producing the binary number 10. This represents a 1 in the twos column and a 0 in the 1s column, or the number 2 (expressed in decimal). Binary addition works like this:

01	10	11
+01	+01	+01
10	11	100

Just as the position of a digit within a decimal number changes its value by a factor of ten (ones, tens, hundreds, thousands, etc.), the position of a binary digit changes its value by a factor of 2. For example, the binary number 0101 indicates a 1 in the 1s column, a 0 in the 2s column, a 1 in the 4s column, and a 0 in the 8s column. The binary number 0101 thus represents the decimal quantity 5. (Fig.C-1 shows binary and decimal equivalences.)

Fig. C-1 Binary
and decimal
equivalences

Binary	Decimal
0000	0
0001	1
0010	2
0011	3
0100	4
0101	5
0110	6
0111	7
1000	8
1001	9
1010	10
1011	11
1100	12
1101	13
1110	14
1111	15

Any decimal number can be represented by binary notation, provided the binary number is long enough. The highest number that can be represented in binary notation is 2^x, where x is the number of places. For example, a binary number with four places can represent any decimal number between 0 and 15 (2^4). The number 15 in binary is 1111: a one in the 8s column, a one in the 4s column, a one in the 2s column, and a one in the 1s column.

Each of these positions in a binary number is called a *bit*, short for *binary digit*. The greater the number of bits, the higher the number we can represent. The bit in the position of highest value in a binary number (usually at the far left) has the greatest effect on the number's value and is called the *Most Significant Bit*, or *MSB*. The bit in the position of lowest value in the binary number (usually the far right column) is called the *Least Significant Bit*, or *LSB*.

Binary notation makes computers and electronic circuits simpler and more practical. The electronic circuit or device need operate in only two states: one or zero, on or off, yes or no. If a voltage is present, we call that binary 1; if no voltage is present, that represents binary 0. These conditions relate to a transistor being fully biased on (binary 1) or fully biased off (binary 0). Similarly, a north-south polarization of a magnetic medium could represent binary 1, and a south-north polarization might indicate binary 0.

In digital audio, the analog signal is represented by a stream of these binary numbers. In the next sections, we'll see exactly how music can be represented by binary numbers.

Sampling and Quantization

Sampling and quantization are the cornerstones of digital audio. These two distinct but interrelated processes form the basis for all digital audio systems. To see how sampling and quantization can preserve an analog audio signal as a series of numbers, let's first look at an audio signal's characteristics.

An analog audio signal is a voltage that varies over time. The faster the variation over time, the higher the audio signal's frequency. The greater the amplitude swings, the louder the signal. The audio signal thus has two properties—time and amplitude—that must be encoded to correctly preserve that signal.

An LP record is a good example of how time and amplitude information are preserved. The side-to-side modulations in the record groove encode the amplitude information; the greater the modulation, the higher the signal amplitude. The time information is encoded by the LP's rotation, which must be the same on playback as when the disc was recorded. If we change the speed of the LP, we change the time relationship and thus the audio signal's frequency.

Digital audio must also preserve the time and amplitude information of an audio signal. But instead of encoding and storing those characteristics continuously as in an LP groove, digital audio preserves time and amplitude in discrete units.

A digital audio system encodes the signal's time information by *sampling* the audio signal at discrete time intervals. The amplitude information is encoded by generating a number at each sample point that represents the analog waveform's amplitude at sample time—a process called *quantization*. Sampling preserves the time information, quantization preserves the amplitude information.

Sampling and quantization produce a series of binary numbers— called *words*—that represent the analog waveform. When those binary words are converted back into voltages with the same timing reference as when they were first sampled, the analog audio waveform is roughly reconstructed. The original waveform is recovered by smoothing the staircase with a low-pass filter. Sampling and quantization thus convert a continuous analog function (the continuously varying voltage of the analog waveform) into a series of discrete binary numbers. Fig.C-2 shows how a continuous analog waveform is converted into binary numbers, then back into a continuous analog waveform.

Fig. C-2 Graphical representation of the signal flow in a complete PCM digitization system

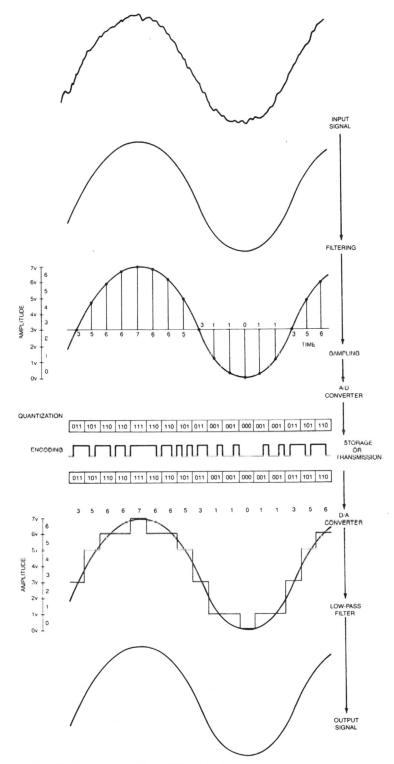

Courtesy Ken Pohlmann, *Principles of Digital Audio*

Sampling Rate, Nyquist Theorem, and Aliasing

The speed at which the samples are taken is called the *sampling rate*, or *sampling frequency*. The sampling rate determines the highest audio frequency that can be correctly encoded. Specifically, the sampling rate must be at least twice as high as the highest audio signal to be preserved. The compact disc format, for example, samples the analog signal at 44,100 times per second (44.1kHz), which provides an audio bandwidth of about 20kHz. Sampling at 96kHz, as in the DVD-Audio format, provides a bandwidth of nearly 48kHz.

This fundamental relationship between sampling frequency and audio bandwidth was stated in the now-famous Nyquist Theorem. In 1928, telegraph engineer Harry Nyquist postulated that in any sampled system, the sampling rate must be at least twice as high as the highest frequency we want to encode.

If we violate the Nyquist theorem and sample a signal with a frequency higher than half the sampling rate, a form of distortion called *aliasing* occurs. Aliasing creates new frequencies in the sampled signal that weren't present in the original signal. Specifically, if we sample a 33kHz sinewave with a 48kHz sampling frequency, a new signal at 15kHz (48kHz minus 33kHz) is created. Once aliasing occurs, there is no way to remove the spurious alias components from the signal. The term *alias* comes from the fact that the incorrectly sampled signal assumes a completely new identity as a lower-frequency signal. Aliasing is sometimes called "foldback" because the incorrectly sampled high-frequency signal is folded back into the audioband.

The only way to prevent aliasing is to never let the sampler see a signal higher in frequency than half the sampling rate. This is accomplished with an *input low-pass filter* that removes all energy above half the sampling frequency. This input filter, called an *anti-aliasing filter*, is an essential part of all digital audio systems. It allows audioband frequencies to pass, but rapidly attenuates the signal just below half the sampling rate. These filters have been a significant source of sonic degradation in digital audio, particularly in early CD releases, when the filters were more crude than they are today.

Armed with this knowledge that the input signal is band-limited, we can address the common question of newcomers to digital audio: What happens to the information *between* the samples? If there are squiggles in the waveform between samples, won't that information be lost by the sampling process?

The answer is that there is *no* information between samples. If the input signal is properly band-limited, those squiggles will be removed by the anti-aliasing filter. And if the appropriate sampling rate is chosen for the filter's cutoff frequency, the sampler will perfectly encode any waveform input to it. In Fig.C-2 shown earlier, the input filter removed all energy above 20kHz (squiggles in the uppermost sinewave) before the signal was sampled.

Let's take the case of a 40kHz sampling frequency and a 20kHz sinewave. Even though the sampler sees only two samples per waveform, that's enough information to perfectly encode that 20kHz sinewave. Fig.C-3 shows the original 20kHz waveform (top) and the resultant waveform after sampling (the squarewave). We know from Appendix A that a squarewave is a sinewave combined with all its odd-order harmonics; these harmonics are represented as the four high-frequency waveforms below the 20kHz squarewave. When these harmonics are removed by an output low-pass filter, we're left with a 20kHz sinewave—the same signal we started with.

Fig. C-3 A 20kHz sinewave sampled at 40kHz produces a squarewave. Low-pass filtering removes the harmonics above 20kHz, recovering the 20kHz sinewave.

(A) 20 kHz input sinewave

(B) 20 kHz sampled square wave

(C) 180 kHz sinewave (ninth harmonic)

(D) 140 kHz sinewave (seventh harmonic)

(E) 100 kHz sinewave (fifth harmonic)

(F) 60 kHz sinewave (third harmonic)

(G) 20 kHz output sinewave (fundamental)

Courtesy Ken Pohlmann, *Principles of Digital Audio*

We can see from this worst-case example that sampling is a perfectly lossless process: the reconstructed waveform is theoretically identical to the input waveform. This is true provided that the input signal is properly band-limited and an appropriate sampling rate for the filter's characteristics is chosen. Digital audio has its problems (which I'm about to discuss), but sampling theory isn't one of them.

One mechanism, however, by which today's standard-resolution digital audio (CD, for example) degrades musical quality is too low a sampling frequency. Although our upper limit of hearing is 20kHz (if you're over 30, 16kHz is a more accurate figure), research has shown that increasing the audio bandwidth from 20kHz to 40kHz improves musical reproduction. Although we can't hear 40kHz sinewaves, removing energy above 20kHz from the signal reduces the music's sense of openness, transient attack, and natural quality. Moreover, the steep digital filtering required with 44.1kHz sampling degrades sound quality, a phenomenon described in Chapter 8 under "Why 44kHz Sampling and 16-Bit Quantization Isn't Enough."

Quantization

We've seen how sampling preserves the time information in an audio signal; now let's look at how quantization encodes the amplitude information.

Quantization generates a binary number that represents the analog waveform's amplitude at sample time. The binary number is a digital representation of the audio signal's analog voltage when the sample is taken.

The number of bits available to encode the audio waveform's amplitude is called the *quantization word length*. Just as the sampling rate determines the digital audio system's bandwidth, the quantization word length determines the digital audio system's dynamic range, resolution, and distortion level. The most common digital audio systems, including the CD, use 16-bit words. High-resolution digital audio is generally defined as word lengths of 20 bits or more. The longer the word length, the greater the fidelity to the original signal.

Quantization word length defines the number of steps available to encode the audio signal. Specifically, the number of steps is 2^x, where x is the number of bits in the word. For example, 16-bit quantization provides 2^{16} steps (65,536) to quantize the analog signal amplitude. An 18-bit system quadruples this figure to 262,144, and a 20-bit quantization word length provides 1,048,576 quantization steps. The longer the word length, the wider the dynamic range, the lower the distortion and noise, and the higher the resolution.

Unlike sampling, which is a lossless process, quantization produces errors in the encoded signal. Converting an infinitely variable analog function into a discrete number is inherently an approximation. This error occurs because the amplitude represented by a given quantization word is virtually never the signal's exact analog voltage. The difference between the analog signal's actual amplitude and the amplitude represented by the quantization word is called *quantization error*.

Fig.C-4 shows how quantization error occurs. The analog amplitude values don't exactly coincide with the values represented by the quantization words. For example, the first sample (the vertical dotted line to the far left) falls between the quantization levels 100111 and 101000. There is no value "100111.25," so the quantizer simply rounds off to the nearest discrete quantization value (100111), even though that number isn't quite correct. The difference between the voltage represented by 100111 (1.3V) and the audio signal's actual voltage (1.325V) is quantization error. When the audio signal is reconstructed, the slightly wrong binary number 100111 will generate a slightly wrong analog amplitude. The result is a distortion of the original waveform.

Fig. C-4
Quantization
error is limited
to one-half LSB.

Courtesy Ken Pohlmann, *Principles of Digital Audio*

The worst case is when the analog amplitude falls exactly between two quantization levels, as occurs at the second sample in Fig.C-4; the difference between the analog amplitude and the quantization word representing that amplitude is the greatest.

Quantization error can be expressed as a percentage of the least significant bit (LSB). At the first sample, the quantization error was one-quarter of an LSB. At the second sample, the error was one-half of an LSB. Note that quantization error can never exceed half the amplitude value of an LSB. Consequently, the smaller the quantization step size, the less the quantization error. Adding one bit to the quantization word length doubles the number of quantization steps and halves the quantization error. Because such a halving represents a difference of 6dB, the signal-to-noise ratio of a digital system improves by 6dB for each additional bit in the quantization word. A digital system with 18-bit quantization will have 12dB less quantization noise than a system with 16-bit quantization.

We can also approximate the signal-to-noise ratio of a digital system by multiplying the number of bits in the quantization word by 6. Sixteen-bit quantization provides a theoretical dynamic range of about 96dB. A 20-bit digital audio system has a dynamic range of about 120dB, or 24dB higher than a 16-bit system.

Quantization error is audible as a rough, granular sound on low-level signals, particularly reverberation decay. Instead of hearing the sound decay into silence, the reverberation decay grows in coarseness and grain as the signal decays. This is because the quantization error becomes a greater percentage of the signal as the signal's amplitude decreases.

This increase in distortion as the signal level drops is unique to digital audio; all analog recording formats exhibit higher distortion at *high* signal levels, such as saturation in analog tape. This situation presents unusual challenges: an increase in distortion as signal level decreases makes that distortion much more audible. Increasing the word length to 20 from 16 bits significantly reduces this problem.

Note that signal-to-noise ratio and distortion figures specified for a digital audio system are with a full-scale signal. Most of the time, a music signal is well below full-scale and therefore closer to the noise floor. The distortion isn't a function of how many bits the system has available, but the number of bits used by the signal at any given moment. This is why distortion and noise are inversely proportional to signal amplitude, and why digital audio has problems with low-level signals.

These factors make setting recording levels in a digital system an art completely different from setting analog recording levels. Ideally, the highest peak over the entire audio program should just reach full-scale digital (using all the bits). If the recording level is set so that the highest peak reaches –6dB, this is equivalent to throwing away one bit of the quantization word, with the attendant 6dB reduction in signal-to-noise ratio. And if the analog signal amplitude is higher than the voltage represented by the highest number, the quantizer simply runs out of bits and repeats the highest number, making the waveform peaks flat. This highly distorted waveform produces an unacceptable "crunching" sound on peaks. If you have a digital-audio recording device with meters, you can look at the recording levels on compact discs by taking the digital output from a CD transport and plugging it into the digital recorder. The recorder's meters will show the exact levels recorded on the CD. If the highest peaks never reach full-scale, some resolution has been needlessly lost.

Note that an audio program with a very wide dynamic range will be closer to the quantization noise floor more of the time than a signal with limited dynamic range. The peaks on the wide-dynamic-range-signal will be set just below full-scale, and the much-lower-level signal will consequently be encoded with fewer bits. This is a particular problem in classical music, which has a very wide dynamic range. This is a strong incentive for recording or mastering engineers to compress the music's dynamic range. In addition, producers of pop music want their records to sound loud in relation to other songs over the radio. Severely limiting the music's dynamic range makes the music loud all the time, but at the expense of dynamics, life, and rhythmic power.

Digital signal levels are referenced to a full-scale signal, which occurs when all the bits are used and no higher signal can be coded. This reference level is called 0dBFS, with FS standing for "full-scale." We may refer to a signal as –20dBFS, meaning it is 20dB below full scale.

Dither

The most extreme case of quantization error occurs when the signal amplitude is less than one LSB (Fig.C-5). This low-level signal isn't encoded at all by the quantizer: the quantizer outputs the same code at each sample point and the information is completely lost (C and D). If the signal does traverse quantization steps, the encoded signal is a squarewave, which represents a significant distortion of the original signal. This suggests that any information lower in amplitude than the LSB will be lost.

Fig. C-5
Quantization error is large relative to a signal traversing only a few quantization steps.

(A) Input sinewave

(B) Quantized square wave

(C) Input sinewave

(D) Quantized DC ouput

Courtesy Ken Pohlmann, *Principles of Digital Audio*

Fortunately, this limit can be overcome by adding a small amount of noise, called *dither*, to the audio signal. Dither allows a quantizer to resolve signals below the LSB, and greatly improves the sound of digital audio.

Fig.C-6 is identical to Fig.C-5, but this time we've added a small amount of white noise to the audio signal. This noise causes the audio signal to traverse quantization levels, allowing the signal to be encoded. The original sinewave is better preserved in the pulse-width modulation signal of Fig.C-6.

Fig. C-6 Dither can alleviate the effects of quantization error.

(A) Dither is added to the sinewave input.

(B) Sinewave is preserved in pulse width modulation.

(C) Dither is added to the sinewave input.

(D) Sinewave is preserved in pulse width modulation.

Courtesy Ken Pohlmann, *Principles of Digital Audio*

Dither reduces quantization artifacts, allows the system to resolve information lower in amplitude than one-half the least significant bit, and makes a digital audio system sound more like analog. Among other benefits, dither improves low-level resolution and smooths reverberation decay. Without dither, reverberation decay becomes granular in texture, then seems to drop off into a black hole. It's ironic that a small amount of analog white noise can greatly improve the performance of digital audio. Still, despite the great advantages of dither, we do end up paying a small penalty in decreased signal-to-noise ratio.

Dither is an odd concept to someone unfamiliar with digital audio; specifically, that adding noise to the audio signal can improve fidelity.

Finally, it should be pointed out that the preceding explanation of sampling and quantization describes a pulse-code modulation (PCM) digital-audio system, the standard encoding method in nearly all professional digital audio and in the compact disc. Other forms of encoding are possible such as Pulse-Width Modulation (PWM) used in the Super Audio CD format. This encoding method is explained in Chapter 8.

Digital Audio Storage

Once the audio signal is in the digital domain, we must store it on some medium. Common storage formats include the compact disc, magnetic tape, magneto-optical discs, and computer hard disks.

One might intuitively conceptualize a digital audio recording system as storing the binary information representing the audio signal directly on the medium. For example, a reflective spot on a CD could represent binary one, a non-reflective spot binary zero. In practice, however, digital audio is always encoded with a modulation scheme. Further, a significant amount of additional information is added to the raw audio data.

Every encoding scheme increases the storage capacity of the medium and facilitates data recovery. The Eight-to-Fourteen Modulation (EFM) encoding scheme used in the CD is a good example of encoding. The disc surface is a spiral track of small indentations called *pits* and flat areas called *land*. A transition from pit to land or land to pit represents binary one; all other surfaces (pit bottom or land) represent binary zero. The pattern of pit and land is created by the EFM encoding: 8 audio bits are converted into 14 bits for storage on the CD. These 14-bit words are linked by 3 "merging" bits to produce 17 bits for 8 audio bits. The result is a specific pattern of ones and zeros that follows certain rules. For example, each binary one is separate from other binary ones by a minimum of two zeros and a maximum of ten zeros. Although EFM encoding more than doubles the number of bits to be recorded, it actually increases the storage capacity of the CD compared to unmodulated coding. Note that both left and right audio channels as well as this additional information are encoded into a single serial datastream.

Fig. C-7 The CD frame format prior to EFM modulation

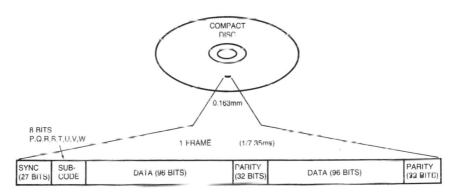

Courtesy Ken Pohlmann, *Principles of Digital Audio*

The compact disc is also a good example of how audio data are mixed with non-audio data and stored on the medium. The CD datastream is formatted into structures called *frames*. A CD frame (Fig.C-7) contains a synchronization pattern to identify the beginning of a block, bits that contain information about the signal (pre-emphasis, elapsed time, data format, etc.), and error-correction information. Between EFM coding, error correction, subcode, and synchronization, only about a third of the data stored on a CD are actual audio data. All digital audio-storage formats add non-audio data and structure the data into clearly defined blocks.

For a full discussion of how audio data are stored and recovered from the compact disc, see the section in Chapter 8 on how CD transports work.

Error Correction

No storage or transmission medium is perfect. LPs have ticks and pops, and analog magnetic tape has imperfections in the magnetic coating that cause a momentary loss of high frequencies. In analog recording, nothing can be done about these errors; we must live with their sonic imperfections.

Digital audio, however, provides an opportunity to make the audio signal virtually impervious to media imperfections. Lost or damaged data can be reconstructed with error-correction techniques. Error correction doesn't merely approximate the missing data; in most cases it can precisely restore the lost information bit for bit. For example, the compact disc's error-correction system can completely correct up to nearly 4000 consecutive missing bits. These errors could result from poor-quality disc manufacturing, or scratches on the disc from mishandling. Without error correction, the CD simply wouldn't function. The official CD specification—called the "Red Book"—allows a Block Error Rate (BLER) of 220 errors per second.

The two principles on which error correction is based are *redundancy* and *interleaving*. Redundant data is information added to the signal that isn't necessary to decode the signal—unless that signal is corrupted. The crudest form of redundancy is simply to store the data twice. Data corrupted in one spot is unlikely to be corrupted at the second storage location. A more efficient technique transmits a *checksum* with the data that indicates if the data has been reliably retrieved. In practice, error-correction schemes are enormously complex.

Digital audio media are subject to two kinds of errors: *bit errors* and *burst errors*. Bit errors are short in duration and easy to correct. Burst errors, however, affect long, consecutive streams of data. Not only is a large chunk of data missing, but the redundant information accompanying that data is also lost and so the chance of correction is reduced.

A technique called *interleaving* increases the possibility that a burst error can be corrected. Interleaving scatters data to different areas of the media. When those data are deinterleaved (put back in the original order), the long burst error is broken up into many shorter errors that are more easily corrected.

If the error is so large that it cannot be completely corrected, the error is *concealed* by approximating the missing data. Some concealed errors may be audible as a *click* or *pop* sound. This is a rare occurrence; the CD's error-correction system is so good that very few discs—even those abused and scratched—have uncorrectable errors.

Digital-to-Analog Conversion

The digital-to-analog conversion process requires recovering the digital audio data from the medium and converting it to analog form.

The recovered datastream must first be demodulated. In the CD format, this involves converting the 14-bit EFM-coded words back into their original 8-bit form. The data are deinterleaved and error correction performed. Synchronization information—essential to data recovery—is no longer needed and is discarded. The subcode information (track number and timing, along with other housekeeping data) is stripped out of the datastream and handled separately from the audio data. All of these functions are performed by the CD transport, which outputs a formatted datastream to the digital processor, which actually converts the signal to analog. (A full description of how a digital processor converts digital data to an analog signal is included in Chapter 8.)

Jitter Explained

In analog recording, speed variations in the recording media cause audible distortion. The classic case is a tape machine's "wow and flutter," speed fluctuations that cause the music's pitch to shift up and down slowly ("wow") or quickly ("flutter"). Digital audio doesn't suffer from wow and flutter; digital audio data can be read from the medium at a varying rate, yet be clocked out at a constant speed. But digital audio does suffer from a distortion-producing mechanism conceptually similar to wow and flutter, called *clock jitter*.

Jitter—timing variations in the clocks that serve as the time-base reference in digital audio systems—is a serious and underestimated source of sonic degradation in digital audio. Only recently has jitter begun to get the attention it deserves, both by high-end designers and audio academics. One reason jitter has been overlooked is the exceedingly difficult task of measuring such tiny time variations—on the order of tens of trillionths of a second. Another reason jitter has been ignored is the mistaken belief by some that if the ones and zeros that represent the music are correct, then digital audio must work perfectly. Unfortunately, getting the ones and zeros correct is only part of the equation. Those ones and zeros must be converted back to analog with extraordinarily precise timing to avoid degrading the signal.

As described in Chapter 8, the series of discrete audio samples are converted back into a continuously varying signal with a digital-to-analog converter (DAC) chip. A DAC takes a quantization word and converts it to a voltage—exactly opposite the function of the A/D converter. All that is required for perfect conversion (in the time domain) is that the samples be input to the DAC in the same order they were taken *and with the same timing reference* as when the samples were created. In theory, this sounds easy—just provide a stable clock to the A/D converter and a stable clock of the same frequency to the D/A converter.

It isn't that easy in practice. If the samples aren't converted back to an analog waveform with the identical timing with which they were taken, distortion of the analog waveform will result. These timing errors between samples are caused by variations in the clock signal that controls *when* the DAC converts the digital words to an analog voltage.

Let's take a little closer look at how the DAC decides *when* to convert the digital samples to analog. In Fig.C-8, the binary number at the left is the quantization word that represents the analog waveform's amplitude when it was first sampled. The bigger the number, the higher the amplitude. (This is only conceptually true—in practice, the data are in 2's complement form, a code that is easier to handle by circuits.) The square-wave at the top is the "word clock," the timing signal that tells the DAC *when* to convert the quantization word to an analog voltage. Assuming the original sampling frequency was 44.1kHz, the word clock's frequency will also be 44.1kHz (or, if the processor uses an oversampling digital filter, some multiple of 44.1kHz). On the word clock's *leading* edge, the next sample (quantization word) is loaded into the DAC. On the word clock's *falling* edge, the DAC converts that quantization word to an analog voltage. This process happens 44,100 times per second (without oversampling). If the digital processor has an 8x-oversampling digital filter, the word-clock frequency will be eight times 44,100, or 352.8kHz.

It is here at the word clock that timing variations affect the analog output signal. Specifically, clock jitter is any time variation between the clock's trailing edges. Fig.C-9 shows perfect and jittered clocks (exaggerated for clarity).

Fig. C-8 The word clock tells the DAC when to convert the quantization words to an analog voltage.

Courtesy *Stereophile*

Now, look what happens if the samples are reconstructed by a DAC whose word clock is jittered (Fig.C-10). The sample amplitudes—the ones and zeros—are correct, *but they're in the wrong places*. The right amplitude at the wrong time is the wrong amplitude. A *time* variation in the word clock produces an *amplitude* variation in the output, causing the waveform to change shape. A change in a waveform's shape is the

Fig. C-9 Word-clock jitter consists of either a random variation or a variation that has a periodic component.

Courtesy *Stereophile*

Fig. C-10 An analog waveform is reconstructed correctly with a jitter-free word clock (top); word-clock jitter results in a distortion of the analog waveform's shape.

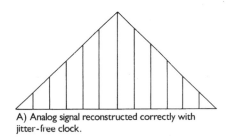

A) Analog signal reconstructed correctly with jitter-free clock.

B) Analog signal reconstructed with jittered clock. (Exaggerated for clarity) Although all the samples have the correct amplitude, because they occur at the wrong time, the reconstructed signal has the wrong shape.

Courtesy *Stereophile*

very definition of distortion. Remember, the word clock tells the DAC *when* to convert the audio sample to an analog voltage; any variations in its accuracy will produce an analog-like variability in the final output signal—the music.

Clock jitter can also raise the noise floor of a digital converter and introduce spurious artifacts. If the jitter has a random distribution (called "white jitter" because of its similarity to white noise), the noise floor will rise. If, however, the word clock is jittered at a specific frequency, artifacts will appear in the analog output as sidebands on either side of the audio signal frequency being converted to analog. It is these specific-frequency artifacts that are the most sonically detrimental; they bear no harmonic relationship to the music, and may be responsible for the hardness and glare often heard from digital audio.

Fig.C-11a is a spectral analysis of a computer-simulated digital processor's output when reproducing a full-scale, 10kHz sinewave with a jitter-free clock. Fig.C-11b is the same measurement, but with 2 nanoseconds (two billionths of a second) of jitter with a frequency of 1kHz on the clock. The plot in Fig.C-11b reveals the presence of discrete-frequency sidebands on either side of the test signal caused by jitter of a specific frequency. The amplitude of these artifacts is a function of the input signal level and frequency; the higher the signal level and frequency, the higher the sideband amplitude in the analog output signal.

Figs. C-11a and b Computer-simulated spectral analysis of a digital processor's output with a jitter-free clock (left), and with 2ns of jitter (right). (Courtesy *Stereophile*)

How much jitter is audible? In theory, a 16-bit converter must have less than 100 picoseconds of clock jitter if the signal-to-noise ratio isn't to be compromised (there are 1000 picoseconds in a nanosecond). Twenty-bit conversion requires much greater accuracy, on the order of 8ps. One hundred picoseconds is one-tenth of a billionth of a second (10^{-10}) — about the same amount of time it takes light to travel *an inch*. Moreover, this maximum allowable figure of 100ps assumes that the jitter is random (white), and does not have a specific frequency that would be less sonically benign. Clearly, extraordinary precision is required for accurate conversion.

Where does clock jitter originate? The primary source is the interface between a CD transport and a digital processor. The master clock signal is embedded in the S/PDIF (Sony/Philips Digital Interface Format) signal that connects the two devices (though it's more accurate to say that the audio data are embedded in the clock). The digital processor recovers this clock signal at the input receiver chip. The typical method of separating the clock from the data and creating a new clock with a *Phase Locked Loop* (PLL) produces *lots* of jitter. Even if the clock is recovered with low jitter, just about everything inside a digital processor introduces clock jitter: noise from digital circuitry, processing by integrated circuits—even a pcb trace.

It's important to note that the only point where jitter matters is at the DAC's word-clock input. A clock that's recovered perfectly but is degraded just before it gets to the DAC is no better than a high-jitter recovery circuit that's protected from additional jitter on its way to the DAC. Conversely, a highly jittered clock can be cleaned up just before the DAC with no penalty.

Digital Signal Processing (DSP)

DSP is the manipulation of an audio signal in the digital domain. DSP opens vast and exciting new possibilities for improving the quality of reproduced sound—possibilities unimaginable with analog techniques.

DSP is nothing more than the mathematical processing of the digital data representing an audio signal. This processing can take many forms, allowing DSP chips to be configured in a wide range of applications. For example, DSP chips can be programmed to be a high-pass and a low-pass filter, thus replacing the capacitors, resistors, and inductors in a loudspeaker crossover. Some loudspeakers accept a digital input, implement the crossovers with DSP, then convert the signal to analog inside the loudspeaker. The advantages of DSP crossovers are significant: the designer can make the crossover frequency and slope exactly as he or she wants it without regard for the limitations of analog crossover components—capacitors, resistors, and inductors. Moreover, the phase response can be precisely controlled, as can the time offset between drivers. In addition to such control, DSP crossovers get analog components out of the signal path for better sound. Such "digital" loudspeakers were pioneered by Meridian Audio.

Distortions in conventional loudspeakers can be corrected by DSP. If we know that a particular loudspeaker has amplitude errors and departures from linear phase response, those errors can be corrected in the digital domain by DSP.

The first commercial consumer product of this genre was the Celestion DLP-600. The DLP-600 is a digital input/output device connected between a CD transport and digital processor that corrects for time and amplitude anomalies in the Celestion SL-600si loudspeaker. The DLP-600 even corrects for reflections from driver mounting bolts and cabinet diffraction by introducing "anti-impulses" that cancel the acoustic reflections.

DSP in Professional Audio

DSP technology is rapidly being applied to all kinds of audio technology. For example, DSP can replace the racks of equipment used for sound reinforcement at amplified concerts. Currently, the equipment in those racks must be patched together with cables to configure the system. If the engineer needs an equalizer, for example, it must be physically patched into the system.

In a DSP-based system, however, there are no racks of specific equipment, only DSP chips that can be configured to perform any task required. The engineer assembles the sound-reinforcement system by dragging icons of particular devices with a mouse across a computer monitor. If he needs an equalizer, he just drags the equalizer icon into the signal path. This action reconfigures the DSP chips to perform equalization. The system's complexity is limited only by the number of available DSP chips. This concept is a revolution in how audio signals are handled and processed.

Perceptual Coding

Storing or transmitting even standard-resolution (16-bit/44.1kHz) digital audio requires a large storage capacity of the recording medium, or wide transmission bandwidth of the broadcast signal. Large storage capacity and wide bandwidth translate to greater expense in delivering digital audio to consumers. Moreover, some technologies are limited in the amount of data they can store or transmit. One example is the MiniDisc, which stores digital audio on a 2.5" disc. Another example is DVD-Video; most of the bandwidth is consumed by the digital video, leaving very little left over for the soundtrack.

This quandary is resolved by reducing the number of bits needed to encode an audio signal. This technique, called *perceptual coding*, attempts to radically reduce the data rate of digital audio signals with minimal effect on sound quality.

Dolby Digital is a good example of why perceptual coding is such a hot field. A 16-bit/44.1kHz digital audio signal (as is found on CD) consumes 705,600 bits per second per channel (16 times 44,100). With Dolby Digital's six discrete audio channels, a conventionally coded film soundtrack would consume a whopping 4,233,600 bits per second (4.23Mbs). This is roughly half the maximum continuous bitrate possible from DVD, leaving very little data for digital video, which has an even more voracious appetite for data capacity. The Dolby Digital perceptual encoder produces a digital audio datastream with a bitrate of just 384,000 or 448,000 bits per second—for all six channels. That's less than one tenth the amount of data without perceptual coding.

Let's look at how this is possible. Perceptual coding exploits idiosyncrasies of human hearing to allocate the available bits to sounds we can hear, and to ignore sounds we're less likely to hear. For example, the psychoacoustic effect of masking (described in Appendix A) prevents us from hearing quiet sounds in the presence of louder sounds. Perceptual coders introduce severe noise and errors into the audio signal because the music is encoded with so few bits. But that noise and distortion are cleverly manipulated so that they are just under the *masking threshold*, or the point below which a sound is inaudible. For example, if most of the musical energy at a given moment is concentrated between 1kHz and 3kHz, the noise will also be concentrated in that frequency band. The noise spectrum is constantly shifting so that the noise "hides" beneath the audio signal. Frequency bands with more information are allocated more bits; those bands with little information are allocated fewer bits. In practice, perceptual coding is vastly more complex.

I was once able to attend a remarkable demonstration of perceptual coding that highlighted how the technology works. I first heard a musical selection that had a signal-to-noise ratio of 13dB—a ridiculously low figure. For comparison, most electronics have signal-to-noise ratios of 80dB or greater. The sound was so noisy and distorted that the music was barely recognizable. I next heard the same music, again with a signal-to-noise ratio of 13dB, but this time it sounded fine. On an objective basis, the two presentations had exactly the same amount of noise. The difference was that in the second presentation, the noise was constantly shifting in spectral content so that it could "hide" beneath the correctly coded musical signal.

As powerful and useful as this technology can be, it has unfortunately been taken to extremes by some researchers in the field. They pronounced early perceptual coders as "transparent" (the perceptually coded signal was indistinguishable from the original), even though they sounded horrible. Moreover, in their zeal to further reduce the data rates, proponents of perceptual coding have sacrificed musical quality. The researchers speak of "psychoacoustic redundancy" and "informational irrelevance" with little regard for preserving the music with the highest fidelity. With this technological power comes hubris; perceptual coding has been promoted as suitable for master-tape archiving, a truly frightening thought. Our musical heritage should be preserved with the best technology, not the most economical.

Perceptual coding has its place: it makes possible reasonably good sound on DVD-Video, provides 74 minutes of playing time on a 2.5" MiniDisc, and can improve the quality of audio sent over the Internet. But keep in mind that perceptual coding was borne out of economics, not a desire to advance the state of the art of music recording and reproduction.

Those readers interested in learning more about digital audio are directed to the excellent *Principles of Digital Audio* by Ken Pohlmann.

Appendix D: The Role of Critical Listening in Evaluating Audio Equipment Quality

The following essay is a newly expanded treatment of my Audio Engineering Society paper of the same name, first presented at the 1991 AES convention in New York. It is published for the first time in this book.

Abstract

Critical observational listening can reveal aspects of audio equipment quality not exposed by traditional measurement techniques. Observational listening impressions are, however, often dismissed as mysticism, even when conducted by conscientious, technically oriented practitioners.

This paper outlines the methods and underlying philosophy of critical listening, explores why critical listening is rejected by some within the scientific audio community, and draws the distinction between serious listening and pseudoscientific claims.

Introduction

To doubt everything or to believe everything are two equally convenient solutions; both dispense with the necessity of reflection. Jules Henri Poincaré as quoted by Bertrand Russell in the preface to *Science and Method*.

The theme of the 91st Audio Engineering Society convention, "Audio Fact and Fantasy—Reckoning With the Realities," reflects the increasing polarization of the audio community over so-called "subjective" and "objective" audio. The conflict is so deep—and so fundamental to audio engineering—that the discourse has become known as "The Great Debate."

At one extreme, audio "objectivists" claim that no audible differences exist between competently designed and built products. This faction holds that "if it can't be measured, it can't be heard." Objectivists reject the listening experience outright, believing that nothing more can be known about audio equipment quality beyond the numbers generated by technical measurement. Those who use the listening experience to judge equipment quality are considered "charlatans" (1), believers in "astrology" (2), and "think the earth is flat." (3) Indeed, the letter from this convention's chairman inviting members to submit papers referred to critical listening observations as "fantasy." (4) Further, objectivists attempt to discredit listening observations by speciously linking critical listening with rejection of physical laws and established scientific fact. (5)

At the other extreme are critical listeners who repudiate any role of science in audio engineering, and who make absurd pseudoscientific claims about the audibility of certain phenomena.

Most critical listeners, however, reject this fringe view and simply trust their ears when making judgments about reproduced sound. To many of these listeners, the audio engineering establishment is made up of soulless technocrats whose narrow and rigid world view excludes a sensitivity to the subtle, yet musically significant, differences between audio components— differences that cannot be measured with existing technology. The objectivists are viewed as bound by theoretical dogma, and constrained by their refusal to accept the reality of direct experience. The objectivists' claim that products with similar technical performance will sound identical is an absurd premise anathema to the experience of hundreds of thousands of critical listeners.

Thus the lines of division are drawn.

The term "subjectivist" has been generally used to describe those who rely on the listening experience to judge sound-reproduction quality—largely because the term represents the polar opposite of "objectivist." In this paper I use the expression "observational listener" [1] because it better describes the process of critical listening.

Any inquiry that attempts to truly understand "The Great Debate" must address the underlying philosophical structures of both positions rather than rehash the same tired arguments. Although documenting observational-listening methodology is useful, a more fruitful approach examines the underlying source of the conflict. In addition to presenting the basic tenets and methods of observational listening, I shall attempt to look beyond the traditional battlegrounds and establish a wider framework for the debate. Indeed, "The Great Debate" is symptomatic of the uncertainty of science's capacity to encompass within its domain all forms of knowledge.

My profession gives me a unique insight into this conflict; I am a full-time reviewer of so-called "high-end" consumer audio products. In the course of my work, I have evaluated the sound qualities of more than 300 products and measured their technical performances. My job has been listening to, and measuring, audio equipment. My experience overwhelmingly indicates that many aspects of audio equipment quality are revealed in the listening room, not in the test laboratory. This simple thesis will be regarded by most audio professionals as a given truth unworthy of debate, yet others will denounce it as heresy and a threat to science's role in audio engineering, and, indeed, a threat to science itself.

This paper will explore why.

Observational Listening: Methods and Criticism

Whenever connoisseurship is found operating within science or technology we may assume that it persists only because it has not been possible to replace it by a measurable grading. — Michael Polanyi, *Personal Knowledge*: *Towards a Post-Critical Philosophy*

Observational listening is an integral part of every facet of audio. From the recording engineer who selects microphones based on their sound to the consumer choosing loudspeakers in a showroom, the observational listening experience plays a powerful role in music recording and reproduction. At every stage in the recording process, countless judgments are made about the quality of the perceived sound. (6)

No one doubts the necessity or utility of observational listening. Yet judgments of sound quality expressed in published product reviews are criticized as capricious, fantasy-inspired, biased, a result of the placebo effect, or influenced by external variables, while value judgments made at every other point in the recording/reproduction chain are accepted without question. Audio equipment reviewers are singled out for attack by objectivists—the "journalistic elite" (7)—even though reviewers employ the identical observational listening methodology as the recording engineer selecting microphones or the violin maker evaluating his creation.

Contrary to the objectivists' misconceptions, much observational listening as practiced by magazine reviewers is conducted under carefully controlled conditions—more controlled, in fact, than the conditions present during many other stages of the music recording and reproduction processes. Levels between components are matched to within 0.1dB or less. Linear differences, such as whether the product is polarity-inverting or not, are accounted for. Listening sessions are conducted daily for weeks or months before the review is written. A wide range of familiar source material is used over long periods of time and over a variety of equipment, precluding the possibility of ascribing a particular characteristic to a component that is actually a characteristic of the recording.

I cannot speak for the profession as a whole, but my listening (and that of my colleagues who write for the same publication) is anything but casual. My listening room was purpose-built from the ground up solely for music listening. Many of my colleagues are active recording engineers and use their own recordings in evaluating equipment. Some are musicians, daily exposed to the ultimate reference of live, unamplified instruments in an acoustic space. All of us became reviewers because of our lifelong dedications to music and music-reproduction technology. We take our responsibility to readers—and to audio truth—seriously; our attitude is the antithesis of caprice or whim. Indeed, the content of this paper exemplifies an approach to observational listening that is anything but cursory, casual, or superficial.

The objectivists dismiss observational listening by claiming the listening setup is sloppy, haphazard, casual, and that the reviewer has no regard for the sonic differences imposed by easily explainable measurable differences. According to this argument, the differences heard among components are nothing more than differences in level or frequency response—objective differences to which reviewers are supposedly oblivious. Further, observational listeners are often characterized as technical know-nothings operating from platforms of ignorance. (8) That may sometimes be the case, but the technically competent and conscientious observational listener should not be condemned by association. Just as there are varying levels of competence in any field, an entire philosophical position—the validity of the listening experience—cannot be summarily dismissed because some of its practitioners fail to uphold the highest standards.

Observational listening impressions reported in product reviews are also attacked because of alleged reviewer bias. But in my own work (and that of my colleagues), the positive or negative tone of a review is based solely on the component's sonic performance. The product's brand name, size, cost, reputation, faceplate thickness, and whether the manufacturer buys advertising play no role in the review's outcome. Although an expensive product from a reputable manufacturer will be expected to sound better than an inexpensive product, any such preconceptions vanish when the products reproduce music. The listening experience is the sole criterion by which a product is judged. Other factors, such as build quality, value, user interface, and compatibility with other products play minor roles, but it is the product's ability to convey the music's meaning that determines the positive or negative tone of the review. It is not unusual for an expensive product from a company with an excellent reputation to receive a negative review, or for a low-priced product to receive a favorable assessment.

Further, there is a high degree of correlation between the descriptions of a particular product's sonic character published by different magazines around the world. Reading several reviews of a product—reviews sometimes published simultaneously—often reveals a clear consensus about the component's specific sonic signature. This evidence that observational listening as practiced by magazine reviewers reveals the unique musical characteristics of individual audio components is dismissed by objectivists who allege premeditated fraud. The resort to conspiracy theories is always the sign of a weak argument.

The entire purpose of observational listening is to discover and report to the magazine's readers how the component affects the musical experience. The magazine's continuing success is predicated on the accuracy of the sonic descriptions and the judgments of the products as determined by the world at large. The growth of high-end magazines—and their increasing commercial success in a marketplace long dominated by publications reflecting an objectivist philosophy—reflects the concurrence between reviewers' and readers' observations and experiences.

Listening vs. Measurement

One of the worst-kept secrets in audio engineering is that what we hear does not always correlate with what we measure. —Richard Heyser

Observational listening, and the connoisseurship employed in its practice, are required to judge audio equipment quality because today's measurement techniques fail to describe how an audio component affects the music-listening experience. Just as a concert piano is best judged by experts who listen to the instrument, music-reproduction technology must be evaluated by musically sensitive listeners trained in recognizing artifacts in reproduced sound. These artifacts are vastly more varied, complex, and subtle than can be described by a set of measurements.

The objectivists' belief that nothing more can be known about an audio component's performance beyond the numbers generated by "objective" measurement implies that quality in an audio component can be unambiguously quantified and expressed by mathematical symbols. Because the entire sum of how a component affects the signal passing through it—down to the smallest detail—is known and measurable, why listen? And because these tests and measurements are completely objective, why interject human subjectivity into the process of determining which audio components have more quality than others?

This objectivist argument is based on two false premises: 1) that scientific inquiry is objective and entirely detached from the individual, and 2) that audio equipment quality can be reduced to a series of mathematical representations.

The first false premise—that objectivity actually exists—is deeply rooted in Western thought. The modern scientific mind likes to think of itself as existing outside nature, a passive and disinterested observer. This paper cannot have the ambition of discussing in depth the illusion of science as a value-free pursuit; instead I refer the reader to the work cited in footnote 8. But a glimmer of the underlying fallacy can be seen when examining the concept of objectivity in audio testing. What do we observe objectively when determining what constitutes "good" performance? The size of the chassis thread screws? How many cycles of the test tone the component reproduced during the test? The color of the resistors? Of course not. Of the virtually infinite range of observations of the component under analysis, some are *chosen* as being greater indicators of "goodness" than others. It is this choice of tests that is in itself a subjective decision.

The scientist, confronted with evidence provided by nature, is guided by *values* when inventing hypotheses. There are no rules, no procedures, and no formalized objective methods for creating hypotheses; they instead spring—apparently spontaneously—from the mind because they have greater *value* than less plausible explanations. The formulation of hypotheses is inherently subjective and driven by value.

But what is "quality" in an audio component? Is it merely the ability to meet certain "objective" criteria? I think not. I propose that audio equipment quality is irreducible to a set of numbers. Audio component quality is defined in the listening room by the component's ability to convey the music's essence and meaning without imposing itself on the communication between artist and listener. Some components produce an intimacy with the music that makes the listener forget the playback system; others seem to do their best to prevent such a reaction. My experience suggests that this fundamental characteristic—perhaps related to the listener's holistic reaction to the reproduced sound—is a much more meaningful indicator of component quality than a set of numbers produced in the test lab.

More specifically, we haven't even begun to understand—much less quantify—the myriad audible differences among components. Such aspects of the musical presentation as soundstage depth, sharpness of instrumental outlines, sense of space between individual instruments, and how well soundstage width is maintained toward the rear of the presentation are far too complex to be measured by existing methods. This isn't to say that these qualities are somehow mystical because they defy measurement. If the sound is different, then the signals must be different. But measurement fails simply because the resolution of today's instruments falls far short of the human auditory system's refinement. Indeed, the measurements in use today were developed decades ago as design tools, not as representations of musical reality. Measurement may one day advance to the point of describing these differences, but that day is probably a long way off.

Oddly, audio is the only field that measures its products in ways that bear absolutely no relation to the way the products are used. Specifically, we frequently use single-frequency test tones to judge technical performance, yet the products will operate on much more complex musical signals. The "Heyser Box" beautifully illustrates this irony. Invented by the late Richard Heyser, the Heyser Box is a small device with one input and one output jack. When subjected to laboratory measurement, the box exhibits flat frequency response and introduces no noise, phase shift, or distortion. Indeed, the box appears to be a straight wire. But when music is put through the box and listened to, the sound is so garbled as to be unintelligible. The secret? A circuit inside the box detects the constant amplitude of test tones and closes a relay connecting input to output. But when a varying-amplitude musical signal is detected, the relay quickly opens and closes, chopping up the signal.

Another shortcoming of attempting to describe equipment quality through measurement is that virtually all laboratory testing assumes that audio components distort signals according to a Markov process. A Markov process, named after Russian mathematician Andrey Andreyevich Markov, ignores the past when considering future values. Specifically, audio testing assumes that previous conditions of the component or test signal have no effect on the component's present behavior. For example, we assume that the component will exhibit identical performance from moment to moment, whether the component has been sitting at idle or processing full-scale signals. But audio components can remember the past: musical transients produce inertial effects in the form of thermal "tails," overshoot, and ringing. Semiconductors can behave differently in the milliseconds after passing a high-level transient signal. The ultimate example of how an audio component's memory of the past affects present performance is the power amplifier that outputs no signal (100% distortion) because its rail fuse had been previously blown by high signal levels.

Music is not test tones. And the audio chain is full of non-Markov processes. Yet the audio engineering establishment clings to the belief that the numbers generated by conventional measurement can somehow describe—down to the smallest detail—every aspect of how that component affects the signal passing through it. Measurement can be useful in a crude sense—a loudspeaker with x sensitivity requires y watts of amplifier power to produce z sound-pressure level, for example. And measurement is essential in guiding the designer toward his goal. But looking at a series of numbers cannot hope to replace the direct experience of listening to music through a product and employing the skills of a sensitive and fully attentive listener in judging the quality of the reproduced sound.

Beyond the physical differences between music and test tones, quantifying audio-equipment performance is destined to fail because measurement excludes the listener's role in music reproduction. Sound is merely vibrating air molecules; the brain processes that vibration into music, then recognizes the music's meaning and, on occasion, finds ecstasy in that meaning. Without this processing within the listener's brain, music doesn't exist.

Richard Heyser illustrated this idea in a treatise for an Audio Engineering Society workshop discussing the nature of distortion: "Now let's consider this: the end product of audio is the listening experience. The end product is the result of perception, cognition, and valuation processes occurring in the mind. What things do we know about such processes? The answer is very little. But there are a few observable facts about this which, when considered for audio, give pause for redefining the concept of distortion. We know, for example, that words which are sung are perceived in a different manner than words which are spoken. Aphasia—the loss of ability to understand or speak words as a result of brain lesion—does not affect music. Where, in our audio technology, can we measure a waveform and distinguish its message as that of language or music? The brain does it. And can we be so presumptuous as to assume that the same measure of distortion which we use for one such waveform (which we cannot identify) must also apply to the other waveform? The left hemisphere of our brains and the right hemisphere play an incredibly complicated role in perception—a role completely ignored whenever we make a simple waveform analysis with audio test equipment."

Do we really have the hubris to believe that the resolution of test instruments developed in the last few decades exceeds that of human hearing acuity, refined through millions of years of evolution? The reluctance to admit that measurements fail to quantify all aspects of audio component behavior stems from a reluctance to accept the limits of our present-day engineering, and indeed, of the limits of science itself.

Skills

One of the most belittling experiences is to deride the "black art" of a craftsman who gets consistent results by a certain ritual which he cannot explain and then to discover that his actions in fact held a deeper technical significance than we understood from our simplified model. —Richard Heyser

Central to "The Great Debate" is the question of science's capacity to encompass within its domain all forms of knowledge. The objectivists hold that understanding reality is a formalized process, which, if its rules are followed, will establish an unambiguous, universal truth. Adherence to the prescribed methods is the only way of revealing nature's secrets. This belief is reflected in the blind-testing methodology, detailed later in this paper. So great is the objectivists' faith in blind testing (and the underlying formalized method on which it is based) that they refuse to listen for themselves. (9) This position reflects a general belief that no forms of knowing exist outside those revealed through the prescribed methods of scientific inquiry.

I propose that other forms of knowing are possible. Many skills, including critical observational listening, fall outside the domain of formalized method and cannot be quantified: these forms of knowledge are "tacit," "unspecifiable," and "inarticulate." (10) The audio engineering establishment dogma rejects as unreal these forms of knowledge because they cannot be measured or quantified.

Polanyi offers two examples of skills that fall outside the formalized domain of science:

It follows that an art which has fallen into disuse for the period of a generation is altogether lost. There are hundreds of examples of this to which the process of mechanization is continuously adding new ones. These losses are usually irretrievable. It is pathetic to watch the endless efforts—equipped with microscopy and chemistry, with mathematics and electronics—to reproduce a single violin of the kind the half-literate Stradivarius turned out as a matter of routine more than 200 years ago. (11)

More specifically, Polanyi describes in objective terms the simple skill of bicycle riding, using the formalized prescriptive language of science:

When he starts falling to the right he turns the handlebars to the right, so that the route of the bicycle is deflected along a curve towards the right. This results in a centrifugal force pushing the cyclist to the left and offsets the gravitational force dragging him down to the right. This maneuver presently throws the cyclist out of balance to the left, which he counteracts by turning the handlebars to the left, so he continues to keep himself in balance by winding along a series of appropriate curvatures. A simple analysis shows that for a given angle of unbalance the curvature of each winding is inversely proportional to the square of the speed at which the bicycle is proceeding.

But does this tell us how to ride a bicycle? No. You obviously cannot adjust the curvature of your bicycle's path in proportion to the ratio of your unbalance over the square of your speed; and if you could you would fall off the machine, for there are a number of other factors to be taken into account in practice which are left out of the formulation of this rule. Rules of art can be useful, but they do not determine the practice of an art; they are maxims, which can serve us a guide to an art only if they can be integrated into the practical knowledge of the art. They cannot replace this knowledge. (12)

Although the physics of riding a bicycle can be expressed and understood rationally, another component is necessary to ride a bicycle—tacit knowledge. Without ever having ridden a bicycle, a person who demonstrated a knowledge of bicycle-riding physics would appear to know how to ride a bicycle. Conversely, the scientifically illiterate person, with absolutely no knowledge of Newtonian physics, could be a bicycling expert yet be unable to express this tacit knowledge. Without moving from the theoretical to the experiential domain, one would be tempted to believe that the person who could articulate the physics of bicycle riding could indeed ride a bicycle while the person who could not express his tacit, inarticulate knowledge, could not.

The example of bicycle riding demonstrates that knowledge gained by studying theory is very different from knowledge gained by experience and practice. Knowledge without experience is empty, devoid of the reality that theory represents. Indeed, science education emphasizes practical experience because there is no substitute for it:

> *The large amount of time spent by students of chemistry, biology, and medicine in their practical courses shows how greatly these sciences rely on the transmission of skills and connoisseurship from master to apprentice.* (13)

Clearly, some forms of knowing fall outside the realm of formalized study. The objectivists' attempt to dismiss the use of personal skills in evaluating audio equipment, and to reduce the art of listening to a prescriptive method (as exemplified by the blind-testing methodology described later), reflects an unawareness of the role inarticulate knowledge plays in all facets of human existence.

The objectivists' rejection of this form of knowledge, coupled with blind faith in the scientific method's infallibility and unlimited capacity to reveal nature's truths, is the very foundation of "The Great Debate."

Language

> *. . . the root cause of the continuing fight between subjective and objective audio. . . is not that either is more correct than the other. . . rather is due to the fact they do not speak the same language.* —Richard Heyser

The dichotomy between the academic engineering establishment and critical listeners is exacerbated by the different language each uses to describe their realities. To the objectivists, who believe that every aspect of an audio component's sonic performance can be measured, quantified, and communicated unambiguously through mathematical symbols, the language of critical listening is nothing more than vague poetic nonsense. Examples of the observational listener's lexicon include the expressions "low-frequency extension," "air," and "bloom." Analyzing these terms' relative abstraction or expressiveness sheds light on why the different languages of audio prevent mutual understanding of each others' positions.

The meaning of the term "low-frequency extension" is easily understood by virtually anyone who has listened to large and small loudspeakers. The expression has meaning because it describes a perception readily experienced in everyday life.

The next term, "air," is meaningful to a smaller percentage of the population because it expresses an aspect of audio quality not consciously recognized by most casual listeners. They may prefer a musical presentation with "air" to one without "air," but they probably couldn't say why. It is abstract to those who haven't consciously discerned this aspect of an audio system's performance.

Finally, "bloom" is even more abstract to most people because it describes a phenomenon not readily encountered, recognized, or discerned in an audio system. The ability of a playback system to reveal "bloom" (a sense of expanding air surrounding instrumental image outlines that follows the note's dynamic envelope) is a subtle refinement rarely differentiated by the vast majority of the music-listening public. The word is absolutely meaningless to those who haven't experienced bloom in a music playback system, yet is highly descriptive to those who have experienced the phenomenon.

To those who associate audio-equipment performance with technical terms and specifications rather than with the listening experience, the lexicon of observational listening appears devoid of substance—worthless jargon designed to obfuscate rather than to enlighten. Conversely, a musician with no technical knowledge of audio reproduction technology would find technical terms and specifications meaningless, bearing absolute no relation to *his* reality.

Both the expressions of observational listeners and the measurement data generated by laboratory testing are symbolic representations of reality. Without direct contact with, and experience in, that reality, its associated lexicon is dismissed as unintelligible. Language must be used repeatedly, consistently, in context, and relate to matters of experience to acquire meaning.

The following passage illuminates the inextricable bond between language and understanding:

An illustration—akin to that of topographic anatomy by which we exemplified the ineffable—may exhibit this dual movement of comprehension in learning a language. Think of a medical student attending a course in the X-ray diagnosis of pulmonary diseases. He watches in a darkened room shadowy traces on a fluorescent screen placed against a patient's chest, and hears the radiologist commenting to his assistants in technical language, on the significant features of the shadows. At first, the student is completely puzzled. For he can see in the X-ray picture of a chest only the shadows of the heart and ribs, with a few spidery blotches between them. The experts seem to be romancing about figments of their imagination; he can see nothing that they are talking about. Then as he goes on listening for a few weeks, looking carefully at the ever new pictures of different cases, a tentative understanding will dawn on him; he will gradually forget about the ribs and begin to see the lungs. And eventually, if he perseveres intelligently, a rich panorama of significant details will be revealed to him; of physiological variations and pathological changes, of scars, of chronic infections and signs of acute disease. He has entered a new world. He still sees only a fraction of what the experts can see, but the pictures are definitely making sense now and so do most of the comments made on them. He is about to grasp what he is being taught; it has clicked. Thus, at the moment when he has learned the language of pulmonary radiology, the student will also have learned to understand pulmonary radiograms. The two can only happen together. Both halves of the problem set to us by an unintelligible text, referring to an unintelligible subject, jointly guide our efforts to solve them, and they are solved eventually together by discovering a conception which comprises a joint understanding of both the words and the things. (14)

By confining one's experience exclusively to technical parameters and excluding the listening experience as a method of evaluating audio equipment quality, objectivists dismiss as nonsense the language used to describe differences between components because they have no experience to which it relates.

Scale

Another problem related to the language used to describe the sound of audio components is the matter of scale. Objectivists claim that perceived differences are magnified out of proportion by ulterior motives. (15) I submit that this question of scale reflects the varying sensitivity of different listeners when exposed to the same musical presentation.

The ability of certain individuals to demonstrate apparently preternatural skills is well documented. These individuals have worked at developing a particular sense, either out of a survival need or merely by practicing it daily in their professions. Examples of these skills are described by Csikszentmihalyi:

> *The flexibility of attentional structures is even more obvious when they are compared across cultural or occupational classes. Eskimo hunters are trained to discriminate between dozens of types of snow, and are always aware of the direction and speed of the wind. Traditional Melanesian sailors can be taken blindfolded to any point of the ocean within a radius of several hundred miles from their island home and, if allowed to float free for a few minutes in the sea, are able to recognize the spot by the feel of the currents on their bodies. A musician structures her attention so as to focus on nuances of sound that ordinary people are not aware of, a stockbroker focuses on tiny changes in the market that others do not register, a good clinical diagnostician has an uncanny eye for symptoms—because they have trained their attention to process signals that would otherwise pass unnoticed.* (16)

Similarly, the audio-equipment reviewer, whose chosen profession is discerning, evaluating, and describing differences between audio components and who practices his skills daily, develops a sensitivity that appears farfetched to someone not similarly attuned. The audible differences reported thus seem overstated to those who have not developed such an ability or who are unaware that such abilities can exist.

These sonic differences in the musical presentation can, however, be appreciated by anyone who enjoys music. The sonically sensitive music lover, who may lack the specialized skill to describe exactly why one component sounds better than another, nonetheless enjoys music more through components with lower levels of electronically or mechanically induced sonic artifacts. This listener simply knows what sounds more like music.

Responsible Reporting and Pseudoscience

Nothing irks the scientific audio community more than reading or hearing about some new audio device or technique that countermands the laws of physics. The world of high-end audio abounds in this nonsense.

Unfortunately, objectivists attempt to discredit all observational listening by linking the entire high-end audio industry and responsible critical listeners to absurd pseudoscientific claims. This "guilt by association" technique is an affront to all serious listeners who repudiate the mumbo-jumbo and pseudoscientific elements of audio. The responsible high-end press, whose allegiance is to its readers, has a duty to expose such fraud for what it is, both in the interests of truth and to protect its readers from buying worthless devices.

There is a regrettable tendency for marketers of some audio products to invent incredible explanations of why a particular device has an audible effect. The phenomenon may be real, but is given a "false interpretation" by its discoverers. The history of science is filled with examples of a real phenomenon being attributed to unlikely and unscientific causes, followed by what Polanyi calls "destructive analysis" by the scientific community before the underlying mechanisms are understood.

The case of hypnotism illustrates the cycle of false interpretation followed by destructive analysis. Franz Mesmer's dissertation at the University of Vienna in 1766 suggested that the gravitational attraction of the planets influenced human health by affecting an invisible fluid found in the human body and throughout nature. This theory evolved into "animal magnetism," wherein the invisible fluid in the body acted according to the laws of magnetism. According to Mesmer, "animal magnetism" could be activated by any magnetic object and manipulated by a trained person. Mesmer was accused of fraud and fled to Paris, where he enjoyed a lucrative practice fueled by patient testimonials. A commission appointed by King Louis XVI to investigate Mesmer's methods reported that Mesmer was unable to substantiate his claims. (17)

Physician John Elliotson later expounded a whole system of laws governing animal magnetism. "He claimed that the magnetism in a glass of water could be graded by dipping one finger into it, or two fingers, or the whole hand. Another 'law' declared that mucous surfaces of the subject, like those of the tongue or eyeball, were capable of receiving a greater mesmeric stimulus than the skin. All this was nonsense and proved to be nonsense. And since the assumption had not yet dawned on anyone that hypnotic suggestion was the effective agent of Mesmerism, the conclusion seemed inevitable that Elliotson's subjects were impostors, who were either deluding him or colluding with him." (18) Elliotson appealed to his attackers to consider the practical evidence of his technique: "I have given the details of 76 painless operations. In the name of common sense and humanity, what more is wanted?" The fact remained that Elliotson's technique did indeed allow him to perform painless surgery.

Polanyi interprets:

Not until the concept of hypnosis was established as a framework for the facts could those facts be eventually admitted as true. Indeed, whenever truth and error are amalgamated in a coherent system of conception, the destructive analysis of the system can lead to correct conclusions only when supplemented by new discoveries. But there exists no rule for making fresh discoveries or inventing truer conceptions, and hence there can be no rule, either, for avoiding the uncertainty of destructive analysis. (19)

Similarly, today's false interpretations of audible phenomenon are subject to the same form of destructive analysis as was applied to hypnotism. Because an effect has no rational explanation it doesn't automatically follow that the effect is nonexistent. Just as hypnotism was a very real effect—yet denounced as fraud—many audio devices can change the character of the reproduced sound. They too are denounced as fraud because the underlying causes are misrepresented, which opens the door to destructive analysis and even ridicule. This trend is exacerbated by the objectivist hubris that no mysteries remain in audio engineering: every aspect of how circuits affect signals is understood down to the smallest scale.

A more recent example of Polanyi's "destructive analysis" bears startling parallels to the case of hypnotism. When the first two-box CD players (separate transport and digital-to-analog converter) were introduced, observational listeners immediately reported hearing differences between cables carrying the digital audio data from the transport to the digital-to-analog converter. In theory, no such audible differences should exist if the cable doesn't change the ones and zeros representing the audio signal. Nonetheless, it became readily apparent to critical listeners that digital cables exhibited an analog-like variability in sound quality. Observational listeners also discovered that cables carrying digital audio were directional; that is, the cable produced a different sound when connected in reverse direction between the data source and the digital-to-analog converter. After ten years of listening experience, the audibility and directionality of digital cables were so obvious that digital cables were no longer the subject of debate among observational listeners.

Objectivists seized on these reports, characterizing them as the height of audiophile lunacy. Proving that cables don't change the digital data is a simple matter. Moreover, the objectivists argued, a computer program doesn't operate differently if run from an external hard disk drive through a cable rather than from an internal disk drive. It was an article of faith among objectivists that if the ones and zeros are the same, the sound must be the same. The question of the audibility of digital cables became a litmus test of one's rationality; anyone who claimed there were differences was subjected to ridicule by some within the audio engineering establishment.[2]

The objectivists' destructive analysis of the digital interface fell prey to Polanyi's principle that destructive analysis is uncertain because it is provides no guidance in making new discoveries about the phenomenon in question. Specifically, subsequent analysis revealed that the digital interface can affect the reproduced sound by introducing timing errors in the clock carried along with the audio signal. These timing errors, known as jitter, are passed to the so-called "word clock" that controls the timing of the conversion of digital samples into analog values at the digital-to-analog converter chip. The cable's bandwidth and characteristic impedance, along with the source's output impedance and receiver's input impedance, all affect the amount of interface-induced jitter, creating an analog-like variability in sound quality. Even though the ones and zeros are the same, the precision of the timing with which those ones and zeros are converted into music was continuously variable, which introduced a continuous variability in sound quality. Computer data are not affected by this variability because they are never converted to an analog form and analyzed by the human brain as sound. It turns out that humans are extraordinarily sensitive to these timing variations, and that jitter is partly responsible for the audible deficiencies of early digital-audio reproduction.

Further, the integrity of the solder joint between the cable and termination can introduce reflections in the cable, which in turn adds jitter. The amount of jitter in the clock at the digital-to-analog converter depends on whether the poor solder joint was at the interface's transmitting or receiving end. In my own measurements of interface jitter, poorly made cables introduced nearly double the amount of jitter depending on which end was connected to the transport. (20). This inquiry confirms observational listeners' reports that digital cables are directional.

The digital interface's capacity for introducing an analog-like variability in sound quality has now been so well researched and documented—in published, peer-reviewed papers written by respected academics—that it has become accepted fact. (21) Indeed, jitter became the audio buzzword of the late 1990s. Virtually every manufacturer of test instrumentation scrambled to add jitter-measurement capability to its laboratory hardware. But the engineering community was alerted to potential problems in the digital interface only by reports from critical listeners unafraid to describe their listening impressions in the face of ridicule by objectivists. Similarly, the phenomenon was first investigated by open-minded researchers who acknowledged the growing body of listening observations that the interface was not sonically transparent.

To observational listeners, an effect is judged real or illusory in the listening room, not according to the effect's theoretical compatibility with established dogma. The jitter example cited above is just one example of many now-established phenomena that would never have been discovered had individuals not investigated them by critical listening. Rather than engage in destructive analysis in an effort to discredit observational listening, the scientific audio community should listen for itself and investigate these phenomena. The idea that nothing more remains to be learned about apparently simple systems (power amplifiers, for example) is ludicrous. Even more ludicrous is the belief that all aspects of the relatively new field of digital audio are fully understood by science. It is ironic that the very individuals equipped with the academic training needed to research these phenomena are the least likely to listen for themselves, and the most likely to dismiss observational listening reports as pseudoscientific nonsense. Indeed, there sometimes seems to be an inverse relationship between an individual's scientific skills and his willingness to listen for himself. [3]

Scientists should ignore claims that are patently absurd; there is only so much research time and money. Similarly, audio journalists should denounce false interpretations for what they are, and indeed many do. But the criterion by which a claim is prejudged patently absurd or a possibility worth investigating should be its audible effect—knowledge gained by first-hand listening experience—not by its compliance with established theory.

The objectivists' "rejection without listening" doctrine is an impediment to the advancement of audio engineering.

The High-End Audio Industry: Fraud, Delusion, or Reality?

If, as objectivists claim, all competently designed and manufactured audio components are sonically identical, then it follows that the entire high-end audio industry is a fraud perpetrated on an unsuspecting public. This view would seem to suggest that the music-listening world needs nothing more than an inexpensive receiver—provided, of course, that it has lots of features and the front-panel markings were easy to read. Indeed, one of the objectivists' objections to high-end audio is how expensive certain components are. They believe the public is being systematically exploited, driven by a high-end audio "journalistic elite" who "irresponsibly" recommend components based on sound quality no different from any cheap, competently designed product. (22)

To subscribe to this theory, one of two premises must also be accepted: 1) that the entire high-end audio industry realizes the components it designs and builds are no better than any others, and are thus engaged in premeditated collusion and fraud to perpetuate their own existence; or 2) that everyone associated with high-quality music reproduction lives in a fantasy world, victim of the same delusions that defraud consumers of their money. Maintaining that no sonic differences exist between competently designed and manufactured products forces one to embrace one of these two scenarios.

Let's take the first premise—that high-end audio companies willfully engage in fraud, knowing that their products sound no better than any others. If that were the case, why would so many of them spend large sums of money on sophisticated computer-assisted electronic design software and hardware? On expensive associated components with which to audition their own products? On continuing education for their designers? Why would they include expensive resistors and capacitors in their products—components sometimes embedded in potted modules never seen by the consumer?

Even a cursory examination of this position reveals its absurdity.

The second possible theory—that high-end product designers and their customers are subject to mass delusion—is equally absurd. Many high-end product designers hold advanced engineering degrees and possess solid scientific backgrounds. Can it be believed that their entire careers and life's work—designing better-sounding equipment—are based on delusion and fantasy? That with every new circuit evaluation in the listening room the designers (and everyone else in the company who listens) consistently hear differences that don't exist? That the superiority of certain capacitor types, passive components, wire, and layout techniques is a figment of the collective imagination, perpetuated through the power of suggestion and deluded journalists? That every consumer who chooses a component based on sound quality is similarly deluded?

I propose that it is more reasonable to believe that audible differences exist between, say, polystyrene and electrolytic capacitors or silver and copper wire, than either the mass-fraud or mass-delusion theories of high-end audio.

Blind Listening Tests

Experience which is not valued is not experienced. . . Value is at the very front of the empirical procession —Robert M. Pirsig, *Lila: An Inquiry into Morals*

At first glance, it would seem that proving or disproving the audibility of a certain phenomenon is a simple proposition: Expose a listener to the two stimuli in question, prevent the listener from knowing the identity of the stimuli, and instruct the listener to correctly identify a particular stimulus. If the listener identifies a particular stimulus with statistically significant reliability, the phenomenon can be considered audible. If the listener cannot identify the particular stimulus under these conditions—with statistical certainty—the phenomenon is considered nonexistent. To objectivists, questions of a phenomenon's audibility begin and end with blind testing.

Blind testing is the cornerstone of objectivist belief. So great is their faith in blind testing's infallibility that they refuse to participate in observational listening themselves. This position is stated unequivocally by Professor Stanley Lipshitz, the most vocal proponent of the objectivist philosophy:

> *. . . I would like to comment briefly on a frequently heard but nonsensical request which the 'subjectivists' make of us 'objectivists'—namely that we undertake tests to substantiate their claims for the audibility of a certain effect. How can you expect someone who professes not to be able to hear something to demonstrate its audibility? The onus clearly falls on those who claim they* can *hear the difference to be willing to subject their claims to the harsh reality of a blind listening test.* Only by doing so *can the validity of some of these assertions be either proven or refuted, and in the process can the field of audio engineering truly be advanced.* (latter emphasis added) (23)

Without firsthand personal knowledge if differences among components exist or not, the objectivists' entire belief structure rests solely on the validity of the blind-testing methodology ("*Only by doing so. . .* "). The objectivists live and die by the blind test.

Clearly, the objectivists consider blind testing as the great exposer of observational listeners' fraud and delusion—the listeners' Achilles' Heel. I propose, however, that the entire blind methodology is the *objectivists'* Achilles' Heel, for it is the sole basis for their position. Any underlying weakness in the blind methodology completely undermines their entire philosophical foundation.

Before I examine the flaws inherent in blind testing, a review of how these tests are performed is illustrative. Blind listening tests are frequently conducted under the following conditions:

1) The experimenter's agenda is often to prove that no audible differences exist rather than to discover if differences do exist. (24)

2) There is an adversarial relationship between listener and experimenter, and the listener is aware that he will be exposed to ridicule if he "fails."

3) The playback system, music, room, and other conditions are foreign to the listener.

4) The experimenter controls all aspects of the test, including the music used, playback level, how long the listener can hear each presentation, how many times the listener can hear each presentation, the rapidity of switching between presentations, and in which musical passage the switching occurs.

5) The experimenter controls the number of successive trials without regard for the listener's fatigue, increasing the number of trials if a trend indicating reliable identification appears.

6) The number of successive trials is excessively high, in an attempt to get a greater statistical sample size.[4]

At one large-scale blind listening test I attended, conducted during an officially sanctioned Audio Engineering Society convention (the 91st), the test conditions revealed more about those conducting the test than about the audible phenomenon in question. This listening test was designed to "discover" if different brands of loudspeaker cables sounded different from one another. Two folding tables at the front of a huge ballroom supported a pair of small domestic loudspeakers designed for a living room, not a space that seats 400. Many in the audience sat to the left of the left loudspeaker or to the right of the right loudspeaker. The loudspeaker positions, and the large distances involved, meant no audience member could hear a soundstage. In addition, the loudspeaker's tonal balance was severely distorted because the loudspeakers had been designed to stand on the floor, not for placement three feet off the ground on flimsy tables. Further, the sound reproduced by the domestic loudspeakers was picked up by microphones worn by panelists (all of whom had just ridiculed the possibility of audible differences between cables), then amplified through the room's public-address system. The audience thus heard the sound from the loudspeakers, then a delayed version of that sound reproduced through the ballroom's public address loudspeakers.

The two individuals who designed and conducted the test are AES members, reputed experts in designing listening tests (indeed, one—David Clark—was made a Fellow of the AES for his work on double-blind testing), and vocal critics of observational listening as practiced in published product reviews. Despite the objections of some audience members about the absurd listening conditions, this "scientific" inquiry into the audibility of loudspeaker cables continued. But listening conditions are of no importance if the outcome is known in advance. The "researchers" subsequently claimed that the data gathered during this test "revealed" no audible differences between cables.

Not surprisingly, tests conducted in this manner (and even those conducted by well-meaning researchers under better conditions) have frequently shown that listeners are unable to identify differences previously heard under other conditions. One must ask, however, if the inability to discriminate under blind testing conditions indicates that the phenomenon doesn't exist, or if these testing procedures interject hidden variables that invalidate the test results.

The question is not a trivial one. If blind testing is inherently flawed as a method of revealing differences, the objectivists' position becomes untenable.

I submit that the methods employed in blind testing, and the conclusions drawn from them, reflect a fundamental misunderstanding of human musical perception. Blind testing is flawed on two levels: the mechanics of the process, and the philosophical underpinnings on which the technique is based.

To begin with the mechanical and procedural flaws of blind testing, the process is a gross distortion of reality in that the conditions present during blind testing are the antitheses of the conditions present during normal music listening. This is another example of the observation cited earlier that audio is the only field that tests its products in ways that bear absolutely no relationship to the ways in which those products are used. An individual's sensitivity to subtle differences is diminished under the stress and completely artificial conditions inherent in blind testing.

Observational listeners employ the "single presentation method" of listening, in which a piece of music is auditioned in its entirety before listening to the same piece again through another component. This technique is in sharp contrast to the rapid back and forth switching employed in blind listening tests. Because of these procedural problems, the interaction between the listener and the test introduces unknown and therefore unquantifiable variables into the experiment. In a discipline that prides itself on recognizing and controlling all experimental variables, it is surprising that the myriad characteristics of human perception have been so studiously ignored.

Among these variables are an individual's ability to maintain sensory sensitivity in the face of excessive stimulation. Research indicates that the limits of consciousness are far lower than previously assumed—limits that are routinely exceeded during blind testing. Csikszentmihalyi writes:

At this point in our scientific knowledge we are on the verge of being able to estimate how much information the central nervous system is capable of processing. It seems we can manage at most seven bits of information—such as differentiated sounds, or visual stimuli, or recognize the nuances of emotion or thought—at any one time, and that the shortest time it takes to discriminate between one set of bits and another is about 1/18 of a second. By using these figures one concludes that it is possible to process at most 126 bits of information per second, or 7560 per minute, or almost half a million per hour. It is out of this total that everything in our life must come—every thought, memory, feeling, or action. It seems like a huge amount, but in reality it does not go that far.

The limitation of consciousness is demonstrated by the fact that to understand what another person is saying we must process 40 bits of information per second. If we assume the upper limit of our capacity to be 126 bits per second, it follows that to understand what three people are saying simultaneously is theoretically possible, but only by managing to keep out of consciousness every other thought or sensation. We couldn't, for instance, be aware of the speakers' expressions, nor could we wonder about why they are saying what they are saying, or notice what they are wearing.

Despite its great powers, attention cannot step beyond the limits already described. It cannot notice or hold in focus more information than can be processed simultaneously. Retrieving information from memory storage and bringing it into the focus of awareness, comparing information, evaluating, deciding—all make demands on the mind's limited processing ability. (emphasis added) (25)

The finite and limited reserve of concentration is depleted by the myriad unfavorable conditions inherent in blind testing, leaving little left to discriminate audible differences, much less to interpret the music's meaning—a subject to which I shall return.

This situation creates a paradox: The harder one tries to discern a difference, the more difficult it becomes to detect that difference. Trying hard consumes so much of Csikszentmihalyi's 40 bits per second that little processing power is left to discriminate audible differences.

A common trick among recording engineers is to tell an anxiety-ridden vocalist about to lay down an overdub that the first run-through of the song is just to set levels and practice—the tape machine won't be recording. Of course, the good engineer knows that this will often be the best performance the artist can give and pushes the "Record" button—to the subsequent relief and gratitude of the artist after realizing the subterfuge. Similarly, subjects undergoing listening tests should be oblivious to any monitoring of their performance—a "triple-blind" test, if you will.

During blind testing, the listener's tendency is to focus on a specific aspect of the presentation to aid him in identifying a particular component. This natural inclination to "try hard" is a fatal mistake because it is diametrically opposed to normal music-listening practice. By concentrating on the specific, the listener becomes oblivious to communication of musical expression—the true indicator of audio equipment quality. It is ironic that legal documents and government regulations, which are carefully designed to be specific and unambiguous, are often the most incomprehensible and devoid of meaning.

Polanyi addresses this question by identifying two types of awareness, the "subsidiary" and the "focal," exemplified by driving a nail with a hammer:

> *When we use a hammer to drive a nail, we attend to both the nail and hammer, but in a different way. We watch the effect of our strokes on the nail and try to wield the hammer so as to hit the nail most effectively. When we bring down the hammer we do not feel that its handle has struck our palm but that its head has struck the nail. Yet in a sense we are certainly alert to the feelings in our palm and the fingers that hold the hammer. They guide us in handling it effectively, and the degree of attention that was given to the nail is given to the same extent but in a different way to these feelings. The difference may be stated by saying that the latter are not, like the nail, objects of our attention, but instruments of it. They are not watched in themselves; we watch something else while keeping intensely aware of them. I have a* subsidiary *awareness of the feeling in the palm of my hand which is merged into my* focal *awareness of my driving in the nail.*
>
> *Subsidiary awareness and focal awareness are mutually exclusive. If a pianist shifts his attention from the piece he is playing to the observation of what he is doing with his fingers while playing it, he gets confused and may have to stop. This happens generally if we switch our focal attention to particulars of which we had been previously aware only in their subsidiary role.*

The kind of clumsiness which is due to the fact that focal attention is directed to the subsidiary elements of an action is commonly known as self-consciousness. A serious and sometimes incurable form of it is "stage-fright", which seems to consist in the anxious riveting of one's attention to the next word—or note or gesture—that one has to find or remember. This destroys one's sense of the context which alone can smoothly evoke the proper sequence of words, notes, or gestures. Stage fright is eliminated and fluency recovered if we succeed in casting our mind forward and let it operate with a clear view to the comprehensive activity in which we are primarily interested. (26)

The mutually exclusive qualities of subsidiary and focal awareness affirm the paradox cited earlier: the harder one tries to hear a difference, the harder that difference becomes to detect. This paradox is expressed in the Zen concept of "effortless effort." I contend that much of an audio component's quality is perceived in this subsidiary awareness, and that focal awareness precludes perception of the component's real measure of quality—the ability to convey the music's meaning.

Sports training has long recognized the mutually exclusive quality of focal and subsidiary awareness:

When [the peak experience] happens on the tennis court, we are concentrating without trying to concentrate. We feel spontaneous and alert. We have an inner assurance that we can do what needs to be done, without having to "try hard." We simply know the action will come, and when it does, we don't feel like taking credit; rather, we feel fortunate, "graced." These moments seem to occur most frequently when players are volleying back and forth at the net. Often the exchange of shots at such short quarters is so rapid that action faster than thought is required. These moments are exhilarating, and the players are often amazed to find that they make perfect placements against shots they didn't even expect to reach. Moving more quickly than they thought they could, they have no time to plan; the perfect shot just comes. . . Quieting the mind means less thinking, calculating, judging, worrying, fearing, hoping, trying, regretting, controlling, jittering, or distracting. (27)

These very same ideas are expressed by the Zen master D.T. Suzuki in his foreword to *Zen in the Art of Archery*:

As soon as we reflect, deliberate, and conceptualize, the original unconsciousness is lost and a thought interferes. The arrow is off the string but does not fly straight to the target, nor does the target stand where it is. Calculation, which is miscalculation, sets in. . .

Man is a thinking reed, but his great works are done when he is not calculating and thinking. "Childlikeness" has to be restored with long years of training in self-forgetfulness. (28)

The parallels between the scientific philosopher's "subsidiary awareness," the tennis pro's "not trying," and the Zen master's "self-forgetfulness" are striking. All three examples demonstrate that our relationship to the physical world, and our actions within it, are manifestly dependent on our state of mind. These independent observations affirm that an individual's mental state is a significant variable in his ability to perform certain tasks. Yet blind listening tests ignore these variables, their promoters clinging naively to the concept of "objectivity."

There is also medical evidence that blind listening tests interject the unquantified variable of human interaction into the test. It is widely known that musical perception occurs in the right half of the brain, analytical reasoning in the left. This has been shown in Positron Emission Tomography (PET) scans, a medical technique used in studying the biochemical processes of organs, particularly the brain. Music listening produces increased right-brain metabolism, analytical reasoning increases left-brain metabolism. (29)

The mental activity forced on the listener by blind-testing methodology—comparing, judging, calculating, trying to retrieve a memory of the previous sound, focusing on the specific, anxiety, fear of failing and of being judged, thinking ahead to the outcome, and thinking of the consequences of success or failure are all left-brain functions. These mental activities—which are never called into play during normal music listening—leave little room for sensitivity to how well the component conveys the music's meaning and value—the true indicator of audio-equipment quality.

The allegation that differences detected under optimum conditions vanish under blind conditions because the difference never existed in the first place should be reexamined with a new appreciation for the psychological variables imposed by the limitations of consciousness. Observational listeners reject blind listening tests not because they are *too* rigorous, but because they are *not rigorous enough*. They fail to take into account the relationship between the listener and the test conditions.

In defense of blind testing, objectivists draw a parallel between audio testing and the undeniable utility of large-scale blind testing of new drugs. The key difference is that drug subjects go about their lives normally whether they receive the drug or a placebo, and need not perform tasks under artificial conditions that influence the effect under study. Blind testing's value in medical research doesn't automatically confer similar value when applied to a completely different field.

When blind listening tests, despite their effect of obscuring audible differences, indicate that an audible phenomenon does exist (a phenomenon denied by objectivists), the results are either incorrectly reported as a null,[5] or judged "not statistically significant." The "disinterested" experimenter often chooses to believe that certain listeners enjoyed an amazing run of luck rather than that they could discriminate a difference the experimenter had previously concluded to be inaudible. For example, during the power amplifier listening tests conducted at the 85th AES convention in Los Angeles, a prominent reviewer of high-end equipment—a trained, skilled listener—identified a particular power amplifier in seven out of seven double-blind trials. His performance was dismissed by the experimenter (David Clark) as that of a "lucky coin." This experimenter explained the use of this term to the reviewer: if one flips a coin enough times, seven heads in a row will appear on occasion. The experimenter was the same individual who organized and conducted the double-blind listening tests of loudspeaker cables at the 91st AES convention described earlier.

It is a greater act of faith to believe that this trained observational listener was "lucky" than to even entertain the possibility that the listener could indeed discriminate between the two power amplifiers. When evidence supports a hypothesis in conflict with one's preconceived ideas, the true scientist will explore that hypothesis and develop additional experiments to verify or refute that hypothesis, not cling tenaciously to prejudice.

One of the strongest indictments of blind listening tests is, ironically, the very test cited by objectivists that "proved" all power amplifiers sound alike. This test "revealed" that power amplifiers as diverse as an output-transformerless tube design, an expensive solid-state unit, and a $220 Japanese receiver were sonically identical. (30) These amplifiers were as different from each other in design and measured performance as one could assemble. The amplifiers differed dramatically in their ability to deliver current to the loudspeaker, their distortion spectra, output impedance (which, with the OTL tube amplifier, would react with the load to introduce frequency response errors of 2dB), dynamic headroom, slew rate, transient intermodulation distortion, and virtually every other measurable grading of amplifier performance. Despite the large measurable differences in these amplifiers, the listeners could not distinguish among them. (31)

Objectivists claim that blind testing is very sensitive to revealing small differences between components. Yet they also claim that differences heard by observational listeners are nothing more than trivial factors such as a slight level difference or frequency response deviation, differences that are easily identifiable and measurable. I quote Stanley Lipshitz:

Certainly blind testing shows up differences very sensitively. If one needs convincing of this all one needs to do is ascertain how small a level difference or frequency response mismatch can be reliably detected under such conditions. One can hear differences on the order of 0.2dB over an octave or so of bandwidth. But, by the same token, this means that if one wishes to hear differences beyond such relatively trivial linear differences (that is, if one wishes to ascertain the presence of audible nonlinear distortions), these linear differences really must first be minimized. If this is not done, the comparison test cannot draw any conclusion beyond the fact that an audible difference existed whose cause could have been nothing more than a simple level or frequency response mismatch. Without further tests, nothing new has been learned. (32)

The objectivists can't have it both ways. If "blind testing shows up differences very sensitively," yet the same methodology led to the absurd conclusion that an output-transformerless tube amplifier, a high-end solid-state design, and a $220 Japanese receiver, all having very different linear performances, were sonically identical, then the inescapable conclusion is that blind listening tests are fundamentally flawed. If blind testing is truly sensitive to revealing differences, why were such gross differences between amplifiers (including frequency response variations of 2dB, an order of magnitude greater than Dr. Lipshitz's claimed 0.2dB audibility threshold) not detected? [6]

An even greater indictment of blind listening tests comes to us from the field of "perceptual" low-bit-rate digital audio coding. A perceptual encoder/decoder (codec) reduces the number of bits required to represent the analog audio signal. A 90% reduction in the bit rate is not uncommon. The massive amount of quantization noise created by encoding a signal with so few bits is theoretically hidden underneath the correctly coded musical signal. No measurement techniques exist that quantify perceptual codec performance; all evaluations must be performed by listening.

When the European Broadcast Union (EBU) needed to choose a codec for digital audio broadcasting throughout Europe, it turned to the Swedish National Radio Company to design and conduct listening tests. Swedish Radio, which is analogous to the UK's BBC, developed an elaborate methodology called "double-blind, triple-stimulus, hidden-reference." A "subject" (listener) would hear three "objects" (musical presentations); presentation A was always the unprocessed signal, with the listener required to identify if presentation B or C had been been processed through the codec.

The test involved 60 "expert" listeners spanning 20,000 evaluations over a period of two years. Swedish Radio announced in 1991 that it had narrowed the field to two codecs, and that "both codecs have now reached a level of performance where they fulfill the EBU requirements for a distribution codec." In other words, Swedish Radio said the codec was good enough to replace analog FM broadcasts in Europe. This decision was based on data gathered during the 20,000 "double-blind, triple-stimulus, hidden-reference" listening trials. (33)

After announcing its decision, Swedish Radio sent a tape of music processed by the selected codec to the late Bart Locanthi, an acknowledged expert in digital audio and chairman of an *ad hoc* committee formed to independently evaluate low-bit rate codecs. Using the same non-blind observational listening techniques described earlier in this paper, Locanthi instantly identified an artifact of the codec. After Locanthi informed Swedish Radio of the artifact (an idle tone near 1.5kHz), listeners at Swedish Radio also instantly heard the distortion. (34)

How is it possible that a single listener, using non-blind observational listening techniques, was able to discover in less than ten minutes a distortion that escaped the scrutiny of 60 expert listeners, 20,000 trials, and elaborate "double-blind, triple-stimulus, hidden-reference" methodology?

Although the procedural problems with blind testing outlined earlier certainly played a role in leading Swedish Radio astray, their assumptions about humans and musical perception (and indeed, about the world in general) were fundamentally flawed. The researchers' lexicon reveals how they view the musical experience: listeners are called "subjects" and musical works are called "objects." By emphasizing an artificial subject/object duality, the oneness between music and listener is destroyed. Is it surprising that a methodology that reduces listeners to "subjects" and musical expression to "objects" fails to understand that musical joy exists in the immediate relationship in which subject and object are not separate?

Blind listening tests subvert the entire reason we listen to music. Music isn't merely an arbitrary collection of pitches of varying amplitude and duration; it is filled with meaning, expression, and feeling. Indeed, there would be no rational reason for listening to music if it were merely an incomprehensible and meaningless assortment of sound. It is the expression of the composer or artists that compels us to listen. The joy of understanding musical expression is what drives the entire audio hardware and music-recording industries; why else would humanity spend billions of dollars a year on audio hardware and recorded music?

It is this expression that some audio components convey better than others. This characteristic of some components is known colloquially as "playing the tune." A component may produce a "good" set of numbers in the test laboratory, but that is no indicator of its ability to express the music's meaning—to "play the tune." This view implies that quality in audio equipment is not strictly inherent in the component itself, but is dependent on the listener's sensitivity to this quality. This sensitivity to musical differences in components is a result of *caring* about the music. If the listener cares, the difference between components will be audible and musically meaningful; if the listener doesn't care, the difference may not be recognized because it has no value. This is why blind listening tests obscure differences between components; the music's meaning has no significance under such conditions. Just as music is not merely a collection of arbitrary pitches of varying amplitude and duration, the interaction between listener and music cannot be reduced to "subjects" and "objects."

Rejecting the roles that meaning, feelings, emotion, and value play in audio science reflects a basic and prevalent misconception about science itself. Scientific method seeks to divorce value from the experimental process in the belief that personal involvement interjects bias and leads to erroneous conclusions. But science is not value free, and other forms of knowing exist that fall outside the formalized domain of science. Music listening is based on value and meaning, the first casualties in the objectivists' blind-listening methodology.

Conclusion

And what is good, Phaedrus,
And what is not good—
Need we ask anyone to tell us these things?
—Robert M. Pirsig, *Zen and the Art of Motorcycle Maintenance: An Inquiry into Values*

The polarization of the audio community over "The Great Debate" is in many ways a false dichotomy. The responsible observational-listening approach—which combines careful controls over the listening procedure, technical understanding, professionalism, and use of highly developed personal skills—is far more rigorous than the method's critics realize. Moreover, the observational listener's contention that musically significant differences exist between audio components—differences that cannot be measured with existing technology—is accepted as a truism by hundreds of thousands of critical listeners, both consumer and professional. Indeed, the vast majority of the AES membership who use their ears professionally accept this reality.[7] Yet this reality, affirmed by the world at large, is dismissed as "fantasy" by a fringe, yet vocal, minority of academicians isolated by theoretical dogma and a refusal to listen for themselves. Unfortunately, it is the very scientists with the skills to explore these phenomena who are most inclined to summarily reject the methods of critical observational listening.

Audio objectivists regard observational listeners as anti-science—advocates of mysticism over rational in inquiry. This perception is utterly false; listeners don't view science as intrusion on their reality, but rather as just one of many tools for advancing the art of audio engineering. Observational listeners see no inherent conflict in their methods; the objectivists' quandary arises from their mistaken belief that any acceptance of listening impressions to judge equipment quality is tantamount to a rejection of rationality itself.[8]

Audio objectivists and observational listeners ultimately share the same goal. But what is that goal? To create equipment that generates a set of measurement numbers in the laboratory that somehow indicates more "goodness"?

No. Our common goal is this: When a faceless listener somewhere in the world sits down before his playback system with his favorite music, he experiences the greatest joy our technology can convey.

Can audio engineering have a higher purpose?

References

1. S.P. Lipshitz, "The Great Debate—Some Reflections Ten Years Later," presented at the Audio Engineering Society 8th International Conference, "The Sound of Audio," May 1990.

2. Comment of participant at the AES 8th International Conference, "The Sound of Audio," May 1990.

3. Comment of participant at the AES 8th International Conference, "The Sound of Audio," May 1990.

4. J. Bruck, open letter to AES members.

5. Ibid.

6. F.E. Toole, "Listening Tests: Turning Opinion into Fact," *Journal of the Audio Engineering Society*, Vol.30 No.6, p.431 (June 1982).

7. S.P. Lipshitz, op. cit.

8. Ibid.

9. Ibid.

10. M. Polanyi, *Personal Knowledge: Towards a Post-Critical Philosophy*, New York, Harper and Row (1958) (First published by The University of Chicago Press, 1958), p.55.

11. Ibid.

12. Ibid.

13. Ibid.

14. Ibid.

15. S.P. Lipshitz, op. cit.

"Many reviewers have, over the intervening years, dabbled with controlled tests and found that many imagined differences seem to vanish under blind conditions. This doesn't surprise anyone who has spent some time trying to get to the bottom of such cases, but does tend to make one cynical about the likelihood of ever resolving the question in the public's mind. After all, the sale of magazines is probably boosted by the controversy, and the more differences between components that reviewers are able to 'perceive' (or imagine that they have perceived) the better it is for their egos and their publishers. In other words, there may be strong ulterior motives for not wishing to resolve the matter."

16. M. Csikszentmihalyi, *Flow: The Psychology of Optimal Experience*, Harper & Row (1990), p.33.

17. *Encyclopedia Britannica*, 1989 edition, Vol.8, p.47.

18. M. Polanyi, op. cit.

19. Ibid.

20. R. Harley, "CD Transport Performance," *Stereophile*, Vol.16 No.11, pp.83-113.

21. M.O. Hawksford and C. Dunn, "Is the AES/EBU/SPDIF Interface Flawed?," AES preprint #3360.

22. S.P. Lipshitz, op. cit.

23. Ibid.

24. Ibid.

25. M. Csikszentmihalyi, op. cit., pp.28-29, 31.

26. M. Polanyi, op. cit.

27. W. T. Gallway, *The Inner Game of Tennis*, Bantam (1974), pp.22-23.

28. E. Herrigel, *Zen in the Art of Archery*, Pantheon (1953), p.vii.

29. A. Stiller, "Toward a Biology of Music," *The Audio Amateur*, One/1990 p.40.

30. I. Masters, "Do All Amplifiers Sound the Same?," *Stereo Review*, January, 1987.

31. C. Grewin, T. Rydén, "Subjective Assessments on Low Bit-Rate Audio Codecs," proceedings of the 10th International AES Conference, "Images of Audio."

32. Recorded comments of Bart Locanthi replayed at the 91st AES Convention workshop on low-bit-rate codecs.

Footnotes

1. The term "observational listening" was coined by Harry Pearson, founder of *The Absolute Sound* magazine. Pearson also invented much of today's widely accepted language used to describe artifacts in reproduced music.

2. John Watkinson, author of six books on digital audio, articulated the idea during a presentation the 10th AES conference "Images of Audio" in London (1991) that if the ones and zeros are the same, the sound must be the same. Making reference to binary

ones and zeros, Watkinson stated, to great laughter from the audience, "Somehow I can't conceive of an audiophile 'one'. . . You can only say that [if the data are identical, the sound is identical] once, which is a problem if you have to publish a hi-fi magazine every month. It leaves an intellectual vacuum. . . When the term 'audiophile' replaced 'hi-fi freak,' I immediately thought of necrophiles (sic) and pedophiles. Perhaps I wasn't far off."

3. Fortunately, some academic researchers see critical listening as an *expansion* of rationality, not a rejection of it. For example, AES Fellow Michael Gerzon wrote in his paper "Limitations of Double-Blind A/B Listening Tests," presented at the 91st AES convention, "Most subjectivists don't deny the possibility of eventually finding objective justifications for what they hear. . . One should take the comments of less cranky subjectivists seriously as at least guides for designing listening-test protocols."

4. S.P. Lipshitz, op. cit.
"It is usually best, rather than conducting a preset number of trials, to monitor the statistics as the trials proceed, and to extend the number of trials if there appears to be a reasonable possibility that a subject is performing somewhat better than random."

5. T. Nousaine, "The Great Debate: Is Anyone Winning?," presented at the 8th Audio Engineering Society Conference "The Sound of Audio," May 1990.
Mr. Nousaine incorrectly stated *Stereophile* magazine's blind power-amplifier listening tests were "falsely reported" as indicating statistical evidence that the listeners could distinguish between power amplifiers. For a more rigorous statistical analysis of the data and an accurate reporting of the results, the reader is referred to the analysis by Professor Herman Burstein in *Stereophile*, Vol.12 No.10 (October, 1989), pp.33-41. Mr. Nousaine also ignored in his paper the positive results of a later blind test performed by Banks and Krajicek at Pomona College using samples of the same two amplifiers and featuring an almost identical methodology. This later test demonstrated statistically significant blind identification of the two amplifiers and was reported in full in *Stereophile* (Vol.12 No.11, November 1989).

6. Many respected academic researchers also question the validity of blind A/B testing. Michael Gerzon stated in his paper "Limitations of Double-Blind A/B Listening Tests," presented at the 91st AES convention, "It would be a disaster if we had protocols that didn't reveal subjective differences that the average consumer would notice in five years' time. I want to indicate possible areas in which normal double-blind A/B protocols may not be adequate to reveal faults that may be audible to even unsophisticated end listeners. I'm going to do this with possible models of how we hear." Gerzon encouraged other researchers to look beyond double-blind testing and "to develop experimental methodology matched to the phenomenon which is being tested," and to "not believe that one simple protocol—double-blind or A/B or ABX—is the answer to all kinds of measurement problems."

Similarly, AES Fellow J. Robert Stuart stated in his landmark papers "Estimating the Significance of Errors in Audio Systems" and "Predicting the Audibility, Detectability and Loudness of Errors in Audio Systems" that "A/B testing using program material and particularly musical program is fraught with difficulties...the author sets out some reasons why the 'objective' approaches of A/B listening and null-testing may be flawed."

7. A survey taken by David Clark at the amplifier listening tests conducted during the 85th AES convention showed that 70% of the AES members in attendance believed audible differences existed between power amplifiers.

This figure alarmed Clark, who stated in his paper "Ten Years of ABX Testing" "This is an amazing response from members of an engineering society who are all undoubtedly aware of the many controlled tests which failed to support the claim. Mechanical, civil or nuclear engineers would certainly be held to a higher level of scientific integrity."

8. The greatest expression of the reconciliation between two apparently disparate modes of thought is found in Robert M. Pirsig's *Zen and the Art of Motorcycle Maintenance: An Inquiry Into Values* (William Morrow & Company). My interpretation of Pirsig's ideas is the foundation of this paper.

Notes

The Richard Heyser quotes are taken from *Time Delay Spectrometry*, a collection of his published papers, available from the Audio Engineering Society (www.aes.org).

Csikszentmihalyi (16) includes the following references relating to the limits of consciousness:

"The first general statement about the number of bits that can be processed simultaneously was by Miller (1956). Orme (1969), on the basis of von Uexkull's (1957) calculations, has figured that 1/18th of a second is the threshold of discrimination. Cognitive scientists who have treated the limitations of attention include Simon (1969, 1978), Kahneman (1973), Hasher & Zacks (1979), Eysenck (1982), and Hoffman, Nelson, and Houck (1983). Attentional demands made by cognitive processes are discussed by Neisser (1967, 1976), Treisman & Gelade (1980), and Treisman & Schmidt (1982). The attentional requirements of storing and recalling information from memory have been dealt with by Atkinson & Shiffrin (1968) and Hasher & Zacks (1979). But the importance of attention and its limitations was already known to William James (1890).

This paper is dedicated to Robert M. Pirsig.

Glossary

A/B comparison A back-and-forth listening comparison between two musical presentations, A and B.

absolute polarity A recording with correct absolute polarity played back through a system with correct absolute polarity will produce a positive pressure wave from the loudspeakers in response to a positive pressure wave at the original acoustic event. Incorrect absolute polarity introduces a 180° phase reversal of both channels. Absolute polarity is audible with some instruments and to some listeners.

AC line-conditioner/protector A device that filters noise from the AC powerline and isolates equipment from voltage spikes and surges. Some AC line-conditioners/protectors also protect equipment from lightning strokes. Home-theater audio equipment is plugged into the AC line-conditioner/protector, and the conditioner is plugged into the wall.

acoustic absorber Any material that absorbs sound, such as carpet, drapes, and thickly upholstered furniture.

acoustic diffuser Any material that scatters sound.

acoustic feedback Sound from a loudspeaker causes a turntable to vibrate; that vibration is converted by the phono cartridge into an electrical signal, which is reproduced by the loudspeaker, which causes the turntable to vibrate even more. This sets up a *feedback loop* in which the vibration feeds on itself, becoming louder and louder. You've probably heard acoustic feedback at an amplified concert as a howl or screech from the PA system.

acoustic panel absorber A device that absorbs low to mid frequencies by diaphragmatic action. That is, sound striking the panel absorber causes the panel to move, converting acoustic energy into a minute amount of heat in the panel.

acoustics The science of sound behavior. Also refers to a room; e.g., "This room has good acoustics."

AC synchronous A motor whose rotational speed is determined by the frequency of the AC voltage driving it. Used in most belt-drive turntables.

AC-3 Another name for Dolby Digital, the 5.1-channel discrete digital surround-sound format. (see "Dolby Digital")

active subwoofer A speaker designed to reproduce only low frequencies, and which includes an integral power amplifier to drive the speaker.

ADC see "analog-to-digital converter"

adjacent-channel selectivity Tuner specification that describes a tuner's ability to reject radio stations adjacent to the desired station.

AES/EBU interface Professional system for transmitting digital audio. An AES/EBU cable is a balanced line and is terminated with XLR connectors. Also found on some consumer products. Named for the Audio Engineering Society and European Broadcasting Union.

agile Sonic description of bass that can follow quickly changing pitches and dynamics.

aggressive Sonic description of a forward presentation that seems to thrust the music on the listener.

air Sonic description of treble openness, or of space between instruments in the soundstage. Contrast with "dull," "thick."

air-bearing tonearm A tonearm in which the armtube floats on a cushion of air.

air-bearing turntable A turntable in which the platter floats on a cushion of air.

alternate-channel selectivity Tuner specification describing a tuner's ability to reject stations two channels away from the desired station.

ambience Spatial aspects of a film soundtrack that create a sense of size and atmosphere, usually reproduced by the surround speakers.

Ambisonics A method of capturing a three-dimensional soundfield and reproducing that soundfield through loudspeakers. Although Ambisonics is compatible with monophonic and stereo reproduction, we generally think of Ambisonics as a multichannel music format.

ampere Unit of electrical current, abbreviated A.

analog An analog signal is one in which the varying voltage is an analog of the acoustical waveform; i.e., the voltage varies continuously with the original acoustical waveform. Contrasted with a digital signal, in which binary ones and zeros represent audio or video information.

analog bypass Input on a digital controller that passes analog input signals to the output without analog-to-digital and digital-to-analog conversions.

analog-to-digital converter A circuit that converts an analog signal to a digital signal. All A/V receivers and A/V preamplifiers that perform Dolby Pro-Logic decoding in the digital domain have a pair of analog-to-digital converters.

analytical Sonic description that describes a component that reveals every nuance in the recording, but in an unpleasant way. An analytical component is rarely musical.

anamorphic A film or video format in which a widescreen image has been "squeezed" horizontally (either with lenses or by digital manipulation) to fit a standard 4:3 aspect ratio. Correct picture geometry is restored on playback by "unsqueezing" the image into its original aspect ratio. The anamorphic format delivers the correct aspect ratio without sacrificing resolution.

anechoic Literally "without echo."

anechoic chamber An acoustically reflection-free room. An anechoic chamber's walls are covered in highly absorbent material so that no sound is reflected back into the room. Used in loudspeaker testing.

anti-skate adjustment Control on a tonearm that adjusts the amount of force applied to the tonearm to counteract the arm's natural tendency to skate (pull inward).

articulate Sonic description of a component that clearly resolves pitches.

aspect ratio The width-to-height ratio of a visual image. Standard television sets have an aspect ratio of 1.33:1. Widescreen television sets (including most HDTV sets) have an aspect ratio of 16:9 (1.78:1).

asynchronous sampling-rate converter Sampling rate converter in which the input and output sampling rates are free-running independently of each other.

atmosphere see "ambience."

audiophile A person who values sound quality in reproduced music.

Audiophilia nervosa Humorous name for a condition in which the listener is constantly fretting over the equipment at the expense of enjoying music.

A/V Short for audio/video. Identifies a component or system as one that processes video as well as audio signals.

A/V input An input on an A/V receiver or A/V preamplifier that includes both audio and video jacks.

A/V loop An A/V input and A/V output pair found on all A/V receivers and A/V preamplifiers. Used to connect a component that records as well as plays back audio and video signals. A VCR is connected to a receiver's or preamplifier's A/V loop.

A/V preamplifier Also called by its more descriptive name of "A/V controller," the A/V preamplifier is a component that lets you control the playback volume and select which source you want to watch. A/V preamplifiers also perform surround decoding.

A/V preamplifier/tuner An A/V preamplifier that includes, in the same chassis, an AM or FM tuner for receiving radio broadcasts.

A/V receiver The central component of a home-theater system; receives signals from source components, selects which signal you watch and listen to, controls the playback volume, performs surround decoding, receives radio broadcasts, and amplifies signals to drive a home-theater loudspeaker system. Also called a "surround receiver."

azimuth In magnetic tape recording, the angle of the heads along the line of the tape, ideally 90°. In LP playback, the angle of the cantilever in relation to the record surface.

baffle The front surface of a loudspeaker on which the drivers are mounted.

balanced connection A method of connecting audio components with three conductors in a single cable. One conductor carries the audio signal, a second conductor carries that audio signal with inverted polarity, and the third conductor is the ground.

banana jack A small tubular connector found on loudspeakers and power amplifiers for connecting speaker cables terminated with banana plugs.

banana plug A common speaker-cable termination that fits into a banana jack.

bandwidth The range of frequencies that a device can process or pass. In reference to an electrical or acoustic device, bandwidth is the range of frequencies between the –3dB points.

bass Sounds in the low audio range, generally frequencies below 500Hz.

bass extension A measure of how deeply an audio system or loudspeaker will reproduce bass. For example, a small subwoofer may have bass extension to 40Hz. A large subwoofer may have bass extension to 16Hz.

bass management A combination of controls and circuits in an A/V receiver, A/V preamplifier, or multi-channel digital audio player (DVD-A and SACD) that determines which speakers receive bass signals.

bass reflex A speaker design with a hole or slot in the cabinet that allows sound inside the cabinet to emerge into the listening room. Bass reflex speakers have deeper bass extension than speakers with sealed cabinets, but that bass is generally less tightly controlled. Also called "vented" or "ported." Contrast with "infinite baffle."

B-Format In Ambisonics, the W (mono pressure signal), X (sides), and Y (front to back) signals. Also refers to these signals along with the Z (height) signal.

bi-amping Using two power amplifiers to drive one loudspeaker. One amplifier typically drives the woofer, the second drives the midrange and tweeter.

big screen A large-screen direct-view television set or rear-projection set. Usually reserved for sets larger than 40".

binaural recording Recording technique in which microphones are placed inside the "ear canals" of a dummy head. The recording contains spatial cues introduced by the dummy head's physical structure. When reproduced through headphones, a binaural recording re-creates the original three-dimensional acoustic space with uncanny realism.

binding post A connection on power amplifiers and loudspeakers for attaching loudspeaker cables.

bipolar speaker A speaker that produces sound equally from the front and the back. Unlike the dipolar speaker, the bipolar's front and rear soundwaves are in-phase with each other.

bipolar transistor Most common transistor type in audio electronics. Name "bipolar" (two poles) comes from fact that current flows through two types of semiconductor material, P and N. Bipolar transistors are either NPN or PNP types, which refers to the polarity of their operating voltages.

bit rate The number of bits per second stored or transmitted by a digital audio or digital video signal. For example, the bit rate of compact disc is 705,600 bits per second per channel. Dolby Digital has a bit rate of 384kbs (384,000 bits per second) for 5.1 channels. MP3 has a bit rate as low as 32kbs per channel. DVD-Audio has a bit rate as high as 4.608 million bits per second per channel. Higher bit rates generally translate to better audio quality. Also called "datarate."

bi-wiring Technique of running two cables to each loudspeaker. One cable is connected to the loudspeaker's woofer input terminals, one to the tweeter's input terminals. Bi-wiring is possible only with loudspeakers with two pairs of input terminals.

bleached Sonic description of a component that emphasizes the upper harmonics of an instrument's sound, while de-emphasizing the lower harmonics and fundamental. A bleached sound is thin, bright, and lacking warmth.

bloom Sonic description of a sense of air around instrumental images.

boomy Excessive bass, particularly over a wide band of frequencies.

boutique brand A product line that appears to be high-end, but actually puts inferior electronics in slick, eye-catching chassis.

break-in Initial period of use of a new audio component, during which time the component's sound improves.

bridging Amplifier-to-loudspeaker connection method that converts a stereo amplifier into a monoblock power amplifier. One amplifier channel amplifies the positive half of the waveform, the other channel amplifies the negative half. The loudspeaker is connected as the "bridge" between the two amplifier channels.

brightness In audio, an excessive amount of treble that adds shrillness to the sound. In video, the amount of light generated by a video display device.

brightness signal More correctly called "luminance" and represented by the letter "Y," the brightness component of a video signal contains all the black-and-white information. A color video signal is a combination of luminance and chrominance (color information).

brittle A midrange or treble character that makes instrumental timbres sound harsh. Contrast with "liquid."

buffer Electronic circuit that isolates one component or circuit stage from another. A preamplifier is a buffer because it acts as an intermediary between source components and a power amplifier. The preamplifier's buffering function relieves the source components of the burden of driving a power amplifier. A digital buffer stores data temporarily in solid-state memory. Digital buffers act as jitter-reduction devices because the output is controlled by a precision clock.

build quality The quality of electronic parts, chassis, and construction techniques of an audio or video component.

bypass test Listening test in which the component under evaluation is alternately removed from and inserted into the signal path in order to assess its sonic characteristics.

calibration The act of fine-tuning an audio or video component for correct performance. In an audio system, calibration includes setting the individual channel levels. In video, calibration means setting a video display device to display the correct color, brightness, tint, contrast, and other parameters.

cantilever Thin tube protruding from a phono cartridge that holds the stylus.

capacitive reactance Property of capacitance that blocks low frequencies but passes high frequencies. Capacitive reactance makes a capacitor behave as a frequency-dependent resistor. Because of capacitive reactance, a capacitor connected to a tweeter allows treble to pass but blocks bass.

capacitor Electronic component that stores a charge of electrons. Reservoir capacitors are used for energy storage in power amplifiers; filter capacitors filter traces of AC from DC power supplies; coupling capacitors connect one amplifier stage to another by blocking DC and allowing the AC audio signal to pass.

capture ratio Tuner specification: the difference in dB required between the strengths of two stations needed before a tuner can lock to the stronger station and reject the weaker one. The lower the capture ratio, the better the tuner.

cartridge demagnetizer Device that removes stray magnetic fields from metal parts inside a phono cartridge.

CAV laserdisc A laserdisc recorded with Constant Angular Velocity, meaning that the disc spins at a constant speed regardless of where on the disc the playback laser is reading. Also called a "standard play" laserdisc because it can store 30 minutes of video per disc side. Contrast with Constant Linear Velocity (CLV).

CD Compact Disc Plastic disc 120mm in diameter that stores up to 80 minutes of music.

CD-4 Compatible Discrete 4. A Quadraphonic format invented by JVC in which the two rear channels are encoded along with the front channels, and a high-frequency (30kHz–50kHz) difference signal allows the rear-channel signals to be demodulated.

CD Recordable Format for recording digital audio on a compact disc. CDR is a "write once" format, meaning that once recorded on, the disc cannot be erased.

CD-Rewritable Recordable CD format that can be rerecorded over multiple times.

center channel In a multichannel audio system, the audio channel that carries information that will be reproduced by a speaker placed in the center of the viewing room between the left and right speakers. The center channel carries nearly all of a film's dialogue.

center-channel mode A setting on A/V receivers and A/V preamplifiers that configures the receiver or preamplifier for the type of center-channel speaker in the system.

center-channel speaker The speaker in a home-theater system located on top of, beneath, or behind the visual image; reproduces center channel information such as dialogue and other sounds associated with onscreen action.

channel balance The relative levels or volumes of the left and right channels in an audio system or individual component.

channel separation A measure of how well sounds in one channel are isolated from the other channels.

chapter stop A marker on laserdiscs or DVDs that provides a search point for randomly accessing that point on the disc. Key scenes in movies are marked with chapter stops, as are individual songs in concert videos.

Chesky 6.0 An alternative multichannel audio technique proposed by Chesky Records using four front loudspeakers and two rear loudspeakers.

chesty A loudspeaker coloration that emphasizes the deep chest sounds in spoken or singing voice.

chrominance (chroma) The color-carrying portion of a video signal. The chroma signal carries color and hue, but no brightness information.

chuffing Sound created by the port of a bass reflex loudspeaker when reproducing low bass at high levels. Caused by large movement of air in the port.

Class-A Mode of amplifier operation in which a transistor or tube amplifies the entire audio signal.

Class-A/B Mode of amplifier operation in which the output stage operates in Class-A at low output power, then switches to Class-B at higher output power.

Class-B Mode of amplifier operation in which one tube or transistor amplifies the positive half of an audio signal, and a second tube or transistor amplifies the negative half.

clipping An amplifier that is asked to deliver more power than it is capable of will flatten the tops and bottoms of the audio waveform, making the peaks appear to be clipped off. Clipping introduces a large amount of distortion, audible as a crunching sound on musical peaks.

clock A signal present in all digital products that acts as a timekeeper.

CLV laserdisc A laserdisc recorded with Constant Linear Velocity, meaning the disc changes speed depending on where on the disc the playback laser is reading. CLV discs spin more slowly when the laser is reading at the outer radius and faster when the laser is reading at the inner radius, thus maintaining a constant velocity as seen by the playback laser. Also called "Extended Play" laserdisc because they can store one hour of video per disc side.

coaxial cable A cable in which an inner conductor is surrounded by a braided conductor that acts as a shield.

coaxial digital output A jack found on CD transports and some CD players that provides a digital audio signal on an RCA jack for connection to another component through a coaxial digital interconnect.

coaxial driver A loudspeaker driver in which one drive unit (typically a tweeter) is mounted inside a second drive unit (typically a midrange).

coherence The impression that the music is an integrated whole, rather than made up of separate parts.

coincident microphones A stereo or multichannel recording technique in which microphones are placed very close to each other. Examples include Blumlein (also called crossed figure-of-eight), XY (crossed cardioids), and MS (middle-side; a forward-oriented omnidirectional or cardioid microphone and a figure-of-eight microphone).

coloration A change in sound introduced by a component in an audio system. A "colored" loudspeaker doesn't accurately reproduce the signal fed to it. A speaker with coloration may have too much bass and not enough treble, for example.

comb filtering A phenomenon that introduces a series of deep notches in the frequency response, usually caused by combining a direct signal with a slightly delayed version of that signal, such as the sidewall reflection from a loudspeaker in a listening room.

common-mode rejection When a balanced signal is input to a differential amplifier, only the difference between the two phases of the balanced signal is amplified. Any noise common to both phases (common mode noise) is rejected by the differential amplifier.

compliance In phono cartridges, a number expressing the cantilever's stiffness. Specifically, compliance is the length of cantilever movement when a force of 10–6 dynes is applied, expressed in millionths of a centimeter. High compliance is any value above 20. Low compliance is any value below 10.

component video A video signal split into three parts: luminance, and two color signals (technically known as Y, B–Y, R–Y). Better-quality DVD players have component-video output; when connected to video display devices with component video input, the result is better picture quality than composite video or S-video connection.

composite video A video signal in which the luminance (brightness, or black-and-white) information and the chrominance (color) information are combined into a single signal. Composite video inputs and outputs appear on RCA jacks.

compression A component of a sound wave in which the air density is greater than normal atmospheric pressure. A woofer cone moving outward creates a compression. One compression and one rarefaction make one complete cycle of a sound wave.

cone The paper, plastic, or metal diaphragm of a loudspeaker that moves back and forth to create sound.

congested A thickening of the sound that makes instrumental images less separate and distinct.

constrained-layer damping Construction method in which a layer or layers of soft materials are placed between layers of harder materials to dissipate vibrational energy.

Consumer Electronics Show (CES) Annual trade show for the consumer electronics industry, held in Las Vegas in early January.

contact cleaner Fluid for removing oxide and dirt from audio jacks and plugs.

continuousness Quality of a musical presentation in which the sound seems a whole, rather than disjointed.

contrast The range between white and black in an image.

control components An audio system's preamplifier is a control component because it adjusts the volume and determines which source you listen to.

controller Another term for an A/V preamplifier.

critical listening The art of evaluating audio equipment quality by careful analytical listening for specific sonic flaws.

crossover A circuit that splits up the frequency spectrum into two or more parts. Crossovers are found in virtually all dynamic loudspeakers, and in A/V receivers and A/V preamplifiers.

crossover distortion see "zero-crossing distortion"

crossover frequency The frequency at which the audio spectrum is split. A subwoofer with a crossover frequency of 80Hz filters all information above 80Hz out of the signal driving the subwoofer, and all information below 80Hz out of the signal driving the main speakers.

crossover slope Describes the steepness of a crossover filter. Expressed as "xdB/octave." For example, a subwoofer with a crossover frequency of 80Hz and a slope of 6dB/octave would allow audio frequencies at 160Hz (an octave above 80Hz) into the subwoofer, but signals at 160Hz would be reduced in amplitude by 6dB. A slope of 12dB/octave would also allow 160Hz into the subwoofer, but the amplitude would be reduced by 12dB. The most common crossover slopes are 12dB/octave, 18dB/octave, and 24dB/octave. Crossover slopes are also referred to as "first-order" (6dB/octave), "second-order" (12dB/octave), "third-order" (18dB/octave), and "fourth-order" (24dB/octave). The "steeper" slopes (such as 24dB/octave) split the frequency spectrum more sharply and produce less overlap between the two frequency bands.

crosstalk see "channel separation"

CRT Cathode-Ray Tube A vacuum tube in which electrons are fired at a screen coated with phosphors that give off light when struck to produce a visible pattern (a picture). Direct-view television sets use a large CRT. Some front-projectors use three small CRTs to project an image.

current The flow of electrons in a conductor. For example, a power amplifier "pushes" electrical current through speaker cables and the voice coils in a loudspeaker to make them move back and forth.

current-to-voltage converter Circuit following the digital-to-analog converter chip that converts the DAC's current pulses to a voltage.

cutoff frequency see "crossover frequency"

DAC see "digital to-analog converter"

DAD see "Digital Audio Disc"

damping factor A number that expresses a power amplifier's ability to control woofer motion. Related to the amplifier's output impedance.

data compression see "perceptual coding"

data rate see "bitrate"

dB see "decibel"

dBFS Decibels referenced to full scale in digital audio. Full scale is the maximum recorded level possible in digital. All digital levels are expressed in dBFS; a signal level 20dB below full scale is –20dBFS.

dBSPL A measurement of loudness (sound-pressure level) in decibels, referenced to the threshold of hearing (0dBSPL).

dBW A measurement of amplifier power in decibels referenced to 1W of output power.

DC (Direct Current) Flow of electrons that remains steady rather than fluctuating. Contrasted with alternating current (AC).

decibel The standard unit for expressing relative power or amplitude levels of voltage, electrical power, acoustical power, or sound-pressure level. Abbreviated dB.

de-emphasis In the compact disc format, a treble boost can be applied during recording (pre-emphasis), and a treble cut during playback (de-emphasis), increasing the signal-to-noise ratio.

depth The impression of instruments, voices, or sounds existing behind one another in three dimensions, as in "soundstage depth."

detail Low-level components of the musical presentation, such as the fine inner structure of an instrument's timbre.

dialogue intelligibility The ability to clearly hear and understand the dialogue in a movie without strain. Dialogue intelligibility is affected by the quality of components in a home-theater system, room acoustics, and how the system is set up.

diaphragm The surface of a loudspeaker driver that moves, creating sound.

dielectric Insulating material inside a capacitor or around a cable.

differential amplifier Electronic circuit that amplifies only the difference between the two phases of the balanced signal.

diffraction The bending of soundwaves as they pass around an object. Also: a re-radiation of sound caused by discontinuities in surfaces near the radiating device, such as the bolts that secure drivers to a speaker cabinet.

diffusion Scattering of sound. Diffusion reduces the sense of direction of sounds, which benefits sound produced by surround loudspeakers.

digital Calculation or representation by discrete units. For example, digital audio and digital video can be represented by a series of binary ones and zeros.

Digital Audio Broadcasting (DAB) Delivery of digitally encoded music via cable TV hookup, satellite dish, or over the air along with a conventional AM or FM broadcast.

Digital Audio Disc (DAD) Unofficial name of the format in which a DVD-Video disc stores two channels of audio at 96kHz with 24-bit word length. No longer used with the introduction of DVD-Audio.

digital audio server Source component that stores music on hard-disc drives and can be programmed to play music by genre or other selection criteria.

Digital Audio Tape (DAT) Format for storing up to two hours of 44.1kHz or 48kHz digital audio with 16-bit resolution on a small cassette tape. Essentially defunct.

digital loudspeaker Loudspeaker incorporating a digital crossover and power amplifiers. A digital loudspeaker takes in a digital bitstream, spits up the frequency spectrum with digital signal processing, converts each of those signals to analog, and amplifies them separately. The individual power amplifiers then power each of the loudspeaker's drive units.

digital preamplifier Audio component that performs source selection, volume control, and other functions in the digital domain.

Digital Satellite System (DSS) A method of delivering high-quality digital video into consumers' homes via an 18" roof-mounted dish.

Digital Signal Processing (DSP) Manipulation of audio or video signals by performing mathematical functions on the digitally encoded signal.

Digital Theater Systems (DTS) A discrete digital surround-sound format used in movie theaters and some home-theater systems. A better-sounding alternative to Dolby Digital. Also called DTS Digital Surround. The DTS format encompasses film soundtracks and music releases.

digital-to-analog converter A chip that converts digital audio signals to analog audio signals. CD players, laserdisc players, DSS boxes, and DVD machines all contain digital-to-analog converters. Also: A stand-alone component in an audio system that converts digital audio signals to analog signals. Also called a digital processor or DAC.

Digital Transmission Content Protection (DTCP) Copy-protection system that allows content owners to control how the content may be copied. Also known as "5C" after the five companies that developed the standard.

digital volume control Digital circuit that adjusts the signal level by performing mathematical computation on the ones and zeros representing the audio signal.

diode Electronic component that allows current to flow in only one direction.

dip A reduction in energy over a band of frequencies. Contrast with peak.

dipolar speaker A loudspeaker that produces sound from the rear as well as from the front, with the front and rear sounds out-of-phase with each other.

direct-coupled Electronic circuit in which no coupling capacitors are in the signal path.

Direct Stream Digital (DSD) Method of digitally encoding music with a very fast sampling rate, but with only 1-bit quantization. Developed by Sony and Philips for the Super Audio CD (SACD).

direct-view Another name for a conventional television set. Called direct-view because you view the image directly on the front of its picture tube.

discrete Separate. A circuit using separate transistors rather than an integrated circuit. A discrete digital surround-sound format contains 5.1 channels of audio information that are completely separate from each other; contrasted with a matrixed surround format such as Dolby Surround, which mixes the channels together for transmission or storage.

dispersion The directional pattern over which a loudspeaker distributes its sound.

dither A small amount of noise added to an audio signal that improves the low-level resolution of digital audio.

Dolby Digital A 5.1-channel discrete digital surround-sound format used in movie theaters and consumer formats. The surround format required on the DVD and HDTV broadcasts.

Dolby Digital EX Surround format that matrix-encodes a third surround channel in the existing left and right surround channels of a Dolby Digital signal. This third surround channel (called "surround back") drives a loudspeaker or loudspeakers located directly behind the listening position for greater spatial realism. Called THX EX in THX-certified products.

Dolby noise reduction Circuitry found in cassette decks that reduces tape hiss. Dolby B provides 10dB of noise reduction at high frequencies; Dolby C provides 20dB of noise reduction at high frequencies; and Dolby S provides 24dB of noise reduction at high frequencies and 10dB at low frequencies.

Dolby Pro Logic A type of Dolby Surround decoder with improved performance over standard Dolby Surround decoding. Specifically, Pro Logic decoding provides greater channel separation and a center-speaker output. A Dolby Pro Logic decoder takes in a 2-channel, Dolby Surround-encoded audio signal and splits that signal up into left, center, right, and surround channels.

Dolby Pro Logic II Pro Logic surround decoder with improved performance and added features compared with older Pro Logic circuits.

Dolby Pro Logic IIx Pro Logic surround decoder that generates the surround-back channel from 2-channel or 5.1-channel sources.

Dolby Surround An encoding format that combines four channels (left, center, right, surround) into two channels for transmission or storage. On playback, a Dolby Pro Logic decoder separates the two channels back into four channels.

downconverted A digital audio signal that has been converted from a higher sampling frequency to a lower sampling frequency. For example, a digital master tape recorded at 96kHz is downconverted to 44.1kHz sampling for storage on a compact disc.

downmix converter A circuit found in DVD players that converts the 5.1-channel discrete Dolby Digital soundtrack into a 2-channel Dolby Surround-encoded signal. A DVD player's downmix converter lets you hear surround sound from DVD if you don't have a Dolby Digital decoder. Also refers to the circuit in all DVD-Audio players that creates, on the fly, a 2-channel mix from the disc's multi-channel signal.

driver The actual speaker units inside a loudspeaker cabinet.

dry Sonic presentation in which the ambience or reverberation is reduced.

DSD see "Direct Stream Digital"

DSP see "Digital Signal Processing"

DSP room correction Technique of removing room-induced frequency-response peaks and dips with digital signal processing.

DTCP see "Digital Transmission Content Protection"

DTS see "Digital Theater Systems"

DTS ES Discrete Surround-sound format that delivers discrete 6.1-channel sound. The additional channel (compared with 5.1-channel sound) drives a loudspeaker or loudspeakers located directly behind the listening position.

DTS ES Matrix Surround-sound format that matrix-encodes a third surround channel into the existing left and right surround channels in a DTS signal.

DTS Neo:6 Decoding circuit developed by Digital Theater Systems for creating 6-channel audio from 2-channel sources. Comes in two flavors: DTS Neo:6 Music and DTS Neo:6 Cinema.

dull Lacking treble energy.

DVD CD-sized disc that can contain digital video (DVD-Video), high-resolution digital audio (DVD-Audio), or computer data (DVD-ROM).

DVD-Audio Subset of the DVD standard that provides for high-resolution, multichannel digital audio on DVD.

DVD-Video Format created for storing movies on a CD-sized disc.

dynamic compression Phenomenon in loudspeaker drivers in which an increase in drive signal results in little increase in acoustic output. Occurs when the driver's voice coil heats.

dynamic range In audio, the difference in volume between loud and soft. In video, the difference in light level between black and white (also called contrast).

dynamic range compressor A circuit found in some Dolby Digital-equipped receivers and preamplifiers that reduces dynamic range. A dynamic range compressor can reduce the volume of peaks, increase the volume of low-level sounds, or both. Useful for late-night listening when you don't want explosions to disturb other family members, but still want to hear low-level sounds clearly.

dyne A unit of force. The threshold of hearing (0dBSPL) represents a pressure on your eardrum of 0.0002 dynes/cm2. A force of 10^{-6} dynes applied to a phono cartridge cantilever will push that cantilever approximately 15 millionths of a centimeter.

edge A harshness in transient musical events such as the initial attacks of percussion instruments.

effective tonearm mass The total mass of a tonearm's moving parts, and where along the tonearm that mass is distributed. Mass near the pivot point only slightly increases a tonearm's effective mass, but the same amount of mass near the tonearm's cartridge end greatly increases the effective mass. A tonearm's effective mass must be matched to the phono cartridge's compliance for optimum performance.

electromagnetic interference (EMI) Disturbance caused by radiation of electromagnetic waves.

electrostatic loudspeaker Loudspeaker in which a thin diaphragm is moved back and forth by electrostatic forces. Contrasted with a dynamic loudspeaker, in which electromagnetic forces move the diaphragm back and forth.

EMI see "electromagnetic interference"

envelopment The impression of being surrounded by sound, such as in a surround-sound system.

equalization In tape or LP record playback, a treble cut to counteract a treble boost applied during recording. Also describes modification of tonal balance by employing an equalizer.

equalizer A circuit that changes the tonal balance of an audio program. Bass and treble controls are a form of equalizer.

etched An unpleasant emphasis on transient musical information, accompanied by excessive brightness.

extension How high or low in frequency an audio component can reproduce sound.

Fast Fourier Transform (FFT) Mathematical technique that converts information from the time domain to the frequency domain.

feedback In amplifier circuits, taking part of the output signal and sending it back to the amplifier's input. Feedback reduces distortion and makes the circuit more stable. (see also "acoustic feedback")

FFT see "Fast Fourier Transform"

filter Electronic circuit that selectively removes or reduces the amplitude of certain frequencies.

filter capacitor Type of capacitor used in power supplies to filter traces of 60Hz AC from the DC supply.

FireWire A high-speed interface that can carry high-resolution digital audio. Officially called IEEE1394, but also known as i.LINK (Sony's trade name). An open standard developed by Apple Computer.

5C see "Digital Transmission Content Protection"

5.1 channels The standard number of channels for encoding film soundtracks. The five channels are left, center, right, surround left, and surround right. The ".1" channel is a 100Hz-bandwidth channel reserved for high-impact bass effects.

flat A speaker that accurately reproduces the signal fed to it is called "flat" because that is the shape of its frequency-response curve. Flat also describes a soundstage lacking in depth.

floorstanding speaker A speaker that sits on the floor rather than on a stand.

flutter echo Back-and-forth acoustic reflections in a room between pairs of surfaces. Think of a pair of facing mirrors, each reflecting light into the other. Flutter echo can be heard as a "pinging" sound after a handclap. Caused by untreated parallel surfaces.

forward A description of a sonic presentation in which sounds seem to be projected forward toward the listener.

frame One complete picture in video. The NTSC television picture is composed of 29.97 frames per second. Half a frame is called a "field."

frequency Number of repetitions of a cycle. Measured in Hertz (Hz), or cycles, per second. An audio signal with a frequency of 1000Hz (1kHz) undergoes 1000 cycles of a sinewave per second.

frequency response A graphical representation showing a device's relative amplitude as a function of frequency.

front-projector A video display device that projects an image from a distance onto a separate screen.

full-range speaker A speaker that reproduces bass as well as midrange and treble frequencies.

gain Number expressing the amount of amplification provided by an amplifier. An amplifier that converts a signal with an amplitude of 0.1V to 1V is said to have a gain of 10.

geometry In cables, the physical arrangement of the conductors and dielectric.

Gracenote CDDB Database identifying album, song title, and artist that can be embedded in digital audio servers, computer-based audio systems, and portable music players, or accessed via the Internet.

grainy Sonic description of a roughness to instrumental or vocal timbres.

harmonic distortion The production of spurious frequencies at multiples of the original frequency. A circuit amplifying a 1kHz sinewave will create frequencies at 2kHz (second harmonic), 3kHz (third harmonic), and so forth.

HDCD see "High Definition Compatible Digital"

HDTV High Definition Television A new digital-video transmission system that is replacing the NTSC video system in use since 1953.

heatsink Large metal device that draws heat away from the interior of an electronic device and dissipates that heat in air. The fins protruding from the sides of power amplifiers are heatsinks.

hierarchical encoding In Ambisonics, a multichannel signal that is scalable to any number of playback channels, including mono and stereo, ensuring compatibility with a wide range of playback systems.

Helmholtz resonator Acoustic device with a small opening that absorbs sound by causing the air in the device to resonate at a particular frequency.

Hertz (Hz) The unit of frequency; the number of cycles per second. Kilohertz (kHz) is thousands of cycles per second.

HiFi Short for High Fidelity, the high-quality audio format used in some VHS machines. A HiFi VCR can provide excellent sound quality. Contrasted with VHS linear tracks, which offer poor sound quality.

high-blend circuit FM tuner feature that automatically switches the signal to monaural when the broadcast signal strength falls below a certain level.

high-cut filter Filter that removes treble energy.

High Definition Compatible Digital (HDCD) Process for improving the sound quality of 16-bit/44.1kHz digital audio on compact disc. An HDCD-encoded disc will play on any CD player, but sounds best when played on a CD player or digital processor equipped with an HDCD decoder.

high-density layer The information layer in a hybrid Super Audio CD that contains high-resolution digital audio.

high-pass filter A circuit that allows high frequencies to pass but blocks low frequencies. Also called a "low-cut filter." High-pass filters are often found in A/V receivers and A/V preamplifiers to keep bass out of the front speakers when you're using a subwoofer.

high-resolution digital audio Generally regarded as digital audio with a sampling rate greater than 48kHz and a word length longer than 16 bits.

home theater The combination of high-quality sound and video in the home.

Home THX A set of patents, technologies, and playback standards for reproducing film soundtracks in the home. THX doesn't compete with surround formats such as Dolby Digital or DTS, but instead builds on them.

hybrid An audio component that combines more than one technology, such as tubes and transistors in the same amplifier, or dynamic and ribbon drivers in the same loudspeaker.

hybrid disc SACD-based disc that is compatible with CD players as well as SACD players. Has two information layers; one layer contains CD-quality audio, the second contains high-resolution audio.

Hz see "Hertz"

IC Integrated circuit. Some products use ICs for processing and amplifying audio signals; higher-quality units use discrete transistors instead.

i.LINK Sony trade name for the IEEE1394 (FireWire) interface.

image specificity Soundstage attribute in which instrumental or vocal images are precisely positioned and clearly defined.

imaging The impression of hearing, in reproduced music, instruments and voices as objects in space.

IMD see "intermodulation distortion"

immediate An immediate musical presentation is somewhat vivid, lively, and forward. Contrast with "laid-back."

impedance Resistance to the flow of AC electrical current. An impedance is a combination of resistance, inductive reactance, and capacitive reactance.

inductive reactance The property of an inductor that increases its opposition to current flow as frequency increases.

inductor Electronic component that increases its opposition to current flow as frequency increases. Many loudspeaker crossovers use a large inductor on the woofer to filter out high frequencies.

infinite baffle A sealed loudspeaker cabinet. The cabinet wraps around the drive units, mimicking a baffle of infinite size. Also called air suspension or acoustic suspension. Contrast with a reflex, or ported, loudspeaker.

infrared (IR) The frequency of light emitted by wireless remote controls.

input impedance The resistance to current flow presented by a circuit or component to the circuit or component driving it. Impedance is a combination of resistance, capacitive reactance, and inductive reactance.

input overload A condition in which a component (typically a preamplifier) produces severe distortion because the signal driving the component is too high in level. For example, connecting a high-output moving-magnet cartridge to a preamplifier's moving-coil input could overload the preamplifier's input, introducing audible distortion.

input receiver Chip or circuit in a digital processor that takes in the S/PDIF datastream, generates a new clock based on that datastream, strips out the audio data, and sends the audio data to the digital filter. Converts S/PDIF to audio data, control data, and a clock.

integer upsampling Increasing the sampling frequency of a digital audio signal by an integer multiple; i.e. 44.1kHz to 88.2kHz (2x) or 176.4kHz (4x). Contrasted with non-integer upsampling; i.e. 44.1kHz to 96kHz.

integrated amplifier Audio product combining a preamplifier and power amplifier in one chassis.

interconnect A cable that carries line-level audio signals (audio interconnect), composite video signals (video interconnect), or S/PDIF-encoded digital audio (digital interconnect.).

intermodulation distortion (IMD) Distortion introduced by amplifier circuits that is the sum and difference of the input signal. For example, an amplifier driven with a mix of 1kHz and 5kHz generates intermodulation-distortion products at 6kHz (the sum of 1kHz and 5kHz) and at 4kHz (the difference between 1kHz and 5kHz). These IMD products then intermodulate with each other to create a nearly infinite series of distortion products.

International Steering Committee Consortium of music-industry representatives who issued a set of guidelines to the consumer-electronics industry expressing their needs in a next-generation music carrier.

interpolation Filling-in missing information with a "best-guess" estimate.

JFET (Junction Field Effect Transistor) A type of transistor often used in preamplifier input stages that differs in internal structure and operation with the more common bipolar transistor.

jitter Timing variations in the clock that synchronizes events in a digital audio system. The clock could be in an analog-to-digital converter that controls when each audio sample is taken. Of more interest to audiophiles is clock jitter in digital audio reproduction; the clock controls the timing of the reconstruction of digital audio samples into an analog signal. Jitter degrades musical fidelity.

jitter-reduction device A component inserted between a digital source such as a CD transport and a digital-to-analog converter. The jitter-reduction device takes in a jittered S/PDIF signal and outputs a low-jitter S/PDIF signal.

Kbs Kilo-bits per second. Thousands of bits per second; a measure of bit rate.

kHz see "kilohertz"

ladder DAC see "multibit DAC"

laid-back Sonic description in which the musical presentation has a sense of ease, with some distance between the listener and the soundstage. A laid-back presentation has been likened to sitting in a distant row in a concert hall. Contrast with "forward" and "immediate."

land The flat areas on a CD surface between the pits. Digital data are encoded in the land-to-pit and pit-to-land transitions.

laserdisc A format for storing analog video signals on a 12" double-sided disc.

LCD projector A projector using three LCD panels and an incandescent light source.

lean Sonic description of a musical presentation lacking midbass. Synonyms are "thin," "lightweight," and "underdamped" (to describe loudspeakers). Contrast with "weighty," "full," and "heavy."

least significant bit (LSB) In binary notation, the bit that has the lowest value. In 16-bit digital audio, the 16th bit has the least effect on the numerical value of the 16-bit word. An example in decimal notation: in the decimal number 15,389, the digit in the ones column (9) has the least effect on the value of the number. Contrast with most significant bit (MSB).

LED (Light Emitting Diode) Solid-state device that emits light when current is passed through it. LEDs are used as indicators on the front panels of many audio components.

letterbox A video image that results from displaying an image of widescreen aspect ratio on a television set of standard aspect ratio. The picture is presented between black bars above and below the image.

level matching Technique of ensuring that two musical presentations are reproduced at exactly the same volume so that more accurate judgments of the audio quality can be reached.

LFE see "Low Frequency Effects"

light-emitting diode see "LED"

lightweight Musical presentation lacking bass energy.

linear An output that varies in direct proportion to the input.

linearity Digital audio specification that describes the amplitude accuracy of a digital-to-analog converter. For example, a DAC driven with a digital signal at –90dBFS may reproduce that level as –88dB; the DAC has a 2dB positive linearity error. That is, the output level doesn't perfectly match the input level.

line doubler Also called a "scan converter," a device that converts an interlaced scanned signal to a progressive scanning signal, and presents those lines to a video display device at twice the frequency of normal NTSC video. Reduces the visibility of scanning lines, particularly in large projected images.

line level An audio signal with an amplitude of approximately 1V to 2V. Audio components interface at line level through interconnects. Contrasted with "speaker level," the much more powerful signal that drives speakers.

line-source loudspeaker Loudspeaker with a tall and narrow dispersion pattern. A tall ribbon driver is naturally a line source, as is a vertical array of point-source drivers. Contrasted with a point-source loudspeaker, which has a shorter, broader dispersion pattern.

liquid Sonic description of a musical presentation lacking shrillness. Usually applied to the midrange, liquidity implies correct reproduction of musical timbre.

litz cable Cable in which many small strands are grouped, with each strand insulated. This technique isolates each strand from the surrounding strands.

loading Method of enclosing a driver (usually the woofer) in a loudspeaker cabinet. Different loading methods include the infinite baffle, bass reflex, and transmission line.

localization The ability to detect the directionality of sounds.

loudspeaker A device that converts an electrical signal into sound. The loudspeaker is the last component of the playback chain.

low-cut filter A circuit that removes bass frequencies from an audio signal. Also called a "high-pass filter."

low-frequency cutoff The point at which a loudspeaker's output drops in the bass by 3dB.

Low Frequency Effects (LFE) A separate channel in the Dolby Digital format reserved for low bass effects, such as explosions. The LFE channel is the ".1" channel in the 5.1-channel Dolby Digital format.

low-pass filter A circuit that removes midrange and treble frequencies from an audio signal. Also called a "high-cut filter."

LP Long-Playing record. Double-sided 12" vinyl disc that stores approximately 25 minutes of audio per side.

LSB see "Least Significant Bit"

luminance The black-and-white, or brightness, component of a video signal. Represented by the letter Y.

lush see "liquid"

luxury products Audio components built with lavish cosmetic design and expensive chassis. Contrasted with value products, which attempt to produce the best sound for the least money.

magneto-optical recording Recording method used in the MiniDisc format, in which magnetic particles are heated by a laser, then magnetized to store digital data.

mass loading Technique of increasing the mass of loudspeaker stands or equipment racks by filling them with sand, lead shot, or other dense material.

matrix A method of encoding four audio channels into two channels for transmission or storage.

Mbs Mega (million) bits per second. A unit of measure for expressing bit rates. MPEG-2 video encoding has a variable bit rate that averages 3.5Mbs.

MD see "MiniDisc"

MDF see "Medium Density Fiberboard"

Medium Density Fiberboard (MDF) Composite wood material from which most loudspeaker cabinets are made.

Meridian High Resolution (MHR) Proprietary high-resolution, multichannel, encrypted digital interface used between products made by Meridian Audio. Sanctioned by the DVD Forum for carrying high-resolution signals from a DVD-A player.

Meridian Lossless Packing (MLP) Data compression system used in DVD-Audio that reduces the bit rate with no loss in quality. The decompressed bitstream is bit-for-bit identical to the original bitstream. Contrasted with "lossy" compression systems that degrade fidelity.

metallic An unpleasant harshness to a sound that is reminiscent of metal being struck.

MHR see "Meridian High Resolution"

midrange Audio frequencies in the middle of the audible spectrum, such as the human voice. Generally the range of frequencies from about 300Hz to 2kHz. Also: a driver in a loudspeaker that reproduces the range of frequencies in the middle of the audible spectrum.

millisecond One one-thousandth of a second.

MiniDisc (MD) Sony-invented format for storing 74 minutes of digital audio on a 2.5" disc encased in a plastic caddy. Designed for portable applications, not as a replacement for the compact disc.

minimonitor A small, stand-mounted loudspeaker.

MLP see "Meridian Lossless Packing"

modular A/V preamplifier An A/V preamplifier built with interchangeable modules for upgrading to future technologies.

modulated Dolby Digital An obsolete form of Dolby Digital required for storing Dolby Digital on laserdisc. The Dolby Digital signal is modulated to an RF signal for storage on the laserdisc, then demodulated on playback. Contrasted with unmodulated Dolby Digital as used in DVD.

monoblock A power amplifier with only one channel.

MOSFET (Metal-Oxide Semiconductor Field Effect Transistor) Type of transistor that is turned on (biased) by voltage rather than current. Contrast with "bipolar transistor."

most significant bit (MSB) In binary notation, the bit that has the highest value. In 16-bit digital audio, the first bit has the greatest effect on the numerical value of the 16-bit word. An example in decimal notation: in the decimal number 15,389, the digit in the ten-thousands column (1) has the most effect on the value of the number. Contrast with least significant bit (LSB).

moving-coil cartridge Transducer that converts stylus motion in a record groove to an electrical signal. Tiny coils attached to the cantilever are moved back and forth in a fixed magnetic field, inducing current flow through the coils.

moving-magnet cartridge Transducer that converts stylus motion in a record groove to an electrical signal. Tiny magnets attached to the cantilever are moved back and forth between fixed coils of wire, inducing current flow through the coils.

MP3 Low-bit-rate coding scheme used in portable audio players and Internet downloads.

MPEG-1 video compression A video encoding method that reduces to 1.4Mbs the number of bits needed to represent the video signal. Provides poor picture quality.

MPEG-2 video compression A much-higher-quality version of MPEG-1 encoding. Used in DSS and DVD. MPEG-2 reduces the data rate of digital video from 168 million bits per second on a master tape to an average of approximately 3 million bits per second on a DVD.

MPX filter A switch on some tuners and cassette decks that invokes a 19kHz filter to remove the 19kHz pilot tone from the broadcast FM signal. An MPX filter is necessary when recording on a cassette deck because the pilot tone can interfere with correct Dolby noise-reduction tracking.

MSB see "Most Significant Bit"

multibit DAC Digital-to-analog converter employing a "ladder" of resistors, each resistor corresponding to one bit in the digital audio word. Each successive resistor value is twice that of the resistor below it on the rung, which allows half as much current flow with each step down the ladder. This resistance-doubling progression follows the binary progression 1, 2, 4, 8, 16, 32, 64, and so forth. Contrast with 1-bit DAC, in which the digital audio signal is represented by pulses just one bit high.

multichannel power amplifier A power amplifier with more than two channels, usually five or seven.

multichannel preamplifier A preamplifier with more than two channels, usually six.

multichannel sound Sound reproduction via more than two channels feeding more than two loudspeakers.

multipath In FM-radio transmission, two or more paths for the signal to travel between transmitter and receiver. Multipath is caused by mountains or buildings that reflect the radio signal; the receiving antenna picks up the directly broadcast signal along with the signal after it has been delayed by the reflections. Multipath introduces audible distortion. Multipath in television transmission is seen as "ghosting" in the picture.

multipath indicator Meter in better FM tuners that indicates the amount of multipath in the received signal.

multi-room A feature on some A/V products that lets you listen to two different sources in two different rooms.

nasal Sonic description of midrange coloration (particularly loudspeakers) that makes vocalists sound congested.

New Old Stock (NOS) Vacuum tubes that have never been used, but haven't been manufactured in a long time (perhaps decades).

Noise shaping Digital audio technique in which quantization noise is shifted to the top octave of the audioband, or above the audioband, thus decreasing the audible noise. Used in 1-bit DACs and Direct Stream Digital.

NOS see "New Old Stock"

NTSC National Television Standards Committee, the body that set our color TV standard in 1953. NTSC has become a descriptive name for television and video signals that conform to this standard. Jokingly referred to as "Never Twice the Same Color."

Nyquist Theorem Expresses relationship between a digital audio system's sampling frequency and the highest audio signal that can be preserved. Specifically, the sampling frequency must be at least twice as high as the highest audio frequency to be recorded. Named for telegraph engineer Harry Nyquist, who published his theorem in 1928.

octave The interval between two frequencies with a ratio of 2:1. The bottom octave in audio is 20Hz-40Hz; the top octave is 10kHz-20kHz.

off-axis response A loudspeaker's frequency response measured at the loudspeaker's sides. Contrast with on-axis, the loudspeaker's response directly in front of the baffle.

offset A bend in a pivoted tonearm that gives the arm an S or J shape and orients the cartridge at 25° relative to the arm.

off-tape monitoring Listening to a tape a split second after it has been recorded. Possible only with a three-head tape recorder.

ohm The unit of resistance to electrical current flow.

Ohm's law Expresses the relationship between voltage, current, and resistance in electrical circuits. If you know two of the values (current and resistance, for example), you can calculate the third value using Ohm's law. Formula is E=IXR, or voltage equal current flow multiplied by the resistance. E stands for electromotive force (voltage); I stands for current (for intensity of electrons); R stands for resistance.

Omnipolar loudspeaker Trademarked name of Mirage Loudspeakers for its loudspeaker design technology that radiates sound in all directions.

on-axis response A loudspeaker's frequency response measured directly in front of the baffle.

one-note bass Sonic description of bass that seems to have just one pitch. Caused by excessive output over a narrow frequency band in loudspeakers. A "boom truck" is one-note bass taken to an extreme.

opaque Impression that the soundstage is cloudy, veiled, or thick. Contrast with "transparent."

output impedance Technically, the change in a component's output voltage in response to a change in load impedance. Practically, a component with a high output impedance can deliver less current to a load than a component with a low output impedance. Low output impedance is desirable.

output stage The last amplifier circuit in an audio component. The output stage in a CD player is an amplifier that drives the preamplifier. In power amplifiers, the output stage delivers current to the loudspeakers.

output transformer Transformer in tubed amplifiers that couples the output stage to the loudspeaker. Output transformers are required in tubed amplifiers to change the amplifier's high output impedance to a lower value that can better drive loudspeakers. The output transformer also blocks DC from appearing at the amplifier's output terminals.

overall perspective Describes a musical presentation's degree for forwardness. An up-front perspective is likened to sitting in row C of a concert hall; a laid-back perspective is likened to sitting in row W.

overdamped Technical term that describes a woofer's motion in reaction to a drive signal, specifically how long the driver continues to move after the drive signal has stopped. An overdamped loudspeaker has lean but articulate bass presentation. Contrast with "underdamped."

overhang In loudspeakers, woofer movement after the drive signal has ceased. In tonearms, the distance from the tonearm's pivot point to the cartridge.

oversampling digital filter Digital audio circuit that removes all energy above half the sampling frequency. An 8x oversampling filter generates seven new samples for each incoming sample, thus increasing the sampling frequency by eight times. Oversampling shifts the spurious images to a higher frequency, where they are more easily filtered.

pace The sense of rhythmic drive or propulsion in music.

palpable Impression that the reproduced instrument or voice is tangible; literally, "touchable."

pan&scan A method of converting a widescreen presentation to an image of standard aspect ratio (4:3) without black bars at the top and bottom of the picture. The camera moves back and forth (panning and scanning) in each scene to show only the most important parts of the image. This results in the left and/or right edges of the image being cut off.

panning The movement of sounds and images from one location to another. Originally a camera term.

passband Range of frequencies allowed to pass by a filter.

passive level control Device that adjusts the volume of an audio system without using amplifiers or other active electronic components such as tubes or transistors. A passive level control is typically a box with a volume control.

passive radiator Diaphragm in some loudspeakers that isn't connected electrically, but is moved by air pressure inside the cabinet created by the woofer's motion. Also called an auxiliary bass radiator (ABR), the passive radiator covers what would have been the port in a reflex-loaded loudspeaker.

passive subwoofer A speaker for reproducing bass frequencies that must be powered by a separate power amplifier. Contrasted with "active" or "powered" subwoofers, which contain an integral amplifier.

PCM see "Pulse Code Modulation"

peak A short-term, high-level audio signal. Also: an excess of energy over a narrow frequency band (contrasted with "dip").

peaky Sonic description of a sound with excessive energy over a narrow frequency band.

pentode Vacuum tube with five elements: the cathode, plate, screen grid, control grid, and suppressor grid. More efficient than the simpler triode vacuum tube.

perceptual coding A method of reducing the number of bits needed to encode an audio or video signal by ignoring information unlikely to be heard or seen.

period The time it takes to complete one cycle of a sinewave.

phantom center-channel mode A setting on A/V receivers or A/V controllers invoked when no center-channel speaker is used.

phantom image The creation of an apparent sound source between two loudspeakers.

phase In a periodic wave, the fraction of a period that has elapsed. Describes the time relationship between two signals.

phase adjustment A control provided on some subwoofers that lets you delay the sound of the subwoofer slightly so that the subwoofer's output is in-phase (has the same time relationship) with the front speakers.

phase angle A measurement of how inductive or capacitive a loudspeaker's impedance is.

phase locked loop (PLL) A electronic circuit that compares the phase of an incoming signal with that of a reference frequency, thereby synchronizing the two signals.

pitch definition The ability to distinguish pitch in reproduced music, particularly in the bass. Some products (especially loudspeakers) obscure the individual pitches of notes.

pits and land Tiny depressions (pits) and flat areas (land) embedded in a CD or DVD that represent digital data.

pivoted tonearm A tonearm in which the cartridge and armtube traverse the record in an arc while maintaining a fixed pivot point. Contrasted with tangential-tracking tonearms.

planar loudspeaker Loudspeaker in which the driver or drivers are mounted in an open panel.

planar magnetic Type of driver in which conductors carrying the audio signal are bonded to a diaphragm. A subset of the ribbon driver, planar magnetic drivers are also called quasi-ribbons.

playback components Broadly speaking, the power amplifier and loudspeakers. Contrasted with source components (tuner, CD player, LP turntable, DVD player, etc.) and control components (preamplifier).

plinth The flat deck of a turntable beneath the platter.

PLL see "Phase Locked Loop"

pneumatic platform Device that isolates components from vibration with compressed air.

point-source loudspeaker Loudspeaker that emits sound from a point in space. Contrast with line-source loudspeaker.

port Opening in a loudspeaker cabinet that channels bass from inside the enclosure to outside the enclosure. Also called a "vent."

ported loudspeaker see "reflex-loaded loudspeaker"

port noise Noise generated by large air flows in a reflex-loaded loudspeaker's port. Also called "chuffing."

power amplifier An audio component that boosts a line-level signal to a powerful signal that can drive loudspeakers.

power bandwidth The range of frequencies over which an amplifier can deliver its rated power.

power handling A measure of how much amplifier power, in watts, a speaker can take before it is damaged.

power output A measure of a power amplifier's ability, in watts, to deliver electrical voltage and current to a speaker.

power supply Circuitry found in every audio component that converts 60Hz alternating current from the wall outlet into direct current that supplies the audio circuitry.

power transformer Device in a power supply that reduces the incoming voltage from 120V to a lower value.

preamplifier Component that receives signals from source components, selects a source for listening, controls the volume, and drives the power amplifier. Literally means "before the amplifier."

pre-preamplifier Component that boosts a tiny signal from a phono cartridge to a higher level for input to a phono preamplifier. Typically used to match a moving-coil cartridge output to a preamplifier designed for a moving-magnet input.

presence The sense that an instrument or voice is actually in the listening room.

presence region Band of frequencies in the midrange that contributes to presence.

psychoacoustics The study of human hearing.

Pulse Code Modulation (PCM) A method of representing an audio signal as a series of digital samples.

Pulse Width Modulation (PWM) A method of representing an audio signal digitally in which the signal's amplitude information is contained in the widths of a single-bit pulse.

punchy Sonic presentation having dynamic impact, particularly in the bass.

push-pull amplifier Amplifier in which pairs of transistors or vacuum tubes are arranged so that one transistor or tube amplifies the positive half of the audio waveform, and the other tube amplifies the negative half. Contrasted with single-ended amplifier.

PWM see "Pulse Width Modulation"

Q for Quality Factor. Numerical value describing woofer resonance in an enclosure. Technically, Q is the woofer's peak resonant frequency divided by the peak's bandwidth.

Quadraphonic Four audio channels. Two Quadraphonic formats were introduced in the early 1970s: the matrix SQ system and the discrete CD-4.

quantization Assigning a discrete numerical value to an analog function. In digital audio, the analog waveform's amplitude is converted to a number (quantized) each time a sample is taken.

quantization error Difference between the actual analog value and the number representing that analog value. Quantization error occurs when the analog value falls between two quantization steps; the quantizer assigns the closest number. Quantization error introduces noise and distortion in digital audio, often heard as a roughness at low signal levels, particularly during reverberation decay.

quantization word length The number of bits created by the A/D converter at each sample point. Compact disc records quantization words 16 bits in length.

quarter-wavelength bass trap Acoustical absorber in which an absorbent material is hung at a distance from a reflective surface. The peak absorption frequency occurs when the distance between the absorbent material and reflective surface is one-quarter the wavelength of sound, and at odd multiples of a quarter wavelength.

quasi-ribbon driver see "planar magnetic"

quieting sensitivity Tuner specification that states the voltage across the antenna required to produce an audio signal with a signal-to-noise ratio of 50dB. Contrast with the less stringent "usable sensitivity."

radiation pattern The way in which a speaker disperses sound.

Radio Data System System for broadcasting text or other data along with an FM radio broadcast. The receiving tuner must be equipped with RDS decoding to display the text or data.

Radio Frequency (RF) Most often refers to spurious noise with energy in the radio-frequency band.

rail The power-supply voltage fed to the audio circuits.

rail fuse Fuse sometimes found on the back of a power amplifier that is in series with the rail. The rail fuse will blow when excessive current is drawn by the amplifier's output stage.

rarefaction A component of a sound wave in which the air density is lower than normal atmospheric pressure. A woofer cone moving inward creates a rarefaction. One rarefaction and one compression make one complete cycle of a sound wave.

RCA jack A connector found on audio and video products. Signals transmitted via RCA jacks include line-level audio, composite video, and component video.

RDS see "Radio Data System"

rear-projection TV A video display device, using three CRT tubes mounted inside a cabinet, that projects its image off a mirror onto a screen mounted at the cabinet front.

rectifier A device that converts AC current into DC current. Found in all power supplies.

rectify To convert AC current into DC current.

Red Book Name for the compact disc specification, derived from the document's red cover. A "Red Book" disc is a conventional CD.

Red Book layer The information layer in a Super Audio CD that contains conventional 16-bit/44.1kHz digital audio.

re-equalization A Home THX technology that reduces the amount of treble on playback so that you hear a more natural-sounding reproduction when a film soundtrack is played back in the home.

reflex-loaded loudspeaker see "bass reflex"

resolution The quality of an audio component that reveals low-level musical information.

resonance Vibration of an object or air that is disproportionate in amplitude to the stimulus. A bell ringing at a certain frequency is an example of resonance; the pitch is the bell's resonant frequency.

reverberation Dense acoustical reflections in an acoustic space that become lower in amplitude and more closely spaced over time. The sound in a room after the sound source has stopped producing sound.

reverberation time The time it takes sound in a room to decrease in amplitude by 60dB. Symbol: RT_{60}.

RF Dolby Digital see "modulated Dolby Digital"

RIAA Recording Industry Association of America

RIAA accuracy Flatness of the RIAA phono equalization circuit in a phono preamplifier.

RIAA equalization A treble boost and bass cut applied to the audio signal when a record is cut; a reciprocal treble cut and bass boost on playback restores flat response. RIAA equalization increases the playing time of an LP (because bass takes up the most room in the record groove) and decreases noise (because the treble cut on playback also reduces record surface noise).

ribbon loudspeaker Loudspeaker in which the diaphragm is electrically conductive and carries the audio signal. Usually made from a long, thin strip of aluminum.

rolled off Sonic description of reduced energy at the frequency extremes (bass or treble). A loudspeaker whose treble is rolled off sounds dull.

rolloff Reduction in energy at the frequency extremes, or the effect of a filter; e.g. the crossover produces a 12dB per octave rolloff above 2kHz.

room correction see "DSP room correction"

room gain Increase in bass level when a loudspeaker plays in a room compared with the loudspeaker's bass level in an anechoic chamber. The room's walls increase the amount of bass heard; the closer to the walls the loudspeaker is placed, the greater the room gain.

room resonance modes Excessive acoustical energy at certain frequencies when the air in a room is excited by the sound of a loudspeaker.

rumble Low-frequency noise associated with LP playback.

SACD see "Super Audio CD"

sampling The process of converting an analog audio signal into digital form by taking periodic "snapshots" of the audio signal at some regular interval. Each snapshot (sample) is assigned a number that represents the analog signal's amplitude at the moment the sample was taken.

sampling frequency The rate at which samples are taken when converting analog audio to digital audio. Expressed in samples per second, or, more commonly, in Hertz; i.e., the CD format's sampling frequency is 44.1kHz.

sampling-rate converter Circuit that changes the sampling frequency of a digital audio signal.

satellite speaker A small speaker with limited bass output designed to be used with a subwoofer.

scan line One sweep of a beam of electrons across a video display device. In the NTSC system, each video frame is composed of 525 scan lines, of which 480 are usable.

scan rate The frequency with which a video display device "paints" scan lines. NTSC video has a scan rate of 15,734 lines per second (525 lines per frame multiplied by 29.97 frames per second).

SCMS see "Serial Copy Management System"

screechy Unpleasant character of upper midrange or treble that makes instruments or voices have some of the sound of noisy car brakes. Most often applied to the sound of violins.

screen The front of a direct-view television's CRT tube, the front of a rear-projector onto which an image is projected, or a separate material onto which a front-projector projects a video image.

SDMI see "Secure Digital Music Initiative"

secondary windings Coils of wire in a transformer that aren't physically connected to the AC line, but that supply voltage and current to the power supply through electromagnetic induction. Power transformers often have multiple secondary windings to increase the isolation between a component's multiple power supplies.

Secure Digital Music Initiative (SDMI) Attempt by the music and electronics industries to develop copy-control safeguards on recorded music.

selectable IF bandwidth A tuner feature that adjusts the bandwidth in the tuner's intermediate frequency (IF) stage for best sound quality and minimum interference from adjacent stations. Found on better tuners.

selectivity Tuner specification describing the tuner's ability to reject unwanted stations. Good selectivity is important to those who live in cities, where stations are closely spaced on the broadcast spectrum.

sensitivity 1) A measure of how much sound a speaker produces for a given amount of input power. Speaker sensitivity is measured by driving a speaker with 1W of power and measuring the sound-pressure level from a distance of 1 meter. 2) A measure of an FM tuner's ability to pull in weak stations. Tuner sensitivity is important if you live a long distance from FM transmitters.

Serial Copy Management System (SCMS) System for preventing second-generation digital copies of copyrighted audio material. A digital recorder equipped with SCMS will record digitally from another source, but that recording cannot then be used as a source for a second-generation recording.

servo An electrical or mechanical system that controls the speed or position of a moving device by forcing it to conform to a desired speed or position. In a servo-controlled turntable, the platter's rotational speed is compared with a reference frequency, and a correction signal is applied to the drive motor to keep the two frequencies identical.

servo-driven woofer A woofer in which an accelerometer (a device that converts motion to an electrical signal) attached to the voice coil sends to an amplifier information about its position and motion. The amplifier then applies a correction signal so that the woofer's motion matches the characteristics of the audio signal.

shielded loudspeaker A loudspeaker lined with metal to contain magnetic energy within the speaker. Shielded loudspeakers are used in home theater because the speakers' magnetic energy can distort a video monitor's picture.

sibilance *s* and *sh* sounds in spoken word or singing.

signal-to-noise ratio Numerical value expressing in decibels the difference in level between an audio component's noise floor and some reference signal level.

silky Sonic description of midrange or treble sounds lacking hardness or glare.

single-ended amplifier Amplifier in which both half-cycles of the audio waveform are amplified by the output tube or transistors. Contrasted with "push-pull amplifier."

single-presentation listening Evaluating audio components by listening to just that component rather than in comparison with other components.

Six-channel input A preamplifier input comprising six discrete jacks that will accept the six discrete analog outputs from a multichannel SACD or DVD-Audio player.

skating Force generated in LP playback that pulls the tonearm toward the record center.

skin effect Phenomenon in cables in which high frequencies travel along the conductor's surface and low frequencies travel through the conductor's center.

slam Sonic description of large dynamic impact in the bass that the listener feels in his body.

Smart Radio see "Radio Data System" (RDS)

smooth Sonic description of a presentation lacking peaks and dips in the frequency response.

soundfield see "soundstage"

sound-pressure level (SPL) A measure of loudness expressed in decibels (dB).

soundstage The impression of soundspace existing in three dimensions in front of or around the listener.

source components Components that provide audio or video signals to the rest of the system. CD players, turntables, and FM tuners are audio source components; VCRs, laserdisc players, DSS dishes, and DVD players are audio/video source components.

source switching Function performed by preamplifier or integrated amplifier that selects which source component's signals are fed to the speakers.

spade lug A speaker termination with a flat area that fits around a binding post.

S/PDIF interface Standardized method of transmitting digital audio from one component to another. Stands for Sony/Philips Digital Interface Format.

speaker see "loudspeaker"

SPL see "Sound-Pressure Level"

SPL meter A device for measuring the Sound-Pressure Level created by an audio source.

sprung turntable A turntable in which the platter and armboard are mounted on a sub-chassis that floats within the base on springs. Contrasted with unsprung turntables.

standing wave Stationary area of high and low acoustical pressure in a room caused by interaction of the sound with the room's boundaries.

stator The element in an electrostatic loudspeaker driver that remains stationary.

step-up transformer Transformer with a higher output voltage than the input voltage. Sometimes used between a moving-coil cartridge and a moving-magnet phono input.

stopband Range of frequencies stopped by a filter.

SQ A Quadraphonic format invented by CBS (which was bought by Sony) in which the rear channels were matrix-encoded into the front channels.

ST-Type optical interface Transmission system for sending digital audio in the S/PDIF format in which the signal is transmitted as light down a glass conductor. An ST-Type optical cable is terminated with locking bayonet connectors. No longer used on modern audio equipment.

stylus Tiny wedge protruding from a phono cartridge's cantilever that rests in the record groove and moves back and forth in response to modulations in the groove.

sub-chassis A component of some sprung turntables in which a platform (the sub-chassis) is suspended from the plinth, and upon which the platter and tonearm are mounted.

subwoofer A speaker designed to reproduce low bass frequencies.

Super Audio CD (SACD) Sony/Philips format for storing CD-quality audio as well as high-resolution digital audio on a CD-sized disc. "Hybrid" SACD discs can be played on conventional CD players as well as SACD players.

surround decoder A circuit or component that converts a surround-encoded audio signal into multiple audio signals that can be amplified. All A/V controllers incorporate surround decoding to convert the Dolby Digital or DTS signals from DVD, satellite, or over-the-air HDTV broadcasts to discrete analog signals.

surround decorrelation A THX technology that makes the sound in the monaural left and right surround channels slightly different, thus increasing the sense of envelopment and diffusion.

surround delay A technique of delaying the signal to the surround channels to increase the apparent separation between the front and surround channels.

surround mode A setting on A/V receivers and A/V preamplifiers that determines what surround decoding or signal processing is performed on the audio signal.

surround receiver see "A/V receiver"

surround sound An audio recording and playback format that uses more than two channels, and is reproduced with more than two loudspeakers, some of which are located behind the listener.

surround speakers Speakers located beside or behind the listener that reproduce the surround channel of surround-sound–encoded audio programs.

S-video A video connection method that keeps the video signal's brightness and color information separate.

sweet spot Point in the listening room where the sound is the best.

system matching The art of combining components to create the most musical system for a given budget.

tangential-tracking tonearm A tonearm in which the entire tonearm and bearing move in relation to the record along a tangent to the record groove. Contrasted with the more common pivoted tonearm that traverses an arc across the record.

taut Sonic description applied to tight, well-defined bass reproduction.

terminated cable A cable employing resistors, inductors, and capacitors in a box on the cable.

terminations The fittings on the end of a cable: RCA plugs, spade lugs, banana plugs, etc.

THD see "Total Harmonic Distortion"

theater pass-through Feature on some preamplifiers that sets the preamplifier to some fixed gain setting (usually unity gain) independent of the volume control setting. Useful in systems with a digital controller.

thick Sonic description of bass with poor pitch definition, or of an opaque soundstage.

thin Lacking bass weight.

three-way speaker A loudspeaker that divides the frequency spectrum into three parts (bass, midrange, treble) for reproduction through three or more drivers.

THX Lucasfilm's set of patents, technologies, and technical/acoustic performance criteria for film-sound reproduction in movie theaters. (see also "Home THX")

THX-certified An A/V product that correctly implements the THX technologies and meets stringent technical performance criteria for film-sound reproduction.

THX EX Surround format that matrix-encodes a third surround channel in the existing left and right surround channels of a Dolby Digital signal. This third surround channels drives a loudspeaker or loudspeakers located directly behind the listening position for greater spatial realism. Called Dolby Digital EX in non-THX-certified products.

timbre The physical quality of a sound.

timbre matching A THX technology that ensures that sounds arriving from the listener's sides have the same timbres as sounds arriving from the front, in order to ensure smooth panning of sounds.

time smearing Phenomenon that occurs in digital filters in which some energy in the audio signal is spread out over time, before and after that signal.

tizzy Excessive upper-treble energy that is also grainy.

toe-in Angling loudspeakers so that they point directly toward the listening position rather than straight ahead.

tonal balance Relative levels of bass, midrange, and treble in an audio component or musical presentation.

TosLink cable An optical cable for carrying digital audio. Most laserdisc players have TosLink digital outputs.

total harmonic distortion (THD) Specification stating the amount of harmonic distortion in an audio component. Called "total" because it is the sum of all the individual harmonic-distortion components created by the component.

tracking error In LP playback, a difference in the stylus/groove relationship between the cutting stylus and playback stylus.

transducer Any device that converts energy from one form to another. Microphones, loudspeakers, and phono cartridges are transducers.

transient A short-lived sound, often at high level. The sound of a snare drum is an example of a musical transient.

transient response The ability of a component to accurately reproduce transient musical events.

transistor Device made from solid semi-conductor material that can amplify audio signals.

transition band Range of frequencies in a filter between the passband (the frequency range passed by the filter) and the stopband (frequency range stopped by the filter).

transmission line A loudspeaker loading technique in which the woofer's rear wave is absorbed in a long duct or labyrinth (the transmission line) inside the enclosure.

transparent Sonic description of a component or system that has very low levels of coloration. A soundstage in which the acoustic space sounds clear rather than veiled.

treble High audio frequencies, generally the range from 3kHz-20kHz.

Trifield A pair of algorithms derived from Ambisonics in which a center-channel signal, and selectively, rear-channel signals, are derived from a 2-channel recording.

triode The simplest vacuum tube, employing just three elements: the cathode, plate, and control grid.

tube see "vacuum tube"

tube damper Device that fits over a vacuum tube to reduce vibration. Some tube dampers also act as heatsinks.

tweeter A speaker driver designed to reproduce treble signals.

two-way speaker A loudspeaker that splits the frequency spectrum into two parts, bass and treble, for reproduction by two or more drivers.

UHJ In Ambisonics, the mono and stereo compatible combination of the W (mono pressure signal), X (sides), and Y (front to back) signals.

ultra-linear A method of operating a pentode vacuum tube that combines the output power of a pentode with the distortion characteristics of a triode. Invented by David Hafler and Herbert Keroes in 1951.

unbalanced connection Connection method in which the audio signal is carried on two conductors, called signal and ground. Contrasted with balanced connection, in which the audio signal is carried on three conductors.

underdamped In loudspeakers, woofer movement after the drive signal has stopped.

uni-polar A loudspeaker that directs its acoustic output in one direction. Contrast with dipolar.

universal disc player Source component that plays CD, DVD-Video, DVD-Audio, and SACD.

unmodulated Dolby Digital A method of storing Dolby Digital that doesn't require modulation to accommodate the laserdisc format. All Dolby Digital signals except those stored on laserdisc are unmodulated.

unsprung turntable Turntable in which the platter and tonearm are connected directly to the turntable base rather than suspended on a sub-chassis. Contrast with "sprung turntable."

upsampling Technique of increasing the sampling frequency of a digital audio signal so that it can be converted to analog from the higher frequency.

uptilted A sound having too much treble and not enough bass.

usable sensitivity Tuner specification that states the voltage across the antenna required to produce an audio signal with a signal-to-noise ratio of 30dB. Contrast with the more stringent "quieting sensitivity."

user interface The controls and displays on a product and their logic and ease of use.

vacuum hold-down Mechanism for achieving tight coupling between an LP and platter by creating a vacuum just above the platter.

vacuum tube Device for amplifying audio in which the active elements are enclosed in a glass envelope devoid of air.

value product Audio component that seeks to achieve maximum sonic performance for the lowest price by cost-effective design and by eschewing expensive chassis.

veiled Impression of a haze or veil between you and the musical presentation. Contrast with "transparent."

vented loudspeaker see "reflex loudspeaker"

vertical tracking angle (VTA) The angle at which the stylus sits in a record's groove. Adjusted by moving the tonearm pivot point up or down.

vertical tracking force (VTF) Pressure applied by gravity to the stylus in a record groove.

vertical venetian-blind effect A change in perceived tonal balance when the listener moves sideways in the listening position when listening to electrostatic loudspeakers.

video display A device that converts a video signal into a visual image.

video monitor A direct-view television set with video input and output jacks.

vivid Musical presentation in which every sound is clearly audible. An overly vivid presentation is analytical and unmusical.

voice coil Coil of wire inside a loudspeaker driver through which current from the power amplifier flows.

volt Unit of electromotive force. The difference in potential required to make one Ampere of current flow through one ohm of resistance. See also "voltage."

voltage Analogous to electrical pressure. Voltage exists between two points when one point has an excess of electrons in relation to the other point. A battery is a good example: the negative terminal has an excess of electrons in relation to the positive terminal. If you connect a piece of wire between a battery's positive and negative terminals, voltage pushes current through the wire. One volt across 1 ohm of resistance produces a current of 1 Ampere.

voltage source Technical description of a power amplifier that can maintain its output voltage regardless of the load impedance.

VTA see "Vertical Tracking Angle"

VTF see "Vertical Tracking Force"

wall-stud resonance Acoustic resonance of a listening room's walls when struck by sound. Occurs only in drywall-on-stud construction.

Watermarking Technique of embedding digital codes disguised as noise in the audio waveform to control how content is copied, and to trace the source of music piracy. Also describes a visible imprint on the surface of a legitimate SACD that disappears on a copy.

watt The unit of electrical power, defined as the power dissipated by 1 Ampere of current flowing through 1 ohm of resistance.

wavelength The distance between successive cycles of a sinewave or other periodic motion.

weighting curve A filter applied to noise or sound-pressure level measurements that approximates the perceived loudness or noise level.

weighty A full and robust bass presentation.

widescreen see "letterbox"

WG4 see "Working Group 4"

woofer Driver in a loudspeaker system that reproduces bass.

Working Group 4 (WG4) Consortium of consumer-electronics industry representatives given the task of developing and formalizing a high-resolution digital audio carrier.

XLR jack and plug Three-pin connector that usually carries a balanced audio signal.

zero-crossing distortion Discontinuity in a musical waveform in push-pull amp.

Index

A

M

STEREO • MULTICHANNEL AUDIO • MUSIC

the abso!ute sound ®

$24 for 1 year (6 issues)

Each issue of *The Absolute Sound* is packed with **expert recommendations, in-depth equipment reviews, product comparisons,** and **advice** for enjoying your home-theater system.

Whether you're looking for a turntable, a CD player, integrated, pre-power amplifiers or speakers, our experts uncover the best products for the money in every price range!

In each issue you'll find:

❑ A special **Buyer's Guide** to the best two-channel and multi-channel components

❑ **Music reviews** by some of the best critics in the country

❑ What you should know about **evaluating** equipment

❑ The latest on **new technologies** such as SACD and DVD-Audio, and much, much more

☐ YES! Send me a subscription to *The Absolute Sound* where I'll get all of the above and I'll receive 6 issues for $24—and **SAVE 43%** off the cover price.

Offer good in U.S. only. Savings based on annual cover price of $41.70. **For Canada US$25 (includes GST). Foreign US$60. Prepaid in US funds only.**

☐ PAYMENT ENCLOSED   ☐ BILL ME

CHARGE MY: ☐ VISA ☐ MC ☐ AMEX   CARD NO. _____ EXP _____

SIGNATURE _____

NAME _____

ADDRESS _____

CITY _____ STATE _____ ZIP _____

E-MAIL ADDRESS_____

Mail your order to: *The Absolute Sound,* PO Box 469039, Escondido, CA 92046
Or call **1-888-732-1625. (760) 245-2809** (outside the US)   3RHT3-2

Acapella Publishing
P. O. Box 1768
Tijeras, NM 87059-1768

ORDER FORM

Name and address:

_____

_____

_____

_____

Ship to:

_____

_____

_____

_____

Daytime Telephone: _____

E-Mail Address: _____

Telephone Orders: Call Toll Free 800-848-5099 (U.S. and Canada)

Have your credit card ready.

Quantity		Unit Cost	Total Amount
	Home Theater For Everyone, 2nd Edition—Soft Cover	$19.95	
	Home Theater For Everyone, 2nd Edition—Hard Cover	$29.95	
	The Complete Guide to High-End Audio, 3rd Edition—Soft Cover	$34.95	
	The Complete Guide to High-End Audio, 3rd Edition—Hard Cover	$44.95	
	Shipping and Handling: $4.95 U.S, $8.95 outside continental U.S. Regardless of quantity		
	Total (enclosed)		

Payment:

☐   **Check or Money Order, sorry no COD**

☐   **VISA, MasterCard, AmEx, Discover**

_____

Card Number

_____

Expiration Date

_____

Signature

_____

Name on Card